HOSPITALITY LAW

HOSPITALITY LAW

Managing Legal Issues in the Hospitality Industry

FOURTH EDITION

STEPHEN BARTH, J.D.

Conrad N. Hilton College of Hotel and Restaurant Management

University of Houston

Attorney and Founder of HospitalityLawyer.com

WILEY

John Wiley & Sons, Inc.

Library of Congress Cataloging-in-Publication Data

Barth, Stephen C.
    Hospitality law : managing legal issues in the hospitality industry / Stephen C. Barth. —4th ed.
       p.   cm.
    Includes index.
    Summary: "Written to help teach hospitality students what they need to know to manage a facility
    legally, safely, and securely"—Provided by publisher.
    ISBN 978-1-118-08563-9 (hardback)
      1. Hotels—Law and legislation—United States.   2. Hospitality industry—Law and legislation—
    United States.   I. Title.
    KF2042.H6B368 2011
    343.73'07864794—dc23
                                                                                2011031190

Printed in the United States of America

10 9 8 7 6 5 4 3 2 1

CONTENTS

PREFACE

Hospitality Law: Managing Legal Issues in the Hospitality Industry, Fourth Edition, was written to help teach hospitality students what they need to know to manage a facility legally, safely, and securely.

In the day-to-day operation of a hospitality facility, it is the manager, not the company attorney, who will most influence the legal position of the operation. Rarely will you find a hospitality manager who is also a licensed attorney. However, professional hospitality managers (and, by extension, their staffs) make decisions every day based on their own interpretation of the law. The quality of these decisions will ultimately determine whether lawyers and the expense of fees, trials, and potential judgments may become necessary. A few examples will help illustrate this fact:

- A restaurant guest is unhappy with the quality of service provided during his meal. He complains to the manager and angrily demands his money back, but his meal has been eaten.
    - Is the guest legally entitled to a refund?

- A hotel guest maintains that a $50 bill she had left on her bedside table was gone when she returned to her room after going out for lunch.
    - Is the hotel required to replace the funds?

- A resort employee is arrested by the local police for driving under the influence of alcohol. He is employed by the hotel as a van driver, but was not on duty at the time of the arrest.
    - Should the hotel suspend his employment?

- A hotel food and beverage director is presented with a bottle of rare and expensive wine as a Christmas gift from her linen vendor.
    - Can she legally accept the gift without threatening her employment status?

- A franchise restaurant owner receives a letter from her franchisor stating that the "casual Friday" dress code policy recently adopted by the owner is in violation of the franchise agreement.
    - Must the owner change her policy?

These examples are just a few of the thousands of legal issues that daily confront hospitality managers. Obviously, it would be very expensive to consult an attorney each time a legal issue arises. It is also true, however, that making the wrong decision in any of these cases could result in tremendous costs in legal fees and settlements, or in costly negative publicity. Because that is true, a hospitality student's and a professional manager's greatest need is to understand how they can act in ways to ensure that they are managing legally in the hospitality industry. *Hospitality Law: Managing Legal Issues in the Hospitality Industry, Fourth Edition,* will show them how.

■ NEW TO THIS EDITION

Organization: The *Fourth Edition* maintains the more logical flow that was developed in the Third Edition. Throughout the book, changes to the law have been updated and revised to ensure that the most current information is presented.

Web exercises: Each of the web exercises has been updated to ensure accuracy and enrich the learning experience. Strategic links have also been added to ensure currency as the law changes between editions.

Access to actual legal cases: Summaries of actual legal cases are still included at the end of each chapter to further illustrate and practically apply the law. Faculty and students are able to access an annual case summary of over 100 of the most significant hospitality case decisions made during a particular year by logging into Resources, then the Academics section on **hospitalitylawyer.com**, where you will also find downloadable PowerPoints and links to the cases cited in the book.

By accessing www.hospitalitylawyer.com/textbook.aspx the reader has the ability to review an annual case summary of more than 100 of the most significant hospitality case decisions from that year. Links to cases in the book are also found here.

International Snapshots are included to give the instructor and students a different perspective on legal issues. Each of these was contributed by practicing attorneys or professionals in their field and describe the differences between U.S. law and the international arena in general or as it compares to a particular foreign country.

Travel and tourism: Continuing the trend on globalization, Chapter 13, "Legal Responsibilities in Travel and Tourism," has an added dimension, including international travel treaties.

Additionally, information on relevant recent events and trends has been added throughout, including:

- ■ Impact of the recent economic collapse on hotel development
- ■ Social media concerns
- ■ Data and guest privacy
- ■ The bedbug invasion
- ■ Allergy, nutrition, and food labeling concerns in the food and beverage arena

■ THE CONCEPTUAL DEVELOPMENTAL PROCESS

After teaching hospitality law for several years, I recognized the need for a different kind of resource that could be used to teach hospitality students what they need to know about managing in today's litigious environment. Accordingly, this book is built around *interactive pedagogy,* which *exposes readers to realistic scenarios.*

Before developing the first edition of *Hospitality Law: Managing Legal Issues in the Hospitality Industry,* a survey of attorneys and human resource directors at the top 100 U.S. hospitality organizations was completed. The participants were asked to identify the primary areas they felt were critical to a hospitality student's legal education and training. The most significant areas of interest focused on the ability to manage correctly and, thereby, reduce the potential for legal liability.

Thus, **preventing liability through a proactive management of the law** is the dominant theme of this textbook. In all cases, where issues of content, writing style, and design were involved, the touchstone for inclusion was simply: "Does this add to a student's ability to do the right thing?" If so, it was considered critical; if not, it was quickly deemed superfluous. For that reason, this book will look and read very differently from any other hospitality law textbook on the market. The legal information in it has been carefully selected and classroom-tested to be clear, understandable, and easy to apply. This book exposes the reader to many realistic scenarios that hospitality managers regularly face.

CREATING AN INTERACTIVE LEARNING ENVIRONMENT

This textbook has been designed as a necessary tool for a hospitality law course that will foster an attitude of *compliance and prevention* in work ethics and personal management philosophy. Compliance and prevention means gaining an understanding of how to prevent or limit your legal liability by complying with legal norms. Instead of approaching the topic of hospitality law from a traditional case study viewpoint, this book provides a necessary understanding of the basic foundations and principles of the laws affecting the hospitality industry. Once the basic principles are understood, the text goes on to provide guidelines and techniques that show how to manage preventively and apply a practical legal awareness prior to taking action.

Much of the book's effectiveness as a learning tool relies on participating in an interactive learning process. Several different types of learning features and exercises intended to help develop a pattern of behavior are included. Their purpose is to teach you to consider the legal implications of day-to-day management activities. Finally, in recognition of the importance of technology, a number of activities showcase the value of the computer as a lifelong learning tool.

Chapter Outline. Each chapter begins with an outline that helps demonstrate how topics fit together in the context of the overall subject.

Opening Vignettes. Each chapter follows the daily routine of a fictional hotel manager, Trisha Sangus, as she grapples with challenges and dilemmas that demonstrate how an understanding of the chapter topic would be critical to a real-life hospitality manager's decision-making ability.

In This Chapter You Will Learn. This section is more than just a list of learning objectives. This feature identifies concrete skills and necessary information that will have been gained after studying the chapter. This demonstrates how the information will be useful in management careers.

Legalese. Legal definitions are provided, written in simple language to help develop the vocabulary and understanding needed to follow the law.

Analyze the Situation. These hypothetical but realistic scenarios illustrate how a legal concept just encountered in the textbook is relevant to situations that are likely to arise in the hospitality industry. In many cases, we have intentionally made the facts ambiguous to present a challenge and encourage thinking through the situation and fostering discussion in the classroom.

Search the Web. Every chapter includes interactive Search the web exercises, which provide URLs to a carefully chosen collection of Internet sites that hospitality managers can use to find guidelines, access information, or learn more about the hospitality industry and the law.

Legally Managing at Work. These sidebars contain practical legal guidelines for managers, covering a variety of situations that directly relate to restaurant and hotel operations. Topics range from recommended steps for managers when responding to guest injuries or health emergencies, to legal guidelines for drawing up contracts, and dealing with the media during an emergency situation.

In this section, checklists, step-by-step procedures, and written forms will demonstrate how to create policies and respond to situations in a manner that will help ensure compliance with the law and protect businesses.

International Snapshot. An attorney or industry professional has compared U.S. legal practices with the same practices in the international community at large or a specific country. This section will create an enhanced perspective.

What Would You Do? These realistic decision-making scenarios ask readers to put themselves in a situation that requires them to apply the legal principles they have learned in the chapter. Many include a concrete activity, and all contain questions that require a personal decision in a set of circumstances that may be faced in future careers.

The Hospitality Industry in Court. Actual legal cases are often used as examples or learning tools in hospitality law course. The challenge lies in selecting cases that effectively illustrate the topic being discussed. Many court cases that become famous are ultimately decided on the basis of procedural issues or legal technicalities, rather than on the facts of the case. Consequently, they are of interest to law students, but much less helpful to hospitality managers.

Each chapter of this book includes summaries of real-life hospitality cases. The cases have been selected specifically to reinforce the *compliance and prevention* theme of the textbook. We encourage looking up the entire case or using the summaries as springboards for assignments or class discussions.

What Did You Learn in This Chapter? The main ideas and objectives of each chapter are briefly summarized here. The summary can be used as a supplement to, but not as a substitution for, a thorough review of the chapter material.

Rapid Review. In addition to traditional end-of-chapter self-evaluation questions, each chapter's Rapid Review also includes specific exercises designed to build writing skills, such as drafting a policy for staff, writing a memo to a supervisor, or perhaps composing a letter to a local government official. Each chapter's Rapid Review also includes at least one assignment that requires use of the Internet.

Team Activity. Employers continue to stress the importance of working in teams. This is especially true for managers at every level, who may be called on to participate on committees or supervise projects with other groups of employees. This textbook provides classroom-tested activities that will stimulate thinking and discussion, while allowing practice of the team-building and social skills needed to succeed as hospitality managers.

▦ INSTRUCTOR'S MATERIALS

To help instructors manage the large number of exercises, activities, and discussion questions posed in this textbook, an ***Instructor's Manual*** (ISBN: 978–1–118–15223–2) is available. Please contact your Wiley sales representative for details. The Instructor's Manual is also available to qualified instructors on the Wiley website at www.wiley.com/college/barth. This site also includes PowerPoint slides.

The **Test Bank** has been specifically formatted for **Respondus**, an easy-to-use software program for creating and managing exams that can be printed to paper or published directly to Blackboard, WebCT, Desire2Learn, eCollege, ANGEL, and other eLearning systems. Instructors who adopt *Hospitality Law, Fourth Edition* can download the Test Bank for free. Additional Wiley resources also can be uploaded into your LMS course at no charge.

———————————

Stay in touch with Stephen Barth. Follow him on Twitter @hospitality_law!

ACKNOWLEDGMENTS

This edition, like the three before it, was truly a community effort. It would be impossible to thank everyone over the years who has provided me with insight or ideas that made this book possible. Accordingly, for those of you I fail to mention personally, please know that it was not an intentional oversight.

A special note of thanks to Allison Jeffcoat for her assistance researching the law and her keen eye for formatting and organization; to the master's candidates at the Hilton College for their suggestions and proof reading; to Jenni Lee at Wiley for her patience and support. Also, of course, many thanks to David Hayes for his contributions to *Hospitality Law*, and for helping to make this book a success.

Special thanks go to those educational professionals whose experience in the classroom, insights, and encouragement served to illumine this text. Reviewers can do a remarkable job of keeping the needs of the student at the forefront of the writing effort, and the following individuals were tremendous in this regard. Truly, this book contains the collective teaching acumen of some of hospitality education's very best, and this Fourth Edition of the textbook is a testament to their skill, commitment, and wisdom.

Tom Atkinson, Columbus State Community College
Diana S. Barber, Georgia State University
Thomas F. Cannon, University of Texas at San Antonio
Edward H. Coon, University of South Carolina
Sybil David, Greenville Technical College
Edward Doherty, Endicott College
Gary M. Donnelly, Casper College
Linda K. Enghagen, University of Massachusetts
William D. Frye, Niagara University
James M. Goldberg, Northern Virginia Community College
Christian E. Hardigree, University of Nevada at Las Vegas
Joseph W. Holland, University of Wisconsin–Stout
Jeffrey P. Ivory, Saint Louis Community College
Barry R. Langford, University of Missouri–Columbia
Charla R. Long, Grand Valley State University
Brenda G. Montgomery, Arkansas Tech University
Craig H. Mueller, St. Louis Community College
Robert Alan Palmer, California State Polytechnic University–Pomona
George J. Pastor, Hillsborough Community College
Walter Rapetski, Asheville-Buncombe Tech Community College
Laurie Salame, University of Massachusetts
Denver E. Severt, Eastern Michigan University
David M. Spatt, Johnson & Wales University
Christian M. Stegmaier, University of South Carolina
John E. Taylor, Brigham Young University, Hawaii

James R. Turley, New York Institute of Technology
Bruce S. Urdang, Northern Arizona University
William B. Werner, University of Nevada at Las Vegas
Peter Yersin, Pennsylvania State University

Thanks, also, to the attorneys and industry professionals who devoted their time and expertise in providing the international snapshots. The book is much better due to their efforts.

Andrew Galeziowski
Caryn Pass
David Comeaux
Elizabeth Demaret
Frank Zaid
Irvin W. Sandman
James Eiler
Perrin Rynders
Rick Barrett-Cuetara
Robert Zarco
San San Lee
John Vernon

This edition is dedicated to my brothers Kenneth, Eric, and Paul and their families' for their infinite, unwavering support, and making me laugh every single day—love you guys!

STEPHEN BARTH, J.D.
Conrad N. Hilton College of Hotel and Restaurant Management
University of Houston
Attorney and Founder of HospitalityLawyer.com,
the Hospitality Law Conference Series, and the
Global Congress on Legal, Safety, and Security Solutions in Travel

CHAPTER 1

PREVENTION PHILOSOPHY

TRISHA SANGUS WAS busy and more than a little frustrated. As the general manager of a 275-room resort hotel, she knew that the peak season was about to begin, and she had no front office manager to handle the supervision of her front desk staff, the reservationists, van drivers, night auditors, and other guest service employees. Without an experienced front office manager, the tourist season could be extremely difficult. She had spent the entire morning on the telephone attempting to do background checks on the three top applicants she had interviewed. Inevitably, she got the same response from all of the past employers she called. Either they would not give out any information about the candidates or they would only tell Trisha the person's name and employment dates. It seemed as if everyone was too cautious to say anything that she could use to help make a good hiring decision. She wondered if it was worth the effort of verifying the employment of her applicants at all.

Her thoughts were interrupted by the telephone. It was her human resource director, asking whether

Trisha had made a decision about purchasing employee workbooks that explained the new tip-reporting requirements, which had changed again, making obsolete the current booklets that had been used for employee training. Trisha asked the director to get a cost estimate on the 75 booklets they would need and promised a decision in the next few days. As she hung up the telephone, Trisha wondered how many of her food and beverage employees were actually in compliance with the new reporting requirements. *It sure seemed easier when the government left people alone*, she thought. On the other hand, it was only fair for employees to pay all the taxes they legally owed.

Trisha looked at her watch and jumped up from behind her desk. Her monthly safety meeting was about to start. The meeting was to be chaired by her director of security, and she knew how important it was to attend. It sent the right message, Trisha thought, for her employees on the Safety Committee to see her at the meetings. It let them know how she felt about the importance of safety and security training. Unfortunately, she had only had time to skim the article "Workplace Violence," which she knew was to make up the major topic of this week's meeting. Lately, it seemed there were too few hours in the day to accomplish all that she had to. Keeping up her own education in the field was getting harder and harder each month.

The last meeting of the day was the most difficult. Sanitation scores on the local Health Department inspections had been going down over the past few months. The violations were not serious, but the scores did tell Trisha that the managers in that department seemed to be letting the small things slip. A quick walk through the kitchen made Trisha aware that the problems remained unresolved. She wondered why the standards seemed to be slipping, despite the fact that her food and beverage director, and indeed most of the food and beverage staff, were long-time property employees.

As Trisha walked back to her office, she reflected on the issues of the day. She had worked hard to become a general manager. She was one of the youngest GMs in her company. The customer contact she so enjoyed, however, seemed to be less and less a part of her daily routine now. Rules, regulations, and paperwork seemed to consume most of her time. She needed to reprioritize her efforts, but so many issues were important that she was not quite sure where to start.

As she flipped through the afternoon mail, she noticed a headline on the front page of the local newspaper: "City Hotel Targeted in Lawsuit." She was familiar with the hotel. Its general manager was one of her friends and colleagues. Trisha knew that it was an important part of her job to minimize the chances of a lawsuit like the one in the paper from happening at her hotel. She wondered if her own efforts were enough, and if not, what she could do to improve them.

IN THIS CHAPTER, YOU WILL LEARN:

1. Why the study of laws related to hospitality is important.
2. The historical origins of the law and its evolutionary nature.
3. A philosophical framework to help prevent legal difficulties before they begin.
4. How to evaluate management actions on an ethical basis.

1.1 THE FUTURE HOSPITALITY MANAGER AND THE LEGAL ENVIRONMENT

Hospitality law is the body of law relating to the foodservice, travel, and lodging industries. That is, it is the body of law governing the specific nuances of transportation, hotels, restaurants, bars, spas, country clubs, conventions, events, and more.[1]

Today, hospitality managers must be multitalented individuals. In addition to knowledge of their own designated area of expertise, such as food and beverage, marketing, accounting, or rooms management, hospitality managers are often called on to assume specialized roles, such as employee counselor, interior designer, facility engineer, or computer systems analyst. Given the complexity of the modern business world, it is simply a fact that the skill level required for success today in this field is greater than it was in the past.

Hospitality management has always been a challenging profession. Whether in a casino, a school lunch program, a five-star hotel, a sports stadium concession program, or myriad other environments, hospitality managers are required to have a breadth of skill not found in many other areas of management. Hospitality managers are in charge of securing raw materials, and producing a product or service and selling it—all under the same roof. This makes them very different from their manufacturing counterparts (who are in charge of product production only) and from their retail counterparts (who sell, but do not manufacture, the product). Perhaps most

---

[1]http://en.wikipedia.org/wiki/Hospitality_law?oldid=0.

important, the hospitality manager has direct contact with guests, the ultimate end users of the products and services supplied by the industry.

Additionally, hospitality managers are called on frequently to make decisions that will, in one manner or another, impact the legal standing of their employers. Robert James, founder of one of the largest hotel contract management companies in the United States, once estimated that 60 to 70 percent of the decisions he made on a daily basis involved some type of legal dimension. This is not to say that hospitality managers need to be *attorneys*. They do not. However, the decisions that they make may or may not increase their organization's chances of needing the services of an *attorney*.

Consider the situation in which a hospitality manager is informed that a guest has slipped and fallen in an area of the dining room containing a salad bar. It appears that the guest had been serving himself and slipped on a piece of lettuce dropped by a previous guest. Was this a simple accident? Could it have been prevented? Is the restaurant responsible? What medical attention, if any, should the manager be prepared to provide? What if the injuries are severe? Should the restaurant be held responsible? Can the restaurant manager be held personally responsible? Most important, what should the manager actually do when the incident is brought to his or her attention? What, if anything, should the employees do? Who is responsible if the employees were not trained in what to do?

From this example, it is clear that the hospitality manager is in a position to profoundly influence the legal position of the operation. Day after day, in hundreds of situations, the actions of hospitality managers will influence the likelihood of the business or the manager becoming the subject of *litigation*.

There is a unique body of law relating to the foodservice, travel, and lodging industries. These laws have developed over time as society and the courts have sought to define the relationship between the individual or business serving as the host and the individual who is the guest. This textbook will give you up-to-date information on the most important of those special laws and relationships. That is not to imply, however, that this book is designed to make you a lawyer. What it will do, if you use it properly, is train you to think like one. It will teach you to consider carefully how the actions taken by you and those you work with will be viewed in a legal context. The industry's very best legal educators, hospitality managers, writers, and reviewers have created this book especially for you. They all speak with one voice when they say, "Welcome to the world of hospitality management!" As an industry, we need your skill, ability, and creativity. This textbook, if studied carefully, will help you become the hospitality manager you deserve to be and that our industry and guests require you to be.

1.2 THE HOSPITALITY MANAGER AND LEGAL MANAGEMENT

Jack P. Jefferies, who served for more than 20 years as legal counsel for the American Hotel and Lodging Association (AH&LA), has stated: "Over 135,000 new federal and state *laws* are issued annually, as well as hundreds of thousands of federal and state administrative rules."[2] With this much change in the *law*, some believe that the topic is too complex to learn in an introductory course or from one book. In addition, they would argue that because the law is constantly changing, even if an individual learned the law today, his or her knowledge would be out of date in a very short time. Although these positions are understandable, they argue for, not against, the future hospitality manager's study of legal management.

Although the law is indeed complex, certain basic principles and procedures can be established that will minimize a manager's chances of encountering legal difficulty.

---

[2]Jack P. Jefferies, *Understanding Hospitality Law*, 3rd ed. (East Lansing, MI: The Educational Institute of the American Hotel and Lodging Association, 1995).

LEGALESE
Attorney: Any person trained and legally authorized to act on behalf of others in matters of the law.

LEGALESE
Litigation: The act of initiating and carrying on a lawsuit. Often, used to refer to the lawsuit itself.

LEGALESE
Law: The rules of conduct and responsibility established and enforced by a society.

Since it is possible to prevent legal difficulty by anticipating it beforehand, it is less important to know, for example, the specific rules of food safety in every city than it is to know the basic principles of serving safe food. No one, not even the best lawyer, can be expected to know everything about every area of the law. In the same way, hospitality managers are not required to have a comprehensive knowledge of every law or lawsuit that impacts their industry. What they must know is how to effectively manage their legal environment. To begin this journey, it is important to grasp three key concepts:

1. Laws have historical origins, and managers need to know them.
2. Laws have an evolutionary nature, based on changes in society.
3. It is possible to use a philosophy of preventative management to manage the legal environment and minimize the chances of litigation.

Historical Origins of the Law

Common law and *civil law* are the two major systems of law in place in the Western world. Common law is the body of law that has descended from the law created in Great Britain and is used in the United States and most countries in the British Commonwealth. Civil law is descended from the law created in the Roman Empire and is used by most Western European countries, as well as Latin America, Asia, and Africa. Although both legal systems certainly defy oversimplification, it can generally be said that common law comes from reviewing past litigation that has been decided by the courts. It is greatly interested in precedent, or what has been decided in previous court cases with similar situations or facts.

In civil law, decisions evolve based on written laws or codes. Judges in civil law feel less bound by what others have decided before them and more compelled by the law as it has been established by government bodies. Given the nearness of countries within Europe, and the influence of the British Empire, it is no wonder that these two great legal systems frequently operated in close proximity, which has often blurred their distinctions. Interestingly, the term *civil law* is actually used in the common law system to refer to private law (or private disputes), as opposed to public or criminal matters.

Common law developed in England following the Norman Conquest. In common law, the principle of *stare decisis* is followed. A decision made by a higher court must be obeyed by all lower courts. In this manner, citizens know which actions are legal and which are punishable. Essentially, the purpose of the common law was to interpret and enforce rules related to the granting of land by the British monarchy to those subjects deemed worthy of such land grants. The barons who received this land would often grant parts of it to those they felt were deserving. The courts that were created at this time were charged with overseeing the peaceful resolution of disputes regarding land, inheritance, marriage, and other issues related to land grants.

Between 1765 and 1769, an Englishman, Sir William Blackstone, wrote four volumes he titled the *Commentaries*. In these books, Blackstone sought to compile a general overview of all the common law of his time. Blackstone's work formed the basis for much of the law in the New World, as his work migrated there with the English colonial settlers. Laws related to those in the hospitality industry were, of course, included.

Despite the anger against Britain that resulted in the Revolutionary War, the colonists of the soon-to-be United States embraced the common law as their favored rules of conduct and responsibility. Blackstone's work was widely used as a textbook in the law schools of the new country, and it influenced many of its early law students, including Thomas Jefferson, John Marshall, James Monroe, and Henry Clay. Inevitably, succeeding generations throughout the history of the United States have taken the common law as they have found it and modified it to meet the needs of their ever-changing society.

LEGALESE

Common law: Laws derived from the historical customs and usage of a society, and the decisions by courts when interpreting those customs and usages.

LEGALESE

Civil law: The body of law (usually in the form of codes or statutes) created by governmental entities that are concerned with private rights and remedies, as opposed to criminal matters.

LEGALESE

Stare decisis: The principle of following prior case law.

Evolutionary Nature of Common Law

It should come as no surprise that a rapidly changing society will often revise its rules of conduct and responsibility. This is true in society as a whole and in how society views the hospitality industry. In the United States of the 1850s, obviously, one would not have been expected to find a law requiring a certain number of automobile parking spaces to be designated for people with disabilities seeking to enjoy an evening meal at the town's finest restaurant, because the world in that era contained neither the automobile nor the inclination of society to grant special parking privileges to those who were disabled. In today's society, we have both. What changed? First, the physical world changed. We now have automobiles, along with the necessity of parking them. More significant, however, is the fact that society's view of how people with disabilities should be treated has changed. Parking ordinances today require designated "disabled" parking spaces, generally located close to the main entrances of buildings to ensure easy access. Not only is it good business to have such spaces, but current laws also mandate that the hospitality manager provide them.

In this case, parking requirements grew out of a law created at the federal government level. The law is called the *Americans with Disabilities Act* (ADA). This act, and its many applications to hospitality, will be discussed in greater detail in Chapter 7, "Legally Selecting Employees." It is mentioned here to illustrate that laws evolve just as society evolves. Changes in society lead to changes in the law.

Laws in the United States may be enacted at the federal, state, and local levels (see Figure 1.1).

> **LEGALESE**
> **Americans with Disabilities Act:** Federal legislation (law) that protects the rights of people with disabilities so that they may be treated fairly in the workplace and have access to places of public accommodation, such as hotels, restaurants, and airplanes.

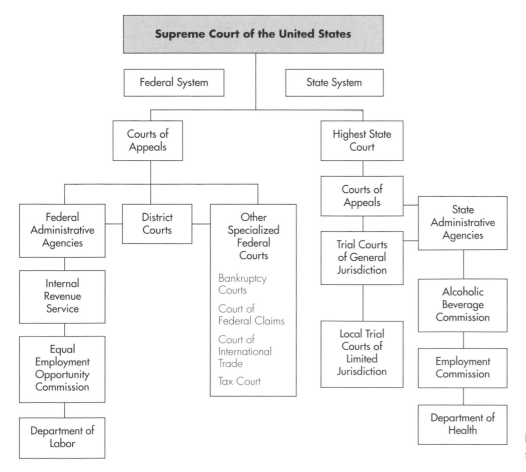

Figure 1.1 The U.S. legal system.

At each of these levels, the laws reflect the changing desires of the citizens and their elected officials. Because society includes members who operate hospitality facilities, *hospitality-related laws* created and modified by society impact those who work in the hospitality industry.

> **Search the Web 1.1**
>
> Go to the Internet. Search for categories related to laws regulating tobacco use and sales in your state and/or city.
>
> Assignment: Draft a one-paragraph essay summarizing the laws governing tobacco use in your state. Are there any special stipulations that a hospitality manager would especially want to be aware of (such as the designation of smoking and nonsmoking areas in a restaurant or public lobby)?

Preventative Legal Management

Future hospitality managers will encounter laws that do not currently exist. How, then, can they be expected to operate their facilities in full compliance with the law throughout their career? Just as important, how can they be expected to manage these facilities in a way that will minimize their chances of doing something illegal? The answer is not to attempt to monitor every legislative body empowered to enact law. The answer is to operate hospitality facilities in a way that combines preventative legal management with sound ethical behavior.

Lessons from the Medical Field

In the medical field, it is widely agreed that it is better to prevent a serious illness beforehand than to treat it after the fact. For example, doctors advise that it is preferable to prevent a heart attack through proper diet, exercise, and the cessation of smoking than for a patient to have a bypass operation after a heart attack has occurred. In the case of prevention, the doctor advises the patient, but it is, in large measure, up to the patient to put into practice the recommendations of the physician.

In a similar vein, it is far better for hospitality managers to operate their facilities in a way that minimizes the risk of litigation, rather than in a manner that exposes their operations to the threat of litigation.

STEM the Tide of Litigation

As noted, the law is not static; in fact, it changes frequently. Managers must stay abreast of these changes so that ultimately, on a daily basis, they integrate their acquired knowledge and awareness of the law into a personal style of management and decision making. The acronym STEM was coined as an easy way to remember the steps in a decision-making process that can assist managers in getting started. It stands for: select, teach, educate, and manage. It is presented here as a way of beginning to "STEM" the tide of litigation. The details of how STEM works are included in the box on page 7.

On any given day, the general manager of a hotel or restaurant in the United States will make decisions about hiring, firing, and/or providing benefits to employees. Other daily tasks might include approving a meeting space contract for a major event to be held on the property, an event that involves the service of alcohol. Decisions regarding if and when to add a lifeguard to the pool area, whether to subcontract parking services to a local valet company, and even the uniform requirements of staff, will all be made by the manager. All of these seemingly independent decisions have a significant common denominator—they all have legal implications.

Whether it is opening a restaurant, operating a country club, or hiring a housekeeper, hospitality managers must be aware of the legal implications of each and every decision they make. It is of vital importance that managers resolve to be fair, to operate within the law, and to manage preventatively. On occasions when they do not, and a lawsuit results, the courts may hold managers *liable* for their inattentiveness.

This philosophy of preventative management becomes even more important when one considers that a great many litigation matters encountered by hospitality operators have a common denominator: a poorly prepared employee. Injuries and the resulting damages, whether financial, physical, or mental, are usually a consequence of an employee who has not been sufficiently taught to perform his or her duties. He or she might make an omission, such as not cleaning up a spill near a salad bar, or might pursue an activity outside the scope of his or her duties, such as sexual harassment or arguing with a customer.

LEGALESE

Liable: To be legally responsible or obligated.

LEGALLY MANAGING AT WORK:

Applying the STEM Process in Hospitality Management

A process can be implemented that will help reduce employee errors and omissions and, therefore, litigation and liability. The process is called STEM, for *select, teach, educate,* and *manage.* It works like this:

1. *Select:* Managers can begin reducing litigation by selecting the right employee for the right job. Managers cannot hire "just anyone" at the last minute. Employees must be selected based on specific job qualifications, written job specifications, and information derived from a thorough investigation of the candidate for the position, whether the employee to be hired is a busperson, waitperson, hostess, door supervisor, or line supervisor.

2. *Teach:* Managers must develop proper training methods for employees, including feedback devices such as competency testing, to ensure that the training is effective.

3. *Educate:* Managers must continuously educate themselves so that they know which topics and procedures must be passed on to employees through effective teaching methods.

4. *Manage:* Effective managers know that if you consistently do things the right way, the chances for mistakes—and, therefore, for litigation—will diminish. Management has been defined as consisting of four functions: planning, organizing, controlling, and motivating. Although all four have legal implications, the STEM process focuses almost exclusively on the motivating function. A manager who creates a supportive work environment will gain the trust and respect of employees, who will then be motivated to do their best work, and thus avoid making errors that could result in litigation.

The recent increasing number of lawsuits is not caused solely by employees, of course. The legal system and some attorneys certainly share the blame. Managers, however, bear most of the responsibility for what has been occurring. When an employee makes a mistake, often it is the result of management error. Either the wrong person was hired for the job, the duties for the job were not effectively communicated to the employee, the employee was not properly trained, or the employee was not effectively supervised or motivated to do the job properly.

To create an environment conducive to motivation, you must first establish trust and respect. When managers make a commitment to employees or guests, they must follow through. They also must be willing to accept responsibility for their mistakes, and to apologize for them when appropriate. Managers must set an example: If managers ask employees to be on time, then managers must also be on time; if managers expect employees to pay for food, beverages, and services, then he or she must also pay for food, beverages, and services. In current parlance, managers must walk the talk!

Finally, all of the planning, organizing, controlling, and motivating in the world will not help if management cannot effectively communicate its vision and plan to the employees who will carry out that vision. The ability to communicate with skill and grace is a critical component of being a successful manager.

Today's culturally diverse workforce will require diverse motivating techniques. Remember that different people are motivated by different incentives. Money is a perfect example. To some, it is a strong motivating factor; others would prefer more time off instead of additional pay. Managers must know their employees and determine—by asking them, if need be—what will motivate them, both as individuals and as a work team. Examples of possible motivational efforts include the following:

- A sales contest with a significant prize
- A parking space with recognition for the employee of the month
- A 50 percent discount on meals at the restaurant
- A card on their birthday
- A written "pat on the back" for a job well done
- Taking the time to ask employees how their day was
- Involving employees in setting goals
- Seeking employee input in developing work schedules
- Listening to their concerns

All of those listed and others are the types of activities a manager should undertake to build the trust and loyalty of employees. If a consensus can be reached on what to do and how to do it, the motivating task becomes much easier.

The goal of STEM is to reduce employee mistakes. By continually encouraging and rewarding good performance, managers can create an environment that will, in fact, reduce the number of times employees make mistakes. Remember that even if a goal may is reached, the efforts of the individual or group still might merit praise. In other words, managers should try to catch their employees doing something right instead of trying to catch them doing something wrong.

It is not possible to manage effectively while sitting behind the desk. Effective managers know that "management by walking around" is alive and well, particularly in a service industry such as hospitality. Of course, an important part of managing is the ability to motivate employees. As much as managers would like all employees to come to the job every day brimming with enthusiasm, the fact is, too often, just the opposite is true. A significant number of employees may dislike coming to work, their jobs, their situation in life, and much more. They must be motivated to perform at the level management has targeted in order to exceed management's own expectations, and, more important, those of the guest.

To recap the STEM process: Select the right employee for the right job; teach employees while creating a training trail; educate management; motivate staff in a positive and nurturing manner. All these efforts will help foster loyalty and goodwill, while reducing the likelihood of litigation.

> ## ≫ ANALYZE THE SITUATION 1.1

A FELLOW SUPERVISOR CONFIDES in you that he has been arrested for a second time in two years for driving under the influence of alcohol. His current case has not yet gone to trial. This supervisor is responsible for the late-night closing of the restaurant in which you both work.

1. Should you discuss this situation with the restaurant's general manager?

2. After reading the next section on Ethics, has your answer changed?

3. Which aspect of STEM is relevant here?

1.3 ETHICS AND THE LAW

It is not always clear whether a course of action is illegal or simply wrong. Put another way, an activity might be legal but still be the wrong thing to do. As a future hospitality manager who seeks to manage his or her legal environment and that of other employees, it is important that you be able to make this distinction.

Ethics refers to the behavior of an individual toward another individual or group. Ethical behavior refers to behavior that is considered "right" or the "right thing to do." Consistently choosing ethical behavior over behavior that is not ethical will go a long way toward avoiding legal difficulty. This is true because hospitality managers often will not know what the law requires in a given situation. In cases of litigation, juries may have to make determinations of whether a manager's actions were ethical or deliberately unethical. How juries and judges decide these questions may well determine their view of a manager's liability for an action or inaction.

Although it is sometimes difficult to determine precisely what constitutes ethical behavior, the following seven guidelines can be very useful when evaluating a possible course of action:

1. *Is it legal?* Does the law or company policy prohibit this activity?
2. *Does it hurt anyone?* Will this action negatively affect any stakeholders?
3. *Is it fair?* Is it fair to all the stakeholders?
4. *Am I being honest?* Are you being honest with yourself and with the company?
5. *Would I care if it happened to me?* Would it bother you if you were the recipient of the action?
6. *Would I publicize my action?* Would you be embarrassed if stakeholders became aware of your action?
7. *What if everyone did it?* Could the business effectively operate in an equitable fashion?

Consider the hospitality manager who is responsible for a large wedding reception in a hotel. The bride and groom have selected a specific champagne from the

LEGALESE

Ethics: Choices of proper conduct made by an individual in his or her relationships with others.

hotel's wine list to be used for their champagne punch. The contract signed by the bride and groom lists the selling price per gallon of the punch but does not specifically mention the name of the champagne selected by the couple. In the middle of the reception, the hotel runs out of that brand of champagne. A less costly substitute is used for the duration of the reception. Neither the bride and groom nor the guests notice the difference. Using the seven ethical guidelines just listed, a manager could evaluate whether he or she should reduce the bride and groom's final bill by the difference in selling price of the two champagnes.

How an individual determines what constitutes ethical behavior may be influenced by his or her cultural background, religious views, professional training, and personal moral code. A complete example of the way someone would actually use the seven ethical guidelines is demonstrated in the following hypothetical situation.

An Ethical Dilemma: Free Champagne

Assume that you are the food and beverage director of a large hotel. You are planning for your New Year's Eve gala and require a large amount of wine and champagne. You conduct a competitive bidding process with the purveyors in your area and, based on quality and price, you place a very large order (in excess of $20,000) with a single purveyor. One week later, you receive a case of very expensive champagne, delivered to your home with a nice note from the purveyor's representative stating how much it appreciated the order and that the purveyor is really looking forward to doing business with you in the years ahead. What do you do with the champagne?

Ethical Analysis

Your first thought might be the most obvious one—that is, you drink it. But, hopefully, you will first ask yourself the seven questions of the ethical decision-making process.

1. Is it legal?

    From your perspective, it might not be illegal for you to accept a case of champagne. However, there could be liquor laws in your state that prohibit the purveyor from gifting that amount of alcoholic beverage. You must also consider whether it is permissible within the guidelines established by the company for which you work. Many companies have established gift acceptance policies that limit the value of the gifts that employees are eligible to accept. In this case, violation of a stated or written company policy may subject you to disciplinary action or even the termination of your employment. Accordingly, you need to be extremely familiar with the ethics policy that has been adopted by the company you are working for. Assuming that it does not violate a law and/or company policy, go to question 2.

2. Does it hurt anyone?

    Well, it probably would not hurt you, unless you drank all of the champagne at once; but, realistically, are you really going to be fair and objective when you evaluate next year's bids, or is your mind going to be thinking back to the case of champagne that you received? Assuming that you do not think that it is hurting anyone, go on to question 3.

3. Is it fair?

    Before answering this question you have to recognize who the stakeholders are in this particular situation. How might others in your company feel about the gift you received? After all, you agreed to work for this firm at a set salary. If benefits are gained because of decisions you make while on duty, should those benefits accrue to the *business* or to *you*? Assuming that you have decided that it is fair for you to keep the champagne, go to question number 4.

4. Am I being honest?

   This question gives you the opportunity to second-guess yourself when you are answering questions 2 and 3. Do you really believe that you can remain objective in the purchasing aspect of your job and continue to seek out the best quality for the best price, knowing that one of the purveyors rewarded you handsomely for last year's choice and may be inclined to do so again?

5. Would I care if it happened to me?

   If you owned the company you work for, and you knew that one of the managers you had hired was given a gift of this magnitude from a vendor, would you question the objectivity of that manager? Would you like to see all of your managers receive such gifts? Would you be concerned if they did?

6. Would I publicize my action?

   If you have trouble remembering the other questions, try to remember this one. Would you choose to keep the champagne if you knew that tomorrow morning the headlines of your city newspaper would read: "Food and Beverage Director of Local Hotel Gets Case of Champagne after Placing Large Order with Purveyor"? Your general manager would see it, other employees would see it, all of the other purveyors that you are going do business with would see it, and even potential future employers would see it.

7. What if everyone did it?

   If you justify your choice of keeping the champagne, consider: Does this process ever stop? What would happen if the executive housekeeper had a bed delivered to her home every time she ordered new bedding for the hotel? What would happen if every time she ordered new washers and dryers, she received a matching set at home?

Alternative Options

What are some of the realistic alternatives to keeping the champagne?

- Return it to the purveyor with a nice note stating how much you appreciate it but that your company policy will not allow you to accept it.
- Turn the gift over to the general manager to be placed into the normal liquor inventory (assuming that the law will allow it to be used this way).
- Donate it to the employee Christmas party.

Use the seven questions to evaluate each of these three courses of action. Do you see any differences?

Codes of Ethics

Some hospitality managers feel it is important to set their ethical beliefs down in a code of ethics. Figure 1.2 is the code of ethics developed by the Club Managers Association of America (CMAA). These managers are involved primarily in the management of private and public country clubs, city clubs, and athletic clubs.

In some cases, a company president or other operating officer will relay the ethical philosophy of a company to its employees in a section of the employee handbook or through a direct policy statement, as illustrated in the ethics statement presented in Figure 1.3, which was created by Hyatt Hotels.

Club Managers Association of America
Code of Ethics

We believe the management of clubs is an honorable calling. It shall be incumbent upon club managers to be knowledgeable in the application of sound principles in the management of clubs, with ample opportunity to keep abreast of current practices and procedures. We are convinced that the Club Managers Association of America best represents those interests, and as members thereof, subscribe to the following code of ethics:

We will uphold the best traditions of club management through adherence to sound business principles. By our behavior and demeanor, we shall set an example for our employees and will assist our club officers to secure the utmost in efficient and successful club operations.

We will consistently promote the recognition and esteem of club management as a professional and conduct our personal and business affairs in a manner to reflect capability and integrity. We will always honor our contractual employment obligations.

We shall promote community and civic affairs by maintaining good relations with the public sector to the extent possible within the limits of our club's demands.

We will strive to advance our knowledge and abilities as Club Managers, and willingly share with other Association members the lessons of our experience and knowledge gained by supporting and participating in our local chapter and National Association's educational meetings and seminars.

We will not permit ourselves to be subsidized or compromised by any interest doing business with our clubs.

We will refrain from initiating, directly or through an agent, any communications with a director, member or official of another club regarding its affairs without the prior knowledge of the Manager thereof, if it has a Manager.

We will advise the national Headquarters, whenever possible regarding managerial openings at clubs that come to our attention. We will do all within our power to assist our fellow club managers in pursuit of their professional goals.

We shall not be deterred from compliance with the Law, as it applies to our clubs. We shall provide our club officers and trustees with specifics of Federal, State and Local laws, statutes and regulations, to avoid punitive action and costly litigation.

We deem it our duty to report to local or national officers any willful violations of the CODE OF ETHICS.

Figure 1.2 CMAA code of ethics.

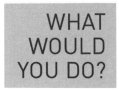

WHAT WOULD YOU DO?

Assume that your local municipality is considering the passage of a law that would prohibit the sale of all tobacco products from the interiors of bars and restaurants but not grocery stores. The restaurant you manage has a cocktail lounge, and cigarettes are both consumed and sold in that section of your restaurant. There is no current effort to prohibit smoking in cocktail lounges such as the one you operate. You are considering whether to address the local government body charged with creating such legislation:

1. What are the major considerations you will think about before you decide to support or oppose the proposed legislation?

2. Will the fact that you do or do not smoke influence your position?

3. Which ethical issues are in play here?

INTRODUCTION

The following statement is designed to reaffirm and further implement Hyatt Corporation's ("Hyatt") standing policy of strict observance of all laws and ethical standards applicable in jurisdictions in which the Corporation conducts its business. This statement is applicable to all of Hyatt's subsidiaries, affiliates and divisions, operating both inside and outside the United States (the "Corporation") and is applicable to all officers and employees of the Corporation. Unless amended by the Board of Directors of Hyatt, this statement and the compliance therewith is subject to no waivers or exceptions in the name of competitive or commercial demands, social traditions, or other local exigencies.

1. Policy Statement to Conduct Business in Accordance with all Laws and Complete Honesty
It is the policy of the Corporation to conduct its business in accordance with all applicable laws and regulations of the jurisdictions in which such business is conducted and to do so with complete honesty and integrity and in accordance with the highest moral and ethical standards.

2. Use of Corporate Assets
No corporate funds, assets, services or facilities (including, for the purposes hereof, without limitation, complimentary items, discounts and amenities), shall be used, directly or indirectly, for any unlawful or unethical purpose. Any question as to the legality or ethics of any contemplated use of corporate funds, assets, services or facilities shall be referred to Hyatt's general counsel.

3. Use of Corporate Assets for Political Purposes
No corporate funds, assets, services, or facilities shall be used, directly or indirectly, for the purpose of aiding, supporting or opposing any political party, association, organization or candidate where such use is illegal or improper under the laws or regulations of the relevant jurisdiction. This includes loans of corporate funds, assets, services or facilities and direct or indirect payments, including reimbursements of employees or third parties for political contributions or payments which they might personally have made. The use of corporate funds, assets, services or facilities for political purposes, in jurisdictions where the same are permitted by law shall not be prohibited if the use shall be with the specific prior written authorization of a senior officer of Hyatt and the advance written approval of Hyatt's general counsel after a determination by him that said use would be lawful and proper in all respects. Employees, may, of course, make personal political contributions as they choose, so long as such contribution is not in violation of any applicable laws, but no employee may be compensated or reimbursed, directly or indirectly, by the Corporation for any such personal contribution.

4. Use of Corporate Assets to Unlawfully Secure or Retain Business
No corporate funds, assets, services or facilities shall be used to secure or retain business where such use is in violation of any applicable law or regulation. Without limitation of the foregoing, no employee shall engage in any form of bribery or kickbacks and no corporate funds, assets, services or kickbacks and no corporate funds, assets, services or facilities shall be used to influence or corrupt the action of any government official, agent or employee, or of any private customer, supplier or other person. The foregoing includes direct and indirect payment (including payments through consultants, suppliers or other third parties) or use of corporate funds, assets, services or facilities in any form to or the benefit of governmental or non-governmental persons including the reimbursement of employees for payments or gifts which they might personally have made.

5. Use of Corporate Assets to Influence Decisions Affecting the Corporation
No corporate funds, assets, services or facilities shall be used in violation of any applicable law or regulation for the purpose of influencing any decision or action affecting the Corporation, including the performance or the timely performance of official duty or action or to ward off or postpone decisions on matters affecting the Corporation. The foregoing includes direct and indirect payments (including payments through consultants, suppliers or other third parties) or use of corporate funds, assets, services or facilities in any form to or for the benefit of governmental or non-governmental persons including the reimbursement of employees for payments or gifts which they might personally have made.

6. Use of Corporate Assets in Violation of Labor Laws
No corporate funds, assets, services or facilities shall be used in violation of any applicable law or regulation concerning labor unions. All labor unions must be dealt with as any normal customer and the extension of special courtesies outside the normal business context is illegal.

Figure 1.3 Corporate policy for Hyatt Hotels.
(Reprinted with permission)

7. Acceptance of Gifts, Payments, Fees or Privileges

Employees of the Corporation are not to solicit or accept gifts, payments, fees, services, special valuable privileges, pleasure or vacation trips or accommodations, loans (except on conventional terms from banks or loan institutions), or other special favors from any organization, person or group that does, or is seeking to do business with the Corporation without prior written approval of the President of Hyatt or the President of Hyatt Hotels Corporation. The foregoing shall not prohibit the acceptance of Christmas gifts (not in cash, bonds, or similar items) of nominal value (generally not exceeding $150.00) where the giving and accepting of such gifts are a normal practice in the business involved and the same is known to and approved by the employee's supervisor. No employees shall accept anything of value in exchange for referral of third parties to any such person, organization or group.

8. Entertainment of Customers, Suppliers, Employees and Business Associates

It is recognized that reasonable and proper entertainment of selected customers, suppliers, prospective employees and business associates, is, at times, in the best interest of the Corporation and is generally proper. However, such entertainment must at all times be in accordance with all applicable laws and regulations and in accordance with the approvals and reporting procedures established by the Corporation. It is further recognized that the furnishing of nominal gifts or the furnishing of corporate services or facilities on a complimentary basis are often in the best interests of the Corporation and are reasonable and proper. However, employees of the Corporation may furnish gifts, services or facilities at company expense, only if the same shall meet all of the following conditions:

a) Gifts in the form of cash, bonds (or similar items) shall not be given regardless of amount except for annual holiday gifts and the like where individual gifts do not exceed $150.00 per year;

b) The furnishing of gifts, services, or facilities are in accord with normally accepted business practices, and comply with the policies of the organization;

c) The practice would be considered reasonable and in accord with generally accepted ethical practices in all governing jurisdictions;

d) The subsequent public disclosure of all facts would not be embarrassing to the Corporation;

e) The practice must be in accordance with all applicable laws and regulations.

9. Use and Disclosure of Company Assets

No undisclosed fund or asset of the Corporation shall be established for any purpose.

10. Accurate Reporting of Financial Statements

No false, artificial or misstated entry shall be made in any of the books, records or financial statements of the Corporation for any reason, and no employee shall engage in any arrangement that results in such prohibited act. All entries on the books and records of the Corporation shall reflect the real nature or purpose of the transaction reported, and no corporate funds, assets, services or facilities shall be used with the intention or understanding that such use, in whole or in part, is for any purpose other than that described by the documents supporting the use in question. In addition, no one should knowingly supply false or artificial or misstated information in any non-financial record of the company.

11. Ownership Interest in Competing Businesses

No employee or member of his or her immediate family who has a key position at Hyatt shall be engaged in or shall have any ownership interest in any firm or business which is in competition with or does business with Hyatt, directly or indirectly, or is otherwise substantially engaged in the business of travel and entertainment.

12. Ownership of Materials, Techniques, Manuals, Systems, Programs, or Information

Training materials, techniques operating manuals, data processing systems, programs, procedures, data-bases, sales and marketing information, marketing strategies, financial information, personnel information, discoveries and inventions including processes, data, lists, systems, products, training materials, operating manuals, and other matters conceived or put into practice while an employee works for Hyatt are the property of Hyatt and not the employee. In addition, this information is not common public knowledge and is therefore considered "Confidential Information." Unauthorized use or disclosure of Confidential Information to a third party may cause irreparable harm to Hyatt. By executing this Disclosure Statement, the employee agrees to maintain the confidentiality of such proprietary information during the period of his/her employment and thereafter. In addition, upon breach of this condition of employment, the employee agrees that he/she shall forfeit any claim that he/she might have to incentive-type compensation of any kind upon such employee's termination from Hyatt. All Hyatt materials and possessions relating to any Confidential Information must be promptly returned upon termination from Hyatt.

Figure 1.3 (Continued)

13. Statements to Auditors

No employee shall make a false or misleading statement to the Corporation's independent auditors or internal auditors, nor shall any employee conceal or fail to reveal any information necessary to make the statements made to such auditors not misleading. In addition, no employee shall make a false or misleading statement to any investigator or other third party representative hired by the Company to investigate any internal or external complaint or business discrepancy.

14. Reporting Requirements and Procedures

Any employee obtaining information of knowledge of any violation of any of the foregoing prohibitions shall promptly report such matter to Hyatt's General Counsel.

15. Policy Questions

Any employee, who has any question regarding the interpretation of or compliance with this policy statement, should discuss the matter with his superior and/or Hyatt's General Counsel.

16. Disciplinary Action

Any employee participating in any violation of this policy statement shall be subject to appropriate disciplinary action.

17. Approval

Any question relating to specific provisions of this policy or any requests for advance-approval decisions with respect to this policy or representations concerning the establishment of funds should be directed to the attention of Hyatt's General Counsel.

Discrimination

Hyatt is committed to providing a work environment that is free of discrimination. In keeping with this commitment, we maintain a strict policy prohibiting unlawful harassment, including sexual harassment. This policy applies to all employees of Hyatt, including supervisors and nonsupervisory employees. It prohibits harassment in any form, including verbal and physical harassment.

Sexual harassment is a behavior which undermines the integrity of the employment relationship. All employees must be allowed to work in an environment free form unsolicited and unwelcomed sexual overtures. Sexual harassment does not refer occasional compliments. It refers to behavior which is not welcomed, which is personally offensive, which reduces morale, and which therefore interferes with employee effectiveness.

Sexual harassment may include actions such as:

- Unwelcomed or unwanted sexual advances. This could include any form of physical contact.
- Requests or demands for sexual favors. This could include subtle or blatant expectations. It also includes pressure or requests for any type of sexual favor accompanied by an implied or stated promise of preferential treatment or negative consequences concerning any aspect of one's employment status.
- Verbal abuse. Conversation that is sexually oriented and that may be expected to be unacceptable to another individual. This could include inappropriate comments about an individual's body or appearance where such comments go beyond a mere compliment; telling "dirty jokes" that may be expected to be offensive; or any other tasteless, sexually oriented comments, innuendoes or actions that offend others.
- Engaging in any type of sexually oriented conduct that interferes with another's work performance or the work environment. This includes extending unwanted sexual attention to someone.
- Creating a work environment that is intimidating, hostile or offensive because of sexually oriented conversation, suggestions, requests, demands, physical contacts or attention.

Normal, pleasant, courteous, mutually respectful and non-coercive interaction between employees is not considered to be sexual harassment. However, sexual harassment is an insidious practice which demeans individuals being treated in such a manner. Hyatt will not tolerate sexual harassment of its employees by anyone—supervisors, employees, clients and/or customers.

Employees who violate this policy are subject to termination. If you observe conduct which you believe is sexual harassment, or if you feel you have been the victim of sexual harassment, please advise you General Manager or Director of Human Resources or Divisional Director of Human Resources.

Figure 1.3 (*Continued*)

Employee Relations

Hyatt greatly appreciates the talent and dedication of employees. As thanks for your commitment, it is our daily practice to treat employees with dignity and respect. Hyatt's employee relations philosophy is extended by the following:

• Competitive wages and benefits
• A clean, pleasant and safe work environment
• A well-trained and knowledgeable management team to assure high quality supervision

We do not discriminate on the basis of race, color, creed, sex, national origin, age or handicap, or any other group protected by law.

To satisfy the diverse needs of our customers, we must function as a team whose goal is to provide our guests with the highest quality of service. As part of our teamwork philosophy, we have a policy of open communication at all times. We feel that it is the best way to effectively deal with the daily challenges and opportunities of our business.

I have read and understand this entire document containing the Hyatt Employee Relations Policy, Discrimination Policy and Corporate Ethics Policy Statement.

I understand that I am responsible as an employee to abide fully with all information contained herein.

If, at any time during my employment, I have a question about Hyatt's Ethics Policy or need to disclose knowledge of a violation or request an approval or waiver, I will promptly notify my General Manager.

Print Name

Signature

Title

Company Location

Date   Social Security Number

Questions, Conflicts of Interest, Requests for Approval or Waivers

---

Figure 1.3 (*Continued*)

Notice that in both the CMAA's code of ethics and in Hyatt's corporate policy, reference is made to the importance of following the law. Laws do not exist, however, to cover every situation that future hospitality managers will encounter. Society's view of acceptable behavior, as well as of specific laws, is constantly changing. Ethical behavior, however, is always important to the successful guidance of responsible and profitable hospitality organizations.

At this point in the remainder of the book—Chapters 2 through 13—there are summaries of actual legal cases involving some component of the hospitality industry and the area of the law that is discussed in the chapter.

There are several ways that you can access the full cases:

1. Go to www.HospitalityLawyer.com and click on Resources, then Academics, then Referenced Cases; then search by case name.

2. Go to the John Wiley & Sons, Inc. (the publisher of this book) website, at www.wiley.com/college/Barth.

3. If you have access to Lexis/Nexus, an online research tool, search for the cases there.

4. If you have access to a law library, ask the librarian for assistance in locating a hard copy of the case.

5. Search other websites such as www.Findlaw.com to see if they host it.

As a manager, you will be called on to make many decisions that have legal consequences. It is unrealistic to expect a manager to know all of the laws that could potentially impact his or her operation. Because litigation is prolific in the hospitality industry and laws change frequently, it is imperative that you develop and practice a management philosophy of prevention, such as STEM.

Just because a law does not prohibit a particular activity does not make it the right thing to do. Accordingly, you should also follow a process that will assist you in determining the ethical implications of a decision, as well as the legal implications, such as the one described in the chapter.

WHAT DID YOU LEARN IN THIS CHAPTER?

After you have studied this chapter, you should be prepared to:

RAPID REVIEW

1. Prepare a five-minute training session for your staff that emphasizes the importance of preventing, rather than reacting to, legal liability. Give an example of a situation where this might arise.

2. Give an example, other than the one mentioned in the text, of a recent change in federal, state, or local law that has impacted the hospitality industry. Explain why you believe the law was enacted and whether you believe it was good legislation.

3. Give a hospitality example of the importance that "selection" makes in the STEM process.

4. Give a hospitality example of the importance of "teaching" in the STEM process.

5. Give a hospitality example of the importance of "education" in the STEM process.

6. Give a hospitality example of the importance of "managing" in the STEM process.

7. A vendor has agreed to clean your hotel carpets at a very competitive price. In a telephone conversation with you, the vendor states that if it gets the contract, members of its staff will "do your home carpets once a year" as a thank you. Apply the seven criteria for ethical behavior to this situation.

8. Using the World Wide Web, locate a state law of any type that relates to business operations. Use your search engine to help. Keywords to use include: "state," "laws," and "business." Describe the law in a one-paragraph essay.

Draft a one-page code of conduct for an independent restaurant with 50 employees. Be prepared to justify your document to the rest of the class.

TEAM ACTIVITY

CHAPTER 2

GOVERNMENT AGENCIES THAT IMPACT THE HOSPITALITY INDUSTRY

2.1 FEDERAL REGULATORY AND ADMINISTRATIVE AGENCIES

Internal Revenue Service (IRS)

Occupational Safety and Health Administration (OSHA)

Environmental Protection Agency (EPA)

Food and Drug Administration (FDA)

Equal Employment Opportunity Commission (EEOC)

Bureau of Alcohol, Tobacco, Firearms and Explosives (ATF)

Department of Labor (DOL)

Department of Justice (DOJ)

U.S. Citizenship and Immigration Services (USCIS)

2.2 STATE REGULATORY AND ADMINISTRATIVE AGENCIES

Employment Security Agency

Alcoholic Beverage Commission (ABC)

Treasury Department/Controller

Attorney General

Public Health Department

Department of Transportation

2.3 LOCAL REGULATORY AND ADMINISTRATIVE AGENCIES

Health and Sanitation

Building and Zoning

Courts and Garnishment

Historical Preservation

Fire Department

Law Enforcement

Tax Assessor/Collector

"TRISHA SANGUS HERE, how can I help you?" Trisha asked as she picked up the telephone in her kitchen. It was a Saturday, one of her days off.

Lance Dani, front office supervisor at the hotel, was on the other end of the line. "Ms. Sangus, I'm really sorry to call you at home, but we have a problem at the front desk. It's Coach Keedy from Northern University. He's ready to check out."

Trisha liked Coach Keedy. His team competed against the local university twice a year, and Trisha considered herself fortunate to have acquired his business. Despite the fact that he brought a large number of energetic college students to her hotel each time he arrived, the students were generally well mannered and caused no difficulty. She certainly welcomed the weekend business they brought to town. Coach Keedy's team had lost the night before, and she knew when that happened, he would take it hard. It tended to be a bit unpleasant for everyone the next day.

"What seems to be the problem?" Trisha inquired.

"Well," Lance replied excitedly, "the coach is refusing to pay his entire bill. He says that, as a nonprofit organization, his college is tax-exempt, and he won't pay the sales tax or the local occupancy tax on his rooms. He's very upset. I asked him for a tax-exemption certificate, but he doesn't have any documentation proving his tax-exempt status. He said any fool would know a college is tax-exempt. Those were his exact words."

I was afraid this might happen, thought Trisha. In the past, her hotel had billed Coach Keedy's school directly for any room charges incurred when the team stayed at the hotel. However, the school recently changed its billing policy. Now, the coaches were expected to pay a team's hotel bill out of their own pockets, then seek reimbursement from the school. While she was sure that the new policy had some financial merit for the school, it was a change that Trisha felt had some distinct operational disadvantages, and this was one of them. When the hotel controller's office billed the school directly, the complex issue of taxation was handled smoothly. The accountants for both the hotel and the school knew the intricacies of tax-exempt status. Dealing with customers across the front desk was another matter.

"How does he want to pay for the charges?" asked Trisha.

"With a personal check," replied Lance. "But he asked me to find a copy of the school's federal tax-exemption document."

Trisha knew that the college where Coach Keedy worked had submitted a federal identification number authorizing a tax exemption. The hotel controller's office had the document on file.

"Okay," said Trisha, "we know the coach represents a tax-exempt institution, and we do have his federal ID number on file, but by law, we're not allowed to deduct the tax if he pays with a personal check. Charge him the tax, just as the regulations require us to do. Explain that you talked to me, and I authorized it. If he wants a further explanation, call me back and I will talk to him and explain why. I also think it would be a good idea for you and me to get together tomorrow to review federal tax-exemption status, state taxes, and local option taxes, such as the occupancy tax. I think I can clear up some misunderstandings you seem to have. Remember, call me back if you have more trouble. See you tomorrow."

"Okay, Ms. Sangus, goodbye," Lance replied as he

slowly hung up the telephone and stepped out of his office to explain the situation to the coach. Lance had a pretty good idea that, despite his best efforts, the coach would still want to talk to his boss. He also had a good idea that tomorrow's meeting with Ms. Sangus would be one in which note taking would be required.

IN THIS CHAPTER, YOU WILL LEARN:

1. How federal governmental agencies are involved in regulating the hospitality industry.
2. How to analyze the various roles of state governmental agencies that regulate the hospitality industry.
3. How to identify local governmental agencies involved in regulating the hospitality industry.
4. How to recognize those national and international agencies and departments charged with monitoring and regulating the travel industry.
5. How to manage conflicting regulations.
6. How to properly respond to an official inquiry or complaint from a regulatory entity.
7. How to keep abreast of regulatory changes.

2.1 FEDERAL REGULATORY AND ADMINISTRATIVE AGENCIES

The hospitality industry is regulated by a variety of federal, state, and local governmental entities. Hospitality managers must interact with these agencies in a variety of different ways, and observe all applicable procedures and regulations established by government. Managers must fill out forms and paperwork, obtain operating licenses, maintain their property to specified codes and standards, provide a safe working environment, and open up their facilities for periodic inspection. The purpose of this chapter is to help you understand the scope of the regulatory process and be able to respond to questions from these regulatory agencies in a way that is both legally correct and sound from a business perspective.

With thousands of federal, state, and local agencies, departments, offices, and individuals regulating business today, it is simply not possible for a hospitality manager to be knowledgeable about all the requirements that may apply to his or her operation. It *is* possible, however, to take these four actions:

1. Be aware of the major entities responsible for regulation.
2. Understand how to resolve conflicting regulations.
3. Be aware of the process for responding to an inquiry or complaint from a regulatory entity.
4. Stay abreast of changes in regulations that affect your segment of the industry.

Internal Revenue Service (IRS)

The Internal Revenue Service (www.irs.gov) is a division of the United States Department of Treasury. The stated mission of the IRS is to "Provide America's taxpayers top-quality service by helping them understand and meet their tax responsibilities, and by applying the tax law with integrity and fairness to all." Although it is unlikely that the agency responsible for collecting taxes will be popular in any country, the right of the IRS to charge an individual with a criminal act makes it deserving of a manager's thoughtful attention.

In the hospitality industry, managers perform two separate roles when interacting with the IRS. A manager is both a taxpayer to the federal government (by paying income tax on the profits of a business) and a tax collector for the federal government (by withholding individual employee taxes on income). The IRS requires businesses to:

■ File quarterly income tax returns and make payments on the profits earned from business operations (Form 941). Taxes must be filed on or before the last day of the month following the end of each calendar quarter.

■ File an Income and Tax Statement with the Social Security Administration on or before the last day of February (Form W-3).

■ Withhold income taxes from the wages of all employees (as specified in Circular E). Withheld employee taxes are deposited with the IRS at regular intervals (Form 8109). Employee withholding taxes must be paid in one of three ways:

1. *Quarterly*, if the total amount of withheld tax for the period is less than $500;

2. *Once a month*, if the total amount of withheld tax is between $500 and $3,000; *or*

3. *Within three working days* of a payroll issuance, if the withheld amount is greater than $3,000.

■ Report all employee income earned as tips (Form 8027), and withhold taxes on the tipped income.

■ Record the value of meals charged to employees when the meals are considered a portion of an employee's income.

■ Record all payments to independent contractors, and file any forms listing those payments (Forms 1096 and 1099).

■ Furnish a record of withheld taxes to all employees on or before January 31 (Form W-2) and maintain copies of this record for four years.

The IRS ensures that businesses pay their taxes through periodic examinations of their financial accounts and tax records. These examinations are called audits. A hospitality manager must respond if the IRS notifies him or her of a forthcoming audit. The manager should also consult a certified public accountant (CPA) or an attorney that specializes in tax audits as soon as possible to ensure that the appropriate documents are prepared and in order.

It would be an oversimplification to state that federal tax laws are complex—they are hugely complex. As a hospitality manager, you may be responsible for submitting or filing the taxes owed by a business, so it is important that you understand the role that you play in ensuring your company's compliance with federal tax laws.

For example, the IRS considers tips and gratuities given to employees by guests of the business as taxable income. As such, this income must be reported to the IRS, and taxes, if due, must be paid on that income. In addition, employers are responsible for assisting the IRS in this reporting process by collecting tip-reporting forms from employees and forwarding the information to the IRS.

Figure 2.1 is a copy of IRS Publication 531. This publication explains the regulations related to an employee's reporting of tipped income. It is a good example of the instructions the IRS gives an individual taxpayer. Note that the IRS explains what is required and how the requirements can be met.

Just as employees have specific responsibilities for reporting tipped income, the employer also has responsibilities imposed by the IRS. For a complete list of a business's tax responsibilities, and to obtain copies of various tax forms, visit the IRS website at www.irs.ustreas.gov and look up employment taxes in the Business tab. Search the Web 2.1 will guide you as you examine these requirements.

IRS Publication 531: Reporting Tip Income

Keeping a Daily Tip Record

Why keep a daily tip record?

You must keep a daily tip record so you can:

- Report your tips accurately to your employer
- Report your tips accurately on your tax return, and
- Prove your tip income if your return is ever questioned.

How to keep a daily tip record.

There are two ways to keep a daily tip record. You can either:

1. Write information about your tips in a tip diary, or
2. Keep copies of documents that show your tips, such as restaurant bills and credit card charge slips.

You should keep your daily tip record with your personal records.

If you keep a tip diary, you can use Form 4070A, Employee's Daily Record of Tips. To get a year's supply of the form, ask the Internal Revenue Service (IRS) or your employer for Publication 1244, Employee's Daily Record of Tips and Report to Employer. Each day, write in the information asked for on the form.

If you do not use Form 4070A, start your records by writing your name, your employer's name, and the name of the business if it is different from your employer's name. Then, each workday, write the date and the following information:

- Cash tips you get directly from customers or from other employees,
- Tips from credit card charge customers that your employer pays you,
- The value of any noncash tips you get, such as tickets, passes, or other items of value,
- The amount of tips you paid out to other employees through tip pools or tip splitting, or other arrangements, and the names of the employees to whom you paid the tips. Do not write in your tip diary the amount of any service charge that your employer adds to a customer's bill and then pays to you and treats as wages. This is part of your wages, not a tip.

Figure 2.1 Reporting tip income.

Search the Web **2.1**

Go online to www.irs.gov.

1. Select: Forms and Publications.

2. Select: Publication Number.

3. Select: Publication 15: Circular E, Employers Tax Guide.

Read the portion of Publication 15 that refers to an employer's responsibilities related to the reporting of tip income by employers.

Occupational Safety and Health Administration (OSHA)

OSHA (www.osha.gov) is an agency in the Department of Labor. It was created in 1970 after the passage of the Occupation Safety and Health Act. The purpose of the act was "to assure, so far as possible, every working man and woman in the nation safe and healthful working conditions." Despite criticism from many in business, OSHA has taken an aggressive role in protecting workers' rights.

All businesses, including hospitality operations, must comply with the extensive safety practices, equipment specifications, and employee communication procedures mandated by OSHA. Specifically, businesses are required to:

■ Provide a safe workplace for employees by maintaining facilities and providing protective clothing, in accordance with OSHA safety and health standards (these standards will vary for different types of workplace environments).

■ Purchase equipment that meets OSHA specifications of health and safety.

■ Establish safety checklists and training programs for employees, especially for those who will operate equipment that may cause injury.

■ Report to OSHA within 48 hours any workplace accidents that result in a fatality or require the hospitalization of five or more employees.

■ Maintain a record of work-related injuries or illnesses (OSHA 200 Log), and file that record once a year. Employers are also required to post an annual summary of the prior year's injuries and illnesses.

■ Schedule at least one employee trained in first aid on each work shift.

■ Display OSHA notices on employee rights and safety in appropriate languages, in places where the notices can be easily read.

■ Provide all employees with access to information on any toxic or harmful substances used in the workplace, and keep records certifying that employees have reviewed the information.

■ Offer hepatitis B vaccinations for employees who may have come into contact with blood or body fluids.

OSHA monitors workplace safety with a large staff of inspectors called compliance officers. Compliance officers visit workplaces during regular business hours and perform unannounced inspections to ensure that employers are operating in compliance with all OSHA health and safety regulations. In addition, compliance officers are required to investigate any complaints of unsafe business practices. Figure 2.2 is an

---

Section 8, Title: INSPECTIONS, INVESTIGATIONS, AND RECORDKEEPING

In order to carry out the purposes of this Act, the Secretary, upon presenting appropriate credentials to the owner, operator, or agent in charge, is authorized:

(1) to enter without delay and at reasonable times any factory, plant, establishment, construction site, or other area, workplace or environment where work is performed by an employee of an employer; and

(2) to inspect and investigate during regular working hours and at other reasonable times, and within reasonable limits and in a reasonable manner, any such place of employment and all pertinent conditions, structures, machines, apparatus, devices, equipment, and materials therein, and to question privately any such employer, owner, operator, agent or employee.

Figure 2.2 OSHA inspection provisions.

excerpt of the Occupational Health and Safety Act that gives the agency authority to enter a business to investigate worker safety.

Hospitality managers have the right to accompany OSHA compliance officers during an inspection, and managers should make it a point of doing so, for two reasons. First, the manager may be able to answer questions or clarify procedures for the compliance officer; and second, the manager should know what transpired during the inspection. Afterward, the manager should discuss the results of the inspection with the compliance officer and request a copy of any inspection reports filed. Generally, inspections are not announced, although the compliance officer must state a specific reason for the inspection.

The penalties for violating OSHA regulations can be severe and costly. Figure 2.3 details the penalties OSHA can assess against a business. Because of the stringent penalties for noncompliance, it is important that hospitality managers ensure that their workplace is safe. As stressed in this book several times, the best way to avoid accidents, lawsuits, and penalties is to adopt a philosophy of preventative management. Where worker safety is concerned, this may be as simple as providing information or as complex as developing an employee-training program.

One example of the type of information OSHA requires to be posted or provided is the material safety data sheet (MSDS). An MSDS is a manufacturer's statement

---

OSHA Act of 1970

Section Title: Penalties

Section Number: 17

(a) Any employer who willfully or repeatedly violates the requirements of section 5 of this Act, any standard, rule, or order promulgated pursuant to section 6 of this Act, or regulations prescribed pursuant to this Act, may be assessed a civil penalty of not more than $70,000 for each violation, but not less than $5,000 for each willful violation.

(b) Any employer who has received a citation for a serious violation of the requirements of section 5 of this Act, of any standard, rule, or order promulgated pursuant to section 6 of this Act, or of any regulations prescribed pursuant to this Act, shall be assessed a civil penalty of up to $7,000 for each such violation.

(c) Any employer who has received a citation for a violation of the requirements of section 5 of this Act, of any standard, rule, or order promulgated pursuant to section 6 of this Act, or of regulations prescribed pursuant to this Act, and such violation is specifically determined not to be of a serious nature, may be assessed a civil penalty of up to $7,000 for each violation.

(d) Any employer who fails to correct a violation for which a citation has been issued under section 9(a) within the period permitted for its correction (which period shall not begin to run until the date of the final order of the Commission in the case of any review proceeding under section 10 initiated by the employer in good faith and not solely for delay or avoidance of penalties), may be assessed a civil penalty of not more than $7,000 for each day during which such failure or violation continues.

(e) Any employer who willfully violates any standard, rule, or order promulgated pursuant to section 6 of this Act, or of any regulations prescribed pursuant to this Act, and that violation caused death to any employee, shall, upon conviction, be punished by a fine of not more than $10,000 or by imprisonment for not more than six months, or by both; except that if the conviction is for a violation committed after a first conviction of such person, punishment shall be by a fine of not more than $20,000 or by imprisonment for not more than one year, or by both.

(f) Any person who gives advance notice of any inspection to be conducted under this Act, without authority from the Secretary or his designees, shall, upon conviction, be punished by a fine of not more than $1,000 or by imprisonment for not more than six months, or by both.

(g) Whoever knowingly makes any false statement, representation, or certification in any application, record, report, plan, or other document filed or required to be maintained pursuant to this Act shall, upon conviction, be punished by a fine of not more than $10,000, or by imprisonment for not more than six months, or by both.

Figure 2.3 OSHA penalties for noncompliance.

(h) (1) Section 1114 of title 18, United States Code, is hereby amended by striking out "designated by the Secretary of Health, Education, and Welfare to conduct investigations, or inspections under the Federal Food, Drug, and Cosmetic Act" and inserting in lieu thereof "or of the Department of Labor assigned to perform investigative, inspection, or law enforcement functions."

(2) Notwithstanding the provisions of sections 1111 and 1114 of title 18, United States Code, whoever, in violation of the provisions of section 1114 of such title, kills a person while engaged in or on account of the performance of investigative, inspection, or law enforcement functions added to such section 1114 by paragraph (1) of this subsection, and who would otherwise be subject to the penalty provisions of such section 1111, shall be punished by imprisonment for any term of years or for life.

(i) Any employer who violates any of the posting requirements, as prescribed under the provisions of this Act, shall be assessed a civil penalty of up to $7,000 for each violation.

(j) The Commission shall have authority to assess all civil penalties provided in this section, giving due consideration to the appropriateness of the penalty with respect to the size of the business of the employer being charged, the gravity of the violation, the good faith of the employer, and the history of previous violations.

(k) For purposes of this section, a serious violation shall be deemed to exist in a place of employment if there is a substantial probability that death or serious physical harm could result from a condition which exists, or from one or more practices, means, methods, operations, or processes which have been adopted or are in use, in such place of employment unless the employer did not, and could not with the exercise of reasonable diligence, know of the presence of the violation.

(l) Civil penalties owed under this Act shall be paid to the Secretary for deposit into the Treasury of the United States and shall accrue to the United States and may be recovered in a civil action in the name of the United States brought in the United States district court for the district where the violation is alleged to have occurred or where the employer has its principal office.

Figure 2.3 (Continued)

>> ANALYZE THE SITUATION 2.1

CARLOS MAGANA WAS A Spanish-speaking custodian working in a health-care facility kitchen. Bert LaColle was the new food and beverage director. Mr. LaColle instructed Mr. Magana to clean the grout between the red quarry kitchen tile with a powerful cleaner that Mr. LaColle had purchased from a chemical cleaning supply vendor. Mr. LaColle, who did not speak Spanish, demonstrated to Mr. Magana how he should pour the chemical directly from the bottle to the grout, then brush the grout with a wire brush until it was white.

Because the cleaner was so strong, and because Mr. Magana did not wear protective gloves, his hands were seriously irritated by the chemicals in the cleaner. In an effort to lessen the irritation to his hands, Mr. Magana decided to dilute the chemical. He added water to the bottle of cleaner, not realizing that the addition of water would cause toxic fumes. Mr. Magana inhaled the fumes while he continued cleaning, and later suffered serious lung damage as a result.

Mr. LaColle was subsequently contacted by OSHA, which cited and fined the facility for an MSDS violation. Mr. LaColle maintained that MSDS statements, including the one for the cleaner in question, were in fact available for inspection by employees.

1. Did the facility fulfill its obligation to provide a safe working environment for Mr. Magana?

2. What should Mr. LaColle have done to avoid an OSHA violation?

detailing the potential hazards and proper methods of using a chemical or toxic substance. The MSDS is intended to inform workers about the hazards of the materials they work with so that they can protect themselves and respond to emergency situations. The law states that employees must have access to MSDSs and be assisted in reading and understanding them. OSHA inspectors are responsible for ensuring that MSDSs are placed in areas accessible to workers.

An OSHA Hazard Communication provides a guide for what a standard MSDS should include:[1]

- The material's identity—including its chemical and common names
- Hazardous ingredients (even in parts as small as 1 percent)
- Cancer-causing ingredients (even in parts as small as 0.1 percent)
- A list of physical and chemical hazards (stability, reactivity) and characteristics (flammable, explosive, corrosive, etc.)
- A list of health hazards, including:
  - Acute effects, such as burns or unconsciousness, which occur immediately; and chronic effects such as allergic sensitization, skin problems, or respiratory disease, which build up over a period of time
  - If the material is a known carcinogen
  - Limits to which a worker can be exposed, specific target organs likely to sustain damage, and medical problems that can be aggravated by exposure
  - Precautions and safety equipment and emergency and first aid procedures
- Specific firefighting information
- Precautions for safe handling and use, including personal hygiene
- The identity of the organization responsible for creating the MSDS, date of issue, and emergency phone number

Figure 2.4 is an excerpt example of an MSDS. The specific product detailed is Jet Dry, a trademarked item distributed by Economics Laboratories for use in commercial dishwashers. The point here is that all hospitality managers must be aware of the sometimes very specific requirements that federal agencies place on them. The requirements can be numerous, and they change frequently. One way to stay current with your obligations as an operator is to log on to OSHA's website (www.osha.gov) and click on What's New.

Environmental Protection Agency (EPA)

The EPA (www.epa.gov) is an independent agency of the federal government. Established in 1970, the EPA's mission is to "permit coordinated and effective government action on behalf of the environment."[2] In the hospitality industry, the EPA serves as a regulator of pesticides, as well as water and air pollution. Care must be taken when discharging waste, particularly toxic waste such as pesticides or cleaning chemicals from laundry areas. In 1996, new amendments were added to the Safe Drinking Water Act of 1974, which is a federal law that empowers the EPA to set standards for drinking water quality and to oversee the states, towns, and water suppliers that implement and enforce those standards. The EPA also monitors indoor air-quality issues (such as smoking in commercial buildings).

Many EPA directives are carried out or implemented by state and local governments, such as state recycling laws and municipal ordinances for trash disposal. Thus,

---

[1]OSHA, *Inspection Procedures for the Hazard Communication Standard*, OSHA CPL 02-02-038 [CPL 2-2.38D], March 20, 1998, Appendix D, "Guide for Reviewing MSDS Completeness," www.osha.gov/pls/oshaweb/owadisp.show_document?p_table=DIRECTIVES&p_id=1551.
[2]U.S. Environmental Protection Agency, *Environmental Merit Awards 2011*, www.epa.gov/region1/ra/ema/pdfs/EMA2011_Program.pdf, p. 9. Accessed July 5, 2011.

ECONOMICS LABORATORY—JET DRY (934984)
MATERIAL SAFETY DATA SHEET

FSC: 6850. NIIN: 00F000893

Manufacturer's CAGE: 85884

Part No. Indicator: A

Part Number/Trade Name: JET DRY (934984)

General Information
Company's Name: ECONOMICS LABORATORY, INC.
Company's Emergency Ph #: (612) 293-2233
Record No. For Safety Entry: 001
Tot Safety Entries This Stk#: 001
Date MSDS Prepared: 01JAN85
Safety Data Review Date: 22JAN85
MSDS Serial Number: BBHKT

Ingredients/Identity Information
Proprietary: YES
Ingredient: PROPRIETARY
Ingredient Sequence Number: 01

Physical/Chemical Characteristics
Appearance and Odor: CLEAR GREEN LIQUID--NO SPECIFIC ODOR.
Boiling Point: 212F
Specific Gravity: 1.022
Solubility in Water: COMPLETE
Percent Volatiles by Volume: 90%

Fire and Explosion Hazard Data
Flash Point: NON-FLAMMABLE
Extinguishing Media: ALL RECOGNIZED METHODS ARE ACCEPTABLE.
Reactivity Data
Stability: YES
Hazardous Decomp Products: OXIDES OF CARBON
Hazardous Poly Occur: NO

Health Hazard Data

Signs/Symptoms of Overexp: MAY CAUSE MINOR EYE IRRITATION, BURNING SENSATION.

Emergency/First Aid Proc: FLUSH EYES WITH PLENTY OF WATER. INGESTION: DO NOT INDUCE VOMITING. DRINK LARGE QUANTITIES OF WATER OR MILK.

Precautions for Safe Handling and Use

Steps if Matl Released/Spill: MOP UP SPILL. WASH AREA WITH WATER.

Waste Disposal Method: CONSULT LOCAL REGULATIONS.

Precautions—Handling/Storing: KEEP FROM FREEZING.

Label Emergency Number: (612) 293-2233

Figure 2.4 An MSDS for Jet Dry.

while you, as a hospitality manager, may have little contact with the federal agency, it is important to be fully aware of your state and local laws in these areas.

Food and Drug Administration (FDA)

The FDA (www.fda.gov) plays an important role in the hospitality industry. It is responsible for ensuring the proper labeling of food and the safety of food. As a food-service manager, you will encounter the work of the FDA whenever you purchase food that has a mandatory FDA nutrition label. In addition, the FDA's Model Food Service Sanitation Ordinance is used by many state and community health departments as a basis for their own foodservice inspection programs. You can find the 2009 FDA Ordinance online at:

- www.fda.gov/Food/FoodSafety/RetailFoodProtection/FoodCode/ FoodCode2009/

Or, if you wish to view a state-adopted Food Service Sanitation Ordinance, you can view the ordinance recently adopted by Montgomery County at:

- www.montgomeryco.com/health/Environmental%20Health/ Food%20Service%20Sanitation%20Ordinance.pdf

Foodservice operators also need to be aware of the FDA's precise definitions governing the use of nutritional and health-related terms. A restaurant that prints phrases such as "low-calorie," "light," or "cholesterol-free" in their menus must make sure that the recipes for those dishes meet the FDA's requirements for those statements. These and other menu-labeling requirements will be discussed more fully in Chapter 12, "Your Responsibilities When Serving Food and Beverages."

Equal Employment Opportunity Commission (EEOC)

The Equal Employment Opportunity Commission was established by Title VII of the Civil Rights Act of 1964 and went into effect on July 2, 1965. Essentially, this agency enforces laws against discrimination in employment. Figure 2.5 lists the specific laws that are enforced by the EEOC. The following general areas fall under the jurisdiction of the EEOC:

- Sexual harassment
- Race/color discrimination
- Age discrimination
- National origin discrimination
- Pregnancy discrimination

Title VII of the Civil Rights Act

Equal Pay Act of 1963

Age Discrimination in Employment Act of 1967 (ADEA)

Rehabilitation Act of 1973, Sections 501 and 505

Titles I and V of the Americans with Disabilities Act of 1990 (ADA)

Civil Rights Act of 1991

Figure 2.5 Laws enforced by the Equal Employment Opportunity Commission.

■ Religious discrimination

■ Portions of the Americans with Disabilities Act

Some of these areas will be discussed in detail in Chapter 8, "Legally Managing Employees." The impact of the EEOC on the daily tasks of the hospitality manager is obvious. Consider, for example, the hotel manager who seeks to schedule a Christian to work on Christmas Day. The hotel is, of course, open. The question that might arise is whether the needs of the manager, who must staff the hotel, should take precedence over those of the worker, who desires a day off on the basis of his or her religious convictions.

Title VII of the Civil Rights Act of 1964 prohibits employers from discriminating against individuals because of their religious beliefs when hiring and firing. The act also requires employers to reasonably accommodate the religious practices of an employee or prospective employee, unless doing so would create an undue hardship upon the employer. Flexible scheduling, voluntary substitutions or swaps, job reassignments, and lateral transfers are examples of accommodating an employee's religious beliefs. The question of whether a manager could "reasonably" accommodate the request of a Christian worker to be off on Christmas Day is complex. The point to be remembered, however, is that managers are not free to act in any manner they desire, but the federal government, through the requirements of the EEOC, also plays a role in the actions of management.

The EEOC also investigates complaints by employees who think they have been discriminated against. Businesses that are found to have discriminated against employees can be ordered to compensate the employee(s) for damages, such as lost wages, attorney fees, and punitive damages.

Bureau of Alcohol, Tobacco, Firearms and Explosives (ATF)

The Bureau of Alcohol, Tobacco, Firearms and Explosives (www.atf.gov) is responsible for enforcing all federal laws and regulations governing the manufacture and sale of alcohol, tobacco, firearms, and explosives; as well as for investigating incidents of arson. Formerly, the entire ATF was housed within the U.S. Department of Treasury, just as the IRS is, because it enforces the payment of federal taxes on the production of alcohol and the sale of alcoholic beverages. However, on January 24, 2003, pursuant to the creation of the Department of Homeland Security, the law enforcement functions of the ATF were transferred to the Department of Justice and the tax and trade functions of the ATF stayed with the Treasury Department under the newly created Alcohol and Tobacco Tax and Trade Bureau (www.ttb.gov).

Hospitality managers will interact with the ATF in the following ways:

■ Retail sellers of alcohol—including bars, restaurants, and hotels—must pay a special federal liquor tax each year (IRS Form 11, Special Tax Return). They will receive a Special Tax Stamp showing proof the tax was paid and must keep this stamp on the premises, available for inspection.

■ Alcohol vendors are not permitted to mix cocktails in advance of a sale and may not reuse emptied liquor bottles to store mixed cocktails.

■ Operators must keep records, invoices, and receipts of all alcohol purchased.

■ Operators must properly dispose of empty liquor bottles and may not reuse or sell them.

In its publication "P-5170.2, Federal Liquor Laws and Regulations for Retail Dealers," published in 1995, the ATF specifically dictates the way liquor retailers should handle empty liquor bottles. An excerpt from P-5170.2 is presented in

---

P-5170.2

Any retail dealer, or agent or employee of such dealer, who refills any liquor bottle with distilled spirits, or who reuses any liquor bottle by adding distilled spirits or any substance (including water) to the original contents is subject to a fine of not more than $1,000 or imprisonment for not more than 1 year, or both.

Disposition of liquor bottles

The possession of used liquor bottles by any person other than the one who emptied the contents thereof is prohibited, except that this prohibition shall not:

(1) prevent the owner or occupant of any premises on which such bottles have been lawfully emptied from assembling the same on such premises

(i) for delivery to a bottler or importer on specific request for such bottler or importer;

(ii) for the destruction, either on the premises on which the bottles are emptied or elsewhere, including disposition for purposes which will result in the bottles being rendered unusable as bottles; or

(iii) in the case of unusual or distinctive bottles, for disposition as collector's items or for other purposes not involving the packaging of any products for sale;

(2) prevent any person from possessing, offering for sale, or selling such unusual or distinctive bottles for purposes not involving the packaging of any product for sale; or

(3) prevent any person from assembling used liquor bottles for the purpose of recycling or reclaiming the glass or other approved liquor bottle material.

Any person possessing liquor bottles in violation of law or regulations is subject to fine of not more than $1,000, imprisonment for not more than 1 year, or both.

Figure 2.6 Refilling, reusing, and disposing of liquor bottles.

Figure 2.6. Note the severe penalties assessed against businesses that do not comply with this regulation. The ATF enforces these regulations with its own officers, who conduct inspections during an operation's regular hours of business. Additional information on the regulations covering the sale of alcohol is included in Chapter 12, "Your Responsibilities When Serving Food and Beverages."

Department of Labor (DOL)

The U.S. Department of Labor (www.dol.gov) was established in 1913 to "foster, promote, and develop the welfare of the wage earners of the United States, to improve their working conditions, and to advance their opportunities for profitable employment."[3]

Today, the department is charged with preparing the U.S. workforce for new and better jobs, and for ensuring the adequacy of America's workplaces. It is responsible for the administration and enforcement of more than 180 federal laws, which govern the protection of workers' wages, health and safety, employment, and pension rights; equal employment opportunity; job training; unemployment insurance and workers' compensation programs; collective bargaining; and collecting, analyzing, and publishing labor and economic statistics. Following is a brief description of some of the principal federal labor-related regulations most commonly applicable to hospitality businesses.

---

[3]U.S. Department of Labor, "The Organic Act of the Department of Labor," March 4, 1913, www.dol.gov/oasam/programs/history/organact.htm. Accessed July 2011.

Wage and Hours

The Fair Labor Standards Act (FLSA) prescribes standards for wages and overtime pay, which affect most private and public employment. The act is administered by the Wage and Hour Division of the Employment Standards Administration. It requires employers to pay covered employees the federal minimum wage and overtime of one-and-one-half times the regular wage. It restricts the hours that children under 16 can work and forbids their employment in certain jobs deemed too dangerous. This agency also establishes guidelines for tip credits, meal credits, and uniform purchases. In Chapter 8, "Legally Managing Employees," we will look at specific provisions of the FLSA that hospitality managers must keep in mind.

Pensions and Welfare Benefits

The Employee Retirement Income Security Act (ERISA) of 1974 regulates employers who offer pension or welfare benefit plans for their employees. This area of the Labor Department is also responsible for reporting requirements for the continuation of health-care provisions, required under the Comprehensive Omnibus Budget Reconciliation Act of 1985 (COBRA).

Plant Closings and Layoffs

These types of occurrences may be subject to the Worker Adjustment and Retraining Notification Act (WARN). WARN protects employees by requiring early warning of impending layoffs or plant closings. WARN is administered by a special division of the Department of Labor.

Employee Polygraph Protection Act

This law, enacted in 1988, bars most employers under most circumstances from using lie detectors on employees or prospective employees. However, the law does permit employers to request that an employee undertake such a test in connection with any ongoing investigation into an incident that resulted in loss to the employer. Results of the lie detector test are not to be shared with anyone except the examiner, the employer, or those so ordered by the courts.

Family and Medical Leave Act

This law, the FMLA, requires employers with 50 or more employees to grant up to 12 weeks of unpaid, job-related leave to eligible employees for the birth or adoption of a child, or for the serious illness of the employee or a family member. These provisions and others that relate to hiring and managing employees are discussed in Chapter 7, "Legally Selecting Employees," and Chapter 8, "Legally Managing Employees."

It is important to note that other federal agencies besides the Department of Labor also enforce laws and regulations that affect employers. As discussed earlier in this chapter, laws that ensure nondiscrimination in employment are generally enforced by the Equal Employment Opportunity Commission. The Taft-Hartley Act, which regulates a wide range of unionization issues, is enforced by the National Labor Relations Board.

Department of Justice (DOJ)

In the United States, the Department of Justice (www.usdoj.gov) is headed by the U.S. attorney general. Although the position of attorney general has existed since the founding of the republic, it was not until 1870 that a separate Department of Justice was created, bringing together under the authority of the attorney general the activities of U.S. attorneys, U.S. marshals, and others. The Justice Department investigates and prosecutes federal crimes, represents the United States of America in court, manages the federal prisons, and enforces the nation's immigration laws.

The Department of Justice also enforces Title III of the Americans with Disabilities Act (ADA), which states that hospitality operations must remove barriers that can restrict access or the full enjoyment of amenities by people with disabilities. The requirements for complying with this section of the ADA are discussed in Chapter 10, "Your Responsibilities as a Hospitality Operator to Guests."

U.S. Citizenship and Immigration Services (USCIS)

Most hospitality managers will interact with the U.S. Citizenship and Immigration Service through its regulation of illegal immigrants. Formerly, these duties were handled by the Immigration and Naturalization Service (INS) under the purview of the Department of Justice, but on March 1, 2003, pursuant to the Homeland Security Act, the INS was dismantled and separated into three component agencies under the Department of Homeland Security. These agencies are the Immigration and Customs Enforcement (ICE), Customs and Border Protection (CBP), which handle immigration enforcement and border security, and the U.S. Citizenship and Immigration Service (USCIS), which handles the administration of benefit applications. These agencies are important to keep in mind when hiring employees because hospitality managers are required to secure identification documents from all those they hire. This is mandated so that jobs will be given only to those legally able to secure them. The precise method of verifying employment eligibility will be discussed in Chapter 7, "Legally Selecting Employees." Penalties for noncompliance in this area can be severe, so it is a good idea to stay well versed in the applicable regulations.

As you have already noticed, in response to the unfortunate incidents occurring on September 11, 2001, the federal government made sweeping changes to many agencies, combining a number of them under the Department of Homeland Security umbrella. This agency is discussed more thoroughly in Chapter 13, "Legal Responsibilities in Travel and Tourism."

2.2 STATE REGULATORY AND ADMINISTRATIVE AGENCIES

Just as the federal government plays a regulatory role in the hospitality industry, so too do the various state agencies. It is important to understand that the states serve both complementary and distinct regulatory roles. The roles are complementary in that they support and amplify efforts undertaken at the federal level, but they are distinct in that they regulate some areas in which they have sole responsibility. Let's take a brief look at some of the state entities that play a significant regulatory role in the hospitality industry. The administrative structure or specific entity name may vary by state, but the regulatory process will be similar.

It is important to note that state and/or local regulations may affect the actions of hospitality managers more often than federal regulations. Codes and ordinances established at the state or local level can often be very strict, and may require investment in equipment or to pay extra diligence in the operation of a facility. The penalties for violating these laws can be just as severe as those at the federal level.

Employment Security Agency

Each state regulates employment and employee/employer relationships within its borders. Generally, items such as worker-related unemployment benefits, worker safety issues, and injury compensation will fall to the state entity charged with regulating the workplace. In addition, in most states, this entity will also be responsible for areas such as providing employment assistance to both employees and employers.

Consider the case of Virgil Bollinger. The hotel where Virgil works is purchased by a new owner, who states that Virgil's sales manager position is no longer needed. In Virgil's state, an employer's account is not charged for *unemployment benefits* if an employee is let go as a result of staff reductions. However, Virgil believes that his employment has been terminated for other reasons, none of which relate to his work performance. It would be the role of the Employment Security Agency to determine to which, if any, unemployment compensation benefits Virgil is entitled.

Workers' compensation is an area of great concern to most hospitality managers. Worker injuries are expensive, in terms of both money and disruption to the workplace. As a hospitality manager, it is important for you to know and follow the state regulations related to workplace safety, and the method for properly documenting and reporting any work-related injury. In each state, worker safety will usually be monitored by a workers' compensation agency, commission, or subdivision of the employment security agency.

> **LEGALESE**
> **Unemployment benefits:** A benefit paid to an employee who involuntarily loses his or her employment without just cause.

> **LEGALESE**
> **Workers' compensation:** A benefit paid to an employee who suffers a work-related injury or illness.

Alcoholic Beverage Commission (ABC)

Although the sale of alcohol is not a requirement for a foodservice or lodging operation, many facilities do offer them for their guests' enjoyment. The nature of alcohol and its consumption, however, subjects the hospitality manager to intense regulation. Generally, this regulation takes place at both the state and local levels. A state's alcoholic beverage commission (ABC) will be responsible for the following areas of control:

- License issuing
- Permitted hours of sales
- Advertising and promotion policies
- Methods of operation
- Reporting of sales for tax purposes
- Revocation of licenses

As a hospitality manager, failure to abide by the regulations required to sell alcoholic beverages lawfully may subject you to criminal prosecution, as well as a civil proceeding (an administrative hearing) before the regulatory body of your state's ABC. In addition, the enactment of *dram shop act* legislation could make a hospitality manager, or the business itself, liable to guests or third parties and their families should significant violations of the alcohol service regulations result in injury to an intoxicated guest, or to persons harmed by an individual who was illegally served. Simply put, providers of alcoholic beverages can be held responsible for the acts of their intoxicated patrons if those patrons were illegally served. Specific techniques related to the proper selling of alcoholic beverages will be fully discussed in Chapter 12, "Your Responsibilities When Serving Food and Beverages."

States are very careful when granting licenses to sell liquor, and they are generally very aggressive in revoking the licenses of operations that fail to adhere to the state's required procedures for selling alcohol. In most states, license revocation can be the result of any of the following:

- Frequent incidents of fighting, disorderly conduct, or generally creating a public nuisance
- Allowing prostitution or solicitation on the premises

> **LEGALESE**
> **Dram shop acts:** Legislation, passed in a variety of forms and in many states, that imposes liability for the acts of others on those who serve alcohol negligently, recklessly, or illegally.

- Drug and narcotic sales or use
- Illegal adult entertainment, such as outlawed forms of nude dancing
- Failure to maintain required records
- Sale of alcohol to minors

Hospitality operators are also responsible for reporting all sales of alcohol to their state's alcoholic beverage commission (ABC). The ABC will perform random audits to determine the accuracy of the information received. Other enforcement tools used by the ABC are to conduct unannounced inspections of the premises where alcohol is sold and/or to intentionally send minors into an establishment to test whether the operator will serve them.

≫ ANALYZE THE SITUATION 2.2

TRIXIE MITCHELL MANAGED THE Dusty Cellar, a bar near a college campus. She was active in her business community and served on the college's Presidential Advisory Board for Responsible Drinking. All servers and bartenders in her facility were required to undergo a mandatory four-hour alcohol service training program before they began their employment and to take a required refresher course each year. Each server was certified in responsible alcohol service by the national office of Ms. Mitchell's hospitality trade association.

On a busy Friday night during the fall football season, one of Ms. Mitchell's servers approached a table with four female patrons. Since all appeared to be near 21 years old, but well under the 35-year-old limit Ms. Mitchell had established for a mandatory identification (ID) check, the server asked to see a picture ID from each guest.

The server checked each guest's ID—verifying the age, hair color, general likeness, and absence of alterations to the ID card—and then requested—in a practice unique to Dusty's—the mandatory recitation by each patron of the birthday and address printed on the ID. Since all four guests passed their ID checks, the server served the patrons. Each guest had three glasses of wine over a period of 90 minutes.

The next day, Ms. Mitchell was contacted by the state ABC and an attorney for the parents of a teenager whose car was involved in an accident with one of the four patrons served the prior night. It had been established that one of the patrons, whose ID had been professionally altered, was 20 years old, not 21. This patron was involved in the auto accident after she left the bar and drove back to her dorm room. The ABC began an investigation into the sale of alcohol to minors, while the attorney scheduled an appointment with Ms. Mitchell's attorney to discuss a settlement based on the potential liability arising from the dram shop act legislation enacted in Ms. Mitchell's state.

1. Did Ms. Mitchell break the law by serving alcohol to an underage student?

2. Are Ms. Mitchell and her business liable for the acts of the underage drinking if her state has enacted dram shop legislation?

Treasury Department/Controller

A state's treasury department is responsible for the collection of taxes levied by that state. For those in the hospitality industry, this can include liquor taxes, sales taxes, occupancy taxes, as well as a wide array of use taxes.

An excellent example of the diversity displayed by the various states in regard to taxation is the document in Figure 2.7, published in 1997 by the Iowa State University purchasing department for its employees. It demonstrates the importance of a thorough understanding of the laws regarding taxation in the state where you will manage a hospitality facility.

A relatively recent development in the United States has caused an expansion of duties for many state treasury departments. In addition to the collection of taxes, these departments or agencies are often responsible for the regulation of their state's lottery and gaming operations. As this segment of the hospitality industry expands, so too will the regulatory efforts of the various state treasury departments. Typical areas of gaming and lottery regulation by treasury departments include licensing, lottery ticket sales, winnings disbursement, and casino operations. Figure 2.8 is an excellent example of the procedures that treasury regulators can mandate in the operation of gaming facilities. In this document, the Michigan Treasury Department identifies some of the written procedures for money handling that must be filed with the department prior to the granting of a casino license.

Attorney General

The state's attorney general is the chief legal officer of the state. In Chapter 3, "Hospitality Operating Structures," you will learn that one responsibility of the attorney general's office is to specify the franchise information required for disclosure in

---

IOWA STATE UNIVERSITY

Iowa State University (ISU), as a state educational institution, is exempt from paying state sales tax or local option sales tax on goods or services purchased in the state of Iowa. We are required to pay hotel/motel taxes. The states listed below also grant tax-exempt status to Iowa State University for goods or services purchased while in their state . . . (however) a form or copy of a letter is usually required.

Iowa State University is tax-exempt in the following states:*

Colorado, Idaho, Illinois, Indiana, Iowa, Kansas, Kentucky, Michigan, Mississippi, Missouri, New York, North Dakota, Ohio, Pennsylvania, Rhode Island, South Dakota, Texas, Wisconsin.

Goods or services purchased by Iowa State University while in the following states are subject to that state's sales tax. Iowa State University is not tax-exempt in the following states:

Alabama, Nebraska, Arizona, Nevada, Arkansas, New Jersey, California, North Carolina, Connecticut, Oklahoma, District of Columbia, South Carolina, Florida, Tennessee, Georgia, Utah, Louisiana, Vermont, Maine, Virginia, Maryland, Washington, Massachusetts, West Virginia, Minnesota, Wyoming.

The following states do not have a general sales tax:

Alaska, Hawaii, Montana, New Hampshire, New Mexico, Oregon.

Last Updated: Friday, March 6, 1998.

*Delaware did not respond with information regarding tax-exempt status.

Figure 2.7 Tax-exempt notice.

that state. If, for example, an entrepreneur were interested in purchasing a franchise, the attorney general's office would regulate the franchisor and franchisee relationship.

Public Health Department

The public health department is generally responsible for the inspection and licensing of facilities that serve food. This department may be self-standing, but it is often associated with or housed in a state department of agriculture.

DEPARTMENT OF TREASURY, MICHIGAN: GAMING CONTROL BOARD

CASINO GAMING: (By authority conferred on the Michigan Gaming Control Board by section 4 of Initiated Law of 1996, as amended, being § 432.204 of the Michigan Compiled Laws)

PART 9. INTERNAL CONTROL PROCEDURES R 432.1901 Rule 902.

The procedures of the internal control system are designed to ensure all of the following: (a) That assets of the casino licensee are safeguarded.

(b) That the financial records of the casino licensee are accurate and reliable.

(c) That the transactions of the casino licensee are performed only in accordance with the specific or general authorization of this part.

(d) That the transactions are recorded adequately to permit the proper recording of the adjusted gross receipts, fees, and all applicable taxes.

(e) That accountability for assets is maintained in accordance with generally accepted accounting principles.

(f) That only authorized personnel have access to assets.

(g) That recorded accountability for assets is compared with actual assets at reasonable intervals and appropriate action is taken with respect to any discrepancies.

(h) That the functions, duties, and responsibilities are appropriately segregated and performed in accordance with sound practices by competent, qualified personnel and that no employee of the casino licensee is in a position to perpetuate and conceal errors or irregularities in the normal course of the employee's duties.

(i) That gaming is conducted with integrity and in accordance with the act and these rules.

History: 1998 MR 6, Eff. June 26, 1998.R 432.1903 Board approval of internal control system. Rule 903.

(1) A licensee shall describe, in a manner that the board may approve or require, its administrative and accounting procedures in detail in a written system of internal control. A written system of internal controls shall include a detailed narrative description of the administrative and accounting procedures designed to satisfy the requirements of these rules. Additionally, the description shall include separate section for all of the following:

(a) An organizational chart depicting appropriate segregation of functions and responsibilities.

(b) A description of the duties and responsibilities of each position shown on the organizational chart.

(c) A detailed, narrative description of the administrative and accounting procedures designed to satisfy the requirements of these rules. Additionally, the description shall include a separate section for all of the following:

(i) Physical characteristics of the drop box and tip box.

(ii) Transportation of drop and tip boxes to and from gaming tables.

(iii) Procedures for table inventories.

(iv) Procedures for opening and closing gaming tables.

Figure 2.8 Lottery control.

(v) Procedures for fills and credits.
(vi) Procedures for accepting and reporting tips and gratuities.
(vii) Procedures for transporting chips and tokens to and from gaming tables.
(viii) Procedures for shift changes at gaming tables.
(ix) Drop bucket characteristics.
(x) Transportation of drop buckets to and from electronic gaming devices.
(xi) Procedures for chip and token purchases.
(xii) Procedures for hopper fills.
(xiii) Procedures for the transportation of electronic gaming devices.
(xiv) Procedures for hand-paid jackpots.
(xv) Layout and physical characteristics of the cashier's cage.
(xvi) Procedures for accounting controls.
(xvii) Procedures for the exchange of checks submitted by gaming patrons.
(xviii) Procedures for credit card and debit card transactions.
(xix) Procedures for the acceptance, accounting for, and redemption of patron's cash deposits.
(xx) Procedures for the control of coupon redemption and other complimentary distribution programs.
(xxi) Procedures for Federal cash transactions reporting.
(xxii) Procedures for computer backups and assuring the retention of financial and gambling operation.

(d) Other items as the board may require.

(2) Not less than 90 days before the gambling operation commences, unless otherwise directed by the board, a licensee shall submit, to the board, a written description of its internal control system that is designed to satisfy the requirements of subrule (1) of this rule.
(3) If the written system is the initial submission to the board, then a letter shall be submitted from an independent certified public accountant selected by the board stating that the licensee's written system has been reviewed by the accountant and is in compliance with the requirements of . . . this rule.
(4) The board shall review each submission required by subrule (2) of this rule and shall determine whether it conforms to the requirements of subrule (1) of this rule and whether the system submitted provides adequate and effective controls for the operations of the licensee.

If the board finds any insufficiencies, then the board shall specify the insufficiencies, in writing, and submit the written insufficiencies to the licensee. The licensee shall make appropriate alterations. A licensee shall not commence gambling operations until a system of internal controls is approved.

Figure 2.8 (Continued)

Hospitality operators must comply with a variety of health codes and regulations that govern many aspects of their business. The most common areas of state health regulation include the following:

■ Standards for the cleanliness of food, and proper procedures for storing, handling, preparing, and serving food
■ Standards for the storage and handling of food supplies
■ Mandated health procedures for employees working with food
■ Standards for the proper care and washing of food equipment, utensils, and glasses
■ Standards for the proper care and washing of hotel bedding and towels, and specified quantities to be furnished to guests
■ Standards for the supply and use of water for guest use (faucets, showers, swimming pools) as well as for cleaning and dishwashing
■ Standards for water and sewage discharge
■ Display of procedures for helping choking victims
■ Regulations for smoking in public places

Penalties for violating state health ordinances vary widely. Sometimes it is a fine, but in other cases, an operation could be shut down entirely. In minor cases, if an operator can correct the violation within a specified time frame, no penalty will be imposed. And, at the end of that time period, the inspector will come back to verify that the appropriate corrections have been made.

Some state or local health departments occasionally furnish a list of health violators to local newspapers or television stations, which could result in unwanted negative publicity for a hospitality operator. This is an added incentive for managers to make sure they are always in compliance with state and local health ordinances.

Department of Transportation

The states' departments of transportation are responsible for a variety of areas that directly impact hospitality managers. Too often, regulators are viewed only as inspectors, rather than allies. This should not be the case. Consider the situation of a restaurant owner who operates a facility on a busy street in a midsized town. The street itself is maintained by the state highway department. During lunchtime, the restaurant's guests have a hard time turning into the restaurant parking lot from the opposite side of the street, because traffic is so heavy that there are few breaks in the traffic stream. The speed limit on the street is relatively high, so the crossing can be dangerous. This manager should approach the state department of transportation with the problem, in an effort to fashion a solution. It may well be that traffic patterns are so heavy that a reduced speed limit or even a turn lane could be justified. Typically, departments of transportation are also responsible for regulating driveways, exits and approaches, and traffic signage, including billboards on highways.

2.3 LOCAL REGULATORY AND ADMINISTRATIVE AGENCIES

Much of the regulatory process you will face as a hospitality manager will take place at the local level. This is a positive situation because it allows local inspectors to personally get to know both you and your facility.

Health and Sanitation

Often, the health and sanitation department is responsible for the local inspection and licensing of facilities that serve food and beverages. Local inspectors may check for compliance with state health and sanitation codes, as well as municipal ordinances. Additional duties may include the mandatory certification of foodservice workers and managers, issuing and revoking licenses, establishing standards for restroom facilities, and certifying a safe water supply.

Building and Zoning

Building and zoning departments issue building permits, and inspect the building prior to, during, and after any construction. They regulate both new building construction and additions or renovations. Standards for lighting, ventilation, restrooms, elevators, and public corridors and entryways may be established by state or local agencies. (In addition, your insurance company may have its own requirements for lighting levels and ventilation systems.) Local zoning ordinances may also regulate outside land use, such as parking spaces and permits for sidewalk or patio dining. Local inspectors will make sure that facilities are in compliance with all state and local building codes.

In addition, these departments often regulate the type of businesses that can be located in specified areas. This regulation is called zoning, and though this process can be contentious, it is generally accepted as necessary for the greater good of communities. Most hospitality professionals would agree, for example, that a bar or nightclub should not be operated in a building adjacent to a school or church.

Zoning officials regulate land use in ways that can benefit hospitality managers, for example, by prohibiting negative businesses from locating next to land reserved for restaurants, hotels, and other commercial use. Imagine your concern, for example, if you were to learn that a private landfill operator had just purchased the vacant lot next to your four-star restaurant and was to begin accepting deposits in 30 days!

In addition to their role in regulating the placement and construction of businesses, local building and zoning officials are typically responsible for the construction and placement of signs outside a business. The regulations controlling the size of, number of, and construction materials required for signs can be quite extensive. Figure 2.9 is an example of a local sign ordinance that you might encounter as a hospitality manager. Note, in particular, the specificity of information required by the business prior to the granting of a sign permit.

Sign Permits, Delta Township

The provisions of this chapter shall be administered by the township building official who shall have the authority to issue sign permits, without which it shall be unlawful to erect or replace any sign, whether freestanding, or mounted on, applied to or painted on a building or other structure.

Sign permits required. No person shall erect, place, structurally alter, or add to any sign without first obtaining a permit to do so in the manner hereinafter provided.

Application procedure. Application for a permit to erect, place, structurally alter or add to a sign shall be made to the township building official, by submission of the required forms, fees, exhibits and information by the owner of the property on which the sign is to be located, or by his agent or lessee. The application shall contain the following information:

1. The property owner's name and address.
2. The applicant's name and address
3. Address and permanent parcel number of the property on which the sign is or will be located
4. Identification of the type of sign (ground, pole, wall, etc.)
5. Name of business or name of premises to which the sign belongs or relates
6. Plans drawn to an accurate, common scale, depicting the following:
7. Dimensions and display area of the proposed sign, based on the definition of display area contained in this chapter
8. For ground signs and pole signs, the setback of the sign from the nearest public or private road right-of-way
9. For ground signs and pole signs, the height of the sign
10. For wall signs, the height and width of the building wall or tenant-controlled portion of building wall to which the sign will be attached.
11. The proposed graphic images and text to be displayed on the sign.

Scope. Sign permits issued on the basis of plans and other information submitted as part of the permit application authorize only the design and construction set forth and described in the permit application, and no other design or construction.

Figure 2.9 Sign permit ordinance.

Inspectors randomly visit businesses to ensure compliance with building and safety codes. Violators can be fined, and if guests or employees injure themselves as a result of a violation, it may result in a lawsuit.

Courts and Garnishment

In most communities, some agency of the court, sometimes called a "friend" of the court, will have the responsibility of assisting creditors in securing payment for legally owed debts. These debts can include a variety of court-ordered payments, such as child-support payments. In cases like these, a hospitality manager may be ordered by the court to *garnish* an employee's wages.

> **LEGALESE**
>
> **Garnish:** A court-ordered method of debt collection in which a portion of a person's salary is paid to a creditor.

Historical Preservation

In some communities, historical buildings, their use, and renovation may be regulated by an agency charged with historical preservation. If you manage a hospitality facility in a historic building, city zone, or community, you might face regulation from the governmental entity charged with preserving the historical integrity of your facility. This might limit the types of alterations or improvements you may make to your facility, or require you to maintain your property in a manner that is consistent with the historical nature of the area.

Fire Department

The local fire department is a critical part of the safety net that hospitality managers offer their guests. Whether it is for a hotel or restaurant, dependable fire safety departments can assist a manager in limiting potential liability through careful adherence to all local fire codes and procedures. Fire departments will normally conduct routine facility inspections, assist local building departments in reviewing plans for new or renovated buildings, ensure that emergency lighting and sprinklers are installed and maintained properly, and offer fire safety training for managers and employees. As a hospitality manager, it is important to know your local fire codes and to make sure that your operation always includes the required number of fire extinguishers, smoke detectors, sprinklers, fans and ventilation ducts, emergency lights, and emergency exit signs. This equipment should be tested periodically to make sure that it is in good working order. The National Fire Protection Association has established national standards for ventilation systems and automatic fire protection systems in commercial kitchens. Insurance companies also have regulations that will determine the type and amount of fire protection equipment you will need for your operation.

Another important role of the fire department is to regulate the number of individuals who are allowed in a particular space at a given time. For example, it would be the fire department that would determine the maximum number of patrons who could be in a hotel ballroom at one time. The capacity of bars, nightclubs, dining rooms, and sleeping rooms are all examples of areas regulated by the local fire department. You have probably noticed signs that indicate the maximum number of people who can safely be in a public space. Often, local laws require these signs to be prominently displayed.

Law Enforcement

Although local police do not generally serve a regulatory role for business, some communities do have local laws or codes that are enforced by the police department, in a city, or by the sheriff's department in a more rural community. As we have seen, liquor laws, for example, are sometimes enforced by the local police. Other areas of interaction may be parking enforcement and the removal of disorderly guests.

Tax Assessor/Collector

Local municipalities obtain a significant portion of their tax revenues from businesses. These taxes may be levied on the basis of property value, sales revenue, or a combination of both. The tax assessor or collector is responsible for the prompt collection and recording of these taxes.

Increasingly, communities are looking to the hospitality industry as a vehicle for raising tax revenue. One such source of tax revenue is the local occupancy, or bed, tax. Essentially, the occupancy tax is a tax on the sale of hotel rooms. It typically will range from 1 to 15 percent of gross room revenue. This tax may be assessed at the state level, local level, or both. In any case, there are typically few waivers for the tax, and its collection is aggressively enforced by the taxing entity.

2.4 REGULATORY INTERACTION AND OVERSIGHT IMPACTING TRAVEL AND TOURISM

The travel industry is heavily regulated, and because it is so large and diverse, the number of groups and organizations responsible for the legal oversight of travel activities is considerable. From the perspective of the hospitality manager, some of the most significant of these include governmental agencies, both at the federal and state levels, and nongovernmental groups that operate internationally to coordinate travel policies, which are discussed later in this section.

U.S. Government Agencies

You have been introduced to federal agencies that have responsibility for regulation and oversight in the hospitality industry. In the following subsections, you will learn about other federal agencies involved in regulation and policy development for the travel industry. The list is long and represents the most significant of the federal groups responsible for monitoring travel activities, but it is not exhaustive. In fact, travel-related activities impact nearly every federal agency. The agencies and departments identified here will, however, give some indication of the many ways in which travel professionals interact with the federal government in the course of their managerial duties. In addition to federal monitoring and control, states, counties, and local governments may all have agencies, departments, and code enforcement professionals that combine to provide additional regulatory oversight.

Federal Trade Commission (FTC)

The Federal Trade Commission is charged with ensuring that the nation's markets are free of restrictions that could potentially harm consumers. In addition, it works to ensure that competition among firms is fair and results in the availability of lower prices and better goods and services. A further role of the FTC is the dissemination of information that consumers can use to make better purchase decisions. To ensure the smooth operation of the free market system, the FTC enforces federal consumer protection laws that prevent fraud, deception, and unfair business practices. The commission also enforces federal antitrust laws that prohibit anticompetitive mergers and other business practices that restrict competition and could harm consumers.

With regard to the travel industry, the FTC has increasingly devoted its attention to protecting consumers by investigating false, misleading, or deceptive advertising, telemarketing fraud, and Internet scams. Although the FTC does not seek to resolve individual consumer problems, it does use information from individual complaints to investigate fraud and initiate law enforcement actions. The FTC also enters Internet, telemarketing, identity theft, and other fraud-related complaints into the Consumer Sentinel, an online database available for use by civil and criminal law enforcement agencies worldwide.

Centers for Disease Control and Prevention (CDC)

The Centers for Disease Control and Prevention (CDC) is the major federal agency operating to protect the health and safety of individuals at home and abroad, as well as to provide information to enhance health decisions. The CDC, located in Atlanta, Georgia, is an agency of the Federal Department of Health and Human Services. Its official mission is to promote health and quality of life by preventing and controlling disease, injury, and disability.

Becoming seriously ill or having a major accident while traveling, especially in a country where the traveler does not speak the local language, is one of many tourists' greatest fears. Travelers may also face health risks of which they are unaware because they simply do not know about travel-related threats to their health and safety in places they have not previously visited. In many cases, some of these threats could be avoided or minimized if the traveler were aware of them. The CDC makes available, on a region-by-region basis, information about health and safety risks for travelers worldwide. In addition, this information includes recommendations for addressing or minimizing these travel-related threats to health and safety.

Search the Web 2.2

One of the most popular services offered by the CDC is its "Travelers' Health" information. It is available online and seeks to inform travelers about the health risks they may encounter when traveling in various parts of the world. To view a sample of the information provided, go to wwwnc.cdc.gov/travel. Under the "Destinations" tab, select a region to find out about the health risks you might encounter in an area of the world you would someday like to visit.

Department of Commerce

The U.S. Department of Commerce is dedicated to the improvement of business, including tourism. It houses the Census Bureau (www.census.gov), which collects economic data on the hotel and restaurant industries, as well as other service businesses. It also houses the United States Travel and Tourism Administration (www.tinet.ita.doc.gov), which was established by the National Tourism Policy Act of 1981. This agency gathers statistics on travel activity and promotes tourism. On February 20, 2003, the Omnibus Appropriation Act for FY 2003 became law. Included in this appropriation was Section 210, which authorized the U.S. Department of Commerce to award grants and make lump-sum payments in support of an international advertising and promotional campaign to encourage individuals to travel to the United States. The Omnibus Appropriation Act both authorized and appropriated $50 million for this campaign, which is, of course, widely supported by those in the travel industry. The Department of Commerce is advised by its Travel and Tourism Promotion Advisory Board (see Figure 2.10), which includes some of the travel industry's most notable businesspeople.

Rossi Ralenkotter
President & CEO
Las Vegas Convention and Visitors Authority

Dawn Drew
Founder & CEO
The M.O.S.T.E., Inc.

Holly Agra
President
Chicago's First Lady Cruises

Richard Anderson
CEO
Delta Air Lines, Inc.

José Andrés
President & Co-Founder
ThinkFoodGroup

Sheila Armstrong
Executive Director
U.S. Cultural and Heritage Tourism Marketing Council

Helane Becker
Senior Vice President
Dahlman Rose & Company

Nich Calderazzo
Vice President Sales and Marketing
RMP Travel

Todd Davidson
CEO
Oregon Tourism Commission

Maryann Ferenc
Founder, President & CEO
Mise en Place, Inc.

Chuck Floyd
COO—North America
Hyatt Hotels Corporation

Sam Gilliland
Chairman & CEO
Sabre Holdings

Figure 2.10 Department of Commerce Travel & Tourism Advisory Board.

Adam Goldstein
President & CEO
Royal Caribbean International

Dr. David Hayes
Director—International Office
Mayo Clinic

Jeremy Jacobs, Sr.
Chairman & CEO
Delaware North Companies, Inc.

Hubert Joly
President & CEO
Carlson Companies

John Klein
CEO
Premium Outlets, a Division of Simon Property Group

David Kong
President & CEO
Best-Western International

Philip Levine
President & CEO
Baron Corporation

Gina Marie Lindsey
Executive Director
Los Angeles World Airports

Chandrakant "C.K." Patel
President
BVM Holdings, Inc.

J. Stephen Perry
President & CEO
New Orleans Convention and Visitors Bureau

Adam Sacks
Managing Director
Tourism Economics

Joseph W. Saunders
Chairman & CEO
Visa, Inc.

Figure 2.10 (Continued)

Douglas Shifflet
Chairman & CEO
D.K. Shifflet & Associates

Ronald Solimon
President & CEO
Indian Pueblo Cultural Center, Inc. and Indian Pueblos Marketing, Inc.

John Sprouls
CEO
Universal Orlando Resort
Executive Vice President
Universal Parks and Resorts

Greg Stubblefield
Exeuctive Vice President & CSO
Enterprise Holdings

Perry John P. Tenorio
Managing Director
Marianas Visitors Authority

George Zimmermann
Vice President
Travel Michigan at the Michigan Economic Development Corporation

Figure 2.10 (*Continued*)

≫ ANALYZE THE SITUATION 2.3

AN ELDERLY COUPLE FROM Canada, traveling in Central/South America, goes on a shopping trip to a local produce market, where the couple buys and consumes some locally grown fruit. Upon returning that evening to the international hotel in the area, which you manage, the husband falls ill and his wife calls your front desk seeking assistance.

1. What is the likely cause of the man's illness?

2. Based on what you know about reasonable care for guests, what action would you expect your management team to take relative to the man's illness?

3. What would your position be if your hotel was later sued by the couple, claiming you had failed to warn them of local health risks?

Department of the Interior (DOI)

In 1849, Congress passed a bill to create the Department of the Interior. Over the course of its history, the DOI has played a changing role in its mission of managing the country's internal affairs. As a result, it has had, at various times, responsibility for the construction of the national capital's water system, the colonization of freed slaves in Haiti, exploration of the western wilderness, oversight of the District of Columbia jail, regulation of territorial governments, management of hospitals and universities, management of public parks, and the basic responsibilities for Native Americans, public lands, patents, and pensions. In one way or another, all of these roles had to do with the internal development of the nation or the welfare of Americans.

In 1916, President Woodrow Wilson signed legislation creating the National Park Service. The act assigned to the new bureau the 14 national parks and 21 national monuments then under the DOI and directed it "to conserve the scenery and the natural and historic objects and the wildlife therein and to provide for the enjoyment of the same in such manner and by such means as will leave them unimpaired for the enjoyment of future generations."[4] The national monuments, generally smaller than the parks, included prehistoric Native American ruins, geologic features, and other sites of natural and cultural significance reserved by presidential proclamations under the Antiquities Act of 1906. Today, this agency sets policy for the National Park Service, which includes some the country's most significant tourism destinations.

> ### Search the Web **2.3**
>
> The National Park Service is in the tourism business. To view its website, where visitors can book tours, go to www.nps.gov/findapark/index.htm.
>
> It is also possible to find information about national parks and nearby communities at www.nationalparkreservations.com.

Department of State

The executive branch and Congress have constitutional responsibilities for U.S. foreign policy. Within the executive branch, the Department of State is the lead U.S. foreign affairs agency, and the secretary of state is the president's principal foreign policy adviser. The Department of State advances U.S. objectives and interests in shaping a safer and freer world through its primary role in developing and implementing the president's foreign policy. The State Department also supports the foreign affairs activities of other U.S. government entities, including the Department of Commerce. In addition, it provides a variety of important services to U.S. citizens traveling abroad, including the issuing of passports and providing travel warnings. Figure 2.11 is an example of the type of warning developed by the Department of State and is available to those traveling internationally.

---

[4]National Park Service, "Organic Act of 1916," www.nps.gov/grba/parkmgmt/organic-act-of-1916.htm. Last updated August 23, 2010. Accessed July 5, 2011.

Travel Warning
U.S. DEPARTMENT OF STATE
Bureau of Consular Affairs
Afghanistan
March 08, 2011

The Department of State warns U.S. citizens against travel to Afghanistan. The security threat to all U.S. citizens in Afghanistan remains critical. This supersedes the Travel Warning for Afghanistan issued August 13, 2010, to remind U.S. citizens of ongoing security risks, including kidnapping and insurgent attacks.

No part of Afghanistan should be considered immune from violence, and the potential exists throughout the country for hostile acts, either targeted or random, against U.S. and other Western nationals at any time. Remnants of the former Taliban regime and the al-Qa'ida terrorist network, as well as other groups hostile to International Security Assistance Force (ISAF) military operations, remain active. There is an ongoing threat to kidnap and assassinate U.S. citizens and Non-Governmental Organization (NGO) workers throughout the country. Afghan authorities have a limited ability to maintain order and ensure the security of Afghan citizens and foreign visitors. Travel in all areas of Afghanistan is unsafe due to military combat operations, landmines, banditry, armed rivalry between political and tribal groups, and the possibility of terrorist attacks, including attacks using vehicular or other improvised explosive devices (IEDs). The security environment remains volatile and unpredictable.

In August 2010 a group of doctors, nurses, and medical practitioners, including six U.S. citizens, was shot and killed near their vehicles in Badakhshan province as they completed a medical aid visit to remote areas in nearby Nuristan province. Also in Badakhshan province in spring 2010, a group of U.S. citizen missionaries who were alleged to be proselytizing in the area encountered hostility and required evacuation from the area by the Ministry of Interior and the U.S. Embassy.

In Kandahar, the assassination campaign against government officials, their associates, or anyone notably linked to the government, continues. The number of attacks throughout the south and southeastern areas of the country is growing as a result of insurgent and drug-related activity, and no part of Afghanistan is immune from violence.

Kabul is also considered at high risk for militant attacks, including rocket attacks, vehicle borne IEDs, and suicide bombings. Five United Nations (UN) workers were killed during an attack on a UN guesthouse in Kabul in October 2009. More than 20 attacks were reported in Kabul over the past year, although many additional attacks were thwarted by Afghan and coalition forces. Recent incidents include the bombing of a Kabul supermarket popular with Westerners and an attack on the Kabul City Center complex, which includes a hotel frequented by foreign visitors. Insurgents have also targeted the offices, convoys, and individual implementing partners of the U.S. Agency for International Development.

The attack against a Kandahar guesthouse on April 15, 2010, along with the UN attack mentioned above, highlights the growing threat against guesthouses. Buildings or compounds that lack robust security measures in comparison to neighboring facilities may be viewed as targets of opportunity by insurgents.

The Kabul-Jalalabad Road (commonly called Jalalabad Road) and the Kabul to Bagram Road are highly restricted for Embassy employees and, if the security situation warrants, sometimes prohibited completely.

Riots and incidents of civil disturbance can and do occur, often without warning. U.S. citizens should avoid rallies and demonstrations; even demonstrations intended to be peaceful can turn confrontational and escalate into violence.

Figure 2.11 U.S. State Department travel warning for Afghanistan.

Ambushes, robberies, and violent crime remain a problem. U.S. citizens involved in property or business disputes — a common legal problem in Afghanistan — have reported that their adversaries in the disputes have threatened their lives. U.S. citizens who find themselves in such situations should not assume that either local law enforcement or the U.S. Embassy will be able to assist them. From time to time, depending on current security conditions, the U.S. Embassy places areas frequented by foreigners off limits to its personnel. Potential target areas include key national or international government establishments, international organizations and other locations with expatriate personnel, and public areas popular with the expatriate community. Private U.S. citizens are strongly urged to heed these restrictions as well and may obtain the latest information by consulting the embassy website below.

From time to time, depending on current security conditions, the U.S. Embassy places areas frequented by foreigners off limits to its personnel. Potential target areas include key national or international government establishments, international organizations and other locations with expatriate personnel, and public areas popular with the expatriate community such as restaurants. Private U.S. citizens are strongly urged to heed these restrictions as well and may obtain the latest information by consulting the Embassy's security announcements website.

The U.S. Embassy's ability to provide emergency consular services to U.S. citizens in Afghanistan is limited, particularly for those persons outside the capital. U.S. citizens who choose to visit or remain in Afghanistan despite this Travel Warning are encouraged to enroll with the U.S. Embassy in Kabul through the State Department's Smart Traveler Enrollment Program (STEP) to obtain updated information on travel and security within Afghanistan. U.S. citizens without Internet access may enroll directly with the U.S. Embassy. Enrolling makes it easier for the Embassy to contact U.S. citizens in case of an emergency. The U.S. Embassy is located at Great Masood Road between Radio Afghanistan and the Ministry of Public Health (the road is also known as Bebe Mahro or Airport Road) in Kabul. The Embassy phone numbers are 93-(0)700-108-001 and 93-(0)700-108-002. For after-hours, life-or-limb emergencies involving U.S. citizens, the Consular Section can be reached at 93-(0)700-201-908; please direct routine consular correspondence to USConsulKabul@state.gov.

Current information on travel and security in Afghanistan may be obtained from the Department of State by calling 1-888-407-4747 toll free in the United States and Canada or, for callers outside the United States and Canada, a regular toll line at 1-202-501-4444. For further information, please consult the Country Specific Information for Afghanistan and the current Worldwide Caution, which are available on the Bureau of Consular Affairs Internet website.

Figure 2.11 (*Continued*)

Search the Web **2.4**

An important service provided by the Department of State is that of issuing travel advisories and warnings to Americans planning to travel outside the United States. Travelers can access these warnings at travel.state.gov/travel/cis_pa_tw/tw/tw_1764.html.

Department of Homeland Security (DHS)

In the months following the terrorist attacks against America on September 11, 2001, 22 previously separate domestic agencies were merged into one department to protect the nation against terrorist threats. This merger created the Department of Homeland Security (DHS). It has a sixfold agenda:[5]

1. Increase overall preparedness, particularly for catastrophic events.
2. Create better transportation security systems to move people and cargo more securely and efficiently.
3. Strengthen border security and interior enforcement and reform immigration processes.
4. Enhance information sharing with our partners.
5. Improve DHS financial management, human resource development, procurement, and information technology.
6. Realign the DHS organization to maximize mission performance.

More specifically, the department is composed of these divisions:[6]

The Directorate for National Protection and Programs works to advance the Department's risk-reduction mission. Reducing risk requires an integrated approach that encompasses both physical and virtual threats and their associated human elements.

The Directorate for Science and Technology is the primary research and development arm of DHS. It provides federal, state, and local officials with the technology and capabilities to protect the homeland.

The Directorate for Management is responsible for Department budgets and appropriations, expenditure of funds, accounting and finance, procurement, human resources, information technology systems, facilities and equipment, and the identification and tracking of performance measurements.

The Office of Policy is the primary policy formulation and coordination component for the Department of Homeland Security. It provides a centralized, coordinated focus to the development of Department-wide, long-range planning to protect the United States.

The Office of Health Affairs coordinates all medical activities of the Department of Homeland Security to ensure appropriate preparation for and response to incidents having medical significance.

The Office of Intelligence and Analysis is responsible for using information and intelligence from multiple sources to identify and assess current and future threats to the United States.

The Office of Operations Coordination and Planning is responsible for monitoring the security of the United States on a daily basis and coordinating activities within the Department and with governors, Homeland Security Advisors, law enforcement partners, and critical infrastructure operators in all 50 states and more than 50 major urban areas nationwide.

The Federal Law Enforcement Training Center provides career-long training to law enforcement professionals to help them fulfill their responsibilities safely and proficiently.

---

[5]Homeland Security, "Department Six-point Agenda," www.dhs.gov/xabout/history/editorial_0646.shtm. Last modified January 26, 2011. Accessed July 5, 2011.
[6]Homeland Security, "Department Subcomponents and Agencies," www.dhs.gov/xabout/structure/. Last modified on May 31, 2011. Accessed July 5, 2011.

The Domestic Nuclear Detection Office works to enhance the nuclear detection efforts of federal, state, territorial, tribal, and local governments, and the private sector and to ensure a coordinated response to such threats.

The Transportation Security Administration (TSA) protects the nation's transportation systems to ensure freedom of movement for people and commerce.

United States Customs and Border Protection (CBP) is one of the Department of Homeland Security's largest and most complex components, with a priority mission of keeping terrorists and their weapons out of the United States. It also has a responsibility for securing and facilitating trade and travel while enforcing hundreds of U.S. regulations, including immigration and drug laws.

United States Citizenship and Immigration Services secures America's promise as a nation of immigrants by providing accurate and useful information to our customers, granting immigration and citizenship benefits, promoting an awareness and understanding of citizenship, and ensuring the integrity of our immigration system.

United States Immigration and Customs Enforcement (ICE) promotes homeland security and public safety through the criminal and civil enforcement of federal laws governing border control, customs, trade, and immigration.

The United States Coast Guard is one of the five armed forces of the United States and the only military organization within the Department of Homeland Security. The Coast Guard protects the maritime economy and the environment, defends our maritime borders, and saves those in peril.

The Federal Emergency Management Agency (FEMA) supports our citizens and first responders to ensure that as a nation we work together to build, sustain, and improve our capability to prepare for, protect against, respond to, recover from, and mitigate all hazards.

The United States Secret Service safeguards the nation's financial infrastructure and payment systems to preserve the integrity of the economy, and protects national leaders, visiting heads of state and government, designated sites, and National Special Security Events.

The policies put in place by the DHS now and in the future will have a significant impact on the way Americans travel, as well as how America receives travelers.

Treasury Department

The U.S. Treasury Department is entrusted with a variety of duties and functions. In addition to collecting taxes and managing currency production and circulation, this department oversees functions in law enforcement, economic policy development, and international treaty negotiation. Travelers are affected by the department's participation in negotiations to reduce barriers to international trade and finance by working through the World Trade Organization (UNWTO), the Organization for Economic Cooperation and Development, and other international trade negotiating teams. In addition, it houses the Office of Foreign Assets Control (OFAC), which administers and enforces economic and trade sanctions, including travel bans, based on U.S. foreign policy and national security goals against targeted foreign countries, terrorists, international narcotics traffickers, and those engaged in activities related to the proliferation of weapons of mass destruction.

Department of Transportation (DOT)

Congress established the Department of Transportation in 1968. Its mission is to develop and coordinate policies that will provide an efficient and economical national transportation system while considering both environmental and national defense needs. The DOT consists of 13 individual operating administrations:

1. Federal Aviation Administration
2. Federal Highway Administration
3. Federal Railroad Administration
4. National Highway Traffic Safety Administration
5. Federal Motor Carrier Safety Administration
6. Federal Transit Administration
7. Maritime Administration
8. Saint Lawrence Seaway Development Corporation
9. Research and Innovative Technology Administration
10. Office of the Secretary of Transportation
11. Office of the Inspector General
12. Pipeline and Hazardous Materials Safety Administration
13. Surface Transportation Board

Although many of the activities of these DOT divisions affect tourism and travelers, the following four are of special note:

1. *Federal Aviation Administration (FAA).* Early economic regulation of airlines by the federal government concerned mainly the airlines' participation in the airmail system. "The Air Mail Act of 1925 allowed the U.S. government to pay airlines for carrying the mail. The McNary–Watres Act of 1930 let the Post Office Department review the accounting practices of these mail carriers," and, as a result, regulation of the airlines began. The airline companies that did not hold government contracts to carry the mail remained unregulated. Thus, from 1930 to 1938, these unregulated companies grew quickly, and competed for passengers by offering low prices. "In 1935 the Federal Aviation Commission recommended that the entire air transportation industry, not just the airmail carriers, be regulated, much as the Interstate Commerce Commission regulated railroads." As a result, the federal government began regulating airfares and decided how many and which airlines could fly between cities. The Federal Aviation Act of 1958 established the Federal Aviation Agency (now the FAA), which added further safety regulations. Due to pressure by consumer groups, however, Congress passed the Airline Deregulation Act of 1978. This act ended most economic regulation in a series of steps over several years. As a result, airlines could offer new routes and drop routes that lost money.[7]

   The federal government also recognized the need to guarantee service to communities where airlines made little or no profit, and where these airlines might want to eliminate service, which would leave travelers in those communities without air transportation. "Under a program called Essential Air Service, airlines were prevented from dropping service to certain communities even though the airlines might not want to keep operating them." In addition, airlines must meet FAA safety standards if they are to be permitted to use airspace. Thus, despite deregulation, the FAA is still heavily involved in air transportation policy. Specifically, the FAA is responsible for the issuance and enforcement of regulations and minimum standards relating to the manufacture, operation, and maintenance of aircraft. In addition, it is responsible for air traffic management, and **thus operates** a network of airport towers, air route traffic control centers, and flight service stations.[8]

---

[7]Roger Mola, "Economic Regulations of Airlines," U.S. Centennial of Flight Commission, www.centennialofflight.gov/essay/Government_Role/Econ_Reg/POL16.htm. Accessed July 5, 2011.
[8]Ibid.

2. *Federal Highway Administration (FHWA)*. The goal of the Federal Highway Administration is to create the best transportation system in the world for the American people and to enhance the country's economic vitality, quality of life, and the environment. The FHWA is headquartered in Washington, D.C., with field offices across the United States. It performs its tasks through the Federal-Aid Highway program, which provides federal financial assistance to the states to construct and improve the National Highway System, urban and rural roads, and bridges. The program provides funds for general improvements and development of safe highways and roads. It also operates the Federal Lands Highway program, which provides access to and within national forests, national parks, Indian reservations, and other public lands. Both of these programs, and the policies set by their administrators, of course, significantly impact vehicle traffic, travel, and tourism in the United States.

≫ ANALYZE THE SITUATION 2.4

TED FLOOD HAD A reservation at the Sleep Right hotel for the night of October 15. According to the reservation policy explained to Mr. Flood at the time he reserved the room from Sleep Right's national reservation system, the nonguaranteed reservation was to be held until 4:00 P.M. the afternoon of Mr. Flood's arrival.

Unfortunately, Mr. Flood's flight to the city where the Sleep Right was located was delayed, because Mr. Flood's plane had to spend four hours on the airport runway because of mechanical difficulties. Mr. Flood was unable to contact the hotel and, as a result, his room was released by the hotel at 4:30 P.M. and sold to another guest at 5:00 P.M. Consequently, the hotel had no rooms available when Mr. Flood, tired and frustrated, arrived at the front desk at 8:00 P.M.

1. What could Mr. Flood have done to avoid his difficulty?

2. What responsibility, if any, does the hotel now have to Mr. Flood?

3. What role did the FAA likely play in this situation?

3. *Federal Railroad Administration*. A common misconception is that the federal government owns and operates the country's rail system. It does not. The Federal Railroad Administration does, however, provide some funding, and thus has some decision-making authority related to the country's intercity rail passenger system. It also administers federal grants to Amtrak (officially known as the National Railroad Passenger Corporation), which is the organization that actually operates much of the nation's rail system.

4. *National Highway Traffic Safety Administration (NHTSA)*. The Highway Safety Act of 1970 established the National Highway Traffic Safety Administration to implement traffic safety programs. It is responsible for reducing deaths, injuries, and economic losses resulting from motor vehicle crashes. It does so by setting and enforcing safety performance standards for motor vehicles and motor vehicle equipment. The NHTSA investigates safety defects in motor vehicles; sets and enforces fuel economy standards;

helps states and local communities reduce the threat of drunk drivers; promotes the use of safety belts, child safety seats, and airbags; and provides consumer information on motor vehicle safety topics. Because of the immense popularity of auto travel in the United States, the NHTSA plays a major role in the travel industry.

Tourism Policy Council (TPC)

As is clear by now, there are many federal agencies whose policymaking affects travel in the United States. The Tourism Policy Council (TPC) is an interagency, policy-coordinating committee composed of the leaders of nine federal agencies and the president of the U.S. National Tourism Organization (USNTO). The TPC members work cooperatively to ensure that the national interest in tourism is fully considered in federal decisions that affect tourism development. The TPC also coordinates national policies and programs relating to international travel and tourism, recreation, and national heritage resources that involve federal agencies. The council works with the private sector and state and local governments on issues and problems that require federal involvement.

International Organizations

The United States is not, of course, the only government interested in promoting safe travel for its citizens, for many countries count on tourism for significant financial contributions to their economies; hence, they, too, are concerned with traveler safety. That means there are a large number of international groups and organizations whose goal is to improve and promote the travel industry worldwide. The result is the creation of travel procedures, policies, and agreements. The following three organizations direct or control some of the most important of these international cooperative efforts.

World Tourism Organization (UNWTO)

The World Tourism Organization is the leading international organization in the field of travel and tourism. It serves as a global forum for tourism policy issues and as a practical source of tourism knowhow and statistics. Its membership includes 154 countries, 7 territories, and 400 affiliate members representing regional and local promotion boards, tourism trade associations, educational institutions, and private-sector companies that include airlines, hotel groups, and tour operators.

The UNWTO has been vested by the United Nations with a central role in promoting the development of responsible, sustainable, and universally accessible tourism. Through tourism, the UNWTO aims to stimulate economic growth and job creation, provide incentives for protecting the environment and cultural heritage, and promote peace, prosperity, and respect for human rights. The UNWTO is best known for demonstrating the economic importance of tourism, and providing the world's most comprehensive tourism statistics. By establishing standards for the reporting of tourism-related information, the UNWTO has created a common base of statistics that enables operators of tourist destinations to compare their success and progress with that of their competitors.

International Civil Aviation Organization (ICAO)

The International Civil Aviation Organization is one of the least known but most important of the many international groups that affect travel policy and procedure.

> WHEREAS the future development of international civil aviation can greatly help to create and preserve friendship and understanding among the nations and peoples of the world, yet its abuse can become a threat to the general security; and
>
> WHEREAS it is desirable to avoid friction and to promote that co-operation between nations and peoples upon which the peace of the world depends;
>
> THEREFORE, the undersigned governments having agreed on certain principals and arrangements in order that international civil aviation may be developed in a safe and orderly manner and that international air transport services may be established on the basis of equality of opportunity and operated soundly and economically;
>
> Have accordingly concluded this Convention to that end.

Figure 2.12 Conclusion of the Convention on International Civil Aviation, Chicago.

On December 7, 1944, 52 countries signed the treaty that resulted from the Convention on International Civil Aviation, which was held in Chicago, Illinois. Figure 2.12 contains an excerpt from that document.

Today, the ICAO is a specialized agency of the United Nations. It develops rules and regulations concerning training and licensing of aeronautical personnel, both in the air and on the ground, communication systems and procedures, rules for the air and air traffic control systems and practices, and airworthiness requirements for aircraft engaged in international air travel, as well as their registration and identification, aeronautical meteorology, and maps and charts.

World Health Organization (WHO)

The World Health Organization, the United Nations' specialized agency for health, was established in 1948. The objective of WHO is the attainment by all peoples of the highest possible level of health. "Health" is defined by WHO as a state of complete physical, mental, and social well-being—not merely the absence of disease or infirmity. International travelers are affected by the work of WHO, especially when visiting nations challenged to provide their own citizens, and thus visitors, with the basic components of healthy food and water supplies.

2.5 MANAGING CONFLICTING REGULATIONS

Given the large number of legislative bodies daily creating new policies, there are surprisingly few instances where regulations are in direct conflict. As a rule, local legislators and public officials will review state guidelines prior to implementing new regulations, just as state regulators will review federal guidelines. In fact, where there are agencies at each governmental level, the federal agency may create model regulations that will then be adopted in whole or in part at the state level, just as the state may take the role of creating model regulations for possible use at the local level.

Consider the case of A. J. Patel. Mr. Patel is the regional manager for a hotel company that operates properties that provide a free continental breakfast to all registered guests. His properties operate in three different states. Mr. Patel must be familiar with the public health codes of three different state and local governments, which means that he must stay abreast of the changing health code regulations of all six entities. His task has been made easier, however, because the federal Food and Drug Administration (FDA) created a Model Food Service Sanitation Ordinance, which is followed, with varying degrees of specificity, by many state and local communities. Figure 2.13 is a section of the Preface to the State of Michigan's "Food Service Sanitation" ordinance. Note the relationship that is detailed among the federal, state, and local regulators.

There will be times when the requirements placed on a hospitality manager will be in conflict with one another. For example, a federal requirement may conflict with a local one. Although this can sometimes be frustrating, it is important to know what you, as a manager, should do in such a situation.

A conflict between regulatory restrictions occurs when one entity sets a standard higher or lower than another. If, for example, a local sanitation code requires all shelving in a kitchen to be 12 inches above the floor, yet the state code allows shelving to be within 6 inches of the floor, the more restrictive regulation will prevail. This is true because, in this case, a shelf 12 inches above the floor satisfies both regulatory bodies. The principle to remember is this: When regulatory demands conflict, the "most restrictive" regulation should be followed.

Michigan's state-local coordinated food service sanitation program regulates fixed, mobile, and temporary foodservice establishments as well as vending machines dispensing certain food and beverages. The program was first launched with passage of Act 269, P.A. of 1968, and has, from the beginning, been based in large part on the U.S. Public Health Service (USPHS) Model Recommendations for Food Service Sanitation. These recommendations are updated as technology, experience, and research dictate.

Michigan's current regulations consist of (1) the enabling legislation, Michigan's Public Health Code, Act 368, P.A. of 1978, Part 129, as amended; (2) the United States Public Health Service Model Foodservice Sanitation Ordinance; and (3) Foodservice Sanitation Rules promulgated under the authority of Section 12909 of the Public Code. The Foodservice Sanitation Section, Division of Environmental Health, Bureau of Environmental and Occupational Health, Michigan Department of Public Health is charged with responsibility for overall administration and coordination of the program and has delegated the authority for enforcement of the statue and administrative rules to local health departments.

Figure 2.13 State of Michigan Food Service Sanitation ordinance.

≫ ANALYZE THE SITUATION 2.5

SHARON ALEXANDER OPERATED THE Texas Saloon, a steakhouse restaurant that also served beer and wine. Sharon's average menu item sold for $10. Employees were allowed to eat one meal during their shift. For those who voluntarily elected to eat this meal, Sharon would deduct $0.25 per hour ($2 per eight-hour shift) from the federal minimum wage rate she paid her entry-level dishwashers, which reflected the reasonable cost of the meal.

Sharon relied on the Fair Labor Standards Act (FLSA) Section 3(m), which states that employers can consider, as wages, "reasonable costs . . . to the employer of furnishing such employees with board, lodging, or other facilities if such boards, lodging, or other facilities are customarily furnished by such employer to his [or her] employees." Sharon interpreted this regulation to mean that she could pay the entry-level dishwashers a rate that, when added to the $0.25 per hour meal deduction, equaled the federal minimum wage.

One day, Sharon was contacted by her state department of employment, which charged that she was in violation of the state minimum wage law. The law stated that "total voluntary deductions for meals and uniforms may not decrease an employee's wages below the federal minimum wage on an hourly basis." Sharon maintained that because she was in compliance with the federal law, she was allowed to take the meal credit against the wages paid to her entry-level dishwashers.

1. Is Sharon in compliance with the compensation laws of her state?

2. Do federal laws, in this case, take precedent over state law?

In some cases, a regulatory agency will influence a hospitality manager's operation in an indirect, but intentional, manner. One example is the Hotel and Motel Fire Safety Act of 1990. The federal government enacted this law because it was hesitant to require many older hotels to incur the expense of adding in-room sprinkler systems to their rooms, yet it still wanted to influence the safety of the traveling public.

The Hotel and Motel Fire Safety Act of 1990 aims to increase the level of fire safety in hotels and motels by discouraging federally funded travel to hotels and motels that do not meet certain minimum fire protection standards. These standards require the installation of automatic sprinkler systems in hotels and motels over three stories in height, and the installation of hard-wired (not battery-operated) smoke detectors in every room of each and every hotel and motel.

In general, the act prohibits federal funding of a meeting, conference, convention, or training seminar that is conducted in a place of public accommodation that does not meet the fire safety requirements of the act. Under the act, states are responsible for submitting data to the U.S. Fire Administration regarding which hotels and motels meet those specified standards. Note that, in this case, the regulatory body, Congress, did not implement a restriction on operating hotels without sprinkler systems; it simply prohibited funding, by the federal government, of any travel to such a hotel.

2.6 RESPONDING TO AN INQUIRY

Despite the best efforts of management, it is not uncommon for a facility to be found in violation of a regulation. Consider the case of Gerry Monteagudo. Gerry has, for many years, heavily decorated the lobby and public areas of his hotel during the Christmas season. This year, shortly after the decorations had been put in place, Gerry received a letter from the local fire chief citing the hotel for three violations of the local fire code. An inspector noticed that some of the holiday lights were illuminated via the use of extension cords. These extension cords are not allowed, by ordinance, in the township where Gerry operates the hotel. In this case, the problem could be quickly rectified by replacing the extension cords with surge protector cords that are allowed by the local ordinance.

At the other extreme, consider the case of the hospitality manager who is notified that the IRS will be conducting an audit of tip-reporting compliance in her facility. The IRS auditors plan to trace the last three years of tips to all employees, and verify that the required employment taxes were paid on those tips. The manager, in assembling three years of paperwork, discovers that not all taxes were paid during the first year, before she assumed management of the facility. A penalty may still be assessed.

As can be seen, some regulatory violations can be very serious. Because that is true, it is a good idea to follow a standard set of procedures anytime a governmental agency raises the question of regulatory noncompliance.

As a manager, you should never willingly violate a legitimate regulation. In most cases, noncompliance is unintentional, and the governmental agency has, as its responsibility, the duty to inform management of violations. Because many of these agencies can have a significant effect on the facility and, in some cases the manager personally, it is best to respond quickly and professionally to any charge of noncompliance.

LEGALLY MANAGING AT WORK:

Recommended Steps for Responding to Inquiries and Complaints by Government Agencies

1. Upon notification of a complaint or violation, document the date and time that all paperwork was received, and be sure to check of correspondence for required deadlines.

   Upon receipt of correspondence from a government agency, the first thing that you or your clerical staff must do is to note on the correspondence itself the date that it was received. This can be done manually, but preferably with a small mechanical stamping device (as shown in Figure 2.14). Be sure that you include the day, month, and year of receipt. This is important because many governmental agencies require you to respond within a certain number of days from the date you received the correspondence.

   As you read the correspondence, be on the lookout for the due dates of responses. Some due dates are measured from the date of receipt; other due dates are measured from the date mailed. For instance, a letter might state, "If you do not respond within 10 days of your receipt of this correspondence, then we will assume that the claimant's position is true and act accordingly." This is known as an automatic default provision. It is imperative that if you

RECEIVED

APR 1 5 2000

BY:_____

Figure 2.14 Date stamp.

intend to respond, you do so within the time frame specified in the correspondence. There is rarely a remedy to missing a deadline for an initial response.

2. **Assess the severity of the complaint. Determine if legal consultation is necessary.**

   As you read the correspondence, you will need to decide if legal counsel should be consulted in order to deal with the complaint raised in the correspondence. Additionally, you will need to decide if the issue raised needs to be referred to your insurance carrier. It may be a good idea to fax the correspondence to your insurance agent to get his or her opinion as to whether or not there might be coverage for the particular concern raised.

   In the event you do forward this matter to your insurance carrier, and the carrier determines that you are covered, ordinarily as part of your coverage, the carrier will provide an attorney to defend the claim. If the carrier denies you coverage, you will need to hire your own counsel. In the event that occurs, or in the event that you determine on your own that you need legal counsel when dealing with a government agency, you may want to consult with, or retain, an administrative law specialist, an attorney who devotes a significant part of his or her practice to handling complaints for alleged violations of government regulations and/or prosecutions by the government.

3. **Develop a plan of action.**

   How you as a manager should respond to a complaint or violation will vary based on whether you have determined that legal assistance is needed.

WITHOUT AN ATTORNEY

- Calendar all response dates, and be sure to allow yourself enough time for mailing.

- Identify all the people who need to be involved in the response, and contact them in a timely fashion to solicit their input.

- Always keep clear, legible copies of anything that you forward as a response to a complaint. In any response that you give, if it is not true or you cannot prove it, do not state it in your response.

- Follow the instructions on the correspondence exactly. If it says that you only have one page to respond, then use only one page. If it says that the response must be typed, then make sure it is typed. If your response needs to be signed and a notary public must notarize your signature, be absolutely certain that it gets done, and make sure that the copies that you keep are copies of the responses after you have signed them and had them notarized.

WITH AN ATTORNEY

- Forward the correspondence immediately to your attorney, together with any supporting documentation that the attorney might need to understand the situation completely. Also, include a list of people who might have knowledge of the situation raised in the correspondence. It is a good idea to include contact information for the attorney. You want to facilitate communication between the attorney and any witnesses who can help present a positive response on your behalf.

- Stay in direct communication with your attorney until the matter is resolved. Just because you have given it to an attorney does not mean it is off of your plate. It is still crucial that you keep up with time deadlines and potential witnesses. For instance, if you know that certain people are going on vacation or you yourself are going on vacation, let the attorney know so that he or she can plan accordingly in the event he or she needs statements of additional information from you or the witnesses.

2.7 MONITORING REGULATORY CHANGE

It is simply not possible to know every governmental regulation that could affect the hospitality industry, and some laws change on a regular basis. Although changes in major federal law are rather well publicized, you cannot be sure that the policies of all federal agencies, state regulators, and local governments will be made known to you. Sources such as www.HospitalityLawyer.com can be very helpful in keeping managers current. The URLs listed in Figure 2.15 can be of help in following legislation at the national level. Reading about the hospitality industry will not only make you a better manager, but will also enable you to keep up with changing regulations.

For those managers employed by a national chain or management company, the parent company can be an excellent source of information on changing regulations. Indeed, one valuable service provided by franchisors to franchisees is regular updates on regulatory agencies and their work.

Because the federal government can play such a major role in regulating the hospitality industry, it is important to have current and rapid access to the actions taken by each of the federal regulatory agencies. Accessing the website addresses provided

---

HOSPITALITY INDUSTRY SAMPLING OF "WORLD WIDE WEB" HOME PAGE ADDRESSES FOR CORPORATE INFORMATION, REPORTS & PUBLICATIONS

HELPFUL LINKS

⇒ Hospitality Lawyer .... www.hospitalitylawyer.com
⇒ Restaurant.com .... www.restaurant.com
⇒ GoToMeeting .... www.gotomeeting.com
⇒ PrivateClubLawyer.com .... www.privateclublawyer.com
⇒ RestarauntLawyer.com .... www.restaurantlawyer.com

Figure 2.15 Hospitality industry web addresses.
Created by Cathleen Baird, director of archives, and maintained by Lateka Grays, supervisor of the Conrad N. Hilton College Library for the University of Houston, students, faculty, and hospitality industry professionals.

⇒ MeetingLawyer.com..www.meetinglawyer.com
⇒ StephenBarth.com...www.stephenbarth.com

LIBRARIES

⇒ Conrad N. Hilton College Library & Archives............ library.culinary.edu
⇒ MD Anderson Library UH .... info.lib.uh.edu
⇒ Harris County Public Libraries .... www.hcpl.lib.tx.us
⇒ Houston Public Libraries .... www.hpl.lib.tx.us
⇒ Library of Congress .... www.loc.gov

MISCELLANEOUS

⇒ Bizlink (Company Research.................................... www.bizlink.org
⇒ Book Directory .... www.bookdirectory.com
⇒ Business.com .... www.business.com
⇒ City of Houston.. www.houstontx.gov
⇒ Evaluating Websites..www.library.cornell.edu/okuref/research/webeval.html
⇒ Find Articles...www.findarticles.com
⇒ Find Law..www.findlaw.com
⇒ USA gov (Links to Government Sites)....................www.firstgov.gov
⇒ Greater Houston Partnership.............................www.houston.com
⇒ Library Spot, Links to Reference..........................www.libraryspot.com
⇒ Reuters..www.reuters.com
⇒ Search Engine Watch..www.searchenginewatch.com
⇒ Texas Work Commission......................................www.twc.state.tx.us
⇒ The Elements of Style (Guide to Grammar and Writing)..www.bartleby.com/141
⇒ Thesaurus.com...www.thesaurus.com
⇒ Webster Dictionary..www.m-w.com
⇒ Citation Machine (APA and MLA citation help)........www.citationmachine.net

HOSPITALITY AND TOURISM ADDRESSES

⇒ (C.H.I.P.S.) Culinary & Hospitality Book Distributor.....www.chipsbooks.com
⇒ AAA Diamond Rating Program...........................ww2.aaa.com/aaa/common/Tourbook/diamonds/whatisthis.html
⇒ ADA Home Page...www.ada.gov
⇒ Atlapedia..www.atlapedia.com
⇒ Aviation Week...www.avationnow.com
⇒ Technology Resource..hoteltechresource.com
⇒ Daily Restaurant Industry News..........................restsurantnewsresource.com
⇒ Boutique Lodging...www.boutiquelodging.com
⇒ Casino Wire...www.casinowire.com
⇒ CIA World Factbook..cia.gov
⇒ Department of Transportation...........................www.dot.gov
⇒ E-Hotelier...www.ehotelier.com
⇒ E-Hospitality...www.e-hospitality.com
⇒ Epicurious..www.epicurious.com

Figure 2.15 (*Continued*)

⇒	Hospitality Trends..	www.htrends.com
⇒	Food Service Central......................................	www.foodservicecentral.com
⇒	Foodservice.com..	www.foodservice.com
⇒	Gaming Commissions......................................	www.gamingfloor.com/Commissions.htm
⇒	Hospitality Industry Resources...........................	www.hospitalitynet.org
⇒	Hotel Chain Links...	www.hotelstravel.com/chains.html
⇒	Hotel Interactive...	www.hotelinteractive.com
⇒	Hotel Online (Daily News, Updates, and Reports).....	www.hotel-online.com/Neo/News
⇒	Houston Health Department Food Page..............	www.houstontx.gov/health
⇒	International Bed and Breakfast Directory...........	www.ibbp.com
⇒	ITA Tourism Industry......................................	www.tinet.ita.doc.gov
⇒	Just Drinks...	www.just-drinks.com
⇒	Just Food..	www.just-food.com
⇒	Las Vegas Statistics, etc.................................	www.lasvegas24hours.com
⇒	Lodging Research..	www.lodgingresearch.com
⇒	Meetings Industry Mall..................................	mim.com
⇒	PKF Texas...	www.pkftexas.com
⇒	Search Hotels..	www.searchhotels.com
⇒	Smith Travel Research....................................	www.smithtravelresearch.com
⇒	Texas Lodging..	www.texaslodging.com
⇒	Texas Travel Research....................................	www.travel.state.tx.us/travelresearch.aspx
⇒	Tourism Research Links (for Researchers, NOT Travelers)..	www.waksberg.com
⇒	Wired Hotelier..	www.wiredhotelier.com
⇒	World Biz...	www.worldbiz.com
⇒	Daily Travel Industry News..............................	www.travelindustrywire.com

Figure 2.15 (Continued)

in each section of this book is a good way to keep up to date on any changes in the law in that particular area.

As a hospitality manager, it is important to stay involved in the hospitality trade association that most closely represents your industry segment. The National Restaurant Association (NRA), the American Hotel and Lodging Association (AH&LA), the American Dietetic Association (ADA), and others regularly provide their memberships with legislative updates. Many of these organizations have state, regional, or local chapters that can be invaluable sources of information.

On a local level, chambers of commerce, business trade associations, and personal relationships with local police, fire, and building officials can help a manager stay up to date with municipal changes.

As a hospitality manager, it is critical that you take an active role in shaping the regulations that affect the industry. Governments, on the whole, attempt to pass regulations that they believe are in the best interests of the communities they represent. The problem arises, however, when the cost in dollars or the infringement on individual rights will far exceed the societal value of implementing a proposed regulation. For example, some consumers feel that it would be a good idea to have 24-hour video surveillance cameras placed in hotel corridors, even if the cost of installing them resulted in higher room rates. Such a camera might be a deterrent to crime and would make them feel safer; however, other guests object to the cameras as an invasion of their privacy. Hotel managers caught in the middle agree that the safety of their guests is a major concern, but they also know that there are less intrusive ways to make people feel safe while respecting their privacy. Without input from the hospitality industry, however, regulators may not be aware of those alternatives and could pass a law that is ultimately not in the best interests of the hotel guest, the lodging industry, or society.

It is only by staying aware of regulatory changes and being committed to proactive participation in the regulatory process through education and leadership that the hospitality industry will continue to flourish.

INTERNATIONAL SNAPSHOT

Immigration

The growing globalization of the world's economy and labor markets, in addition to amplifying concerns regarding security, has increased the awareness of immigration issues for everyone. For employers in the hospitality industry, who want to secure "the best and the brightest" as well as meet the needs of a labor-intensive industry, these issues are especially acute. They must accomplish these goals while remaining in compliance with complicated immigration laws, rules, regulations, and processes.

Globally, the process of employing noncitizens in a given country typically requires some sort of sponsorship by an in-country employer. (One significant exception is certain European Union nations, which do allow for employment of nationals of other EU nations.) By and large, time-limited work authorization or work permits are available to noncitizens in highly skilled professions, to corporate transferees or those filling managerial/executive positions, and to certain entrepreneurs/investors. In many countries, permanent residence status is also available, allowing a noncitizen to work and remain in a given country permanently, typically after having been a lawful resident in the country for several years. The availability of temporary work authorization or permanent residence status for noncitizens who work in low-skill or unskilled positions is far less common.

In the United States, the immigration system classifies persons into two primary categories: citizens, born in the United States, born to a U.S. citizen parent, or naturalized as U.S. citizens; and aliens, which essentially accounts for everyone else. The alien group is further divided into two primary segments: immigrants, who are aliens coming to the United States permanently or indefinitely (the terms "lawful permanent resident" and "green card holder" are used to describe persons authorized to remain indefinitely, for the remainder of their lives in the United States, subject to certain conditions), and nonimmigrants, who are aliens coming to the United States for a defined time period (e.g., three years) and for a definitive purpose (e.g., to work in a professional capacity for a U.S. employer.)

Typically, most nonimmigrants are limited to employment with a specific employer. For example, professional (specialty occupation or H-1B) workers employed in a capacity requiring a bachelor's degree or higher are generally limited to employment with their employer sponsor. Likewise, L-1 intracompany transferees (managerial or specialized-knowledge persons transferred by a multinational corporation from an office overseas to a U.S. office) are limited to employment within the multinational organization. The U.S. system also has a limited H-2B temporary worker nonimmigrant classification available to even unskilled workers. An employer must establish a short-term or seasonal need and demonstrate the unavailability of U.S. workers via a labor market test to employ such nonimmigrants. The most common use of this classification in the hospitality industry occurs at seasonal resort properties during the high season.

Unlike many other countries, permanent residence is not available to persons based on any particular period of U.S. residence but instead depends on specifically qualifying under existing family relation–based or employment-based categories. Most employment-based permanent residence cases require an employer to demonstrate the unavailability of a qualified, willing, and able U.S. citizen or lawful permanent resident worker, a labor market test known as labor certification. More senior or specialized persons can sometimes be sponsored without the need for labor certification.

Following the elimination of the Immigration and Naturalization Service (INS) as a separate department, the Department of Homeland Security (DHS) was established in 2003 and assumed all INS responsibilities. U.S. Citizenship and Immigration Services (USCIS), a bureau within the DHS, handles the majority of functions that were once completed by the INS, including nonimmigrant and immigrant (permanent resident) petitions. The DHS U.S. Immigration and Customs Enforcement (ICE) handles enforcement of federal immigration laws and customs laws, including I-9/IRCA.

Provided by Andrew Galeziowski of Ogletree and Deakins Law Firm, Atlanta, Georgia. www.ogletreedeakins.com

WHAT WOULD YOU DO?

After the highly publicized death of a college student, a local sports bar in your town lost its liquor license for 60 days. The student had consumed 21 shots of alcohol on his birthday and later died in his dorm room from alcohol poisoning. The bar was crowded, and because the shots had been purchased by a variety of friends of the victim, the bar manager and staff were not aware of the impending problem. Subsequently, the college's student newspaper published editorials warning against the perils of binge drinking and accused the management of the facility of negligence or indifference.

Sorrow in the community and outrage in the local press prompted the mayor of the city in which you operate your own Italian restaurant/pizzeria to propose a local ordinance banning the sale of more than three drinks per day to any individual. A drink, under the ordinance, would be defined as a 12-ounce beer, a 4-ounce glass of table wine, or a 1-1/2-ounce shot of liquor.

Violators would face a fine of $5,000 per incident. Enforcement would fall to the local police. It is widely known in the community that the mayor, generally a strong promoter of business, is a nondrinker, and support for the ordinance is strong because of the accident.

As the elected president of your local restaurant association, you have been asked to address the proposed ordinance at the next meeting of the city council. Develop a plan of action and outline for your address to the city council. In your essay, answer the following four questions:

1. What issues will you consider as you prepare your statement to the city council?
2. What message do you believe the majority of citizens in your community will support?
3. Where will you turn for advice and counsel in preparing your statement?
4. Will it make a difference to you if you know that the local television station will cover the council meeting?

To emphasize the importance of a hospitality operator knowing about OSHA and its hazardous materials definition, consider the case of *Halterman v. Radisson Hotel Corp.*, 523 S.E.2d 823 (Va. 2000).

FACTUAL SUMMARY

John Halterman (Halterman) was permanently injured while working for a Radisson Hotel (Radisson) in Alexandria, Virginia. H&H, the company Halterman worked for, was hired by Radisson to do some welding repairs to washing machines in the laundry facility of the hotel. The machines contained residue of a product called Liquid Lusterfixe, an acidic laundry detergent. None of the Radisson employees warned Halterman about the presence of the chemical. However, Radisson did maintain a display unit for material safety data sheets (MSDSs) on one wall of the laundry room. Those sheets listed all hazardous chemicals and their effects on humans.

During the welding process, the heat from Halterman's welding electrode caused the Lusterfixe to turn into a toxic gas. Halterman spent anywhere from 30 to 45 minutes welding on the machines without any protective breathing equipment. He breathed in unknown quantities of the gas while he worked on the washing machines. In all, the repairs took several hours to complete.

Halterman was in good health when he began the work. By the time he left the hotel, he had developed a cough. His cough worsened over the next few days, and he became short of breath. A doctor diagnosed him as having acute chemical pneumonitis. The gaseous compound he inhaled was known to cause pneumonitis. Eventually, he developed interstitial fibrosis, or scarring of the lungs. Halterman lost about one-third of his lung capacity.

Halterman sued Radisson Hotel for failing to maintain the laundry room in a safe manner and for failing to warn him about the presence of Liquid Lusterfixe, a hazardous chemical. He also sued Radisson for violation of the Hazard Communication Standard (HCS) of the Occupational Safety and Health Act (OSHA). Under OSHA, an employer is required to implement a written system for warning employees about hazardous chemicals used on the work site. Radisson was required to tell its employees and the employer of other employees about the existence of the MSDS display unit.

QUESTION FOR THE COURT

The question for the court was whether Radisson violated the HCS provision of OSHA. Halterman argued Radisson did not communicate the hazardous nature of the working conditions to him. Radisson responded by claiming it was not required by the statute to warn him about the hazard but was merely obligated to inform his employer of the existence of the MSDS display unit.

DECISION

The court ruled in favor of Radisson, holding that the only obligation under the statute was to communicate the existence of the MSDS display to Halterman's employer. Although Radisson had a duty to inform its own employees of hazardous chemicals present at the work site, there was no such duty for employees of other companies working at the hotel.

MESSAGE TO MANAGEMENT

Become familiar with your obligations under OSHA and meet them. Your employee's safety and the safety of others are at stake. Despite this ruling, the best practice is to make all aware of known dangers.

WHAT DID YOU LEARN IN THIS CHAPTER?

Federal, state, and local governments all pass laws and regulations that can potentially impact a hospitality operation. These laws and regulations are enforced by administrative agencies at all three levels of the government. Hospitality managers need to be familiar with the most common agencies and the areas of the industry that they regulate. In order to comply with these regulations, hospitality managers may be required to file forms, submit to inspections, apply for licenses, operate their business in a specified manner, and maintain their facilities and equipment in good working order.

Many government and nonprofit agencies publish guidelines for managers that can help you take the necessary steps to keep your facility in compliance with various regulations. In situations where federal, state, or local laws conflict with one another, the most restrictive regulation is the one that must be followed.

If you receive a complaint from a government agency, it is important that you take the appropriate steps to respond to the complaint in a timely fashion, respond in the manner requested, and develop a satisfactory plan of action. You may also choose to consult with an attorney or your insurance company, depending on the nature and severity of the complaint.

Government publications and websites, industry trade associations, and local community groups are common sources of information that hospitality managers can turn to for information on changing laws and regulations.

RAPID REVIEW

After you have studied this chapter, you should be prepared to:

1. Analyze the role of at least three federal entities that regulate the hospitality industry. Why do you think the federal government feels the need to be involved with regulation in each of these three areas?

2. Tip reporting is mandatory. Create a memo to a restaurant staff describing why they should comply.

3. Secure a material safety data sheet and compare its content to the list of required items detailed in this chapter.

4. Review the protected classes identified by the EEOC and determine if others should be added.

5. List five reasons a state's alcoholic beverage commission might revoke a liquor license. Prepare a five-minute bartender training session that addresses one of these reasons and how a restaurant or bar might avoid the difficulty.

6. Discuss the role of at least four of the eight federal regulatory bodies examined in this chapter.

7. Define the roles of the UNWTO, the IACO, and the WHO as they relate to travel.

8. Using the Internet, locate the home page of your state hotel and restaurant association. Secure the name of the person in the organization responsible for monitoring regulatory changes affecting the hospitality industry, and cite one such recent change in your state.

9. Go to www.HospitaltyLawyer.com and review the OSHA summary update in the Safety and Security Library.

TEAM ACTIVITY

In teams, list as many (at least ten in each category) local, state, and federal regulatory agencies that you would have to be concerned with if you were contemplating opening a country club in your community, with the following amenities: golf, tennis, pools, full-service restaurant, banquet facilities, and service of alcohol.

CHAPTER 3

HOSPITALITY BUSINESS STRUCTURES

"THANKS FOR MEETING with me," said Chris Joseph. "When Professor Laskee suggested I call you, I wasn't sure if you would find time for me. You sure have a nice-looking hotel!"

"Thank you," said Trisha Sangus, general manager of the property. "I always liked Professor Laskee. He was one of my favorites. I learned a lot from him. Anything I can do for him is truly my pleasure. How can I help you?"

"Well," Chris replied earnestly, "I want to start my own restaurant!"

"Great!" replied Trisha. "How can I help?"

"I have some questions," Chris replied. "Do you think it is better to do this all on my own or to have partners? And can you give me any tips on securing funds? I don't have enough money to do it all by myself. I have some capital but probably not enough to do the entire project. I do have some friends and family who can help. Also, I have been thinking about an independent place, but maybe a franchise makes more sense for my first restaurant. What do you think?"

"Time out," said Trisha with a smile. "First things first. I think it's wonderful that you want your own place. Owning a restaurant can be one of the most rewarding things you will ever do. I admire your enthusiasm. If you truly love serving people, and enjoy hard work, you'll make it!"

"I know I will," replied Chris.

"That's great. Confidence is important," said Trisha. "But let me ask you, have you considered the possibilities for structuring your business?"

"What do you mean, 'structuring'?" asked Chris.

"Well, let's look at your first question: to have a partner or go it alone. Your decision will be affected by how you like to work and the amount of control you want to retain, but it will also affect how much freedom you have if you decide to sell the business. An accountant can advise you there, but you should know your options."

"Okay," said Chris. "I'll look into that. What about incorporating? Is that a good idea? For liability, I mean."

"Incorporating can reduce your personal liability if things don't work out, but there are other ways to do that, and some of them are less expensive. But they do have limitations. An attorney can help you there; but again, you should understand your options."

"How about taxes?" asked Chris. "Are there differences there? I'd want to put most of the restaurant's earnings back in the business, at least for the first few years."

"Reinvesting in your business is smart," said Trisha, "and you are right to consider taxation. The type of organizational structure you select will definitely affect your tax rates."

"Wow," said Chris. "Selling, liability, taxes . . . what else is affected by the structure I choose?"

"Capital," replied Trisha. "Most people have to raise or borrow money to start their businesses."

"That would be me!" said Chris with a laugh.

"That's okay," said Trisha. "I don't know of a successful businessperson who has zero debt. It isn't what you owe; it's your ability to repay it. And creditors will look at your business and operating structures to determine, in part, how likely you will be able to repay them."

"Will franchisors look at that, too?" asked Chris.

"Absolutely," replied Trisha. "Look, Chris, you want to make your own place happen. You can do it. But let me give you some reading material, then let's get together again next week. Sound good?"

"Sounds great," replied Chris. "I want to do this right, and I really appreciate your experience, and your willingness to help."

"Just remember," said Trisha with a smile, "free advisors always get a good table!"

"You got it," said Chris. "The best in the house."

IN THIS CHAPTER, YOU WILL LEARN:

1. The importance of selecting the proper organizational and operational structures for a hospitality business.
2. The various organizational business structures used in the hospitality industry.
3. The most common operational business structures used in the hospitality industry.
4. The responsibilities and obligations created by an agency relationship.

3.1 THE IMPORTANCE OF BUSINESS STRUCTURE

One of the most appealing aspects of the hospitality industry is the opportunity for owning your own business. Whether they are interested in owning restaurants or hotels, one establishment or a whole chain, self-ownership is a strong factor in many people's excitement about the field of hospitality.

When individual entrepreneurs elect to start their own business, they face a variety of decisions about location, product offerings, and financing, to name but a few elements. An extremely important decision, and one that will affect the future success or failure of the business, is that of their *organizational structure* and their *operating structure*. In this chapter, you will learn about the most common types of organizational and operating structures used in the hospitality industry.

Organizational structure refers to the legal formation of the business entity. It represents the relationship between the business owners and the outside world. This legal formation is important because the courts and all levels of government treat businesses and their owners differently, based on their organizational structure. Therefore, it is important to select an organizational structure that works to the advantage of both the business and its owner.

Operating structure refers to the relationship between a business's owners and its management. The composition of a business's management can be just as important as its type of structure. Operating structures of different hospitality organizations vary greatly. For example, the individual owner of a restaurant may, in fact, also manage it on a day-to-day basis. In another operating structure, however, a hotel may actually be owned by one legal entity, be managed by another legal entity, and have contractual relationships about precisely how it is to be managed with yet another legal entity.

To understand better the importance of structure, consider the case of John Graves, an individual who, after years of working for a national restaurant chain, wishes to open his own restaurant. Depending on the type of organizational structure John selects, the income tax he must pay on profits will vary considerably. In addition, the limits of his personal liability for the debts of his business will be directly influenced by the organizational structure he chooses.

Banks and other sources of capital will often make decisions on the worthiness of lending to a business venture based on the organizational structure. As well, investors may make investment decisions based on the organizational structure selected by a business's owners. Vendors may also determine whether to extend credit to a business based, in part, on its organizational structure.

Equally as important, an individual's ability to sell or transfer ownership of the business will be affected by the organizational structure selected. As you have learned, the organizational structure selected for a business is important, and a variety of organizational structures are available to an entrepreneur. The most common ones are discussed in section 3.2.

It is also important to determine where the business will be formed in order to get the most benefit out of the laws available to businesses. Generally speaking, business entities are governed by state law, and these requirements often vary from state to state. Thus, it is important to know which state law governs the requirements of a business entity.

The applicable law that governs a business entity is determined by which state the entity is formed in, which in most cases is easily determined by where that entity—say, a corporation—has filed its creation documents. A corporation has the ability to choose the state in which it will be incorporated, which does not necessarily have to be the state in which it is physically located, and a corporation has the ability to incorporate in multiple states.

Some uniformity does, in fact, exist amongst the state laws, however, because of the overwhelming number of business entities that decide to incorporate in the state of Delaware. In order to attract revenue, Delaware has created a set of laws that are extremely favorable to business entities that decide to incorporate in that state. In fact, a significant amount of Delaware's state revenue directly comes from business entity incorporation filings and fees. Thus, the Delaware business laws have become a sort of model standard that most states adopt as their own state's laws, and business owners should be aware of this standard in not only choosing which type of business entity to create but also choosing exactly where to create it.

LEGALESE
Organizational structure: The legal entity that owns a business.

LEGALESE
Operating structure: The relationship between a business's ownership and its management.

3.2 COMMON HOSPITALITY ORGANIZATIONAL STRUCTURES

Sole Proprietorship

A *sole proprietorship* is the simplest of all organizational structures. In this structure, a single individual owns all of the business and is responsible for all of its debts. The majority of small businesses in the United States are sole proprietorships. Examples in the field of hospitality could include a local hamburger stand, a doughnut shop, or perhaps a small bed and breakfast. In a sole proprietorship, the personal assets of the owner can be used to pay any losses, taxes, or damages resulting from lawsuits against the business. There is no personal protection from any of the risks associated with owning a business. Put another way, the *sole proprietor* has unlimited liability for the indebtedness of his or her business.

Profits in a sole proprietorship are taxed at the same rate as the owner's personal income tax. Each year, the owner files a tax return listing the proprietorship's income and expenses. Any profit or loss is reported on the individual owner's tax return. If the owner has income not directly related to the business, losses from the business can be used to reduce the overall amount of income subject to taxation.

Should the owner of a sole proprietorship wish to sell the business or pass his or her ownership rights on to others, he or she is free to do so.

Sole proprietorships can be started simply by opening a bank account to keep track of the business's income and expenses. Because the owner will have unlimited liability, lenders to a sole proprietorship evaluate the financial position of the owner carefully before providing capital to the business.

If the owner of a sole proprietorship is operating under an "assumed name," a name other than his or her own, an assumed-name certificate should be filed with the local government. Thus, if David Daniels began operating a diner and called it Davey's Diner, the term Davey's Diner would be the trade name. Accordingly, the assumed-name certificate filed with the local government would let anyone know that when they do business with Davey's Diner, they are actually doing business with David Daniels, or, put another way, they are doing business with David Daniels d/b/a (doing business as) Davey's Diner.

Any entity operating under an assumed name—not just sole proprietorships—should file a certificate disclosing the ownership and ownership structure of the operation. In many states, filing this certificate is required by law.

General Partnership

A *general partnership* is similar to a sole proprietorship, except that it consists of two or more owners who agree to share the responsibility for the operations, financial performance, and liability of the business. Partnerships are formed through oral or written contracts. Generally, these agreements will specify the contributions and responsibilities of each partner:

- How much money each partner will contribute to the business
- How much time each partner will contribute to the business
- Who will make decisions on how the business is operated
- How profits will be divided
- How losses will be shared
- A procedure for transfer of ownership, if one or more partners wishes to sell his or her portion of the business or becomes unable to participate as a partner

In hospitality, partnerships are occasionally used to begin small operations; but as the risk of liability increases, the operations are better served by converting to one of the limited liability structures discussed later in the chapter.

As in a sole proprietorship, the partners in a general partnership have unlimited liability for the indebtedness of the business. Additionally, the partners are liable jointly and severally for the partnership's debt; that is, they are liable jointly as partner/owners, but they are also liable severally, meaning that one partner alone could be liable for the entire amount of the debt. Thus, even if the partnership is owned on a 50–50 basis, should one partner be unable to pay his or her portion of the debt, the other partner will be liable for the entire amount of the debt. If loans are needed to establish the business, potential lenders will evaluate the personal assets of each partner. Profits from the business are distributed to the partners and taxed at the same rate as the owners' personal income tax.

Partnership agreements can be simple or complex, but as described in Chapter 4, "Business Contracts," because they are complex contracts, they are best documented in writing. This is particularly important when addressing the transfer of ownership rights by one or more partners.

Consider the case of Greg Larson and Mike Haley, who have been equal partners for 20 years in a business that operates a ski run and lift for a resort hotel in Wisconsin. This year, at age 50, Greg would like to sell his portion of the partnership to his daughter. If there were nothing in the partnership agreement prohibiting such a sale, Greg would be free to transfer his half of the business to his daughter. If, however, there is language in the partnership agreement that allows the remaining partner the right of first refusal, Mike would be able to purchase the other half of the business himself, should he so desire, before Greg has the right to sell it to anyone else.

Limited Partnership (LP)

While a sole proprietorship has only one owner, and a general partnership may consist of several owners, a *limited partnership (LP)* consists of two classes of owners: the *limited partner* and the *general (or managing) partner*. The limited partner is simply someone who invests money in the partnership. The general partner may or may not be an investor but serves as the business's operating and financial manager.

Many successful hotel chains began as limited partnerships. A limited partnership is so named because of the "limits" it places on the limited partner's liability. As a general rule, liability will be limited if a partner is not directly involved in the day-to-day managerial decision making of the business. The legal principle involved is one of control. A general partner exercises control over day-to-day operations but as a result bears unlimited liability for any debts or damages incurred by the business. A limited partner risks only his or her investment in the business but must give up the control of that investment in exchange for a limitation on the amount of liability. In fact, if a limited partner becomes actively involved in the business's managerial decision making, the state may revoke the limited partnership's protected status, which would then subject the limited partner to potential unlimited liability for the debts of the business.

The taxation on the profits of a limited partnership is similar to the taxation requirements of general partnerships. The profits are distributed to the partners and taxed at the same rate as the owner's personal income tax.

The limited partnership is a special type of business arrangement provided for by state law. Most states require specific forms to be filed with the secretary of state or some other government official in order for a business to be granted limited partnership status. A limited partnership is closely regulated by the state in which it operates, and it is the state that permits limited partners to invest in a business and be exempt from a large share of the liability should the business fail. Most states require a written limited partnership agreement to be filed as well. Even in a state where it is not required, it is a good idea to have an attorney draw up an agreement prior to the start-up of the business.

LEGALESE
Limited partnership (LP): A business organization with two classes of owners. The limited partner invests in the business but may not exercise control over its operation, in return for protection from liability. The general or managing partner assumes full control of the business operation but can also be held liable for any debts the operation incurs.

LEGALESE
Limited partner: The entity in a limited partnership relationship who is liable only to the extent of his or her investment. Limited partners have no right to manage the partnership.

LEGALESE
General (or managing) partner: The entity in a limited partnership relationship that makes the management decisions and can be held responsible for all debts and legal claims against the business.

≫ ANALYZE THE SITUATION 3.1

NICHOLAS KOSTANTY FORMED A limited partnership with his father-in-law, Ray Sweeney, to open an upscale French restaurant in a Midwestern town. Mr. Kostanty was the general partner and owned 75 percent of the business. Mr. Sweeney, with 25 percent ownership, was the limited partner and invested $100,000. After one year, difficulties in the restaurant's operation caused business to drop off, and Mr. Kostanty called Mr. Sweeney for advice.

After hearing of the difficulties, and concerned with the security of his investment, Mr. Sweeney traveled from Arizona to Indiana to visit the operation. Upon observing the operation for two days, the two partners decided to launch a large and expensive television ad campaign to increase flagging sales. Mr. Sweeney designed the campaign with the help of Seelhoff Advertising and Video, a local advertising agency specializing in television commercials.

Despite an immediate increase in sales, over time, volume continued to decline, and finally, three months after the ad campaign was launched, the restaurant closed its doors. Total debts at the time the restaurant closed equaled $400,000, with assets of the partnership totaling only $200,000. Included in the debt was $150,000 owed to the advertising agency. The agency sought payment directly from Mr. Sweeney. Mr. Sweeney, claiming that his liability was limited to the $100,000 he had previously invested in the business, refused to pay any additional money. The Seelhoff Advertising Agency sued the limited partnership, as well as Nicholas Kostanty and Ray Sweeney individually.

1. By hiring the advertising agency, did Mr. Sweeney forfeit his limited partner status?

2. Is Mr. Sweeney liable for the outstanding debts of the limited partnership?

LEGALESE

Corporation: A group of individuals granted a charter, legally recognizing them as a separate entity with rights and liabilities distinct from those of its members.

LEGALESE

Shares: Fractional portions of a company in which the owner of the portion has voting rights and rights to a respective fraction of the assets of the company.

C Corporation

A *C corporation*, often referred to simply as a *corporation*, is formed when groups of individuals elect to band together to achieve a common purpose. When they do, the corporation has a legal identity completely separate from that of its individual owners. A corporation is empowered with legal rights that are usually reserved only for individuals, such as the right to sue and be sued, own property, hire employees, or loan and borrow money. Corporations are different from sole proprietorships or partnerships in that it is the corporation itself, rather than the individual owners, that is liable for any debts incurred. This is a powerful advantage. Accordingly, as an operation becomes more complex, and the risk of liability becomes greater, incorporating becomes a sound business practice. Today, many of the major hotel and restaurant companies are incorporated (e.g., Marriott, McDonald's, Hilton, Hyatt, Yum! Brands).

The actual owners of a corporation are called shareholders because they own *shares*, or portions, of the business. Legally, shareholders have the power to determine a corporation's direction and the way it is managed. In reality, though, in many cases individual shareholders may have little influence on the way a corporation is run. Shareholders elect directors who oversee the business and hire managers for day-to-day operations (many of these directors and managers may be shareholders themselves). A shareholder is not liable for the debts or other obligations of the corporation, except to the extent of any commitment that was made to buy its shares. Shareholders also have a right to participate in the distribution of any residual assets of the corporation if it is ever dissolved, once all liabilities have been paid off.

A C corporation gets its name from Chapter C of the United States Internal Revenue Code (IRC). Although C corporations eliminate individual liability, they also have a significant disadvantage. Profits from a C corporation are taxed twice. The first tax is levied on the profits the corporation earns. After those taxes are paid, the after-tax profits that remain can be distributed to the corporation's shareholders in the form of *dividends*. The individual owners are then required to pay income taxes on those dividends. It is important to note that the corporation must pay taxes on its profits even if those profits are not distributed to the corporation's owners.

> **LEGALESE**
>
> **Dividend:** A portion of profits received by a shareholder, usually in relation to his or her ownership (shares) of a corporation.

Corporations are taxed at different rates from those of individuals, and the taxes they pay may be affected by special rules that allow certain business expenses to be deducted from revenues prior to establishing the corporation's taxable income.

Consider the case of Michelle Rogen, an entrepreneur who wishes to establish a company providing part-time security guards for restaurants and nightclubs. Ms. Rogen has an inheritance of $1 million that she holds in her name in various bank accounts. She would like to use $100,000 of her funds to begin her business. Because of her concern for potential liability, Ms. Rogen selects her business structure carefully. A sole proprietorship or a general partnership would not provide any liability protection for her. A limited partnership would also be ineffective because Ms. Rogen, as the business manager, would have to take on the general partner's role, and thus her liability would still be unlimited.

Ms. Rogen selects a C corporation structure, which will limit her liability to only the assets of the corporation. If the company is successful, however, it will pay a corporate tax (at a higher rate than Ms. Rogen would have to pay as an individual on those profits), and then Ms. Rogen must pay her own individual tax on any profits she removes from the business. This double taxation is a powerful disadvantage of the C corporation structure.

C corporations are ordinarily more costly to establish and administer than sole proprietorships and general partnerships, but their ability to limit liability makes them very popular. To establish a corporation, the officers of the business must file "articles of incorporation" with either the secretary of state or a corporate registrar's office in the state in which the business will be incorporated. These articles will disclose the officers and board of directors of the corporation, as well as the number of shares the company is authorized to sell initially.

S Corporation

There is a type of corporation that avoids the double taxation inherent in a C corporation. This is known as an *S corporation*, and it also gets its name from the U.S. tax code. An S corporation is also known as a subchapter S corporation.

The S corporation format makes good sense for many hospitality businesses, such as family-owned operations. There are several requirements for establishing and maintaining an S corporation status:

> **LEGALESE**
>
> **S corporation:** A type of business entity that offers liability protection to its owners and is exempt from corporate taxation on its profits. Some restrictions limit the circumstances under which an S corporation can be formed.

- There is a limit of no more than 100 shareholders.
- Only one class of stock is issued.
- All shareholders must be U.S. citizens or residents.

■ All shareholders must be individuals, trusts, or estates, rather than partnerships or corporations.

■ Some types of corporations such as financial institutions, insurance companies, or domestic international sales corporations are not eligible.[1]

An S corporation provides the same liability protection offered by a C corporation but must be established with the agreement of all shareholders. This is done by filing a form with the Internal Revenue Service that has been signed by all of the corporation's shareholders, to signify their agreement to elect S status.

In an S corporation, any profits from the business are distributed directly to the shareholders in proportion to their ownership of the corporation. The profits are reported on the individual owners' income tax returns and are taxed at the individuals' taxable rates, which is similar to the favorable taxation treatment of a partnership; however, shareholders also receive the liability protection of a corporation.

It is also important to remember, however, that income from an S corporation is taxable even if it is not distributed to the shareholders. For example, assume two brothers open a microbrewery and select the S corporation structure. Profits from the bar in the first year are $50,000. The brothers decide they want to use all of the profits from the first year to expand their marketing efforts in the second year. The brothers still, however, must pay individual taxes on the first year's profits in proportion to their ownership in the S corporation.

In addition to filing the S election form with the federal government, in some instances, the state in which the business operates may also require notification. Some states do not recognize the S corporation for state income tax purposes, but do recognize it for liability purposes. Generally speaking, the restrictions on an S corporation make it most suitable for smaller companies, especially those in which the owners are also the employees and managers.

Limited Liability Company (LLC)

The *limited liability company* (LLC) is a form of corporation created under state (rather than federal) law. To fully understand the LLC, let's first recall the disadvantages of the business structures examined so far. If someone starting a new business chooses to establish it as a partnership, it is taxed only once but obligates the owners to part or all of the liability and risk involved in operating the business. A limited partnership is also only taxed once, but the liability of the general partner is unlimited A corporation offers liability protection but features double taxation and complex administrative regulations. An S corporation could be selected to avoid double taxation, but the restrictions on an S corporation can be significant.

The limited liability company is a fairly new type of entity, created by some states to combine the best features of a corporation with the simplicity of a partnership. Under the typical LLC statute, the members (similar to shareholders in a corporation or partners in a partnership) are all protected from the company's debts, unless they undertake personal responsibility for a debt, such as personally guaranteeing a loan for the business. Thus, a member can serve as the company's owner or manager, yet still protect his or her personal assets from liability.

The LLC is governed by an operating agreement, which is similar to a partnership agreement. It sets the rules for managing the company, as well as the rights and responsibilities of the members.

If formed properly, the Internal Revenue Service will treat the LLC as a partnership for tax purposes; thus, there is no double taxation. However, in some states, the LLC will have to pay state income taxes on its profits. If the LLC is not formed properly or within the guidelines established by the state in which it does business, the IRS may consider the LLC to be a corporation for tax purposes.

Depending on the state in which it does business, the LLC may have to pay a filing fee or an annual registration fee. The LLC has become the preferred type of

---

[1]Internal Revenue Service, "S Corporations," www.irs.gov/businesses/small/article/0,,id=98263,00.html. Last reviewed December 15, 2010. Accessed July 2, 2011.

organizational structure in the hospitality industry, particularly for independent operators and many franchisees. Its characteristics and advantages are well suited to hospitality operators who are able to elect such a structure.

Like all organizational structures, the limited liability company should be selected only after seeking the advice of a business attorney and tax advisor.

Another entity is available in most states. Known as the limited liability partnership (LLP), it provides limited liability for its partners, as well as retaining the tax advantages of a general partnership. However, this particular entity is more often used for professional partnerships, such as doctors, lawyers, or engineers, rather than for individuals seeking to enter into a general business operation.

Figure 3.1 summarizes the important differences among the types of organizational structure we have looked at.

Sole Proprietorships

Liability	Unlimited personal liability.
Tax Liability	Owner pays.
Tax Rate	Individual.
To Transfer Ownership	No restrictions.
Number of Owners	One.

General Partnerships

Liability	Unlimited personal liability.
Tax Liability	Partners pay, even if profits are not distributed.
Tax Rate	Individual.
To Transfer Ownership	Per partnership agreement.
Number of Owners	At least two.

Limited Partnerships (LP)

Liability	General Partner has no limited liability protection. Limited Partners have limited liability protection unless provided otherwise.
Tax Liability	Partners pay, even if profits are not distributed.
Tax Rate	Individual.
To Transfer Ownership	Per partnership agreement. Generally, an assignee cannot become a limited partner without majority consent.
Number of Owners	At least two.

C Corporations

Liability	All shareholders have limited liability protection unless otherwise provided.
Tax Liability	Corporation taxed on profits, shareholders taxed on dividends.
Tax Rate	Corporate rate on profits, individual rate on dividends.
To Transfer Ownership	No restrictions for transferring shares.
Number of Owners	All shareholders share limited liability.

S Corporations

Liability	All shareholders have limited liability protection unless otherwise provided.

Figure 3.1 Organizational structures summary chart.

Figure 3.1 (Continued)

Tax Liability	Shareholders pay, even if profits are not distributed.
Tax Rate	Individual
To Transfer Ownership	There are no transfers to an ineligible shareholder. Cannot exceed 75 shareholders.
Number of Owners	All shareholders have limited liability.
Limited Liability Companies (LLC)	
Liability	All members have limited liability protection from the debts of the LLC, unless otherwise provided. Some question exists as to whether states that do not have the LLC form will respect the limited liability of members.
Tax Liability	Members pay, even if profits are not distributed.
Tax Rate	Individual
To Transfer Ownership	Generally, an assignee cannot become a full member without majority consent.
Number of Owners	No restrictions, but at least two members to gain partnership level taxation. May be taxable as a corporation if it has more than 500 members.

3.3 COMMON HOSPITALITY OPERATING STRUCTURES

Now that you understand the manner in which ownership of hospitality operations can be structured, it is equally important to understand the varied manner in which these businesses are managed and operated.

Owner-Operator

Assume that you wished to start your own restaurant. If you proceeded to do so, it is very likely that, regardless of the organizational structure you select, you will also want to manage your restaurant. If you do select an *owner-operator* structure, you would join the ranks of literally thousands of hospitality businesses operated under this model.

Owner-operators may own a single small business or they may own multiunit facilities in several geographic areas. In many cases, the owner-operator structure is used by families that pass restaurants or lodging facilities on to new generations of hospitality managers. In fact, most towns and cities are home to one or more "family-run" businesses that have served their communities for multiple generations.

The actual organizational structures used by owner-operators may vary from single proprietorship to various forms of partnerships and corporations. As the independent owner-operator of your own business, you will have complete freedom to implement any policies, procedures, and products you feel are appropriate. Drawbacks, however, include the possible insufficiency of marketing influence or public recognition, reduced purchasing power, and a lack of operational support (something that business owners without a lot of experience may find valuable or necessary). In many cases, independent business operators who start businesses experience markedly lower expenditures on both initial investment and promotion than do some other operational structures; however, their long-term survival rate is typically lower than with some other operational structures.

Franchise

When customers see facilities with well-established business names such as Hilton, Big Boy, Subway, Marriott, and the like, they may assume that the company that owns these businesses is also its operator. In fact, however, in most cases, the owners of these businesses are not owner operators, but rather, they have elected to enter into a *franchise* relationship.

According to the International Franchise Association, a franchise exists when one party allows another to use its name, logo, and system of business to generate sales and profits. One of the earliest franchisors was the Singer Sewing Machine Company, which set up dealers shortly after the Civil War to sell and repair its sewing machines. McDonald's is a present-day classic example of how, without tremendous personal wealth, an entrepreneur named Ray Kroc could take an idea and quickly spread it coast to coast, then around the world. Many companies turn to franchising as a system for expansion because they can do so rapidly with a minimum amount of capital and with the assistance of top-notch operators. However, in return, the company must be willing to share its revenues with those operators.

In a franchise operating structure, the actual owner of a hospitality facility (the *franchisee*) agrees to operate that facility in a specific manner in exchange for the franchise. A franchise can take many forms, but, as stated previously, it is generally the right to use the name, trademark, and procedures established by the *franchisor* for the sale of a product or service in a specific geographic area.

In a typical franchise operating structure, an owner gives up part of his or her freedom to make operational decisions in exchange for the franchisor's expertise and the marketing power of the franchisor's brand name. The owner of a doughnut franchise, for example, gives up the right to make doughnuts according to any recipe she

> **LEGALESE**
> **Franchise:** A contract between a parent company (franchisor) and an operating company (franchisee) to allow the franchisee to run a business with the brand name of the parent company, as long as the terms of the contract concerning methods of operation are followed.

> **LEGALESE**
> **Franchisee:** The person or business that has purchased and/or received a franchise.

> **LEGALESE**
> **Franchisor:** The person or business that has sold and/or granted a franchise.

≫ ANALYZE THE SITUATION 3.2

AFTER FIVE YEARS OF effort, you develop a unique style of roasting pork that is extremely popular in your hometown. You own and operate five units called Porkies that sell this product. Each unit costs $175,000 to develop. Total sales of each unit average $600,000, with a net profit margin of 10 percent per unit.

A friend of yours discusses your success with you and suggests the possibility of opening five new stores in his or her hometown. Your friend wants to know what you would charge to sell your recipe and your standard operating procedure (SOP) manual, as well as the use of the name Porkies.

1. How would you determine a fair price for your experience?

2. If your friend is successful, causing the name of Porkies to be even better known, thus resulting in greater demand for franchises, should your friend share in future revenue from franchise sales?

3. What are the ethical issues at play here?

chooses but gains the national recognition of a well-known "name" for her doughnut products. The use of the franchise as an operating structure is extremely common in the hospitality industry.

If a business owner elects to operate a franchise, he or she can gain the marketing support of an established trademarked name; credibility with potential investors, lenders, customers, and vendors; and, in many cases, assistance with operational problems that are encountered. Of course, these advantages come with a price. Typically, the franchisor will charge the franchisee an initial fee, plus a percentage of gross revenue. In addition, both parties will sign a legal agreement, which outlines the duties and responsibilities of both the franchisor and franchisee. This franchise agreement is often referred to as a *licensing agreement*, because the franchise company (*licensor*) is granting the right, or *license*, to operate as one of its franchisees (*licensee*).

The operating agreement requirements and other legal aspects of buying and utilizing the franchise operating structure are complex. In Chapter 5, "Significant Hospitality Contracts," we will look closely at those mandatory disclosures and arrangements that relate to franchising. Here, what is important to remember is that operating a business as a franchise is simply one of several operating structures available to a business owner.

The primary advantage to buying a franchise is that doing so allows a business's owners to acquire a brand name with regional or national recognition. In many cases, affiliation with a strong brand name will increase a business's sales and thus its profitability. However, the charges for using the name of the franchisor's brand increase as the perceived quality of the brand name increases. The total fees paid by the business owner to the brand owners are related to the strength of the brand name and the revenue that the name will likely bring. Although the fees related to a franchise agreement are sometimes negotiable, they will, on average, equal 3 to 15 percent of a business's gross sales revenue.

In addition to increased sales levels, affiliation with a brand affects the ability of a business's owner to secure financing. When owners seek financing from banks or other lending institutions, they often find that these lenders will look more favorably on those businesses that elect this operating structure than those that do not. Additional advantages, depending on the franchisor selected, may include assistance with on-site training, advice on purchasing items for sale, and reduced operating costs resulting from vendors who give brand operators preferred pricing.

The greatest advantage to a franchisor of entering into a franchise agreement with a business owner is the increase in fee payments to the brand that will result from the agreement. Like all businesses, franchise companies desire growth. The greater the number of businesses that operate under a single brand name, the greater, in general, the value of the name—and, thus, the fees that can be charged for using that name. In addition, each additional business that affiliates with a brand helps to pay for the fixed overhead of operating that brand. Therefore, additional properties operating under the same brand name result in greater profits for the franchise company.

For a business owner, there are also disadvantages associated with purchasing a franchise. Although there is no question that consumers often prefer the consistency associated with buying a franchised product or service, the manager of such a facility may be hampered by franchisor rules and regulations that do not take into account local needs and tastes. For example, having grits on a breakfast menu may make tremendous sense for an operation in a southern state but may make no sense at all for the same type of unit in the Northeastern portion of the United States. If a franchisor is not sensitive to the needs of local clientele, the franchisee may have a difficult time achieving success.

Local conditions can affect more than menu items. Returning to the example of McDonald's as a franchise model, in his book *Grinding It Out*, Ray Kroc speaks of the difficulties he encountered persuading the McDonald brothers to allow the modifications he required to adjust his building design from one that was successful in California to one that could survive the frigid winters of Illinois.[2] The best franchisors allow their franchisees to make adjustments for local conditions, while maintaining the integrity of the franchise concept. Thus, business owners who select this operating structure should be very familiar with the operating procedures of their franchisors.

Management Contracts

In many cases, those who own a business are not the same individuals as those who want to manage a business. Either these nonoperating business owners can hire individual managers to operate their businesses, or, if they desire, they can select a *management company* to do so. When they do, they will enter into a *management contract* with the chosen management company.

In some cases, investors who are not experienced in hospitality management simply elect to hire a qualified company to run their businesses. In other cases, the owners of a business have absolutely no interest in managing or even in the continued ownership of it. For example, assume that a bank has loaned money to a restaurant owner to start a business. The owner opens the restaurant but, over time, fails to make the required loan repayments. As a result, the bank is forced to repossess the business. In a case such as this, the bank, which is now the restaurant's owner, will likely close it, or, if it feels it is best, seek a company to manage the restaurant until it is put up for sale and purchased by a new owner.

The hotel industry, because it is cyclical, sometimes experiences falling occupancy rates and revenues. Sometimes these cycles result in properties that fall into receivership and lenders who face the consequence of becoming involuntary owners. In cases such as these, effectively managing a hotel may simply mean optimizing the property's value while offering it for sale.

Interestingly, the operating relationship that exists when a hotel owner signs a management contract with a hotel management company is very different from that of a restaurant owner who does not wish to operate the restaurant. Typically, in the restaurant business, the owner of a restaurant who elects not to operate it, but wishes to continue ownership, will often lease the space to another restaurateur. In that situation, the business entity that leases the restaurant pays the restaurant's owner an agreed amount and assumes responsibility for all the expenses associated with operating the business. If the restaurant makes money, the benefit goes to the person(s) who leased the space. If the restaurant loses money, the same person(s) is (are) responsible for the loss.

Unlike the restaurant business, in most cases, hotel owners find they cannot lease their properties to management companies. Rather, it is the management company that receives a predetermined monthly fee from the hotel's owners in exchange for operating the property, and it is the owners who assume a passive position regarding operating decisions, while at the same time assuming responsibility for all operating expenses, and debt service. The fees charged by management companies to operate a hotel vary, but commonly range between 1 and 5 percent of the hotel's monthly revenue. Thus, regardless of the hotel's operating performance, the management company is paid the fee for its services and the hotel's owners receive the profits (if any) after all expenses are paid. Just as the legal agreements, governing franchises can be complex, so too can be those related to management contracts and leases. As a result, these also will be examined in more detail in Chapter 5.

LEGALESE

Management company: An entity that, for a fee, assumes responsibility for the day-to-day operation of a business.

LEGALESE

Management contract: The legal agreement that defines the responsibilities of a business owner and the management company chosen to operate the owner's business.

---

[2] Ray Kroc, *Grinding It Out: The Making of McDonald's* (Chicago: Contemporary Books, 1977).

REITs

LEGALESE

REIT: Short for "real estate investment trust," a very special form of business structure in which the owners of a business are generally prohibited from operating it.

Some ownership and operating structures are quite unique. One of these is the real estate investment trust (*REIT*). A REIT is a form of business ownership that, in many cases, expressly forbids the owner of a business from operating it. Thus, for example, an individual REIT could own 300 hotels but not be allowed to serve a customer breakfast in any of them!

As a REIT, a company can own hotel properties but in most cases must lease them to operating companies. A real estate investment trust is a private or public corporation (or trust) that enjoys special status under the U.S. tax code. That status allows the REIT to pay no corporate income tax as long as its activities meet statutory tests that restrict its business to certain commercial real estate activities. Most states honor this federal treatment and, as a result, also do not require REITs to pay state income tax.

The REIT is a popular ownership model for hotels because the Real Estate Investment Trust Act of 1960 set up three key provisions when it created REITs:

LEGALESE

Condominium: A multiple-unit complex (i.e., hotel, apartment house, office building), the units of which are individually owned with each owner receiving a recordable deed to the individual unit purchased, including the right to sell that unit and sharing in joint ownership of all common grounds, hallways, and on-site facilities.

1. Owners that operate as REITs pay no tax on corporate income.
2. In order to get that tax break, REITs must pay out at least 90 to 95 percent of every dollar in income to their shareholders in the form of dividends.
3. Companies can pass the tax savings from the dividend deduction on to shareholders, making REITs an attractive investment.

Although the details of how a REIT is established (there are actually several varieties of REIT) are beyond the scope of this text, it is important for hospitality managers to understand that, especially in the lodging industry, the REIT is a common business structure.

Condo Hotels

LEGALESE

Fractional ownership:
A purchase arrangement in which a condominium owner purchases the use of his or her unit for a portion (fraction) of a year.
The fraction may be defined in terms of the number of days per year (e.g., 30, 60, etc.) or very specific days and/or months (e.g., January 1 through March 31). Individual units purchased under such an arrangement are commonly known as fractionals.

An increasingly popular hotel structure, and thus an increasingly common hotel organizational/operating structure, is the *condominium* or "condo" hotel (sometimes also referred to as a mixed-use property).

In 2005, Smith Travel Research reported that there were 227 condo hotel projects in the development pipeline, representing more than 93,000 units (rooms); a number of hotel rooms close to the average annual supply of new rooms built in a "normal" year.[3] As of March 2006, condo hotel rooms made up nearly 20 percent of the hotel rooms under development in the United States. Given the latest economic downturn, the development of condos has slowed dramatically, along with the entire hotel development industry. Unfortunately, there is not universal agreement on the definition of a condo hotel. A "condo" hotel can refer to many types of hotel operating structures, ranging from a traditional hotel with residential condominiums next door, or on the top few floors, to properties where some or all of the hotel rooms have actually been turned into condominiums and are then sold to individual owner/investors. These owners may own their condominium units entirely, or they may have purchased *fractional ownership*.

Condo hotels differ from traditional condominium complexes in that, in a condo hotel, owners who are not staying in their units on a given night have the option of placing the unit in a rental "pool." Under such a pooled rental program, the condo owner's unit is sold as a traditional hotel unit. Revenue from the sale is then shared, according to a previously agreed upon formula, between the unit's owner and the entity responsible for administering the rental program.

---

[3]"The Condo Hotel Boom," *Global Hospitality Advisor* (January 2006), p. 1. Available at www.jmbm.com/.../lookup/...=/GHG%20Advisor%20Jan%202006%20.pdf. Accessed July 2, 2011.

It is easiest to understand the increased popularity of condo hotels when they are viewed from the perspective of the hotel's developer. In contrast to a traditional hotel developer who normally faces many years of operation before a significant return on capital can be expected, a condo hotel developer expects to sell some or all of the guestrooms constructed to individual unit owners prior to, or immediately upon, completion of the hotel. As a result, the condo hotel developer is able to realize significant financial returns several years earlier than the developer of a traditional hotel is. As well, construction loans for condominiums are often less expensive and easier to obtain than traditional hotel construction loans. In summary, the condo hotel developer expects, and thus far has been achieving, higher rates of return than those rates achievable by traditional hotel development.

In completed condo hotel projects, the business operating structure employed typically takes one of two forms. In the first, the project's developer retains ownership of, and typically manages, the revenue generating areas such as restaurants, lounge, meeting space and the like. In such an arrangement, the operating structure employed may be that of an owner-operator, a management contract, or even a franchise. In the second case, all of the hotel's commercial areas are turned over to and operated by a *condominium homeowners' association (CHOA)*.

Although CHOAs are usually elected in a democratic manner, it may also be true that the condo owners elected simply are not experienced in hotel operations management. This is true for both revenue-generating areas such as room rental and restaurant and bar operations, and the basic maintenance of the facility.

Figure 3.2 is a partial list of some of the non–revenue-generating areas of a condo facility for which a CHOA would typically be responsible. From the information in

LEGALESE

Condominium homeowners' association (CHOA): A group of condo owners, elected by all of the condo owners in a project, to interpret, develop, and implement the policies and procedures required to effectively manage their condominium complex.

ROOF REPAIR AND REPLACEMENT

PAINTING AND WATERPROOFING

INSURANCE

INTERIOR DECORATING

POOL MAINTENANCE

LANDSCAPE MAINTENANCE

TREE PRUNING

ALARM MAINTENANCE

GENERATOR MAINTENANCE

ELEVATOR MAINTENANCE

IRRIGATION MAINTENANCE

LAKE MAINTENANCE

PLUMBING, ELECTRICAL AND GENERAL MAINTENANCE

BUILDING RESTORATION MANAGEMENT

AIR CONDITIONING

CONCRETE WORK

LIGHTING

ASPHALT WORK

SECURITY

SIGNAGE

WALLS AND FENCES

Figure 3.2 Typical responsibilities of a CHOA.

that list, it is easy to see that inexperienced members of a CHOA would face many challenges in effectively operating a condo hotel. Despite that fact, however, the CHOA is increasingly common. With current development trends, it will continue to be an increasingly prevalent form of hospitality operating structure.

3.4 THE AGENCY RELATIONSHIP

As you have learned, the ownership of hospitality businesses can be maintained utilizing a variety of organizational structures. As well, these businesses are managed under a variety of operating structures. Sole proprietorships, partnerships, and corporations are all subject to the federal and state laws governing employer–employee relationships.

It is also true that owner-operators, franchisors, franchisees, and management companies are subject to the laws governing employer–employee relationships. This is important to understand because the conduct of a business's employees, regardless of organizational or operating structure, will directly affect the liability (or potential liability) of a business. Hospitality owners need to keep laws regarding employee relationships in mind when deciding on an organizational or operating structure for their business, and then choose the structure that will best allow them to absorb any liabilities incurred by the employees of the organization.

In the United States, regardless of the business structure selected, the relationship between businesses and their hired help usually takes the form of one of three concepts:

1. Master–servant
2. Agent–principal
3. Independent contractor

Figure 3.3 summarizes the characteristics of each relationship.

The Master–Servant Relationship

Returning to the previous example of John Graves, the man who wanted to begin his own restaurant, we can examine these relationships and the special rights and responsibilities they involve. It is highly unlikely that John will be able to operate his new restaurant entirely by himself. John would more than likely need to hire bartenders, wait staff, and kitchen help. When he hires people to fill these positions, he is creating a master–servant relationship: John is the master and his employees are the servants. Traditionally, in the law, the term *servant* was used to describe employees who performed manual labor. They were not generally in a position to act and/or make decisions on behalf of the master or employer when dealing with third parties. The master–servant relationship implies that the employee is under the direct control of the employer, and since the employers are presumed to be in control of their employees, employers are generally held responsible for the behavior of the employees when they are working. To illustrate, assume that a groundskeeper was directly hired by John to maintain the grassy areas, parking lots, and landscaping around his restaurant. This employee would likely be assigned a variety of groundskeeping tasks, including cutting grass. Assume further that, while mowing, the worker inadvertently ran the mower over a rock, and that the rock was discharged, with great force, into the parking lot where it struck the side of a parked car, resulting in significant damage to that customer's car. John, as this groundskeeper's employer,

Relationship	Characteristics
Master-servant	Also known as the employer-employee relationship, where the servant is the employee whose performance is controlled by the employer.
Agent-principal	An agent is empowered to act on behalf of or for the principal, with some degree of personal discretion, and the principal is ordinarily responsible for the conduct and obligations undertaken by the agent.
Employer-independent contractor	The employer has very little control, if any, over the conduct of the independent contractor; accordingly, the independent contractor is not an employee and usually not an agent (however, one could hire an independent contractor specifically to be an agent, such as a real estate agent or an attorney).

Figure 3.3 Three types of employer–employee relationships.

will be directly responsible for the actions of this employee and the damage he or she has caused.

The Agent–Principal Relationship

John could also hire someone to act as his general manager. In this instance, some of the general manager's work might be under the direct control of John, but the general manager might also be empowered to make decisions on behalf of the restaurant, and to enter into contracts on behalf of the restaurant. When employees act on behalf of the *principal*, they are usually referred to as *agents* of the principal. Agents have a fiduciary duty (responsibility) to act in the best interests of the principal. In this instance, the agent would be the general manager, and the principal would be John and his restaurant business. In general, a contract is used to specify the specific terms of a principal–agent relationship.

In many cases, the distinction between the agent–principal relationship and the master–servant is quite blurred. As empowerment becomes more widespread in hospitality workplaces, this distinction may fade altogether. Servants who are given more discretion and more authority will be more frequently categorized as agents. The distinction becomes important when you are trying to assess the responsibility of the employer for the acts of the employee. For example, assume that a restaurant customer becomes violently ill from food poisoning that is later linked to unsanitary practices by a kitchen employee in John's restaurant. If the relationship is considered a master–servant relationship, John could be held legally responsible for the guest's injuries under the concept of *respondeat superior*.

LEGALESE
Principal: Employer, the person hiring and directing employees (agents) to perform his/her/its business.

LEGALESE
Agent: A person authorized to act for or to represent another, usually referred to as the principal.

LEGALESE
Respondeat superior: Literally; "let the master respond," a legal theory that holds the employer (master) responsible for the acts of the employee.

In this example, the servant in the master–servant relationship does not have the ability to speak on behalf of John or the restaurant, and thus will not be considered an agent. However, if the servant did have independent decision-making capabilities, then the employee could be classified as an agent. In the agent–principal relationship, the principal is ordinarily responsible for the behavior of the agent, as well as for any significant, or even insignificant, promises or obligations undertaken by the agent on behalf of John or the restaurant. Thus, if the general manager of the restaurant (the agent) enters into a long-term contract to purchase meat from a particular purveyor, John and the restaurant will be responsible for fulfilling the obligations undertaken by the contract (assuming that the contract is in proper form, as discussed in Chapter 4, "Contract Basics."

Because principals are held responsible for the actions of their agents, agents have a *fiduciary responsibility* to act in the best interest of their principals.

The agent generally has five duties:

LEGALESE

Fiduciary responsibility: The requirement that agents act in the best interest of their principals.

1. *Utmost care:* The agent is bound to a very high standard to ensure the maximum protection of the principal's interest.
2. *Integrity:* The agent must act with fidelity and honesty.
3. *Honesty and duty of full disclosure:* The agent must make honest and full disclosure of all facts that could influence in any way the principal's decisions, actions, or willingness to follow the advice of the agent.
4. *Loyalty:* The agent is obligated to refrain from acquiring any interest adverse to that of a principal without full and complete disclosure of all material facts and obtaining the principal's informed consent. This precludes the agent from personally benefiting from secret profits, competing with the principal, or obtaining an advantage from the agency for personal benefit of any kind.
5. *Duty of good faith:* The agent must act with total truthfulness, absolute integrity, and total fidelity to the principal's interest.

Because of the master–servant and agent–principal relationships, it is very important that hospitality operators carefully select and train their employees. If you, as a hospitality owner or manager, are responsible for selecting employees who will represent or make decisions on behalf of your operation, you must trust the decision-making capability of those individuals, as well as their integrity to act in the best interests of the operation when they are making decisions and/or entering into contracts.

In Chapters 7, "Legally Selecting Employees," and 8, "Legally Managing Employees," you will learn how to properly select and manage employees under current federal and state employment laws, and see some ways that you can minimize the risk of liability by using effective employee selection and training techniques.

The Independent Contractor

LEGALESE

Independent contractor: A person or entity that contracts with another to perform a particular task but whose work is not directed or controlled by the hiring party.

Back to John. From time to time, he may also need to hire individuals or other companies to come in and perform specialized tasks that are outside the day-to-day operations of his restaurant. For instance, he may need to repaint the exterior walls of the building that houses the restaurant. John could hire an individual painter or a company that provides painting services. This type of relationship would involve an *independent contractor* relationship.

Usually, employers are not liable for the behavior of independent contractors, and independent contractors cannot ordinarily bind employers to obligations that they have made. The general rule is that the more control that the worker retains,

≫ ANALYZE THE SITUATION 3.3

THE GREAT FOX WATERPARK and Resort, located in the Wisconsin Dells area of Wisconsin, has received an invoice from Lion Distributing of Reisterstown, Maryland. The invoice is for ten cases of pool chemicals delivered to the resort two weeks ago. The invoice states Mr. Mark Bell, the resort's head lifeguard, ordered the chemicals. The price on the invoice is three times the normal price paid for chemicals of this type (which are normally purchased from a local vendor).

When questioned by the hotel's accounting office about the purchase, Mr. Bell states that all he recalls is that he was working one day and received a telephone call in which the caller asked for the "right" shipping address for the resort. The confirmation of address was needed, the caller maintained, because an office mix-up had resulted in some shipments of products purchased by its customers being misdelivered. Mr. Bell provided the caller with the hotel's correct shipping address.

Despite the obvious overcharge, the vendor refuses to accept the shipment back, claiming Mr. Bell, as an agent of the resort, had authorized the purchase of the chemicals. The vendor threatens a lawsuit if their invoice is not paid. Upon investigation, it is determined that one of the ten cases of product has, at this time, already been used.

1. Assume that Mr. Bell did not ordinarily purchase pool chemicals for the resort. Is the resort responsible for paying the invoice?

2. Assume that Mr. Bell did in fact ordinarily purchase pool chemicals for the resort. Is the resort then responsible for paying the invoice?

3. What steps would you suggest that the resort's owners take to prevent being victimized by potential invoice frauds of this type?

- Degree of control or direction over the worker: The greater control, the higher probability that it is an employer-employee relationship.

- The workers' investment in the enterprises: Does the worker provide his or her own tools and materials, or are they provided by the employer? If provided by the worker, that is evidence of an independent contractor.

- Opportunity for profit and loss: Employees are ordinarily guaranteed a wage, whereas an independent contractor, such as a painter, usually bids a job for a set amount and then has to perform the job efficiently to make a profit.

- Permanency of the work relationship: Most employees have a permanent, consistent relationship, full- or part-time with one employer; independent contractors work with many different employers and usually on a random basis.

- Are the workers' services an integral part of the employer's operation? A plumber that comes in every few months is not an integral component of the day-to-day operations; dishwashers, servers, front desk clerks, housekeepers are integral components.

Figure 3.4 Methods of assessing employer liability.

the more likely that the worker will be characterized as an independent contractor. Figure 3.4 displays some of the characteristics utilized by courts and government agencies to help determine whether a specific relationship is one of an employer–employee (master–servant) or that of an employer–independent contractor.

To illustrate the importance of understanding the differences in employer–employee relationships, return to the previous lawn-mowing example. This time, however, assume that John hired a lawn service company to care for the grass around his restaurant. In this case, John's relationship with the lawn service company would be that of an employer–independent contractor. As a result, if an employee of the lawn service company inflicted the same damage to a customer's car that was described

INTERNATIONAL SNAPSHOT

A Comparative Overview of Business Entities in the Hotel Industry

UNITED STATES

Traditional hotels in the United States operate as a variety of entities under a variety of models. Most often, they take the forms of corporations or limited liability companies rather than partnerships.
Limited liability companies offer added protection for officers and directors above that of a normal corporation. Among these entities, there are both publicly traded companies, such as Hilton, and privately held companies, such as Hyatt.

There is a greater variety among the operation structures of the various hotels. The major distinction can be drawn between a traditional hotel model and a condo hotel model. Traditional hotels have many different forms of management and franchise agreements, but all follow the basic model that there is one central owner for the entire property. Condo hotels, which have become significantly more popular in recent years, have many units owned by many people but typically managed by one entity. A third group has made a greater footprint in the market recently, the hybrid hotel, where some units are condos, typically full-time residences, and the remainder is traditional hotel rooms. Both the W Hotels and Ritz-Carlton Hotels have properties with this new hybrid structure.

CHINA

I. Rapid Growth in the Hotel Industry
As China prepared for the impending 2008 Summer Olympic Games in Beijing, its hotel industry experienced tremendous growth. Traditional hotels are, in light of China's breakneck economic development, in the fast lane for expansion. According to the "2006 Chinese Traditional Hotel Research Report" compiled by the National Development and Reform Commission of China, the number of traditional hotels exceeded 600 by the end of 2005.

In comparison, development of condo style hotels does not enjoy the same level of fast pace. Because of the lack of clear private ownership laws and regulation with respect to condo style hotel units, buyers are faced with greater risks. However, Chinese condo hotel buyers might be more receptive to the risks of condo style hotel units, given the fact that the Private Property Law went into effect in October 2007.

II. Business Entities in the Hotel Industry

Most hotels in China are organized under the Company Law of People's Republic of China.
The Company Law became effective on January 1, 2006, governing two types of business entities: limited liability companies and joint stock companies.

Currently, no foreigners are permitted to invest directly through joint stock companies, and their direct investments are required to be operated via the vehicle of limited liability companies. As reported by the China Franchise and Chain Store Association, 74 percent of the growth of the leading traditional hotel brands in China is achieved through direct operation, and franchised traditional hotels are less than 1 percent of all franchises in China.

Provided by John Vernon, Partner with VernonGoodrich, LLP (Copyright April 1, 2007 John M. Vernon).

earlier, it would be the lawn service, not John's restaurant, that would be liable for repairing the damages to the customer's vehicle.

Chapters 9 through 13 examine the different types of circumstances under which hospitality operations may be held liable in a court of law, and identify some preventive measures that managers can take to minimize the risk of litigation. Although we strive throughout this book to emphasize managerial practices that will promote safe and legal operations (and prevent the possibility of a lawsuit), accidents or misunderstandings will invariably occur, and at those times, a well-chosen business structure may provide the hospitality owner with a higher degree of protection against liability than one that was poorly chosen.

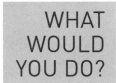

WHAT WOULD YOU DO?

Assume that you are responsible for approving commercial loans at a bank where you are the senior lending official. You are approached by two hospitality management college graduates, each with three years' management experience acquired after they completed their studies. They are seeking a loan slightly in excess of $1 million to establish a restaurant in the community. The funds will be used to lease land, facilities, and equipment, as well as for renovation, inventory, salaries, and other start-up costs.

Write an essay that answers the following questions:

1. Will the organizational structure selected by the partners have an impact on your decision to extend the loan?

2. Will the operating structure selected by the partners have an impact on your decision to extend the loan?

3. What other factors would influence your decision?

4. Would it make a difference to you if the partners were requesting the loan to complete a franchise agreement with an established and successful franchisor?

5. What additional information might you request if the partners were seeking the loan to operate as an independent restaurant? Would it matter if the loan were for an existing restaurant, as opposed to a new start-up?

To see how a court views the legal relationship between a franchisor and a franchisee, consider the case of *Allen v. Greenville Hotel Partners, Inc.* 409 F.Supp 2d 672 (D.S.C. 2006).

THE HOSPITALITY INDUSTRY IN COURT

FACTUAL SUMMARY
Multiple guests suffered severe injuries by a fire started by an arsonist while they were staying at a Comfort Inn hotel. The Plaintiffs brought suit for personal injuries and wrongful deaths against Choice Hotels (Choice), the franchisor, and against Comfort Inn, the franchisee.

QUESTION FOR THE COURT
The question for the court was whether the franchise agreement between Choice Hotels, the franchisor, and Comfort Inn, the franchisee, was such that it gave Choice a right to control the day-to-day operations of the Comfort Inn. If Choice was held to have a right to control over Comfort Inn's operations, then it could be held vicariously liable for injuries suffered by patrons and guests due to Comfort Inn's negligence. If Choice had no right to control, then liability for Comfort Inn's negligence would not be appropriate. The Plaintiffs claimed that Choice had been negligent for failing to provide proper security and fire protection for the Comfort Inn, and Choice had

the right to control the daily operations of the Comfort Inn because the franchise agreement gave Choice a right to enforce trademark standards designed to maintain uniform appearance and service throughout the Choice Hotel chain.

DECISION

The court ruled in favor of Choice, holding that Choice did not control Comfort Inn's daily operation or security and fire systems. The rules and regulations provided in the franchise agreement were a way to ensure a similar experience in all Comfort Inns, and therefore maintain the public goodwill of the Choice franchise. The court held that this regulation in the agreement was not enough to show Choice's control over the operations of the Comfort Inn, nor did it specifically control the hotel security and fire systems, which were the specific causes of the injuries in this case. Thus, Choice was not found liable for Comfort Inn's negligence.

MESSAGE TO MANAGEMENT

Franchisors need to be cautious when considering the extent of control over the franchised operations in the franchise agreement.

WHAT DID YOU LEARN IN THIS CHAPTER?

Establishing the appropriate business structure for a hospitality operation is a decision that requires owners or managers to consider the amount of liability risk they are willing to absorb, the willingness to pay taxes on the operation's profits, and the degree of control they wish to exercise over the business. There are a variety of business structures to choose from, each offering different benefits to the business operator. Your business may not fit within the parameters established for particular structures, so your choices may be limited.

However you choose to operate your business, you will rely on others to represent the interests of your business. To varying degrees, you will be responsible for their decisions and acts. Determining the types of employees and agents that will be needed for your business operation, and the degree of control they will have, is an important liability consideration that must be factored into your choice of an organizational structure.

RAPID REVIEW

After you have studied this chapter, you should be prepared to:

1. Identify those organizational structures that result in paying income taxes based on distributed, as compared to earned, profits. Explain the advantages of each approach.

2. Identify those operating structures that affect the amount of control an owner has over the day-to-day operations of a business. Explain the advantages and limitations of each structure.

3. Explain the phrase *respondeat superior*, in terms of liability and business structure. Describe a real situation in which the phrase takes on meaning.

4. Compose a letter to a potential lender addressing only the issue of why the organizational and business structures you have selected for your new business group make it advantageous for the lender to grant you the loan you have requested.

5. State the defining characteristics of six types of organizational structures used in the hospitality industry as they relate to:

    Taxes
    Liability
    Financing
    Transfer of ownership

6. Explain the concept of fiduciary responsibility and ethics as they relate to the general manager of a hospitality operation.

7. Describe the two primary operating structures utilized by condo hotels.

8. Discuss the concept of a franchise as it relates to reducing an owner's risk of failing in a business.

9. Identify the best organizational structure and operational structure for the business you would most like to own, and explain why they would be best.

Assume that the decision has been made to start a new chain of sub-type sandwich shops. Assume also that investor funding is available to construct five such stores.

TEAM ACTIVITY

1. Divide the group into six teams.

2. Three of the teams are responsible for suggesting possible organizational structures for the chain. Each team should discuss the advantages and disadvantages of the structure they suggest.

3. The remaining three teams are responsible for choosing possible operational structures for the chain. Each team should discuss the advantages and disadvantages of the structure they suggest.

CHAPTER 4

CONTRACT BASICS

OKAY, LANCE DANI thought, as he hung up the telephone, *it's only 11:00 A.M. Nothing to get upset about . . . yet. I'm sure Ms. Sangus will know what to do.*

Lance was the new front office supervisor at the hotel managed by Trisha Sangus. Generally, he considered himself very good at resolving guest-related difficulties, but he knew that this one was not going to be easy. He had personally handled the room reservation for Tom and Sarah Barry because he knew how important it was. The Barrys' wedding had been held in the hotel the previous night, and the food and beverage staff had performed flawlessly. The newlyweds had checked into the hotel's spectacular bridal suite around 11:30 P.M., and had even called down to the front desk to say thank you for the complimentary champagne Mr. Dani had arranged to be placed in their room. But that was yesterday. He hoped that they would be just as happy in a few hours.

Lance again reviewed the two room reservations facing him on his desk. He had asked that they both be printed in hard copy so he could study them carefully.

Mr. Tom Barry

Arrival: Friday, November 3; Departure Saturday, November 4

Room Type Reserved: Bridal Suite, #417

Confirmation Number: 458Y31

Mr. Patrick Farmer

Arrival: Saturday, November 4; Departure Sunday, November 5

Room Type Reserved: Bridal Suite, #417

Confirmation Number: 463Y75

"No problem," he had thought, but that was before the Barrys' call of a few minutes ago stating that Northeast Airlines had canceled all flights out of the city due to a severe snowstorm, and they would require their room for one more night. Lance reviewed the second reservation. No question about it, the Farmers would be arriving soon. Preparations were currently underway for their wedding, which was also to be held in the hotel. Two guests, both VIPs, only one spectacular bridal suite. Time to see the general manager.

As usual, Trisha took the news calmly, and began gathering the facts of the situation. "Do we have any unsold rooms for tonight?" she asked.

"We have 34 arrivals scheduled for tonight, with 26 available rooms," replied Lance. "Twenty reservations are credit card guaranteed, 14 have a 6:00 P.M. hold. With the storm, we may lose a few more arrivals than normal, but you can count on some unanticipated stay-overs also. I originally forecasted for 10 total no-shows."

"Did you confirm the Farmers' reservation for the bridal suite?"

"Yes," said Lance, "it's part of their group contract."

"How many members of the Farmers' group block have reserved?"

"They have picked up 90 percent of their 20-room block."

"Deposit?"

"One thousand dollars."

Trisha thought for a moment, then said, "We have a confirmed reservation for the Farmers, and remember that they have a contract with us to host their reception and dinner tonight. I'm meeting with the chef and the food and beverage director at noon to review the preparations. The reception and dinner have a value to the hotel of over $10,000 in food and beverage sales. We certainly don't want to upset those guests. In addition, we have an extremely important stay-over guest in the bridal suite, which the Farmers also have reserved. It seems clear to me that we have only one choice. I'm sure you know what to do, Lance. Let's make sure we do it right."

As Lance left the general manager's office, he was not at all sure he knew what to do. He certainly was not sure how to avoid a serious difficulty with one or both of the hotel's two very important customers. All he knew for sure was that he wished he had a second bridal suite. What was most confusing, he thought, was exactly who had a right to the bridal suite. As he arrived back at his office, Jodi, his front desk agent, peeked her head around his door and knocked softly.

"Mr. Dani," she began. "There is a Mr. Farmer here. He knows he's early, but he has requested an early check-in. I told him I would need to get an okay from you. What should I tell him?"

IN THIS CHAPTER, YOU WILL LEARN:

1. The two basic types of valid business contracts.
2. The four essential components that must be present to create a valid contract.
3. The purpose of the Uniform Commercial Code (UCC).
4. The consequences of breaching an enforceable contract.
5. How to avoid legal difficulties related to contracts before they arise.

4.1 INTRODUCTION TO CONTRACTS

LEGALESE

Contract: An agreement or promise made between two or more parties that the courts will enforce.

In any society, the members of the society choose to abide by rules designed to enhance the quality of life of that group. Violations of the rules are typically met with some form of negative consequence imposed by group members. In some cases, rules of conduct are passed down to successive generations by societal customs and mores. In other cases, the rules are expressly stated in the written laws governing the society. One important job of the courts is the enforcement of societal laws. It is also the job of the courts to enforce *contracts*.

Business Contracts

Generally speaking, litigation in the hospitality, or any other, industry arises because the *plaintiff* believes one of the following to be true:

- The *defendant* did something he or she was not supposed to do.
- The defendant did not do something he or she was required to do.

Surprisingly, it can sometimes be perplexing for hospitality managers to know precisely what is expected of them when serving guests. It can also be just as difficult to know what should reasonably be expected of the vendors and suppliers with which the manager interacts. Business contracts, and the laws surrounding them, have been established so that both parties to an agreement can more clearly understand exactly what they have agreed or promised to do. This is important for many reasons; however, one of the most important, as the majority of participants in lawsuits (regardless of their outcome!) will attest, is avoiding legal difficulties, which is very much preferable to settling those difficulties in court.

Verbal and Written Contracts

Hospitality managers, in the course of their normal duties, make a great number of promises and enter into a multitude of agreements on a daily basis. Although effective managers enter into these agreements in good faith, any number of problems or misunderstandings can arise that may prevent promises from being fulfilled.

Valid contracts may be established either in writing or verbally. In most cases, written contracts are preferred over verbal contracts because it is easier to clearly establish the precise responsibilities of each party when those responsibilities are completely spelled out. In addition, time can cause memories to fade, businesspeople may change jobs or retire, and recollections, even among the most well-intentioned of parties, can differ. All of these factors can create discrepancies in verbal contracts.

> **LEGALESE**
> **Plaintiff:** The person or entity that initiates litigation against another. Sometimes referred to as the claimant, petitioner, or applicant.

> **LEGALESE**
> **Defendant:** The person or entity against which litigation is initiated. Sometimes referred to as the respondent.

›› ANALYZE THE SITUATION 4.1

IN RESPONSE TO A telephone inquiry, Vincent's Tree Service offered to trim an apple tree on the lawn outside the front lobby of the Olde Tyme Prime Rib restaurant, for a fee of $500. Mr. Wilbert, the restaurant's manager, agreed to the price and a start date of Monday. At noon on Monday, Vincent's informed Mr. Wilbert that the job was completed. The tree trimming went fine, but a large quantity of branches and leaves from the tree were left neatly piled near the tree's base. When Mr. Wilbert inquired about the removal of the debris, Vincent's stated that removing it had never been discussed and was not included in the quoted price. Mr. Wilbert agreed that the topic of removal was never discussed but stated that it is generally assumed that when a company trims a tree, it will remove the brush it generates; therefore, he refused to pay until the brush was removed.

1. Which party's position seems most valid to you? Why?

2. How would you suggest the issue be resolved between these two contracting parties?

Interestingly, despite the fact that written contracts have many distinct advantages over verbal agreements, in the hospitality industry, most transactions with guests are established orally, rather than in writing. For example, when a potential customer calls a restaurant to order a pizza for home delivery, a contract is established via telephone. The guest agrees to pay for the pizza when delivered, just as the restaurant agrees to prepare and deliver a high-quality product. It simply would not be practical to get such an agreement in writing. Likewise, the guest who calls a restaurant and makes a reservation for eight people at 7:30 P.M. on a Friday night does not usually get a written agreement from the restaurant stating that it accepts the responsibility to provide a table for that group. The guest simply makes a verbal request, and that request is either accepted or denied based on the space available at the restaurant.

There are many cases in which transactions with guests or other businesses are actually confirmed in writing. In Chapter 5, "Significant Hospitality Contracts," you will review, in detail, some of the most important types of written contracts used in the hospitality industry.

Perhaps the most common example of a written, ordinarily enforceable, contract related to hospitality guests is the registration card, which is signed by guests when they stay at a lodging facility. Figure 4.1 shows such a card used by Holiday Inn. Note that, while most written contracts are actually signed by both contracting parties, only the guest signs this type of contract. Also, the responsibilities of the hotel are not clearly stated on the registration card, although they have been clearly established over time by common law. These responsibilities will, however, be discussed fully in Chapter 9, "Your Responsibilities as a Hospitality Operator."

⟫ ANALYZE THE SITUATION 4.2

JEREMY MOSS'S CREDIT CARD was billed $450.00 by the Langford Inn.

The charge was a "no-show" charge that resulted from Mr. Moss not arriving at the hotel on a night that "he" had reserved, via the hotel's website, two rooms (at $225.00 each). The hotel had been sold out that night, and the rooms, in keeping with hotel policy, had been held for Mr. Moss until 4:00 A.M. the next morning.

Mr. Moss contacts the hotel when he receives his credit card statement and protests that he never made the reservations. The reservation data collected on the website lists Mr. Moss's actual address and his home telephone number, as well as the credit card number billed by the hotel.

Mr. Moss, however, still maintains that he did not make the reservation, and thus demands that the "no-show" billing be removed from his card.

1. Do you believe the hotel is justified in charging Mr. Moss for the no-shows?

2. How could this hotel prevent such misunderstandings in the future?

Guest Name					
XXXXXXXXXXXX XXXXXXXXX					

Room Number	Room Type	Room Status	Arrival Date		Departure Date
XXXX	XXXX	X	mm/dd/yy		mm/dd/yy

Room Rate	Second Rate	Mkt/Seg	# of Guests	Sp. Svc.	ETA
XXXXXXXXXX	XXXXXXX	X-XXXX	X	XXXXX	

Confirmation Number	Reservation Number		ID	Time
XXXXXXXXX	XX-XXXXX-X		XXX	XXXXXX

Company
XXXXXXXXXXXXXXXXXXXXXXXXX

Address
XXXXXXXXXXXXXXXXXXXXXXXX

Address
XXXXXXXXXXXXXXXXXXXXXXXX

City	State	Zip
XXXXXXXXXXXXXXXXX	XX	XXXXXXXXX

Telephone Number	Advanced Deposit
(XXX) XXX-XXXX	

Settlement Code	Account	Description		Approval
X	XXXXX			

Alliance Code	Alliance Number		Priority Club Level
XXX	XXXXXXXXXXXXXXX		XXXXXXXXXXXXXXX

Comments
XXXXXXXXXXXXXXXXXXXXXXXXXXXXXXXXXXXXXXXXXXXXXXX

HOLIDAY INN ANYTOWN
123 MAIN STREET
ANYTOWN, ZZ 12345-6789
Phone: (000) 000-0000
Fax: (000) 000-0000

Please notify a Guest Service Representative if there are any errors on this record of your registration. We want to make certain that your name and room number are correct so that your mail and messages can reach you promptly.

Independently owned by and operated by XXXX

UPON CHECKING OUT, MY ACCOUNT WILL BE SETTLED BY:

- ☐ Visa
- ☐ MasterCard
- ☐ American Express
- ☐ Discover
- ☐ Diners / Carte Blanche
- ☐ CASH
- ☐ Other

NOTICE

LIABILITY FOR LOSS OF ANY MONEY, JEWELRY OR OTHER VALUABLES IS LIMITED BY LAW. IF YOU ARE NOT FAMILIAR WITH THE LAW IN THIS AREA, YOU SHOULD READ THE NOTICE POSTED AT THE DESK OR IN THE ROOMS.

I AGREE THAT MY LIABILITY FOR THIS BILL IS NOT WAIVED AND AGREE TO BE HELD PERSONALLY LIABLE IN THE EVENT THAT THE INDICATED PERSON OR COMPANY FAILS TO PAY FOR ANY PART OR THE FULL AMOUNT OF THESE CHARGES. I AGREE THAT IF AN ATTORNEY IS RETAINED TO COLLECT THESE CHARGES, I WILL PAY ALL REASONABLE ATTORNEY FEES AND COSTS INCURRED.

SIGNATURE

Please Note:

A safe deposit box is available for the protection of your valuables. The hotel's liability is limited pursuant to general business law.

TRANSPORTATION REQUEST

Guest Name / Contact _____
Number of Persons _____ Group _____
Date Service Required _____ Time Service Required _____

FROM Airport   **TO Airport**

Airline _____   Airline _____
Flight # _____   Flight # _____
Terminal _____   Terminal _____

Special Instructions _____

Make of Auto / Color	License No.
Year	State

Figure 4.1 Guest registration card.
Copyright 1999 Bass Hotels & Resorts, Inc. All rights reserved.

When dealing with vendors, suppliers, and others who provide services to the hotel, verbal contracts are quite common. When a hospitality operation does business with a vendor that has an excellent reputation, a typical verbal contract can be established in as simple a manner as a telephone call. If, for example, the manager of a restaurant is required by state or local law to have the fire extinguisher system above the deep-fat fryers inspected twice a year, the agreement to do so may not be committed to writing each time an inspection is made. Perhaps the same company has been performing the inspection for several years. Indeed, it may be that in order to efficiently schedule its staff, the inspection company, rather than the restaurateur, decides on the exact day of inspection. In this case, the presence of the inspector, access provided to the facility, the invoice for services performed, and a written inspection report all serve as indications that a verbal agreement to inspect the restaurant was in existence, even if no written agreement exists.

4.2 COMPONENTS OF AN ENFORCEABLE CONTRACT

LEGALESE

Enforceable contract:
A contract recognized as valid by the courts and subject to the court's ability to compel compliance with its terms.

All contracts, whether verbal or written, must include specific components that will make them legally *enforceable* in a court of law. If any of the components are missing, the courts will consider the contract unenforceable.

To be enforceable, a contract must be legally valid, and it must consist of an offer, consideration, and acceptance.

Capacity and Legality

Not all agreements or promises made between two or more parties are legally valid. If, for example, a child who is ten years old "agrees," even in writing, to host 100 of his friends at the local amusement park, the park owner would have no recourse if the ten-year-old subsequently neglected to arrive with his friends and pay the admission fees. The reason, logically, is that society requires a party to a contract to be of a minimum age before he or she can legally commit to the promises made in the contract. In most cases, minors do not meet the minimum age requirement; therefore, any contract they enter into would be considered unenforceable by the courts. In addition, an individual who does not have the mental capacity to understand what the terms of the contract entail will not be able to enter into an enforceable contract. This incapacity could be due to a variety of reasons, from mental illness to inebriation.

Even if the parties to a contract are considered legally capable, the courts will not enforce a contract that requires the breaking of a law. If, for example, a gourmet restaurant contracts with a foreign supplier to provide an imported food product that has not entered the country with the proper inspections, the courts will not enforce the contract because the activity involved—that is, the selling of uninspected food products—is itself illegal. Agreements to perform illegal acts are not enforceable. Thus, to be considered legally enforceable, a contract must be made by parties who are legally able to contract, and the activities specified in the contract must not be in violation of the law.

Offer

LEGALESE

Offer: A proposal to perform an act or to pay an amount that, if accepted, constitutes a legally valid contract.

Given that two or more parties are legally capable of entering into a contract, and that the contract involves a legal activity, the second component required in a legally enforceable contract is an offer.

The *offer* simply states, in as precise a manner as possible, exactly what the offering party is willing to do, and what he or she expects in return. The offer may include specific instructions for how, where, when, and to whom the offer is made. The offer may include time frames or deadlines for acceptance, which are either clearly stated or implied. In addition, the offer will generally include the price or terms of the offer.

When a guest enters a restaurant and reads the menu, he or she is reading a series of offers from the restaurant manager. While the menu may state, "16-Ounce Roast Prime Rib of Beef, $22.95," the contract offer could be stated as, "The restaurant will provide prime rib, if you, the guest, will agree to pay $22.95 for it."

When a school foodservice director places an order for produce with a vendor, the offer is similar. The foodservice director offers to buy the necessary products at a price quoted by the vendor. The reason that an offer is a required component of a contract is clear. The offer sets the term and responsibilities of both parties. The offer states, "I will promise to do this, if you will promise to do that."

Returning to the tree-trimming case referred to in Analyze the Situation 4.1, you can see why the offer is so important in a contract. In that example, the restaurateur and the tree service had differing ideas on precisely what constituted the offer. In fact, a great deal of litigation today involves plaintiffs and defendants who seek the court's help to define what is "fair" in regard to a legitimate offer, when those offers have not been clearly spelled out. It is important to note also that the courts will enforce contracts that have reasonably identifiable terms, even if those terms are heavily weighted in favor of one of the parties. Because of this, it is a good idea to clearly understand all of the terms of an offer prior to its acceptance. By doing so, the effective hospitality manager can help minimize his or her potential for litigation.

Consideration

An important part of the contract is *consideration*, which can best be viewed as something of value, such as the payment or cost of the promises of performance agreed to in a contract. For a contract to be valid, consideration must flow both ways. In the case of the prime rib dinner just mentioned, the consideration by the restaurant is the prime rib. The guest, by ordering the prime rib, is agreeing to pay $22.95 as consideration. Similarly, an airline that offers to transport a passenger round trip does so for a specific fare, which, in this case, is the consideration. The airline provides the trip and the guest pays the fare.

Consideration may be something other than money. If a restaurant agrees to host an employee Christmas party for a professional decorating company in exchange for having the company decorate its restaurant for Christmas, the consideration paid by the restaurant would be the hosting of the employee Christmas party, while the consideration paid by the decorator would consist of the products and services required to decorate the restaurant.

Another type of consideration often employed in the hospitality industry is the temporary or permanent use of property. When a hotel advertises a specific rate for the rental of a room, that rate is the consideration to be exchanged for the overnight use of the room.

When that same hotel company purchases a piece of land to build a new property, it will likely exchange money for the right to build on or own the property.

Consideration can also be the promise to act or not act. When the board of directors of a country club agrees to employ a club manager for a certain annual salary, the club provides consideration in the form of money, while the club manager's consideration consists of the work (acts) that he or she will do while managing the club. In some cases, consideration requires that one of the contracting parties does not act. Suppose that a couple buys an established restaurant from its current owner. The restaurant's name, as well as the original restaurant owner, is well known in the local area. Consideration in the sales contract may well include language that prohibits the original owner from opening a restaurant with a similar name in the immediate vicinity for a specified period of time. In this case, the consideration requires the original owner not to act in a specific manner.

LEGALESE
Consideration: The payment/value exchanged for the promise(s) contained in a contract.

A hotel may rent a room for $25, $250, or $2,500 per night should it so choose. The guest has a right to agree or not agree to rent the room. As long as both parties to a legitimate contract are in agreement, the amount of the consideration is not generally disputable in court. Indeed, should an individual who is competent wish to sell a piece a land he or she owns for $1 (perhaps to a charitable group), the courts will allow it, regardless of the appraised value of the land. The important point here is that the courts will ordinarily not deem a contract unenforceable simply because of the size of the consideration. It is the agreement to exchange value that establishes mutual consideration, and thus the contract's enforceability, not the magnitude of the value exchanged.

Acceptance

Because it takes at least two parties to create a contract, a legal offer and its consideration must be clearly accepted by a second party before the contract comes into existence. It is important to note that the *acceptance* must mirror exactly the terms of the offer in order for the acceptance to make the contract valid. If the acceptance does not mirror the offer, it is considered a *counteroffer* rather than an acceptance. When an acceptance that mirrors the offer is made, an *express contract* has been created.

An offer may be accepted orally or in writing, unless the offer itself specifies the manner of acceptance. In both cases, however, it must be clear that the terms of the offer were in fact accepted. It would not be fair, or ethical, for a wine steward to ask if a diner would like an expensive bottle of wine, and then, because the diner did not say no, assume that the lack of response indicated an acceptance of the offer. In that circumstance, the diner should not be required to pay for the wine. In the same manner, a contractor who offers to change the light bulbs on an outdoor sign for a restaurant cannot quote a price to the restaurant manager and then proceed to complete the job without a clear acceptance by the manager.

➤➤ ANALYZE THE SITUATION 4.3

JOANNA HART WAS OFFERED a position as director of foodservice for the independent school district of Laingsford. She received a written offer of employment on the first of the month, with a stipulation that the offer would be in effect until the 15th of the month. If Ms. Hart were to accept the employment offer, she would have to sign the employment contract and return it to the Laingsford superintendent of schools before the offer expired on the 15th. Upon reading the details of the contract, Ms. Hart felt that the salary identified in the letter was too low, and thus she adjusted it upward by $5,000, initialing her change on the contract copy. She then returned the offer letter to the schools superintendent with a cover letter, stating she was pleased to accept the position as detailed in the contract. The contract arrived by mail in the office of the superintendent on the 14th of the month, at which time, the superintendent called Ms. Hart to express his regret that she had rejected the employment offer. During the telephone call, Ms. Hart realized that the superintendent would not accept her salary revision proposal, so instead she verbally accepted the position at the original rate of pay. The superintendent, however, declined her acceptance, stating that the original employment offer no longer existed.

1. Does the school have the legal right to withdraw its offer of employment? Why or why not?

Legal acceptance may be established in a variety of ways. In the hospitality industry, these generally take the form of one of the following:

1. **Verbal or nonverbal agreement.**

   In its simplest form, acceptance of a contract offer can be done verbally, with a handshake or even with an affirmative nod of the head. If, for example, a guest in a cocktail lounge orders a round of drinks for his table, he is verbally agreeing to the hotel's unspoken, but valid, offer to sell drinks at a specific price. If, when the drinks are consumed, the guest is asked if he would like another round, and he nods his head in an affirmative way, he will be considered to have accepted the offer of a second round. Acceptance may also be implied by conduct. If a guest at a delicatessen stands in line to order coffee, and while doing so sees a display of breakfast muffins that are clearly marked for sale, unwraps a muffin and begins to eat it while waiting in line, her actions would imply the acceptance of the deli's offer to sell the muffin.

2. **Acceptance of a deposit.**

   In some cases, a hospitality organization may require a deposit to accompany, and thus affirm, the acceptance of an offer. If, for example, a hotel is offering a two-night package over New Year's weekend, it may decide that the offer to rent a room for that period specifies an acceptance that must be made in the form of a nonrefundable guest deposit.

3. **Acceptance of partial or full payment.**

   In some cases, full or partial prepayment may be required to demonstrate acceptance of an offer. This concept of payment prior to enjoying the benefits of the contract is not at all unusual. Theaters, amusement parks, and cinemas are all examples of contracts that are affirmed via prepayment. It is the right of hotels and restaurants to make full or partial prepayment a condition of their contracts. It is the right of the guests, however, to refuse this contract offer and take their business elsewhere should they wish to do so.

4. **Agreement in writing.**

   In many cases, the best way to indicate acceptance of an offer is by agreeing to the offer in writing. As mentioned previously, a large number of management/guest contracts in the hospitality industry are made orally. Dinner reservations and hotel reservations made over the telephone are quite common. When the sum of money involved is substantial, however, even these reservation contracts should be confirmed in writing, if at all possible. In most cases, the confirmation of an offer in writing provides more than just proof of acceptance. Because most people are more cautious when their promises are committed to paper, a written contract acceptance is often accompanied by a summary of the terms of contract. This helps prevent confusion. For example, when a hotel guest asks the hotel to send written confirmation of a room reservation, that confirmation document would include such information as:

   Name of the guest
   Date of arrival
   Date of departure
   Room rate
   Type of room requested
   Smoking or nonsmoking preference
   Number of guests in room
   Type of payment agreed to (e.g., cash, credit card, and debit card)
   Hotel cancellation policy

It is generally one or more of the preceding elements of a reservation that are in dispute when guests claim that the hotel has made an error in their reservation. It is clear that the number of disputes over hotel-guest contract terms would be greatly reduced with the increased use of written documentation of acceptance.

In today's business environment, agreement in writing can take several forms. The fax machine allows rapid confirmation, and revision, of contract terms. This machine has become an indispensable component in the hospitality manager's effort to manage his or her legal environment. Electronic mail (email) is even more popular as a quick and effective way to accept contract terms in writing. Email has the advantage of allowing both parties to revise documents directly as they are passed back and forth. As well, a record (the email string) is maintained of changes and revisions as they occur. Last, the regular U.S. Postal Service has traditionally been recognized as a legally binding method of providing written acceptance of contracts.

To illustrate the importance of this concept, consider, for example, the food vendor that is promoting a special sale on boneless hams for the Christmas holidays. The vendor sends an email to all of its clients. In the email, an offer for the sale of the hams is made that includes a 20 percent price reduction if orders of the hams exceed $100,000 and "payment is made by November 1."

A cafeteria chain's purchasing agent receives the email and decides to take advantage of the offer. The agent prints the email, fills in the email order form's blank spaces to indicate the amount of product to be purchased, and places it in an envelope, along with a check for the full purchase amount (including the discount). The printed email form and check are mailed, and the envelope is postmarked on November 1 by the postal service. The purchasing agent will be considered to have met the terms of the contract and to have responded within the prescribed time frame because the acceptance was postmarked on the first of the month. However, if the vendor had stated, "Acceptance must be received in our offices by November 1," then the acceptance would not have been in time. Again, this points out the importance of clarity and specificity when agreeing to any contract terms.

Search the Web 4.1

Go to www.yahoo.com.

1. Under Search, type: "hospitality contracts."
2. Search for stories related to contracts and contract negotiations that are making headlines in the news, nationally or in your area.
3. Print out one of the articles, and be prepared to summarize it in class.

4.3 THE UNIFORM COMMERCIAL CODE

LEGALESE

Uniform Commercial Code (UCC): A model statute covering such issues as the sale of goods, credit, and bank transactions.

Although hospitality managers encounter a wide variety of business contracts, two of the most common are those related to buying the goods and services needed to operate their businesses (purchase agreements) and those related to selling goods and services to their customers (sales contracts).

It is important that the hospitality manager become familiar with purchase agreements and sales contracts for two reasons: because they are used frequently in the industry, and because a very special code of laws exists to help facilitate business transactions that are carried out using sales contracts. The *Uniform Commercial Code (UCC)* was developed to simplify, modernize, and ensure consistency in the laws regulating the buying and selling of personal property (as opposed to land), any loans granted to expedite those sales, and the interests of sellers and lenders. The rules of the UCC, first developed in 1952, were designed to add fairness to the process of transferring property, to promote honesty in business transactions, and to balance the philosophy of *caveat emptor* by giving buyers, sellers, and lenders a measure of protection under the law.

The main purposes of the UCC are:

1. To simplify, clarify, and modernize the law governing commercial transactions.
2. To permit the continued expansion of commercial transactions.
3. To provide for consistency in the law regarding the sale and financing of personal property in the various jurisdictions (municipalities, counties, and states).

The UCC comprises 11 articles, or topic areas:

Article 1	General Provisions
Article 2	Sales Contracts
Article 2A	Leases
Article 3	Commercial Paper
Article 4	Bank Deposits and Collections
Article 4A	Funds Transfers
Article 5	Letters of Credit
Article 6	Bulk Transfers
Article 7	Warehouse Receipts, Bills of Lading, and Other Documents of Title
Article 8	Investment Securities
Article 9	Secured Transactions; Sales of Accounts and Chattel Paper

The UCC governs many aspects of the hospitality manager's work, including the selling of food and drink, the buying and selling of goods (personal property), and the borrowing and repayment of money. Accordingly, you need to become familiar with its basic concepts. For example, when purchasing goods under contract, the UCC has three basic requirements:

1. Sales of more than $500 must be in writing and agreed to by both parties.
2. The seller has an obligation to provide goods that are not defective and that meet the criteria and terms set forth in the contract.
3. The buyer has an obligation to inspect the goods that were purchased, to make sure they conform to the terms of the contract, and to notify the seller immediately of any discrepancies.

The important thing to keep in mind about the UCC is that it is a law that requires you to fulfill any promises made in a purchasing or sales contract. If a restaurant enters into an agreement to buy 50 heads of lettuce from a food wholesaler on or before a specified date, then that wholesaler is obligated to deliver 50 heads of lettuce on time, and the restaurant is obligated to pay for it.

The UCC protects the interests of buyers by requiring that goods or products offered for sale be fit for use and free of any known defects. In other words, the food wholesaler cannot deliver 50 heads of spoiled lettuce to the restaurant, or it will not have fulfilled the terms of the sales contract. Likewise, the UCC also protects the interests of sellers by requiring that buyers inspect all goods after receiving them and inform the seller immediately of any defects. Thus, the restaurant cannot claim three months after the fact that the lettuce it received was spoiled, and then refuse to pay the outstanding bill. It must notify the food wholesaler immediately of the spoiled lettuce or live with the consequences.

The UCC is a very complex law with many requirements that hospitality managers must be aware of. In Chapter 6, "Legally Managing Property," we will look closely at Articles 2 and 9 when we discuss the legal aspects of buying and selling property. Then, in Chapter 12, "Your Responsibilities When Serving Food and Beverages," you will learn how the UCC regulates the wholesomeness of the food and beverages that are sold in restaurants and other hospitality operations.

>> ANALYZE THE SITUATION 4.4

THE SMOKING BONES BBQ restaurant serves an excellent spinach salad as an accompaniment to its popular chicken and rib dishes. Michelle Brennan, the restaurant's manager, purchases, from a local vendor, all of her produce, including fresh spinach used in the salads.

Unfortunately, one of Michelle's guests becomes ill after eating at her restaurant. The source of the illness is traced directly to the fresh spinach used in the restaurant's salads. In fact, upon further investigation, it is determined that the spinach, when delivered to the restaurant's produce vendor, was already infected with E. coli bacteria that matched a strain identified in cattle manure used to fertilize the spinach field.

1. According to the UCC, a seller has a responsibility not to sell defective products. Who, in this example, is the seller?

2. Assume that you were the guest sickened by the bacteria. Who do you believe should be held responsible for the damages you incurred?

3. What specific steps could Michelle take to help prevent incidents such as the one described here from reoccurring in her restaurant?

LEGALESE

Breach of contract: Failure to keep the promises or agreements of a contract.

LEGALESE

Force majeure: Greater force; a natural or human-induced disaster, through no fault of the parties to the contract, that causes a contract to not be performed.

4.4 PREVENTATIVE LEGAL MANAGEMENT AND CONTRACTS

Breach of Contract

In some cases, the agreements and promises made in a contract are not kept. When this happens, the party that has not kept its agreement is said to be in *breach of*, or to have breached, the terms of the *contract*.

Sometimes, it is simply not possible to fulfill the obligations set forth in a contract. Guests who stay past their previously agreed-on departure dates may make it difficult for a hotel to honor upcoming room reservations. Diners who stay longer than anticipated may do the same to restaurant guests who hold dinner reservations. Events of *force majeure* such as acts of nature, or war, government regulations, disasters, strikes, civil disorder, the curtailment of transportation services, and other emergencies may make keeping the promises of a hospitality contract impossible. This can happen to either party. A hotel that is closed because of a hurricane, as sometimes happens on the southern and eastern coasts of the United States, may well be unable to service the guests it had planned to host. Likewise, if an air traffic controllers' strike closes all major airports, guests flying to a convention in Las Vegas may be unable to arrive in time for their room reservations. Adding a force majeure clause to a contract allows the parties to both specify what will happen should a force majeure event occur and identify some types of force majeure events that will trigger the clause.

Voluntary breach of contract occurs when management elects to willfully violate the terms of the contract. In most cases, however, it is unwise to voluntarily breach a contract. When it is done, it usually means that the breaching party should not have agreed to the contract terms in the first place.

There can be a variety of reasons for breaching a contract, and the consequences of such a breach can be very serious, even if the breach was unavoidable. Consider the case of the hotel that contracts to cater a couple's wedding reception. The contract to provide dinner, a cash bar, and a room with a dance floor is agreed upon in January for a wedding that is to take place in early June. In late May, the hotel is sold, and the new owner immediately applies to the state liquor control board for a transfer of the liquor license. The control board requires a criminal background check of the new owner, which will take 60 days to complete. As a result, the hotel must operate for that period of time without a liquor license. The contract to provide a cash bar for the wedding is now breached, and the wedding party threatens litigation for the hotel's failure to keep its agreement. It may be that the breach just described could not have been avoided, but the negative effect on the wedding party is real, as is the threat of litigation and loss of customer goodwill.

Remedies and Consequences of Breaching an Enforceable Contract

If a contract's terms are broken, and the contract is enforceable, the consequences can be significant. The plaintiff can pursue a variety of options when it is clear that the other party has breached a contract.

Suit for Specific Performance

When this option is selected, the party that broke the contract is taken to court, with the plaintiff requesting that the court force the defendant to perform the specific contract terms that have not been performed, or to refrain from engaging in some activity that is prohibited by the contract. A simple example might be a franchisee who has met all the terms and conditions of a franchisor and has signed a franchise agreement but at the last minute is told that he or she will not be granted the franchise because the franchisors themselves wish to build and operate on the designated site. In this case, the potential franchisee could bring legal action to force the franchisor to keep its promise and grant the franchise.

Liquidated Damages

Often, the language of a contract will call for a specific penalty if the contract terms are not completed on an agreed-on date. If, for example, a building contractor has agreed to complete the repaving of an amusement park's parking lots by the beginning of the park's season, penalties may be built into the contract itself if the job is not finished on time. Indeed, the contractor may have offered the penalty option as an incentive to win the contract. Liquidated damages refer to these penalty payments. When a contract is breached, the liquidated *damages* could be imposed.

LEGALESE

Damages: Losses or costs incurred due to another's wrongful act.

Economic Loss

When damages have not been specifically agreed on in the terms of the contract, the party that has created the breach may still be held responsible for damages. Consider the plight of the travel agency that contracts with a hotel for 100 sleeping rooms during the Christmas season for a tour group traveling to Hawaii. Upon arrival, the group finds that the hotel is oversold and thus the reserved rooms are not available. Because the hotel has breached the contract, the travel agency may bring litigation against the hotel claiming that the reputation of the agency itself has been damaged due to the hotel's contract breach. In addition, the agency may be able to recover the costs required to provide alternative housing for its clients. Few would argue that angry vacationers are good for business, and thus the agency may stand a good chance of recovering significant economic damages. These damages, if awarded, would be the responsibility of the hotel to pay, as a direct result of the contract breach.

Alternative Dispute Resolution

LEGALESE
Arbitration: A process in which an agreed-on, independent, neutral third party (the arbitrator) renders a final and binding resolution to a dispute. The decision of the arbitrator is known as the "award."

Often, there is honest disagreement over the meaning of contract terms. When this is the case, it may be difficult to determine which, if either, of the parties is in breach of the contract. When that occurs, the parties, or in some cases the courts, will elect to use dispute resolution techniques aimed at clearing up confusion or resolving the situation. Dispute resolution may also be used in other controversies, such as those involved with personal injury, employment, or labor disputes.

The two most common types of dispute resolution techniques are *arbitration* and *mediation*. In arbitration, the arbitrator is an independent, unbiased individual who works with the contracting parties to understand their respective views of the contract terms. The arbitrator then makes a decision that is binding on each party. In mediation, the mediator, who is again an independent, unbiased reviewer of the facts, helps the two parties come to an agreement regarding the issues surrounding the contract terms. Although the mediation process is a voluntary one, and neither party is bound by the recommendations of the mediator, mediation can be an extremely effective way to bring a contract dispute to resolution.

LEGALESE
Mediation: A process in which an appointed, neutral third party (the mediator) assists those involved in a dispute with resolving their differences. The result of mediation, when successful, is known as the "settlement."

Statute of Limitations

It is important to understand that if you intend to use the courts to enforce a contract, you must do so in a timely manner. There are specific laws that set out maximum time periods in which the courts are legally permitted to enforce or settle contract disputes. These laws are normally referred to as *statutes of limitations*. Generally, the statute of limitations for written contracts is four years from the date of the breach; however, this is an area where exceptions apply and where state laws sometimes vary. As a hospitality manager, you should become familiar with your state's statute of limitations on contracts.

LEGALESE
Statute of limitations: Various laws that set maximum time periods in which lawsuits must be initiated. If the suit is not initiated (or filed) before the expiration of the maximum period allowed, then the law prohibits the use of the courts for recovery.

Preventing Breach of Contract

It is generally best to do all that is possible to avoid breaching an enforceable contract. As with any litigation, prevention is typically better than attempting to manage the negative consequences that may result from a contract breach. Preventing breach of contract may not always be possible. In most cases, however, the hospitality manager can avoid breaching contracts by following specific steps before and after entering into a contractual agreement. The steps listed below can help minimize the chance of litigation in the future.

LEGALLY MANAGING AT WORK:

Eight Steps to Follow When Entering into Contracts

1. Get it in writing.

The single most important thing a hospitality manager can do to avoid contract breach is to get all contracts in writing whenever possible. Many hospitality contracts are, by their nature, verbal contracts. Generally speaking, however, the verbal contracts for dining reservations or food delivery tend to be rather simple ones. When the relationship between the contracting parties is more complex, it is nearly impossible to remember all the requirements of the contract unless the contract is committed to writing. For example, the standard contract for a hotel to provide sleeping rooms to airline crews staying overnight may run 50 typed pages or more. Obviously, it would not be possible to recall all the details of such an agreement without having that agreement in writing. A manager and his or her staff can only fulfill the terms of a contract if those terms are known and readily available for review.

Because many contracts are complex, it is sometimes advisable to have these contracts reviewed by an attorney before agreeing to their terms. This can best be done if the contract is a written one. Changes, corrections, and improvements can be made only if the attorney can see the terms of the agreement and read what will truly be required of the client.

Last, it is a simple fact that the representative parties to a contract may change, but the contract can still be used. For example, the contract between a waste hauler and a hospital to provide trash removal service to the hospital's foodservice facility will continue, even if the manager of that facility is transferred, quits, or retires. In such a situation, the terms of the trash removal contract need to be established in writing, both as a professional courtesy to the incoming manager and as a service to the foodservice facility itself.

2. Read the contract thoroughly.

The number of individuals and hospitality managers who sign contracts without thoroughly reading them is surprising, given that it simply is not possible for the managers or staff of a hospitality organization to fulfill all of their contractual responsibilities unless they know exactly what those responsibilities are. Just as important, it is not possible to hold vendors and suppliers accountable for the full value of their products and services unless contract language is known and understood.

Consider the case of the hotelier who plans a beach party during a spring break weekend. This manager contracts one year in advance with a talent agency to provide a popular and expensive band that will play at the hotel during the two-day party. A fee is agreed on and the agent sends the hotelier a standard performance contract. Upon reading the contract carefully, the hotelier discovers the following paragraph:

The agent, on behalf of himself and the entertainers, hereby authorizes the hotel and its advertising agency to use all publicity information, including still pictures, and biographical sketches of any and all entertainers supplied by the agent. These pictures and information may be used in any media, including television, radio, newspapers, and the Internet, that is deemed appropriate by the hotel. Agent further agrees that all such publicity information will be made available to the hotel no later than 30 days before the first performance.

It is the hotelier's opinion that 30 days is not nearly long enough to advertise the event. In fact, at least six months of lead time is required to advertise in some of the spring break magazines that will be distributed on college campuses across the country. In this case, a single sentence in a much longer document could have a tremendous impact on the economic success of the entire spring break event. It is highly likely that the talent agent will, under the circumstances, agree to provide the publicity material in a time frame acceptable to the hotel. It is important to note, however, that it required a careful reading of the entire contract and the hotelier's experience in the field of advertising to detect this potential difficulty.

Reading a written contract thoroughly before signing it is an important activity that must be undertaken to prevent contract breach. If it is determined that the hospitality manager simply does not have the time to read a complex contract in its entirety, then the contract should be referred to an attorney for review. Many managers refer any contract that exceeds a specific dollar amount or length of time to an attorney. The important concept to remember, however, is that all contracts must be read carefully. It is the manager's responsibility to see that this is done.

3. Keep copies of all contract documents.

When agreements proceed as planned, contract language causes little difficulty. When there is disagreement or failure on the part of either party, however, contract language can be critical. It has been said, tongue in cheek, that "the large print giveth and the fine print taketh away." Because it is never possible to determine whether a contract will be trouble-free, it is a good idea to keep a copy of all contracts that are signed. If the contract is a verbal one, it is a good idea to make notes on the significant agreement points and then file these notes.

Many hospitality operators find that it is best to keep a separate section in their files devoted specifically to contracts. Others place contracts in individual customer or vendor files, and some do both. Regardless of the filing approach, if the contract is easily available for review when clarification is needed, the likelihood of contract breach will be reduced.

4. Use good faith when negotiating contracts.

Good faith is a term used to designate an individual's honest belief that what he or she is agreeing to do can, in fact, be done. In a hotel manager's case, this can be as simple a concept as deciding that the hotel will accept no contracts for room reservations unless it, in good faith, believes that guestrooms can be provided.

It is always best to carefully weigh the commitments of any contract. Many times, contracts are breached because one of the contracting parties finds it impossible to perform the obligations. While circumstances can change, and no one can be perfectly clear about the future, it is worth noting that a careful, realistic assessment of contract capability and capacity can go a long way in avoiding contract breach.

5. Note and calendar time deadlines for performance.

When a contract requires specific actions to be taken by or on designated dates, it is a good idea to list those dates in calendar form so that there can be no mistaking precisely when performance is required. It is especially helpful to create these timelines prior to signing a contract. In this way, any potential conflicts or impossibilities can be detected before it is too late. Many lawsuits involving contracts are initiated because one party did not do what he or she agreed to do in a timely manner. Noting and calendaring time deadlines can help prevent this from occurring.

6. Ensure the performance of third parties.

Many times in the hospitality industry, a manager must rely on others to fulfill some portion of a contract. Consider, for example, the hotel that hosts a meeting for a nonprofit organization of health-care workers. In order to secure the contract for the sleeping rooms and meeting space required by the group, the hotel agrees to provide audiovisual services for the meetings.
Like many hotels, this hotel uses a third-party vendor to provide the audiovisual equipment. Obviously, a failure on the part of this third-party vendor can result in a failure on the part of the hotel to keep its promises. While it is not possible to prevent such an occurrence, it is important to recognize that when the use of third parties will be required, contract language addressing the third party's possible failure to perform should be included.

7. Share contract information with those who need to know, and educate staff on the consequences of contract breach.

Often, managers negotiate contracts that their employees must fulfill. However, an employee's ability to honor contract terms is directly related to his or her knowledge of those terms. Consider, for example, the hotel sales department that works very hard to prepare a bid to house the flight crews of a major airline that must layover in the hotel's city. The contract is won, and the crews begin to stay in the hotel. A portion of the contract relates to the cashing of personal checks. While the hotel's normal policy prohibits cashing personal checks over $25, the airline contract calls for the hotel to cash the personal checks of airline crew members for up to $100. These checks are guaranteed by the airline itself. Unless every desk agent and night auditor, as well as the management team at the front desk, are aware of this variation in policy, problems can occur. All it would take is the refusal by one uninformed or newly hired desk agent to cash a check, and the hard work of the sales department could be severely compromised.

8. Resolve ambiguities as quickly and fairly as possible.

Despite the best of intentions of both parties, contractual problems can arise. When they do, it is important that they be dealt with promptly and in an ethical manner. By doing so, a potentially damaging situation may be resolved quickly and amicably.

Consider the case of a tour bus company that contracts to stop at a midpriced downtown hotel on its way to Florida. The tour operator has a contract for rooms and meals; it is in writing, and the conditions are clearly spelled out. Upon check-out, however, the tour operator is surprised to find that the hotel has added a parking charge for the bus to the operator's bill. The tour operator protests that no such charge was part of the contract, and thus they should not have to pay it. The hotel points out that nothing in the contract states that parking would be provided free of charge, and thus the bill is owed. In a case like this, honest people can agree to disagree about the intent of the original contracting parties. Had the issue come up prior to signing the contract, the matter might have been quickly resolved. At this point in the process, resolution is important because the reputation of the hotel and its integrity may well be more important than the small amount involved in the parking charge. It is the responsibility of management to weigh the costs of litigation in both time and money, before making a decision to fairly resolve a contract dispute.

By attempting to put himself or herself in the position of the other party and trying to understand that party's concerns, the manager may be able to find a compromise that is fair to all concerned and that will help reduce the possibility of litigation.

Forecasting Contract Capacity

You have learned that contracts, whether verbal or written, commit the parties to the contract to very specific legal obligations. As a result, managers must carefully consider the implications before they agree to enter into contracts. One of the most difficult tasks facing the hospitality manager is that of forecasting contract capacity; in other words, knowing exactly how many contracts for products and services to accept on any given day or night. It is important to remember that a guestroom or dinner reservation, even if made orally, could be a valid contract. While some legal experts would argue that a contract does not exist until a deposit or form of payment has been supplied, the majority of legal scholars would agree that a contract is established when the guest makes a reservation and the restaurant or hotel accepts that reservation in a manner consistent with its own policies. Therefore, if a hotel or restaurant accepts only reservations that are guaranteed with either a deposit or a credit card number, at that facility, the contract will not be said to exist until that deposit is received or the credit card number is supplied. If, on the other hand, the hospitality facility regularly accepts reservations on an exchange of promise basis (i.e., the guest agrees to show up and the facility agrees to provide space), a contract does indeed exist at the time the reservation is made, and the hospitality facility can be held accountable if it does not honor its part of the contract.

To illustrate the difficulty encountered by hospitality professionals, consider the situation facing the food and beverage director of a large public golf course and country club. At that club, Mother's Day brunch is the busiest meal of the year. The club dining room seats 300. The average party stays 90 minutes while eating. The club will serve its traditional Mother's Day buffet from 11:00 A.M. to 2:00 P.M. Reservations are required, and historical records indicate that, on average, 15 percent of those making reservations will not show up (are no-shows), for a variety of reasons. The club does not require either a deposit or a credit card number to hold a reservation. The challenge for the food and beverage director is to know just how many reservation contracts to accept. If too few contracts are accepted, guests will be told the facility has sold out, yet the club's revenue will not have been maximized because more guests could have been served. If too many contracts are accepted, guests may not be able to be served at the time they have reserved or, possibly, may not be served at all, because there is no place to seat them. In the former situation, the club has not maximized its profit potential; in the latter, it may not be able to fulfill its contractual promises.

Some segments of the hospitality industry are very different from many other businesses because of the highly perishable nature of their products. For example, a hotel room that goes unsold on a given night can never be sold, on that night, again. An unoccupied cruise ship's berth on the day the ship is set to sail could also never be sold in the future. The same is true of unoccupied airline seats at the time a plane takes off.

In a like manner, in the restaurant segment of the hospitality industry, a table for five at a Mother's Day brunch can likely be sold only once or twice on that day. If the table goes unsold, the revenue lost cannot be easily recouped. This is different from most retail environments, where excess inventory can be discounted if management so desires. Obviously, the cost of no-shows at the hotel, cruise ship company, airline or country club would be passed on to other guests in the form of higher room rates, travel costs, or menu prices. Clearly, this is a difficult situation for both the hospitality operators and their guests.

Years ago, the airline industry tried to address the problem of no-shows by over-forecasting its contract capacity. Air carriers would accept far more reservations for seats on its flights than actually existed. In a precedent-setting piece of litigation, Ralph Nader sued Allegheny Airlines in 1973 for intentionally over-booking a flight on which he had reserved a seat.[1] Nader won the lawsuit; and due in part to his

---

[1] *Nader v. Allegheny Airlines, Inc.* 365 F. Supp. 128 (1973); reversed 512 F.2d 527; cert. Granted 96 S.C. 355.

litigation, in 1997, the Civil Aeronautics Board required the airline industry to inform consumers of their rights whenever an airline must "bump," or deny seating to, a passenger on its reserved and ticketed flights. The lesson for the hospitality industry is quite clear: If widespread overforecasting of contract capacity takes place, and consumers suffer, the federal or state government may step in with mandated remedies for guests and regulated operational procedures for the hospitality industry.

Establishing an Effective Reservation Policy

The solution to the problem of forecasting contract capacity in the hospitality industry is to make a clear distinction among reservations that are confirmed, guaranteed, and nonguaranteed, and to take reasonable steps to reduce no-show reservations. In some facilities, the no-show rate for reservations made is as high as 50 percent. In an effort to address this issue in a legally responsible and morally ethical way, future hospitality managers and the entire industry should begin adopting and educating consumers about the precise definition of a *confirmed reservation*.

A confirmed reservation can be made orally or in writing. In the restaurant business, it is common to hold a reservation for 15 to 20 minutes past the originally agreed-on time. Thus, if a dinner reservation is made for 8:00 P.M., the manager will hold space for the dinner party until 8:15 P.M. or 8:30 P.M., depending on the restaurant's policy. If the guests do not arrive by that time, they will have breached the reservation contract and be considered a no-show. In the hotel business, confirmed rooms are generally held until 4:00 P.M. or 6:00 P.M., after which the guest, if he or she has not arrived, is considered a no-show.

The difficulty involved in collecting monies due when a guest no-shows a confirmed but *nonguaranteed reservation* is significant. As a practical matter, collections on nonguaranteed reservations are almost never undertaken. On the one hand, there is no doubt that the guest who verbally reserves a table for dinner on a Friday night and then no-shows the reservation has broken a contract promise. The problem, however, is that initiating a lawsuit for a sum as small as a party of five's dinner bill is truly prohibitive in both time and money. On the other hand, guests also find that they have little recourse when a restaurant denies their confirmed but nonguaranteed reservations. The courts have been hesitant to force restaurants to pay heavy penalties if they refuse to honor a nonguaranteed reservation, even when there is clear evidence that the reservation was the result of a legitimate contract.

To prevent these types of problems, hotels and restaurants should strive to accept all or nearly all of their reservations as *guaranteed reservations*, and accept nonguaranteed reservations only on an as-needed basis. For example, a popular restaurant may accept dinner reservations on a busy weekend only if the reservations are accompanied by a credit card number that will be billed if a guest should no-show. Similarly, while it is easy to understand that a hotel in Indianapolis could likely require payment in full to reserve a room during the busy Indianapolis 500 race weekend, all hotels have the legitimate option of insisting that all guestroom reservations include billing information (i.e., valid credit or debit card numbers) that would allow for the guest's billing in the event the guest no-shows his or her reservation.

What is called for is a reasoned response on the part of both parties. Guests must understand that a reservation requires the setting aside of space that could be sold to another. Hospitality managers should train their reservation agents to explain that guests will be given a confirmed reservation only if they agree, in advance, to guarantee that reservation.

Three major points should be clearly explained to the guest before agreeing to the guaranteed reservation contract:

1. The hotel or restaurant will honor the reservation and will never knowingly offer to rent space for which it already has valid, guaranteed reservations.

2. The cancellation policy of the hospitality facility will be explained at the time of the confirmed reservation so that it is clearly understood by the guest.

LEGALESE

Confirmed reservation:
A contract to provide a reservation in which the provider guarantees the guest's reservation will be honored until a mutually agreeable time.
A confirmed reservation may be either guaranteed or nonguaranteed.

LEGALESE

Nonguaranteed reservation:
A contract to provide a confirmed reservation where no prepayment or authorization is required.

LEGALESE

Guaranteed reservation:
A contract to provide a confirmed reservation in which the provider guarantees the guest's reservation will be honored regardless of time of arrival, but stating that the guest will be charged if he or she no-shows the reservation. Prepayment or payment authorization is required.

3. Payment in accordance with the reservation contract will be made by the guests in the event that they no-show the reservation.

It is interesting to note that the state of Florida passed a law that says hotels will be fined if they deny space to any guest who has guaranteed a reservation by paying a deposit (as set by the hotel). Because most people would agree that knowingly accepting more guaranteed reservations than can be accommodated is ethically questionable, it is important that those in the hospitality industry work hard to ensure that a reservation, once confirmed, is honored.

Even when reservations are guaranteed with a deposit, no-shows can present a legal challenge in the hospitality industry. For customer relations purposes, few hospitality managers are willing to take a no-show guest to court to recover the money lost from holding a reservation. The time and legal expense, as well as the possible loss of goodwill, is simply too great. Naturally, guests do not like to be billed for services they did not use, even if they have contracted for them. Differences of opinion and possible litigation can arise, especially when a hospitality manager takes an aggressive stance in billing no-show guests for their confirmed reservations.

It might appear that the billing of guaranteed no-show reservations would be fairly straightforward. It is not. Even when policies on billing no-shows are clearly explained, difficulties will arise and judgment calls will have to be made. Consider the following situations in which the front office manager of a midscale corporate hotel must decide whether to bill guaranteed reservations that have been designated as no-shows by her automated front office property management system (PMS):

- Francine Dulmage arrived one day early for her confirmed guaranteed reservation, but since she was already in the hotel, she did not think to cancel her original reservation. The property management system listed Francine as a no-show the following night.

- A guest, Ryan Thomas, arrived at the hotel, claiming he had a reservation, but none was found under his name. The guest was checked in as a "walk-in," that is, a guest with no prior confirmed reservation. That evening, the property management system identified the reservation of Thomas Ryan as a no-show.

- Peggy Richards, who had guaranteed her reservation with a credit card, was told that in order to avoid a charge to her card, she would need to cancel her reservation by 4:00 P.M. on the day of arrival. She canceled at 4:20 P.M., because her cell phone was out of range at 4:00 P.M. Her company is the hotel's largest client.

- Bart Stephens, a regular at the hotel, checks in with a reservation he made for himself. That night, the property management system identifies a Mr. Stevens as a no-show. On further investigation, the front office manager finds that the hotel reservationist had misspelled the name on a second reservation made by Mr. Stephens's secretary, who could not recall whether she or Mr. Stephens was supposed to have reserved his room. The credit card number used to reserve the room for Mr. Stevens belongs to Mr. Stephens.

- For the past ten years, the Scotts family of Tennessee has held its annual reunion in the same hotel. This year, 18 rooms have been reserved by Mr. and Mrs. Scotts. All of the rooms are confirmed reservations, guaranteed with Mr. Scotts's credit card. When Mr. and Mrs. Scotts check into the hotel, their group totals 17, not 18, different parties. When asked if they will need the eighteenth room, Mr. Scotts says no, a death in the family has reduced their need to 17 rooms this year, and unfortunately in future years as well. He apologizes for not contacting the hotel prior to his arrival. That night, the property management system identifies one room for Mr. Scotts as a no-show.

As these examples illustrate, it may be difficult or even impossible to eliminate all no-shows. They are an inevitable part of the hospitality industry. However, it is in the best interest of any hospitality facility that must forecast contract capacity to do so as effectively as possible.

LEGALLY MANAGING AT WORK:

Reducing No-Show Reservations

The following steps can help improve managerial accuracy in the forecasting process. In addition, they will help reduce the chance of litigation when contractual obligations related to reservations cannot be fulfilled.

1. Become known as a facility that honors its confirmed reservations. If you choose to overbook, advise your guests of the practice and the potential consequences to them. Establish a consistent policy for placing guests in other comparable properties in the event it is not possible to honor a confirmed reservation.

2. Whenever possible, document all reservations in writing.

3. Put all policies related to making guaranteed reservations and the billing of no-shows in writing. Follow these written policies. For more ways to protect your operation from no-show reservations, review the recommended practices in Figure 4.2, which MasterCard distributes to hospitality operators.

MasterCard Guaranteed Reservations Best Practices

1. Take the cardholder's account number, card expiration date, name embossed on the card, and address.
2. Confirm the room rate and location.
3. Issue the cardholder a reservation confirmation number, and advise the cardholder to retain it.
4. Explain the hotel's no-show policy.
5. Confirm the details of the reservation in writing/by fax, including your guarantee policy, cancellation procedure, and billing statement for no-shows.
6. Explain to cardholders that if they fail to cancel by the agreed-upon time, their MasterCard will be charged for the night, plus applicable tax.
7. Upon cancellation of a reservation, retain the cancellation number.
8. Communicate to cardholders in writing that you have initiated a billing to their credit card for their no-show, including all pertinent information, a copy of the sales draft, and the hotel's reservation policy.
9. In the event of a no-show, the hotel must complete a sales ticket filling in the cardholder's name, account number, expiration date, date of no-show, assigned room number, and merchant ID number; and must write "guaranteed reservation/no-show" in place of the cardholder's signature; and follow the usual authorization procedures.
10. Remember, that if a cardholder who has guaranteed a reservation by use of a MasterCard arrives within the specified period (until check-out time the next day), the lodging facility is obligated to provide a room.

Figure 4.2 MasterCard guaranteed reservations best practices.

INTERNATIONAL SNAPSHOT

International Contracts

With the increasing number of hotels and restaurants expanding outside of the United States and the number of non-U.S. vendors that are transacting with those hotels and restaurants, there is an increasing need for managers to be aware of issues that arise in transborder transactions.

In addition to the "normal" contractual provisions otherwise identified in this section of this chapter, a manager should keep certain issues in mind when contracting with a non-U.S. party or for performance of work or services outside of the United States. Although each jurisdiction is different and has its own requirements, the following checklist can be used to identify potential areas that require additional thought:

1. *Clarity:* Take care to fully and accurately describe the performance required under the agreement. Carefully record any discussion in writing. Keep all prior correspondences to ensure that there is a record of what was discussed. Also, do not take anything for granted, and remember that there may be cultural and language variances that contribute to the need for more specificity. Make sure that both parties have a clear expectation of performance, and specify the language to be used for the agreement.

2. *Currency risk issues:* Specify in the agreement the type of currency used to pay for the transaction in question. Give preference to the currencies that are stable. And in long-term contracts (or contracts that are performed over time), it is advisable to agree on a specific exchange rate if the agreement contemplates the use of local currency as part of the business activity (e.g., guests at a hotel in a non-U.S. country pay in the currency of that country).

3. *Local law issues:* Consult a local lawyer on issues of local law. This is particularly important when business activities are being performed in countries other than the United States. Certain activities and practices that are otherwise permitted in the United States may be specifically prohibited in other countries. For example, there may be certain foreign exchange restrictions prohibiting transfers of certain amounts out of a country without first complying with notification or permit requirements.

4. *Dispute resolution:* As there are no international courts to resolve transborder business and commercial issues, and because litigation is quite costly, it is important that any international contracts contain provisions that provide for a mechanism to resolve matters in case of a dispute. This avoids confusion in the event of default. More and more often, parties rely on the resolution by senior executives of the contracting parties as a first step. If no resolution can be reached at that step, then the dispute resolution provision may call for arbitration by the International Chamber of Commerce or mediation by an expert familiar with the industry of the contracting parties. The key is that the terms of the arbitration and mediation must be spelled out. To ensure the clarity of such terms, a lawyer familiar with international dispute resolution should be consulted.

5. *Choice of law/venue:* Make sure that that the agreement clearly states which laws govern the transaction. Will it be the laws of one of the parties or of a neutral location? Note that on certain issues, such as real estate, labor, or foreign exchange control issues, you may need to rely on local law. The laws of another jurisdiction, however, can still be elected to govern the other parts of the transaction or the agreement reached between the parties. Also, in case arbitration fails, it is important to agree on the venue of the lawsuit. Because of the transborder nature of transactions, parties often agree in the agreement to a location (often neutral) where the litigation can be initiated and carried out. One word of caution: Make sure that the courts of the venue chosen have the capability to apply the laws specified in the agreement.

The foregoing is only a representative list of issues to consider in the context of an international contract. As always, local laws and customs should be reviewed and consulted, along with the fundamental contract principles otherwise discussed in this chapter and other parts of the book.

Provided by San San Lee of the Law Offices of San San Lee, Los Angeles, California. www.sansanlaw.com

WHAT WOULD YOU DO?

Assume that you manage a 300-room hotel. Your local university football team is playing a home game on Saturday, and the demand for rooms far exceeds supply. Your no-show rate on reservations for the past three football games has been 8, 12, and 9 percent, respectively. Currently, you have 100 nonreserved rooms.

Prepare a brief (half-page) report describing how you would answer the following questions.

1. How many room reservation contracts are you willing to accept?

2. Should you require that all reservations be confirmed?

3. What factors will you consider as you make your decision? What strategies will you employ to reduce no-shows? Write a short (half-page) essay answering questions 4 and 5 that follow, drawing from your personal perspective.

4. You and your family are traveling out of state to attend one of your school team's away football games. Upon arrival, the hotel where you have a confirmed reservation denies you a room because it has none available. What do you think the hotel should do for you?

5. What if no other rooms were available within a 50-mile radius of the hotel you originally booked?

THE HOSPITALITY INDUSTRY IN COURT

To see how courts typically treat exculpatory clauses, consider the case of *Hanks v. Powder Ridge Restaurant Corp.*, 276 Conn. 314, 885 A.2d 734 (Conn. Sup. Crt., 2005).

FACTUAL SUMMARY

Plaintiff Gregory Hanks traveled to Powder Ridge Ski Resort to snowtube. Prior to snowtubing, Powder Ridge patrons are required to sign a "Waiver, Defense, Indemnity and Hold Harmless Agreement, and Release of Liability" ("Agreement"). The Agreement stated that by signing the Agreement, the patron acknowledged the inherent risks of snowtubing and that he assumed all risks associated with snowtubing. The Agreement further stated that the patron would defend, indemnify, and hold harmless the Defendants from any claims or lawsuits, including negligence claims.

Plaintiff signed the Agreement on behalf of himself and four children he brought with him. While snowtubing, Plaintiff suffered injuries when his foot became caught between the snowtube and the manmade bank of the snowtubing run. Plaintiff underwent multiple surgeries to repair his injuries.

Plaintiff thereafter filed suit against Defendant Powder Ridge alleging that Defendants negligently caused his injuries.

QUESTION FOR THE COURT

The question for the court was whether the enforcement of the exculpatory Agreement, which would release a snowtube operator from liability for personal injuries sustained as a result of the operator's negligent conduct, would violate public policy. The court examined several factors, including whether Plaintiffs and Defendants enjoyed similar bargaining power. Defendants argued that they did not enjoy a superior bargaining power because snowtubing is a voluntary activity and not an essential public service. Therefore, Plaintiff did not have to participate in snowtubing.

DECISION

Even though the court found that the Defendants had a "well-drafted" Agreement, the court held that the Agreement violated public policy. Therefore, Defendants' argument that the Agreement released them from liability failed.

MESSAGE TO MANAGEMENT
Even a "well-drafted" Agreement with an exculpatory clause may not insulate you from liability.

Contracts are used in the hospitality industry to govern the many different promises and business transactions entered into on a daily basis. Contracts can take one of two forms, verbal or written. To be enforceable in a court of law, a contract must be for a legal purpose, entered into by competent parties, and include an offer, consideration, and acceptance.

The Uniform Commercial Code (UCC) is the law regulating contracts related to buying and selling. This code gives protection to buyers, sellers, and financial lenders when goods are purchased under contract. Because reservations are considered to be a type of contract, it is important that hospitality managers develop reservation policies that will allow them to fulfill the promises made to their guests, while maximizing their own revenue in the event that guests do not honor their reservations.

A breach of contract occurs when one of the parties is unable to fulfill the obligations set forth in a contract. When this occurs, the injured party may go to court and receive damages or some other type of remedy. The best way for managers to prevent a breach of contract is by thoroughly understanding their rights and obligations under the contracts they agree to, and by taking the necessary steps to fulfill those requirements.

After you have studied this chapter, you should be prepared to:

1. Describe two hospitality situations in which a verbal contract is superior to a written contract, and explain why you believe it to be so.

2. Discuss "legality" as a major component required of an enforceable contract. Give a hospitality example where legality comes into question.

3. Using the Internet, go to the home page of a national hotel chain. Evaluate the hotel chain's reservation-booking system from a legal perspective. Address specifically the concept of consideration.

4. You are the general manager of a midsized hotel. Draft a memo for your front desk staff describing the rationale and policy for billing guests with a confirmed reservation who do not arrive at the hotel to use their rooms.

5. Give a hospitality example that illustrates why it is so important to establish acceptance of an offer prior to the formation of a contract.

6. On a busy weekend, you have forecasted that 10 percent of your dining room reservations will no-show. Create notes that you would use to explain to your reservationist why he or she should continue to book reservations when you are past capacity.

7. Consider the concept of "statute of limitations," as it relates to a guest who has experienced an unsatisfactory meal in your restaurant. At what point do you believe the guest would lose his or her right to protest the quality of products (menu items) purchased from you. Defend your answer.

8. You purchased a warranty for your telephone system that provides 24-hour response time from the vendor. Draft a letter to the vendor protesting the breach of contract that resulted when it took three days for you to get service. Remember that your goal is to have a professional relationship with the vendor, as well as a working telephone system.

TEAM ACTIVITY

Divide into three teams, with each team assigned to one of the following roles:

Hotel

Guest

Judge

Have each team read the following scenario, then answer their individual questions below:

The sales department at the Remington Hotel made a mistake. It booked two weddings, for the same night, in the Grand Ballroom. The error was not uncovered until six weeks prior to the weddings. A clerical error in the sales office resulted in the overbooking. The second party booked in the ballroom has now been informed that there is no acceptable, alternative space available in the hotel. The estimated revenue that would have been generated from the second wedding was approximately $30,000 (300 guests @ $100.00 each).

For the Hotel's team:

1. What level of compensation for the guest do you feel is appropriate due to your hotel's contract breech?

2. Assume that the only available, comparable, and alternative site for the overbooked guest's wedding reception would cost the guest $40,000. What level of compensation for the guest do you now feel would be appropriate due to the hotel's contract breech?

For the Guest's team:

1. What are some expenses you will incur (in addition to the alternative hotel's actual charges) because of the wedding's venue change (i.e., additional printing costs for new invitations, guest relocation costs, and the like)?

2. Assume that the only available, comparable, and alternative site for your wedding reception would cost you $40,000. What level of total compensation do you now feel is appropriate due to the hotel's contract breech?

For the Judge's team:

1. Assume that the only available, comparable, and alternative site for the overbooked guest's wedding reception would cost that guest $40,000. Assume that the contracting wedding party also indicates that they would spend an additional $5,000 for reasons directly related to the wedding's venue change. What level of compensation for the guest do you feel would be appropriate due to the hotel's contract breech?

2. In addition to the costs indicated in #1 above, assume that the guests also made a claim for an extra $25,000 to compensate them for the time, effort, and embarrassment related to the wedding's venue change. What level of compensation for the guest do you feel would be appropriate due to the hotel's contract breech?

CHAPTER 5

SIGNIFICANT HOSPITALITY CONTRACTS

"YOU REALLY SHOULD look into buying them," said Latisha Austin. "Our guests absolutely love them!"

The "them" Latisha was referring to were the mattresses and box springs that made up the new line of Peaceful Sleep bedding Latisha had just purchased for her 117-room limited-service hotel.

It was a beautiful, sunny Thursday afternoon, and Trisha Sangus and Latisha had decided to meet at the Walnut Hills Country Club to play a round of golf and talk "shop." Trisha loved to play golf and so did Latisha. Trisha also enjoyed Latisha's company and their conversations.

As they chatted at the first tee, awaiting their tee time, Latisha was telling Trisha about the new line of mattresses that had recently been made part of the upgraded bedding standard for all Sleep Well hotels.

Latisha was the general manager of the Sleep Well property in the same town that Trisha's hotel was located. Mr. Larsoon, a real estate developer who had limited hotel experience but possessed excellent business sense, owned it. Trisha knew Mr. Larsoon well because, earlier in her career, she had worked for a time as the front office manager of the Sleep Well. Mr. Larsoon was an honest businessperson and had taught Trisha much before he retired.

"Of course, they were expensive," continued Latisha, "but we really have had lots of good comments on them."

"Are those the Perfect Sleep mattresses I read about last week in *Hotel Monthly?*" asked Trisha.

"No—mine are Peaceful Sleep," replied Latisha, "Perfect Sleep are the ones advertised by the Town Park Hotels. My franchise service manager says our mattresses are better."

"How did you choose the supplier of the ones you bought?" asked Trisha.

"That's the best part," replied Latisha, "Select Hotels—our franchisor—set it up so we had our own line of mattresses made by Thompson Mattresses. They designed them just for us. So I just bought the beds from them."

"Thompson also makes the Perfect Sleep," said Trisha. "How did Sleep Well pick that vendor?"

"I don't really know," replied Latisha. "I just got an e-mail announcing the bedding upgrade, then another announcing that we could buy direct from the factory."

"What were the actual mattresses specs?" asked Trisha. "Did you try to buy them locally?"

"We didn't get specs, just the brand name of the mattresses—that made it really easy, so I didn't look for a local manufacturer. Besides, with the whole company buying the beds direct, I'm sure we all got a better price for them than I could have gotten locally."

How many Sleep Wells are there?" asked Trisha.

"I think there are a little over 2,000," replied Latisha.

"Just out of curiosity," Trisha asked, "what do you think would have happened if you had bought alternative mattresses? I mean, ones of the same or better quality than the ones you did buy, but from a different manufacturer?"

"Oh, we couldn't have done that," replied Latisha. "If we didn't meet the brand standards, we'd lose points on our biannual Inspection Quality score. You must remember that!"

Trisha remembered well how excited and nervous everyone at Latisha's hotel got when the Sleep Well "inspector" made the twice-yearly property visit. The actual score the hotel received on its inspection was always very important to the general manager and reflected a variety of factors, one of which was that individual property's adherence to the franchisor's ever-changing brand standards.

"Well," said Latisha, as she approached the white tees and readied her ball, "You really should look into them. You really can't go wrong in this business when you're trying to give your guests as comfortable a night's sleep as possible."

"Perfect Sleep or Peaceful Sleep, the Thompson Company certainly created clever names and clever marketing programs," thought Trisha. Trisha actually had no doubt that the new beds Latisha had purchased were, in fact, comfortable. She also had no doubt, however, that if she were managing the Sleep Well, she would have been uncomfortable recommending their purchase to Mr. Larsoon.

IN THIS CHAPTER, YOU WILL LEARN:

1. Contract clauses commonly utilized in hospitality contracts.
2. The purpose of a franchise contract (franchise agreement).
3. The purpose of a management contract (management operating agreement).
4. Important forms of meeting space contracts used in lodging operations.
5. Important forms of group rooms contracts used in lodging operations.

5.1 SPECIFIC CONTRACT CLAUSES

In the previous chapter, you learned about basic business contracts. Many of the contracts used in the hospitality and tourism industries are very similar to those used in other industries; these include contracts regarding employment, routine facilities and grounds maintenance, equipment purchases, employee insurance, and accounting services, to name but a few areas. There are, however, some unique and very specialized hospitality- and tourism-related contracts and contract terminology you will likely encounter during your hospitality career. In this chapter, you will learn about this industry-specific terminology, as well as some types of specialized contracts.

Types of Specialized Contracts

Although it is not possible to list all of the potential types of specialized contracts hospitality managers may confront, the following four types deserve special explanation because of their widespread use in the hospitality industry. Each of these contract/agreement types is examined in detail later in this chapter.

Franchise-related Contracts

As you learned in Chapter 3, in a franchise arrangement, the owner of a hospitality facility, (the franchisee) agrees, in exchange for a franchise, to operate the business in a specific manner approved by the franchisor. The actual franchise contracts utilized in the selection, purchase, and implementation of franchise operating agreements are highly regulated and very detailed. Unless very carefully created and thoroughly read, these intricate agreements can often be misconstrued or misinterpreted by the contracting parties. Therefore, it is important to fully understand their intent and complexity.

Management Operating Agreements

A management contract, or as it is very commonly known, a management *operating agreement*, is created when the owner of a hospitality facility allows another party to assume the day-to-day operation of that facility.

Hospitals, school foodservices, campus dining operations, and business dining facilities are commonly operated under management contracts. Hotels, from the smallest to the largest, can also be operated in this manner. In an operating agreement (management contract) the facility owner allows the management company to make the operational decisions that are necessary for the facility to effectively serve its clientele. Typically, a management contract will set forth, in great detail, the period that the agreement will be in effect, the payment terms, the responsibilities of each party, and the stipulations by which the arrangement can be ended, as well as a variety of legal and operational issues. These agreements are typically very detailed and, as a result, understanding their basic components as well as areas of possible contention is very important.

> **LEGALESE**
> **Operating agreement:**
> A contract that details the areas of responsibilities of the owner of a business and the entity selected by the owner to operate the business. Also referred to as a "management contract."

Meeting Space Contracts

Although many limited-service hotel's guestroom contracts consist only of individual or group rooms sales agreements, full-service hotels will enter into many meeting space contracts in addition to their individual and group room contracts. Especially in larger hotels with significant amounts of meeting, event, and convention space, not only are meeting space contracts common, but also their proper management is essential to the profitability of their respective properties.

Hotels are not the only segment within the hospitality industry that utilizes meeting and space contracts. Convention centers, country clubs, restaurants, and catering halls are just a few of the many hospitality industry facilities that routinely rent space and may provide meetings related services to their guests. Such facilities must carefully detail, via a contract, the services they will provide their guests, as well as the terms under which they will provide them.

In many cases, the contract terms for meetings are negotiated between a hotel and one or more professional *meeting planners.*

Meeting planners annually buy large numbers of sleeping rooms, as well as reserve significant amounts of meeting and catering space. Meeting planners may negotiate group room contracts, meeting space contracts, or both combined into one contract. These individuals may represent a variety of corporations, groups, and organizations. They are sophisticated buyers of hotel products who often use comparison-shopping

> **LEGALESE**
> **Meeting planners:** A group of professionals that plan and organize meetings and events for their employers and clients.

techniques, and who can heavily influence a hotel's reputation based on their experience with it. It is not unusual for hotels to designate one (or more) very experienced staff members to deal exclusively with this group of professionals. As a result, understanding how these contracts are actually negotiated and developed is essential to hospitality managers in a variety of industry segments.

Search the Web 5.1

Meeting Professionals International (MPI) is the world's largest association of meeting planning professionals, with over 20,000 members. You can learn more about this group by visiting its website at www.mpiweb.org.

Note the large number of educational services it offers. Many of these are designed to help the members better negotiate and administer the meetings contracts they execute with the hotels they select for their meetings.

Group Lodging Contracts

A group rooms contract is developed when an individual or organization requires a large number of hotel rooms. Nearly all hotels rely, to some degree, on group business to help maximize their room sales revenue. The situations in which group rooms are sold can be as varied as an agreement with an airline to provide overnight accommodations for flight crews, to group meetings and conventions, and family weddings. In Chapter 4, "Business Contracts," you learned that hotels are required to honor individual guestroom reservations because when such reservations are made, they constitute valid business contracts. As well, when group reservations are made, a unique type of contract is created, and hotels must also honor these.

Group room contracts are different, in many ways, from individual room contracts, and they frequently contain distinctive features that must be well understood by hoteliers. Group room contracts are common because many hotels require that any room request exceeding a total of 10 sleeping rooms per night be confirmed by a written contract. The reason is simple: When a guest requests a large number of rooms, he or she may expect a discount for each room purchased. This is often agreeable to the hotel, but the precise conditions under which the discount is to be offered are best confirmed with a written contract. Furthermore, a group rooms contract may be drawn up months or years before the rooms will actually be used. This is often the case for large convention hotels that may contract for rooms and space several years ahead of time. A written contract guarantees that the sponsoring group will have the amount of rooms they need and the hotel can expect to receive revenue for the use of its rooms for a certain period of time. In this chapter, you will learn how group lodging contracts should be structured.

In addition to the unique types of contracts that are found in the hospitality industry, there are also industry-specific words and phrases that must be understood if contracts of these special types are to be properly created and their terms accurately followed. These special types of contract wording are known as essential *clauses*.

In the next portion of this chapter, you will examine essential contract clauses that hospitality managers should carefully examine in all of the contracts they execute; as well as those provisions utilized in the contracts they negotiate when they

LEGALESE

Clause (contract): A distinct contract provision or stipulation.

sell products and services to their customers and guests, and the essential clauses they utilize when they contract to purchase their own business-related products and services. When you understand all of these, you will be ready to learn more about specialized hospitality and tourism contracts.

Since business contracts can cover a variety of offer and acceptance situations, their form and structure can vary considerably. That said, all hospitality contracts should contain certain essential clauses, or stipulations, that a manager should identify and review carefully before entering into the contract relationship. These essential clauses are actually not specific wordings; rather, they are areas or terms of the agreement that should be clearly spelled out, to ensure that both parties to the contract understand them completely. The reason for including these clauses in contracts, and for reviewing them carefully, is to prevent ambiguity and misunderstanding.

Essential Clauses for Providing Products and Services to Guests

It is always better to settle potential difficulties before agreeing to a contract than to be forced to resolve them later, and perhaps create ill will or significant legal problems. Reviewing the following essential clause areas in contracts, before agreeing to their terms, can help you do just that.

Length of Time the Contract Price Terms Exist

When an offer is made, it generally will include the price proposed by the seller. It is just as important to clearly establish exactly how long that price is to be in effect. When issuing coupons, for example, the manager of a quick-service restaurant (QSR) will want to clearly inform consumers of the coupon's expiration date. If a hotel's director of sales grants a particular corporation a special discounted room rate based on anticipated rooms sales, it is important to note the length of time that the reduced rate will be in effect. When any offer for products or services includes a price, the wise hospitality manager will specify the time frame for holding, or honoring, that price.

Identification of Who Is Authorized to Modify the Contract

Unanticipated circumstances can cause guests to change their plans at the last minute. This is especially true in lodging, where group rooms or meeting contracts may be modified during the group's stay. A typical situation would be one in which an organization signs a contract for meeting space. In one of the meeting rooms, an invited speaker requests that a liquid crystal display (LCD) projector and projection screen (items not included in the original contract) be provided for his use. If, acting on the request of the speaker, the hotel provides the equipment, the contracting organization may later refuse to pay for it. Although the equipment was in fact provided, the invited speaker was not authorized to modify the original contract.

It is always important to identify, prior to agreeing to contract terms, exactly who will be given authority to modify the contract should the need arise. It is also best to require that any modifications to the contract be in writing wherever practical.

Deposit and Cancellation Policies

Hotels often require deposits before they will reserve sleeping rooms for guests. It is important to remember that hotel rooms are an extremely perishable commodity. Room nights cannot be "saved up" by hotel managers in anticipation of heavy demand, nor can their numbers be quickly increased in the face of heightened actual

Figure 5.1 Cancellation clause.

Cancellation Clause

If arrangements for the event are canceled in full, a fee consisting of a percentage of the total anticipated revenue outlined in this contract will be charged. The fee is determined by the length of time between written notification of the cancellation and the scheduled arrival date as follows:

0–31 days prior to arrival	100% of anticipated revenue
32–90 days prior to arrival	75% of anticipated revenue
91–180 days prior to arrival	50% of anticipated revenue
181–365 days prior to arrival	25% of anticipated revenue

Anticipated revenue may include room, meal, gratuities, telephone, and hotel-provided services, as well as taxes due on recovered sums.

---

demand. Consequently, hotel managers must be very careful to ensure that rooms reserved by a guest will in fact be purchased by the guest. The portion of a contract that details an operation's deposit and cancellation policies is critical both to the hotel and to the guest, and thus must be made very clear.

Deposits guarantee reservations. Typically, a deposit equal to the first night's room and tax bill will be required on group lodging contracts and some individual room reservations. This deposit may be required at the time of the contract's signing or 30 days prior to the group's arrival. For most individual room reservations, a credit or debit card number from a valid payment card is the method used to guarantee the reservation. In other cases, personal checks or certified checks may be required.

Cancellations of reservations can occur for a variety of reasons. If the hotel is to have a fair cancellation policy, it must consider the best interests of both the hotel and the guest, and the policy must be clearly stated in the contract. This is true whether the contract is oral or written. Generally, failure to cancel a guaranteed reservation by the agreed-on time will result in forfeiture of an advanced deposit or one night's room and tax, billed to the payment card number that was given to guarantee the reservation.

When groups are very large and the revenue expected from the group's stay at the hotel is substantial, cancellation penalties can be more tightly defined. Figure 5.1 illustrates the type of clause used in a convention hotel to protect the hotel from last-minute cancellations of an entire group.

Allowable Attrition

LEGALESE

Attrition: Reduction in the number of projected participants or attendees.

Allowable *attrition* refers to the amount of downward variance that may be permitted in a contract before some type of penalty is incurred on the part of the guest.

Attrition, then, is simply the loss of previously estimated guest counts. Consider, for example, the individual guest responsible for hosting a large family reunion in his or her city. When the guest first approaches the hotel to reserve sleeping rooms and space for meals, the family reunion might be months away. The guest will want to know the specifics of room rates to be charged, as well as prices for meals. Both of these charges, however, might depend on the "pick-up," or actual number of served guests. This is true because, in most cases, the larger the number of sleeping rooms sold or meals provided, the lower the price. At the time of the contract signing, however, the actual number of guests to be served is likely unknown. The guest responsible for planning the reunion may estimate 200 attendees when planning the event, but at the reunion, only 100 individuals attend. Allowable attrition clauses inform both parties of the impact, on price, of a reduced number of actual guests served.

Allowable Attrition Clause

The Hotel agrees to hold ample inventory to accommodate the rooms reserved in this Group Rooms Contract. In doing so, the Hotel may be put in a position to turn away other groups that may request rooms for the same dates. Therefore, the Hotel limits the amount of attrition or reductions in the contracted room block. Additional reductions will be billed at 100% of the contracted room and tax.

91 days or more prior to arrival	50% of room block
61–90 days or more prior to arrival	20% of room block
31–60 days or more prior to arrival	10% of room block
Less than 31 days prior to arrival	2% of room block

For all meal and meeting functions, the Hotel reserves the right to move groups to a room with capacity equal to the actual number of guests to be served.

Figure 5.2 Allowable attrition clause.

Figure 5.2 is an example of an allowable attrition clause in a group lodging contract. Notice that both parties to the contract are clearly informed about the consequences of reduced pick-up on the part of the guests. In addition, the clause has a statement clearly indicating that if the size of the group is reduced by too much, the hotel may relocate the meal or meeting space of the group. This is particularly important in a facility with restricted meeting space, where there might be only one large ballroom. If guests reserve this room based on a large estimate, which then fails to materialize, the hospitality manager might have no choice but to move the group to a smaller room, thus freeing the larger room for potential resale.

It is important to remember that guests often overestimate the projected attendance at their functions. If hospitality managers do not consider the impact of attrition, their operations may be hurt by this common guest tendency. As attrition disputes are becoming more common, meeting planners are insisting that contracts also include clauses that hold the hotel accountable for using diligence to resell any rooms unused by the meeting to reduce the damages caused by exceeding the allowable attrition.

Indemnification for Damages

To indemnify means to secure against loss or damage. Indemnity language is important when a hotel contracts with an organization whose individual members will occupy rooms designated under a group contract. In one situation, an organization of law enforcement officers contracted with a hotel to hold its annual convention. During the course of the convention, a few members of the organization became intoxicated and caused some damage to the physical property of the hotel. The question then arose: Who should be held responsible for the damages? The law enforcement organization, the individual officers, and the cities that employed them were all considered possible sources of damage reimbursement.

It is important to make clear exactly who will be responsible if damages to rooms or space should occur. Although significant damage during a guest's stay is certainly the exception rather than the rule, the possibility of consequential damage does exist and should be addressed. A general clause covering this area in a group rooms contract might read as follows:

The group shall be liable for any damage to the hotel caused by any of its officers, agents, contractors, or guests.

Payment Terms

Although payments and terms for payment might seem relatively straightforward, in the hospitality industry, contract payment terms can sometimes become quite complex. Consider the case of a visiting college basketball team. The head coach reserves sleeping rooms and agrees to pay for the rooms with a college-issued credit card. One of the players, however, makes several hundred dollars' worth of long-distance telephone calls from his hotel room. Who is responsible for this payment? Further, how can the hotel hope to collect the monies due to it? The best way to address problems such as these is to clearly and precisely state the terms of payment and the responsibility for all expenses incurred.

Dining establishments generally require a cash, check, or credit/debit card payment at the time of meal service. In the lodging industry, payment can take a variety of forms:

- Individual guest pays all charges.
- Company or group pays all charges.
- Payment in full is required prior to arrival.
- Hotel directly bills the company or group for room and tax only.
- Hotel directly bills the company or group for all charges.
- Individual guest pays incidentals (e.g., telephone, meals, movies, laundry, and parking).
- Multiple guests are all billed to one common master bill.

Note that in the preceding example, if the coach's contract called for the group to pay all charges, then the college would indeed be responsible for the long-distance telephone charges. If the contract included a clause in which individuals pay for incidentals, then the individual player would be held responsible for the charges. The importance of using precise language to prevent ambiguity should be apparent.

Performance Standards Related to Quantity

Previously, we discussed ways for hospitality managers to address the problem of attrition and no-shows. But what of the guest whose actual numbers exceed the original estimate? If, for example, a catering hall anticipates serving 200 guests, but 225 people arrive to attend the event, the operation may face space and production shortages. Because this type of situation is also common, many operators will prepare food and create place settings in the dining room for a number of guests larger than the contracted guest count. This approach prevents frantic, last-minute attempts to meet an unanticipated demand.

While there is no industry standard established, many operators find that agreeing to prepare for 5 percent more guests than the contracted number is a good way to balance the potential needs of the guest with the actual needs of the operation. When the operation agrees to a performance standard related to quantity, this standard should be clearly stated in the contract.

When providing for products and services in the vastly diverse hospitality industry, additional essential clauses may be required based on the type and style of the hospitality facility. When that is the case, management should identify these potential problem areas and address them each and every time a contract is executed.

Essential Clauses for Purchasing Products and Services

Just as there are essential and important components of a contract that state when the hospitality manager is responsible for providing products and services, it is equally critical to ensure that essential clauses are in place when hospitality managers contract to purchase or receive products and services. Here, too, it is in the best interest of both parties to get all contractual arrangements in writing. Listed next are some of the important contractual elements to be considered before executing a purchasing contract.

Payment Terms

Some of the most significant components of a contract for buying products and services are the payment terms. Consider the case of the restaurateur who wants to purchase a new roof for her restaurant. She gets three bids from contractors, each of whom quotes her a similar price. In one case, however, the builder wants full payment prior to beginning work. In the second case, the builder wants half the purchase price prior to beginning the job and the balance upon a "substantial completion" of the work. In the third case, payment in full is required within 30 days after completion of the job. Obviously, in this case, the payment terms could make a considerable difference in which contractor gets the bid.

Required down payments, interest rates on remaining balances, payment due dates, and penalties for late payments are points that should be specified in the contract, and reviewed carefully.

Delivery or Start Date

In the case of some delivery dates, a range of times may be acceptable. Thus, when purchasing sofas, a hotel could insert contract language, such as "within 60 days of contract signing" as an acceptable delivery date clause. In a like manner, food deliveries might be accepted by a kitchen "between the hours of 8:00 A.M. and 4:00 P.M."

In some cases, the delivery or start date may be unknown. Consider, for example, the following contract clause written when a hotel agreed to lease part of its lobby space to a flower shop. The time it would take to get the shop stocked and operational was unknown, and thus the start date of the lease could not easily be determined. The delivery/start clause here is part of that longer contract document. In the section titled "Start Date," it reads:

> The initial Operating Term of this agreement shall commence at 12:01 A.M. on the first day the Flower Shop is open for business and terminate at 11:59 P.M. on the day preceding the tenth (10th) anniversary thereof; provided, however, that the parties hereto may extend this agreement by mutual consent for up to two (2) terms of five (5) years each.

Note that, though the actual start date was uncertain, the language identifying precisely when the start date was to occur was unmistakable. In all cases, it is important that a start date be present and that it be clear.

Completion Date

Completion dates let the contracting parties know when the contract terms end. In the case of a painter hired to paint a room, this date simply identifies when the painter's work will be finished. If the contract is written to guarantee a price for a product purchased by a restaurant, the completion date is the last day that price will be honored by the vendor.

It is often difficult to estimate completion dates. This is especially true for construction contracts when weather, labor difficulties, or material delays can affect timetables. Despite these difficulties, completion dates should be included whenever products or services are secured.

Some contracts are written in such a manner that the completion or stop date of the contract is extended indefinitely unless specifically discontinued. The following clause is taken from an agreement to cooperatively market hotel rooms with a discount hotel broker. Note the language related to the contract's extension:

> Unless otherwise noted in the contract, this participation agreement between the hotel and Tandy Discount Brokerage automatically renews on an annual basis unless cancellation is received in accordance with established publication period deadlines.

Self-renewing contracts are common, but must be reviewed very carefully by management prior to acceptance of their terms. It is important to calendar (identify for future attention) any action required by management to discontinue a self-renewing contract so that critical dates will not be missed.

Performance Standards

Performance standards refer to the quality of products or services received. This can be an exceptionally complex area because some services are difficult to quantify. The thickness of concrete, the quality of carpeting, and the brand or model of a piece of equipment can, for example, be specified. The quality of an advertising campaign, a training program, or interior design work can be more difficult to evaluate.

The effective hospitality manager should quantify performance standards in a contract to the greatest degree possible. With some thought, and help from experts in the topic the contract is about, great specificity may be determined. Consider the foodservice manager who wishes to purchase canned peach halves. A purchase specification, such as the following, could be included as part of the purchase contract:

> Peaches, yellow cling halves, canned. U.S. Grade 3, (Choice), packed 6, number 10 cans per case, with 30 to 35 halves per can. Packed in heavy syrup, with 19 to 24 Brix; minimum drained weight, 66 ounces per number 10 can, with certificate of grade required.

Recall that under the Uniform Commercial Code (UCC), a vendor is contractually obligated to provide goods that are fit for use and free of defects. Clauses that specify performance standards in a purchasing contract give both buyers and sellers an added level of protection, because the extra details will clearly spell out the expectations of both parties, with regard to the nature and quality of the goods transferred.

Licenses and Permits

Obtaining licenses and permits, which are normally required for contracted work, should be the specific responsibility of the outside contracting party. Tradespeople, such as plumbers, security guards, air conditioning specialists, and the like, who must be licensed or certified by state or local governments, should be prepared to prove they indeed have the appropriate credentials. However, it is the responsibility of the hospitality manager to verify the existence of these licenses, if they are required to perform the terms of a contract. In addition, a photocopy of these documents should always be attached to the contract itself. Figure 5.3 is an example of a general clause related to the issue of licenses and permits.

Indemnification

LEGALESE
Indemnification: To make one whole; to reimburse for a loss already incurred.

Accidents can happen while an agreement is being fulfilled. In order to protect themselves and their organizations, hospitality managers should insist that the contracts they execute contain *indemnification* language similar to this example:

> Contractor hereby agrees to indemnify, defend, and hold harmless the restaurant and its officers, directors, partners, employees, and guests from and against any losses, liabilities, claims, damages, and expenses, including, without limitation, attorneys' fees and expenses that arise as a result of the negligence or intentional misconduct of Contractor or any of its agents, officers, employees, or subcontractors.

Licenses and Permits Clause

The contractor represents and warrants that it has in effect all licenses, permits, and other authorizations or approvals necessary to provide the services from all applicable governmental entities, and that such licenses and permits shall be maintained and in full force and effect for the length of this contract. The revocation, suspension, or withdrawal of any license, permit, authorization, or approval shall be immediately reported in writing by the contractor, and in such an event, the contract will be suspended. The contractor shall provide evidence that all such licenses, permits, and other authorizations are in effect at the signing of this contract and at any time during its length at the request of the owner.

Figure 5.3 Licenses and permits clause.

To better understand indemnification, consider the case of Melissa Norin, the manager of a restaurant located near an interstate highway. Melissa hired Twin Cities Signs Company to change the lights in a 60-foot-high road sign advertising the restaurant. While completing this work, a Twin Cities truck collided with a car parked in the restaurant's parking lot. The car owner approached Melissa, demanding that the restaurant pay for the car's damages. Without an indemnification clause in the contract for services with Twin Cities, Melissa's restaurant might incur expenses related to the accident.

Certainly, it is a good idea to have all contracts reviewed by legal counsel, but because of the significance of indemnification, this clause in a contract should be written only by a competent attorney.

Nonperformance Clauses

Often, it is a good idea to decide beforehand what two parties will do if the contract terms are not fulfilled. In the case of purchasing products and services, the simple solution may be for the hospitality manager to buy from a different vendor. If, for example, a fresh-produce vendor who has contracted with a group of family-owned restaurants frequently misses delivery deadlines or delivers poor-quality products, the nonperformance solution might simply be to terminate the contract. Language would need to be written into the contract that would address the rights of the restaurant group to terminate the agreement if the vendor consistently performed unsatisfactorily.

In some cases, nonperformance on the part of the vendor can have an extremely negative effect on the hotel or restaurant. If, for example, a hotel books a well-known entertainer as a major component in a weekend package, the failure of that entertainer to perform as scheduled would have a significant negative impact on the hotel. It is very likely that the reputation of the hotel would suffer, because it promised its guests something it did not deliver. The guests are likely to demand refunds in such a situation, and the potential that one or more of them could bring litigation against the hotel is very real.

In addition to the costs incurred due to unhappy guests, the cost of replacement entertainment might be quite high if the original entertainer canceled on short notice. Figure 5.4 is an example of nonperformance contract language that might be used to protect the hotel in such a case.

When nonperformance by a vendor will cause a negative effect on the hospitality operation, it is critical that language be included in the contract to protect the operation. The protection may be in general terms, such as the clause below, or it may be quite specific. A common way to quantify nonperformance costs is to use a "dollars-per-day" penalty. In this situation, the vendor is assessed a penalty of agreed-on "dollars per day" if it is late in delivering the product or service.

> ### Entertainer Nonperformance Clause
>
> The "Entertainer" recognizes that failure to perform hereunder may require Hotel to acquire replacement entertainment on short notice. Therefore, any failure to provide the agreed-upon services at the times, in the areas, and for the duration required hereunder shall constitute a default, which shall allow the Hotel to cancel this contract immediately on oral notice. The "Entertainer" and or his or her agent shall be liable for any damages incurred by the Hotel, including without limitation, any costs incurred by the Hotel to secure such replacement entertainment.

Figure 5.4 Entertainer nonperformance clause.

Dispute Resolution Terms

In some cases, it is a good idea for contracting parties to agree on how to settle any disputes that may arise before they actually occur. To do so, several issues may need to be addressed. The first is the location of any litigation undertaken. This is not a complex issue when both parties to the contract and their businesses are located in the same state. When the contract is between two parties that are not located in the same state, contract language such as the following could be inserted into the contract:

> This agreement shall be governed by and interpreted under the laws of the State of _____ [location of business].

Additional terms may include the use of agreed-on, independent third parties to assist in problem resolutions. Litigation costs are another area of potential disagreement that can be addressed before any contract problems arise. Language such as the following makes clear who is responsible for the costs associated with contract litigation:

> Should any legal proceedings be required to enforce any provisions of this Agreement, the prevailing party shall be entitled to recover all of its costs and expenses related thereto, including expert witness' and consultants' fees and attorneys' fees.

Exculpatory Clauses

LEGALESE

Exculpatory clause (or contract): A contract, or a clause in a contract, that releases one of the parties from liability for his or her wrongdoings.

In addition to the essential elements related to providing and receiving products and services just listed, some hospitality managers would add an *exculpatory clause*, especially when providing products and services to guests. These clauses seek to exculpate, or excuse, the hospitality operator from blame in certain situations. An example would be a sign in a pool area that states "Swim at Your Own Risk," or a clause in a meeting space contract that states "Operator not responsible for materials left in meeting rooms overnight." Although these clauses may help reduce litigation, it is important to understand why this is so. Exculpatory clauses generally cause guests to exercise greater caution. Warning signs or contract language that cause guests to be more careful truly will work in the favor of both guests and the hospitality organization. In addition, some parties to a contract may accept the exculpatory statement as legal truth. That is, they will assume that they have somehow given up their right to a claim against the hospitality organization because of the exculpatory clause's language.

It is very important to note, however, that the courts have not generally accepted the complete validity of exculpatory clauses. In some cases, they do in fact exculpate; in others, they do not. Consequently, exculpatory clauses have the disadvantage of sometimes providing a false sense of security to the operator. In summary, these clauses can be useful, but they should not be relied upon to absolve the operator of his or her reasonable responsibilities to care for the safety and security of guests.

≫ ANALYZE THE SITUATION 5.1

LAUREEN STATTE WAS A guest at the Vacation Inn Express, a mid-priced, limited service hotel in an urban area. When she checked into the hotel, she inquired about the availability of a workout room. Upon receiving assurances that the hotel did indeed have such an area, Ms. Statte checked into the hotel, put away her luggage, changed into workout attire, and proceeded to the workout area.

Upon entering the workout room, she noticed a sign prominently posted near the entrance to the workout room stating: "Hotel Not Liable for Any Injuries Incurred During Workouts."

According to her attorney, Ms. Statte lifted deadweights for approximately 10 minutes, and then mounted a treadmill. As an experienced treadmill user, she started slowly, gradually increasing the treadmill's speed. Shortly after beginning the treadmill workout, Ms. Statte fell backward into a plate-glass window that was approximately 2 feet behind the treadmill. The glass shattered, and shards from the glass severely injured Ms. Statte.

Ms. Statte's attorney claimed the accident was the fault of the hotel because the treadmill was too close to the window, and the hotel neglected to outfit the windows with safety glass. As its defense, the hotel pointed out the presence of the exculpatory clause sign, clearly posted, that Ms. Statte agreed she had read prior to beginning her workout.

1. Do you believe a guest who has agreed to be responsible for her own injuries during a workout has also agreed to be responsible for them in the presence of significant negligence on the part of the hotel?

2. As the hotel manager, how might you resolve this dispute?

3. Could a lawsuit have been prevented?

5.2 FRANCHISE CONTRACTS

In Chapter 3, you learned that franchising is a business strategy that allows one business entity to use the logo, trademarks, and operating systems of another business entity for the benefit of both. Because of the potential for abuse, the laws and contract language that govern the advertising for sale and purchase of franchises are closely regulated and complex. As well, the language of the franchise agreements that control the actions of franchisor and franchisee are typically very detailed and, as a result, must be well understood by both of these parties.

Purchasing a Franchise

Evaluating and purchasing a franchise is a very complex undertaking. This can be made even more difficult if the companies selling franchises are not open and honest in the description of their offerings. In the past, some franchisors, in some industries, were fraudulent or deceptive in their claims. Because of this, detailed regulations and laws have been enacted that specify *disclosure* requirements that franchisors must follow when, as shown in the example in Figure 5.5, they advertise their franchise for sale.

The Franchise Rule

The Federal Trade Commission (FTC), through its mandate to regulate unfair or deceptive trade practices, is the government agency assigned the task of regulating the offering of franchises. To do so, the FTC requires all franchisors to supply information that it feels is necessary for a potential franchisee to make an informed buying decision. (The types of information that franchisors must disclose will be discussed later in this section.) It is important to note that while the FTC requires that certain information be disclosed, it does not verify the accuracy of that information. Figure 5.6 is a statement from the FTC that must be prominently displayed on the cover or first page of a disclosure document, which the franchisor is required to supply to anyone considering purchasing a franchise.

In the mid-1970s, the FTC developed a document titled "Disclosure Requirements and Prohibitions Concerning Franchising and Business Opportunity Ventures," which took effect on October 21, 1979. Commonly known as the Franchise Rule, it establishes detailed disclosure requirements for franchisors. Figure 5.7 is an excerpt from the FTC Franchise Rule. Note the very specific information it requires franchisors to disclose.

Revised Franchise Rule

In January 2007, the Federal Trade Commission approved amendments to the Franchising Trade Regulation Rule. The changes were optional from July 1, 2007, until July 1, 2008. After July 1, 2008, the changes became mandatory for all franchisors. The major changes in the new Franchise Rules occur in the areas of disclosures and exemptions.

The rules governing the content of the disclosures, as well as the substance of the disclosures, have been changed. Franchisors must now disclose franchisor-initiated litigation against franchisees. Additionally, franchisors no longer have to disclose franchise brokers. If current or former franchisees have signed confidentiality clauses in franchisor agreements in the last three years, the disclosure document must contain language about the existence of such clauses. However, the most significant change is the requirement of a fully reconciled summary of the inflow and outflow of franchised and company-owned outlets over the course of each year. Safeguards are in place to avoid double-counting certain events.

Procedures for disclosures have changed, as well. Franchisors can now deliver the disclosure document not only in hard copy or CD-ROM format but also through email or through the franchisor's website. The disclosure document must be delivered no later than 14 calendar days before the franchisee signs any agreement or pays any money. Last, the final franchise agreement must be disclosed to the franchisee at least seven calendar days before the franchisee executes it.

Crystal's Coneys and Chips

The International Franchise Leader in Coney Dogs and Fries

Crystal's Coneys and Chips is the worldwide segment leader in take-out Coney dogs and freshly made French fries (chips). There's a good reason why. Our franchisees realize that the support, training, and marketing assistance available through Crystal's Coneys and Chips (CC&C) ensure them the highest possible return on investment. It's true in Frankfort, Kentucky, as well as Frankfurt, Germany!

America and the world love Coney dogs and chips. At CC&C we have developed the very best recipes for both of these popular items. This means strong customer counts and strong revenues. Strong revenues mean a strong bottom line, and that's why our franchisee retention rate is second to none in the industry.

Ninety percent of our 500-plus stores are franchisee-owned and -operated. CC&C operates only 10 percent of them. That's why we know that listening to you, not competing with you, makes us both successful.

We can assist in site selection, financing, and start-up. Our franchise fees and start-up costs are low. If you are serious about your future in the Coney dog and chips market, e-mail Maureen Pennycuff, international director of franchise sales at *mpennycuff@cc&c.com,* or visit our Web site at

www.cc&c.com

This is the one franchise opportunity that you can't afford to miss!

Figure 5.5 Fictional representation of the type and style of information typically placed in an advertisement for a franchise that would be found in the hospitality trade press.

Federal Trade Commission Warning Statement

To protect you. we've required your franchisor to give you this information. *We haven't checked it and don't know if it's correct.* It should help you to make up your mind. Study it carefully. While it includes some information about your contract, don't rely on it alone to understand your contract. Read all of your contract carefully. Buying a franchise is a complicated investment. Take your time to decide. If possible, show your contract and this information to an advisor like a lawyer or an accountant. If you find anything you think may be wrong or anything important that's been left out, you should let us know about it. It may be against the law.

There may also be laws on franchising in your state. Ask your state agencies about them.

Figure 5.6 Franchise warning statement.

FTC Franchise Rule [Excerpt]

Title 16—Commercial Practices; Revised as of January 1, 1986

CHAPTER I—FEDERAL TRADE COMMISSION

SUBCHAPTER D—TRADE REGULATION RULES

PART 436—DISCLOSURE REQUIREMENTS AND PROHIBITIONS CONCERNING FRANCHISING AND BUSINESS OPPORTUNITY VENTURES

16 CFR 436.1

In connection with the advertising, offering, licensing, contracting, sale, or other promotion in or affecting commerce, as "commerce" is defined in the Federal Trade Commission Act, of any franchise, or any relationship which is represented either orally or in writing to be a franchise, it is an unfair or deceptive act or practice within the meaning of section 5 of that Act for any franchisor or franchise broker:

(a) To fail to furnish any prospective franchisee with the following information accurately, clearly, and concisely stated, in a legible, written document at the earlier of the "time for making of disclosures" or the first "personal meeting":
  (1)
    (i)   The official name and address and principal place of business of the franchisor, and of the parent firm or holding company of the franchisor, if any;
    (ii) The name under which the franchisor is doing or intends to do business; and
    (iii) The trademarks, trade names, service marks, advertising or other commercial symbols (hereinafter collectively referred to as "marks") which identify the goods, commodities, or services to be offered, sold, or distributed by the prospective franchisee, or under which the prospective franchisee will be operating.
  (2) The business experience during the past 5 years, stated individually, of each of the franchisor's current directors and executive officers (including, and hereinafter to include, the chief executive and chief operating officer, financial, franchise marketing, training and service officers). With regard to each person listed, those persons' principal occupations and employers must be included.
  (3) The business experience of the franchisor and the franchisor's parent firm (if any), including the length of time each:
    (i)   Has conducted a business of the type to be operated by the franchisee;
    (ii) Has offered or sold a franchise for such business;
    (iii) Has conducted a business or offered or sold a franchise for a business:

Figure 5.7 FTC Franchise Rule excerpt

       (A) operating under a name using any mark set forth under paragraph (a)(1)(iii) of this section, or

       (B) involving the sale, offering, or distribution of goods, commodities, or services which are identified by any mark set forth under paragraph (a)(1)(iii) of this section; and

    (iv) Has offered for sale or sold franchises in other lines of business, together with a description of such other lines of business.

  (4) A statement disclosing who, if any, of the persons listed in paragraphs (a) (2) and (3) of this section:

    (i) Has, at any time during the previous seven fiscal years, been convicted of a felony or pleaded nolo contendere to a felony charge if the felony involved fraud (including violation of any franchise law, or unfair or deceptive practices law), embezzlement, fraudulent conversion, misappropriation of property, or restraint of trade;

    (ii) Has, at any time during the previous seven fiscal years, been held liable in a civil action resulting in a final judgment or has settled out of court any civil action or is a party to any civil action:

       (A) involving allegations of fraud (including violation of any franchise law, or unfair or deceptive practices law), embezzlement, fraudulent conversion, misappropriation of property, or restraint of trade, or

       (B) which was brought by a present or former franchisee or franchisees and which involves or involved the franchise relationship; Provided, however, That only material individual civil actions need be so listed pursuant to this paragraph (4)(ii), including any group of civil actions which, irrespective of the materiality of any single such action, in the aggregate is material;

    (iii) Is subject to any currently effective State or Federal agency or court injunctive or restrictive order, or is a party to a proceeding currently pending in which such order is sought, relating to or affecting franchise activities or the franchisor-franchisee relationship, or involving fraud (including violation of any franchise law, or unfair or deceptive practices law), embezzlement, fraudulent conversion, misappropriation of property, or restraint of trade.

Such statement shall set forth the identity and location of the court or agency; the date of conviction, judgment, or decision; the penalty imposed; the damages assessed; the terms of settlement or the terms of the order; and the date, nature, and issuer of each such order or ruling. A franchisor may include a summary opinion of counsel as to any pending litigation, but only if counsel's consent to the use of such opinion is included in the disclosure statement.

  (5) A statement disclosing who, if any, of the persons listed in paragraphs (a) (2) and (3) of this section at any time during the previous 7 fiscal years has:

    (i) Filed for bankruptcy;

    (ii) Been adjudged bankrupt;

    (iii) Been reorganized due to insolvency; or

    (iv) Been a principal, director, executive officer, or partner of any other person that has so filed or was so adjudged or reorganized, during or within 1 year after the period that such person held such position in such other person. If so, the name and location of the person having so filed, or having been so adjudged or reorganized, the date thereof, and any other material facts relating thereto, shall be set forth . . .

The Rule is a trade regulation rule with the full force and effect of federal law. The courts have held it may only be enforced by the FTC, not private parties. The FTC may seek injunctions, civil penalties and consumer redress for violations.

The Rule is designed to enable potential franchisees to protect themselves before investing by providing them with information essential to an assessment of the potential risks and benefits, to meaningful comparisons with other investments, and to further investigation of the franchise opportunity.

The Rule, formally titled "Disclosure Requirements and Prohibitions Concerning Franchising and Business Opportunity Ventures," took effect on October 21, 1979, and appears at 16 C.F.R. Part 436.

Figure 5.7 (Continued)

The amended rules have exempted certain franchise relationships. Purchases by owners, officers, or managers of franchisors are not covered by the new rules. If the franchisee has been in business for five years and has a net worth of $5 million, then the new Franchise Rules do not apply. If the franchisee's initial investment is larger than $1 million (excluding the value of the real estate and any amounts provided by franchisor), then the new rules do not apply. Last, the amended rules do not apply if the franchise location is outside the United States.

For more information, please visit www.ftc.gov/opa/2007/01/franchiserule.shtm.

Search the Web **5.2**

Visit www.ftc.gov/bcp/franchise/16cfr436.shtm.

Read the entire FTC Franchise Rule (16 CFR Part 436), to familiarize yourself with its requirements, and then write a one-page bulleted summary of the rule.

The Franchise Rule imposes six different requirements in connection with the "advertising, offering, licensing, contracting, sale, or other promotion" of a franchise:

1. *Basic disclosures:* Franchisors are required to give potential investors a basic disclosure document at the earlier of the first face-to-face meeting or ten business days before any money is paid or an agreement is signed in connection with the investment (Part 436.1(a)).

2. *Earnings claims:* If franchisors make earnings claims, whether historical or forecasted, they must have a reasonable basis for those claims, and evidence supporting the claims must be given to potential investors in writing at the same time as the basic disclosures (Parts 436.1(b)–(d)).

3. *Advertised claims:* The rule affects only promotional ads that include an earnings claim. Such ads must disclose the number and percentage of existing franchisees that have achieved the claimed results, along with cautionary language. The use of earnings claims in promotional ads also triggers required compliance with the rule's earnings claim disclosure requirements (Part 436.1(e)).

4. *Franchise agreements:* The franchisor must give investors a copy of its standard-form franchise agreement and related agreements at the same time as the basic disclosures; and final copies intended to be executed at least five business days before signing (Part 436.1(g)).

5. *Refunds:* Franchisors are required to make refunds of deposits and initial payments to potential investors, subject to any conditions on refundability stated in the disclosure document (Part 436.1(h)).

6. *Contradictory claims:* Although franchisors are permitted to supply investors with any promotional or other materials they wish, no written or oral claims may contradict information provided in the required disclosure document (Part 436.1(f)).

The Franchise Offering Circular

Some states have franchise investment laws that require franchisors to provide presale disclosures, known as franchise offering circulars (FOCs) to potential franchisees. These states treat the sale of a franchise like the sale of a security. They typically prohibit the offer or sale of a franchise within their governance until a company's FOC has been filed of public record with, and registered by, a designated state agency.

Those states with disclosure laws give franchise purchasers important legal rights, including the right to bring private lawsuits for violation of the state disclosure requirements. The FTC keeps a record of those states that require franchisors to provide FOCs. Potential franchise purchasers who reside in states that have these requirements should contact their state franchise law administrators for additional information about the protection these laws provide.

The FOC is a document designed to encourage the purchase of a franchise. These circulars generally will follow a format patterned after the FTC's Franchise Rule. It is important to remember, however, that the FTC does not verify, as factual, the information contained in a circular. Because this is true, the documents making up the FOC should, like all contracts, be read very carefully.

The following information must be included in an FOC. This information is requested by states that require FOCs, in accordance with guidelines established by the FTC. After reading these items, you may realize that these state requirements are almost identical to the FTC's own disclosure requirements in the Franchise Rule:

- A description of the franchisor and the type of license it is offering
- The business experience of the franchise company's owners and/or managers
- Initial fees, continuing fees, and royalties if required
- Initial investment estimates
- The licensee's obligations
- The licensor's obligations
- Policies about the geographic territory protected by the license agreement
- Restrictions on what the licensee may sell and how it may be sold
- Renewal and termination policies
- Transfer of ownership policies
- Claims regarding average earnings or profitability of current franchisees
- Locations of current franchisees
- A sample franchise (license) agreement
- Any information required by a specific state (e.g., California, Utah, or Maine)
- The name and address of the legal representative of the franchisor

Additional items may be included based on state law, FTC requirements, and the specific nature of the franchise. Again, it is important to remember that one of the goals of the FOC is to facilitate the selling of franchises. As with any disclosure, those who prepare it should be honest, or they face possible litigation for deception. Similarly, those who read the document for purposes of purchasing a franchise should be prepared to verify, to the greatest degree possible, the information it contains.

Franchise Contracts

If, after reviewing the FOC, an owner elects to execute a contract with a franchisor, then the two parties will sign a special form of hospitality contract called a *franchise agreement*.

The franchise agreement is the document that actually regulates the relationship between franchisee and franchisor. It is important to ensure that the information in the circular is consistent with that found in the franchise agreement. Because the franchise agreement details the rights and responsibilities of both the franchisor and franchisee, the document will directly address the following topics:

License granted
Franchisee responsibilities

LEGALESE

Franchise agreement:
A special hospitality contract that details the responsibilities of both parties (franchisor and franchisee) involved in the operation of a franchise.

Franchisor responsibilities
Proprietary rights
Audit requirements
Indemnification and insurance requirements
Transfer of ownership policies
Termination policies
Renewal options
Relationship of the parties to the contract
Areas of protection
Terms of the agreement (start and stop dates)

The franchise agreement is a critical contract in that it spells out in detail the rights and responsibilities of both the franchisor and franchisee. As such, it should be carefully read and examined by an attorney. For a hospitality manager whose responsibilities include operating a franchise, either as an owner or as an employee hired by the owners, it is imperative that the contract terms be followed. If they are not, the franchisor may have the right to terminate the contract.

It is important to understand that, in most cases, franchise companies do not actually own the hotels operating under their brand names. Franchise companies such as these own, instead, the right to sell the brand name and determine the standards that will be followed by those hotel owners who do elect to affiliate with their brands. With the ownership of a hotel vested in one business entity and the responsibility for brand standards resting with another business entity, it is not surprising that conflict can arise between the hotel's owners and the brand managers. For example, assume that the managers of a given brand decide that the bedding for their brand, and thus the mattresses, bedspreads, sheet quality standards, and pillow sizes, are not in keeping with the quality of that provided by competing brands. The brand managers may have the authority, under the franchise agreement, to require affiliated hotel owners to update their bedding. The owners, however, facing significant purchase and replacement costs for bedding that is in perfectly good condition, but that has been declared "substandard" by the brand managers, might attempt to resist the purchase of the new items. In fact, franchised hotel owners may disagree with their brand managers about numerous operating issues.

Because franchisors are generally in a stronger bargaining position than the franchisee, the franchise agreement is often heavily weighted in favor of the franchisor. However, like any contract, the franchise agreement is a negotiable document. Up-front fees or application fees, monthly royalties, areas of protection, required purchases, or renovations to facilities are all contract areas that can be negotiated prior to signing the franchise agreement. Difficulties and misunderstandings can arise between franchisors and franchisees, even when details seem to be clearly spelled out in the contract. Some of the most glaring areas of tension center on specific ways of operating the business, and balancing the needs of the franchisee with those of the franchisor.

The franchise agreement is, in the final analysis, simply a contract between the brand's managers and the hotel's owners. As such, it is negotiable. The stronger the position of each side, the more power each will bring to the negotiating process. It is always in the best interest of the business's owners to be represented by an attorney during the franchise agreement finalization period because these agreements are detailed and complex. In the opinion of many, franchise agreements, which are drafted by the franchisor, tend to be written in the favor of the franchisor. Because this is true, owners should carefully read every line of the franchise agreement to determine exactly what they must do to stay in compliance with the agreement, as well as the penalties that will be incurred if they do not stay in compliance.

To become familiar with some of the many areas of potential conflict between the manner in which franchisors and franchisees interpret management agreement terms and clauses, follow the instructions in Search the Web 5.3.

Selling a Franchise

Selling a nonfranchised business is sometimes complex. However, selling a franchise can be even more difficult, because, in most franchise contracts, the sale of a franchise will generally require approval from the franchisor. The franchisor's rationale is clear: It is in their best interest to ensure that any owner who takes over a franchise indeed meets the requirements the franchisor has set out for its franchisees. This is, of course, a legitimate interest. It results, however, in a situation that places restrictions on the seller.

In some cases, the franchisor retains the *right of first refusal* in a franchise sale. In other cases, such as that in Figure 5.8, the franchisor will insert a clause in the franchise agreement that requires notification in the event of a pending sale. Should the new buyer elect not to renew the franchise, the franchisee may have to pay a termination fee to the franchisor.

When an independent restaurant or lodging facility owner elects to sell his or her business, he or she is free to determine a suggested selling price, advertise that

LEGALESE

Right of first refusal: A clause in a contractual agreement between two parties in a business relationship in which one party, upon termination of the business relationship, can exercise the right to buy the interest of the other party before those rights can be offered for sale to another.

Search the Web **5.3**

Go to www.hospitalitylawyer.com.

1. Select: Resources.

2. Select: Academics.

3. Select: Hospitality Law Textbook Support.

4. Select: Click Here for Fourth Edition Reference Cases.

5. Select "Joint Franchisor-Franchise Relations by Robert Zarco, Richard Barrell-Cuetara, and Andrew Loewinger Presented at the Third Annual Hospitality Law Conference."

6. Review this article, and be prepared to discuss it in class.

Notification/Nonassumption Clause

In no event shall owner offer the hotel through public auction or through the media of advertising, either in newspapers or otherwise, without first obtaining the written consent of franchisor, which shall not be unreasonably withheld.

If in the event of the sale of the hotel the purchaser fails to assume owner's obligations hereunder, or in the event franchisor shall have elected to terminate this agreement, then owner agrees to pay to franchisor as liquidated damages and not as a penalty, no later than the closing, or 10 days following the effective date of such termination, a termination fee in an amount equal to the greater of 12 times the average monthly fees earned by the franchisor during the preceding 12 months or 12 times the basic fees projected in the current year's operating budget.

Figure 5.8 Right of first refusal clause.

Agency Relationship Clause

The franchisee is an independent contractor. Neither the franchisee nor franchisor is the legal representative or agent of the other. No partnership, affiliate, agency, fiduciary responsibility, or employment relationship is created by this agreement.

Figure 5.9 Agency relationship clause.

the business is for sale, and sell the business as he or she sees fit. When a franchisee wants to sell his or her business, however, the franchisor often requires that the buyer sign the current franchise agreement, which most often contains materially different financial terms from those in the selling franchisee's agreement. What the buyer is buying is often different from what the seller is selling.

Owning a franchise is an effective way for many entrepreneurs to improve their odds of success when starting a business. Investigating the many different alternatives available from various franchisors is an important part of this process. From a legal standpoint, the manager of a franchise operation has the dual burden of operating in such a way as to satisfy both the owners of the operation and the franchisor. When conflicts occur between the best interests of the ownership and those of the franchisor, it is important to remember where the agency relationship lies. In fact, language inserted by the franchisor in a franchise agreement is typically very clear about that issue, as can be seen in Figure 5.9.

5.3 MANAGEMENT CONTRACTS

In Chapter 3 you learned that some hospitality business owners choose to allow another entity to operate their businesses. When they do so, the terms and conditions of the operating arrangement are documented in a management contract, or as it is also known, a *management agreement*.

Management companies are common in all segments of the hospitality industry. As a result, a great number of hospitality managers will, during their careers, work directly or indirectly with a management company. Because that is true, it is important that you understand how management companies are structured, the manner in which the management contracts (agreements) under which they operate are developed, and the unique relationship that results when an owner selects a management company to operate a franchised business.

Management Companies

A management company is an organization formed for the express purpose of managing one or more businesses. Management companies may be classified in a variety of ways, such as the industry segment in which they operate, their geographic location, and their size. From a legal perspective, however, one important way to classify management companies is by the ownership interest they have in the businesses they operate. This relationship can take a variety of forms, including these four:

1. *The management company is neither a partner nor an owner of the business it manages.* In this situation, the business's owners simply hire the management company. This is common, for example, when lenders

---

LEGALESE

Management agreement: The legal agreement that defines the responsibilities of a business owner and the management company chosen to operate the owner's business. Also known as a "management contract."

involuntarily take possession of a business. In other cases, the management company may, for its own philosophical reasons, elect to concentrate only on managing properties and will not participate in business investing (ownership).

2. *The management company is a partner (with others) in the ownership of the business's they manage.* Although this common arrangement exists in many segments of hospitality, it is especially popular within the hotel industry. Frequently, in this situation, the management company either buys or is given a portion of business ownership (usually 1 to 20 percent), and then assumes the management of the property. Those business owners who prefer this arrangement feel that the partial ownership enjoyed by the management company will result in better performance by them. However, if the business experiences losses, the management company will share in these losses, and this fact can help serve as a motivator for the management company!

3. *The management company only manages businesses it owns.* Some management companies form simply to manage the businesses they themselves own. These companies want to participate in business as both investors and managers. Clearly, an advantage of this situation is that the management company will benefit from its own success if the businesses it manages are profitable. If the company is not successful, however, it will be responsible for any loses incurred in its operations.

4. *The management company owns, by itself, some of the businesses it manages, and owns a part, or none at all, of others it manages.* To understand better the complexities of the various scenarios under which a management company can function, consider a very successful hotel management company operating in a large city. The company decides to vary its ownership participation in the businesses it manages, depending on the individual hotel it manages. Thus, in this example, the hotel management company might:
   - Own 100 percent of one or more hotels it manages.
   - Manage and be a partial owner of other hotels.
   - Manage, but not own any part of, yet another hotel property.

In each of the situations just described, it is important, as you learned previously, for hospitality managers actually employed by the management company to clearly understand the fiduciary responsibilities that accompany their employment (see Chapter 3).

Types of Management Contracts

Not surprisingly, there are as many different contracts between those who own businesses and the management companies they employ to manage them as there are businesses under management contract. Each business owner might, depending on the management company selected, have a unique management contract, or operating agreement, for every business owned. In some cases, these contracts may include preopening services provided before the business is officially open and may even include activities related to the sale of the business.

Management contracts can be complex and their terms subject to diverse interpretation. In his 1980 book *Administration of Hotel and Restaurant Management Contracts*, James Eyster detailed many of the components typically included in hospitality management agreements. Considered a classic work in the field of management contracts, it is an excellent examination of the complexities of hospitality contracts and issues. This is so because, while times have changed since 1980, and certainly, each specific management contract is different, many of the negotiable issues identified in Eyster's book must still be addressed by owners and prospective management companies when they are discussing a potential management agreement:

- The length of time the agreement is to be in effect
- Base fees to be charged
- Incentives fees earned or penalties assessed related to operating performance
- Contract terms in the event of the business's sale
- Management company investment required or ownership required
- Procedures for early termination by either party
- Procedures for extending the contract
- Exclusivity (Is the management contract company allowed to operate competing businesses?)
- Reporting relationships and requirements (how much reporting detail is required and how frequently will reports be produced)
- Insurance requirements of the management company (who must carry the insurance and how much)
- Employee status (Are the business's employees employed by the owner of the business or the management company?)
- The control, if any, that the owner has in the selection or removal of the business's management personnel

The interests of hotel owners and the management companies they employ frequently conflict, and these conflicts can sometimes become highly publicized. On the surface, it would seem that the interests of a business owner and the management company selected to operate its business would always coincide. Both the owner and management company, it would seem, are interested in operating a profitable business. In fact, however, disputes arise because business owners will typically seek to minimize the fees they pay to management companies (because reduced fees yield greater owner profits), while management companies, of course, seek to maximize their fees.

Owners who hire management companies often have serious disagreements with those companies over whether the businesses they manage are indeed operated in the best interest of the owners. There are various reasons for these disagreements. For example, in a typical management contract, the owner absorbs the costs of management company errors. Unlike a lease arrangement, in a management contract it is generally the owner, not the management company, that is responsible for all costs associated with operating the business. As a result, the unnecessary costs incurred as a result of any errors in marketing or operating the business are borne not by the management company making the errors but, rather, by the business's owner.

For another example of potential owner/management company conflict, consider that recent lawsuits filed by owners against management companies focus on the issue of how management companies purchase goods and services for the businesses they manage. Management companies in the hospitality industry are responsible for purchasing billions of dollars worth of products, including, for example, food, furniture, fixtures, in-room amenity items, computers, and software, as well as services such as insurance, long-distance telephone, credit card processing, and payroll preparation services. Difficulties can arise when management companies, who are authorized by their management contracts to make purchases on behalf of owners, reap the benefits that accrue to large volume buyers. In some cases, large management companies have negotiated contracts with literally hundreds of manufacturers and suppliers. These contracts produce millions of dollars of rebates directly from the vendors back to the management company. The management company may retain these rebates and, in fact, may even operate their purchasing departments as separate profit centers. In other cases, the management company may have an equity investment in some of the vendors companies, or in the most egregious of cases, may even own the vendor company outright. Although these types of arrangements are not automatically illegal, they must be disclosed to the owners of the businesses for whom the management company is under contract and to whom is owed a fiduciary duty.

It is important to remember that agency law requires agents to place their principals' interest over their own, precludes agents from competing with their principals, and precludes self-dealing. That is, agents might not operate on their own behalf without disclosure to and approval of their principals. If rebates received by a management company, as in this example, are not disclosed to the business's owner, they might cease being rebates and simply become vendor *kickbacks*.

> **LEGALESE**
>
> **Kickback:** A secret rebate of part of a purchase price, given by the seller, to the buyer, in exchange for the buyer's influence in the purchasing decision.

Search the Web 5.4

Go to www.hospitalitylawyer.com.

1. Select: Resources.
2. Select: Academics.
3. Select: Hospitality Law Textbook Support.
4. Select: Click Here for Fourth Edition Reference Cases.
5. Select "Management Contracts Litigation Update by David Moseley Presented at the Third Annual Hospitality Law Conference."
6. Review this article, and be prepared to discuss it in class.

Ethical issues arise when a management company directly receives a benefit (discounts, commissions, or rebates) based on purchases made on an owner's behalf. Should those benefits accrue to the owner or the management company? The answer should be clearly spelled out in the management contract.

Management Contracts for Franchised Properties

As you have learned, a hospitality business, and especially hotels may:

- Operate as a franchise
- Operate under a management contract

As well, a business may operate as a franchise and be operated under a management contract. Just as special legal issues arise when operating a business as a franchise and when operating under a management contract, issues also arise when operating a franchise business under a management contract. To better understand the legal issues that may occur in an operating arrangement that includes both a franchise and management company, it is instructive to examine, as an example, the hotel segment of the hospitality industry.

Hotel owners often find themselves in some level of conflict with, or, at the very least, in disagreement with, franchisors about how to best manage the franchised brand; as well as how to operate the individual hotels making up the brand. For example, assume that the franchisor for a hotel brand has, as a brand standard, established breakfast hours for the hotel's complimentary continental breakfast to be from 6:00 A.M. to 9:00 A.M. Assume, also, that the hotel is operated, for its owners, under a management contract.

The hotel's owners have instructed the management company to begin the breakfast at 7:00 A.M., rather than 6:00 A.M. on the weekends, to reduce labor costs. If the management company follows the directive of the brand managers, it has violated the owner's wishes (but fulfilled the terms of the franchise agreement); however, if it follows the clear instructions of the hotel's owner, it will be in violation of a brand standard and thus the owner's franchise agreement.

When owners instruct management companies to violate or ignore brand standards, the resulting influence on the hotel's relationship with the brand can be negative. Alternatively, when brand managers seek a management company's compliance with acts that may be in the best interest of the brand managers, but not necessarily the hotel's owners, difficulties may also arise. This will, in most cases, be true despite the claims of franchisors that all of their actions are undertaken in the best interest of the brand's franchisees.

Even when a hotel's owners do not intentionally initiate brand-related conflict with their management companies, it can still occur. For example, assume that those brand managers responsible for selling franchises to owners were successful in convincing a hotel's owners to reflag (choose a new brand) their property. Assume also that this owner employs a management company to operate the hotel.

After one year of operation, the owner complains to the franchise company that the number of reservations received through the franchisor's national reservation center is not consistent with the amounts verbally promised by the brand's sales representatives. In fact, complain the owners, the volume of reservations received is only about one-half of that promised. In cases such as these, it is not at all unusual (and in fact is most likely), that the brand managers will claim that it is the management company operating the hotel, and not the brand, that is the cause of the shortfall. Not surprisingly, the management company is highly unlikely to agree with this assessment. The potential for resulting conflict is clear. This is simply one example of possible brand versus management company conflict.

As you learned, sometimes a management company owns all or part of the hotel it operates. In most arrangements, however, the management company does not own the hotel it operates. The result is that, in some cases, conflicts arise between the management company and the brand (but not the business's owner). Many management companies have excellent relations with the brands they manage for owners, while others do not. This results because, at times, some of the wishes or even the directives of the brand managers are in conflict with the perceived best interest of the management company.

For example, a franchise company might, in an effort to promote business, send to a management company managed hotel several large, exterior banners, that advertise a special rate or hotel feature. Obviously, the brand wants these signs displayed on the property. The management company's sales philosophy, however, might not include hanging large exterior banners around the hotel because it believes such banners cheapen the image of the hotel. Because of this belief, the banners are not displayed. The resulting conflict is actually easy to understand from the perspective of either entity. The conflict should not, however, be allowed to escalate and significantly damage the relationship between the franchisor and management company because that could easily result in real harm to the long-term best interest of the business and its actual owners.

5.4 CONFERENCE SERVICES CONTRACTS

For many hospitality businesses, and especially for hotels, well-executed contracts related to conference services are vital to the operation's profitability. Conference services contracts are unique in that they are typically executed between a hospitality business and a group. Group business is critical to the success of many hospitality businesses, but it is especially important to hotels and conference centers. Interestingly, however, there is no universally accepted definition of *group* business. Groups may, for example, consist of tour groups, sports teams, conventions, trade shows, corporate training meetings, wedding parties, and special travel packages marketed by the hotel's sales department and other multiroom night users. Despite the specific characteristics of a group, or its reason for meeting, *conference services contracts* detail the terms and conditions of the group's meeting arrangements.

One of the most important components of conference services contracts is the language used to establish and assign responsibility for the group's *master bill.*

Master bills are helpful when one member of the group is responsible for paying all hotel charges. If, for example, a company sponsors a training session for of its employees, it is likely to be most convenient for that company's accountant to pay one invoice for meeting space, meals, and hotel rooms rather than to reimburse individuals for their individual costs. Similarly, a coach traveling with a sports team will likely find a master bill to be the best way to pay for the team's rooms. Master bills, however, and their management are frequently one of the areas of greatest conflict in conference services contracts.

For most hospitality businesses, conference services contracts will take one of two basic forms: meeting and space contracts and group lodging contracts. In many cases, a group may utilize both a hotel's meeting space and its lodging facilities. In such cases, the contract between the group and the hotel will, by necessity, include components found in each of the two basic types of conference services contracts.

Meeting Space Contracts

Although limited-service hotels primarily contract for the sale of sleeping rooms, full-service hotels, as well as conference centers and some other hospitality organizations also offer guests the ability to reserve meeting space, meeting rooms, exhibition halls, and food and beverage services. For example, a large, full-service hotel might contract with a nonprofit organization to provide sleeping rooms, meeting space, and an exhibit hall for the use during the association's annual convention. When this occurs, the rental rate for the space may be tied to the number of sleeping rooms used by the group during its meeting; in other cases, however, the price of the meeting space is not related to the use of sleeping rooms. Since most hotels have limited meeting space, and that space is used primarily as an enticement to sell sleeping rooms, experienced hotel managers must carefully contract for the sale of this space. The meeting space contract utilized by a hotel or conference center allows the manager to set precisely the terms and conditions on the sale of its valuable meeting space and services. Figure 5.10 provides an example of the level of detail typically found in such contracts.

> **LEGALESE**
>
> **Conference services contract:** An agreement that details the space, products, and services to be provided to a group before, during, and after its meeting.

> **LEGALESE**
>
> **Master bill:** A single folio (bill) established for a group that includes specifically agreed-on group charges. Sometimes called a "master folio," "group folio," or "group bill."

Group Lodging Contracts

Although the meeting and space contracts developed by full-service hotels sometimes include provisions for sleeping rooms as well, contracts for "sleeping rooms only" are very common in hotels that do not offer meeting space. Moreover, even full-service hotels frequently have clients who only want to rent sleeping rooms and require few, if any, of the services offered by the hotel. In cases such as these, a group lodging contract will be created to describe the very specific conditions under which the group will hold and pay for the rooms it desires.

MEETING CONFIRMATION

DATE:

ORGANIZATION:

CONFERENCE:

GROUP CONTACT:

TITLE:

PHONE: FAX:

ADDRESS:

KEY DUE DATES: For your convenience, we have listed key dates mentioned within this Meeting Confirmation for your reference. Please review the corresponding sections for further information.

Acceptance/Signed Meeting Confirmation

Credit Arrangements/Completed Credit Application

Reservation Cutoff

Program Details/Menu Selections

Three Days Prior to Scheduled Events

Food and Beverage Guarantees

PROGRAM SPECIFICS:

DATES:

DAY:

DATE:

SINGLES:

DOUBLES:

CONCIERGE:

Figure 5.10 Group meeting contract.

Check-in time is 4:00 P.M.; check-out time is 12:00 P.M.; late checkout is $15.00 per hour until 4:00 P.M., after which time a full day's charge will apply. Complimentary luggage storage is available.

GUESTROOM RATES

Singles:

Doubles:

Concierge Level: $40 additional

Early Arrival:

Late Departure:

The above room rates are subject to prevailing taxes, which are currently at 17%.

DAY MEETING PACKAGE RATES (for all meeting attendees):

Subject to 8.25% sales tax and 20% service charge

This DAY GUEST PACKAGE RATE includes:

Lunch (Aspen Dining Room): Lunch is available for seating at 11:30 A.M. or 12:30 P.M.

Meeting Room Supplies: Room setup, pads, pencils, ice water pitchers, and hard candies.

Continuous Beverage Service (7:30 A.M.–5:00 P.M.): Coffee, decaf, tea, assorted sodas, and bottled water.

Community Refreshment Breaks

Morning Break (7:30 A.M.–10:30 A.M.): Assorted baked goods (varies daily), sliced fresh fruit, assorted mini-yogurts and orange juice.

Afternoon Break (2:00 P.M.–4:00 P.M.): Assorted afternoon snacks, fresh baked cookies or brownies of the day, candy, whole fresh fruit, and lemonade.

Standard Audio Visual

10–25 people: 2 flipcharts (including markers and masking tape), data projector, screen, podium and easel.

26–50 people: 2 flipcharts (including markers and masking tape), 2 data projectors, 2 screens, standard microphone, VCR/DVD player, easel, and message board.

51–75 people: 3 flipcharts, 2 data projectors, 2 screens, standard microphone, VCR/DVD player, easel, and message board.

76+ people: 4 flipcharts, 2 data projectors, 2 screens, standard microphone, lavaliere microphone, VCR/DVD player, easel, and message board.

RESERVATIONS

Procedure

We understand that reservations will be made with a rooming list. A copy of our rooming list is enclosed. The rooming list is to be returned to our office before the cutoff date.

Cutoff Date

All reservations must be received no later than_____. At that time, any uncommitted rooms in your guest room block will be released for general sale,

Figure 5.10 (Continued)

and future reservations will be subject to space and rate availability. A payment guarantee will be required to continue holding guest rooms.

Billing

Arrangements have been made for all individuals to pay for their room, taxes; and incidental charges, and for all group charges be placed on a master account to be paid by the booking organization.

FUNCTION ARRANGEMENTS

We have reserved meeting space as outlined below. Meeting rooms are not held on a 24-hour basis unless otherwise noted. A conference services manager personally assigned to your account will be contacting you to discuss and finalize your exact room setup requirements, menu selections, and audiovisual equipment needs.

Please advise us of all changes to your agenda so that we may best serve your specific program requirements. Should there be a significant reduction in attendees, we serve the right to adjust function space accordingly.

Day	Date	Time	Function	Setup	Attendance

MEETING ROOM RENTAL

The charge for meeting space will be_____ per break-out per day.

FUNCTION GUARANTEES

A final guarantee of the number of meeting attendees and/or catered food functions is due no later than three (3) business days prior to each scheduled event. This guarantee represents the minimum guest count for billing purposes and may not be reduced after this time.

CREDIT ARRANGEMENTS

Upon our accounting department's approval of your credit application, your master account will be direct-billed. Our credit terms are "Net due upon receipt of invoice" with interest charged at 1.5% on all balances over 30 days of billing date.

CREDIT APPLICATION

Credit application due:_____

RECEIVING/HANDLING OF PACKAGES

Incoming materials for your meeting should arrive at the hotel no more than three (3) days prior to your meeting date. Packages for your meeting should be addressed to the attention of your hotel service manager, and list the name and date of your meeting. If more than one package is sent, please indicate the number of packages sent by listing, for example, "package 1 of 3" or "package 2 of 3." Five (5) or fewer boxes will be delivered complimentary to your meeting room. There is a $1.50 handling and delivery charge for six (6) or more boxes.

CANCELLATION

Acknowledgement of a definite commitment by the Hotel will in good faith, continue to protect the facilities and dates agreed, to the exclusion of other business opportunities. Therefore, the commitment of space and dates is of specified value to the Hotel. Due to the great difficulty in reselling guest

Figure 5.10 (Continued)

rooms and conference space on short notice, cancellation of the entire program will be subject to an assessment according to the following schedule:

0 to 30 days prior to arrival. Full payment on total number of guest rooms, meeting charges, package plans, and any estimated banquet revenues as booked for the duration of the dates agreed upon.

31 to 60 days prior to arrival	75% of the above
61 to 90 days prior to arrival	50% of the above
91 to 180 days prior to arrival	30% of the above
181 days to 1 year prior to arrival	15% of the above
Signing date to one year prior to arrival	10% of above

ATTRITION

The rates and the availability for this program are based on the contracted guest-room block. Therefore, reduction in the guestroom block will be subject to an assessment according to the following schedule:

Up to 60 days prior to arrival: 10% can be reduced without any fee. Additional rooms over the 10% will be charged for one-night guestroom revenue.

60 to 31 days: 10% of the existing block can be reduced without any fee. Additional rooms over the 10% will be charged two nights guestroom revenue.

0 to 30 days prior to arrival: 5% of the existing guestroom block can be reduced without any fees. Rooms reduced over 5% will be charged for the full number of nights they were contracted for.

PROGRAM ALTERATION CONTINGENCY

This agreement has been based on the sequence of days, number of agreed-upon guestrooms, and function requirements specified, If these requirements are significantly changed, we reserve the right to alter the terms and conditions of this contract, including assessment of cancellation fees and availability of specified rooms and rates.

ACCEPTANCE

If the above details meet with your approval, please sign this letter agreement and return to us by_____. If an approved agreement is not received by the above option date, the Hotel will release the tentative space reserved.

We sincerely appreciate the opportunity to serve_____. You can be assured of the effort of our entire staff and my personalized attention to help make your meeting and stay most enjoyable and successful.

ACCEPTANCE BY CLIENT

Name:_____

Title: _____

Date:_____

ACCEPTANCE BY HOTEL

Name:_____

Title: _____

Date:_____

Figure 5.10 (Continued)

A well-developed group lodging (rooms) contract will include detailed language about a variety of items including:

■ The total number of rooms and room nights to be held for the group

■ The group's arrival and departure dates

■ Negotiated group rates by specific room type or run of house (any room type)

■ The *cut-off date* or reservations rooming list due date

■ Reservations procedures

■ Complimentary rooms (if any) to be credited to the to the master bill

■ Disclosure of all fees (including any early departure fees, no-show fees, and the like)

■ All room taxes, surcharges, and, if applicable, extra person charges

■ Rates applicable to rooms booked after the cut-off or reservations due date

■ Whether reservations booked by the groups members for dates just before or just after the group's stay will be counted in the total, cumulative room block

■ If there is an early departure fee, who will advise each guest of the policy and whether fees count toward attrition fees, if any

■ How room rates will be calculated if the contract is signed prior to the establishment of the group's final room rates

> **LEGALESE**
>
> **Cut-off date:** The date on which any rooms contracted, and thus held for sale, but not yet picked up (reserved) by the group are returned to the hotel's general rooms inventory.

The existence of group lodging contracts is certainly not new, but the Internet has made this contract type increasingly more complex to develop and, for hoteliers, more difficult to negotiate properly. To better understand why this is so, consider the situation in which a group contracts with a hotel to provide the group's members with sleeping rooms for a date one year in the future. The hotel establishes the rate the group members will pay, and the individual members are to call into the hotel to make their own reservations from the block (group of rooms) reserved for the members.

Assume that, one month prior to the group's arrival, all of the rooms reserved for them have been picked up (reserved) by the group's members. Assume also, however, that the hotel is not full, and its revenue managers elect to offer, online and through the hotel's franchise-affiliated website, a room rate lower than the one offered to the group. Despite the overwhelming tendency of travelers to equate the online rate with the rate at which they have reserved their own room, such rates are not easily comparable. This is because the estimated cost of group giveaways and allowances must be factored into the room rate quoted to the group. As well, when the requests of a group room buyer involve a large amount of meeting space and/or significant numbers of complimentary rooms or services, the hotel may quote a room rate for the block that is equal to or even higher than the hotel's normal transient room rate.

As illustrated in this example, as a myriad of travel websites offer more choices and become easier to use, individuals attending meetings are discovering they can often obtain lower room rates for their stays than the rate that had been quoted to their group. In addition, independent travel companies have begun to aggressively target meetings and convention attendees with e-mails and faxes offering cheaper rooms at nonheadquarters (group host) hotels. As a result, as in this example, a hotel's own revenue managers may lower room rates when a group is meeting in the hotel (e.g., by posting discounted rates on Internet travel sites such as Expedia or Travelocity) to the detriment of the hotel. Inevitably, group members book these lower-priced rooms rather than the ones originally blocked for the group. The result is that the group may not get credit for booking the number of rooms it had originally reserved, thus triggering potential rate increases or penalties. In response, savvy meeting planners have begun to demand the insertion of clauses into their group lodging contracts that exert increased control over room rates that hotels may charge during the period of the group's stay in the hotel. The reason they seek to do so is easy to understand.

Of course, hotel revenue managers seek to maximize the revenue generated by each of their available rooms (RevPAR). Meeting planners, however, will respond negatively when, for example, a group's negotiated rate of $200.00 per night is listed in the group lodging contract but, for the same time period, the hotel's revenue managers list $125.00 per night rooms on an Internet travel site simply because they believe that "any room sale is better than no sale." In a case such as this one, heavily discounting rooms during a time of a group's meeting will likely:

- Upset the group's leadership, because it will appear to the group's members that its leaders were poor negotiators who were "outsmarted" by the hotel.

- Upset the hotel's sales representative responsible for servicing the group, because rather than appearing to have given the group a "good rate," the hotel's sales representative will now appear to have taken advantage of the group. The result is a loss of credibility on the part of the sales representative and the hotel.

- Create hard feelings and accounting difficulties as meeting planners attempt to receive the concession or "comp" terms promised in their group lodging contracts. These difficulties arise because, in many cases, a group's members will in fact have purchased the total number of room nights the group contracted to buy. However, because the hotel's yield management decisions drove attendees away from the group block (but not away from the hotel) the attendees' room night purchases were not counted as part of the group block pick-up.

The language utilized in developing conference services contracts is among some of the most complex and rapidly changing in the hospitality industry. This is so because meeting planners representing group space and sleeping room buyers are sophisticated professionals, as are their hotel counterparts. As a hospitality manager, it is important to be aware of, and fully understand, the essential contract clauses currently used in conference services contracts. To learn more about these critically important clauses, follow the instructions found in Search the Web 5.5.

Search the Web 5.5

Visit www.hospitalitylawyer.com.

1. Select: Resources.

2. Select: Academics.

3. Select: Hospitality Law Textbook Support.

4. Select: Click Here for Fourth Edition Reference Cases.

5. Select "APEX Meeting Contracts Accepted Practices" provided by the Convention Industry Council.

6. Review this article, and be prepared to discuss it in class.

≫ ANALYZE THE SITUATION 5.2

MELISSA IS THE CONVENTION services director at her city's civic (convention) center. The center has been contracted to host a large press conference to announce the intention of the Republican senator representing her state to run for reelection. Despite Melissa's best efforts, the senator's office is very unhappy with the physical condition of the civic center.

"This is awful," says the senator's chief of staff. "The carpet is worn and the interiors need painting. This isn't how the center looked six years ago when we booked our reelection announcement speech. It's too late to move the press conference now, but there is no way the senator is paying the contracted amount for this space. It's just six years after we selected you, and now the conditions are terrible!

Despite the fact that the civic center is, indeed, six years older than it was at the time of the contract signing, it is not materially different, and Melissa suspects that the complaint about the condition of the facilities is merely a ploy, initiated by the senator's chief of staff, to receive a reduction on the senator's conference services bill.

Assume that you are Melissa.

1. What would be your response to the senator's aide?

2. Assume that Melissa is responsible for drafting the contracts for all of the civic center's space requests that are to take place five or more years in the future. What would you do to ensure that guests such as these were not, in the future, able to make the claim that the facilities they contracted for previously were not the same as those they actually received on the date of their meeting?

INTERNATIONAL SNAPSHOT

A Comparison of Franchise Disclosure Requirements under U.S. Law and International Law*

INTRODUCTION

Due to the widespread increase in franchising as a method of doing business, there has been a tremendous increase in franchise legislation both in the United States and internationally. Specifically, in addition to the United States, the following 12 countries have enacted franchise disclosure laws: (1) Australia; (2) Brazil; (3) Canada, Alberta Province; (4) Canada, Ontario Province; (5) China; (6) France; (7) Indonesia; (8) Malaysia; (9) Mexico; (10) Romania; (11) South Korea; and (12) Spain. Both the United States and the foreign jurisdictions regulate franchising and offer protections to prospective franchisees through presale disclosures, which take the form of a Uniform Franchise Offering Circular (UFOC) in the United States.

ITEMS TO BE DISCLOSED

The UFOC contains 23 broad categories of disclosure items. Of these items, the only ones that are either required or recommended to be disclosed in all of the foreign jurisdictions are the basic franchisor

information, ongoing fees, and investment costs. The other items of disclosure (i.e., franchisor management, bankruptcy, franchisor and franchisee obligations, exclusive territory, franchisor financing, franchisee outlets, and trademark information) are required only in some of the jurisdictions.

The second main difference between the United States and the foreign jurisdictions deals with public figures (persons whose names or physical appearance are generally known to the public in the geographic area where the franchise will be located). In the United States, information pertaining to public figures must be disclosed, whereas the foreign jurisdictions do not require such disclosure.

The third difference between U.S. and international disclosures deals with earnings information. Specifically, only Australia requires such disclosure, while Canada, France, and Romania recommend the disclosure of earnings information. Meanwhile, earnings information is a mandatory disclosure in the United States.

The fourth distinction involves the disclosure of the franchise agreement in the UFOC. In the United States, the franchise agreement must be included in the UFOC,

*Some of the factual information contained in this article was obtained from the following publication: Andrew P. Loewinger and Michael K. Lindsey, "International Franchise Disclosure Laws" (Conference Proceedings of the ABA Forum on Franchising, Scottsdale, Arizona, 2002).

whereas only six of the foreign countries require the franchise agreement to be disclosed.

The last major difference between the U.S. and foreign disclosure requirements centers on the franchisor's financial situation. In the United States, the franchisor's financial statements must be included in the UFOC. In contrast, only about two-thirds of the foreign jurisdictions require the franchisor's financial condition to be disclosed.

DISCLOSURE REQUIREMENTS IN CHINA

Franchising is still in its early stages in China. Currently, franchising is regulated through the "Trial Implementation Measures of the Administration of Franchise Operations" (the "Measures"), which were primarily established to standardize franchise operations and to protect the legal rights of the franchisor and franchisee.

Since franchising is not a predominant method of doing business in China, the disclosure requirements under Chinese law are minimal. Specifically, only the following items are either required or recommended to be disclosed in China:

Franchisor information

Initial fees

Ongoing fees

Investment information

Supplier information

Franchisor duties

Current and past franchisees

Financial statements

Receipt

None of the remaining items are required to be disclosed under Chinese law.

OTHER DIFFERENCES

These examples demonstrate just a few of the differences between United States and foreign jurisdictions with respect to presale disclosures. Other differences center on who is required to provide disclosures, who is required to receive disclosures, and when the disclosures are required. Further, there are differences between the U.S. and foreign laws as to the exemptions and exclusions under the franchise laws. In sum, before investing in a franchise, a potential franchisee should seek the advice of an experienced franchise attorney to review the franchisor's business and to prevent any overreaching by the franchisor.

Provided by Robert Zarco and Himanshu M. Patel of the law firm of Zarco Einhorn & Salkowski, P.A., Miami, Florida. www.zarcolaw.com.

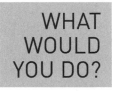

WHAT WOULD YOU DO?

Assume that you are the group sales manager at the Claremont hotel. John Pingston is one of your clients. Mr. Pingston, a professional meeting planner, works for a meeting planning company that was selected by the American Society of Hospitality Teachers (ASHT) to choose a hotel for that society's annual meeting.

At your hotel, like many others, the purchase of all hotel room nights is accompanied by the awarding, to the buyer, of major airline frequent flier credits (points). Mr. Pingston agrees to select the Claremont for the ASHT meeting but then states that, as the person responsible for "buying" the rooms, the airline award miles that accompany the room sales should be granted to him personally rather than to the ASHT, and, in fact, he strongly implies that if he is not granted the frequent traveler airline miles, he will move the contract for the group's 700 total room nights to one of the Claremont's competitors.

1. Would you grant the mileage award points to Mr. Pingston? Why or why not?
2. Assume that you granted the bonus miles to Mr. Pingston.
   a. Who do you feel would be more embarrassed by the disclosure that you did so? The planner or your hotel?
   b. If you decided to do so, to whom should you disclose Mr. Pingston's "booking bonuses"?
      i. The CEO of the planner's company?
      ii. The ASHT board of directors?
      iii. The membership of the ASHT?

THE HOSPITALITY INDUSTRY IN COURT

The following two case studies involving hospitality firms revolve around the interpretation of contracts. First consider *Marriott Hotel Services, Inc. v. National Vacation Resorts*, 2008 WL 2690060 (Cal. App. 2008).

FACTUAL SUMMARY

National Vacation Resorts (Classics) entered into a group rooms contract with Marriott Hotel Services (Marriott). Marriott agreed to provide hotel rooms to Classics for a room commitment of 1,360 rooms over a course of several days in 2005. The contract included an Attrition clause stating that if less than 85 percent of the total room nights were used, then Classics would pay liquidated damages that totaled the difference between 85 percent of the total room nights and Classics' actual room usage, multiplied by the average room group rate. Preceding the Attrition clause, however, was a Group Room Rate clause that stated, "On or before December 22, 2004, Classics may release up to 25 rooms per night from the room block at no penalty. If Classics exercises this option, Marriott has the right to revoke the Marius Meeting Room for the purpose of booking an additional group. The following Attrition clause will then apply to the revised room block."

In July 2005, Marriott informed Classics that there was an outstanding balance on the contract, which included an $81,030 charge for a shortfall of 370 rooms. Marriott demanded payment of the outstanding balance, and Classics asserted that the Attrition clause did not apply because it did not release the 25 rooms as stated in the group room rate clause.

ISSUE FOR THE COURT

The issue in this case was whether Classics' interpretation of the contract would apply, resulting in the application of the Group Room Rates clause being condition precedent to the application of the Attrition clause. Classics contended that the Attrition clause that Marriott sought shortfall damages under only applied to a revised room block. Specifically, Classics stated that under the Group Room Rates clause in the contract, which preceded the Attrition clause, the Room Attrition clause would only apply if Classics had released 25 rooms, and thus revised the room block. If Classics' interpretation was correct, then Classics would not be responsible for the outstanding balance on the contract because it had not released the 25 rooms, and thus the condition precedent to the Attrition clause had not occurred. If not, then Classics would be liable under the Attrition clause for the room shortfall by reading the contract in its entirety.

DECISION

The court disagreed with Classics' position, and relied on settled contract interpretation standards stating that Classics' interpretation of the contract was only relevant if the contractual language is reasonably susceptible to differing interpretations. In this case, Classics only offered a subjective interpretation of the contract that was not disclosed during negotiations, and thus did not constitute competent extrinsic evidence to support their interpretation. Thus, since the interpretation evidence was inadmissible, there was no conflict of interpretation regarding the Attrition clause. The court read the contract as a whole, and in its plain language, found that the purpose of the clauses was clear. Under the Group Room Rates clause, Classics was given an option to reduce the room number in the room block in order to minimize the financial impact of an anticipated shortfall. The Attrition clause would apply and functionally penalize Classics if the anticipated shortfall was more that 15 percent of the revised room block number. Thus, the Attrition clause was always effective, but Marriott had simply given Classics a 15 percent cushion that, if timely invoked, could lessen some of the burden of an anticipated shortfall.

MESSAGE TO MANAGEMENT

Be sure to clearly understand what each party expects from the clauses negotiated in a contract. If you are unsure, bring up your concerns during negotiations to clarify the contract language, because courts are extremely unwilling to rewrite a signed and negotiated contract that has objectively clear terms.

Second, consider *Hyatt Corp. v. Women's Int'l Bowling Cong., Inc.*, 80 F. Supp. 2d 88 (W.D.N.Y. 1999).

FACTUAL SUMMARY

The Women's International Bowling Congress (WIBC) made convention arrangements with the Hyatt Regency of Buffalo, New York (Hyatt). Under the agreement, Hyatt would hold a block of rooms for WIBC convention attendees. The convention attendees would be financially responsible for their own rooms. WIBC made a request to Hyatt for additional rooms to be held under the convention block. Hyatt agreed to hold the additional rooms, and attempted to insert clauses into the revised agreement requiring WIBC to guarantee all rooms would be filled and obligating WIBC to pay for any unused rooms. WIBC did not sign the revised agreement but instead offered a substitute agreement that made no mention of a guarantee to fill all rooms or an obligation to pay for unused rooms. The substitute agreement proposed by WIBC was signed by both parties and incorporated into the convention contract. The convention attendees used only about half of the rooms held by Hyatt. Hyatt sued WIBC to recover compensation for the unused rooms. WIBC refused to pay for the rooms and asserted it was never obligated to do so.

QUESTION FOR THE COURT

The question for the court was whether the contract obligated WIBC to pay for unused rooms held by Hyatt for the convention room block. The court was first faced with whether the contract was unclear. In deciding whether WIBC was obligated to pay for unused the rooms, the court would only look to the terms of the contract if the language was clear. No outside evidence could be presented by the parties unless the terms of the contract were unclear and additional explanation was needed. Hyatt argued it was reserving a block of rooms for WIBC. In using the term "reserve," Hyatt attempted to show WIBC meant to pay for unused rooms. However, the actual term used in the contract was "hold." WIBC argued the term "hold" made it clear no financial obligation was intended. Instead, the rooms were to be held by Hyatt for the individual convention attendees to reserve and pay for.

DECISION

The district court ruled in favor of WIBC. The court held the contract language was clear or unambiguous. It also held the use of the term "hold" meant WIBC was under no obligation to use all of the rooms in the room block or pay for unused rooms.

MESSAGE TO MANAGEMENT

The contracts must spell out clearly and unequivocally the intentions of the parties. Use illustrations, if need be, to clearly establish the scope of the agreement.

Although the content of any contract signed by a manager is important, in the hospitality industry, the wording found in some forms of hospitality-specific contracts is especially important. As a result, hospitality managers know that there are essential phrases (clauses) that their contracts should contain. This is true both for contracts relating to the goods and services hospitality managers provide to their guests and for the products and services they themselves purchase. Individuals who undertake

> WHAT DID YOU LEARN IN THIS CHAPTER?

responsibility for signing contracts of these types must know and understand these clauses well.

Just as the wording found in some hospitality contracts is especially significant, some hospitality contracts types are especially important to managers. Franchise-related contracts are one type of agreement that is of special importance to hospitality managers. Critical components of these varied contracts can include very specific terms related to purchasing a franchise, operating a franchised business, and selling a franchise.

Management contracts, or management agreements, comprise another contractual area of special significance to hospitality managers. This is so because a great number of management companies operate hospitality businesses for these business's owners. As a result, the contracts between the owners of a business and those who manage it can take many forms. Often, these contracts are complex and very detailed. Because this is so, hospitality managers must pay very close attention to the conditions and terms of management agreements. This is especially the case when the management contract describes an agreement for operating an owner's franchised business.

Finally, in the segment of the hospitality industry that routinely rents meeting space or sleeping rooms to guests, there are additional contract features that are unique. Meeting and space contracts, as well as group lodging contracts, are especially significant contract types encountered by many hospitality managers.

RAPID REVIEW

After you have studied this chapter, you should be prepared to:

1. List and describe those clauses essential to contracts utilized when providing products and services to guests.
2. List and describe those clauses essential to contracts utilized when purchasing hospitality products and services.
3. Explain to potential buyers of a franchise the importance of the Franchise Rule.
4. List three advantages and three disadvantages to operating a business under a franchise agreement.
5. Explain the various arrangements under which management companies operate businesses.
6. Identify potential sources of conflict you might face if, for its owner, you operated, under a management contract, a franchised business such as a restaurant, hotel, or car rental facility.
7. Identify at least three essential contract clauses that protect a hotel when contracting to provide space and food products for a large wedding party.
8. Log on to the Hospitalitylawyer.com "Best in Class" segment identified in Search the Web 5.5. When you arrive, review the terms required for ADA compliance. List the responsibilities of meeting planners, as well as the meeting venue they select, for ensuring conformity with its basic provisions.

TEAM ACTIVITY

With your team, obtain a copy of a group meeting and space contract from a hotel in your area. Identify the following clauses in the contract:

Indemnification
Oral modification
Acts of nature
Guarantees (attrition)

Changes, additions, and modifications
Liquor liability
Americans with Disabilities Act (ADA)
Ownership
Duty to mitigate damages
Termination
Construction and remodeling
Service fees versus gratuities

If you cannot find one or more of these clauses, is the contract deficient? Why or why not?

CHAPTER 6

LEGALLY MANAGING PROPERTY

THE STAFF MEETING had been going well. Trisha Sangus, general manager of the hotel, sat at the head of the conference table. The heads of sales and marketing, food and beverage, security, engineering, front office, and housekeeping were all in attendance, as was the property controller.

Trisha enjoyed the weekly meeting. It gave her a chance to learn from each of her colleagues, as well as to help her to guide their development. She knew that several of them had an interest in someday serving as a general manager, and she realized that an important part of her job was helping to give them the skills and knowledge they would need in their future careers. Some of them were almost ready for the next level of management, while others still had to master some of the basics they would have to face as a general manager.

Trisha was about to launch into a discussion of a proposed change she wanted to make in the type of background music playing in the lobby area when Walter Lott, the chief maintenance engineer, spoke up: "Ms. Sangus, I almost forgot—the garage called this morning on the van."

"This won't be good," thought Trisha. The hotel's 17-passenger van was only three years old but had already accumulated over 250,000 miles, due to a constant series of trips transporting guests to and from the airport. Maintenance costs had been averaging $500 a month. Fortunately, the van's engine had been holding up well, given its high number of miles. The van drivers had noticed a defective headlight in yesterday's daily inspection, and while the van was in the shop, the chief engineer had asked the service technician to investigate a periodic slippage in the transmission that prevented the van from accelerating properly.

Walter Lott continued, "It's the transmission alright, and the drive shaft. I think we can get it back in service for about $2,500, but I wanted to check with you first."

"Let's buy a new van," said Mr. Dani, the front office supervisor. "The old one is really starting to show its age."

"It's not in the capital budget," said Ms. Waldo, the controller, with a sigh.

"Well," said Mr. Ray, director of security, "if it stops running completely, you'll just have to use the 'Somewhere Account'!"

As the laughter died down, Mr. Dani asked, "What's the Somewhere Account?"

Trisha replied wryly, "It's the account we use when we have to find the money somewhere, because we have no choice. It's a figure of speech."

"How about a lease?" asked the executive housekeeper.

"That's too expensive," said the food and beverage director. "It's like renting an apartment instead of buying a house. Always buy, that's what my father told me."

"I thought leasing was less expensive," the executive housekeeper replied. "That's what my car dealer told me."

"Don't we save on taxes by leasing?" asked Mr. Dani.

"I wouldn't lease," said the food and beverage director, "unless the auto dealer pays for the repairs; otherwise, it's too expensive."

"But I thought we didn't have the funds anyway," said the sales and marketing director.

"Ms. Waldo said we don't have the capital funds in the budget," Trisha replied. "There are other funds. But before we do decide to lease or buy a new van—if that's in fact what we should do—we need to talk about the differences between leasing and buying."

Trisha knew her one-hour meeting was about to become a two-hour gathering, but she also knew, from the comments around the table, that her staff needed to understand some basics about property, leasing, and buying.

"Listen," she began. "There is a world of difference between buying and leasing a van, or anything else the hotel needs. I'll tell you why. . . ."

IN THIS CHAPTER, YOU WILL LEARN:

1. The difference between real property and personal property.
2. The function of the Uniform Commercial Code when buying property.
3. The role of liens and financing statements in protecting rights of buyers and sellers in purchasing property.
4. How to evaluate the purchase-versus-lease decision from a legal perspective.
5. How to avoid infringement of trademark, patent, copyright, and concept rights.

6.1 INTRODUCTION TO PROPERTY

In the hospitality industry, when a hotel manager is away from the hotel, it is common to say that he or she is "off property." Property, in this sense, refers to the grounds and building of the hotel. At the same time, when a guest enters the pool area, he or she may see a sign that states, "Towels are provided for your convenience, but are the property of the hotel." In this case, property refers to a physical asset owned by the hotel. With so many different meanings and uses of the word, property, and its legal characteristics, is an extremely important concept for a hospitality manager to understand.

In the hospitality industry, there are two types of property the future manager must learn to administer:

- Real property
- Personal property

Within the category of personal property, the two subtypes are tangible and intangible property, as shown in Figure 6.1. A tangible item is one that can be held or touched. Thus, furniture is a tangible form of property, as are land, equipment, food inventories, and a variety of other materials needed to effectively operate a hospitality facility. Intangible items are those that cannot be held or touched but have real value, although that value can sometimes be difficult to establish, such as the goodwill of a business.

Understanding the way the law views property is important because it affects how property ownership disputes and claims are settled, the rights of an individual to use the property as they see fit, and even how ownership of the property is allowed to be transferred.

The law treats *real property* differently from *personal property*, and these distinctions are critical for managers to understand.

Real Property

Real property refers to land and all things that are permanently attached to land. *Real estate* is a related term that is frequently used when referring to real property.

Certainly, the trees on a country club's land are part of its real estate. So, too, are the ponds, streams, and grassy areas that make up the golf course. *Improvements* are features such as fences, sewer lines, and the like, which are changes or additions to land that make it more valuable.

Fixtures

Although at first observation it appears simple to determine what is real property and what is personal property, at times it is quite complex. This difficulty comes from trying to distinguish between items that were intended to be improvements that are "permanently attached" to the land, as opposed to simply being placed on the land.

Clearly, a chimney built into the golf course clubhouse would be considered permanently attached to the clubhouse building. But would a fan placed on the floor of

LEGALESE
Real property: Land and all the things that are permanently attached to it.

LEGALESE
Personal property: Tangible and intangible items that are not real property.

LEGALESE
Real estate: Land, including soil and water, buildings, trees, crops, improvements, and the rights to the air above, and the minerals below, the land.

LEGALESE
Improvements: An addition to real estate that ordinarily enhances its value.

REAL	PERSONAL
	Tangible
	Intangible

Figure 6.1 Property types.

the dining room be considered permanent? Would a fan affixed to the chimney to improve heat circulation be considered real property? Would it matter exactly how the fan was attached? The answer to these more complex questions comes with an understanding of the legal terms *chattel* and *fixture*.

▶▶ ANALYZE THE SITUATION 6.1

JAY GEIER PURCHASED A cinnamon roll franchise from a franchisor. To house the operation, he purchased a small, but ideally located, building from David Stein. The two individuals agreed on a fair price, then both Mr. Geier and Mr. Stein signed the sales contract. Mr. Geier was to take possession of the property on March 1.

On the morning of February 28, Mr. Geier arrived at the property to take some exterior measurements he would need in order to get a contractor's bid on resurfacing the parking lot. He observed Mr. Stein removing a window air conditioning unit from the small manager's office at the rear of the building.

Mr. Geier protested that the air conditioner should not be removed, as it was part of the sale. Mr. Stein replied that the air conditioner was his personal property and was never intended to be sold with the building, nor was it specifically mentioned in the sales contract.

1. Can Mr. Stein be permitted to take the air conditioner?

2. Would the air conditioner be considered real or personal property?

3. Should the air conditioner have been mentioned in the sales contract?

A fan set on the floor of a dining room would not be considered real property because it is clearly movable. Thus, it would instead be classified as chattel. In contrast, a fan that has been permanently installed in the fireplace itself would be considered a fixture. Fixtures include all the things that are permanently attached to property, such as ceiling lights, awnings, window shades, doors, and doorknobs. It is important to note that it is possible to remove an item that has been permanently attached to real property. Thus, a ceiling fan that has been permanently installed in a dining room could, of course, be removed. However, from a legal standpoint, an item that is to remain with the property would ordinarily be identified as a fixture.

Questions often arise as to whether certain fixtures and/or improvements are to be considered real property or treated as personal property. The general rule is: If an item can be removed without damaging any real property, the item is generally considered to be personal property. When the issue is not clear, it is best to consult with an attorney skilled in this area of the law.

Personal Property

Anything that is not real property is personal property, and personal property is anything that isn't nailed down, dug into, or built into the land. A restaurant on an acre of ground is real property, but the tables and chairs in the dining room are not. A restaurant building permanently attached to a plot of land is real property. A van used for catering that is parked in the restaurant's parking lot is not.

As previously stated, personal property can be considered either *tangible* or *intangible*. Tangible property is the type that we most often think of when referring to goods owned by a company or individual. Tangible property can be thought of as all of those items that can easily be moved from one location to another. Automobiles, furniture, artwork, and food inventories are all examples of personal property.

Intangible property can be just as valuable as any real estate or tangible personal property. Intangible property includes items such as franchise rights, trademarks, money, stocks, bonds, and interests in securities. A share of Hilton Corporation stock is a tangible piece of paper, but its real value emanates from the fact that it represents an intangible shareholder interest in the Hilton Corporation. Money is also a form of intangible property. A five-dollar bill is a tangible piece of paper, but it represents an intangible interest in the monetary system used in the United States.

To appreciate the importance of intangible property, consider the case of Stanley Richards. Stanley invents a seasoning salt for beef, which chefs around the world agree is spectacular. His wife, Ruth, creates a small, stylized cartoon drawing of a cow for the label of his seasoning. Stanley consults an attorney, who helps the Richards apply for and receive the exclusive right to use Ruth's drawing in their business. Stanley's product is a huge success. Soon, the stylized cow is associated worldwide with creativity, good taste, and uncompromising quality. Millions of people immediately recognize the cow drawing and what it represents. Stanley is approached by a multinational seasoning company that produces seasonings for poultry, pork, and fish. The company would like to use Ruth's drawing on its own products. The company feels that having the drawing prominently displayed on its own products would improve market awareness of its nonbeef seasonings.

The right to use the stylized drawing of the cow, so valuable in this case, is an example of an intangible property right. Although the drawing of the cow itself is easily duplicated and worth only a few cents, what the stylized cow drawing represents is extremely valuable and may not simply be taken from the Richards without their agreement; they, and they alone, have the right to determine how this property can be legally used.

It is important to note that a partnership or company, as well as an individual, can own personal property. Thus, the word "personal" designates that the property is not "real" property. Essentially, personal property could be considered all property that is not "real" or real estate.

6.2 PURCHASING PROPERTY

For the hospitality manager, the buying, leasing, or selling of property occupies a great deal of time. The foodservice director at an extended-care facility will buy property from vendors, such as food, supplies, and equipment, then turn around and sell some of that property—in this case, the food—to the residents of the facility. At the same time, other equipment for the operation may be leased, such as a dishwasher or a soda-dispensing machine. On a much larger scale, the director of operations for a large hamburger chain may be responsible for buying or leasing land on which to put new stores, and buying or leasing the equipment that will go into the new stores, as well as selling off real and personal property that the company no longer needs.

Purchasing Real Property

In order to sell property legally, the seller must have a legal *title* to that property. It is the responsibility of the buyer to verify this right, however; otherwise, the buyer may find after the purchase that he or she does not legally own the property at all!

Whether the hospitality manager is purchasing real or personal property, the establishment of title to the property being purchased is the responsibility of the manager. And although it might appear that title to lands and real estate would be very simple to verify, the process can, in fact, be quite complex.

LEGALESE

Tangible property: Personal property that has physical substance and can be held or touched. Examples include furniture, equipment, and inventories of goods.

LEGALESE

Intangible property: Personal property that cannot be held or touched. Examples include patent rights, copyrights, and concept rights.

LEGALESE

Title: The sum total of all legally recognized rights to the possession and ownership of property.

LEGALESE

Deed: A written document for the transfer of land or other real property from one person to another.

LEGALESE

Warranty deed: A deed that provides that the person granting the deed agrees to defend the title from claims of others. In general, the seller is representing that he or she fully owns the property and will stand behind this promise.

LEGALESE

Quitclaim deed: A deed that conveys only such rights as the grantor has. This type of deed transfers the owner's interest to a buyer, but does not guarantee that there are no other claims against the property or that the property is indeed legally owned by the seller.

LEGALESE

Title search: A review of land records to determine the ownership and description of a piece of real property.

LEGALESE

Bill of sale: A document under which personal property is transferred from a seller to a buyer.

Deeds

Title to real property can be transferred from an owner in a variety of ways, such as through marriage, divorce, death, an act of the courts, bankruptcy, gift giving, or sale. A *deed* is the formal document used to transfer ownership of real property from one person or entity to another. A deed will consist of the date, the names and descriptions of the parties involved in the transfer, the consideration, a full description of the property, and any exceptions to the transfer.

Deeds may be either *warranty deeds* or *quitclaim deeds*. The laws governing deeds vary from state to state; thus, it is important to make sure that legal title to the real property is provided in the deed.

When there is any doubt as to the legitimacy of the title to a prop-erty, it is sometimes necessary to conduct a *title search*.

Title Insurance

Even when the ownership of a piece of property is well established through a title search, it is advisable for a buyer to purchase title insurance. Title insurance is a critical part of any commercial or private purchase of real estate. This insurance helps protect the interests of the buyer should another individual claim ownership of a piece of property after the buyer has completed the sale. Title insurance will cover any losses as the result of these claims.

Some common instances where title insurance has protected a buyer include:

Forgery
Improper court proceedings
Survey mistakes
Missing heirs
Unfiled liens

Some inexperienced managers confuse title insurance with loan policy insurance. Loan policy insurance protects a lender (such as a bank) from claims against title to the real property, while title insurance protects the buyer.

To illustrate the importance of title insurance, consider the case of William Clark. Mr. Clark has a daughter named Kimberly. When her father dies, Kimberly inherits a piece of land outside a major city. Mr. Clark did not leave a will, but the house he lived in, and the land it rested on, was passed on to Kimberly, his only living heir, by state law. Thirty years later, Kimberly Clark sells the land to Brian Lee, who builds a restaurant on the site. Five years later, Joshua Davidson produces a lien and a will that, he claims, was signed by Mr. Clark. The will clearly states that Mr. Clark wished to leave the land not to his daughter, but to Mr. Davidson, to settle an old debt. In this case, Mr. Lee's claim to the land may be questionable. Title insurance would protect Mr. Lee if the newly produced will were in fact proved to be valid.

Purchasing Personal Property

For the future hospitality manager, purchases of personal property will, in most cases, vastly exceed purchases of real estate. Because this is true, it is very important to have a thorough understanding of the law and practices surrounding the transfer of ownership of personal property.

Bill of Sale

A *bill of sale* is the formal document used to transfer ownership of personal property from one individual or entity to another. As shown in Figure 6.2, the following items are included in a bill of sale:

■ Name of seller
■ Name of buyer

BILL OF SALE

I, _____, of [name of firm, if appropriate], in the County of
_____, State of _____, in consideration of _____
dollars ($_____), to be paid by _____, of [name of firm
if appropriate], the receipt of which is hereby acknowledged, do hereby
grant, sell, transfer, and deliver to _____ and his [or her]
heirs, executors, administrators, successors, and assigns, forever, the following:

(Description of Property)

I hereby warrant that I _____ [or name of firm, if appropri-
ate] am the lawful owner of the Property, that it is free from all encum-
brances; that I have the right to sell the property; and that I will warrant
and defend my right to legally convey it against any lawful claims or demands by anyone.
In witness, whereof, I_____, hereunto set my hand, this
___ day of_____ 20_____.

Seller _____

[Signature of individual or authorized representative of firm]

Figure 6.2 A bill of sale.

- Consideration
- Description of the property
- Statement of ownership by seller
- Date of sale

Because a bill of sale is a contract, it can take many forms. In the hospitality industry, it is common for a buyer to agree to buy a certain type of good from a vendor on a regular basis. Consider the case of Renee Miller, the director of housing and food-services at a state-supported university. Renee knows she will need a large amount of ground beef throughout the school year, but because she has limited freezer space, she must take delivery of the beef on a monthly basis. To negotiate the best possible price, she places all of her ground beef business with the same meat wholesaler. Renee executes a special contract for sale of goods with the seller to ensure that the quality, price, and terms she has agreed upon are maintained throughout the year (see Figure 6.3).

A contract developed to transfer ownership of personal property is common when the property cannot be viewed at the time of sale, as in Renee Miller's case, or when the property has not yet been manufactured. For example, if a hotel orders custom-made drapes and bedspreads, they may not be manufactured by the seller until a contract for their sale has been signed by both parties. As is the case with all contracts, the contract for sale of goods should be carefully examined by both the buyer and seller.

It is important to determine exactly when the transfer of ownership occurs in a sale of personal property. Generally, goods are shipped FOB, which means, "free on board." When used, the term refers to the fact that shippers are responsible for the care and safety of goods until they are delivered to the buyer's designated location. Transfer of ownership occurs not at the time of sale in this case but upon delivery.

Notice that in both the bill of sale and the more formal contract for the sale of goods, the seller is not required to provide a title when transferring ownership. This is different from the sale of real property, where a title (deed) is a required part of the transaction. Unlike real property, ownership of personal property is generally assumed by its possession, and it is not customary for the seller to prove his or her ownership rights by a title. An exception to this rule is the sale of motor vehicles.

CONTRACT FOR SALE OF GOODS

Agreement made and entered into this [date] _____, by and between _____ [name of seller], of [address] _____ [city] _____, [state] _____ , herein referred to as "Seller," and [name of buyer] _____, of [address] _____ [city] _____ , [state] _____, herein referred to as "Buyer."

  Seller hereby agrees to transfer and deliver to Buyer, on or before [date] _____, the following goods:

DESCRIPTION OF GOODS

CONSIDERATION TERMS

Buyer agrees to accept the goods and pay for them in accordance with the terms of this contract. Buyer agrees to pay for the goods at the time they are delivered and at the place where he [or she] receives the goods. Goods shall be deemed received by Buyer when delivered to address of Buyer as described in this contract. Until such time as goods have been received by Buyer, all risk of loss from any casualty to said goods shall be on Seller.

  Seller warrants that the goods are now free from any security interest or other lien or encumbrance, that they shall be free from same at the time of delivery, and that he [or she] neither knows nor has reason to know of any outstanding title or claim of title hostile to his [or her] rights in the goods.

  Buyer has the right to examine the goods on arrival and has [number] of days to notify Seller of any claim for damages on account of the condition, grade, or quality of the goods. The notice must specifically set forth the basis of his [or her] claim, and that his [or her] failure to either notify Seller within the stipulated period of time or to set forth specifically the basis of his [or her] claim will constitute irrevocable acceptance of the goods.

  This agreement has been executed in duplicate, whereby both Buyer and Seller have retained one copy each, on [date] _____.

_____   _____
Buyer   Seller

[Signatures]

Figure 6.3 Contract for sale of goods.

Stolen Property

In the case of stolen property, even though possession implies ownership, it does not equate to the lawful right to sell. There is no criminal penalty imposed by law if a buyer innocently purchases stolen goods from a seller who purports to own those goods. However, in the event the rightful owner takes steps to reclaim his or her goods, the innocent buyer would have no recourse except to go back to the thief; that is, the buyer could file a lawsuit against the thief for the return of any money paid. In reality, the ability of the buyer to identify and help prosecute the thief is often minimal. Obviously, it is in the hospitality manager's best interest to buy only from reputable sellers.

  A restaurant or hotel manager may be punished if it can be shown that he or she knowingly purchased stolen goods. Although it might be easy to trace stolen goods, it is more difficult to determine if a buyer, in fact, knew the goods were stolen. However, frequently it can be inferred from circumstances surrounding the purchase.

  A buyer is violating federal law if he or she knowingly purchases stolen goods, and those goods have: (1) a value of over $5,000 and (2) been a part of interstate commerce.

The term *interstate commerce* merely refers to the movement of property from one state into another state. In order to commit a federal offense, a person must know that the property had been stolen, but he or she need not know that it was moving through interstate commerce.

>> ANALYZE THE SITUATION 6.2

AS THE OWNER OPERATOR of a popular Italian restaurant, controlling costs is an important part of your day-to-day activities. Costs of labor, food, and equipment are your direct responsibility. Profit margins are good, but controlling costs is a constant challenge.

At a meeting of the local chapter of the state restaurant association, you see your friend Wayne, who excitedly tells you about a purchase he has just made. Wayne owns and operates an upscale steakhouse in your town. He purchased 50 full-sized stainless-steel line pans for $2 each from a passing "liquidator." Wayne tells you that he jumped at the chance to buy them because when new, the line pans cost $75 each.

When you inquire about the seller, Wayne says that two men simply arrived at his restaurant in a small pick-up truck, with a variety of equipment and small wares in the uncovered back.

"Best of all," Wayne says with a wink, "as soon as I washed them and put them in with my regular stock, there was no way anyone could tell the difference between the ones I just purchased from the ones I already had!"

Talk at the restaurant association meeting centers on rising food costs and the likelihood of having to raise menu prices. Several operators state that they are seriously looking at price increases. You, too, have been considering such a move. Wayne tells the group that at his place, "We are going to hold the line on price increases this year."

1. If you had needed them, would you have purchased the pans?

2. What are the legal issues at play here? What ethical issues are at play?

3. If the "sellers" in this scenario are caught and confess to selling stolen merchandise, do you think that Wayne will get to keep his pans?

Because of the severe penalties involved, the prudent hospitality manager will avoid purchasing any property that is sold at far below its real value, is sold at odd times or by questionable salespersons, or is sold when there is doubt as to its origin. If something appears too good to be true, it generally is, and thus should be avoided.

Warranty

Those who sell property often find that any promises they make about that property can help to better sell it. For example, if the human resources manager at the corporate office of a franchise company decides to purchase a copy machine, the promises, or *warranties*, made by the copy machine's manufacturer may play a significant role in the machine selected. If two copy machines cost approximately the same amount, but the manufacturer of one warrants that it will provide free repairs if the machine

LEGALESE

Warranty: A promise about a product made by either a manufacturer or a seller that is a part of the sales contract.

breaks down in the first two years, while the other manufacturer does not, the warranty of the first manufacturer would probably be a deciding factor in the selection of the copy machine.

When evaluating the final warranty offer, the following questions should be considered: Before signing any contract for the purchase of goods, it is a good idea to determine what warranties, if any, are included in the purchase. When purchasing real property, a deed helps explain exactly what is included with the purchase. In a similar manner, a warranty helps explain exactly what rights are included in a purchase of personal property. It is important to remember that a warranty is part of the sales contract. That is, the intangible rights a warranty offers the buyer are just as real as the property itself.

Because they are part of the contract, it is always important to make sure that any warranties offered verbally are documented in the sales contract. Warranties can be considered to be either expressed or implied. An express warranty is created when a manufacturer makes a statement of fact about the capabilities and qualities of a product or service. These statements can be made either by a salesperson or in promotional literature. Examples include statements such as: "This copier will make 35 copies per minute," or "This dishwasher uses six gallons of water for each rinse cycle."

When a seller makes claims about the capabilities of a product or service being offered, that seller is obligated under the law to deliver a product that meets all of the capabilities described. Because express warranties are considered to be part of the sales contract, the law enforcing the truthfulness of warranties is the Uniform Commercial Code, which you read about in Chapter 4, "Business Contracts." When a buyer relies on factual representations to purchase a product or service, and those statements later prove to be false, then a breach of the sales contract has occurred. Under Article 2 of the UCC, the buyer may be entitled to recover damages from the seller.

The UCC further protects the interests of buyers by requiring that any products sold be fit for use and free of defects. Thus, even if a seller does not specifically claim that his or her products are free of defects, a buyer would expect that any product purchased would be in good working order. This type of unwritten expectation is called an *implied warranty*.

Under Article 2 of the UCC, personal property that is sold must conform to two implied warranties. One implied warranty is that the item is fit to be used for a particular purpose. This is known as an implied warranty of fitness. The second implied warranty is that the item will be in good working order and will adequately meet the purposes for which it was purchased. This is called an implied warranty of merchantability.

In many states, consumers can enforce their rights with respect to implied warranties for up to four years after a purchase. This means that, for the first four years of a product's life, the seller is liable for any defects or breakdowns of his or her product, including the implied warranties established by the UCC.

The seller has the right to disclaim, or negate, any express or implied warranties by inserting language into the sales contract. The UCC has drafted standard contract clauses that can be used for those situations. As with any sales contract, the disclaimer must be in writing and must be agreed to by both parties.

Just as price is a negotiable part of any contract, so, too, are warranties. It is a good idea to try to negotiate additional warranties before making a purchase. Before buying personal property, it is imperative to understand the warranty offer and to compare warranties from competing brands before making a purchase. Effective hospitality managers seek to negotiate the longest, strongest, most comprehensive warranty possible, and insist that the warranty be in writing.

Managers should try to include as much of the following information as possible in the warranty in order to ensure maximum protection:

1. How long is the warranty?
2. When does the warranty begin?
3. Will it include the charges for the parts and/or labor to make the repairs?

LEGALESE

Implied warranty: An unwritten expectation that a product purchased is free of defects.

4. What parts of the purchase are covered by the warranty?

5. Can you lose the warranty if you do not follow manufacturer guidelines for routine service and maintenance, and who can perform these tasks?

6. Where is authorized service performed?

7. Who pays to deliver the defective product to the repair area?

Figure 6.4 is an example of a warranty a hotel manager might encounter when buying dishwashers for a new extended-stay facility. Notice the promises that are made by the dishwasher's manufacturer.

DISHWASHER WARRANTY

FULL ONE-YEAR WARRANTY

For one year from date of original purchase, we will provide, free of charge, parts and service labor in your place of business to repair or replace any part of the dishwasher that fails because of a manufacturing defect.

FULL TEN-YEAR WARRANTY

For ten years from date of original purchase, we will provide, free of charge, parts and service labor in your place of business to repair or replace the tub or door liner if it fails to contain water because of a manufacturing defect such as cracking, chipping, peeling, or rusting.

LIMITED SECOND-YEAR WARRANTY

For second year from date of original purchase, we will provide free of charge, replacement parts for any part of the water distribution system that fails because of a manufacturing defect. Associated inlet and drain plumbing parts are not covered by this warranty. You must pay for the service trip to your place of business and service labor charges.

This warranty is extended to the original purchaser and any succeeding owner for products purchased for in the 48 mainland states, Hawaii and Washington, DC. In Alaska, the warranty is the same except that it is LIMITED because you must pay to ship the product to the service shop or for the service technician's travel costs to your place of business.

All warranty service will be provided by our Factory Service Centers or by our franchised Customer Care servicers during normal working hours. Check the White Pages for XXXX COMPANY OR XXXX COMPANY FACTORY SERVICE.

What Is Not Covered

Service trips to your place of business to teach you how to use the product.

Read your Use and Care material. If you then have any questions about operating the product, please contact your dealer or our Consumer Affairs office at the address below, or call, toll-free: 1-800-xxx-xxxx.

Improper Installation. If you have an installation problem, contact your dealer or installer. You are responsible for providing adequate electrical, plumbing, and other connecting facilities.

Replacement of fuses or resetting of circuit breakers.

Cleaning or servicing of air gap device in drain.

Failure of the product if it is used for other than its intended purpose.

Damage to product caused by accident, fire, floods, or acts of God.

WARRANTOR IS NOT RESPONSIBLE FOR CONSEQUENTIAL DAMAGES.

Some states do not allow the exclusion or limitation of incidental or consequential damages, so the above limitation or exclusion may not apply to you. This warranty gives you specific legal rights, and you may also have other rights, which vary from state to state. To know what your legal rights are in your state, consult your local or state consumer affairs office or your state's attorney general.

Figure 6.4 Manufacturer's warranty.

6.3 FINANCING THE PURCHASE OF PROPERTY

The buying and selling of property is fairly straightforward when the buyer pays the seller the entire purchase price all at once. It is more complicated, however, when the buyer decides to pay for property over time. Consider the case of Bill Humphrey. Mr. Humphrey operates a 400-room hotel in the downtown area of an extremely large city. Mr. Humphrey determines that the ice machines in his hotel must be replaced. The cost will be in excess of $100,000. His controller advises him that the hotel cannot afford to purchase the ice machines for cash at this time, but could afford to make monthly payments toward the purchase price. Mr. Humphrey approaches the hotel's bank, explains the problem, and secures a loan to purchase the ice machines.

In this scenario, a number of problems could arise. What if the hotel cannot make its loan payments? What rights would the bank then have? Could it retake possession of the ice machines? These and other complications can arise any time personal property is financed.

Debtor and Creditor Relationship

LEGALESE

Lien: A claim against property that gives the creditor (lien holder) the right to repossess and/ or sell that property if the debtor does not repay his or her debt in a timely manner.

A *lien* is the right of a person to retain a lawful interest in the property of another until the owner fulfills a legal duty. If, for example, a restaurateur purchases new tables and chairs from a seller, but elects to pay one half of the purchase price at the time the tables are delivered and the other half over a period of six months, the seller would retain a lien on the tables and chairs. That is, the seller would maintain a lawful ownership interest in the chairs until they were paid for in full. Of course, since the tables and chairs are housed in the restaurant, the restaurateur would also have partial ownership and rights to the property. In this scenario, two parties have legitimate and legal claims to the ownership of the tables and chairs. This complex relationship of dual ownership can be made easier to grasp with a better understanding of collateral and liens.

Collateral and Liens

LEGALESE

Collateral: Property that is pledged to secure the repayment of a debt.

LEGALESE

Perfect a lien: To make a public record of a lien, or to take possession of the collateral.

Collateral is an asset a person agrees to give up if he or she does not repay a loan. A lien is a claim against the property (the collateral) used to ensure payment of a debt. Liens can be recognized by contract, from general trade practices, or implied by law.

The process of legally recording a contractual lien is known as "making the lien *perfect*," or *perfecting the lien*. The possessor of a lien, who files the appropriate records with the proper public office, is known as a secured creditor. This type of creditor has a superior right to possession of the collateral or any proceeds if the collateral is sold.

Perfecting a lien implied by law is done by taking possession of the property. If, for example, an in-room air conditioning unit is taken to a repair facility, the repaired unit will normally stay in the possession of the service facility until payment for the repairs has been made.

Other liens include judgment liens, which are those ordered by the courts, and landlord liens, whereby a landlord can secure payment of rent by taking a tenant's property if necessary. In most states, mechanics or persons who furnish materials for buildings are entitled to a lien. In some states, these claims must be filed in the office of the clerk of the court, or established by a suit brought within a limited time. Upon the subsequent sale of the building, these liens, if properly filed, are paid.

Mortgages and Deeds of Trust

When financing the sale of real property, the creditor will generally insist on securing the debt with a lien backed by collateral. In most cases, the lien will be filed on the real property being purchased. For example, if Marion Pennycuff wishes to purchase land and a building in which to house a café, he could secure funding for this purpose from a bank, providing his financial position is good. Marion would actually buy the real property with money loaned by the bank, and the bank would file for a *mortgage* lien on the property. In this instance, the land and building would serve as collateral for the loan. In some states, a *deed of trust* is a substitute for a mortgage lien, but it serves an identical purpose.

If Marion should decide to sell the property before he has completely repaid his mortgage, a buyer would not be able to obtain a clear title to the property, until the original mortgage was completely repaid.

Assume, however, that Marion wished to borrow the $100,000 to begin a consulting company, instead of purchasing the land and building. It is most likely that the bank would still require Marion to provide collateral to secure the loan. This collateral could be in the form of real or personal property that Marion owned, including intangible personal property such as stocks or bonds.

Security Agreements

When creditors retain some legal rights of ownership in a piece of personal property, they are said to have a *security interest* in that property.

When personal, rather than real, property is involved, creditors protect and establish their interest by means of a security agreement. The *security agreement* is an arrangement similar to the mortgage or deed of trust. In it, the creditor makes a loan, and the debtor agrees to pay back the loan in a timely fashion. If the debtor doesn't, then the creditor has the right to seize the personal property, sell it, and apply the money generated by the sale to the debt. The debtor is still responsible for any remaining balance.

Article 9 of the Uniform Commercial Code is the law that regulates purchases made using security agreements and that gives a creditor the right to take back property that the debtor either cannot or will not pay for. As with other areas, the UCC requires debtors and lenders to follow specific procedures in order to finance the purchase of property in a way that is legally binding and that will be upheld by the courts. For example, because it is a contract, the security agreement must include a written description of the property that is being purchased, and must be signed by both parties.

Financing Statements

Under UCC rules, in order for a security agreement to fully protect the creditor, it must be perfected. This is generally done by preparing and filing a financing statement. A *financing statement* is the tool used in most states to record (perfect), a lien on personal property. These statements are typically filed with either the secretary of state's office and/or the local county recorder of records. To perfect their lien, creditors file a financing statement, or UCC-1 form, with the appropriate official. The filing of the UCC-1 form publicly states that a lien exists on a particular piece of personal property.

Unless otherwise indicated, the financing statement remains in effect for five years. When the loan has been paid off, the debtor can request a termination statement that clears the financing statement from the public records.

Figure 6.5 is a copy of the UCC-1 form currently in use. Note that it lists the debtor, the creditor (secured party), and a description of the property that serves as the collateral.

If a creditor has been asked to use a piece of personal property as collateral for a loan, he or she can review the financing statements on file at the office of the governmental agency retaining these records. If creditors find that no previous liens have been recorded against the property, they can be assured that they will have perfected their interest in the property when they properly file a UCC-1 on that property.

LEGALESE

Mortgage: The pledging of real property by a debtor to a creditor to secure payment of a debt.

LEGALESE

Deed of trust: Used in some states instead of a mortgage. A deed of trust places legal title to a real property in the hands of a trustee until the debtor has completed paying for the property.

LEGALESE

Security interest: A legal ownership right to property.

LEGALESE

Security agreement: A contract between a lender and borrower that states that the lender can repossess the personal property a person has offered as collateral if the loan is not paid as agreed.

LEGALESE

Financing statement: A formal notice of a lien being held on personal property, required under the Uniform Commercial Code in most cases. Also called a UCC-1 because of its form number in the UCC.

UCC FINANCING STATEMENT
FOLLOW INSTRUCTIONS (front and back) CAREFULLY

A. NAME & PHONE OF CONTACT AT FILER [optional]

B. SEND ACKNOWLEDGMENT TO: (Name and Address)

THE ABOVE SPACE IS FOR FILING OFFICE USE ONLY

1. DEBTOR'S EXACT FULL LEGAL NAME - insert only <u>one</u> debtor name (1a or 1b) - do not abbreviate or combine names

1a. ORGANIZATION'S NAME			

OR

1b. INDIVIDUAL'S LAST NAME	FIRST NAME	MIDDLE NAME	SUFFIX

1c. MAILING ADDRESS	CITY	STATE	POSTAL CODE	COUNTRY

1d. TAX ID #: SSN OR EIN	ADD'L INFO RE ORGANIZATION DEBTOR	1e. TYPE OF ORGANIZATION	1f. JURISDICTION OF ORGANIZATION	1g. ORGANIZATIONAL ID #, if any	NONE

2. ADDITIONAL DEBTOR'S EXACT FULL LEGAL NAME - insert only <u>one</u> debtor name (2a or 2b) - do not abbreviate or combine names

2a. ORGANIZATION'S NAME			

OR

2b. INDIVIDUAL'S LAST NAME	FIRST NAME	MIDDLE NAME	SUFFIX

2c. MAILING ADDRESS	CITY	STATE	POSTAL CODE	COUNTRY

2d. TAX ID #: SSN OR EIN	ADD'L INFO RE ORGANIZATION DEBTOR	2e. TYPE OF ORGANIZATION	2f. JURISDICTION OF ORGANIZATION	2g. ORGANIZATIONAL ID #, if any	NONE

3. SECURED PARTY'S NAME (or NAME of TOTAL ASSIGNEE of ASSIGNOR S/P) - insert only <u>one</u> secured party name (3a or 3b)

3a. ORGANIZATION'S NAME			

OR

3b. INDIVIDUAL'S LAST NAME	FIRST NAME	MIDDLE NAME	SUFFIX

3c. MAILING ADDRESS	CITY	STATE	POSTAL CODE	COUNTRY

4. This FINANCING STATEMENT covers the following collateral:

5. ALTERNATIVE DESIGNATION [if applicable]: ☐ LESSEE/LESSOR ☐ CONSIGNEE/CONSIGNOR ☐ BAILEE/BAILOR ☐ SELLER/BUYER ☐ AG. LIEN ☐ NON-UCC FILING

6. ☐ This FINANCING STATEMENT is to be filed [for record] (or recorded) in the REAL ESTATE RECORDS.   Attach Addendum   [if applicable] | 7. Check to REQUEST SEARCH REPORT(S) on Debtor(s) [ADDITIONAL FEE]   [optional] ☐ All Debtors ☐ Debtor 1 ☐ Debtor 2

8. OPTIONAL FILER REFERENCE DATA

FILING OFFICE COPY — NATIONAL UCC FINANCING STATEMENT (FORM UCC1) (REV. 07/29/98)

Figure 6.5 Financing statement excerpt from Uniform Commercial Code.

It is common in the hospitality industry to buy personal property with a loan from a third-party creditor, such as a bank, or to have the purchase price financed over time by the seller. If, for example, you, as a manager, wish to purchase $30,000 worth of cash registers for a new restaurant, you have three options:

1. *Pay seller purchase price in full.* No UCC-1 required.
2. *Borrow purchase price from a third-party lender (such as a bank), and pay seller in full.* The third-party lender (bank) files UCC-1 on the cash registers, evidencing its lien on the registers.
3. *Convince seller to finance purchase price over time.* The seller files UCC-1 on the cash registers, evidencing its lien on the registers.

6.4 LEASING PROPERTY

Just as it is common to buy personal property in the hospitality industry, it is equally common to *lease* it. Both real and personal property can be leased.

Because a lease is a type of contract, it must clearly indicate the item to be leased, the price or rent to be paid, and the consent of the two parties to the lease—the *lessor* and *lessee*. A lease is different from a purchase of property in that leases transfer possession, rather than ownership. It is critical that hospitality managers fully understand the essential terms of any leases they enter into, and the differences inherent in leasing, rather than owning, a piece of property.

Essential Lease Terms as a Lessor

Hospitality managers take on the role of a *landlord* when they designate specific space in their hotel or restaurant to be operated by a *tenant*. Historically, hotels would lease lobby space to businesses that would interest their guests. Thus, tailors, dressmakers, jewelers, furriers, and the like would occupy hotel space and provide additional revenue for the property. Additionally, parking lot operators might lease the hotel's parking spaces.

More recently, in an effort to satisfy guest demands for regional or nationally known restaurants, some hotels have begun leasing their entire foodservice operations. In addition, airports and shopping malls have become landlords for well-known, or "branded," foodservice concepts that appeal to a variety of guests.

When hospitality managers take on the role of landlord, it is critical that the lease contracts they enter into be reviewed by legal counsel prior to signing. An attorney can help ensure that the duties of both landlord and tenant are clearly spelled out in the lease, and that in the event of a breach of the agreement, appropriate remedies are available to the landlord. Consider the case of Michael Singh. Mr. Singh serves as the general manager of a 400-room hotel. Mr. Singh elects to lease his gift shop to an elderly couple with excellent references, and they operate the gift shop successfully for several years. Through no fault of their own, illness causes the couple to become less prompt in opening the gift shop. In fact, on a few days within the past two months, the shop has not opened at all. Mr. Singh knows that the couple's continued inability to open the store could severely damage the hotel's business. The rights of the hotel and the tenant in a situation like this must be clearly documented, so that the hotel manager can take appropriate steps to remedy the problem.

The hospitality lease, especially for real property, is generally different from that of an ordinary landlord and tenant relationship. When a landlord leases a home or apartment, the day-to-day use of that property is normally not subject to the inspection of the landlord. For the hotel operator, however, a lease is drawn up with the expectation that the space will be used for an activity that enhances the financial well-being of the hotel under terms contained in the lease. Thus, operating hours, products sold, and even pricing strategies may be contained in a hospitality

LEGALESE

Lease: A contract that establishes the rights and obligations of each party with respect to property owned by one entity but occupied or used by another.

LEGALESE

Lessor: The entity that owns the property covered in a lease.

LEGALESE

Lessee: The entity that occupies or uses the property covered in a lease.

LEGALESE

Landlord: The lessor in a real property lease.

LEGALESE

Tenant: The lessee in a real property lease.

manager's lease when he or she serves as landlord. While a residential landlord may not impose him or herself unduly on a tenant, the hospitality manager has a responsibility to make sure the tenant operates in compliance with the lease, since the tenant's actions can be helpful or harmful to the success of the entire hotel.

The following areas of a lease agreement deserve special attention when a hospitality manager assumes the role of the lessor (or landlord).

Length of Lease

The lease length is important in that it directly affects rent amounts. Landlords prefer leases that are long because they minimize vacancies and guarantee a steady source of revenue for the use of the space. Increasingly, tenants also prefer long leases to avoid the rent increases that often occur when leases are resigned. However, a lease that is too long may prevent a landlord from raising the rent when necessary. In a like manner, the tenant may find that his or her business grows beyond the ability of the leased space to contain it, and a move to a larger space is required. In all cases, the lease length should be established to meet both the short-term and long-term interests of both parties.

Lease start dates, or occupation dates, should be clearly established in the lease agreement. Often, lessees will want early access to the space in order to install fixtures and make improvements. The number of days required to complete this work can be significant, and the party responsible for rent during that time period, or whether rent is to be paid at all, should be clearly spelled out.

Although it is less common that hospitality managers find themselves as lessors of personal property, sometimes it does occur. An example would be the resort hotel that rents bicycles to its guests. This rental arrangement provides an excellent service to guests but creates special liability issues for the hotel. These issues will be discussed in Chapter 10, "Your Responsibilities as a Hospitality Operator to Guests."

Rent Amount

Lease payments on real property are typically of four distinct types, based on the payment responsibilities of the lessee:

- A "net" lease is one in which the lessee pays some or even all of the taxes due on real property, in addition to the base rent amount.
- In a "net net" lease, the lessee pays for both taxes and insurance as required by the lessor.
- In a "net net net," or triple-net, lease—the most common type in the hospitality industry—the lessee pays for all of the costs associated with occupying the property, including building repairs and maintenance.
- In a "percentage" lease, tenants pay a fixed percentage of their gross revenue as part of their lease payment. Although some fixed charges might also apply, the unique feature of this lease is its variability. Thus, a hotelier might charge the gift shop lessee monthly rent based on the sales achieved by the gift shop. In this way, rent payments are lower when business is slow for the shop but increase as the business and the lessee succeeds.

It is important that both landlord and tenant understand the costs for which they will be responsible. When leasing personal property, the hourly, daily, monthly, or quarterly payments required should be clearly identified in the lease agreement.

Subleasing Rights of Tenant

Most lessees realize that conditions can change, and they may not be able to or want to fulfill all of the lease terms specified in the lease agreement. Consider for example, the shopkeeper who leases space for a flower shop in an urban hotel. The shopkeeper is very successful and elects to sell her rights to the flower shop space to open a larger shop in a different part of the city. In this situation, the shopkeeper will want to *sublet*—that is, to transfer or assign to another—her interest in the hotel lease to a new shopkeeper.

The concern of the hotel, as the lessor, is that the new shopkeeper must be able to meet the requirements set forth in the lease. For this reason, it is a good idea for the lessor (hotel manager) to insist that any sublessee demonstrate his or her financial strength and integrity before the lessor approves the sublease arrangement.

While it would not be reasonable for the lessor to have complete say over who the sublessee may be, it is also not reasonable for the choice of sublessee to be left solely in the hands of the original tenant. Accordingly, leases should address this issue with a clause acknowledging the right of the lessee to sublease, but only with the landlord's written consent. The clause should also state that the landlord's consent cannot be unreasonably withheld.

Insurance

Landlords are favorite targets for litigation. If a tenant is negligent, and the result is injury to an individual, the lessor must be protected. The size and types of policies that the lessor should require the lessee to purchase vary, but in all cases the lessor should insist that:

- The lessee's insurance carriers must be acceptable to the lessor.
- Copies of the insurance policies should be delivered to the lessor at the time of the lease signing.
- Lessees and their insurance companies should be required to give prior notice to the lessor if the policies are canceled, withdrawn, or not renewed.

In addition, landlords, when preparing leases, may insert exculpatory type clauses that seek to limit their liability. As seen previously, these clauses may not provide complete protection, but they can sometimes be helpful. It is best to have a commercial insurance agent or attorney who is experienced in insurance to review lease provisions and insurance policies to ensure that both lessor and lessee have adequate insurance coverage for the responsibilities allocated to each by the lease agreement.

Termination Rights

Leases may be terminated for a variety of reasons, but these reasons must be clearly spelled out as part of the lease. If, for example, a tenant is delinquent in paying rent, the lessor can require that the premises be vacated. Most landlords will allow the payment to be made a few days later without penalty. This grace period should be clearly identified in the lease, as well as any penalties that will be assessed if the payment is tendered beyond the grace period.

Disturbances, violation of operating hours, significant damage to the property, and failure to abide by lease terms may all be justification for termination. However, while the reasons might be valid, they will not justify an *eviction* unless those reasons are distinctly identified in the lease.

When you, as a hospitality manager, serve as a landlord, the quality of the tenants who supply services to your guests can reflect well or poorly on the overall operation. Capable tenants who operate their businesses in a professional manner can be a real asset to a hospitality property; inexperienced or less-qualified tenants can cause great difficulty. When serving as a lessor, it is imperative that the hospitality manager examine the essential lease terms discussed in this section to ensure the best possible chance of the lessee's, and the lessor's, success.

Essential Lease Terms as a Lessee

When a hospitality manager takes on the tenant role in a lease arrangement, the lease may be for either real or personal property. When Mike Keefer decided to open a steakhouse, he discovered that his own favorite steakhouse was, in fact, for sale.

LEGALESE

Sublet: To rent property one possesses by a lease, to another. Also called subleasing.

LEGALESE

Eviction: The procedure that a lessor uses to remove a lessee from physical possession of leased real property, usually for violation of a significant lease provision, such as nonpayment of rent.

Rather than sell Mike the restaurant, the owner agreed to lease the land, building, and equipment to him in exchange for a percentage of the restaurant's gross sales. This arrangement provided Mike with a lower-cost entry into the restaurant business, and provided the landlord with continued ownership of the restaurant property.

Whether the hospitality manager leases land, buildings, or equipment, such as dishwashers, icemakers, and beverage machines, it is important that an attorney review the provisions of the lease prior to signing. The following items deserve the hospitality manager's special attention when leasing real or personal property.

Landlord Representation and Default

When a tenant leases real property, or an individual leases personal property, it is generally assumed that the lessor has the legal right to lease the property for its intended purpose. The issue of landlord representation and truthfulness, however, can become complex. Consider the case of the restaurateur who examined a property for use as a restaurant. The landlord stated in the lease that the space could lawfully be operated as a "restaurant." After the lease was executed, the restaurateur found that the restaurant's proximity to a school prevented him from obtaining a liquor license. The community zoning laws prohibited selling alcohol near a school. Thus, the landlord's representation that the space could be used as a restaurant was true, but only if that restaurant elected not to serve alcohol. The lesson here is that, as a tenant, any representation made by the landlord about the fitness of property for its intended purpose should be independently verified.

A related concern for lessees is the rights they have if the landlord should lose possession of the property through default. If, for example, a tenant pays his or her rent on time, but the landlord defaults on loans in which the property served as collateral, the rights of the lessee should be addressed in the lease. A clause can be inserted in the lease that guarantees that the tenant's lease will be undisturbed. This is an area of the lease that is best carefully reviewed by legal counsel.

Expenses Paid by Landlord

Whether the lease negotiated is a net, a net net, a triple net, a percentage lease, or some combination thereof, disputes over covered expenses are a common source of landlord/tenant disagreement. Because the landlord has limited ability to reduce expenses during periods of financial difficulty, there are few options available to the landlord when costs must be reduced. If electricity is to be paid by the landlord, it represents a significant expense and should be addressed directly by the hospitality operator. A restaurant consumes a large amount of electricity through cooking equipment, dishwashing, and air conditioning. The lease should clearly identify whether any limits are set on the quantity of electricity that can be used, as well as the types and capacities available.

HVAC is the acronym for heating, ventilation, and air conditioning. In both a net and a net net lease, the repair and maintenance of these items are part of the lease arrangement and are ordinarily paid for by the landlord. The services provided for HVAC maintenance and repair can be critical and should be included in the lease, along with a schedule of times when the services are available.

≫ ANALYZE THE SITUATION 6.3

SANDY AZNOVARIO LEASED A corner space in a shopping center to operate Olde Style Buffet, an all-you-can-eat buffet geared toward senior citizens and families. The buffet was especially popular on weekends, and its best business was done on Sundays, before and after people in the community normally attended church.

Kathy Miley was the landlord for the shopping center. She and Sandy signed a net net lease, clearly stating that maintenance and repair of the HVAC system would be the responsibility of the shopping center's commercial real estate company.

On Easter Sunday, the Buffet's busiest day of the year, the head cook reported to Sandy that the overhead exhaust system in the kitchen was not working, and the kitchen was becoming unbearably hot, smoky, and humid. Sandy called the landlord's leasing office and heard a recorded message stating the office was closed because of the Easter holiday. Sandy then contacted Beatty's 24-hour Emergency HVAC Repair Service, which sent a representative, who examined the HVAC system, then replaced a broken fan belt on the rooftop exhaust fan.

Sandy submitted the bill from Beatty's, including a triple-time labor charge for holiday service, to Kathy Miley's company for payment. Kathy refused to pay the bill, stating that Beatty's was not the authorized HVAC service company used by Miley, nor did the lease specifically state that HVAC service would be provided on holidays.

1. Who is responsible for this bill?

2. What could have been done beforehand to keep this conflict from occurring?

Like HVAC service and repair, cleaning services, if provided as part of the lease payment, should be clearly identified, and a schedule of cleaning times should be attached to the lease itself. The number of times the restroom is cleaned daily, as well as a definition of "cleaning," should be provided. Does it include floor mopping and the cleaning of toilets and mirrors each time? Or does the cleaning involve only removing large paper debris from the floors? Obviously, a guest will have a different experience under these two alternatives.

It is the responsibility of the hospitality manager who leases space to determine precisely what he or she will get in the way of services included, and expenses paid for, by the landlord.

Terms of Renewal

The terms under which a tenant may renew his or her lease should be of utmost importance to the hospitality manager who finds himself or herself in the role of lessee.

Consider the situation of David Berger. David is the district real estate manager for a chain of muffin shops. As part of his job, David negotiates leases for the company's 800-square-foot operations. More than property leases are managed by David. One of his prime concerns when negotiating a lease is the provision for renewal. If David selects a successful site, he will seek to renew his lease with as little upward change in rent as possible. If the site is less successful, he may elect not to renew the lease, or do so only with a significant reduction in lease payments.

It is important to note that a landlord has no obligation to continue a lease that has expired. Because of that, David often encounters landlords who wish to dramatically increase the rent payments for spaces where the muffin shops have shown great success. To prevent this, David insists that renewal formulas limiting rent increases to an acceptable amount be written into each lease when it is originally signed.

Normally, a lease can be extended only upon written notice from the lessee. Leases can, however, be written in such a way so as to renew automatically, unless terminated in writing by one of the parties to the lease.

Rights of the Landlord

Most tenants understand that a landlord will have the right to periodically inspect their property. This should, however, be allowed only at reasonable hours, and with reasonable notice. Of even more importance to most tenants is the right of a landlord to lease to a competing business.

Leasing to Competing Tenants

Consider the case of a landlord with a large, 30-store shopping center. It is in the best interest of the landlord to fill all the space with high-quality tenants. The space might even be large enough to house more than one hospitality operation—for example, a bagel shop and a pizzeria.

If, however, the landlord rents space in the shopping center to an upscale bakery, would it be fair for that same landlord to rent space in the same shopping center to a second upscale bakery? Unless the lease of the first bakery expressly prohibits it, the landlord would have the right to lease space to a direct competitor. Although few landlords will give a tenant veto power over any new tenants, it is reasonable to expect that a landlord will allow a tightly drawn definition of any future competitor, in order to help ensure the success of a tenant considering the leasing of space.

Deposits, Damages, and Normal Wear and Tear

Normally, a landlord will require a deposit payment for the lease of real property. Landlords who lease personal property may also require deposits to ensure the return of the leased item in good condition. The amount of the deposit should be clearly spelled out in the lease.

Certainly, tenants must be held responsible for damages they incur on leased property. Tenants should not, however, be responsible for the normal wear and tear associated with the use of a piece of property. Difficulties can arise when the definition of normal wear and tear varies between landlord and tenant. Because it can be a source of conflict, the more detail that can be added to this section of the lease, the less likely it is for litigation to result. Dates by which a landlord must return a deposit upon lease termination, and the appropriate method of resolving disputes about owed amounts, should also be included.

Unfortunately, legal clashes between landlord and tenant are common occurrences. They can be reduced if both parties to the lease carefully consider the essential lease terms that most directly affect the success of the lessor and lessee relationship. When vacancies are high, landlords may be willing to negotiate on terms they otherwise would reject. Likewise, if space is in short supply, tenants may be in a weaker negotiating position. Carefully reviewing lease terms is always a good idea and one that the hospitality manager would be well advised to undertake only with the aid of a qualified attorney.

The Buy-versus-Lease Decision

The decision to purchase or lease a piece of property is an important one. Managerial philosophy can play a large part in this decision. Regardless of whether one elects to own or merely utilize property, the decision has wide-ranging effects on a number of business issues. The most important effects are addressed in the next Legally Managing at Work discussion.

Often, the decision to lease rather than purchase property is an economic one. A new passenger van for a hotel may cost over $30,000. If the van is purchased, the hotel has undertaken a *capital improvement*. Payments for the van are not deductible as a business expense on the monthly profit and loss (P&L) statement. The value of the van, however, may be *depreciated* over a period of time fixed by law.

LEGALLY MANAGING AT WORK:

Legal Considerations of Buying versus Leasing

1. Right to use

Purchase	**Lease**
Unlimited use in any legal manner seen fit by the owner.	Use is strictly limited to the terms of the lease.

2. Treatment of cost

Purchase	**Lease**
Property is depreciable in accordance with federal and state income tax laws.	Lease payments are deductible as a business expense, according to federal and state tax laws.

3. Ability to finance

Purchase	**Lease**
The property may be used as collateral.	The property may not generally be used for collateral.

4. Liability

Purchase	**Lease**
Owner is liable.	Lessee and/or lessor may be liable.

5. Improvements

Purchase	**Lease**
Implemented as desired by owner.	Improvements limited to those allowed by lease terms.

6. Termination

Purchase	**Lease**
Ownership passes to estate holders.	Right to possess concludes with termination of lease contract.

7. Default

Purchase	**Lease**
Lender retains down payment and/or may foreclose on the property.	Lessor retains deposit and/or lender may evict and pursue balance of lease. With personal property, the lessor may reclaim the leased item.

LEGALESE

Capital improvement: The purchase or upgrade of real or personal property that results in an increased depreciable asset base.

LEGALESE

Depreciation: The decrease in value of a piece of property due to age and/or wear and tear.

If a hotel operator wants to replace the air filters located in the ceiling of an atrium-style lobby four times a year, it makes little sense to purchase the mechanical lifts necessary to do the job. These pieces of equipment can be leased for a day and the task can be completed.

By contrast, if a restaurateur wants to operate a restaurant in a prime location in a mall food court, he or she may have no option other than leasing, because the mall owner is not likely to sell the restaurateur the space needed to operate, but rather, will lease the space under a *commercial lease*.

The owner of a piece of property has rights that a lessee does not enjoy. In some cases, however, the effective hospitality manager, for a variety of reasons, may find it desirable to lease a piece of property. In either case, it is important to know and protect the rights associated with each type of property's possession.

6.5 RESPECTING INTELLECTUAL PROPERTY RIGHTS

Some of the most important, and personal, property rights protected by law are those that relate to *intellectual property*—personal property that is both intangible and conceptual.

In the hospitality industry, some managers violate intellectual property rights by using, but not paying for, the intellectual property of others. Good managers both avoid infringing on the property rights of others and pay for those intellectual items they legitimately use to assist their business.

When an individual creates something that is unique and valuable, his or her right to enjoy the financial proceeds of that creation is protected by laws related to trademarks, patents, copyrights, and trade dress. It is important to note that intellectual property maintains its status even after the death of the person who created the property.

Trademark

Trademarks are used to identify the producer, manufacturer, or source of a product. They are frequently used in the hospitality industry. The reason is clear: Guests like to see name-brand products in use by the establishments they frequent. Well-established trademarks, or *marks*, as they are sometimes called, let consumers know precisely whose product they are buying or being served. For example, many restaurants find it convenient to serve ketchup directly from the bottle. As a consumer, a bottle manufactured and labeled by Heinz will elicit a much different response from one manufactured by Bob. When consumers see the Heinz name on the label, they associate the ketchup with the quality represented by the Heinz Company. An unscrupulous foodservice manager who buys Bob's ketchup, and then puts it in a Heinz bottle, violates not only food safety laws, discussed later in this text, but trademark property rights laws as well.

The owner of a trademark has the right to prevent others from using that mark, if the owner was the first to use it in the respective marketplace. When a trademark has been properly applied for and received, no other person may manufacture or sell any article using the same or similar signs, marks, wrappers, or labels.

Trademark law protects the public by making consumers confident that they can identify brands they prefer and can purchase those brands without being confused or misled. Trademark laws also protect hospitality managers by ensuring that they are getting the quality they are paying for.

Patent

When an inventor creates something new, he or she may apply for a *patent* on the invention. If, for example, a restaurateur invents a piece of kitchen equipment that can easily peel and remove the center from a large Spanish onion, that restaurateur would

LEGALESE

Commercial lease: A lease that applies to business property.

LEGALESE

Intellectual property: Personal property that has been created through the intellectual efforts of its original owner.

LEGALESE

Trademark: A word, name, symbol, or combination of these that indicates the source or producer of an item. Sometimes called a mark.

LEGALESE

Patent: A grant issued by a governmental entity ensuring an inventor the right to exclusive production and sale of his or her invention for a fixed period of time.

be able to quickly produce one of today's most popular appetizer items. It would not be fair for another restaurateur to see that piece of equipment and proceed to manufacture it for sale him- or herself if the first restaurateur had applied for, and received, a patent on that piece of equipment.

The U.S. Patent and Trademark Office is the federal entity responsible for the granting of patents. An inventor, as the owner of the patent, has the right to exclude any other person from making, using, or selling the invention covered by the patent anywhere in the United States for 17 years from the date the patent is issued. If an inventor has applied for, but not yet received, a patent, he or she may use the term "patent pending" or "patent applied for."

Copyright

A *copyright* is the set of rights given to reproduce and use intellectual property. For example, the writer of a song has a right to compensation any time that song is performed. If a singer takes the song, records it, and then sells the recording, the copyright laws would require the singer to fairly compensate the songwriter who wrote the song's music and lyrics.

Copyright protection was considered so important that the founding fathers of the United States specifically granted the new Congress the responsibility of regulating copyrights. Figure 6.6 is an excerpt from the United States Constitution that addresses the issue of copyrights.

The owner of a copyright has the right to prevent any other person from reproducing, distributing, performing, or displaying his or her work for a specific period of time. The Copyright Act of 1976 states that copyrighted work can be a literary work, musical work, dramatic work, pantomime, choreographic work, pictorial work, graphic work, sculptural work, motion picture, audiovisual work, sound recording, or computer program. Most of the items found on the Internet are copyrighted also, including the text of websites, contents of e-mail, and sound and graphic files.

In 1998, President Clinton signed the Digital Millennium Copyright Act (DMCA) into law. The DMCA amends the Copyright Act of 1976 and incorporates two major international treaties: the World Intellectual Property Organization (WIPO) Copyright Treaty and the WIPO Performances and Phonograms Treaty. The DMCA's main effect is to heighten the penalties for copyright infringement over the Internet, and to criminalize the production and distribution of circumvention technology, and the act of circumvention, whether or not copyright infringement is involved.

When an individual has been granted a copyright, he or she is said to be the *copyright owner*. Copyright laws exist in foreign countries as well as the United States.

In some cases, under the doctrine of fair use, it is legal to use a copyrighted work without permission from the owner, but the purpose of such utilization is very important. A copyrighted work used for commentary, news reporting, teaching, scholarship, or research, is normally not an infringement of a copyright because it is an educational, rather than a commercial, use of the work.

LEGALESE

Copyright: The legal and exclusive right to copy or reproduce intellectual property.

LEGALESE

Copyright owner: A person or entity that legally holds a right to intellectual property under the copyright laws.

The Constitution of the United States of America

Article 1, Section 8

The Congress shall have the power:

to promote the progress of science, and the useful arts, by securing, for limited times, to authors and inventors, the exclusive right to their respective writings and discoveries.

Figure 6.6 Excerpt from the U.S. Constitution.

In the hospitality industry, it is critical that copyrighted works be used only when appropriate authorization has been received, particularly when the use of a copyrighted work—such as the broadcasting of a boxing match—will provide a direct economic benefit to the hospitality establishment. Generally speaking, the courts are aggressive enforcers of copyright laws; thus, it is a good idea to be very clear about the origin and ownership of potentially copyrighted works before they are used in a manner to produce income and profit.

Trade Dress

LEGALESE

Trade dress: A distinct visual image created for and identified with a specific product.

Although the rights related to *trade dress* are actually a part of those rights related to trademarks, in the hospitality industry, they merit separate discussion. A trade dress is a very special and unique visual image.

Trade dress includes color schemes, textures, sizes, designs, shapes, and placements of words, graphics, and decorations on a product or its packaging. In the hospitality industry, an entire restaurant may be created in such a way as to be protected under the laws related to trade dress. The laws in this area can be murky. Certainly, no one restaurant chain has an exclusive right to operate a restaurant with a "down home" theme. A trade dress question arises, however, when one restaurant chain uses the same items to create that feel as does its competitor.

Italian, Mexican, French, and American restaurants, to name a few, all have unique characteristics associated, not with the product served, but with the feel and visual image of the establishment. Trade dress protection allows the creative restaurateur to protect his or her aesthetic ideas in an industry that highly rewards innovation and creativity. For an excellent examination of the trade dress issue, do the following Search the Web exercise. It involves the case of two Mexican-style restaurants, one of which was accused of a trade dress violation.

Search the Web **6.1**

Enter lp.findlaw.com.

1. Select: Cases and Codes.
2. Select: US Supreme Court.
3. Select: Party Name Search.
4. In the Search field type: "Two Pesos."
5. Select: "Two Pesos, Inc. v. Taco Cabana, Inc., 505 U.S. 763 (1992)."

Review the intangible property rights Supreme Court case involving Two Pesos, Inc. and Taco Cabana, Inc. Be prepared to describe in class the items of similarity between the two businesses on which the court based its decision.

Preventing Intellectual Property Rights Infringement

LEGALESE

Public domain: Property that is owned by all citizens, not an individual.

In order to prevent infringing on the rights of intellectual property owners, the United States Patent and Trademark Office maintains a database of registered patents and trademarks. Consult that database if there is any question of whether a mark or an invention is in the *public domain*.

If a company does not take care, its trademarks can become part of the public domain. "Aspirin" is often mentioned as a word that began as a trademarked term but later passed into such common usage that the courts would no longer enforce the property rights of the word's creator. A common word, used frequently by society, cannot become the subject of trademark protection.

Although most hospitality managers can, through thoughtful planning, avoid infringing on patent and trademark rights, copyright issues are more complex. Consider the case of the corporation that owns a theme park with a variety of thrill rides. One of the most popular is a seated ride where four passengers share a padded car that progressively goes faster and faster, traveling up and down on a circular track. The ride is fast, loud, and popular with teenagers. Hundreds of flashing lights and loud music, played by 25 broadcast-quality speakers, are an important ingredient in this ride. The corporation is free to put any type of lighting around the ride that it feels would be appropriate. However, the company is not free to broadcast any music it wishes over the speakers in conjunction with the ride, unless the music is used in compliance with U.S. copyright laws. Figure 6.7 shows the section of the United States legal code that deals with the infringement of copyright.

U.S. Code, Title 17, Section 504

Sec. 504. Remedies for infringement: Damages and profits

In General. - Except as otherwise provided by this title, an infringer of copyright is liable for either:

(1) The copyright owner's actual damages and any additional profits of the infringer, as provided by subsection (b); or

(2) Statutory damages, as provided by subsection (c).

    (b) Actual Damages and Profits. The copyright owner is entitled to recover the actual damages suffered by him or her as a result of the infringement, and any profits of the infringer that are attributable to the infringement and are not taken into account in computing the actual damages. In establishing the infringer's profits, the copyright owner is required to present proof only of the infringer's gross revenue, and the infringer is required to prove his or her deductible expenses and the elements of profit attributable to factors other than the copyrighted work.

    (c) Statutory Damages.

(1) Except as provided by clause (2) of this subsection, the copyright owner may elect, at any time before final judgment is rendered, to recover, instead of actual damages and profits, an award of statutory damages for all infringements involved in the action, with respect to any one work, for which any one infringer is liable individually, or for which any two or more infringers are liable jointly and severally, in a sum of not less than $750 or more than $30,000 as the court considers just.

For the purposes of this subsection, all the parts of a compilation or derivative work constitute one work.

(2) In a case where the copyright owner sustains the burden of proving, and the court finds, that infringement was committed willfully, the court in its discretion may increase the award of statutory damages to a sum of not more than $150,000. In a case where the infringer sustains the burden of proving, and the court finds, that such infringer was not aware and had no reason to believe that his or her acts constituted an infringement of copyright, the court in its discretion may reduce the award of statutory damages to a sum of not less than $200. The court shall remit statutory damages in any case where an infringer believed and had reasonable grounds for believing that his or her use of the copyrighted work was a fair use under section 107, if the infringer was:

    (i) an employee or agent of a nonprofit educational institution, library, or archives acting within the scope of his or her employment who, or such institution, library, or archives itself, which infringed by reproducing the work in copies or phonorecords; or

    (ii) a public broadcasting entity which or a person who, as a regular part of the nonprofit activities of a public broadcasting entity (as defined in subsection [g] of section 118) infringed by performing a published nondramatic literary work or by reproducing a transmission program embodying a performance of such a work.

Figure 6.7 U.S. Code Title 17, Section 504.

Copyright laws in the United States give songwriters and publishers the right to collect royalties on their intellectual property whenever their songs are played in public. Note that the law allows the owner of the copyright to recover the profits made by any group that unlawfully uses copyrighted material.

Whether a hospitality manager plays songs in an establishment on CDs, television, tape, or in a live performance, the owners of the song have a right to royalties. This is because federal copyright laws state that playing copyrighted music in a public place constitutes a performance. When copyrighted music is performed in public, hospitality managers are in violation of the law if they do not pay the royalties due the owners of the music that has been played.

Of course, it would be extremely difficult for the practicing hospitality manager to know exactly who owns the rights to a particular piece of music. Most of the songs played in the United States are licensed by either Broadcast Music, Inc. (BMI); the American Society of Composers, Authors, and Publishers (ASCAP); or SESAC, which originally stood for the Society of European Stage Actors and Composers, but now is referred to solely by its acronym, pronounced SEE-sack. In order to play a given piece of music, a fee must be paid to the licensor that holds the right to license the music in question. Fee structures are based on a variety of factors, but the average restaurant, playing background music seven days a week, would be expected to pay only a few hundred dollars per year for the right to broadcast most of the music available for play. If the hospitality manager refuses or neglects to pay the fees rightfully due a licensing group, he or she can be subject to fines or prosecution.

Congress has determined that any facility that plays its background music on a piece of equipment that could normally be found in a home will not be held to the normal copyright infringement rules if they do not charge admission to hear the music. Certainly, it is not the intent of the copyright laws to prohibit turning on a simple radio or television in a public place. In 1998, President Clinton signed the Fairness in Music Licensing Amendment, a law that allowed small restaurants an exemption from some licensing fees. The law took effect in January 1999.

The specific provisions of the amendment providing for the free broadcast of music and video are quite clear. Restaurants under 3,750 square feet can play as many televisions and radios as they desire without paying royalty fees. There is no restriction on the size of the television that may be installed in a restaurant of this size. For specific information, visit www.copyright.gov. For restaurants larger than 3,750 square feet, if the owner applies for and receives an exemption, the restaurant may play up to four televisions (no more than one per room), and use up to six speakers (no more than four per room). The television sets cannot be larger than 55 inches.

Many hospitality venues utilize jukeboxes for their patrons' entertainment. It is ordinarily the provider of the jukebox who has the burden of paying the royalties for the music included in the jukebox, but this should be spelled out in the agreement prior to the installation of the jukebox.

Just as music is covered by copyright laws, so too are the broadcasts of such groups as the National Football League (NFL), Major League Baseball (MLB), the National Basketball Association (NBA), and others. The right to air these broadcasts is reserved by the group creating the programming, and the hospitality manager who violates their copyrights does so at great risk. If you have any doubt about the legality of your intended broadcasts, contact the broadcast company (i.e., cable operator) or the owner of the broadcasted product (NFL, Time Warner, etc.) to clarify the circumstances under which you may broadcast and to get written permission to do so.

For hotels, the broadcasting of in-room videos or movies on demand is treated in a similar way to jukeboxes in restaurants. The providers of the service to the hotel operator are ordinarily responsible for paying the royalties from showing the product. Again, this needs to be clarified in the agreement between the provider of the service and the hotel operator.

INTERNATIONAL SNAPSHOT

U.S. Hotel Companies Seeking Trademark Protection May Now File in the United States for Protection Abroad

Most well-known hotel companies earn their profits primarily by managing and franchising hotels, thereby allowing the hotels to operate under the hotel company's "flags." These flags (such as Westin, Marriott, and Hilton) are trademarks. They represent a way of doing business, the hotel company's valuable relationships with its customers, and, in essence, the company's power to deliver economic performance to a hotel. Hotel companies, therefore, consider their trademarks to be among their most valuable assets.

Valuable assets must be protected, and trademarks are no exception. Trademarks are usually protected by registering them in the jurisdictions where they are used. These registrations must then be renewed at intervals prescribed by the laws of the applicable jurisdiction.

Hotel companies often operate hotels internationally. This means that, to protect their marks, they should, at a minimum, register and renew their registrations in each country where the hotels are located. They should also consider "registering defensively" in countries where there is a high "knock-off" risk. Before November 2, 2003, the registration process required a U.S. hotel company to engage in a country-by-country registration process. One shortcut registration process has existed for some time: Companies may register for and obtain a European Community Trade Mark (ECTM), which provides protection in all countries of the European Union for the cost of a single application. But as of that date, U.S. companies were given an additional shortcut alternative to the country-by-country registration process. On November 2, the United States became the fifty-ninth country to implement the Madrid Protocol.

The Madrid Protocol is a treaty that allows trademark holders to file a single application covering all 60 protocol member countries. The resulting International Registration permits some applicants to greatly reduce costs associated with multiple international trademark applications.

Like any trademark protection regime, the Madrid Protocol has disadvantages as well as advantages:

■ One-stop Madrid filings through the U.S. Trademark Office are more convenient and initially less costly than filing multiple international applications.

■ International registrations offer the same scope of protection as a registration in the applicant's home country. Because U.S. trademark law requires applicants to describe the goods covered by their marks more narrowly than that of other countries, an international registration based on a U.S. application will give a U.S. trademark holder narrower protection in some other countries than non-U.S. trademark owners would receive.

■ Because an international application must be based on an original "home country" application, if a U.S. applicant's original U.S. application is refused by the Patent and Trademark Office, or fails for any other reason within five years, the entire international application based on it will also fail. An applicant may refile applications in each individual country while retaining the original filing date, but the fees and costs associated with the original protocol application will be lost.

■ If member country trademark offices raise substantive objections to applications for an international registration, local counsel will be necessary to resolve each such objection.

■ Madrid filings do not cover countries that are not members of the Madrid Protocol. Some important countries that are not members include Canada and most of Central and South America.

Whether a company should seek international registration under the Madrid Protocol depends heavily on the countries where the company needs protection. If, for example, the company expects to use its mark solely in Europe and the United States, a European Community Trade Mark will provide protection in all countries of the European Union for the cost of a single application, and the costs and benefits of prosecuting a ECTM application will be generally more favorable than those associated with a Madrid filing. If, however, the company requires broad, worldwide protection, an international application may be the best overall approach.

Provided by Irvin W. Sandman, Esq., and Robert C. Cumbow, Esq., of Graham & Dunn's Hospitality, Beverage, and Franchise Team, Seattle, Washington. www.grahamdunn.com.

Assume that you are the food and beverage (F&B) director at a full-service hotel in a large East Coast college town. Your general manager, Mr. Peterson, is planning to have a large event centered on this year's Super Bowl. As the F&B director, you are an integral part of the event planning committee. One of the teams in the NFL final is from the state in which your hotel is located, so fan interest is very high.

Mr. Peterson proposes an event that will be held in the hotel's Grand Ballroom, which can hold 700 people. The festivities will begin at 3:00 P.M. on Super Bowl Sunday, with the televised pregame show, a darts tournament, and a Mexican food buffet. At 6:30 P.M., the game is to be shown on five 60-inch TV screens that will be placed around the ballroom. The chief maintenance engineer has assured Mr. Peterson that the sets can be mounted on the ballroom's walls. The evening will conclude with a postgame "victory" party, which will end around midnight.

During one of the planning meetings, the discussion centers on the admission price that will be charged. The issue of reserved seating is raised by Scott Haner, director of sales and marketing. He believes that corporate clients of the hotel will be more inclined to attend if they can be assured good seats near the large-screen televisions.

1. As a hospitality professional, what issues must you consider prior to finalizing this Super Bowl party event?
2. If Mr. Peterson elects to charge a $20 fee for seats close to the large screens, but only $5 for seats farther away from the screens, would your opinion be different? Why or why not?
3. What are the responsibilities of the management team in this scenario?

THE HOSPITALITY INDUSTRY IN COURT

To understand just how possessive movie studios can be about their copyrights and how extensive the litigation can be in this area of the law, examine the following two case studies. First, consider *National Football League v. McBee & Bruno's, Inc.* 792 F.2d 726 (8th Cir. 1986).

FACTUAL SUMMARY

The National Football League and the St. Louis Cardinals (NFL) brought suit against McBee & Bruno's, Inc. (Bruno), owner of several St. Louis restaurants, for violations of federal copyright law when their restaurants broadcast the Cardinals' home games, which the NFL had "blacked out," or not broadcast within 75 miles of the Cardinals' home playing field.

The NFL maintains and manages contracts for all of its collective teams, including the Cardinals, with the major television networks. One clause of these network contracts specifies that any NFL games that are not sold out within 72 hours of game time will be blacked out of the broadcasting area.

All NFL games are telecast by the television networks in the following manner: television cameras present at the game capture the game play while announcers offer commentary from a sound booth. Then both the audio and the video signal are transmitted and combined together at an earth station outside of the stadium. The combined signal, or uplink, is sent to a satellite, which then transmits the signal, now a downlink, to a network control panel in Long Island. The downlink is termed a "clean feed" because it contains no images other than those broadcast from the stadium. After the downlink, the clean feed is sent to the television network studios, where commercials and other images are added, creating a "dirty feed." The dirty feed is retransmitted to the satellite and downlinked again to local broadcast stations, which add in local content and finally broadcast the game on the air.

Bruno owned sports bar restaurants within the 75-mile blackout area in St. Louis, and each sports bar had a satellite dish antenna that was capable of intercepting the clean feed downlinked from the satellite. Bruno, in fact, intercepted the clean feed and broadcast blacked-out games it in all but two of its sports bars.

QUESTION FOR THE COURT

The issue for the court was whether Bruno's broadcast of the clean feed transmission was considered a violation of the Copyright Act, or if it qualified for the home-use exemption for transmitting copyrighted materials. The home-use exemption provides that "no copyright liability can be imposed for 'communication of a transmission embodying a performance by the public reception of the transmission on a single receiving apparatus of a kind commonly used in private homes.'" Bruno argued that satellite dishes fall within the exception because satellite dishes are commonly found within homes. Thus, the court had to determine how likely it was for the average patron watching a blacked-out Cardinals game at Bruno's to have the ability to watch the game at home.

DECISION

Ultimately, the court found in favor of the NFL because a District Court finding stated that, at the time, most satellite dishes were owned by commercial establishments, rather than families for home use, and those that were found in homes did not have the capability to intercept the satellite transmission clean feed. Thus, Bruno was found liable for copyright infringement from its pirated broadcast of the blacked-out games, because they could not find safe harbor under the home-use exception.

MESSAGE TO MANAGEMENT

Be aware that the contract rights of others can affect the management decisions of an unrelated hospitality venue. Just because your venue possesses a particular technological capability that is not available to the remainder of the public, as a manager, you should consult an attorney to determine the legal ramifications before using such technology.

Next consider the case of *Home Box Office, Inc. v. Pay TV of Greater New York, Inc.* 467 F. Supp. 525 (E.D.N.Y., 1979).

FACTUAL SUMMARY

In 1974, Home Box Office, Inc. (HBO) contracted with Microband National Systems, Inc. (Microband) to distribute HBO subscription television service to areas in and around New York City. HBO transmitted its service from atop the Empire State Building to various points throughout New York City. Microband received the signal with special equipment, converted the signal, and distributed it to individual households. Microband subcontracted the distribution service to other companies. Pay TV of Greater New York, Inc. (Pay TV) was one of those distribution companies.

Pay TV signed an agreement with Microband in October 1975 to distribute HBO services in Queens County for as long as Microband's contract continued with HBO. Pay TV claimed that it entered the agreement, believing it would eventually take the place of Microband as the main distributor. Pay TV repeatedly requested the right to distribute HBO services in other areas around New York City. HBO denied these requests, despite Pay TV's investment of money and effort in securing new service areas. In May 1976, Microband ended the agreement with HBO. HBO and Pay TV entered into negotiations for Pay TV to have exclusive distribution rights in the King and Bronx County areas as well as the already existing rights in Queens County.

By July 1976, no agreement was reached, but Pay TV continued to distribute services in Queens County and even expanded into other areas. In February 1977, HBO demanded in writing that Pay TV stop transmitting HBO service completely. A final attempt to reach an affiliation agreement failed, and in August 1978, HBO advised Pay TV it was transmitting HBO service without authorization ("pirating"). HBO advised

Pay TV the transmission was illegal, and if it did not stop, a lawsuit would be filed. HBO filed suit in December 1978. At the time of the lawsuit, Pay TV continued transmitting to over 8,000 customers, collecting $75,000 per month. No payment was made to HBO by Pay TV. HBO asked for a temporary injunction to stop Pay TV from transmitting HBO service.

QUESTION FOR THE COURT

The question for the court was whether Pay TV could be ordered to stop intercepting and transmitting the HBO signal. HBO argued Pay TV was violating Section 605 of the Communications Act of 1934 (the act). Under Section 605, anyone intercepting and using signals not intended for the general public was violating the act. Pay TV admitted Section 605 applied to the suit between it and HBO, but argued that HBO consented to the interception of the signal. Pay TV also argued HBO waited too long to ask for an injunction. Finally, Pay TV argued that HBO was suffering harm for which money damages could compensate. With this argument, Pay TV could pay HBO damages but continue to transmit the service while the lawsuit was taking place.

DECISION

The court ruled Pay TV was pirating services and found no evidence that HBO consented to the illegal transmission. The court also held HBO was not too late in seeking an injunction, and money damages would not repair the harm being done by Pay TV. Pay TV was ordered to cease transmission.

MESSAGE TO MANAGEMENT

Pirating (or profiting from) broadcasts not meant for distribution to the general public (or without a license from the distributor, e.g., NFL) is illegal and can subject you to serious economic liability.

WHAT DID YOU LEARN IN THIS CHAPTER?

Property can be classified into several different categories. Real property refers to land and all the things attached to the land. Fixtures are personal items that were once separate but are now considered to be real property. Most items other than land are classified as personal property, which includes both tangible and intangible property. It is important to understand the difference among the categories of property, because different methods of financing the purchase of property exist for each category.

When property is transferred from one owner to another, specific types of documents and sales contracts are used to ensure the legality of the purchase and to protect the buyer and seller. Warranties, or advertised claims about the performance or quality of a product, are often treated as part of the sales contract. Thus, a seller is obligated by law to back up any warranties made. The Uniform Commercial Code offers protection under the law to both buyers and sellers of personal property, as well as to financial lenders.

A lease is a contract that transfers possession, but not ownership, of a piece of property. Leasing real and personal property is a common occurrence in the industry today. Whether a hospitality manager assumes the role of a lessor (landlord) or lessee, it is important to make sure that the lease agreement contains essential terms that will spell out the details of the agreement, and offers adequate protection to both parties.

Trademarks, patents, copyrights, and concept rights are all protected under the law. Hospitality operators must make sure that they are in compliance with laws governing the serving of brand-name products; the use or creation of concepts, logos, or images; and the public broadcasting of music and video.

After you have studied this chapter, you should be prepared to:

1. Restate the difference between real and personal property, and give five hospitality examples of each.

2. Secure a bill-of-sale form, and check it for the six critical information items listed in this chapter. List additional items on the bill of sale, and describe why you believe each is included.

3. Prepare a memo for your staff that lets them know the difference between a deed and a bill of sale. Include an explanation of when each would be used.

4. Secure a copy of an express warranty, and analyze it for differences with an implied warranty.

5. Using the Internet, locate a lender who finances hospitality operations. Determine the current interest rate for a $1 million unsecured loan.

6. Choose a popular, independent, local restaurant. Write a two-page description of that property that you feel defines its trade dress.

7. Assume that your operation is considering whether to buy or lease a beer-dispensing system from your vendor. Your boss has asked you to prepare a memo addressing the legal aspects of the decision. Prepare a one-page memo that addresses the major issues.

8. Give a hospitality example of each of the following:

   Trademark
   Patent
   Copyright
   Trade dress

After reviewing Section 6.4 on leases, form teams of two, then pair up with another team. One team will represent the hotel; the other team will act as a potential tenant. Each team will have 15 minutes to review their position, after which 45 minutes will be used to negotiate the terms of a leasing agreement, using the following information:

- The space to be leased occupies 5,000 square feet in a hotel.
- The potential tenants are looking for a primary 10-year lease to open a restaurant/nightclub.
- Average rental rate in the area is $10 per square foot for a three-year lease.
- The space is a shell only (walls, roof, dirt floor).

Make the best deal you can. Be sure to address the rental rate, finish-out allowance, lease term, and other issues raised in your reading and class discussions. If all issues are not resolved, discuss the terms of the last offer made.

CHAPTER 7

LEGALLY SELECTING EMPLOYEES

"OKAY, LAURA," SAID Trisha Sangus brightly. "Where are we on the hiring of the new sales manager?"

Laura O'Leary, the director of sales and marketing at Trisha's hotel, was very pleased. Three weeks ago, she had successfully presented the hotel's owners with a proposal to expand the nine-member sales staff to ten, and the owners had accepted her recommendation. Now, Laura was heading the search for just the right candidate.

It was important to Trisha that the selection of a candidate for the new sales position go smoothly, and with some speed, because she wanted to demonstrate to the owners that their decision had been a good one. Trisha had discussed the new position with Laura at great length. The city was becoming a popular destination for several association meetings and annual conventions. Although the hotel had ample meeting and banquet facilities, this new market had gone virtually untapped. Trisha was convinced that the right person and the right strategy could make a huge difference in the number of rooms and meetings booked. The result on the hotel's bottom line could be significant as well.

"I know you have held some interviews," said Trisha. "I'd like to review the resumes of your three finalists." Laura gave Trisha the file containing the resumes.

"We have three candidates who meet the criteria we established," Laura explained. "Each is very different from the other, and each has strengths and weaknesses. On the whole, I'm very pleased with our choices."

Trisha rapidly scanned the resumes, along with the notes that Laura had taken during the candidates' interviews. She, Laura, and Michael Pinnard, the new human resource director, had come up with several important interview questions for this particular search.

Strengths	Limitations
Candidate One: Beverly	First position in sales
Four-year degree in HRI from State University	
Candidate Two: Pat	Outside responsibilities
Five years' hotel sales experience	Professional appearance
Candidate Three: Leon	Limited computer skills
Two-year associate's degree	
Two years' hotel sales experience	

"I haven't ranked the candidates in order of preference, but I would like you to see candidates number one and three," said Laura. "I think either one could do a great job."

"I'm curious about your comments on candidate two," said Trisha. "I understand the strength, but help me be clear on the weaknesses. Let's start with the 'outside responsibilities.'"

"Well," Laura began, "it has to do with children." She paused. "I know what you are thinking," said Laura, as she watched Trisha arch an eyebrow in response to her comment. "We certainly didn't ask Pat if she was married or had children. But when we asked her about the ability to work past five o'clock, she replied that she had four children at home, ranging from 8 to 14 years old, and that, given advanced notice, arranging for child care was certainly possible."

Laura looked earnestly at Trisha Sangus, then continued, "You know Trisha," said Laura, "we don't always know when our staff will have to work late. Site tours can pop up anytime. And client dinners can drag on and on. I told the candidate that sometimes we knew ahead of time and sometimes we did not. I was just being honest."

Trisha was well aware of the hours involved in hotel sales. She had spent four years as a director of sales and marketing. She adjusted the rim of her glasses, and carefully reviewed Pat's resume. "Now help me understand the professional appearance comment."

"Well," Laura said, "you know how you stress that we should be professional looking at all times?"

Trisha smiled slightly. She knew that she was perceived in the hotel as a stickler for detail. Staff uniforms were required to be pressed and clean, and nametags had to be fastened straight, and Trisha's reaction in the staff meeting when a junior manager proposed "casual Friday" for the hotel's administrative staff was still talked about. In short, Trisha expected management personnel to look sharp at all times.

"Well," Laura continued, "this candidate wore no makeup at all—no nail polish, no lipstick, not even a little blush! I think our customers expect a higher level of sophistication than that."

Trisha looked at Laura. There was no doubt that well-groomed Laura did in fact present the appearance Trisha had come to associate with a professional salesperson.

"At times like this," Trisha thought, *"it's nice to have a human resource director in the hotel who is both knowledgeable and a good communicator,"* so she called him. "Michael," she said, as the HR director picked up the telephone, "can you step in here for a minute? And bring your calendar. I think Laura will want to schedule some information sessions for her and her staff. And I want to schedule three interviews."

IN THIS CHAPTER, YOU WILL LEARN:

1. To utilize job descriptions, qualifications, and other tools for legally selecting employees.
2. To avoid charges of discrimination by knowing the classes of workers that are protected under the law.
3. To understand the procedure for verifying the work eligibility of potential employees before offering them employment.
4. To distinguish the rights of both employers and employees under the at-will employment doctrine.
5. To understand the concept of collective bargaining and the legal obligations when interacting with labor unions.

7.1 EMPLOYEE SELECTION

Legally selecting and managing a staff can be a very challenging task in today's complex world of laws and regulations. Some managers, especially those with many years of experience, believe that finding, maintaining, and retaining a qualified, service-oriented staff is every manager's most difficult task. It is true that the challenges of managing people are generally greater than those involved in managing technologies or products. People are complex and are affected by so many non–work-related issues that you will find it both difficult and rewarding to be a leader to your staff.

The law is very specific regarding what you, as an employer, can and cannot do as you secure your workforce. Both you and your workers have rights that affect the employment relationship. In the next two chapters, we'll look at how to select and manage employees in accordance with the law.

As an employer, you will have wide latitude in selecting those individuals whom you feel would best benefit your business. However, it is critical that you develop an employee selection procedure that ensures fairness and compliance with the law (to avoid the risk of a discrimination lawsuit), while also allowing you to hire the best possible candidate for the job.

One tool that managers use to make good hiring decisions is the job description, which they then use as a basis for establishing a list of job qualifications that each candidate should possess.

Job Descriptions

Before an employee can be selected to fill a vacant position, management must have a thorough understanding of the essential functions that the employee will need to perform. These are contained in the *job description*. Legally, only those tasks that are necessary to effectively carry out the responsibilities and perform the tasks required in the job should be used in the description.

Job descriptions need not be long. In most cases, a single typewritten page or two will be sufficient to detail the information that makes up the body of a job description. Figure 7.1 is a sample of a job description used in the hospitality industry. The description includes the job title, reporting relationship, tasks, and competencies required for the job.

The job description serves a dual role. It is important from an operational perspective in that it helps supervisors and the HR department keep track of the changing responsibilities of workers. However, it is also important from a legal perspective in that it may need to be produced in court to demonstrate that an employer fairly established the requirements of a job prior to selecting the candidates to fill those jobs.

LEGALESE

Job description: A written, itemized listing of a specific job's basic responsibilities and reporting relationships.

> **Position Title:** Executive Chef
>
> **Reports To:** Food and Beverage Director
>
> **Position Summary:** The department head responsible for any and all kitchens in a foodservice establishment. Ensures that all kitchens provide nutritious, safe, eye-appealing, properly flavored food. Maintains a safe and sanitary preparation environment.
>
> **Tasks:**
>
> 1. Interviews, hires, evaluates, rewards, and disciplines kitchen personnel as appropriate.
> 2. Orients and trains kitchen personnel in property and department rules, policies, and procedures.
> 3. Trains kitchen personnel in food production principles and practices. Establishes quality standards for all menu items and for food production practices.
> 4. Plans and prices menus. Establishes portion sizes and standards of service for all menu items.
> 5. Schedules kitchen employees in conjunction with business forecasts and predetermined budget. Maintains payroll records for submission to payroll department.
> 6. Controls food costs by establishing purchasing specifications, storeroom requisition systems, product storage requirements, standardization recipes, and waste control procedures.
> 7. Trains kitchen personnel in safe operating procedures of all equipment, utensils, and machinery. Establishes maintenance schedules in conjunction with manufacturer instructions for all equipment. Provides safety training in lifting, carrying, hazardous material control, chemical control, first aid, and CPR.
> 8. Trains kitchen personnel in sanitation practices and establishes cleaning schedules, stock rotation schedules, refrigeration temperature control points, and other sanitary controls.
> 9. Trains kitchen personnel to prepare all food while retaining the maximum amount of desirable nutrients. Trains kitchen personnel to meet special dietary requests, including low-fat, low-sodium, low-calorie, and vegetarian meals.
>
> Source: Anonymous

Figure 7.1 Sample job description.

LEGALESE

Job qualifications: The knowledge or skill(s) required to perform the responsibilities and tasks listed in a job description.

If you review Figure 7.1 carefully, you will see that the job description does not mention the physical or mental abilities required to perform the job. The role of the job description is to define the job itself, while the role of the *job qualification* is to define the personal attributes required to satisfactorily perform the job.

Job Qualifications

Once you know exactly what kinds of tasks employees must perform in a given job, it is possible to create a list of the skills or knowledge they must possess in order to successfully perform those tasks. These skills should be written down and attached to the job description. If a potential job candidate is not selected for employment, and later elects to bring legal action against you, it will be critical that you can show how each component of your job qualification list is driven by, or logically flows from, the job description.

Job qualifications can consist of both physical and mental requirements. It is important to remember that the job qualifications list must not violate the law nor include any characteristics that would unfairly prevent a class of workers from successfully competing for the position. If, for example, a hotel groundskeeper listed a height of 6 feet as a job qualification for a grass cutter, that qualification would be considered inappropriate, because there are minority groups that would have difficulty meeting it. The courts might interpret this job qualification as one that unfairly limits the potential for a minority candidate to secure the job. Even though the groundskeeper might be able to show that the tools normally used by the groundskeeping employees were located on shelves most easily reached by those who were 6 feet tall or taller, it is highly unlikely that this occupational qualification could stand up under the scrutiny of the courts, unless the groundskeeper could prove that a height of 6 feet was a *bona fide occupational qualification (BFOQ)*.

To establish that a qualification is, in fact, a bona fide occupational qualification, you must prove that a class of employees would be unable to perform the job safely or adequately, and that the bona fide occupational qualification is reasonably necessary to the operation of the business. In the case of the groundskeeper, simply moving the tools or making the reasonable accommodation of providing a short ladder would open the job to candidates of any height, and probably would prevent a discrimination lawsuit. The following types of qualifications are examples that are appropriate in jobs where knowledge or skill is a necessary requirement of the job.

Physical attributes necessary to complete the duties of the job, such as:

The ability to lift a specific amount of weight
Education
Certifications
Registrations
Licensing
Language skills
Knowledge of equipment operation
Previous experience
Minimum age requirements (for serving alcohol or working certain hours)

> ## ≫ ANALYZE THE SITUATION 7.1

CRUZ VILLARAIGOSA OWNS AND manages The Cruz Cantina, a lively bar and dance club that serves Cuban and other Caribbean-style cuisine. The club has a dance floor, has small tables, and serves outstanding food.

Cruz's clientele consists mainly of 20- to 40-year-old males, who frequent the Cantina for its good food as well as the extremely low-cut, Spanish-style blouses worn by the young female servers who bring the food and drinks to the tables. The Cruz Cantina advertises to women and families, as well as to young men, but the reputation of the facility is predicated upon the physical attractiveness of the women whom Cruz has hired to serve the guests, and the uniforms these servers wear.

Cruz employs women and men of all races and nationalities, but all food and drink servers are female. When Cruz elects not to hire a young man for a job as a server, Cruz is contacted by the young man's attorney. The attorney alleges the young man has been illegally denied a server's job at the Cantina because of his gender, and that sex cannot be a bona fide occupational qualification for a food and beverage server position.

LEGALESE

Bona fide occupational qualification: A job qualification, established in good faith and fairness, that is necessary to safely or adequately perform the job.

Cruz replies that her operation employs both men and women, but that one necessary job qualification for all servers is that they be "attractive to men," and that the qualification of "attractiveness to men" is a legitimate one, given the importance of maintaining the successful image, atmosphere, and resulting business the Cantina enjoys. She maintains that the servers not only serve food and beverages but also play a role in advertising and marketing the unique features of the Cantina. Cruz also maintains that attractiveness is indeed an occupational characteristic that she can use to promote her facility, citing modeling agencies and TV casting agents as examples of employers who routinely use attractiveness as a means of selecting employees. Cruz states that her right to choose employees she feels will best benefit her business is unconditional, as long as she does not unfairly discriminate against a protected class of workers.

1. Do you think that the requirement that servers be "attractive to males" is a bona fide occupational requirement, and "necessary" for the continued successful operation of The Cruz Cantina?

2. If you were on a jury, would you allow Cruz to hire female servers exclusively, if she so desired? Why or why not?

3. What damages, if any, do you feel the male job applicant not selected for employment at the Cantina would be entitled to?

Applicant Screening

When choosing potential applicants for employment, hospitality managers generally utilize some or all of the five major selection devices:

1. Applications
2. Interviews
3. Preemployment testing
4. Background checks
5. References

Applications

The employment application is a document completed by the candidate for employment. It will generally list the name, address, work experience, and related information of the candidate. The requirements for a legitimate, legally sound application are many; however, in general, the questions should focus exclusively on job qualifications and nothing else. Most hospitality companies will have their employment application reviewed by an attorney who specializes in employment law. If, as a manager, you are responsible for developing your own application, it is a good idea to have the document reviewed by a legal specialist prior to its utilization.

It is important that each employment candidate for a given position be required to fill out an identical application, and that an application be on file for each candidate who is ultimately selected for the position. Figure 7.2 is a sample of a legally sound

FOUR SEASONS
Hotels and Resorts
www.fourseasons.com

We are an Equal Opportunity Employer
Complying with all applicable Federal and State Laws

Please Type or Print

DATE TODAY _____

LAST NAME	FIRST	MIDDLE

SREET ADDRESS

CITY	STATE	ZIP

PHONE-HOME	PHONE-WORK

TO VERIFY PREVIOUS EMPLOYMENT, PLEASE INDICATE IF YOU HAVE WORKED UNDER A DIFFERENT NAME.

POSITION(S) DESIRED	☐ FULL TIME ☐ PART TIME ☐ ON-CALL/CASUAL

SALARY DESIRED	DATE AVAILABLE FOR WORK

SOCIAL SECURITY NUMBER

ARE YOU PRESENTLY EMPLOYED? ☐ YES   ☐ NO
IF YES, MAY WE CONTACT YOUR CURRENT EMPLOYER? ☐ YES ☐ NO

DO YOU HAVE A LEGAL RIGHT TO WORK IN THE U.S.? ☐ YES   ☐ NO

IF YOU HAVE WORKED FOR FOUR SEASONS HOTELS BEFORE, PLEASE STATE WHEN AND WHERE:

EMPLOYMENT RECORD

List your previous experience beginning with your most recent position.

(Include military experience as a job.)

PLEASE FILL-IN COMPLETELY, DO NOT USE "SEE RESUME"

#1 EMPLOYER	
ADDRESS	PHONE
STARTING POSITION	STARTING SALARY
LAST POSITION	FINAL SALARY
DATES EMPLOYED From: To:	SUPERVISOR
DUTIES	
REASON FOR LEAVING	

#2 EMPLOYER	
ADDRESS	PHONE
STARTING POSITION	STARTING SALARY
LAST POSITION	FINAL SALARY
DATES EMPLOYED From: To:	SUPERVISOR
DUTIES	
REASON FOR LEAVING	

#3 EMPLOYER	
ADDRESS	PHONE
STARTING POSITION	STARTING SALARY
LAST POSITION	FINAL SALARY
DATES EMPLOYED From: To:	SUPERVISOR
DUTIES	
REASON FOR LEAVING	

#4 EMPLOYER	
ADDRESS	PHONE
STARTING POSITION	STARTING SALARY
LAST POSITION	FINAL SALARY
DATES EMPLOYED From: To:	SUPERVISOR
DUTIES	
REASON FOR LEAVING	

Figure 7.2 Employment application from the Four Seasons Hotel, Houston (Reprinted with permission).

EDUCATION AND SKILLS (answer only if job related)

		DIPLOMA / GED
HIGH SCHOOL DEGREE OR GED EQUIVALENCY		☐ YES ☐ NO

	NAME	GRADUATED	MAJOR
COLLEGE		☐ YES ☐ NO	

OTHER EDUCATION / TRAINING:
(List any special skill(s) related to the job you are applying for)

AVAILABILITY

ARE THERE ANY HOURS, SHIFTS, OR DAYS OF THE WEEK THAT YOU WILL NOT BE ABLE TO WORK? YES NO

IF YES, PLEASE STATE DAYS AND REASON:

I AM WILLING AND ABLE TO WORK:

☐ FULL TIME ☐ PART TIME ☐ TEMPORARY/SEASONAL

☐ ON-CALL/CASUAL ☐ DAYS ☐ EVENINGS ☐ OVERNIGHT

☐ WEEKENDS ☐ HOLIDAYS ☐ OVERTIME

ARE YOU CAPABALE OF PERFORMING THE ESSENTIAL FUNCTIONS OF THE JOB YOU ARE APPLYING FOR WITH OR WITHOUT REASONABLE ACCOMODATION?

☐ YES ☐ NO

HOW WERE YOU REFERRED TO FOUR SEASONS? PLEASE BE SPECIFIC. ☐ ADVERTISEMENT ☐ INTERNET ☐ ON YOUR OWN

NAME OF SCHOOL: NAME OF COMPANY EMPLOYEE: NAME OF AGENCY:

OTHER:

DO YOU HAVE RELATIVES OR ACQUAINTANCES WORKING IN THE HOTEL? ☐ YES ☐ NO
IF YES, PLEASE LIST THEIR NAMES & RELATIONSHIP:

IF UNDER AGE 18, INDICATE DATE OF BIRTH:

IF APPLYING FOR A JOB INVOLVING ALCOHOLIC BEVERAGE SERVICE, ARE YOU AT LEAST AGE 21? ☐ YES ☐ NO

HAVE YOU EVER BEEN CONVICTED OF A FELONY? ☐ YES* ☐ NO DO YOU HAVE FELONY CHARGES PENDING AGAINST YOU? ☐ YES ☐ NO

IF YES, PLEASE GIVE DATES AND DETAILS:

*CONVICTION OF A FELONY WILL NOT NECESSARILY DISQUALIFY YOU FROM EMPLOYMENT.

CERTIFICATION AND SIGNATURE – Please read carefully.

I declare that my answers to the questions on this application are true, and I give Four Seasons Hotels the right to investigate all references and information given. I agree that any false statement or misrepresentation on this application will be cause for refusal to hire or immediate dismissal. I affirm that I have a genuine intent and for no other purposes in applying for a job with Four Seasons Hotels. I agree that my employment will be considered "at will" and may be terminated by this company at any time without liability for wages or salary except for such as may have been earned at the date of such termination unless or until superseded by specific written employment contract. If requested by management at any time, I agree to submit to a search of my person or of any locker that may be assigned to me and I hereby waive all claims for damages on account of such examination. I understand that Four Seasons Hotels is a Drug Free Workplace and has a policy against drug and alcohol abuse and reserves the right to screen applicants and test for cause. I acknowledge that if I need reasonable accommodation in either the application process or employment I should bring the request to the attention of the Human Resources department.

I authorize you to make such legal investigations and inquiries of my personal employment, criminal history, driving record, and other job related matters as may be necessary in determining an employment decision. I hereby release employers, schools or persons from all liability in responding to inquiries in connection with my application.

I understand that an offer employment and my continued employment are contingent upon satisfactory proof of my authorization to work in the United States of America.

CONFIDENTIAL MATERIAL AND THE PROPERTY OF
FOUR SEASONS HOTELS LIMITED

SIGN HERE:_____ DATE:_____
      (APPLICANT'S SIGNATURE)   MONTH/DAY/YEAR

Figure 7.2 *(Continued)*

employment application used by the Four Seasons Hotel, Houston. Note, specifically, how the questions are related to previous work history and job qualifications.

Interviews

From the employment applications or resumes submitted, some candidates will be selected for the interview process. It is important to realize that the types of questions that can be asked in the interview are highly restricted, because job interviews, if improperly performed, can subject an employer to legal liability. If a candidate is not hired based on his or her answer to—or refusal to answer—an inappropriate question, that candidate has the right to file a lawsuit.

The Equal Employment Opportunity Commission (EEOC) suggests that an employer consider the following questions in deciding whether to include a particular question on an employment application or in a job interview:

- Does this question tend to screen out minorities or females?
- Is the answer needed in order to judge this individual's competence for performance of the job?
- Are there alternative, nondiscriminatory ways to judge the person's qualifications?

As a manager, you must be very careful in your selection of questions to ask in an interview. In all cases, it is important to remember that the job itself dictates what is an allowable question. Questions should be written down and followed. In addition, supervisors, coworkers, and others who may participate in the interview process should be trained to avoid questions that could increase the liability of the facility.

Generally, age is considered to be irrelevant in most hiring decisions; therefore, date-of-birth questions are improper. Age is a sensitive preemployment question, because the Age Discrimination in Employment Act protects employees 40 years old and older. It is permissible to ask an applicant to state his or her age if he or she is younger than 18 years old because that age group is permitted to work only a limited number of hours each week. It is also important when hiring bartenders and other servers of alcohol, who must be above a state's minimum age for serving alcohol.

Race, religion, and national origin questions are also inappropriate, as is the practice of requiring that photographs of the candidate be submitted prior to or after an interview.

Questions about physical traits such as height and weight requirements have been found to violate the law because they eliminated disproportionate numbers of female, Asian-American, and Spanish-surnamed applicants.

If a job does not require a particular level of education, it is improper to ask questions about an applicant's educational background. Applicants can be asked about their education and credentials if these are indeed bona fide occupational qualifications. Certainly, it is allowable to ask a potential hotel controller if he or she has a degree in accounting, and which school granted that degree. Asking a potential table busser for the same information would be inappropriate.

It is permissible to ask an applicant if he or she uses drugs or smokes. It is also allowable to ask a candidate if he or she is willing to submit to a voluntary drug test as a condition of employment.

Questions concerning whether an applicant owns a home potentially discriminate against those individuals who do not own their own homes. Questions concerning the type of discharge received by an ex-military applicant are improper, because a high proportion of other than honorable discharges are given to minorities.

Safe questions can be asked about a candidate's current employment, former employment, and job references. In most cases, questions asked on both the application and in the interview should focus on the applicant's job skills, and nothing else. Figure 7.3 contains some guidelines, developed by the EEOC, for asking appropriate interview questions.

Subject	Inappropriate Questions (May Not Ask or Require)	Appropriate Questions (May Ask or Require)
Gender or marital status	• Gender (on application form) • Mr., Miss, Mrs., Ms.? • Married, divorced, single, separated? • Number and ages of children • Pregnancy, actual or intended • Maiden name, former name	• In checking your work record, do we need another name for identification?
Race	• Race? • Color of skin, eyes, hair, etc. • Request for photograph	
National Origin	• Questions about place of birth, ancestry, mother tongue, national origin of parents or spouse. • What is your native language? • How did you learn to speak [language] fluently?	• If job-related, what foreign languages do you speak?
Citizenship, immigration status	• Of what country are you a citizen? • Are you a native-born U.S. citizen? • Questions about naturalization of applicant, spouse, or parents.	• If selected are you able to start work with us on a specific date? If not, when would you be able to start? • If hired, can you show proof that you are eligible to work in the United States?
Religion	• Religious affiliation or preference • Religious holidays observed • Membership in religious organizations	• Can you observe regularly required days and hours of work? • Are there any days or hours of the week that you are not able to work? • Are there any holidays that you are not able to work?
Age	• How old are you? • Date of birth	• Are you 21 or older? (for positions serving alcohol)
Disability	• Do you have any disabilities? • Have you ever been treated for (certain) diseases? • Are you healthy?	
Questions that may discriminate against minorities	• Have you ever been arrested? • List all clubs, societies, and lodges to which you belong. • Do you own a car? (unless required for the job) • Type of military discharge. • Questions regarding credit ratings, financial status, wage garnishment, home ownership.	• Have you ever been convicted of a crime? If yes, give details (If crime is job-related, as embezzlement is to handling money, you may refuse to hire). • List membership in professional organizations relevant to job performance. • Military service: dates, branch of service, education, and experience (if job-related).

Figure 7.3 Guidelines for conducting a job interview.
Source: Jack E. Miller, John R. Walker, Karen Eich Drummond, Supervision in the Hospitality Industry, *Fifth Edition. Hoboken, NJ: John Wiley & Sons, Inc., 2007.*

Preemployment Testing

Preemployment testing is a common way to improve the employee screening process. Test results can be used, for example, to measure the relative strength of two candidates.

In the hospitality industry, preemployment testing will generally fall into one of the following categories:

- Skills tests
- Psychological tests
- Drug screening tests

Skills tests were among the first tools used by managers to screen applicants in the employment process. In the hospitality industry, skills tests can include activities such as typing tests for office workers, computer application tests for those who use word processing or spreadsheet tools, or food production tasks to test culinary artists.

Psychological testing can include personality tests, tests designed to predict performance, or tests of mental ability. For both skills tests and psychological tests, the important rule to remember is this:

> If the test does not have documented validity and reliability, the results of the tests should not be used for hiring decisions.

Preemployment drug testing is allowable in most states, and can be a very effective tool for reducing insurance rates and potential worker liability issues. A drug-free environment tends to attract better-quality employment candidates, with the resulting impact of a higher-quality workforce. There are, however, strict guidelines in some states as to when and how people can be tested. A document with language similar to that found in Figure 7.4 should be completed by each candidate prior to drug testing, and the signed document should be kept on file with the employee's application form.

If preemployment drug testing is to be used, care must be taken to ensure the accuracy of the testing. In some cases, applicants whose erroneous test results have cost them a job have successfully sued the employer. The laws surrounding mandatory drug testing are complex. If you elect to implement either a preemployment or postemployment drug-testing program, it is best to first seek advice from an attorney who specializes in labor employment law in your state.

Employee Consent Form for Drug Testing

I agree, fully and voluntarily to submit to a urinalysis or blood test conducted by _____ for a drug screen as a condition of my consideration for employment. I understand that failing to meet the standards established for this test may result in the disqualification of further consideration of my application. Lastly, I understand that these results will be used only as the basis for an employment decision and will not be shared with any individual or organization outside the company.

The undersigned represents that he or she has read this information in its entirety and understands it.

Employee Signature _____   Date _____

Employer Witness Signature _____   Date _____

Figure 7.4 Employee consent form for drug testing.
Adapted from Foodservice Safety and Security Managers Handbook, *by the National Restaurant Association Educational Foundation. Reprinted with permission.*

Background Checks

Increasingly, hospitality employers are utilizing background checks prior to hiring workers in selected positions. It has been estimated that as many as 30 percent of all resumes and employment applications include some level of falsification. Because this is true, employers are spending more time and financial resources to validate information supplied by a potential employee. Common verification points include the following:

Name
Social Security number
Address history
Education/training
Criminal background
Credit reports

LEGALESE

Negligent hiring: Failure on the part of an employer to exercise reasonable care in the selection of employees.

Background checks, like preemployment testing, can leave an employer subject to litigation if the information secured during a check is false or is used in a way that violates employment law. In addition, if the information is improperly disclosed to third parties, it could violate the employee's right to privacy. Not conducting background checks on some positions can, however, subject the employer to potential litigation under the doctrine of *negligent hiring*.

Consider the case of Holly Rosecrans. Ms. Rosecrans is the assistant general manager of a country club in Florida. One of her responsibilities is the selection and training of pool lifeguards, which are required in her facility by local statute. Each lifeguard must be certified in cardiopulmonary resuscitation (CPR). Ms. Rosecrans interviews a candidate who lists the successful completion of a CPR course as part of his educational background. If Ms. Rosecrans does not verify the accuracy of the candidate's statement, and if a death results because the lifeguard did not have CPR training, the club might well be held liable for the death of the swimmer.

Using background checks as a screening tool does involve some risk, as well as some responsibility. Employers should search only for information that has a direct bearing on the position a candidate is applying for. In addition, if a candidate is denied employment on the basis of information found in a background check, the employer should provide a candidate with a copy of that report. Sometimes, candidates can help verify or explain the content of their own background checks. Reporting agencies can make mistakes, and if you rely on obviously false information to make a hiring decision, it may put your organization at risk.

In all cases, a candidate for employment should be required to sign a consent form authorizing an employer to conduct a background check. Figure 7.5 is a sample consent form that could be used to document this authorization.

References

In the past, employment references were a very popular tool for managers to use in the screening process. But in today's litigious society they are much more difficult to obtain. Although many organizations still seek information from past employers about an employee's previous work performance, few sophisticated companies will divulge such information. It is important to note that some employers have been held liable for inaccurate comments that have been made about past employees. In addition, there are companies that specialize in providing job searchers with a confidential, comprehensive verification of employment references from former employers. Thus, employers are becoming more cautious about supplying information on employees who have left their organization.

To help minimize the risk of litigation related to reference checks, it is best to secure the applicant's permission in writing before contacting an ex-employer. Employers must be extremely cautious in both giving and receiving reference

---

Employee Consent Form for Background Checks and Application Verification

I agree, fully and voluntarily to checks related to:

1. (e.g., Criminal History)

2. (e.g., School Attendance Record)

as well as checks on information I have supplied in my employment application.

I understand that failing to meet the standards established for these checks as well as falsification of information on my application may result in the disqualification of further consideration of my application. Lastly, I understand that the results of these background checks and the accuracy of my application will be used only as the basis for an employment decision and will not be shared with any individual or organization outside the company.

The undersigned represents that he or she has read this information in its entirety and understands it.

Employee Signature _____   Date _____

Employer Signature _____   Date _____

Figure 7.5 Employee consent form for background checks.
Adapted from Foodservice Safety and Security Managers Handbook *by the National Restaurant Association Educational Foundation. Reprinted with permission.*

information. Employers are usually protected if they give a truthful reference; however, that does not mean these employers will be spared the expense of defending a *defamation* case brought by an ex-employee.

If, for example, an employer giving a reference states that an ex-employee was terminated because he or she "didn't get along" with his or her coworkers, the employer might have to be able to prove the truthfulness of the statement, as well as show proof that all of the blame for the difficulties were the responsibility of the ex-employee.

To minimize the risk of a lawsuit, you should never reply to a request for information about one of your ex-employees without a copy of that employee's signed release authorizing the reference check. How much you choose to disclose about an ex-employee is your decision; however, your answers should be honest and defendable. Also, it is best never to disclose personal information such as marital difficulties, financial problems, or serious illness, because you could be sued for invasion of privacy. Many employers today give only the following information about past employees:

> Employer's name
> Ex-employer's name
> Date(s) of employment
> Job title
> Name and title of person supplying the information

If a prospective employee provides letters of reference, always call the authors of reference letters to ensure that they did in fact write them. When possible, it is best to put any request for reference information in writing, and ask that the response be in written form. If a verbal response is all you can get, document the conversation; write down as much of the dialogue as possible, including the name of the party you spoke to and the date and time the contact occurred.

Even with authorization, many employers are reluctant to give out information about former employees. If this happens, simply ask if the company would rehire that worker. The response to that question, combined with the information received from other employers, should help to determine the accuracy of the information given by the applicant.

> **LEGALESE**
>
> **Defamation:** False statements that cause someone to be held in contempt, lowered in the estimation of the community, or to lose employment status or earnings or otherwise suffer a damaged reputation.

The selection of the right employee for the right job is a specialized area of human resources, and the hospitality manager will often be able to rely on a human resources department or personnel director for assistance when undertaking this important task. For the independent entrepreneur, it is critical that the entire employee selection process be reviewed by an expert in employment law and continually monitored for compliance with established procedures.

Wording of Classified Advertisements

One final aspect of employee selection that you must be aware of involves the wording of classified ads that you might place in newspapers or journals when announcing a job opening. As with job descriptions and qualifications, it is important that the terms you use in a classified ad do not exclude or discriminate against individuals. Federal law prohibits the use of words or phrases that might prevent certain types of people from applying for an advertised position. Phrases to avoid include references to age ("ages 20 to 30"), sex ("men" or "women"), national origin, and religion. There are a limited number of cases where a bona fide job qualification might limit the type of person who could apply, and that can be mentioned. In general, however, employers should focus their classified ads on a description of the job and any applicable educational, licensing, or background requirements needed.

7.2 DISCRIMINATION IN THE SELECTION PROCESS

Although employers are free to hire employees as they see fit, they are not free to unlawfully discriminate against people in their employment selection. Employment discrimination laws have been established to protect certain classes of people from unfair or exclusionary hiring practices.

The Fifth and Fourteenth Amendments of the U.S. Constitution limit the power of the federal and state governments to discriminate. The Fifth Amendment has an explicit requirement that the federal government not deprive any individual of "life, liberty, or property," without the due process of the law. Though discrimination by employers in the private sector is not directly addressed in the Constitution, it has become subject to a growing body of federal and state laws, which were passed in recognition of the personal freedoms guaranteed by the Constitution. Although many antidiscrimination statutes affect employee selection, the most significant are:

Civil Rights Act of 1964; Title VII
Americans with Disabilities Act; Title I
Age Discrimination in Employment Act

Civil Rights Act of 1964, Title VII

LEGALESE

Interstate commerce: Commercial trading or the transportation of persons or property between or among states.

Title VII of the Civil Rights Act of 1964, and its resulting amendments, applies to employers with 15 or more employees who are engaged in *interstate commerce*. Figure 7.6 presents the original language of the bill that relates to employee selection.

The act prohibits discrimination based on race, color, religion, sex, or national origin. Sex includes pregnancy, childbirth, or related medical conditions. The act makes it illegal for employers to discriminate in hiring, and in setting the terms and conditions of employment. Labor organizations are also prohibited from basing membership or union classifications on race, color, religion, sex, or national origin. The law also prohibits employers from retaliating against employees or candidates who file charges of

Civil Rights Act of 1964
UNLAWFUL EMPLOYMENT PRACTICES

SEC. 2000e-2. [Section 703]

(a) It shall be an unlawful employment practice for an employer

(1) to fail or refuse to hire or to discharge any individual, or otherwise to discriminate against any individual with respect to his compensation, terms, conditions, or privileges of employment, because of such individual's race, color, religion, sex, or national origin; or

(2) to limit, segregate, or classify his employees or applicants for employment in any way which would deprive or tend to deprive any individual of employment opportunities or otherwise adversely affect his status as an employee, because of such individual's race, color, religion, sex, or national origin.

(b) It shall be an unlawful employment practice for an employment agency to fail or refuse to refer for employment, or otherwise to discriminate against, any individual because of his race, color, religion, sex, or national origin, or to classify or refer for employment any individual on the basis of his race, color, religion, sex, or national origin.

(c) It shall be an unlawful employment practice for a labor organization

(1) to exclude or to expel from its membership, or otherwise to discriminate against, any individual because of his race, color, religion, sex, or national origin;

(2) to limit, segregate, or classify its membership or applicants for membership, or to classify or fail or refuse to refer for employment any individual, in any way which would deprive or tend to deprive any individual of employment opportunities, or would limit such employment opportunities or otherwise adversely affect his status as an employee or as an applicant for employment, because of such individual's race, color, religion, sex, or national origin; or

(3) to cause or attempt to cause an employer to discriminate against an individual in violation of this section.

Figure 7.6 Excerpt from the Civil Rights Act of 1964.

discrimination against them, who refuse to comply with a discriminatory policy, or who participate in an investigation of discrimination charges against the employer.

One outcome of the Civil Rights Act was the formation of the Equal Employment Opportunity Commission, which oversees and enforces federal laws regulating employer/employee relationships. The EEOC investigates complaints by employees who think they have been discriminated against. Businesses that are found to have discriminated can be ordered to compensate the employee(s) for damages such as lost wages, attorney fees, and punitive damages.

In later amendments, the Civil Rights Act was expanded to include *affirmative action* requirements. Affirmative action constitutes a good-faith effort by employees to address past and/or present discrimination through a variety of specific, results-oriented, procedures. This is a step beyond equal opportunity laws like Title VII, which simply ban discriminatory practices. State and local governments, agencies of the federal government, and federal contractors and subcontractors with contracts of $50,000 or more—including colleges and universities—are required by federal law to implement affirmative action programs.

Employers have used a variety of techniques for implementing affirmative action plans. These include:

- Active recruiting to expand the pool of candidates for job openings.
- Revising the selection tools and criteria to ensure their relevance to job performance.
- Establishing goals and timetables for hiring underrepresented groups.

LEGALESE

Affirmative action:
A federally mandated requirement that employers who meet certain criteria must actively seek to fairly employ recognized classes of workers. (Some state and local legislatures have also enacted affirmative action requirements.)

Originally, affirmative action activities were intended to correct discrimination in the hiring and promotion of African Americans and other people of color. Now, affirmative action protections are being applied to women, and some government jurisdictions have extended affirmative action provisions to older people, the disabled, and Vietnam-era veterans. The goal of affirmative action is to broaden the pool of candidates and encourage hiring based on sound, job-related, criteria. The result is a workforce with greater diversity and potential for all.

In addition to the Civil Rights Act, many states also have their own civil rights laws, which prohibit discrimination. Sometimes, the state laws are more inclusive than the Civil Rights Act, in that they expand protection to workers or employment candidates in categories not covered under the federal Civil Rights Act, such as age, marital status, sexual orientation, and certain types of physical or mental disabilities. State civil rights laws may also have stricter penalties for violations, including fines and/or jail time. As a hospitality manager, you should know the provisions of your state's civil rights law.

≫ ANALYZE THE SITUATION 7.2

JETTA WONG IS THE owner and manager of the Golden Dragon oriental restaurant. The restaurant is large, inexpensive, and enjoys an excellent reputation. Business is good, and the restaurant serves a diverse clientele.

Ms. Wong places a classified ad for the table busser in the employment section of her local newspaper. The response is good, and Ms. Wong narrows the field of potential candidates to two. One is the same ethnic background as Ms. Wong and the rest of the staff. The second candidate is Danielle Hidalgo, the daughter of a Mexican citizen and an American citizen. Ms. Hidalgo was born and raised in the United States.

While both candidates are pleasant, Ms. Wong offers the position to the candidate who matches the background of the restaurant and Ms. Wong. Her rationale is that, since both candidates are equal in ability, she has a right to select the candidate she feels will best suit her business. Because it is an oriental restaurant, Ms. Wong feels diners will expect to see oriental servers and bussers. No one was discriminated against, she maintains, because Ms. Hidalgo was not denied a job on the basis of race, but rather on the basis of what was best for business. Ms. Wong simply selected her preference from among two equal candidates. Ms. Wong relates her decision to Ms. Hidalgo.

Ms. Hidalgo maintains that she was not selected because of her Hispanic ethnic background. She threatens to file a charge with the EEOC unless she is offered employment.

1. Do you think Ms. Hidalgo was denied the position because of her ethnicity?

2. In the situation described here, does Ms. Wong have the right to consider race as a bona fide occupational qualification?

3. How should Ms. Wong advertise jobs in the future to avoid charges of discrimination?

Americans with Disabilities Act

On July 26, 1990, the Americans with Disabilities Act (ADA) was enacted. The ADA prohibits discrimination against people with disabilities in the areas of public accommodations, transportation, telecommunications, and employment. The ADA is a five-part piece of legislation; Title I focuses primarily on employment.

There are three different groups of individuals who are protected under the ADA:

1. An individual with a physical or mental impairment that substantially limits a major life activity. Some examples of what constitutes a "major life activity" under the act are: seeing, hearing, talking, walking, reading, learning, breathing, taking care of oneself, lifting, sitting, and standing.
2. A person who has a record of a disability.
3. A person who is "regarded as" having a disability.

Employers cannot reduce an employee's pay simply because he or she is disabled, nor can they refuse to hire a disabled candidate if, with reasonable accommodation, it is possible for the candidate to perform the job. Employers are also required to post notices of the Americans with Disabilities Act and its provisions in a location where they can be seen by all employees.

Even with the passage of the ADA, an employer does not have to hire a disabled applicant who is not qualified to do a job. The employer can still select the most qualified candidate, provided that no applicant was eliminated from consideration because of his or her qualified disability.

Although the law in this area is changing rapidly, the following conditions, among others, currently meet the criteria for a qualified disability, and are protected under the ADA:

- AIDS
- Cancer
- Cerebral palsy
- Tuberculosis
- Heart disease
- Hearing or visual impairments
- Alcoholism
- Epilepsy
- Paralysis

Conditions that are not currently covered under ADA include:

- Kleptomania
- Disorders caused by the use of illegal drugs
- Compulsive gambling
- Sexual behavior disorders
- Nonchronic conditions of short duration such as a sprain, broken limb, or the flu

The ADA has changed the way employers select employees. Questions on job applications and during interviews that cannot be asked include the following:

- Have you ever been hospitalized?
- Are you taking prescription drugs?

- Have you ever been treated for drug addiction or alcoholism?
- Have you ever filed a workers' compensation insurance claim?
- Do you have any physical defects, disabilities, or impairments that may affect your performance in the position for which you are applying/interviewing?

In situations where a disabled person could perform the duties of a particular job, but some aspect of the job or work facility would prevent the applicant from doing so, the employer may be required to make a reasonable accommodation for the worker.

An employer has provided reasonable accommodation when it has made existing facilities readily accessible to individuals with mobility impairments or other disabilities, and restructured a job in the most accommodating manner possible to allow a disabled individual to perform it. The employer is not obligated to provide a reasonable accommodation where such accommodation would result in undue hardship to the employer. Generally speaking, an undue hardship occurs when the expense of accommodating the worker is excessive or would disrupt the natural work environment. The law in this area is vague; thus, any employer who maintains that accommodating a worker with a disability would impose an undue hardship should be prepared to document such an assertion. After investigation, the EEOC issues a "right to sue" letter to an employee if it concludes that an employer is in violation of the ADA.

LEGALLY MANAGING AT WORK:

Accommodating Disabled Employees

To reduce the risk of an ADA noncompliance charge related to reasonable accommodation, follow these guidelines:

1. Can the applicant perform the essential functions of the job with or without reasonable accommodation? (You can ask the applicant this question.)

   If no, then he or she is not qualified and is therefore not protected by the ADA. If yes, go to question 2.

2. Is the necessary accommodation reasonable? To answer this question, ask yourself the following: Will this accommodation create an undue financial or administrative hardship on the business?

   If yes, you do not have to provide unreasonable accommodations. If no, go to question 3.

3. Will this accommodation or the hiring of the person with the disability create a direct threat to the health or safety of other employees or guests in the workplace?

   If yes, you are not required to make the accommodation and have fulfilled your obligation under the ADA.

Search the Web **7.1**

Go to www.eeoc.gov.

1. Under About EEOC, select: Laws, Regulations, Guidance, & MOUs.
2. Select: EEOC Policy Guidance.
3. Select: Enforcement Guidances and Related Documents.
4. Select: Revised Enforcement Guidance: Reasonable Accommodation and Undue Hardship Under the Americans With Disabilities Act.
5. From the document displayed, determine:
   a. What must an employer do after receiving a request for a reasonable accommodation?
   b. Is the restructuring of a job to meet the needs of a disabled person considered a reasonable accommodation?

For additional information on job accommodation under the ADA, log on to the Job Accommodation Network for the ADA at janweb.icdi.wvu.edu.

One ADA provision that foodservice employers should be aware of concerns employees and job applicants who have infectious and communicable diseases. Each year, the U.S. Department of Health and Human Services publishes a list of communicable diseases that, if passed on through the handling of food, could put a foodservice operation at risk. Employers have the right not to assign to or hire an individual who has one of the identified diseases for a position that involves the handling of food, but only if there is no reasonable accommodation that could be made to eliminate such a risk.

Age Discrimination in Employment Act

The Age Discrimination in Employment Act of 1967 (ADEA) protects individuals who are 40 years of age or older from employment discrimination based on age. The ADEA's protections apply to both employees and job applicants. Under the ADEA, it is unlawful to discriminate against a person because of his or her age with respect to any term, condition, or privilege of employment—including hiring, firing, promotion, layoff, compensation, benefits, job assignments, and training.

The ADEA applies to employers with 20 or more employees, as well as to labor unions and governmental agencies. The ADEA makes it unlawful to include age preferences, limitations, or specifications in job notices or advertisements. As a narrow exception to that general rule, a job notice or advertisement may specify an age limit in the rare circumstances where age is shown to be a bona fide occupational qualification (BFOQ) reasonably necessary to the essence of the business, or a minimum age qualification to legally perform the job.

7.3 VERIFICATION OF ELIGIBILITY TO WORK

Even after an employer has legally selected an applicant for employment, the law requires the employer to take at least one more action before an employee can begin work. The employer must determine that the worker is, in fact, legally entitled to hold the job. Verification of employment status takes two major forms. The first is verification of eligibility to work, the second is verification of compliance with the child labor laws.

Immigration Reform and Control Act

The Immigration Reform and Control Act (IRCA) was passed in 1986. The act prohibits employers from knowingly hiring illegal persons for work in the United States, either because the individual is in the country illegally or because his or her immigration and residency status does not allow employment. The law also applies to employers who, after the date of hire, determine that an employee is not legally authorized to work but continue to employ that individual.

Under provisions of the IRCA, employers are required to verify that all employees hired after November 6, 1986, are legally authorized to work in the United States. Unlike many other federal laws, IRCA applies to organizations of any size and to both full- and part-time employees. The act requires that when an applicant is hired, a Form I-9 must be completed (see Figure 7.7).

Form I-9 is often misunderstood. Its purpose is to verify both an employee's identity and his or her eligibility to work; thus, it serves a dual role. The Department of Homeland Security via USCIS (United States Citizenship and Immigration Services) imposes severe penalties on employers who do not have properly completed I-9s for all employees. USCIS has been very meticulous in its audits, issuing large fines for even minor errors such as incorrect dates.

Every employee hired is required to complete an I-9 when beginning work; specifically, the employee is required to fill out Section 1 of the form. The employer is then responsible for reviewing and ensuring that Section 1 is fully and properly completed. At that time, the employer will complete Section 2 of the I-9 form.

Figure 7.8 details the documents that can be used in completing an I-9. It is important to note that the documents used to verify eligibility and identity must be originals. To ensure compliance, employers will often remind individuals to bring necessary identification documents with them on their first day of employment. If an employee cannot produce the appropriate documents within 21 days of being hired, the employer is obligated by law to terminate that individual.

The employer's part of the Form I-9 must be completed within three business days, or at the time of hire if the employment is for less than three days. Each completed I-9 should be kept for three years after the date of employment, or one year after the employee's termination, whichever is longer. Keep all I-9s readily available, as they must be presented to the USCIS within 72 hours upon request.

An employer's good-faith effort in complying with the verification and record-keeping requirements will ensure its defense if any charges surface that the organization knowingly and willingly hired a person who was not legally authorized to work. It is prudent practice to follow the letter of the law in this area, as fines as high as $10,000 per illegal employee can be levied against the business by the government. To ensure compliance, more and more hospitality employers are using the e-verify system found at: www.uscis.gov.

Department of Homeland Security
U.S. Citizenship and Immigration Services

OMB No. 1615-0047; Expires 03/31/07
Employment Eligibility Verification

INSTRUCTIONS
PLEASE READ ALL INSTRUCTIONS CAREFULLY BEFORE COMPLETING THIS FORM.

Anti-Discrimination Notice. It is illegal to discriminate against any individual (other than an alien not authorized to work in the U.S.) in hiring, discharging, or recruiting or referring for a fee because of that individual's national origin or citizenship status. It is illegal to discriminate against work eligible individuals. Employers **CANNOT** specify which document(s) they will accept from an employee. The refusal to hire an individual because of a future expiration date may also constitute illegal discrimination.

Section 1- Employee.
All employees, citizens and noncitizens, hired after November 6, 1986, must complete Section 1 of this form at the time of hire, which is the actual beginning of employment. **The employer is responsible for ensuring that Section 1 is timely and properly completed.**

Preparer/Translator Certification. The Preparer/Translator Certification must be completed if Section 1 is prepared by a person other than the employee. A preparer/translator may be used only when the employee is unable to complete Section 1 on his/her own. However, the employee must still sign Section 1 personally.

Section 2 - Employer.
For the purpose of completing this form, the term "employer" includes those recruiters and referrers for a fee who are agricultural associations, agricultural employers or farm labor contractors.

Employers must complete Section 2 by examining evidence of identity and employment eligibility within three (3) business days of the date employment begins. If employees are authorized to work, but are unable to present the required document(s) within three business days, they must present a receipt for the application of the document(s) within three business days and the actual document(s) within ninety (90) days. However, if employers hire individuals for a duration of less than three business days, Section 2 must be completed at the time employment begins. **Employers must record: 1)** document title; **2)** issuing authority; **3)** document number, **4)** expiration date, if any; and **5)** the date employment begins. Employers must sign and date the certification. Employees must present original documents. Employers may, but are not required to, photocopy the document(s) presented. These photocopies may only be used for the verification process and must be retained with the I-9. **However, employers are still responsible for completing the I-9.**

Section 3 - Updating and Reverification.
Employers must complete Section 3 when updating and/or reverifying the I-9. Employers must reverify employment eligibility of their employees on or before the expiration date recorded in Section 1. Employers **CANNOT** specify which document(s) they will accept from an employee.

- If an employee's name has changed at the time this form is being updated/reverified, complete Block A.

- If an employee is rehired within three (3) years of the date this form was originally completed and the employee is still eligible to be employed on the same basis as previously indicated on this form (updating), complete Block B and the signature block.

- If an employee is rehired within three (3) years of the date this form was originally completed and the employee's work authorization has expired **or** if a current employee's work authorization is about to expire (reverification), complete Block B and:

- examine any document that reflects that the employee is authorized to work in the U.S. (see List A **or** C),

- record the document title, document number and expiration date (if any) in Block C, and

- complete the signature block.

Photocopying and Retaining Form I-9. A blank I-9 may be reproduced, provided both sides are copied. The Instructions must be available to all employees completing this form. Employers must retain completed I-9s for three (3) years after the date of hire or one (1) year after the date employment ends, whichever is later.

For more detailed information, you may refer to the Department of Homeland Security (DHS) Handbook for Employers, (Form M-274). You may obtain the handbook at your local U.S. Citizenship and Immigration Services (USCIS) office.

Privacy Act Notice. The authority for collecting this information is the Immigration Reform and Control Act of 1986, Pub. L. 99-603 (8 USC 1324a).

This information is for employers to verify the eligibility of individuals for employment to preclude the unlawful hiring, or recruiting or referring for a fee, of aliens who are not authorized to work in the United States.

This information will be used by employers as a record of their basis for determining eligibility of an employee to work in the United States. The form will be kept by the employer and made available for inspection by officials of the U.S. Immigration and Customs Enforcement, Department of Labor and Office of Special Counsel for Immigration Related Unfair Employment Practices.

Submission of the information required in this form is voluntary. However, an individual may not begin employment unless this form is completed, since employers are subject to civil or criminal penalties if they do not comply with the Immigration Reform and Control Act of 1986.

Reporting Burden. We try to create forms and instructions that are accurate, can be easily understood and which impose the least possible burden on you to provide us with information. Often this is difficult because some immigration laws are very complex. Accordingly, the reporting burden for this collection of information is computed as follows: **1)** learning about this form, 5 minutes; **2)** completing the form, 5 minutes; and **3)** assembling and filing (recordkeeping) the form, 5 minutes, for an average of 15 minutes per response. If you have comments regarding the accuracy of this burden estimate, or suggestions for making this form simpler, you can write to U.S. Citizenship and Immigration Services, Regulatory Management Division, 111 Massachuetts Avenue, N.W., Washington, DC 20529. OMB No. 1615-0047.

NOTE: This is the 1991 edition of the Form I-9 that has been rebranded with a current printing date to reflect the recent transition from the INS to DHS and its components.

EMPLOYERS MUST RETAIN COMPLETED FORM I-9
PLEASE DO NOT MAIL COMPLETED FORM I-9 TO ICE OR USCIS

Form I-9 (Rev. 05/31/05)Y

Figure 7.7 Form I-9.

Department of Homeland Security
U.S. Citizenship and Immigration Services

OMB No. 1615-0047; Expires 03/31/07

Employment Eligibility Verification

Please read instructions carefully before completing this form. The instructions must be available during completion of this form. ANTI-DISCRIMINATION NOTICE: It is illegal to discriminate against work eligible individuals. Employers CANNOT specify which document(s) they will accept from an employee. The refusal to hire an individual because of a future expiration date may also constitute illegal discrimination.

Section 1. Employee Information and Verification. To be completed and signed by employee at the time employment begins.

Print Name: Last | First | Middle Initial | Maiden Name

Address (Street Name and Number) | Apt. # | Date of Birth (month/day/year)

City | State | Zip Code | Social Security #

I am aware that federal law provides for imprisonment and/or fines for false statements or use of false documents in connection with the completion of this form.

I attest, under penalty of perjury, that I am (check one of the following):
☐ A citizen or national of the United States
☐ A Lawful Permanent Resident (Alien #) A _____
☐ An alien authorized to work until _____
(Alien # or Admission #) _____

Employee's Signature | Date (month/day/year)

Preparer and/or Translator Certification. *(To be completed and signed if Section 1 is prepared by a person other than the employee.) I attest, under penalty of perjury, that I have assisted in the completion of this form and that to the best of my knowledge the information is true and correct.*

Preparer's/Translator's Signature | Print Name

Address (Street Name and Number, City, State, Zip Code) | Date (month/day/year)

Section 2. Employer Review and Verification. To be completed and signed by employer. Examine one document from List A OR examine one document from List B and one from List C, as listed on the reverse of this form, and record the title, number and expiration date, if any, of the document(s).

List A	OR	List B	AND	List C
Document title:				
Issuing authority:				
Document #:				
Expiration Date (if any):				
Document #:				
Expiration Date (if any):				

CERTIFICATION - I attest, under penalty of perjury, that I have examined the document(s) presented by the above-named employee, that the above-listed document(s) appear to be genuine and to relate to the employee named, that the employee began employment on (month/day/year) _____ **and that to the best of my knowledge the employee is eligible to work in the United States. (State employment agencies may omit the date the employee began employment.)**

Signature of Employer or Authorized Representative | Print Name | Title

Business or Organization Name | Address (Street Name and Number, City, State, Zip Code) | Date (month/day/year)

Section 3. Updating and Reverification. To be completed and signed by employer.

A. New Name (if applicable) | B. Date of Rehire (month/day/year) (if applicable)

C. If employee's previous grant of work authorization has expired, provide the information below for the document that establishes current employment eligibility. Document Title: | Document #: | Expiration Date (if any):

I attest, under penalty of perjury, that to the best of my knowledge, this employee is eligible to work in the United States, and if the employee presented document(s), the document(s) I have examined appear to be genuine and to relate to the individual.

Signature of Employer or Authorized Representative | Date (month/day/year)

NOTE: This is the 1991 edition of the Form I-9 that has been rebranded with a current printing date to reflect the recent transition from the INS to DHS and its components.

Form I-9 (Rev. 05/31/05)Y Page 2

Figure 7.7 *(Continued)*

LISTS OF ACCEPTABLE DOCUMENTS

LIST A		LIST B		LIST C
Documents that Establish Both Identity and Employment Eligibility	**OR**	**Documents that Establish Identity**	**AND**	**Documents that Establish Employment Eligibility**

LIST A

Documents that Establish Both Identity and Employment Eligibility

1. U.S. Passport (unexpired or expired)

2. Certificate of U.S. Citizenship *(Form N-560 or N-561)*

3. Certificate of Naturalization *(Form N-550 or N-570)*

4. Unexpired foreign passport, with *I-551 stamp or* attached *Form I-94* indicating unexpired employment authorization

5. Permanent Resident Card or Alien Registration Receipt Card with photograph *(Form I-151 or I-551)*

6. Unexpired Temporary Resident Card *(Form I-688)*

7. Unexpired Employment Authorization Card *(Form I-688A)*

8. Unexpired Reentry Permit *(Form I-327)*

9. Unexpired Refugee Travel Document *(Form 1-571)*

10. Unexpired Employment Authorization Document issued by DHS that contains a photograph *(Form I-688B)*

OR

LIST B

Documents that Establish Identity

1. Driver's license or ID card issued by a state or outlying possession of the United States provided it contains a photograph or information such as name, date of birth, gender, height, eye color and address

2. ID card issued by federal, state or local government agencies or entities, provided it contains a photograph or information such as name, date of birth, gender, height, eye color and address

3. School ID card with a photograph

4. Voter's registration card

5. U.S. Military card or draft record

6. Military dependent's ID card

7. U.S. Coast Guard Merchant Mariner Card

8. Native American tribal document

9. Driver's license issued by a Canadian government authority

For persons under age 18 who are unable to present a document listed above:

10. School record or report card

11. Clinic, doctor or hospital record

12. Day-care or nursery school record

AND

LIST C

Documents that Establish Employment Eligibility

1. U.S. social security card issued by the Social Security Administration *(other than a card stating it is not valid for employment)*

2. Certification of Birth Abroad issued by the Department of State *(Form FS-545 or Form DS-1350)*

3. Original or certified copy of a birth certificate issued by a state, county, municipal authority or outlying possession of the United States bearing an official seal

4. Native American tribal document

5. U.S. Citizen ID Card *(Form I-197)*

6. ID Card for use of Resident Citizen in the United States *(Form I-179)*

7. Unexpired employment authorization document issued by DHS *(other than those listed under List A)*

Illustrations of many of these documents appear in Part 8 of the Handbook for Employers (M-274)

Form I-9 (Rev. 05/31/05)Y Page 3

Figure 7.7 *(Continued)*

DOCUMENTS THAT ESTABLISH EMPLOYMENT ELIGIBILITY

Social Security card
An original or certified copy of a birth certificate issued by a state, county, or municipal authority
Unexpired INS employment authorization
Unexpired reentry permit (INS Form I-327)
Unexpired Refugee Travel Document (INS Form I-571)
Certificate of Birth issued by the Department of State (Form FS-545)
Certificate of Birth Abroad issued by the Department of State (Form DS-1350)
United States Citizen identification (INS Form I-197)
Native American tribal document
Identification used by Resident Citizen in the United States

DOCUMENTS THAT ESTABLISH IDENTITY ONLY

State driver's license or identification card containing a photograph
School or university identification card with photograph
Voter's registration card
United States military identification card or draft record
Identification card issued by federal, state, or local governmental agencies
Military dependent's identification card
Native American tribal documents
United States Coast Guard Merchant Mariner card
Driver's license issued by a Canadian government authority

DOCUMENTS THAT ESTABLISH IDENTITY AND EMPLOYMENT ELIGIBILITY

Current United States passport
Alien Registration Receipt Card (INS Form I-151.)
Resident Alien Card (INS Form I-551), which must contain a photograph of the bearer
Temporary Resident Card (INS Form I-688)
Employment Authorization Card (INS Form I-688A)

Figure 7.8 Form I-9 qualifying documents.

Fair Labor Standards Act of 1938

The Fair Labor Standards Act of 1938 (FLSA) protects young workers from employment that might interfere with their educational opportunities or be detrimental to their health or well-being. It covers all workers who are engaged in or producing goods for interstate commerce or who are employed in certain enterprises. Essentially, the law establishes that youths 18 years and older may perform any job, hazardous or not, for unlimited hours, subject to minimum wage and overtime requirements.

Children aged 16 and 17 may work at any time for unlimited hours in all jobs not declared hazardous by the U.S. Department of Labor. Hazardous occupations include working with explosives and radioactive materials; operating certain power-driven woodworking, metalworking, bakery, and paper-products machinery; operating various types of power-driven saws and guillotine shears; operating most power-driven hoisting apparatuses including nonautomatic elevators, forklifts, or cranes; most jobs in slaughtering, meat-packing, and rendering plants; the operation of power-driven meat-processing machines when performed in wholesale, retail, or service establishments; most jobs in excavation, logging, and sawmilling; roofing, wrecking, demolition, and shipbreaking; operating motor vehicles or working as outside helpers on motor vehicles; and most jobs in the manufacturing of bricks, tiles, and similar products.

Youths aged 14 and 15 may work in various jobs outside school hours under the following conditions:

- No more than three hours on a school day, with a limit of 18 hours in a school week.

- No more than eight hours on a nonschool day, with a limit of 40 hours in a nonschool week.

- They cannot work before 7:00 A.M. or after 7:00 P.M., except from June 1 through Labor Day, when the evening hour is extended to 9:00 P.M.

- A break must be provided after five contiguous hours of work.

Workers 14 and 15 years of age may be employed in a variety of hospitality jobs, including cashiering, waiting on tables, washing dishes, and preparing salads and other food (although cooking is permitted only at snack bars, soda fountains, lunch counters, and cafeteria-style counters), but not in positions deemed hazardous by the U.S. Department of Labor. As with other types of employment law, there are stiff penalties for employers who violate provisions of the Fair Labor Standards Act. Employers can be fined between $1,000 for first-time violations and $3,000 for third violations. Repeat offenders can be subject to fines of $10,000, and even jail terms.

All states have child labor laws as well. Employers in most states are required to keep on file documents and/or permits verifying the age of minor employees. When both state and federal child labor laws apply, the law setting the more stringent standard must be observed. Federal child labor laws are enforced by the Wage and Hour Division of the U.S. Labor Department's Employment Standards Administration. State and local child labor laws can vary, so it is best to confirm the specifics of the child labor laws in your own state by contacting your local state employment agency.

7.4 THE EMPLOYMENT RELATIONSHIP

The laws related to employment, like those in other areas, are fluid, and they change to reflect society's view of what is "fair" and "just," for both the *employer* and the *employee*. For example, in 1945, an employer in the United States could refuse to hire an individual on the basis of his or her race or religion. The employer would have had no fear of liability for such a decision, either from the government or the potential employee. Today, a decision to refuse employment on the basis of race or religion would subject the employer to legal liability both from the government and the spurned job candidate.

At-Will Employment

The right of employers to hire and terminate employees as they see fit is still a fundamental right of doing business in the United States. In most states, the relationship you create when you hire a worker is one of *at-will employment.*

Simply put, the doctrine of at-will employment allows an employer to hire or dismiss an employee at anytime, if the employer feels it is in the best interest of the business. However, employers are still subject to the antidiscrimination laws reviewed earlier in this chapter (and addressed further in Chapter 8, "Legally Managing Employees"). Assume, for example, that you have legally hired four full-time bartenders for a club you manage. Business becomes slow, and you elect to terminate one of the bartenders. The doctrine of at-will employment allows you to do so. Further, the doctrine allows you to reduce your bartender staff even if you have not experienced a downturn in business. You might elect to do so if you felt that you could secure the services of a better bartender, should you need one. Generally speaking, any worker can be fired for cause (i.e., misconduct associated with the job). The at-will employment doctrine allows employers to dismiss a worker without cause.

LEGALESE

Employer: An individual or entity that pays wages or a salary in exchange for a worker's services.

LEGALESE

Employee: An individual who is hired to provide services to an employer in exchange for wages or a salary.

LEGALESE

At-will employment: An employment relationship whereby employers have a right to hire any employee, whenever they choose, and to dismiss an employee for or without cause, at any time; the employee also has the right to work for the employer or not, or to terminate the relationship at any time.

As an employer, your actions can affect the at-will employment status of your workers (e.g., by explicitly entering into an employment contract or making promises to keep an employee on for a year). In order to preserve the maximum flexibility for your business, it is important that you maintain your at-will employment status to cover all staff members that you select and manage. The scope of the at-will employment doctrine varies among different states, so you should familiarize yourself with the requirements placed on employers in the state in which you operate. These requirements are available from the state agency responsible for monitoring employer/employee relationships.

Labor Unions and Collective Bargaining

LEGALESE

Collective bargaining agreement (CBA):
A formal contract between an employer and a group of employees that establishes the rights and responsibilities of both parties in their employment relationship.

In some hotels and businesses, certain categories of employees may belong to an organized labor union. Unions were formed to protect the rights of workers and to establish specific job conditions that would be agreed to and carried out by employers and employees. In this type of arrangement, a group of employees will elect to make one collective employment agreement with an employer that will outline specific characteristics of their job position, such as the wage, hourly rate of pay, or limits on the hours per day or week that can be worked. The agreement would cover anyone employed in that position. This type of employment agreement is called a *collective bargaining agreement (CBA)*, and can also be referred to as a "union contract."

The terms and conditions set forth in a CBA are developed using a process of collective bargaining between the employer and employees. Generally, the members of a labor union working for a specific company (or industry) will elect a representative, who will negotiate the terms and conditions of a collective bargaining agreement for the entire group. The bargaining process is carried out according to rules established by the National Labor Relations Act of 1935, which guarantees the right of employees to organize and bargain collectively, or to refrain from collective bargaining. To enforce this act and oversee the relationship between employers and organized labor, Congress created an independent federal agency known as the National Labor Relations Board (NLRB). The NLRB has five principal functions:

1. *Conduct elections.* The NLRB allows private-sector employees to organize bargaining units in their workplace, or to dissolve their labor unions through a decertification election.
2. *Investigate charges.* Employees, union representatives, and employers who believe that their rights under the National Labor Relations Act have been violated may file charges alleging unfair labor practices at their nearest NLRB regional office.
3. *Seek resolutions.* When a charge is determined to have merit, the NLRB will explain the decision and offer the charged party an opportunity to settle before a formal complaint is issued.
4. *Decide cases.* On the adjudicative side of the NLRB are 40 administrative law judges and a board whose five members are appointed by the president and confirmed by the Senate.
5. *Enforce orders.* The majority of parties voluntarily comply with orders of the board. When they do not, the agency's general counsel must seek enforcement in the U.S. Courts of Appeals. Parties to cases also may seek review of unfavorable decisions in the federal courts.

The NLRA identifies the activities and practices that would be considered "unfair." Employers are forbidden to:

■ Threaten employees with loss of jobs or benefits if they join or vote for a union or engage in protected concerted activity.
■ Threaten to close the plant if employees select a union to represent them.

- Question employees about their union sympathies or activities in circumstances that tend to interfere with, restrain or coerce employees in the exercise of their rights under the Act.

- Promise benefits to employees to discourage their union support.

- Transfer, lay off, terminate, assign employees more difficult work tasks, or otherwise punish employees because they engaged in union or protected concerted activity.

- Transfer, lay off, terminate, assign employees more difficult work tasks, or otherwise punish employees because they filed unfair labor practice charges or participated in an investigation conducted by NLRB.

Under the law, employers are also protected from unfair labor practices that might be undertaken by a union. Examples of prohibited activities by union representatives include:

- Threats to employees that they will lose their jobs unless they support the union.

- Seeking the suspension, discharge, or other punishment of an employee for not being a union member, even if the employee has paid or offered to pay a lawful initiation fee and periodic fees thereafter.

- Refusing to process a grievance because an employee has criticized union officials or because an employee is not a member of the union in states where union security clauses are not permitted.

- Fining employees who have validly resigned from the union for engaging in protected concerted activities following their resignation or for crossing an unlawful picket line.

- Engaging in picket line misconduct, such as threatening, assaulting, or barring nonstrikers from the employer's premises.

Striking over issues unrelated to employment terms and conditions or coercively enmeshing neutrals into a labor dispute. It is up to the individual employer, union, or employee to request assistance from the NLRB in cases of unfair labor practices, or to hold an election that may unionize a job position. Complaints must be filed with the NLRB within six months of the alleged unfair activity. A representative from the NLRB will investigate the complaint. If the complaint is justified, and the parties have not taken steps to settle or withdraw the complaint, then the NLRB will hold a hearing. If an unfair labor practice is found to have occurred, then the NLRB will issue an order demanding that the unfair labor practice stop, and may also require the guilty party to take steps to compensate the injured party through job reinstatement, by payment of back wages, or by reestablishing conditions that were in place before the unfair activity took place. Either party may appeal the order in federal court.

Under the NLRA, employees have the right to form unions and bargain collectively. Once a union is established, new employees hired for a specific position may be required to join the union that represents that job position. However, many states have passed "right to work" laws that stipulate that an employee is not required to join a union if hired for a given position, even if other employees holding that position are unionized. As a manager, you should learn if your state has a "right to work" law.

For managers, a collective bargaining agreement should be treated in the same manner as any other formal contract. Its provisions should be read, understood, and followed. Membership in a union may give employees certain freedoms or conditions as part of their jobs, but employees still must be accountable for their work, and managers are still responsible for ensuring that employees perform their jobs properly, safely, and in accordance with the company's established policies and procedures. If problems do surface, a hospitality manager should consult with his or her company's designated union representative. Most CBAs have specific conditions for hiring new employees for a given position. As a manager, you should review and know this segment of the CBA especially well.

≫ ANALYZE THE SITUATION 7.3

WALTER HORVATH IS THE executive housekeeper at the Landmark Hotel. This 450-room historic property caters to leisure travelers. Occupancy at the hotel is highest on the weekends.

Like many hotels in large cities, the housekeeping staff is difficult to retain. Turnover tends to be high, and the labor market tight. Mr. Horvath works very hard to provide a work atmosphere that enhances harmony and encourages employees to stay. Although he has little control over wage scales, his general manager does allow him wide latitude in setting departmental policies and procedures, as long as these do not conflict with those of the management company that operates the Landmark.

Housekeepers in Mr. Horvath's department highly prize weekends off, yet these are the busiest times for the hotel. In a staff meeting, Mr. Horvath and the housekeepers agreed to implement a policy that would give each housekeeper alternating weekends off, with the stipulation that those housekeepers who are working on weekends might be required to work overtime to finish cleaning all the rooms necessary to service the hotel's guests. The housekeepers agreed to this compromise, and the policy was written into the department's procedures section of the employee handbook, which all new housekeeping employees must read and sign prior to beginning work.

When the holiday season approaches, Mr. Horvath finds that his department is seriously understaffed. The hotel is filling to capacity nearly every weekend as guests flock to the city to do their Christmas shopping. During a job interview with Andreanna White, Mr. Horvath mentions the alternating weekend policy for housekeepers. Ms. White states that the she is the choir director for her church. "I could," she says, "miss alternating Sunday mornings, because I could arrange a substitute. Working overtime on Sundays, however, would cause me to miss both the morning and evening services, and I would not be willing to do that. I could, however, work an eight-hour day of Sundays with no problem, because then I could go to either the morning or evening service."

1. Should Mr. Horvath hire Ms. White, despite her inability to comply with the departmental policy in place at the hotel?

2. If Mr. Horvath hires Ms. White, can he still enforce the alternating weekend policy with currently employed housekeepers, who also might prefer not to work overtime on Sundays?

3. Do you believe Ms. White's choir director position warrants an exception to the departmental policy?

4. How should Mr. Horvath advertise position vacancies in the future?

INTERNATIONAL SNAPSHOT

Canadian Employment Laws

If you operate a hotel anywhere in Canada, you need to consider employment-related laws in the province or territory where the hotel is located. The following is a summary of some important differences between U.S. and Canadian laws.

No "Employment at Will"

The U.S. concept of employment at will described elsewhere in this book does not exist in Canada. In Canada, both employment standards legislation and the common law require an employer that terminates an employee's employment without just cause to provide certain entitlements.

Under employment standards legislation in each province, an employer must provide an employee notice of termination of employment or pay in lieu of notice (usually one week per year of service to a maximum of eight weeks; more for group terminations), unless the employee is terminated for willful misconduct or willful neglect of duty. Some jurisdictions also require an employer to pay severance pay in addition to providing notice. For example, in Ontario, an employee with five or more years of service with an employer that has an annual payroll of at least $2.5 million is entitled to one week's pay per year of service up to a maximum of 26 weeks.

The common law requires that an employer provide an employee "reasonable" notice of termination or pay in lieu of notice unless just cause exists, there is a clear agreement otherwise, or a union represents the employee. Reasonable notice for each employee is determined on a case-by-case basis and depends on a number of factors, such as the employee's position, age, and length of service, and the availability of similar employment elsewhere. Reasonable notice at common law almost always exceeds the notice required by applicable legislation.

Pregnancy and Parental Leave

Whereas the U.S. Family and Medical Leave Act (FMLA), as further discussed in Chapter 8, requires an employer to provide an employee up to 12 weeks of unpaid leave, employment standards legislation in all Canadian jurisdictions require an employer to provide up to at least 52 weeks of pregnancy and parental leave. In addition, the right to pregnancy and parental leave applies to all employees in Canada, not just to those employed by employers with 50 or more employees (as provided by the FMLA).

Discrimination and Harassment

Prohibitions against discrimination and harassment in employment under various U.S. statutes, such as Title VII of the Civil Rights Act of 1964, the Americans with Disabilities Act, and the Age Discrimination in Employment Act of 1967, may be found in each province's or territory's human rights legislation (e.g., in Ontario, the Human Rights Code). Canadian human rights legislation in all jurisdictions prohibit discrimination and harassment on the basis of sex, disability, age, race, national or ethnic origin, color, religion or creed, marital status, and sexual orientation.

An employee in Canada may not file a civil action for discrimination, as is permitted in the United States. An employee may complain only to an administrative tribunal in the province he or she works, which adjudicates complaints. Administrative tribunals across Canada have wide powers to order reinstatement of employees, to require an employer to take steps to prevent discrimination and harassment, and to award monetary compensation. Monetary awards, however, are generally much lower than U.S. jury awards.

There are other significant differences between Canadian and U.S. employment laws. Local legal counsel can help to ensure that you are in compliance with all applicable laws. Other Canadian employment-related laws with which you should comply include:

- *Employment standards legislation*, which regulates minimum wages, hours of work, breaks, overtime pay, vacation and holidays with pay, entitlements on termination, and leaves of absence.
- *Labor relations legislation*, which governs certification/decertification of unions and collective bargaining.
- *Occupation health and safety legislation*, which governs an employer's obligation to provide a safe workplace.

- *Statutory workers' compensation/workplace safety and insurance legislation,* which governs an employer's obligations respecting workplace injuries and accidents.
- *Pay equity and employment equity legislation,* which require equal pay for equal work and equal employment opportunities for employees.

For more information on any Canadian employment law issues, contact James R. Hassell or Patricia S. W. Ross of the Employment and Labor Law Department of Osler, Hoskin & Harcourt LLP Barristers & Solicitors, P.O. Box 50, 1 First Canadian Place, Toronto, Ontario,

M5X 1B8, (416) 362-2111. Or log on to www.osler.com, Osler, Hoskin & Harcourt's website, which contains numerous articles on Canadian labor and employment law: canadaonline.about.com/od/labourstandards/Canada_Employment_and_Labour_Standards.htm for links to Ministry of Labour websites across Canada that provide information on employment standards, health, and safety, and labor relations; and to www.ohrc.on.ca, for Ontario's Human Rights Commission, and links to other human rights agencies across Canada.

Provided by James R. Hassell and Patricia S.W. Ross of Osler, Hoskin & Harcourt LLP, Toronto, Ontario. www.osler.com.

WHAT WOULD YOU DO?

Alex Bustamante is applying for the position of executive chef at the hospital where you serve as director of human resources. The hospital has more than 800 beds, and the meal service offered to patients and visitors alike is extensive. Patients in this facility are extremely ill, and because of their weakened condition, dietary concerns are an important consideration.

While reviewing Mr. Bustamante's work history with him during an interview, he states that he was let go from his two previous positions for "excessive absence." When you inquire as to the cause of his excessive absence, Mr. Bustamante offers that it was due to the effects of alcoholism, a condition with which he has struggled for over ten years, but for which he is currently undergoing weekend treatment and attending meetings of Alcoholics Anonymous (AA). He states that he never drank while at work but sometimes missed work because he overslept or was too hung over to go in. His past employers will neither confirm nor deny Mr. Bustamante's problem. Both simply state that he had worked for them as an executive chef and that he was no longer employed by their organizations.

Based on his education and experience, Mr. Bustamante is clearly the best-qualified candidate for the vacant executive chef's position. However, based on his life history, his ability to overcome his dependence on alcohol is, in your opinion, clearly questionable. Your recommendation on Mr. Bustamante's hiring will likely be accepted by the manager of dietary services.

1. Have you broken the law by inquiring into Mr. Bustamante's difficulty in prior positions?
2. Is Mr. Bustamante protected under the ADA?
3. If Mr. Bustamante were hired but needed three days off per week to undergo treatment, would you grant that accommodation? Under what circumstances?
4. How do the rights of Mr. Bustamante and the concept of negligent hiring mesh in this instance?

To understand how difficult it is to interpret and comply with antidiscrimination laws, consider the case of *Schurr v. Resorts Int'l Hotel*, 196 F.3d 486 (3d Cir. 1999).

FACTUAL SUMMARY

Karl Schurr (Schurr), a white male, worked on a part-time basis as a light and sound technician for Resorts International Hotel (Resorts), a New Jersey casino and hotel. In 1994, a full-time position became available for which Schurr applied. He was one of five applicants for the position. Resorts narrowed down the pool to Schurr and one other candidate, Ronald Boykin, a black male. Both candidates were qualified for the position and were regarded as equally qualified by Resorts.

A New Jersey law was in effect requiring all casino license holders to take affirmative action measures to ensure equal employment opportunities. In short, the regulations required the casinos in New Jersey to employee a certain percentage of women and minorities in specific job categories throughout the casino organization. The job for which Schurr and Boykin applied was in the technician category. Under the regulations, 25 percent of Resorts technicians were to be minorities. At the time Schurr and Boykin applied, only 22.25 percent of the technicians working for Resorts were minorities.

In an attempt to comply with state law and state casino regulations, the management for Resorts hired Boykin over Schurr on the basis of race. Bill Stevenson, the director of show operations and stage manager for Resorts, stated he was obligated to pick the equally qualified minority candidate in order to put Resorts in line with state employment goals. Schurr filed a complaint with the Equal Employment Opportunity Commission for discrimination on the basis of race and sued Resorts for a violation of Title VII of the Civil Rights Act of 1964.

QUESTION FOR THE COURT

The question for the court was whether the consideration of race as a factor in hiring was a remedial measure allowed under Title VII. Schurr argued the use of race as factor in hiring was a violation of Title VII. Resorts claimed the use of race was a nondiscriminatory component of its affirmative action plan designed to increase minority representation in certain job categories, hence fell under the remedial section of Title VII. The remedial aspect of Title VII was designed to cure past discrimination and inequities in minority hiring. Schurr argued Resorts' affirmative action plan and the casino regulations were not based on evidence of historic or current discrimination in the casino industry.

DECISION

The court held the affirmative action plan used by Resorts and the New Jersey law violated Title VII. The plan was not based on historic or current discrimination in the casino industry or in the technician job category. Since there was no evidence of past or current discrimination, Resorts' affirmative action plan was not necessary in the technician job category.

MESSAGE TO MANAGEMENT

The law in this area is extremely complex. Before implementing an affirmative action policy that discriminates on the basis of a protected class, be sure to have it thoroughly scrutinized for compliance with Title VII and current EEOC guidelines.

For a discussion of at-will employment in the state of Illinois, and a touchy discrimination case, consider the case of *Riad v. 520 South Michigan Avenue Assocs*, 78 F. Supp. 2d 748 (N.D.Ill. 1999).

FACTUAL SUMMARY

Nady Riad (Riad) was a general manager for the Congress Hotel (Congress) in Chicago, Illinois. Riad was an Egyptian-born naturalized American. He was recruited by the company managing the hotel, Hostmark Investor Limited Partnership (Hostmark), in part because of his excellent reputation in the hotel industry. As part of the recruitment process, Riad was offered a competitive salary that included participation in an incentive bonus program. If the Congress met certain performance goals under Riad's management, he would be entitled to a fairly large bonus upon approval by the owner of the Congress. Riad accepted the position on an employee-at-will basis.

The Congress Hotel was owned by 520 S. Michigan Avenue Associates Limited (520). The majority owner of 520 was Albert Nasser (Nasser). Nasser is Jewish and was educated in Israel. Shlomo Nahmias (Nahmias) worked for 520 as the owner's representative at the Congress Hotel. Nahmias is also Jewish and was born in Israel.

During his time at the Congress, Riad improved the performance and the financial outlook of the hotel. The exact amount was disputed but the improvement was significant. Pursuant to his employment agreement, Riad believed he was entitled to and did ask for a bonus. Nahmias, acting as the owner's representative, denied his request, stating the Congress was in bankruptcy. Riad instead asked for a pay increase, which was also denied. During his tenure at the Congress Hotel, Riad never received a bonus or a pay increase despite consistently strong employment reviews.

Riad's Egyptian heritage was a possible factor in his being denied pay increases and bonuses. Nahmias made several references to Riad being an Arab managing a Jewish-owned hotel. In front of several employees, Nahmias made several derogatory comments about Riad and his Arab or Egyptian heritage. Eventually, Riad was fired from the Congress despite his excellent performance and the improved financial position of the Congress. Riad sued 520 for employment discrimination on the basis of race.

QUESTION FOR THE COURT

The questions for the court were, one, whether Riad presented sufficient direct evidence of discrimination and, two, whether Riad presented enough evidence for an indirect case of discrimination. Riad argued that Nahmias, who had the power to hire and fire hotel employees, was motivated by race in making decisions regarding Riad's employment. Nahmias and Nasser argued isolated comments about the race of an individual were not enough to show discrimination. They argued there was no connection between the statements and the decision to terminate Riad's employment.

Riad also argued there was evidence of indirect discrimination. Riad argued he was a member of a protected class, was performing his job adequately, and suffered adverse consequences. Again Nasser and Nahmias argued there was no evidence.

DECISION

The court held that Riad presented evidence of both direct and indirect discrimination. Nasser and Nahmias used Riad's race to make an employment decision and were liable to him for damages.

MESSAGE TO MANAGEMENT

Discrimination on the basis of a protected class (in this case, race) does not have a place in the hospitality industry. Establishing a proactive policy of diversity and inclusion via mutual respect can help prevent outcomes such as this one.

Today, you cannot just hire anyone, and many different laws have been passed that affect the way in which you can legally hire and manage employees. Tools, such as written job descriptions, job qualifications, employment applications, and an established employee selection process that contains written guidelines for conducting interviews, preemployment tests, background checks, and reference checks are all used by the companies to ensure—and document—that they are selecting employees in compliance with the law.

It is illegal to discriminate against protected classes of workers in the job selection process. The Civil Rights Act of 1964 outlaws discrimination on the basis of race, color, religion, sex, or national origin. The Age Discrimination in Employment Act protects individuals 40 years old and older from discrimination based on age. The American with Disabilities Act not only protects those with disabilities from discrimination in the selection process but also requires companies to make reasonable accommodations to facilities or job responsibilities that will permit disabled individuals to work in a given job.

A last step before assigning someone to your workforce is to ensure that he or she is eligible to be employed in the United States by complying with the requirements of the Immigrations Reform and Control Act.

The at-will employment doctrine defines the rights of employers and employees in most states, unless an employment contract modifies that relationship. Labor unions are associations of workers that join together to bargain as a unit with management or business ownership. Collective bargaining agreements establish the regulations and the terms that must be followed by both unionized employees and nonunion managers during the employment relationship.

WHAT DID YOU LEARN IN THIS CHAPTER?

RAPID REVIEW

After you have studied this chapter, you should be prepared to:

1. Identify at least three exceptions to the at-will employment doctrine, and prepare a rationale for each exception's existence.

2. Create a description for your most recent job. Use that information to create a job qualifications list for the same job.

3. Appraise the pros and cons of refusing to supply detailed performance information about past employees to those who call for reference checks on them.

4. Use the Internet to determine the union organization in your home state or country that represents the largest number of hospitality workers.

5. Discuss the relationship between affirmative action and diversity awareness.

6. Develop your rationale for determining whether a visually impaired individual, whose sight is fully corrected by prescription glasses, falls under the protection of the ADA.

7. Create a checklist that could be used by a restaurant for complying with the requirements of the Immigration Reform and Control Act (IRCA).

8. Using the Internet, find the state or local agency that regulates child labor laws in your hometown, and compile a list of positions in the hospitality industry that could not be filed by 14- and 15-year-olds under its regulations.

TEAM ACTIVITY

In teams, draft a job description for a hospitality line position (dishwasher, server, front desk agent, etc.) of your choice. List at least five qualifications the potential employee must have; then identify and list the selection tools (i.e., references, tests, drug screenings) that you would use to match the right applicant with the job described.

CHAPTER 8

LEGALLY MANAGING EMPLOYEES

THE VOICE CAUGHT Trisha Sangus's ear as she rounded the basement stairwell and arrived at the hotel's security department offices.

"So these two guys' car breaks down . . . outside a farmhouse way in the country, see, and they go up to the door . . ."

Jon Ray, director of security, was the first one of the group of four men to see Trisha, the hotel's general manager. Jon was a retired policeman and one of the hotel's best department heads. He had done a lot to improve the safety and security of the hotel's physical assets since his arrival three years ago. Trisha knew that all of the guests were safer because of his innovative security efforts.

"Hello Ms. Sangus," Jon called out as the other three men glanced her way. Eric, the security guard who had been speaking, stopped and was now busily attempting to brush an imaginary piece of lint off his shirt. Tom, one of his coworkers, began talking somewhat loudly about the big ballgame that had been played the night before.

"Hello Tom, Eric, Leon," said Trisha as the three security staff members began to drift away from the group.

"Hi, Ms. Sangus," they replied, and then they were gone.

"Busy morning?" Trisha asked.

"The usual," Mr. Ray replied a bit offhandedly. Then, as he looked at Trisha, he stated, "Just the guys being guys. I'm sure in housekeeping the same kinds of stories are being told by their staff. You know, you can't dictate to employees what kind of jokes they like. As you know, most of my guys are ex-cops. They've seen and heard it all."

"I suppose that's true," replied Trisha slowly. "Jon, the story Eric was about to tell, do you think I would find it funny?"

"Well," Mr. Ray replied cautiously, "how can anyone be sure what amuses a person today? In my department, these guys probably would find the joke funny. Certainly not offensive. But they know better than to tell an off-color story around a lady."

"Interesting," thought Trisha as she returned to her office. She agreed with Jon. She didn't think any of his security staff would find a "farmer's daughter" joke offensive. She was also sure that none of the men would tell such a joke in the presence of a female staff person. And there had never been a complaint filed against anyone in Jon's department. On further reflection, however, Trisha realized that she, and the hotel, faced a serious problem. She picked up the telephone to call Jon.

"Jon," she began, "I'm concerned about employee safety in the hotel. As director of security, and a member of the management team, you should be concerned, too. I need you up here immediately."

"I'll come up as soon as I finish the morning report," Mr. Ray replied.

"No, Jon, not later, now!" she said firmly, as she hung up the telephone.

"I wonder what happened," thought Mr. Ray, as he hurried to Trisha's office. Whatever it was, it must have been big!

IN THIS CHAPTER, YOU WILL LEARN:

1. To differentiate between an employment agreement and an employee manual.
2. To establish a nondiscriminatory work environment.
3. To implement a procedure designed to eliminate sexual harassment and minimize the risk of penalties resulting from charges of unlawful harassment.
4. To legally manage the complex areas of employee leave, compensation, and performance.
5. To respond appropriately to unemployment claims.
6. To summarize and list the employment records that must be maintained to meet legal requirements.

8.1 EMPLOYMENT RELATIONSHIPS

After you have legally selected an employee for your organization, it is a good practice to clarify the conditions of the employment agreement with that employee.

All employers and employees have employment agreements with each other. The agreement can be as simple as an hourly wage rate for an hour's work and at-will employment for both parties. An agreement is in place even if there is nothing in writing or if work conditions have not been discussed in detail. *Employment agreements* may be individual, covering only one employee or, as discussed in the last chapter, they may involve groups of employees. Generally, employment agreements in the hospitality industry are established verbally, or with an offer letter.

> **LEGALESE**
>
> **Employment agreement:** The terms of the employment relationship between an employer and employee that specifies the rights and obligations of each party to the agreement.

Offer Letter

Offer letters, when properly composed, can help prevent legal difficulties caused by employee or employer misunderstandings. As their name implies, offer letters detail the offer made by the employer to the employee. Some employers believe offer letters should be used only for managerial positions, but to avoid difficulties, all employees should have signed offer letters in their personnel files. Components of a sound offer letter include:

- Position offered
- Compensation included
- Benefits included (if any)
- Evaluation period and compensation review schedule
- Start date
- Location of employment
- Special conditions of the offer (e.g., at-will relationship)
- Reference to the *employee manual* as an additional source of information regarding employer policies that govern the workplace
- Signature lines for both employer and employee

> **LEGALESE**
>
> **Employee manual:** A document written to detail the policies, benefits, and employment practices of an employer.

Consider the case of Antonio Molina. Antonio applies for the position of maintenance foreman at a country club. He is selected for the job and is given an offer letter by the club's general manager. In the letter, a special condition of employment is that Antonio must submit to, and pass, a mandatory drug test. Though Antonio can sign the letter when it is received, his employment is not finalized until he passes the drug test.

Additional rules that Antonio will be expected to follow, or benefits that he may enjoy while on the job, will be contained in the employee manual.

Employee Manual

In most cases, the offer letter will not detail all of the policies and procedures to which the employer and employee agree. These are typically contained in the employee manual. The manual may be as simple as a few pages or as extensive as several hundred pages. In either case, an important point to remember is that employee manuals are often referenced by the courts to help define the terms of the employment agreement if a dispute arises. The topics covered by an employee manual will vary from one organization to another. However, some common topic areas include:

General Policies
- Probationary periods
- Performance reviews
- Disciplinary process
- Termination
- Attendance
- Drug and alcohol testing
- Uniforms
- Lockers
- Personal telephone calls
- Appearance and grooming

Compensation
- Pay periods
- Payroll deductions
- Tip-reporting requirements
- Timekeeping procedures
- Overtime pay policies
- Meal periods
- Schedule posting
- Call-in pay
- Sick pay
- Vacation pay

Benefits
- Health insurance
- Dental insurance
- Disability insurance
- Vacation accrual
- Paid holidays
- Jury duty
- Funeral leave
- Retirement programs
- Duty meals
- Leaves of absence
- Transfers
- Educational reimbursement plans

Special Areas
- Policies against harassment
- Grievance and complaint procedures

- Family medical leave information
- Dispute resolution
- Safety rules
- Security rules
- Emergency preparedness

Employee manuals should be kept up to date, and it should be clearly established that it is the employer, not the employee, who retains the right to revise the employee manual.

Many companies issue employee manuals with a signature page, where employees must verify that they have indeed read the manual. This is a good idea, as it gives proof that employees were given the opportunity to familiarize themselves with the employers' policies and procedures. It is also a good idea to use wording similar to the following on a signature page. The wording should be emphasized in a type size larger than the type surrounding it.

The employer reserves the right to modify, alter, or eliminate any and all of the policies and procedures contained in this manual at any time.

An additional precaution taken by many employers is the practice of giving a written test covering the content of the employee manual before the employee begins work. The employee's test results are kept on file.

To clarify for employees that their status is "at-will," each page of the employee manual should contain the following wording at the bottom center of each page: "This is not an employment contract." A more formal statement should be placed at the beginning of the manual, such as:

This manual is not a contract, expressed or implied, guaranteeing employment for any specific duration. Although [the company] *hopes that your employment relationship with us will be long term, either you or the company may terminate this relationship at any time, with or without cause or notice.*

The employee manual must be very carefully drafted to avoid altering the at-will employment doctrine. The document should be carefully reviewed by an employment attorney each and every time it is revised.

8.2 WORKPLACE DISCRIMINATION AND SEXUAL HARASSMENT

As noted in the last chapter, various laws prohibit discrimination on the basis of an individual's race, religion, gender, national origin, disability, age (over 40), and in some states and communities, sexual orientation.

Although the federal government has taken the lead in outlawing discrimination in employment practices, many states, and even some towns and cities, also have antidiscrimination laws, which must be followed. In general, the state laws duplicate practices that are outlawed under federal law, such as discrimination based on race, color, national origin, and so on. It is important for a hospitality manager to know the provisions of a state civil rights law for several reasons.

Many state discrimination laws add other categories to the list of prohibited behavior, which are not covered under federal law, such as discrimination on the basis of marital status, arrest record, or sexual orientation. Also, while federal civil rights laws apply to businesses engaged in interstate commerce (which includes most restaurants and hotels), many state laws extend to other types of businesses, such as bars, taverns, stores, and "places of public accommodation." State discrimination laws are enforced by state civil rights agencies, which can assess severe penalties to businesses found in violation of the law. These penalties could include fines, prison terms, or both.

Some companies may also expand the protections that their workers receive under the law. As you saw in Chapter 1, "Prevention Philosophy," Hyatt's policy on conduct and ethics clearly states that its employees will not be discriminated against on the basis of their sexual preference. Since Hyatt Hotels are operated in many states and communities where the law does not prohibit Hyatt from discriminating on the basis of one's sexual preference, Hyatt has voluntarily broadened the protections for its workforce.

These prohibitions of discrimination in the employment area apply when selecting employees for a given job, as well as after they have been hired. With such a wide diversity of employees in the hospitality industry, it is not surprising that a variety of attitudes about work, family, and fellow employees will also exist. Managers cannot dictate conformity in all areas of their employees' value systems. However, as a manager, you are required to prevent discrimination by your staff, coworkers, and even third parties, such as guests and suppliers.

Preventing Discrimination

Workplace discrimination is enforced by the Equal Employment Opportunity Commission (EEOC). Applicants and employees can bring claims of discrimination to the EEOC and/or their state's counterpart to the EEOC (e.g., the Texas Commission on Human Rights), which will investigate the charges and issue a determination of whether they believe discrimination has occurred. It is important to keep in mind that if a discrimination charge is filed, the EEOC has the authority to examine all policies and practices in a business for violations, not just the circumstances surrounding a particular incident. If there is sufficient evidence of discrimination, the EEOC will first work with employers to correct any problems and try to voluntarily settle a case before it reaches the courts.

If a settlement cannot be worked out, the EEOC may file a lawsuit on behalf of the claimant or issue the claimant a right-to-sue letter. If the EEOC does not determine that unlawful discrimination occurred, then the claimant may accept that finding or privately pursue a lawsuit against the employer.

Penalties for violating Title VII of the Civil Rights Act can be severe. Plaintiffs have the right to recover back wages, future wages, the value of lost fringe benefits, other compensatory damages, attorneys' fees, as well as injunctive relief such as reinstatement of their job and the restoration of their seniority. In addition, federal fines for violating Title VII can be up to $50,000 (for businesses with fewer than 100 employees) to $300,000 (for corporations with 500 employees or more).

As we have stressed repeatedly, the best way to avoid litigation is by preventing incidents before they occur. Where discrimination is concerned, this involves making sure that your company's policies, and your own actions as a manager, do not adversely impact members of a protected class.

Some of the more common areas of potential conflict in the hospitality industry concern matters of appearance and language. For example, employers are permitted to require their employees to wear uniforms or adhere to certain common grooming standards (such as restrictions on hair length or wearing jewelry); provided that all employees are subject to these requirements and that the policies are established for a necessary business reason. Although the courts have not outlawed the establishment of "English-only" rules in business, lawsuits have occurred when such companies discriminate against people who have pronounced accents or who do not speak English fluently, especially in job positions where speaking English would not be considered a bona fide occupational qualification.

Managing Diversity

Beyond preventing acts of overt discrimination, managers have a legal obligation to establish a work environment that is accepting of all people. The failure to establish such an environment is recognized by the courts to be a form of discrimination. Racial slurs, ethnic jokes, and other practices that might be offensive to an employee should not be tolerated.

As a manager, your ability to effectively work with people from diverse backgrounds will significantly affect your success. According to Gene M. Monteagudo, former manager of diversity for Hyatt Hotels International, "It is no longer possible to achieve success in the hospitality industry, either in the United States or abroad, unless you can effectively manage people in a cultural environment vastly different from your own." Recognition of the differences among individuals is the first step toward effectively managing these differences. This can be confusing in a society that increasingly equates equality with correctness. The truth is that people are different in many cultural aspects; however, it is also true that "we do not have to be twins to be brothers." In other words, just because we are equal under the law does not mean that we are the same.

One of the great myths of management today is that, because workers are equal under the law, all workers must be treated exactly the same. This is simply wrong. The effective manager treats people equitably, not uniformly. If one worker enjoys showing pictures of her grandchildren to a unit manager, it is okay for that manager to show an interest in them. If another worker prefers privacy, it is equally acceptable for the manager not to ask that employee about his or her grandchildren. Is this more complicated than treating both workers exactly the same? Of course it is. And it may be considered confusing by some. The key to remember here, however, is that the unit manager, by recognizing the real differences between the two employees, and acting on those differences accordingly, is treating them both equitably. That is, they are both being treated with respect for their own system of cultural values.

As you consider the diversity issue in greater detail, you will realize that the recognition of cultural differences is not a form of racism at all, but, rather, the first step toward harmony. The true racist is not the person who notices real cultural differences, but, rather, the person who ignores them. The culturally unaware foodservice manager who does not recognize, for example, the uniqueness and importance of the Asian worker's culture, denigrates that culture in much the same way as the individual who is openly critical of it. In the hospitality industry, the management of cultural diversity and the inclusion of all people in all aspects of the business will remain an important fact of operational and legal life.

Sexual Harassment

By their very nature, hospitality organizations are vulnerable to allegations of sexual harassment. Because this is true, it has become increasingly important that managers be informed about the attitudes and conduct that fall under the classification of sexual harassment. Currently, federal and state law recognizes two types of sexual harassment:

- *Quid pro quo* sexual harassment, in which the perpetrator asks for sexual favors in exchange for workplace benefits from a subordinate, or punishes the subordinate for rejecting the offer.

- Hostile environment harassment, in which the perpetrator, through language or conduct, creates an intimidating or hostile working environment for individuals of a particular gender. In a subtler way, this also occurs when "freezing out" tactics are used against employees or when employees are shunned or relegated to an outer office or desk with little or nothing to do, thus inhibiting all communication.

Title VII of the federal Civil Rights Act, as amended in 1972, prohibits sexual harassment in the workplace. The penalties for violating sexual harassment laws are the same as those for other types of civil rights violations. Claimants can recover lost wages, benefits, and attorneys' fees, and can be reinstated in their jobs. Many states have also adopted laws to protect employees from sexual harassment, which may carry additional fines or penalties.

> **LEGALESE**
> **Quid pro quo:** Latin term for "giving one thing in return or exchange for another."

Employer Liability

Behavior that once may have been tolerated in the workplace is no longer acceptable. The result has been an explosion of sexual harassment claims, pitting employee against supervisor, employee against another employee, women against men, and men against women, and even same-sex complaints.

In an important decision for employers, on June 26, 1998, the United States Supreme Court, in the case of *Faragher v. City of Boca Raton*, ruled on the circumstances under which an employer may be held liable under Title VII of the Civil Rights Act of 1964, 42 U.S.C., Section 2000e, for the acts of a supervisory employee whose sexual harassment of subordinates created a hostile work environment amounting to employment discrimination.

The court held that an "employer is subject to *vicarious liability* to a victimized employee for an actionable hostile environment created by a supervisor with immediate (or successively higher) authority over the employee." In this case, the court found that "uninvited and offensive touching," "lewd remarks," or "speaking of women in offensive terms" was enough to create a hostile employment environment.

The court then determined that if this type of harassment occurs by a supervisor, the employer may avoid liability by raising an affirmative defense, if the following necessary elements are met:

- The employer exercised reasonable care to prevent and promptly correct any sexually harassing behavior.
- The plaintiff employee unreasonably failed to take advantage of any preventive or corrective opportunities provided by the employer.

The court also held that if a supervisor's harassment ultimately results in a tangible employment action, such as an employee's termination, demotion, or reassignment, the employer is not entitled to claim the affirmative defense just described, and the employer will be held strictly liable for any acts of sexual harassment by its supervisors.

The result of this ruling is that the main, and oftentimes only, legal defense for supervisors to allegations of sexual harassment is to demonstrate a history of preventive and corrective measures. Therefore, it is crucial that every hospitality employer have, at a minimum, an employee manual that outlines the company's sexual harassment policy. This policy should be reviewed by an attorney to determine if it is legally sufficient.

Zero Tolerance

In order to guard against the liability that results from charges of discrimination or harassment, and to ensure a high-quality workplace for all employees, hospitality organizations should institute a policy of zero (no) tolerance of objectionable behavior. Listed here are some of the measures that companies institute to create a zero tolerance environment:

- Clear policies that prohibit sexual harassment in the workplace
- Workshops to train supervisors and staff how to recognize potentially volatile situations and how to minimize potentially unpleasant consequences
- Provisions and avenues for seeking and receiving relief from offensive and unwanted behavior
- Written procedures for reporting incidents and for investigating and bringing grievances to closure

Of course, employers should not develop a zero tolerance policy toward harassment merely to avoid lawsuits. However, by creating a clear policy statement that includes severe penalties for violation, companies can demonstrate a good-faith effort to promote a safe, fair, work environment. An effective sexual harassment policy should include the following:

- A statement that the organization advocates and supports unequivocally a zero tolerance standard when it comes to sexual harassment.

LEGALESE

Vicarious liability: A party's responsibility for the acts of another that result in an injury, harm, or damage. (See also *respondeat superior.*)

- A definition of the terms and behaviors discussed in the statement.

- A description of acceptable and unacceptable behaviors; that is, no sexually suggestive photographs, jokes, vulgar language, or the like.

- An explanation of the reasons for the existing policy.

- A discussion of the consequences for unacceptable behavior. You should probably list sexual harassment as a punishable offense in all company handbooks and manuals. Types of disciplinary action available to the company should be stated as consequences for sexual harassment or hostile environment offenses.

- Specific identification of the complaint procedures to be followed by an employee.

- Several avenues for relief or ways to bring a complaint or concern(s) to the attention of management. If all grievances must be cleared through the supervisor and he or she is the culprit, you have not helped.

- Identification, by name, of the employer representative to whom complaints should be reported. This should be to someone who is not in an employee's chain of command. With the current state of the law, it is preferable to direct complaints to the personnel or human resources manager, with an alternative reporting procedure for employees in that department.

- A clear statement that all complaints and investigations will be treated with confidence. All investigative materials should be maintained in separate files with very limited and restricted access.

- A clear statement that the employer prohibits all forms of harassment and that any complaints by employees of other forms of harassment based on any protected category will be addressed under the antiharassment policy.

Although a policy statement is a good beginning, it will not be effective unless it is adopted by managers and communicated to all employees. Most companies reprint their policy on sexual harassment in their employee manual. Other companies have taken additional steps: posting the policy in common areas, such as in lunchrooms and on bulletin boards, and discussing the policy at new employee orientations and other personnel meetings.

A training program is one of the most effective ways an employer can foster a safe working environment and ensure compliance with the law. All employees should participate in a sexual harassment training program, initially during orientation and thereafter on a regular basis. Some of the most effective training techniques include role-playing exercises, group and panel discussions, videos, behavior modeling, and sensitivity training. It is also important that employees become fully familiar with the avenues for seeking relief, should they ever feel uncomfortable because of someone else's behavior. Employees with any kind of supervisory responsibility should be trained to identify circumstances that could be perceived as harassment, and understand both the company's policy and their role in preventing unwelcome behavior and responding seriously to any complaints.

While training is important, it is even more important to evaluate the effects of training. This can be done by administering tests to employees before and after they participate in a training program, keeping the results, and documenting the number of harassment complaints received as well as taking care to note whether the number of complaints has gone up or down. If the feedback shows that a training program is ineffective, change the program. If the feedback shows that an individual was unable to learn the demonstrated skills or follow company guidelines, then either retrain or terminate the employee; otherwise, you may risk a negligent retention claim, because based on the feedback you received, you should have known that this employee would violate company standards or regulations. A jury might conclude that termination of the employee would have prevented the incident that prompted the lawsuit.

Opposing attorneys will not walk away from a case just because you have a policy in place and state that training has occurred. They will want to see that training did in fact occur, what kind of training it was, and whether or not the training was effective. In order to win a lawsuit that accuses you of ineffective training, you must be able to document a training "trail" and be able to show those materials to a jury. Keep records of every seminar and workshop that is conducted, and note the people who attended. If you used supporting materials such as videos or handouts, keep copies of them. If you solicited feedback after the workshop in the form of test results or employee evaluations, keep them on file. Why? Because, unfortunately, it is rarely the truth that wins lawsuits; it is usually the evidence that prevails.

≫ ANALYZE THE SITUATION 8.1

JOSEPH HARPER WAS A cook at the HillsTop resort hotel. He was 61 years old, and had been employed by the resort for over 25 years. Sandra Shana was the new human resource director for the facility. As part of her duties, Ms. Shana conducted the hotel's sexual harassment training program for all new employees, as well as management. The training sessions used up-to-date material provided by the resort's national trade association, and Sandra worked hard to evaluate the effectiveness of the training for both employees and management.

Mr. Harper attended three training sessions in the space of five years. When he was approached by Ms. Shana to schedule another training session he stated, "I don't know why I have to go through this again. It's nonsense and a waste of time. I have gone three times, and it's dumber each time I attend!" Mr. Harper had been heard to make similar comments each time he attended the training sessions, and once even challenged the trainers about the "political correctness" of the training. In addition, he had been heard making similar comments in the employee breakroom while other employees were in the room. No staff member of the resort had ever formally accused Mr. Harper of sexual harassment, however. The HillsTop resort stated in its employee manual that is an "at-will" employer.

1. As the human resource director, would you recommend either the discipline or termination of Mr. Harper based on his comments?

2. If the resort, and Mr. Harper specifically, were named in a guest-initiated lawsuit alleging harassment, and found liable, would you recommend disciplinary action against the human resource director or the resort's general manager for failing to act?

3. Does Mr. Harper have the right to openly express his opinion about the resort's harassment training while at work?

Investigating a Complaint

Unfortunately, even the most thorough prevention effort will not preclude all offensive behaviors. You must, therefore, have a procedure in place to deal with these incidents. This procedure must be strictly followed. Employees must be confident that they can come forward with their concerns without fear of ridicule, retaliation, or job loss.

When a complaint is lodged, or when inappropriate activity is brought to the attention of management, the employer should act immediately. At the time of the complaint, the employer should obtain the claimant's permission to start an investigation. Written consent forms, such as the one displayed in Figure 8.1 are recommended. Note that the form asks for permission to disclose the information to third parties, if necessary, so that a thorough investigation can be conducted.

Often, the circumstances surrounding a claim of sexual harassment are very personal. There are occasions when an employee launches a complaint, then later changes his or her mind or asks if the investigation can be conducted under certain conditions. As a manager, you need to be sensitive to an employee's emotions, but you must not allow them to interfere with a company's established investigation policies. Employees have the right to withdraw a complaint, but if they do so, you should have them sign a form, such as the one shown in Figure 8.2, stating that they no longer wish to pursue the matter and that they are comfortable having no further action taken.

In some situations, it may be necessary to pursue action, in spite of the employee's refusal to continue. For example, the facts brought to management's attention might be so serious that a company would need to consider taking some sort of immediate remedial action, such as the suspension or termination of the alleged harasser.

Investigation Consent Form

I. Name: _____

II. Position and Title: _____

III. Facts of Situation (attach as many pages as necessary):

_____

_____

_____

_____

_____

_____

IV. I hereby request that the company investigate the facts set forth above. I also authorize the company to disclose as much of the facts set forth above as necessary to pursue the investigation. I also understand and acknowledge that the company shall use due diligence in keeping this matter as confidential as possible. I recognize, however, that in the course of the investigation the information may need to become public to do a thorough investigation.

Signature _____ Date _____

Employee

Figure 8.1 Investigation consent form.

Request for No Further Action

I. Name: _____

II. Position and Title: _____

   On the ____ day of _____ 200__, I previously completed a consent form which, among other things, requested that the company investigate certain facts stated by me, a copy of which is attached to this document. I have now decided that it would not be in my best interest to pursue this matter, and am comfortable with my environment in the workplace, as it presently exists. I have been made aware that in the event that I become uncomfortable, I can seek the assistance and support of the company at any time, and have been encouraged to do so. At this time, however, I am requesting that at least for my benefit, no further action be taken in this regard, and I fully understand that an investigation for my benefit shall not take place. I do understand, however, that the company, after having been made aware of these circumstances, may elect to pursue an investigation on its own behalf and for the benefit of other employees.

Signature _____ Date _____
                                    Employee

Figure 8.2 Request for no further action.

Failure to do so could subject the company to liability for keeping the individual if he or she acts inappropriately again and management could not intervene. It is important to remember that just because an employee does not agree to formally complain or to follow through on a complaint, the employer is not relieved from the responsibility of providing a safe working environment.

If the complainant takes the position that the mere presence of the alleged harasser causes anxiety and distress, do not as an interim measure transfer that employee to another job or position. Suggest a couple of days off with pay while you investigate the complaint. A transfer tends to undermine the confidence of the victim, particularly after being told that there would be no retaliation for bringing the concern to the attention of management.

If you choose to undertake an investigation, be sure to do so thoroughly. An ineffective investigation could subject you to legal liability just as if no such investigation took place. When conducting an investigation, employers should exercise discretion in selecting the employees who will be interviewed. It is advisable to confine the investigation to the circle of the alleged victim's immediate coworkers who witnessed the incident, or who were privy to the claimant's situation and confidence. The objective is to garner as much information as possible in order to conduct an even-handed and fair investigation. The questions contained in Figure 8.3 are a few that you might want to consider asking those who are not directly involved in an allegation. Interviewers should be tactful and alert to the interviewees' attitude, and be cognizant of their relationship with the victim as well as the alleged harasser. Witnesses should be reminded of the sensitive nature of the investigation and of the importance of maintaining confidentiality. Always conduct the interviews in private. The results should be discussed with the accused in a nonthreatening manner. To maintain the integrity of the process, individuals identified by the accused who might be able to disprove the allegations should be contacted and interviewed.

1. Have you noticed any behavior that makes people uncomfortable in the workplace?
2. Did it involve sexual or ethnic matters? Would you mind sharing with me who was involved?
3. What is the general atmosphere of the work environment?
4. Do you consider any employees or supervisors to be chronic complainers?
5. Do you think some people are treated differently from others for reasons that are not job-related?
6. Do you feel as if any employees receive the benefit of favoritism for reasons other than job performance?
7. Have you noticed any personality conflicts?
8. Will you let me know if you think of anything else?

Figure 8.3 Possible questions for interviewees not directly involved.
Adapted from Jossen Jared, Investigating Sexual Harassment. In Litigating the Sexual Harassment Case, *the American Bar Association, 1994.*

At all times, the investigation should be carefully and accurately documented. Conversations and interviews with witnesses should be recorded in writing, and whenever possible, signed statements should be obtained. A record of the decision made after the investigation should also be on file. References to the claim should not, however, appear in a personnel file; unless the offender has been issued a disciplinary action after a thorough investigation. A separate investigation file should be kept, and that file should be retained for as long as the statute of limitations on sexual harassment claims specifies. (That period can be as long as two years from the date an incident has occurred.)

Resolving a Complaint

In order to avoid liability, an employer must offer evidence that a complaint of sexual harassment was investigated thoroughly, and that the employer undertook prompt remedial action to end the harassing conduct. The Equal Employment Opportunity Commission (EEOC) recognizes effective remedial action to include the following steps:

1. Prompt and thorough investigation of complaints
2. Immediate corrective action that effectively ends the harassment
3. Provision of a remedy to complainants for such harassment (e.g., restoring lost wages and benefits)
4. Preventive measures against future recurrences

Should the results of an investigation remain inconclusive, or if, after an investigation, no corrective or preventative actions are taken, then the victim has the right to file a lawsuit against the employer. However, if an employer punishes an accused harasser without having conclusive evidence to back up a claim, then the alleged harasser has the right to file a defamation lawsuit, or an invasion of privacy action against the employer. If the results of an investigation prove inconclusive, then the best actions to take are to: advise the alleged harasser that the investigation was inconclusive, inform all employees of the organization's zero tolerance policy of sexual harassment, spell out the consequences for failure to abide by that policy, and conduct sensitivity training programs. If there is a resolution to the investigation, have the complainant sign a resolution form, if possible, such as the one shown in Figure 8.4.

Resolution of Complaint

I. Name:_____

II. Position and Title: _____

III. On the ____ day of _____ , 200 __ , I previously completed a form, which alleged facts regarding the environment in the workplace, a copy of which is attached to this document. I have been made aware of the results of the investigation by the company, as well as its proposed resolution of this matter, which I understand to be as follows:

(i). The alleged harasser shall undergo sensitivity training.

(ii). The alleged harasser shall be suspended without pay for five (5) days beginning on the ____ day of _____ and ending on the ____ day of ____, 200__.

(iii). It is agreed by both parties that the alleged harasser shall return to work at the time stated above, but only after having undergone the sensitivity training.

I am satisfied with the resolution as set forth above, and understand fully that in the event the matter is not completely resolved by the foregoing actions, I have been encouraged to bring my concerns to the company for immediate attention.

Signature _____ Date _____

Employee

Figure 8.4 Resolution of complaint form.

Third-Party Harassment

Third-party sexual harassment occurs when someone outside the workforce harasses an employee or is harassed by an employee. Some examples might be a supplier harassing an employee, a guest harassing an employee, or an employee harassing a guest. In the case of *EEOC v. Sage Realty Corporation,* a federal court in New York held the real estate company responsible when one of its employees violated federal law by terminating a female lobby attendant who refused to wear a uniform that she considered too revealing. She felt that wearing the uniform had caused her to be the victim of lewd comments and sexual propositions from customers and the general public.

In the hospitality industry, where the interaction between guests and employees is a critical component of the business, the risks of third-party harassment are especially great. The adage "the customer is always right" does not extend to harassment. The law clearly states that employees do not have to tolerate, nor should they be subjected to, offensive behavior. This means that employers have a responsibility to protect their employees from third-party harassment.

This is especially troublesome when one considers that managers have limited control over guests, and that it is a natural desire to want to hold on to the customers' business and goodwill. From a legal and practical perspective, however, employees should know that they have the right to speak up when they are subject to unwelcome behavior, and managers should act quickly and reasonably to resolve any situations that do occur.

Liability Insurance

It is important to remember that zero tolerance does not necessarily mean zero claims of harassment. Incidents will occur. Because this is true, employers, especially in the hospitality industry, should purchase liability insurance that includes coverage for illegal acts of discrimination, including internal and third-party sexual harassment. This coverage is not provided in ordinary liability insurance policies; it must be specifically requested. The insurance should cover the liability for acts of the employer, acts of the employees, and any damages that may not be covered by workers' compensation policies.

8.3 FAMILY AND MEDICAL LEAVE ACT

A highly significant piece of federal legislation that greatly impacts employee management in the hospitality industry is the Family and Medical Leave Act of 1993 (FMLA), and its amendments. The U.S. Department of Labor's Employment Standards Administration, Wage and Hour Division, administers and enforces the FMLA. The FMLA entitles eligible employees to take up to 12 weeks of unpaid, job-protected leave each year for specified family and medical reasons. The FMLA applies to all government workers and private sector employers that employ 50 or more employees within a 75-mile radius. It is important to note that the 50 employees need not all work at the same location. For example, a multiunit operator whose total workforce equals or exceeds 50 employees within a 75-mile radius is covered by the act.

To be eligible for FMLA benefits, an employee must have worked for the employer for a total of at least 12 months and have worked at least 1,250 hours over the previous 12 months. A covered employer must grant an eligible employee up to a total of 12 workweeks of unpaid leave for:

- The birth of a child, and to care for the newborn child within one year from birth
- The placement with the employee of a child for adoption or foster care, and to care for the newly placed child within one year of placement
- To care for the employee's spouse, child, or parent who has a serious health condition
- A serious health condition that makes the employee unable to perform the essential functions of his or her job
- Any qualifying exigency arising out of the fact that the employee's spouse, son, daughter, or parent is a covered military member on "covered active duty"

Spouses who work for the same employer are jointly entitled to a combined total of 12 workweeks of family leave for the birth or placement of a child for adoption or foster care, and to care for a parent (not a parent-in-law) who has a serious health condition.

Alternatively, the FMLA allows for military caregiver leave, which entitles the employee to 26 workweeks of leave within a single 12-month period for the purpose of caring for a covered servicemember with a serious injury, if that covered servicemember is the spouse, son, daughter, parent, or next of kin to the employee.

Under some circumstances, employees may take FMLA leave intermittently—which means taking leaves in blocks of time or reducing their normal weekly or daily work schedule. FMLA leave may be taken intermittently whenever medically necessary to care for a seriously ill family member or because the employee is seriously ill and unable to work.

A covered employer is required to maintain group health insurance coverage for an employee on FMLA leave, if the insurance was provided before the leave was taken, and on the same terms as if the employee had continued to work. In most cases, the employee is required to pay his or her share of health insurance premiums while on leave.

Upon return from FMLA leave, an employee must be restored to his or her original job or an equivalent one. An equivalent job need not consist of exactly the same hours but must include the same pay and level of responsibility. Some exceptions are made under the law, especially for salaried or "key" staff personnel.

Employees seeking to use FMLA leave may be required to provide:

■ Thirty-day advance notice of the need to take FMLA leave, when the need is foreseeable

■ Medical certifications supporting the need for leave due to a serious health condition

■ Second or third medical opinions, if requested by and paid for by the employer

■ Periodic reports during FMLA leave regarding the employee's status and intent to return to work

Covered employers must post a notice approved by the secretary of labor explaining rights and responsibilities under the FMLA. An employer that willfully violates this posting requirement may be subject to a fine of up to $100 for each separate offense. Also, employers must inform employees of their rights under the FMLA. This information can be included in an employee manual, when one exists. In some cases, provisions for leaves of absence are also part of a labor union's collective bargaining agreement, and managers should be aware of those provisions.

8.4 COMPENSATION

Generally, employers are free to establish wages and salaries as they see fit. In some cases, however, the law affects the wage relationship between employer and employee. For example, the Equal Pay Act, passed in 1963 by the federal government, provides that equal pay must be paid to men and women for equal work, if the jobs they perform require "equal" skill, effort, and responsibility, and are performed under similar working conditions. An employee's gender, personal situation, or financial status cannot serve as a basis for making wage determinations. In addition to equal pay for equal work, there are a variety of other laws that regulate how much an employer must pay its employees. In the hospitality industry, these laws have a broad impact.

Minimum Wage and Overtime

LEGALESE

Minimum wage: The least amount of wages that an employee covered by the FLSA or state law may be paid by his or her employer.

As mentioned in the previous chapter, the Fair Labor Standards Act (FLSA) established child labor standards in the United States. In addition, it established the *minimum wage* that must be paid to covered employees, as well as wage rates that must be paid for working overtime. The FLSA applies to all businesses that have employees who are engaged in producing, handling, selling, or working on goods that have been moved in or manufactured for interstate commerce. Some, but not many, hospitality operations may be too small to be covered under the FLSA. To be sure, a small business owner should check with the local offices of the Wage and Hour Division, listed in most telephone directories under U.S. Government, Department of Labor, Wage and Hour Division (www.dol.gov/whd).

The minimum wage is established and periodically revised by Congress. Nearly all hospitality employees are covered by the minimum wage, but there are some exceptions. The FLSA allows an employer to pay an employee who is under 20 years of age a training wage, which is below the standard minimum, for the first 90 consecutive calendar days of employment. Also, tipped employees can be paid a rate below the minimum, if the tips they report plus the wages received from the employer equal or exceed the minimum hourly rate.

Some states have also established their own minimum wages. In those states, employees are covered by the law most favorable to them (in other words, whichever wage is higher, state or federal). The differences in state laws can be significant. Compare the current federal minimum compensation provisions in Figure 8.5 with those of several other states. You can see that each state has a great deal of latitude in enacting its own wage and overtime laws.

The FLSA does not limit the number of hours in a day or days in a week an employee over the age of 16 may work. Employers may require an employee to work more than 40 hours per week. However, under the FLSA, covered employees must be paid at least one and one-half times their regular rates of pay for all hours worked in excess of 40 in a workweek.

Some employees are exempt from the overtime provision of the FLSA. These include salaried professional, administrative, or executive employees. Recently, the DOL has instituted its FairPay Overtime Initiative, which was created to assist employers in understanding the FairPay rules and guidelines for overtime eligibility. Go to www.dol.gov/whd/regs/compliance/fairpay/main.htm for the most current information on eligibility and potential exemptions.

Wage and Hour Division investigators stationed throughout the country carry out enforcement of the FLSA. When investigators encounter violations, they recommend changes in employment practices in order to bring the employer into compliance, and may require the payment of any back wages due employees. Employers who willfully or repeatedly violate the minimum wage or overtime pay requirements are subject to civil penalties of up to $1,000 per violation. Employees may also bring suit, when the Department of Labor has not, for back pay, and other compensatory damages, including attorney's fees and court costs.

State	Minimum Wage	Overtime Hours	Maximum Tip Credit	Rest Breaks
Federal	$7.25/hour regular rate	1.5 times	$3.02/hour	None required
Oregon	$8.50/hour regular rate	1.5 times	None Allowed	10 minutes per 4 hours worked
South Carolina	No state law	No state law	No state law	No state law
Vermont	$8.15/hour	1.5 times, but hotels and restaurants are exempt	$4.20/hour	No state law

Remember that whenever a state law or regulation is different from the federal law or regulation, the law or regulation most favorable to the employee must be followed.

Figure 8.5 Variances in federal and state compensation provisions.

Tipped Employees

The hospitality industry employs a large number of individuals who customarily receive *tips* in conjunction with their work duties. On the one hand, some employees, such as hotel housekeepers, may receive tips only occasionally. Food servers, on the other hand, often receive more income in tips than their employer pays them in wages.

Search the Web 8.1

Go to the Internet and enter www.dol.gov.

1. Select: Search.
2. Enter: State Minimum Wages in the search box.
3. Select: Minimum Wage Laws in the States from the search results.
4. Select: The state where you live or go to school.
5. Identify the minimum wage rate for workers in your state.
6. Identify the overtime provisions (referred to as premium pay) for workers in your state.
7. Identify any exemptions or exceptions that relate to the hospitality industry.

Because the minimum wage and the laws related to it change on a regular basis, it is a good idea to regularly contact your local office of the Wage and Hour Division, listed in most telephone directories under U.S. government, Department of Labor, Employment Standards Administration, for legal updates.

The FLSA defines tipped employees as individuals engaged in occupations in which they customarily and regularly receive more than $30 a month in tips. The employer may consider tips as part of wages, but the employer must pay at least $2.13 an hour in direct wages. If an employer elects to use the tip credit provision, they must inform the employee in advance, and must be able to show that the employee receives at least the applicable minimum wage when direct wages and the tip credit allowance are combined. If an employee's tips combined with the employer's direct wages of at least $2.13 an hour do not equal the minimum hourly wage, the employer must make up the difference. Also, employees must retain all of their tips, except to the extent that they participate in a valid tip pooling or sharing arrangement.

Consider the case of Lawson Odde. Lawson is employed in a state that has adopted the federal minimum wage guidelines, which is a minimum wage of $7.25 per hour. Under the law, his employer is allowed to consider Lawson's tips as part of his wages, thus the employer is required to pay Lawson at least $2.13 per hour, and take a *tip credit* for the remainder of the wages needed to comply with the law. However, if Lawson does not make enough money in tips to equal $5.12, the remainder of the minimum wage amount less the hourly wage already paid by the employer, then the employer must pay Lawson the remaining difference so that Lawson is paid a minimum wage.

Like the minimum wage and the requirements for overtime pay, state laws regarding tipped employees and allowable tip credits can also vary. Figure 8.5 details some selected differences in how state and federal laws consider tip credits. It is important to remember that because tips are given to employees, and not employers, the law carefully regulates the influence that you, as an employer, have over these funds. In fact, if an employer takes control of the tips an employee receives, that employer will not be allowed to utilize the tip credit provisions of the FLSA. For more information on tipped employees, read "Uncovering the Mysteries of the Tip Wage" by Terrence Robinson, found at: www.hospitalitylawyer.com/index .php?id=72.

LEGALLY MANAGING AT WORK:

Calculating Overtime Pay for Tipped Employees

Tipped employees are generally subject to the overtime provisions of the FLSA. The computation of the overtime rate for tipped employees when the employer claims a tax credit can be confusing to some managers. Consider, for example, a state in which the minimum wage is $8.00 per hour and the applicable overtime provision dictates payment of one and one-half the normal hours rate for hours worked in excess of 40 hours per week. To determine the overtime rate of pay, use the following three-step method:

1. Multiply the prevailing minimum wage rate by 1.5.
2. Compute the allowable tip credit against the standard hourly rate.
3. Subtract the number in step 2 from the result in step 1.

Thus, if the minimum wage were $8.00 per hour, and the allowable tip credit were 50 percent, the overtime rate to be paid would be computed as:

1. $8.00 × 1.5 = $9.00
2. $8.00 × 5.0 = $3.00
3. $9.00 − $3.00 = $6.00 overtime rate

Tip Pooling

In some hospitality businesses, employees routinely share tips. Consider, for example, the table busser whose job includes refilling water glasses at a fine dining establishment. If a guest leaves a tip on the table, the size of that tip will certainly have been influenced by the attentiveness of the busser assigned to that table. The FLSA does not prohibit *tip pooling*, but it is an area that employers should approach with extreme caution. A tip, by its nature, is given to an employee, not the employer. In that way, a tip is different from a *service charge* that is collected from the guest by the employer and distributed in the manner deemed best by the employer.

LEGALESE
Service charge: An amount added to a guest's bill in exchange for services provided.

> ### Tip-Pooling Consent Form
> 1. Employee name
> 2. Date
> 3. A complete explanation of the facility's tip-pooling policy
> 4. The statement: "I understand the tip-pooling procedures and procedures stated above, and agree to participate in the tip-pooling and redistribution program."
> 5. Employee signature line below the preceding statement

Figure 8.6 Tip-pooling consent form.

Generally speaking, when a tip is given directly to an employee, management has no control over what that employee will ultimately do with the tip. An exception to this principle is the tip-pooling arrangement.

Tip pooling/sharing is a complex area, because the logistics of providing hospitality services is sometimes complex. When a hostess seats a guest, a busser—who has previously set the table—provides water and bread, a bartender provides drinks, and a member of the waitstaff delivers drinks and food to the table, the question of who deserves a portion of the tip can become perplexing.

Employers are free to assist employees in developing a tip-pooling/sharing arrangement that is fair, based on the specific duties of each position in the service area. This participation should be documented in the employee's personnel file. The tip-pooling/sharing consent form should include the information presented in Figure 8.6.

Because it involves compensation, even well-constructed, voluntary tip-pooling arrangements can be a source of employee conflict. In addition, state laws in this field do vary, so it is a good idea to check with your state trade association or Wage and Hour Division regulator to determine the regulations that apply in your own area.

›› ANALYZE THE SITUATION 8.2

STEPHEN ROSSENWASSER WAS HIRED as a busser by the Sportsman's Fishing Club. This private club served its members lunch and dinner, as well as alcoholic beverages. Stephen's duties were to clear tables, replenish water glasses, and reset tables for the waitstaff when guests had finished their meals. Stephen's employer paid a wage rate below the minimum wage, because they utilized the tip credit portion of the FLSA minimum wage law.

When he was hired, Stephen read the tip-pooling policy in place at the club and signed a document stating that he understood it and voluntarily agreed to participate in it. The policy stated that, "All food and beverage tips are to be combined at the end of each meal period, and then distributed, with bussers receiving 20 percent of all tip income."

John Granberry, an attorney, was a club member, and a guest who enjoyed dining in Stephen's assigned section, because Stephen was attentive and quick to respond to any guest's needs. Mr. Granberry tipped well, and the dining room staff was aware that Mr. Granberry always requested to be seated in Stephen's section.

One day after Mr. Granberry had finished his meal, had added his generous tip to his credit card charge slip, and had begun to depart; he stopped Stephen in the lobby of the club, and gave him a $20 bill, with the words, "This is for you. Keep up the good work." A club bartender observed the exchange.

Stephen did not place Mr. Granberry's tip into the tip pool, stating that the gratuity was clearly meant for him alone. Stephen's supervisor demanded that Stephen contribute the tip to the pool. Stephen refused.

1. Is Stephen obligated to place Mr. Granberry's tip into the tip pool?

2. If Stephen continues to refuse to relinquish the tip, what steps, if any, can management take to force him to do so?

3. Can Stephen voluntarily withdraw from the tip-pool arrangement and still maintain his club employment?

Taxes and Credits

Employers are required to pay taxes on the compensation they pay employees and to withhold taxes from the wages of employees. Federal and state statutes govern the types and amounts of compensation taxes that must be paid or withheld. In some cases, tax breaks, called credits, are granted to employers or employees. While these taxes and credits can change, the most important employee taxes are the following:

Income tax: Employers are required to withhold state and federal income taxes from the paychecks of nearly all employees. These taxes are paid by the employee, but collected by the employer and forwarded to the Internal Revenue Service (IRS) and state taxation agency. The amount that is to be withheld is based on the wage rate paid to the employee and the number of federal income tax dependents and deductions the employee has indicated he or she is entitled to. It is important to remember that tips are considered wages for income tax purposes if they are paid by cash, check, or credit card, and amount to more than $20.00 per calendar month.

FICA: Often called Social Security taxes, the Federal Insurance Contribution Act (FICA) taxes to fund the Social Security and Medicare programs. Both employers and employees are required to contribute to FICA. FICA taxes must be paid on the employee's wages, which include cash wages and the cash value of all remuneration paid in any medium other than cash. The size of the FICA tax and the amount of an employee's wages subject to it are adjusted on a regular basis by the federal government.

FUTA: The Federal Unemployment Tax Act (FUTA) requires employers, but not employees, to contribute a tax based on the size of the employer's total payroll. Again, it is important to remember that payroll includes tip income and remuneration paid in forms other than cash.

EIC: The Earned Income Credit (EIC) is a refundable tax credit for workers whose incomes fall below established levels. The credit increases for families with two or more children, for families with a child under one year old, and for families that pay for health insurance for their children. Most workers entitled to the EIC choose to claim the credit when they file their federal income taxes. However, employees who elect to submit a Form W-5 (Earned Income Credit Advance Payment Certificate) have the option of getting the money in advance by receiving part of the credit in each paycheck (see Figure 8.7). Employers are required to include the EIC in the paycheck of any employee who submits a W-5,

20**10** Form W-5

 **Department of the Treasury**
Internal Revenue Service

Instructions

Purpose of Form

Use Form W-5 if you are eligible to get part of the earned income credit (EIC) in advance with your pay and choose to do so. See *Who Is Eligible To Get Advance EIC Payments?* below. The amount you can get in advance generally depends on your wages. If you are married, the amount of your advance EIC payments also depends on whether your spouse has filed a Form W-5 with his or her employer. However, your employer cannot give you more than $1,830 throughout 2010 with your pay. You will get the rest of any EIC you are entitled to when you file your 2010 tax return and claim the EIC.

If you do not choose to get advance payments, you can still claim the EIC on your 2010 tax return.

What Is the EIC?

The EIC is a credit for certain workers. It reduces the tax you owe. It may give you a refund even if you do not owe any tax.

Who Is Eligible To Get Advance EIC Payments?

You are eligible to get advance EIC payments if **all four** of the following apply.

1. You (and your spouse, if filing a joint return) have a valid social security number (SSN) issued by the Social Security Administration. For more information on valid SSNs, see Pub. 596, Earned Income Credit (EIC).

2. You expect to have at least one qualifying child and to be able to claim the credit using that child. If you do not expect to have a qualifying child, you may still be eligible for the EIC, but you cannot receive advance EIC payments. See *Who Is a Qualifying Child?* beginning on this page.

3. You expect that your 2010 earned income and adjusted gross income (AGI) will each be less than $35,535 ($40,545 if you expect to file a joint return for 2010). Include your spouse's income if you plan to file a joint return. As used on this form, earned income does not include amounts inmates in penal institutions are paid for their work or amounts received as a pension or annuity from a nonqualified deferred compensation plan or a nongovernmental

section 457 plan. Generally, earned income also does not include nontaxable earned income, but you can elect to include nontaxable combat pay in earned income.

4. You expect to be able to claim the EIC for 2010. To find out if you may be able to claim the EIC, answer the questions on page 2.

How To Get Advance EIC Payments

If you are eligible to get advance EIC payments, fill in the 2010 Form W-5 at the bottom of this page. Then, detach it and give it to your employer. If you get advance payments, you must file a 2010 Form 1040 or 1040A income tax return.

You may have only one Form W-5 in effect at one time. If you and your spouse are both employed, you should file separate Forms W-5.

This Form W-5 expires on December 31, 2010. If you are eligible to get advance EIC payments for 2011, you must file a new Form W-5 next year.

> **TIP** *You may be able to get a larger credit when you file your 2010 return. For details, see* Additional Credit *on page 3.*

Who Is a Qualifying Child?

A qualifying child is any child who meets all four of the following conditions.

1. The child is your son, daughter, stepchild, foster child, brother, sister, half brother, half sister, stepbrother, stepsister, or a descendant of any of them (for example, your grandchild, niece, or nephew). An adopted child is always treated as your own child. An adopted child includes a child lawfully placed with you for legal adoption. A foster child is any child placed with you by an authorized placement agency or by judgment, decree, or other order of any court of competent jurisdiction.

2. The child is under age 19 at the end of 2010 and younger than you (or your spouse, if filing jointly); or under age 24 at the end of 2010, a student, and younger than you (or your spouse, if filing jointly); or any age and permanently and totally disabled. A student is a child who during any 5 months of 2010 (a) was enrolled as a full-time student at a school or (b) took a full-time, on-farm training course given by a school or a state, county, or local government

(continued on page 3)

▼   *Give the bottom part to your employer; keep the top part for your records.*   ▼
------------------------------------ Detach here ------------------------------------

Form **W-5**

Department of the Treasury
Internal Revenue Service

Earned Income Credit Advance Payment Certificate

▶ **Use the current year's certificate only.**
▶ **Give this certificate to your employer.**
▶ **This certificate expires on December 31, 2010.**

OMB No. 1545-0074

20**10**

Print or type your full name	Your social security number

Note. *If you get advance payments of the earned income credit for 2010, you* **must** *file a 2010 federal income tax return. To get advance payments, you* **must** *have a qualifying child and your filing status must be any status* **except** *married filing a separate return.*

1   I expect to have a qualifying child and be able to claim the earned income credit for 2010 using that child. I do not have another Form W-5 in effect with any other current employer, and I choose to get advance EIC payments   ☐ Yes ☐ No

2   Check the box that shows your expected filing status for 2010:
☐ Single, head of household, or qualifying widow(er)   ☐ Married filing jointly

3   If you are married, does your spouse have a Form W-5 in effect for 2010 with any employer? . . . . .   ☐ Yes ☐ No

Under penalties of perjury, I declare that the information I have furnished above is, to the best of my knowledge, true, correct, and complete.

Signature ▶   Date ▶

Cat. No. 10227P

Figure 8.7 Form W-5.

Questions To See if You May Be Able To Claim the EIC for 2010

⚠ **CAUTION** You **cannot** claim the EIC if you file either Form 2555 or Form 2555-EZ (relating to foreign earned income) for 2010. You also **cannot** claim the EIC if you are a nonresident alien for any part of 2010 unless you are married to a U.S. citizen or resident, file a joint return, and elect to be taxed as a resident alien for all of 2010.

1 Do you expect to have a qualifying child? Read *Who Is a Qualifying Child?* that starts on page 1 before you answer this question. If the child is married, be sure you also read *Married child* on page 3.

☐ **No.** 🛑 You may be able to claim the EIC but you **cannot** get advance EIC payments.
☐ **Yes.** *Continue.*

⚠ **CAUTION** If the child meets the conditions to be a qualifying child of both you and another person, see *Qualifying child of more than one person* on page 3.

2 Do you expect your 2010 filing status to be married filing a separate return?

☐ **Yes.** 🛑 You **cannot** claim the EIC.
☐ **No.** *Continue.*

TIP If you expect to file a joint return for 2010, include your spouse's income when answering questions 3 and 4.

3 Do you expect that your 2010 earned income and AGI will each be less than: $35,535 ($40,545 if married filing jointly) if you expect to have one qualifying child; $40,363 ($45,373 if married filing jointly) if you expect to have two qualifying children; or $43,352 ($48,362 if married filing jointly) if you expect to have three or more qualifying children?

☐ **No.** 🛑 You **cannot** claim the EIC.
☐ **Yes.** *Continue.* But remember, you **cannot** get advance EIC payments if you expect your 2010 earned income or AGI will be $35,535 or more ($40,545 or more if married filing jointly).

4 Do you expect that your 2010 investment income will be more than $3,100? For most people, investment income is the total of their taxable interest, ordinary dividends, capital gain distributions, and tax-exempt interest. However, if you plan to file a 2010 Form 1040, see the 2009 Form 1040 instructions to figure your investment income.

☐ **Yes.** 🛑 You **cannot** claim the EIC.
☐ **No.** *Continue.*

5 Do you expect that you, or your spouse if filing a joint return, will be a qualifying child of another person for 2010?
☐ **Yes.** You **cannot** claim the EIC.
☐ **No.** You may be able to claim the EIC.

Figure 8.7 *(Continued)*

agency. A school includes a technical, trade, or mechanical school. It does not include an on-the-job training course, correspondence school, or Internet school.

3. The child lives with you in the United States for over half of 2010. But you do not have to meet this condition if (a) the child was born or died during the year and your home was this child's home for the entire time he or she was alive in 2010, or (b) the child is presumed by law enforcement authorities to have been kidnapped by someone who is not a family member and the child lived with you for over half of the part of the year before he or she was kidnapped. Also, temporary absences, such as for school, vacation, medical care, or detention in a juvenile facility, count as time the child lived with you. Members of the military on extended active duty outside the United States are considered to be living in the United States.

4. The child does not file a joint return for 2010 (or files a joint return for 2010 only as a claim for refund).

Married child. A child who is married at the end of 2010 is a qualifying child only if the child meets the four conditions just listed and:

1. You can claim him or her as your dependent, or

2. You are the custodial parent and would be able to claim the child as your dependent, but the noncustodial parent claims the child as a dependent because:

a. You signed Form 8332, Release/Revocation of Release of Claim to Exemption for Child by Custodial Parent, or a similar statement, agreeing not to claim the child for 2010, or

b. You have a pre-1985 divorce decree or separation agreement that allows the noncustodial parent to claim the child and he or she gives at least $600 for the child's support in 2010.

Other rules may apply. See Pub. 501, Exemptions, Standard Deduction, and Filing Information, for more information on children of divorced or separated parents.

Qualifying child of more than one person. Even if a child meets the conditions to be a qualifying child of more than one person, only one person can treat that child as a qualifying child for 2010 and take, if otherwise eligible, all of the following tax benefits using that child: the child's dependency exemption, the child tax credit, head of household filing status, the credit for child and dependent care expenses, the exclusion for dependent care benefits, and the EIC. No other person can take any of these six tax benefits unless he or she has a different qualifying child. To determine which person can treat the child as a qualifying child, the following rules apply.

• If only one of the persons is the child's parent, the child is treated as the qualifying child of the parent.

• If the parents do not file a joint return together but both parents claim the child as a qualifying child, the IRS will treat the child as the qualifying child of the parent with whom the child lives for the longer period of time in 2010. If the child lives with each parent for the same amount of time, the IRS will treat the child as the qualifying child of the parent who has the higher AGI for 2010.

• If no parent can claim the child as a qualifying child, the child is treated as the qualifying child of the person who has the highest AGI for 2010.

• If a parent can claim the child as a qualifying child but no parent does so claim the child, the child is treated as the qualifying child of the person who has the highest AGI for 2010, but only if that person's AGI is higher than the AGI of any of the child's parents who can claim the child.

Subject to the rules just described, you and the other person(s) may be able to choose which of you treats the child as a qualifying child. For example, if you, your 3-year-old child, and your mother all live together and your child's other parent does not live with you, you can treat your child as a qualifying child, or you can choose to let your mother do so if her AGI is higher than yours. For details, more examples, and a special rule for divorced or separated parents, see Pub. 596.

 Caution. *A qualifying child whom you use to claim the EIC must have a valid social security number unless he or she is born and dies in 2010.*

What if My Situation Changes?

If your situation changes after you give Form W-5 to your employer, you will probably need to file a new Form W-5. For example, you must file a new Form W-5 if any of the following applies for 2010.

• You no longer expect to have a qualifying child. Check "No" on line 1 of your new Form W-5.

• You no longer expect to be able to claim the EIC for 2010. Check "No" on line 1 of your new Form W-5.

• You no longer want advance payments. Check "No" on line 1 of your new Form W-5.

• Your spouse files Form W-5 with his or her employer. Check "Yes" on line 3 of your new Form W-5.

Note. If you get advance EIC payments and find you are not eligible for the EIC, you must pay back these payments when you file your 2010 federal income tax return.

Additional Information

How To Claim the EIC

If you are eligible, claim the EIC on your 2010 tax return. See your 2010 tax return instruction booklet.

Additional Credit

You may be able to claim a larger credit when you file your 2010 Form 1040 or Form 1040A because your employer cannot give you more than $1,830 throughout the year with your pay. You may also be able to claim a larger credit if you have more than one qualifying child. But you must file your 2010 tax return to claim any additional credit.

Figure 8.7 *(Continued)*

but are not required to verify the worker's eligibility for the credit. The extra money for EIC payments does not come from the employer but is deducted from the income and payroll tax dollars they would normally be required to deposit with the IRS.

WOTC: The Work Opportunity Tax Credit was enacted in 1996 to replace the expired Targeted Jobs Tax Credit. The WOTC gives employers a tax credit of up to $2,100 for hiring certain disadvantaged workers, including certain disabled persons, recipients of Aid to Dependent Children, qualified veterans, qualified ex-felons, youths living in urban empowerment zones, some summer workers, and food-stamp recipients.

As a hospitality manager, it is critical that you keep up to date with the compensation, taxes, and credit legislation enacted at both the federal and state level. Certainly, all taxes that are due should be paid, but the hospitality industry often employs workers who are eligible for tax credits. In addition, employing certain individuals may make the employer eligible for tax credits as well.

8.5 MANAGING EMPLOYEE PERFORMANCE

Most employees come to a job with the expectation that they can complete or learn to complete the tasks assigned to them. In the hospitality industry, some of the workers hired are entering the workforce for the first time, while others may have many years of experience. Regardless of ability or background, to effectively manage employee performance, employers must have a valid and defensible system of employee evaluation, discipline, and, if necessary, termination.

Evaluation

Employee evaluation is often used in the hospitality industry as a basis for granting pay increases, determining who is eligible for promotion or transfer, or as a means of modifying employee performance. Unfortunately, the subjective nature of many employee evaluation methods makes them susceptible to misuse and bias. When the employee can demonstrate that the evaluation system is biased against a class of workers specifically protected by the law, the liability to the employer can be great.

In most larger hospitality companies, the human resource department will have some type of form or procedure in place for use in employee evaluations. In smaller organizations, the process may be less formalized. In all cases, however, the hospitality manager must use great care to ensure that all employees are evaluated on the basis of their work performance, and nothing else. Therefore, it is critical that you base evaluations only on previously established criteria and expectations, such as the job descriptions discussed in Chapter 7, "Legally Selecting Employees."

A false negative employee evaluation that results in loss of employment for the employee subjects the employer to even greater liability. *Wrongful termination* is the term used to describe the unlawful discharge of an employee. The at-will employment status that exists in most states does not mean employers are free to unfairly evaluate employees, then use the results of the evaluation as the basis for a termination.

> **LEGALESE**
> **Employee evaluation:**
> A review of an employee's performance, including strengths and shortcomings; typically completed by the employee's direct supervisor.

> **LEGALESE**
> **Wrongful termination:**
> A violation, by the employer, of the employment relationship resulting in the unlawful firing of the employee.

Discipline

Companies have the right to establish rules and policies for their workplace, as long as those rules do not violate the law. Even potentially controversial policies such as drug testing or surveillance have been upheld by the courts, provided that those policies do not discriminate against or single out specific groups of employees.

Workplace rules should be properly communicated and consistently enforced. The communication process can include written policies and procedures (including an employee manual), one-on-one coaching, and formal training sessions. The enforcement process is just as important a part of the discipline process as is training. If, for example, a restaurant manager, in violation of stated sanitation policies, allows the cook to work without an effective hair restraint on Monday, it will be difficult for the employee to understand why the rule is enforced on Tuesday.

Many organizations implement a policy of *progressive discipline* for employees. This system is used for minor work rule infractions, and some major ones.

≫ ANALYZE THE SITUATION 8.3

GERRY HERNANDEZ WORKED AS a breakfast cook at a large day-care facility. His attendance and punctuality were both good. Written into the facility's employee manual (which all employees sign when they begin their employment) was the following policy: "To be fair to the facility, your fellow employees, and our clients, you must be at your work station regularly and on time."

Gerry had worked at the facility for 10 months when, one day, he was 15 minutes late for work. While Gerry was aware of the facility work rule regarding punctuality, Gerry's supervisor, Pauline Cooper, rarely enforced the rule. Employees who were 5 to 20 minutes late may have been scolded, but no disciplinary action was usually taken, unless, according to Ms. Cooper, the employee was "excessively" tardy. She preferred to, in her words, "cut some slack" to employees, and thus was considered one of the more popular supervisors.

On the day Gerry was late, a variety of problems had occurred in the kitchen. Frozen food deliveries arrived early and no cook was available to put them away; the sanitation inspector arrived for an unannounced inspection; and the rinse agent on the dish machine stopped functioning so dishes had to be washed by hand. Ms. Cooper was very angry, so when Gerry arrived at work, she terminated him, stating, "If you can't get here on time, I don't need you here at all!"

The next day, Gerry filed suit against the day-care facility claiming that he was terminated because of his ethnic background. Ms. Cooper and the day-care facility countered that Gerry was an at-will employee, and thus the facility had the right to terminate employees as they see fit, especially when the employee was in violation of a communicated work rule.

1. Does Ms. Cooper have the right, under at-will employment, to terminate Gerry?

2. If Ms. Cooper has no records documenting her actions in cases similar to Gerry's, is it likely she will be able to help defend her organization against a discrimination charge?

3. How would you advise Ms. Cooper to handle tardy employees in the future?

In a progressive disciplinary system, employees pass through a series of stages, each designed to help the employee comply with stated organizational workplace rules.

Progressive disciplinary systems usually follow five steps:

LEGALESE

Progressive discipline:
An employee development process that provides increasingly severe consequences for continued violation of workplace rules.

1. *Verbal warning.* In this first step, the employee is reminded/informed of the workplace rule and its importance. The employee is clearly told what constitutes a violation and how to avoid these violations in the future.

2. *Documented verbal warning.* In step 2, the supervisor makes a written record of the verbal reprimand, and the document is signed by both the supervisor and employee. One copy is given to the employee and one copy is retained in the employee's file.

3. *Written warning.* An official, written reprimand is the third step, generally accompanied by a plan for stopping the unwanted behavior and a setting forth of consequences if the behavior does not stop. This document is placed in the employee's file.

4. *Suspension.* In this step, the employee is placed on paid or unpaid leave for a length of time designated by management. A record of the suspension, its length and conditions, is placed in the employee's file.

5. *Termination.* As a last option, the employee is terminated for continued and willful disregard of the workplace rule.

In all of these steps, a written record of the action is required. Figure 8.8 is an example of a form that can be used to document the steps in the progressive discipline process.

Not all incidents of workplace rule violations are subject to progressive discipline. Destruction of property, carrying weapons, falsifying records, substance abuse while on the job, and some safety violations may be cause for immediate termination; in fact, failure to do so may place the employer in greater legal risk than not terminating the employee. Employers should make it clear that they reserve the right to immediately terminate an employee for a serious workplace violation as part of the progressive disciplinary procedure.

Termination

Although states and the federal government give employers wide latitude in the hiring and firing of workers, the at-will employment doctrine does not allow an employer unrestricted freedom to terminate employees. An employer may not legally terminate an employee if it is done:

1. *In violation of company employee manuals or handbooks.* Failure to follow the procedures outlined in employee manuals and handbooks may result in legal action against the employer because of the implied contract such documents may establish.

2. *To deny accrued benefits.* These benefits can include bonuses, insurance premiums, wages, stock or retirement options, and time off with pay. If, however, the employee is fired for cause, the firing may be legal, and the accrued benefits may be forfeited.

3. *Because of legitimate illness or absence from work.* This is especially true if the employee was injured at work and has filed a workers' compensation claim. Should the absence become excessive, however, the employer may be able to force the employee to accept disability status.

Employee's Progressive Performance Review

Date _____

Employee's Name: _____

Employee's Position: _____

Type of Action for this Discussion:

____ Oral Warning   ____Written Warning   ____ Probation   ____ Suspension

Employer's view of the violation: _____

_____

_____

Employee's view of the violation: _____

_____

_____

Is the employee being placed on probation?   ___No   ___Yes, until what date: ___/___/__

Is the employee being suspended?   ___ No   ___Yes, until what date: ___/___/__

What specific action steps have been agreed upon between the employee and supervisor to improve and/or resolve the violation? (action steps and date):   _____

_____

_____

I have reviewed and discussed this performance violation with my supervisor and understand the terms listed above to correct my performance.

_____   _____
Employee's signature   Date

_____   _____
Employer's representative signature   Date

_____   _____
Signature of Human Resources witness   Date

Figure 8.8 Progressive discipline form.

4. *For attempting to unionize coworkers.* Some employers are reluctant to allow this type of activity to occur, but it is a right protected by federal law.

5. *For reporting violations of law.* In some states, private business *whistle-blowers protection acts* have been passed to ensure that employees who report violations of the law by their employers will not be terminated unjustly. These laws penalize employers that retaliate against workers who report suspected violations of health, safety, financial, or other regulations and laws.

6. *For belonging to a protected class of workers.* Employers may not fire an employee because he or she is over 40; is of a particular race, color, religion, gender, or national origin; or is disabled. In addition, employers may not treat these workers any differently than they would those workers who are not members of a protected class.

7. *Without notice.* This is true under some circumstances related to massive layoffs or facility closings. In general, larger employers are covered by the Worker Adjustment and Retraining Notification (WARN) Act. WARN provides protection to workers, their families, and their communities by requiring employers to provide notification 60 calendar days in advance of plant closings and mass layoffs. A covered plant closing occurs when a facility or operating unit is shut down for more than six months or when 50 or more employees lose their jobs during any 30-day period at the single site of employment.

   Consider the case of the Mayflower Hotel, a large, independent facility employing 150 people. The hotel is purchased by new owners on June 1. On June 2, the new owners announce that all employees will be terminated from employment by the old owners, then rehired by the new. But employees will be subject to review before rehiring. In such a circumstance, the WARN Act would allow any employees who prefer not to work for the new company the time required to secure other employment.

8. *If the employee has been verbally promised continued employment.* The courts have ruled, in some cases, that a verbal employment contract is in effect if an employer publicly and continually assures an employee of the security of his or her employment.

9. *In violation of a written employment contract.* This is true whether the contract is written for an individual worker or the worker is a member of a labor union that has a collective bargaining agreement (CBA).

In some cases, an employer may be called on to produce evidence that an employee was terminated legitimately and legally. The seven guidelines in the upcoming Legally Managing at Work section can be used to ensure that terminations are defensible, should the need arise.

LEGALLY MANAGING AT WORK:

Guidelines for Conducting Defensible Employee Terminations

1. **Conduct and document regular employee evaluations.**

   It is the rare employee whose performance becomes extremely poor overnight. Generally, employee performance problems can be identified in regular employee evaluation sessions. These evaluations should be performed in a thoughtful, timely manner, with an opportunity for employee input. These written evaluations should be reviewed by upper management to ensure consistency between and among reviewers.

2. **Develop and enforce written policies and procedures.**

   As a manager, you may set yourself up for accusations that your discharge policies are unfair if you cannot show that employees were told, in writing, of the organization's rules of employee conduct. All employees should be given a copy of any employment rules, both because it is a good employment practice and to help avoid potential lawsuits. Employees should be given the chance to thoroughly review these rules and ask questions about them, and then they should be required to sign a document stating they have done so. This document should be placed in the employee's personnel file.

3. **Prohibit "on-the-spot" terminations.**

The hospitality industry is fast-paced, and tensions can sometimes run very high. Despite that, it is never a good idea to allow a supervisor or manager to terminate an employee without adequate consideration. This is not to say that a violent employee, for example, should not be required to leave the property immediately if his or her presence poses a danger to others. It does say, however, that terminations made in the heat of the moment can be very hard to defend when the emotion of the moment has subsided.

4. **Develop and utilize a progressive disciplinary system.**

Make sure that each step of the disciplinary process is reviewed by at least one person other than the documenting manager and the employee. A representative from the human resources department is a good choice, or in small properties, the general manager of the facility.

5. **Review all documentation prior to discharging an employee.**

Because of the serious nature of employee termination, it is a good idea to thoroughly review all documentation prior to dismissing an employee. If the evidence supports termination, it should be undertaken. If it does not, the organization will be put at risk if the discharge is undertaken despite the lack of documentation. If a progressive disciplinary process is in place, each step in that process should be followed every time. In this way, you can defend yourself against charges of discriminatory or arbitrary actions.

6. **When possible, conduct a termination review and exit interview.**

Employees are less likely to sue their former employers if they understand why they have been terminated. Some employers, however, make it a policy to refuse to tell employees why they have been let go, citing the at-will status of employment as their rationale. Each approach has its advantages and disadvantages. An employee who is shown documented evidence of his or her consistent, excessive absence, along with the results of a well-implemented progressive discipline program, is less likely to sue, claiming unfair treatment because of nonrelated demographic issues such as gender, race, ethnicity, and other protected class status.

7. **Treat information regarding terminations as confidential.**

In the most common case, an employee's discharge will be initiated by the employee's supervisor or manager, and should be reviewed prior to implementation by the immediate superior of that supervisor or manager. The actual exit interview may be witnessed by a representative from human resources or a second manager.

Employee termination reflects a failure on the part of both the employer and employee. The employee has performed in a substandard manner, but perhaps the employer has improperly selected or poorly trained and managed that person. The details of these failures need not be shared with those who do not have a need to know. Nothing is gained; in fact, greater employer liability is incurred when management shares details of an employee's termination with others.

In-House Dispute Resolution

The cost of a lawsuit is very high. In the case of employment litigation, many companies have found that the cost of defending themselves against the charges of an unfair employment practice is extremely high, often exceeding the amount of the employee's claim of damages. For example, a simple dispute where an employee asks for damages in the amount of $5,000 may cost the employer five times that amount to defend the charge.

The cost to employees to pursue such an unfair employment claim is high also. Because the employee who charges an employer with an unfair practice is often no longer employed, the employee may face great legal expense at a time he or she can least afford to do so.

Cases involving unfair employment practices may drag on for years, which not only increases legal expenses but can also diminish the likelihood of an amicable settlement between employer and employee. By the time the litigation has been completed, several years may have passed, much expense may have been incurred on both sides, the personal relationship between the employee and employer has been damaged, and both sides may well have come to realize that having one's day in court is often too long in coming and too expensive to undertake.

Because of the disadvantages just listed, a system of resolving disputes between employers and employees that is gaining widespread acceptance is the *in-house dispute resolution* process.

The in-house dispute resolution process is a management tool that seeks to provide three benefits:

> **LEGALESE**
>
> **In-house dispute resolution:** A program, funded by employers, that encourages the equitable settlement of an employee's claim of unfair employment, prior to or without resorting to litigation.

1. *Fairness to employees.* This is achieved by involving employees in the development and implementation of the program. At a corporate level, employers should realize that the purpose of an in-house dispute resolution program is the prevention of litigation, not the winning of every dispute.

2. *Cost savings to employers.* The in-house dispute resolution program should result in reduced costs for employers. It is also important to realize that costs can be measured in terms beyond legal fees.

3. *Timely resolution of complaints.* An in-house dispute resolution program grants, as its greatest advantage, the ability to deal quickly with a problem. Sometimes, this can save the employee/employer relationship and get the employee back to work feeling that his or her concern has been heard and that the employer really cares about him or her, something that rarely happens at the conclusion of a lawsuit.

A well-designed in-house dispute resolution program can have an extremely positive effect on an organization if it is established and operated in the proper manner. Here are four features of an effective in-house dispute resolution program:

1. *Development with employee input.* Employees and employers generally will work toward developing a program that is easy to access, is perceived as fair, provides a rapid response, and includes a legitimate appeal procedure.

2. *Training for mediators.* Those individuals who will hear and help resolve disputes should be specially trained in how to do so. In some companies, these individuals are called *ombudspersons.* Effectively trained mediators can resolve up to 75 percent of all worker complaints without litigation. The resolutions can range from a simple apology to reinstatement and substantial monetary damages.

3. *Legal assistance for employees.* The best programs take into account that employees may need advice from their own legal counsel, and thus payment for this advice is provided. While it might seem strange to fund the legal counsel of an employee in a work-related dispute, the reality is that costs savings will occur if an amicable solution to the problem can be developed.

4. *Distinct and unique chain of command for appeal.* Sometimes, the original finding of the review process will be perceived by the employee as unfair. When this is the case, employees need to know that they can appeal the decision, without further complicating their relationship with the company. Also, they need to be assured that such an appeal will be heard by those who are unbeholden to the first decision maker. Obviously, not all employees will be satisfied with the resolution of their complaint. In addition, some areas such as workers' compensation claims may not be included in the program.

8.6 UNEMPLOYMENT CLAIMS

Of the many costs related to maintaining a workforce, the cost of unemployment insurance is one of the largest and most difficult to administer. The *unemployment insurance* program is operated jointly by the federal and state governments. Each state imposes different costs on employers for maintaining the state's share of a pool of funds for assisting workers who have temporarily lost their jobs.

Figure 8.9 details the contribution rate charged to employers in the state of Ohio in 2009, 2010, and 2011. It is presented as an example of a method used by several states to charge higher taxes to those employers that cause more of the fund pool to be used, and less to those with fewer claims. Thus, two restaurants with identical sales volume, but very different experiences in maintaining staff, can pay widely different unemployment tax rates based on how well they manage their staffs and their *unemployment claims.*

Contribution Rates
    For 2009, 2010 and 2011 the ranges of Ohio unemployment tax rates (also known as contribution rates) are as follows:

	2009	2010	2011
Lowest Experience Rate	0.7%	0.5%	0.7%
Highest Experience Rate	9.4%	9.4%	9.6%
Mutualized Rate	0.4%	0.2%	0.4%
New Employer Rate	2.7%	2.7%	2.7%
*Construction Industry	5.8%	6.0%	6.4%
Delinquency Rate	11.8%	11.8%	12.0%

*except construction

Figure 8.9 Unemployment tax rates for Ohio.
Source: Ohio Job and Family Services, available at jfs.ohio.gov/ouc/uctax/rates.stm.

Rate Notification

Contribution Rate Determinations are mailed for the coming calendar year on or before December 1. The tax rate is also printed on the employer's Quarterly Tax Return (JFS-20125), which is mailed to employers quarterly for *reporting* and payment of taxes due. To determine how much tax is due each quarter, multiply the rate by the total *taxable wages* you paid during the quarter.

Experience Rate

Once an employer's account has been chargeable with benefits for four consecutive calendar quarters ending June 30, the account becomes eligible for an experience rate beginning with the next calendar year. The experience includes taxable wages reported, contributions paid (including voluntary payments) and benefits charged. Unemployment taxes paid are credited to an employer's account. Unemployment benefits paid to eligible claimants are charged to the accounts of the claimant's employers during the base period of the claim. These factors are recorded on the employer's account and are used to compute the annual tax rate after the employer becomes eligible for an experience rate.

Due to recent economic conditions and the resulting increase of unemployment claims filed, the Ohio Unemployment Compensation Trust Fund is more than sixty percent below the "minimum safe level" as of the computation date of the 2011 rates (The "minimum safe level" is, in essence, the balance required in the UC Trust Fund to fund a moderate recession). Therefore, the tax rate schedule in effect for 2011 includes an across the board minimum safe level increase to protect the financial integrity of the trust fund. This increase will help re-build the trust fund to the appropriate level. The additional taxes paid as a result of the minimum safe level increase are credited fifty percent (50%) to the mutualized account and fifty percent (50%) to the employer's account.

The experience rate shown on the Contribution Rate Determination is a combined total of the employer's individual experience rate and the minimum safe level increase.

Mutualized Rate

A separate account, known as the mutualized account, is maintained for the primary purpose of recovering the costs of unemployment benefits that were paid and not chargeable to individual employers for a variety of reasons. When the mutualized account has a negative balance, the costs are recovered and the money restored to the account through a mutualized tax levied on all employers who are eligible for an experience rate. The mutualized tax is used solely for the payment of unemployment benefits.

As of the computation date for the 2011 rates, the mutualized account had a negative balance and a mutualized rate of four-tenths of one percent (0.4%) was levied on all employers who were eligible for an experience rate. The mutual rate is shown on the Contribution Rate Determination. The additional taxes paid as a result of mutualized rate will be credited one hundred percent (100%) to the mutualized account to recover the costs of unemployment benefits charged to the account.

New Employer Rate

If an employer's account is not eligible for an experience rate, the account will be assigned a standard new employer rate of 2.7% unless the employer is engaged in the construction industry, in which case the 2009 rate is 5.8%, the 2010 rate is 6.0% and the 2011 rate is 6.4%.

Figure 8.9 *(Continued)*

Delinquency Rate

Employers who did not furnish the wage information necessary for the computation of their 2011 experience rate by September 1, 2010, were assigned a contribution rate equal to one hundred twenty-five percent (125%) of the maximum experience rate possible for 2011. However, if the employer files the necessary wage information by December 31, 2010, the rate will be revised to the appropriate experience rate.

Penalty Rate

Employers who file the necessary wage information after December 31, 2010, but within 18 months after that date, will have their 2011 rate revised to one hundred twenty percent (120%) of the rate that would have applied if the employer had timely furnished the wage information.

Figure 8.9 (*Continued*)

A worker who submits an unemployment claim does not automatically qualify for payments. The employer has the right to challenge this claim. It is important to remember that each successful claim will have an impact on the employer's experience rate, which is the rate by which future contributions to the unemployment fund are determined. Thus, it is in your best interest, as an employer, to protest any unjust claim for unemployment benefits made by your ex-employees.

Criteria for Granting or Denying Benefits

Each state will set its own criteria for determining who is eligible for unemployment benefits. Variances can occur based on answers to any of the following questions:

- How soon can the unemployed worker petition for benefits?
- When will any allowable payments begin?
- What will the size of the payments be?
- How long will the payments last?
- What must the unemployed worker do in order to qualify and continue receiving benefits?
- How long does the employee have to work for the former employer in order to qualify for assistance?

Generally speaking, an employee who quits his or her job for a nonwork-related reason is not eligible for benefits. Employees who are terminated, except for good cause associated with their work performance, generally are eligible. Again, the laws in this area are complex and vary widely; thus, it is a good idea to thoroughly understand who is eligible for unemployment benefits in the state where you work. This can be accomplished by visiting a branch of your state agency responsible for administering unemployment compensation benefits.

The following are common examples of acts that usually justify the denial of unemployment benefits based on employee misconduct:

- Insubordination or fighting on the job
- Habitual lateness or excessive absence
- Drug abuse on the job
- Disobedience of legitimate company work rules or policies
- Gross negligence or neglect of duty
- Dishonesty

Claims and Appeals

If the state agency responsible for granting unemployment benefits receives a request for unemployment assistance from an unemployed worker, the employer will be notified and given a chance to dispute the claim. It is important that you, as an employer, respond to any unemployment claims or requests for information in a timely manner.

An employer should not protest legitimate unemployment benefit payments. It is appropriate, however, to protest those that are not legitimate. Employers often have difficulty proving that workers should not qualify for unemployment benefits, even in situations that might seem relatively straightforward. In addition, the state unemployment agents who determine whether or not to grant benefits often initially decide in favor of the employee. If an employer does not agree with the state's decision, that employer has the right to appeal.

In an appeal of unemployment benefits, each party has the right to take these steps:

1. Speak on his or her own behalf.
2. Present documents and evidence.
3. Request that others (witnesses) speak on his or her behalf.
4. Question those witnesses and parties who oppose his or her position.
5. Examine and respond to the evidence of the other side.
6. Make a statement at the end of the appeals hearing.

An unemployment hearing is often no different from a trial. Witnesses must testify under oath. Documents, including personnel information, warnings, and performance appraisals, are submitted as exhibits. The atmosphere is usually not friendly. You must organize your case before the hearing to maximize your chances of success. If you have elected to have a lawyer help you, meet with him or her before the hearing to review your position.

Decisions are not typically obtained immediately after the hearing. You will probably be notified by mail of the judge's decision. If you lose the decision, read the notice carefully. Most judges and hearing examiners give specific reasons for their rulings, and this information may help you avoid claims in the future.

Search the Web 8.2

Go online to www.stateofflorida.com.

1. Select: Florida Business.
2. Select Labor & Employment.
3. Select: Unemployment Compensation.
4. Click on the Appeals tab.
5. Select: Frequently Asked Questions about the Appeal Process.

Review the FAQs supplied by the State of Florida, and then answer the following questions:

1. To whom does an employer appeal an unemployment insurance claim in the state of Florida?
2. How long does the average appeals hearing last?
3. Is the hearing recorded? Why or why not?

⟩⟩ ANALYZE THE SITUATION 8.4

CAROLYN MOREAU WAS EMPLOYED for nine years as a room attendant for the Windjammer Hotel. The hotel was moderately busy during the week and filled up with tourists on the weekends.

In accordance with hotel policy, Carolyn submitted a request on May 1 for time off on Saturday, May 15, to attend the graduation ceremony of her only daughter. The hotel was extremely short-handed on the weekend of the 15th due to some staff resignations and a forecasted sell-out of rooms. Carolyn's supervisor denied her request for the day off. Carolyn was visibly upset when the schedule was posted and she learned that her request had been denied. She confronted her supervisor and stated, "I am attending my daughter's graduation. No way am I going to miss it!" The supervisor replied that she was sorry, but all requests for that particular weekend off had been denied and Carolyn was to report to work as scheduled.

On the Saturday of the graduation, Carolyn called in sick four hours before her shift was to begin. The supervisor, recalling the conversation with Carolyn, recorded the call-in as "unacceptable excuse," and filled out a form stating that Carolyn had quit her job voluntarily by refusing to work her assigned shift. The supervisor referred to the portion of the employee manual that Carolyn signed when joining the hotel. The manual read, in part:

Employees shall be considered to have voluntarily quit or abandoned their employment upon any of the following occurrences:

1. Absence from work for one (1) or more consecutive days without excuse acceptable to the company;

2. Habitual tardiness;

3. Failure to report to work within 24 hours of a request to report.

Carolyn returned to work the next day to find that she had been removed from the schedule. She was informed that she was no longer an employee of the hotel. Carolyn filed for unemployment compensation. In her state, workers who voluntarily quit their jobs were not eligible for unemployment compensation.

1. Do you believe Carolyn was terminated or that she resigned from her position?

2. Do you believe Carolyn is eligible for unemployment compensation?

3. Whose position would you prefer to defend in the unemployment compensation hearing? Why?

8.7 EMPLOYMENT RECORDS AND RETENTION

Several federal and state agencies require employers to keep employee records on file, or to post information relative to employment. Although the number of requirements is large and can frequently change, the following examples will illustrate the type of responsibility employers have for maintaining accurate employment records.

Department of Labor (DOL) Records

Every employer subject to the Fair Labor Standards Act (FLSA) must maintain the following records for every employee:

- Employee's full name and social security number
- Address, including zip code
- Birthdate, if younger than 19
- Sex and occupation
- Time and day of week when employee's workweek begins
- Hours worked each day
- Basis on which employee's wages are paid (e.g., "$9 per hour," "$440 a week," "piecework")
- Regular hourly pay rate
- Total daily or weekly straight-time earnings
- Total overtime earnings for the workweek
- All additions to or deductions from the employee's wages
- Total wages paid each pay period
- Date of payment and the pay period covered by the payment

DOL Records on Employee Meals and Lodging

Every employer that makes deductions from wages for meals, uniforms, or lodging must keep records substantiating the cost of providing these items. For example, David Pung manages a cafeteria in the southwest. As part of his employees' compensation, they are allowed one meal per four-hour work shift. Employees who participate in this meal program are charged a rate of $0.25 per hour worked, or $1.00 per meal. David must document both the deductions he makes for the meal (according to the preceding list), and the cost of providing the meal. Since it is impossible to determine the cost of each employee's meal, David uses a method whereby the cost of the meal is determined by the following formula:

1. Total food sales less gross operating profit
2. Equals cost of all meals provided
3. Divided by total meals served (including all employee meals)
4. Equals cost per meal served

David documents this cost on a monthly basis, using his profit and loss statement as the source of his sales and gross operating profit figures, and using a daily customer count as his total number of meals served. Generally, the DOL will provide a good deal of latitude as to how an employer computes the cost per employee meal or costs of providing other services. These costs must be computed and maintained in the employer's records.

DOL Records for Tipped Employees

All employers must keep the following records for tipped employees:

■ A symbol, letter, or other notation placed on the pay records identifying each employee whose wage is determined in part by tips.

■ Weekly or monthly amount reported by the employee, to the employer, of tips received.

■ Amount by which the wages of each tipped employee have been deemed to be increased by tips as determined by the employer (not in excess of 40 percent of the applicable statutory minimum wage). The amount per hour that the employer takes as a tip credit shall be reported to the employee in writing each time it is changed from the amount per hour taken in the preceding week.

■ Hours worked each workday in any occupation in which the employee does not receive tips, and total daily or weekly straight-time payment made by the employer for such hours.

■ Hours worked each workday in occupations in which the employee receives tips and total daily or weekly straight-time earnings for such hours.

In larger organizations, the payroll department will maintain the records required by the DOL. It is important to remember, however, that it is the facility manager who is responsible for producing these records, if required to do so by the DOL. Under current DOL rules, employers must maintain their records for the following time periods.

For Three Years

■ Collective bargaining agreements

■ Sale and purchase records

■ From the date of last entry, all payroll records

■ From the last effective date, all certificates, such as student certificates

For Two Years

■ From the date of last entry, all employee time cards

■ All tables or schedules used to compute wages

■ All records explaining differences in pay for employees of the opposite sex in the same establishment

DOL Records on Family and Medical Leave

The federal Family and Medical Leave Act (FMLA), requires employers to maintain the following records for at least three years:

■ Employee name, address, and position

■ Total compensation paid to employees

■ Dates FMLA-eligible employees take FMLA leave

■ FMLA leave in hours, if less than full days are taken at one time

■ Any documents describing employee benefits or employer policies regarding the taking of FMLA leave

Immigration-Related Records

As discussed in Chapter 7, the Immigration Reform and Control Act (IRCA), requires employers to complete an employment eligibility verification form (Form I-9) for all employees hired after November 6, 1986. Employers must retain all I-9 forms for three years after the employee is hired or one year after the employee leaves, whichever is later.

Records Required by the ADEA

The federal Age Discrimination in Employment Act (ADEA) requires that employers retain employee records that contain the employee's name, address, date of birth (established only after the hiring decision), occupation, rate of pay, and weekly compensation. In addition, records on all personnel matters, including terminations and benefit plans, must be kept for at least one year from the date of the action taken.

As can be seen from the list of recordkeeping requirements just given, these stipulations in the hospitality industry are varied, complex, and sometimes overlapping. As a manager, it is important for you to ensure that your facility's recordkeeping is current and complete. An employment attorney who specializes in hospitality employment law can be very helpful in ensuring compliance in this area.

8.8 EMPLOYMENT POSTERS

Often, regulatory agencies will require that certain employment-related information be posted in an area where all employees can see it. The following regulations demonstrate that fact:

- DOL regulations require that every employer subject to the FLSA post, in a conspicuous place, a notice explaining the FLSA. Posters can be obtained by contacting a regional office of the DOL.

- EEOC regulations require that every employer subject to Title VII of the Civil Rights Act of 1964 and the Americans with Disabilities Act of 1990 post in a conspicuous place a notice relating to discrimination prohibited by such laws. These posters may be combined, and they can be obtained by contacting a regional office of the EEOC.

- OSHA regulations require that every employer post in a conspicuous place a notice informing employees of the protections and obligations under OSHA. Posters can be obtained by contacting a regional office of OSHA.

- DOL regulations require that every employer post in a prominent and conspicuous place a notice explaining the Employee Polygraph Protection Act of 1988. Posters can be obtained by contacting a regional DOL office.

- DOL regulations require that every employer subject to the Family and Medical Leave Act post in a conspicuous place in the establishment a notice (as shown in Figure 8.10) explaining this federal leave law. Posters can be obtained by contacting a regional DOL office.

8.9 WORKPLACE SURVEILLANCE

Surveys by the American Management Association reveal that up to 43 percent of U.S. businesses monitor their employees electronically. Some common procedures include listening in on phone calls, reviewing voicemails, monitoring email and computer files (such as sites visited on the Internet), or some form of video surveillance. That number grows even higher if you add in the companies that monitor their employees in other ways such as by conducting locker, bag, and desk searches.

Unfortunately, there is no one national policy that you can look to for guidance regarding privacy in the workplace. Many companies believe that they are protecting their proprietary business interests by monitoring employees and their work product. Additionally, as companies establish work conduct guidelines (such as zero tolerance sexual harassment policies) to comply with the law, monitoring employees enables the employer to ensure compliance. Even though the law is difficult to pin down in this area, a few general principles can be established by reviewing a cross-section of federal and state laws and court cases.

EMPLOYEE RIGHTS AND RESPONSIBILITIES
UNDER THE FAMILY AND MEDICAL LEAVE ACT

Basic Leave Entitlement

FMLA requires covered employers to provide up to 12 weeks of unpaid, job-protected leave to eligible employees for the following reasons:

- For incapacity due to pregnancy, prenatal medical care or child birth;
- To care for the employee's child after birth, or placement for adoption or foster care;
- To care for the employee's spouse, son or daughter, or parent, who has a serious health condition; or
- For a serious health condition that makes the employee unable to perform the employee's job.

Military Family Leave Entitlements

Eligible employees with a spouse, son, daughter, or parent on active duty or call to active duty status in the National Guard or Reserves in support of a contingency operation may use their 12-week leave entitlement to address certain qualifying exigencies. Qualifying exigencies may include attending certain military events, arranging for alternative childcare, addressing certain financial and legal arrangements, attending certain counseling sessions, and attending post-deployment reintegration briefings.

FMLA also includes a special leave entitlement that permits eligible employees to take up to 26 weeks of leave to care for a covered servicemember during a single 12-month period. A covered servicemember is a current member of the Armed Forces, including a member of the National Guard or Reserves, who has a serious injury or illness incurred in the line of duty on active duty that may render the servicemember medically unfit to perform his or her duties for which the servicemember is undergoing medical treatment, recuperation, or therapy; or is in outpatient status; or is on the temporary disability retired list.

Benefits and Protections

During FMLA leave, the employer must maintain the employee's health coverage under any "group health plan" on the same terms as if the employee had continued to work. Upon return from FMLA leave, most employees must be restored to their original or equivalent positions with equivalent pay, benefits, and other employment terms.

Use of FMLA leave cannot result in the loss of any employment benefit that accrued prior to the start of an employee's leave.

Eligibility Requirements

Employees are eligible if they have worked for a covered employer for at least one year, for 1,250 hours over the previous 12 months, and if at least 50 employees are employed by the employer within 75 miles.

Definition of Serious Health Condition

A serious health condition is an illness, injury, impairment, or physical or mental condition that involves either an overnight stay in a medical care facility, or continuing treatment by a health care provider for a condition that either prevents the employee from performing the functions of the employee's job, or prevents the qualified family member from participating in school or other daily activities.

Subject to certain conditions, the continuing treatment requirement may be met by a period of incapacity of more than 3 consecutive calendar days combined with at least two visits to a health care provider or one visit and a regimen of continuing treatment, or incapacity due to pregnancy, or incapacity due to a chronic condition. Other conditions may meet the definition of continuing treatment.

Use of Leave

An employee does not need to use this leave entitlement in one block. Leave can be taken intermittently or on a reduced leave schedule when medically necessary. Employees must make reasonable efforts to schedule leave for planned medical treatment so as not to unduly disrupt the employer's operations. Leave due to qualifying exigencies may also be taken on an intermittent basis.

Substitution of Paid Leave for Unpaid Leave

Employees may choose or employers may require use of accrued paid leave while taking FMLA leave. In order to use paid leave for FMLA leave, employees must comply with the employer's normal paid leave policies.

Employee Responsibilities

Employees must provide 30 days advance notice of the need to take FMLA leave when the need is foreseeable. When 30 days notice is not possible, the employee must provide notice as soon as practicable and generally must comply with an employer's normal call-in procedures.

Employees must provide sufficient information for the employer to determine if the leave may qualify for FMLA protection and the anticipated timing and duration of the leave. Sufficient information may include that the employee is unable to perform job functions, the family member is unable to perform daily activities, the need for hospitalization or continuing treatment by a health care provider, or circumstances supporting the need for military family leave. Employees also must inform the employer if the requested leave is for a reason for which FMLA leave was previously taken or certified. Employees also may be required to provide a certification and periodic recertification supporting the need for leave.

Employer Responsibilities

Covered employers must inform employees requesting leave whether they are eligible under FMLA. If they are, the notice must specify any additional information required as well as the employees' rights and responsibilities. If they are not eligible, the employer must provide a reason for the ineligibility.

Covered employers must inform employees if leave will be designated as FMLA-protected and the amount of leave counted against the employee's leave entitlement. If the employer determines that the leave is not FMLA-protected, the employer must notify the employee.

Unlawful Acts by Employers

FMLA makes it unlawful for any employer to:

- Interfere with, restrain, or deny the exercise of any right provided under FMLA;
- Discharge or discriminate against any person for opposing any practice made unlawful by FMLA or for involvement in any proceeding under or relating to FMLA.

Enforcement

An employee may file a complaint with the U.S. Department of Labor or may bring a private lawsuit against an employer.

FMLA does not affect any Federal or State law prohibiting discrimination, or supersede any State or local law or collective bargaining agreement which provides greater family or medical leave rights.

FMLA section 109 (29 U.S.C. § 2619) requires FMLA covered employers to post the text of this notice. Regulations 29 C.F.R. § 825.300(a) may require additional disclosures.

For additional information:
1-866-4US-WAGE (1-866-487-9243) TTY: 1-877-889-5627
WWW.WAGEHOUR.DOL.GOV

U.S. Wage and Hour Division

U.S. Department of Labor | Employment Standards Administration | Wage and Hour Division   WHD Publication 1420 Revised January 2009

Figure 8.10 Employee rights under the Family and Medical Leave Act of 1993.

Whether or not a particular monitoring technique is legal usually depends on four factors:

1. *Did the employee have a legitimate expectation of privacy as to the item searched, or the information, conversation, or area monitored?* In an employee lounge, probably not; in a restroom, absolutely!

2. *Has the employer provided advance notice to the employees, and/or obtained consent for the monitoring activity from the employee?* If so, it is difficult for employees to argue that they had an expectation of privacy.

3. *Was the monitoring performed for a work-related purpose, and was it reasonable given all of the circumstances?* Generally, the courts have allowed searches and monitoring that seem to be necessary for operating a business (e.g., protecting trade secrets, enforcing policies and procedures, and ensuring high-quality service levels).

4. *Was the search or monitoring done in a reasonable or appropriate manner?* Was it discriminatory? In other words, was it only utilized on a minority work subgroup?

If you do elect to monitor specific activities of employees, adopting the Employee Privacy Policy in Figure 8.11 is a good way to minimize any misunderstandings or legal difficulties. Let your employees know exactly what is expected of them, and give them a chance to question any part of your policy about which they are unclear. Because the laws in this area are complex and vary by location, it is a good idea to have your attorney review your company's monitoring/privacy policy before it is implemented.

Policy Regarding Employee Privacy

The Company respects the individual privacy of its employees. However, an employee may not expect privacy rights to be extended to work-related conduct or the use of company-owned equipment, supplies, systems, or property. The purpose of this policy is to notify you that no reasonable expectation of privacy exists in connection with your use of such equipment, supplies, systems, or property, including computer files, computer databases, office cabinets, or lockers. It is for that reason the following policy should be read; if you do not understand it, ask for clarification before you sign it.

I, _____, understand that all electronic communications systems and all information transmitted by, received from, or stored in these systems are the property of the Company. I also understand that these systems are to be used solely for job-related purposes and not for personal purposes, and that I do not have any personal privacy right in connection with the use of this equipment or with the transmission, receipt, or storage of information in this equipment.

I consent to the Company monitoring my use of company equipment at any time at its discretion. Such monitoring may include printing and reading all electronic mail entering, leaving, or stored in these systems.

I agree to abide by this Company policy and I understand that the policy prohibits me from using electronic communication systems to transmit lewd, offensive, or racially related messages.

_____   _____
Signature of employee   Date

Figure 8.11 Employee privacy policy.

Obviously, it is in the best interest of both employers and employees to work together to create a workplace that is productive for management and fair to all employees. As a hospitality manager, your legal liability will definitely be affected by your ability to achieve this goal. Figure 8.12 summarizes some of the most significant federal laws related to human resources management. Following the guidelines presented in this chapter will help you manage your operation legally and reduce your risk of liability.

Equal Pay Act of 1963 →	Prohibits pay differences for men and women doing equal work.
Title VII of the Civil Rights → *Act of* 1964 (as amended)	Prohibits discrimination in employment based on race, color, religion, sex, or national origin.
Age Discrimination Employment → *Act of* 1967 (as amended)	Prohibits discrimination in employment against persons over 40; restricts mandatory retirement.
Occupational Safety and → *Health Act of* 1970 (OSHA)	Establishes mandatory safety and health standards in workplaces.
Vocational Rehabilitation → *Act of* 1973	Prohibits discrimination in employment based on physical or mental disability.
Pregnancy Discrimination → *Act of* 1978	Prohibits employment discrimination against pregnant workers.
Immigration Reform and → *Control Act of* 1986	Prohibits knowing employment of illegal aliens.
Americans with Disabilities → *Act of* 1990	Prohibits discrimination against a qualified individual on the basis of disability.
Civil Rights Act of 1991 →	Reaffirms Title VII of the 1964 Civil Rights Act, reinstates burden of proof by employer, and allows for punitive and compensatory damages.
Family and Medical Leave → *Act of* 1993	Allows employees up to 12 weeks of unpaid leave with job guarantees for childbirth, adoption, or family illness.

Figure 8.12 Overview of significant laws impacting the management of employees.
Source: John R. Schermerhorn Jr. Management, 6th ed, New York: John Wiley & Sons, Inc.,1999. Used by permission.

INTERNATIONAL SNAPSHOT

Managing Employees Abroad

Today's hoteliers may be called on to travel to different countries to manage hospitality facilities. The laws and regulations governing employment are different in every country, sometimes in ways that are subtle, but just as often in ways that are fundamental. Some of the most common and most obvious examples are described here.

THE NATURE OF THE EMPLOYMENT RELATIONSHIP

In most places in the United States, an employer or employee may terminate the employment relationship at any time, for any lawful reason or no reason at all; this is often referred to as "employment at will." Although this notion seems natural in the United States, it often does not apply overseas.

To the contrary, many countries have laws that are much more protective of employees' right to retain their employment. Such laws may explicitly define the permissible reasons for terminating the employment relationship, or they may more broadly prohibit termination except in the most egregious of circumstances. There may be more intensive regulation of layoffs for economic or operational reasons (sometimes called "retrenchment" or "redundancy").

In some cases, an employer may simply be prohibited from terminating the employment relationship; if the law is violated, the government may require that the employee be reinstated. In other cases, the employer can end the relationship by the payment of a defined monetary amount, sometimes called "redundancy payments."

Work Permits

Some countries protect their citizens' right to work by prohibiting the employment of foreigners except with special permission of the government. Employers may be required to look first to the local population for all employment needs at every level. Sometimes permits are easily obtainable for executive-level management or for persons with rare skill sets. Often, though, the employer will be required to demonstrate its efforts to hire employees within the jurisdiction before permits are issued. As a result, it may be more difficult, and it may take more time, to fill key vacancies.

Application of U.S. Laws in Foreign Countries

Employers based in the United States (or controlled by U.S. companies) that employ U.S. citizens in locations outside of the country are subject to most of the antidiscrimination laws discussed earlier in this chapter with respect to those U.S. citizens. The United States' discrimination laws do not apply to noncitizens of the United States in operations outside the United States.

Conversely, multinational companies that operate in the United States are subject to the laws of the United States to the same extent as U.S. employers. Just as managers familiar with U.S. employment laws must be aware of potentially drastic differences in employment laws (and the respective effect on operations) when they move abroad, those entering the United States must adjust to the differences in this country, as compared to the places from which they came.

Other Differences

These examples demonstrate just a few of the more common and obvious differences between U.S. employment laws and those that may be typical in other countries. There are likely to be other significant differences in such areas as minimum wages and methods of compensation, required compliance with government welfare benefits programs, workplace safety standards, and taxation schemes. Upon beginning work in any foreign country, every manager should quickly become familiar not just with local customs and practices but with the laws that must be observed with respect to the hotel's employees.

Written by David Comeaux. Provided by David Comeaux of the Ogletree and Deakins Law Firm, St. Thomas, Virgin Islands. www.ogletreedeakins.com.

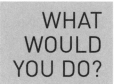

WHAT WOULD YOU DO?

Naomi Yip is the sous chef at one of the city clubs managed by Clubs International, a company that specializes in the operation of golf, city, and other private clubs. The company manages over 50 clubs nationally. Naomi has been with the organization for five years and is considered one of the company's best and brightest culinary artists.

Thomas Hayhoe is the executive chef at the club where Naomi works and is Naomi's immediate supervisor. Naomi's annual evaluations have been very good, and she has been designated as "ready for promotion" in her past two evaluations. In January, Naomi announces she is pregnant and her due date is in July. In March,

Chef Hayhoe completes his annual evaluation of Naomi. He does not recommend her for promotion to executive chef, Naomi's next step up, citing, "the extraordinary demands on time placed on an executive chef within the Clubs International organization," which he claims Naomi will be unable to meet. Chef Hayhoe also cites conversations he has overheard with Naomi in which she declares, "I'm looking forward to spending as much time as possible with my baby."

Clubs International has just been awarded the contract to operate a new and lucrative account, the Hawk Hollow Golf Club. Assume that you were the human resource director advising the company's vice president of operations.

1. Do you feel Chef Hayhoe's evaluation of Naomi is valid?

2. Based on Chef Hayhoe's recommendation, would you recommend Naomi for the executive chef's position at the new account?

3. How would you respond if the new client objected to the appointment of Naomi based on her pregnancy?

THE HOSPITALITY INDUSTRY IN COURT

To understand how important it is to do a thorough investigation and take employee complaints seriously, consider the case of *Romero v. Howard Johnson Plaza Hotel*, 1999 U.S. Dist. Lexis 15264 (S.D.N.Y. 1999).

FACTUAL SUMMARY

Rose Romero (Romero) was a guestroom attendant for Howard Johnson Plaza Hotel (Howard Johnson). Romero was employed with Howard Johnson from 1987 until 1993. During her employment she was sexually harassed by a number of her coworkers on a number of occasions. In one incident, a male coworker responded to a request made by Romero with a string of vulgar comments. Another incident involved Romero and an intoxicated male coworker, who approached Romero stating he knew "how to please a woman" and then exposed himself. Romero reported some of the incidents to supervisors, the general manager of the hotel, security, her union, and ultimately the police.

After Romero made a complaint to the police, the management of Howard Johnson sent the male coworker involved a letter stating the company's policy on sexual harassment. The letter also stated the allegations made by Romero could neither be confirmed nor denied due to the absence of a third-party witness. Romero also requested a union meeting be held so she could discuss her harassment claims. The meeting was conducted publicly, with several of her alleged harassers present. Despite the meeting and a reminder of Howard Johnson's harassment policy for the parties involved, the harassment continued.

After several fabricated reprimands, and at least two suspensions based on false accusations, Romero left Howard Johnson in 1993. She sued Howard Johnson, two of her former coworkers, and three managers for sexual harassment.

QUESTION FOR THE COURT

The court was faced with at least two questions in this case. The first was whether Romero waited too long after the last incident of sexual harassment to bring her lawsuit against the defendants. Under Title VII of the Civil Rights Act of 1964, a person claiming workplace harassment or a hostile work environment must file a charge with the Equal Employment Opportunity Commission (EEOC) within 300 days of the unlawful action. Romero filed her claim with the EEOC on June 13, 1993. Howard Johnson argued Romero could not file complaints about incidents prior to August 22, 1992, and most of the incidents occurred before then. Romero argued that all of the incidents were part of an ongoing act of discrimination and could be considered a continuing violation. Romero also argued she was subjected to a hostile work environment, which involves a continuing pattern of discrimination or sexual harassment rather than one isolated event.

The second question for the court concerned the liability of Howard Johnson. Romero argued Howard Johnson created the hostile work environment because it either failed to provide a reasonable avenue for complaints or knew about the harassment and did nothing to stop it. If Howard Johnson created or contributed to a hostile work environment, it was liable for the misconduct also.

DECISION

The court decided Romero was subjected to a hostile work environment and that the sexual harassment was a continuing violation. Therefore she could sue based on all of the past incidents. The court also found evidence Howard Johnson either knew or should have known of the harassment and failed to stop it.

MESSAGE TO MANAGEMENT

Harassment of any kind must not be tolerated in the workplace.

To understand the Supreme Court's view of an employer's obligation regarding prevention of sexual harassment, consider the case of *Faragher v. City of Boca Raton*, 524 U.S. 775 (1998).

FACTUAL SUMMARY

Throughout college, Beth Ann Faragher (Faragher) worked part-time and during the summers for the Parks and Recreation Department of Boca Raton, Florida (Boca Raton). While employed as a lifeguard from 1985 to 1990, Faragher was supervised by Bill Terry, David Silverman, and Robert Gordon. Terry and Silverman inappropriately touched female lifeguards, including Faragher, and regularly made lewd comments and sexual advances toward the female lifeguards. In 1986, the city of Boca Raton instituted a sexual harassment policy, but it is unclear whether the entire Parks and Recreation Department received a copy of the policy. Faragher and other female lifeguards mentioned the harassment to Gordon in conversation but never made formal complaints. In 1990, a complaint was finally initiated by a former lifeguard, which resulted in disciplinary action against Terry and Silverman. In 1992, Faragher filed suit against the city of Boca Raton, Terry, and Silverman, alleging a Title VII hostile work environment claim.

QUESTION FOR THE COURT

The question for the court was whether an employer (Boca Raton) could be held liable for the acts of its supervisory employees (Terry and Silverman) whose sexual harassment of a subordinate created a hostile work environment. Faragher argued the sexual harassment and discrimination was so widespread the city of Boca Raton either knew or should have known of the conduct of Terry and Silverman. Therefore, she argued, the city of Boca Raton was liable for the conduct of Terry and Silverman. Boca Raton argued the conduct of Terry and Silverman was outside the normal job functions for which they were hired and was so unreasonable the city was not responsible.

DECISION

The court held in favor of Faragher and found the city of Boca Raton liable for the conduct of Terry and Silverman. But it also found that Boca Raton could claim a potential defense. If the employer (Boca Raton) exercised reasonable care to prevent and correct any sexually harassing behavior, and if the employee-victim failed to take advantage of any preventive or corrective measures provided, then the employer would not be liable for sexual harassment.

MESSAGE TO MANAGEMENT

Create a policy of zero tolerance; educate your employees as to what constitutes appropriate and inappropriate behavior, provide a path of relief for victims, investigate all claims promptly, and hold people accountable for their actions.

It is a good practice to define the employment relationship between employers and employees. The agreement can be spelled out in an offer letter. An employee manual can help employees understand what is expected from them, as well as set out policies and procedures for the workplace.

WHAT DID YOU LEARN IN THIS CHAPTER?

Just as you cannot discriminate illegally in the selection process, you cannot discriminate after someone has been hired. Both federal and state civil rights laws exist to protect employees against discrimination in the workplace. You must invoke a zero tolerance policy for sexual harassment and other forms of illegal discrimination. Educate your employees about appropriate and inappropriate behavior. You must also be prepared to do a thorough investigation if inappropriate behavior is brought to your attention.

The Family and Medical Leave Act (FMLA) allows most employees of larger companies to take time off to address personal issues such as the birth of a child or to take care of an injured servicemember.

Compensation for employees is a complex area, particularly in the hospitality industry, as it is labor-intensive and the primary beneficiary of the tip credit toward the minimum wage. Utilizing an objective method to evaluate employees can help to reduce potential litigation for discrimination and wrongful termination. Establishing an in-house dispute resolution program can also reduce potential liability from employee conflict or disputes. Unemployment insurance is available for employees who are discharged without cause related to the workplace (i.e., layoffs).

Certain records and documents (e.g., applications and payroll information) must be retained for a certain length of time. Also, several posters that outline employee rights in several areas must be displayed prominently in the workplace.

RAPID REVIEW

After you have studied this chapter, you should be prepared to:

1. Compose an employment offer letter that does not jeopardize the at-will employment status of an assistant manager of a quick-service restaurant.

2. Draft a voluntary tip-pooling arrangement for use in a sports bar that employs both bartenders and waitstaff. Assume that 75 percent of sales are generated in the seating area and 25 percent are generated at the bar itself.

3. Define the following concepts as they relate to sexual harassment.

   Zero tolerance
   Prevention
   Investigation
   Resolution

4. Use the Internet to look up and identify whether tip pooling is permitted in the state where you work or go to school. Cite your information source and the path to get there.

5. Contrast the concepts of at-will employment and wrongful termination.

6. List and discuss four advantages of an in-house dispute resolution plan.

7. Discuss the pros and cons of tying an employer's unemployment insurance tax rate to the number of claims successfully filed by ex-employees.

8. Detail a procedure for establishing the "cost" of providing lodging to summer college students employed by a theme park and living in dormitory-style housing provided by the park. Explain why this cost is important.

TEAM ACTIVITY

In teams, put yourself in the position of the human resources director of the XYZ Hotel. It has come to your attention through the employee grapevine that one of your male executive housekeepers is making romantic overtures to several of the female housekeepers. How will you handle this situation? Be as specific as possible, given the page-length limitation (two pages, double-spaced). Address all issues and concerns, including yours and those of the accused, as well as privacy, and, finally, recommend a solution.

CHAPTER 9

YOUR RESPONSIBILITIES AS A HOSPITALITY OPERATOR

" L ET ME SEE the incident report," said Trisha Sangus, as she took the document from the hand of Director of Security Travis Daniels. She studied the paper carefully. As a hotel general manager, she had seen dozens of reports of guests who had, or claimed to have had, an accident that could put the hotel at some legal risk. Trisha reviewed every incident report involving guests, and her insurance company was glad she did. Despite the cheerful holiday music playing in the background, Trisha knew a guest incident could mean a troubled holiday for the hotel.

"What's the background on this incident?" she asked.

"Well," began the security director, "as I understand it, Larry Nolan checked into the hotel around 11:00 P.M. last night. I verified that with the front desk manager. Our front desk system notes the time of check-in. Some time after 1:00 A.M., Isaac, one of the night auditors, heard a thud, a brief shout, and a clattering of ice near the lobby elevator. When he went to the elevator entrance, he saw Mr. Nolan lying on the floor near the ice machine, with an ice bucket on the ground and ice all around."

"He slipped on the ice?" Trisha asked "No," said the director, "he claims he slipped on a Christmas ornament that had fallen from a wreath that was hanging on the wall about 3 feet from the ice machine. I talked to him by telephone in his room this morning. He said his cousin was a lawyer, and he was going to sue!"

"Was it a glass ornament?" Trisha interrupted.

"Yes. It was hanging about 9 feet above the ground."

"Did you investigate?" Trisha continued. "Had the ornament in fact fallen and broken?"

"Unfortunately, yes; I checked myself," said the director. All our decorations have four ornamental balls except this one. It has three, and a spot where it appears one was once attached. I think Mr. Nolan was probably right. The bulb did fall."

"What about Lance Dani, the manager on duty?" Trisha asked. "Did he file his manager-on-duty [MOD] closing report?"

"Yes," replied the director. "I have it here. Mr. Dani did the last rounds of the hotel at midnight, just as our procedures dictate. His report is signed and dated."

"Those rounds include checking the ice machine areas for leaks. Did Lance put his initials by that portion of the checklist?"

"Yes, he did," replied the director.

"And did he note a broken ornament?" Trisha asked as she reached across her desk for the MOD report.

"No," said the director. "The bulb must have fallen after midnight. A bad break for the hotel."

"Well," replied Trisha, "we make our own breaks generally. I'll call the insurance company and file a report. That's standard procedure, but frankly, I don't believe Mr. Nolan has much of a liability claim against the hotel, thanks to Lance doing his job right. But this will be a good time to review our accident procedures at the daily staff meeting."

As the director of security left her office, Trisha was glad everyone had performed well in the case of this accident. She had been in hotels where the staff had not been as well trained, and the results, as she knew, could be disastrous, for both the hotels and their managers' careers.

IN THIS CHAPTER, YOU WILL LEARN:

1. To differentiate between the types of legal duties required of a hospitality operator, and the consequences of the failure to exercise reasonable care in fulfilling these duties.
2. To evaluate operational activities in light of their impact on guest safety and potential legal damages.
3. To understand how a lawsuit is initiated and moves through the U.S. court system.
4. To create a checklist of the steps that should be initiated immediately following an accident.

9.1 DUTIES AND OBLIGATIONS OF A HOSPITALITY OPERATOR

Duties of Care

LEGALESE

Duty of care:
A legal obligation that requires a particular standard of conduct.

Hospitality operators owe a *duty of care* to those individuals who enter their establishments. Some duties of care are rather straightforward. For example, a restaurateur has a duty of care to provide food that is safe and wholesome for guests. While hospitality operators are not required to be insurers of their guests' safety, and are generally not held liable for events they could not reasonably foresee, they are required to act prudently and use reasonable care, as defined later in this chapter, to fulfill their duties of care.

Because of the wide variety of facilities they operate, hospitality managers can encounter a variety of duties of care. These include the duties:

1. *Provide a reasonably safe premise.* This would include all public space, the interior of guestrooms, dining rooms, and the exterior space that make up the operator's total physical facility.

2. *Serve food and beverages fit for consumption.* This duty of care is shared with those who supply products to a foodservice operator, and would also include the techniques used by an operator to prepare and serve food or beverages.

3. *Serve alcoholic beverages responsibly.* Because of its extreme importance, this duty of care will be examined separately in Chapter 12, "Your Responsibilities When Serving Food and Beverages."

4. *Hire qualified employees.* This duty must be satisfied to protect yourself against charges of negligent hiring and other potential liabilities.

5. *Properly train employees.* This duty must be satisfied to protect yourself against charges of negligent staff training.

6. *Terminate employees who pose a danger to other employees or guests.* This duty must be satisfied to protect yourself against charges of negligent employee retention.

7. *Warn of unsafe conditions.* When an operator is aware, (or, in some cases, should be aware) of conditions that pose a threat to safety (such as a wet floor or broken sidewalk), those conditions must be made obvious to the guest.

8. *Safeguard guest property, especially when voluntarily accepting possession of it.* In the hospitality industry, guests may retain control of their own property (such as when they take an item into their hotel room) or the operator may take possession of it (such as when a guest's car is valet-parked, a coat is checked, or valuables are deposited in a hotel's safety deposit box). In each case, the law will detail the duty of care you must exercise to protect guests' property.

ANALYZE THE SITUATION 9.1

ALAN BRANDIS ARRIVED AT the Golden Fox restaurant for a Friday-night fish fry. During his meal, a severe thunderstorm began, which caused the ceiling of the men's restroom to leak. After finishing his meal, Alan entered the men's room to wash his hands. He slipped on some wet tile, which was caused by the leak in the roof. Alan struck his head during the fall and was severely injured.

One week later, Alan's attorney contacted the owners of the Golden Fox with a claim for damages. The restaurant owners maintained the fall was not their responsibility, claiming they were not the insurers of guest safety. Although the owners knew of the condition of the roof, they said it leaked only during extremely heavy thunderstorms and was too old to fix without undue economic hardship. Most important, because the storm was not within their control, the owners maintained that it was not reasonable to assume they could have foreseen the severity of the storm, and thus they could not be held liable for the accident.

1. Was the severity of the storm a foreseeable event?

2. What duty of care is in question here?

3. Did the restaurant act prudently?

4. Are the restaurant's defenses valid? Why or why not?

Standards of Care

In fulfilling the duties of care just detailed, you must exercise a *standard of care* appropriate to the given situation. An appropriate standard of care is determined, in part, on the level of services a guest would reasonably expect to find in a hospitality facility. For example, a guest departing on a seven-day cruise of the Pacific would reasonably expect that the ship's staff would include a full-time doctor. The same guest visiting a quick-service restaurant at 11:00 P.M. would not expect to find a doctor on hand. In both cases, it is possible that a guest could suffer a heart attack and require medical care. The ship's standard of care, however, would include medical treatment, while the restaurant's would not.

Many disputes involving liability and negligence in the hospitality industry revolve around the question of what an appropriate standard of care should be. Like the law itself, these standards are constantly evolving. Generally speaking, you as a hospitality manager are required to apply the same diligence to achieve your standards of care as any other reasonable hospitality manager in a similar situation. Because standards are constantly changing, and because the standard of care you apply may be assessed during litigation by people who are not familiar with you or your operation, you must strive to stay abreast of changing procedures and technology. To help you do that, refer back to the continuing education components of the STEM principles discussed in Chapter 1, "Prevention Philosophy."

9.2 THEORIES OF LIABILITY

Despite the best efforts of management, accidents involving people can and do happen in hospitality facilities. Employees and guests are subject to many of the same risks in a hospitality facility that they are subject to outside the facility. For example, it is just as possible to trip and fall in a restaurant parking lot as it is to fall in a grocery store parking lot. It is not your responsibility as a hospitality manager to ensure that accidents never happen in your facility; that would be impossible. It is your responsibility to operate in a manner that is as safe as possible, and to react responsibly when an accident does occur. If you do not, the legal system is designed to hold you and your operation accountable.

Reasonable Care

Hospitality managers must strive to provide an environment that is safe and secure. For example, a hotel manager who rents a room with a lock on the door should be responsible for ensuring that the lock is in proper working order. A guest would reasonably expect the hotel to provide a lock that was in working order. In fact, the concept of reasonability is so pervasive in law that it literally sets the standard of care that hospitality organizations must provide for their employees and guests. That standard is embodied in the concept of *reasonable care*.

Essentially, reasonable care requires you to correct potentially harmful situations that you know exist, or that you could have reasonably foreseen. The level of reasonable care that must be exercised in a given situation can sometimes be difficult to establish. In the case of the manager supplying a guestroom with a working lock, the standard is quite clear. It becomes complex, however, when the guest actually uses the lock. What if the guest does not use the lock properly, or forgets to use it at all? What if the guest abuses the lock to the point where it does not function and then has a theft from his or her room? Clearly, in these cases, the guest bears some or all of the responsibility for his or her own acts.

The doctrine of reasonable care places a significant burden on you as a hospitality manager. It requires that you use all of your skill and experience to operate your facility in a manner that would be consistent with that of a reasonable person (or manager) in a similar set of circumstances.

Torts

A *tort* is a wrong against an individual, in the same way that a crime is a wrong against the state. For example, a patron who drinks too much in a bar and then drives a motor vehicle is guilty of driving under the influence (DUI) of alcohol, a crime against the state. If that same driver causes an accident that injures another motorist, the intoxicated driver would be guilty of a tort, that is, an act that results in injury to another.

There are two types of torts: intentional and unintentional. Intentional torts include:

- Assault
- Battery
- Defamation
- Intentional infliction of emotional distress

Unintentional torts include:

- Negligence
- Gross negligence

Negligence is the most common unintentional tort.

Many legal actions a hospitality manager will experience are those that involve torts. The following sections explain the main types of torts committed against patrons, and those a hospitality manager will most likely face.

Negligence

A person or organization who has not used reasonable care in a situation is deemed to have been *negligent*. Assume, for example, that a guest dives into a resort swimming pool and injures her neck. She thought the pool was deep enough for diving, but the point at which she jumped was only 4 feet deep. The pool was not marked in any way to indicate the water's depth. If a lawsuit follows, and a judge later decides that the resort knew, or could have foreseen, that its guests might dive into the pool, the resort could be found negligent; that is, it did not do what reasonable facility operators would do to protect their guests, such as posting signs prohibiting diving, or installing visible depth markers.

LEGALESE
Reasonable care:
The degree of care that a reasonably prudent person would use in a similar situation.

LEGALESE
Tort: An act or failure to act (not involving a breach of contract) that results in injury, loss, or damage to another (e.g., negligence is an unintentional tort, whereas battery, physically touching someone, is usually an intentional tort).

LEGALESE
Negligent (negligence):
The failure to use reasonable care.

Negligence is said to legally exist when the following four conditions have been met:

1. A legal duty of care is present.
2. The defendant has failed to provide the standard of care needed to fulfill that duty.
3. The defendant's failure to meet the legal duty was the *proximate cause* of the harm.
4. The plaintiff was injured or suffered damages.

LEGALESE

Proximate cause:
The event or activity that directly contributes to (causes) the injury or harm.

In the hospitality industry, managers not only are responsible for their own actions but, under the doctrine of respondeat superior, also can be held accountable for the work-related acts of their employees. In some cases, managers are even held responsible for the acts of their guests or guests of their guests. The degree of responsibility that a hospitality manager might have for the acts of others ordinarily depends on the foreseeability of the act. If a dangerous act or condition was foreseeable, and no action was taken to warn patrons or prevent the accident, then liability will usually attach.

It is important to note that negligence can result from either the failure to do something or because something was done that probably should not have been. In the swimming pool example, the resort's negligence was the result of a failure to act. But what if the pool's depth was 4 feet and the resort incorrectly marked it as 8 feet? In this situation, if a guest dives into the pool and is injured, the resort's negligence would be the result of a specific inappropriate action it took, not inaction.

An operator can be considered negligent even when he or she is only partially responsible for the harm caused to another. Consider the case of a man who slips on an icy sidewalk in front of a restaurant and falls into a heavily trafficked street, where he is subsequently hit by a car. The fall may have caused only minor injuries by itself, but an even greater injury occurred because he was struck by the car. It is likely that the owner of the sidewalk will face potential charges of negligence, even if the majority of the damages suffered by the injured man were caused by the car, not the fall itself.

Gross Negligence

LEGALESE

Gross negligence:
The reckless or willful failure of an individual or an organization to use even the slightest amount of reasonable care.

When an individual or organization behaves in a manner that demonstrates a total disregard for the welfare of others, the act is deemed to be *gross negligence*. The distinction between negligence and gross negligence is an important one, for a simple reason: The penalty is usually greater in a situation involving gross negligence than one involving ordinary negligence. That is because an operator found to have been grossly negligent may be assessed punitive damages (discussed later in the chapter) to serve as an example and to deter others from committing the same act. Often, it is difficult to determine the difference between negligence and gross negligence. The difference in the eyes of a jury, however, can be millions of dollars in an award to a party that can prove it was harmed as a result of the reckless action or inaction of the operator.

>> **ANALYZE THE SITUATION 9.2**

PAUL AND BEATRICE METZ took their 11-year-old daughter Christine on a weekend skiing trip; they stayed at the St. Stratton ski resort. The St. Stratton owned and maintained four ski trails and a ski lift on its property.

One morning, Mr. and Mrs. Metz were having coffee in the ski lodge while their daughter was riding the ski lift to the top of the mountain. On the way up, the car containing Christine Metz and one other skier jumped off its cable guide and plunged 300 feet down the mountain. As a result of the fall, Christine was permanently paralyzed from the neck down.

The Metzs filed a lawsuit against the resort. Their attorney discovered that the car's connections to the cable were checked once a year by a maintenance staff person unfamiliar with the intricacies of ski cable cars. The manufacturer of the cable car recommended weekly inspections, performed by a specially trained service technician.

The ski resort's corporate owners maintained that all skiers assumed risk when skiing, that the manufacturer's recommendation was simply a recommendation, and that their own inspection program demonstrated they had indeed exercised reasonable care. In addition, they maintained that Christine's paralysis was the result of an unfortunate accident for which the cable car's manufacturer, not the resort, should be held responsible.

1. Did the resort exercise reasonable care?

2. What level of negligence, if any, was present? Ordinary negligence? Gross negligence?

3. What amount of money do you think a jury would recommend the resort be required to pay to compensate Christine Metz for her loss, if it is found to have committed a tort against her?

4. Are the resort's defenses valid ones? Why or why not?

Contributory and Comparative Negligence

Sometimes guests, through their own carelessness, can be the cause or partial cause of their own injury or harm. In legal parlance, this is called *contributory negligence*. Consider the case of the wedding guest who attends an evening reception at a local country club. In the course of the evening, the guest leaves the clubhouse and wanders onto the golf course. Because the course is not lit at night, the guest trips over a railroad tie used to define the tee box on the third hole. The guest may claim that the club should have marked the railway tie as a hazard, and that it should have reasonably foreseen that guests would leave the clubhouse and walk on the golf course. The club's attorney, however, is likely to maintain, and rightly so, that walking at night on an unlighted golf course is dangerous and the guest did not exercise reasonable care. Although many variables may determine the final outcome of this situation, the courts have held that the contributory negligence of the injured party can reduce an operator's liability for the damages suffered. Judges and juries will be able to compare the negligence of the plaintiff and the defendant when assessing responsibility for the injuries.

The doctrine of *comparative negligence* has become an acceptable way in which to recognize that reasonable care is a responsibility shared by both hospitality

LEGALESE

Contributory negligence:
Negligent conduct by the complaining party (plaintiff) that contributes to the cause of his or her injuries.

LEGALESE

Comparative negligence:
Shared responsibility for the harm that results from negligence. The comparison of negligence by the defendant with the contributory negligence of the plaintiff. Also known as comparative fault.

operators and those who claim to have been injured by them. If the court determines, for example, that a plaintiff was 25 percent responsible (contributory negligent) for his or her injuries, and the defendant was 75 percent responsible, the amount of damages awarded to the plaintiff would be reduced by 25 percent. The laws that determine comparative negligence vary widely across the 50 states. What is important for you, as a hospitality manager, to remember is to not overlook evidence of negligence on the part of the injured party during your investigation of an incident.

Strict Liability

LEGALESE

Strict liability:
Responsibility arising from the nature of a dangerous activity rather than negligence or an intentional act. Also known as absolute liability or liability without fault.

In some cases, a hospitality organization can be found liable for damages to others even if it has not acted negligently or intentionally. This is because some activities are considered to be so dangerous that their very existence imposes a greater degree of responsibility on the part of the person conducting the activity. For example, if an amusement park elected to train a wild tiger as part of its promotional activities, it would be held responsible for the tiger's actions, even if the park could not be proved to be negligent in the tiger's handling. This is true because keeping dangerous animals in close proximity to people is, in itself, a dangerous activity, and one that was voluntarily undertaken by the amusement park. In these types of circumstances, those who engage in the activity are judged not by their actions, but by the nature of the activity itself, which creates absolute, or *strict liability.*

> **Search the Web 9.1**
>
> Go to www.findlaw.com.
> 1. Select: "Accidents & Injuries" in the Individual Issues section under Learn About the Law.
> 2. Type: Your state and city in the Location field.
> 3. Select: Find Lawyers.
> 4. Select the name of an attorney practicing in your city.
> 5. Contact the attorney's office by telephone or letter and ask if he or she can help you understand how the state and/or local courts view comparative negligence in his or her practice area.

In the hospitality industry, the greatest operational threat imposed by strict liability is that involved with the serving of food and beverages. Recently, the courts have more often begun using the doctrine of strict liability to penalize those who sell defective food and beverages. The position of the courts is that the selling of unwholesome food and beverages is, in itself, so dangerous that those who do so, even unwittingly, will be held to a limited form of strict liability.

Intentional Acts

LEGALESE

Intentional act:
A willful action undertaken with or without full understanding of its consequences.

Although the law makes a distinction between negligence and gross negligence, it reserves the greatest sanctions for those who not only do not exercise reasonable care but also commit *intentional acts* that cause harm to others. If the employees of an innkeeper intentionally invade the privacy of a guest (e.g., viewing guest behavior in a guestroom via a hidden video camera), the innkeeper is subject to severe liability, including punitive damages.

To illustrate this concept, consider this situation: It is late Friday night, about 11 P.M., and your bar is packed—210 people at last count. Your fire occupancy limit is 125, but nobody pays attention to those signs. So far, the night has been fairly peaceful. You finally have a chance to sit down for a moment, so you take a seat at the end of the bar where you can see what's going on, and you ask your bartender to pour you a long, tall, cold ginger ale.

The drink arrives, and as it touches your lips—flash!—out of the corner of your eye, you see a flurry of activity. Two guys are fighting, and really going at it. You grab one guy and the bouncer grabs the other. There is blood all over the face of the guy you grabbed, and he is wailing. You notice a broken beer mug on the table. Three girls are screaming hysterically and wiping blood off their clothes and skin.

You finally get things calmed down, transport the injured patron to the hospital, and start collecting information. You find out:

- The fight started when a guy asked one of the girls to dance; she declined, and everyone at the table, including the subsequently injured patron, began laughing.
- The guy who asked the girl to dance took offense, picked up an empty beer mug, and smashed it into the face of "Mr. Laughter."
- The two guys had never seen each other before.
- The girls had never seen the "dancer" before the incident occurred.

Are you financially responsible for the injuries? Historically, the courts have decided that a hospitality operator is not responsible for damages suffered by a patron that were caused by the intentional actions of a third party, when the third party is a customer or guest. The courts' rationale is that the intentional or criminal act of a third party could not be foreseen by the operator; therefore, it would be impossible for the operator to take any precautions or preventative measures to keep it from happening.

Crimes against Guests

Recently, however, the courts in many jurisdictions have concluded that if violent acts previously occurred on a property, or even if the property is in a "high-crime zone," an incident and resulting injury could be considered foreseeable. Hence, the operator might be held responsible if it failed to use reasonable care in managing the establishment. Additionally, courts have concluded that even though no crime has previously occurred, in some instances a property has the duty to provide additional security, and can be found negligent if they do not. Some courts have awarded high-dollar judgments against hospitality facilities for negligent security. Consider the Van Blargen case, where an assault victim sued and recovered $500,000 from the hotel property he patronized. Van Blargen was assaulted in a private outdoor area while he was walking back to his room. Since the court likened the pool area to a private passageway, because of the surrounding foliage and landscape enclosures, it determined that the hotel had a duty to provide heightened security in such a private area.

Negligence Per Se

The barroom brawl just described does not provide enough facts to discern whether the incident and resulting injury were foreseeable by the operator. But what is readily apparent from the facts is the concept of *negligence per se*.

You may recall that the bar had more than the allowed number of patrons. Is this negligence per se? Quite possibly. The injured patron's attorney will certainly argue that the occupancy restrictions should have been maintained, not just for fire

> **LEGALESE**
>
> **Negligence per se:**
> When a rule of law is violated by the operator; such violation of a rule of law is considered to be so far outside the scope of reasonable behavior that the violator is assumed to be negligent.

regulations, but for physical safety as well. The occupancy restrictions would have helped to maintain order. More than likely, an expert in building safety or club management would concur.

It could also be argued that the excessive occupancy contributed to the likelihood of a fight breaking out on the premises, and that likelihood would have been foreseeable by the operator. In other words, fights, altercations, and injuries are more likely to occur when there is not enough space between patrons (another reason for restrictive occupancy rules).

The moral of this story is, follow the law. It is tempting to pack the house, but there can be dire consequences if an injury occurs and you have violated an ordinance, such as excessive occupancy or serving an underage customer. Always obey local, state, and federal laws.

9.3 LEGAL DAMAGES

If an injured party suffers a demonstrable loss as a result of a tort, the law requires that the entity responsible for the loss be held accountable. The process for doing so is by awarding damages to the injured party. There are two types of damages for personal injuries most likely to be encountered by a hospitality manager: compensatory damages and punitive (or exemplary) damages.

Compensatory damages are actual, identifiable damages that result from wrongful acts. Examples of actual damages include doctor, hospital, and other medical bills, pain and suffering, lost income as a result of an injury, or the actual cost of repairing damage to a piece of real or personal property. The recovery of these damages is said to "compensate" the injured party for any out-of-pocket costs incurred as a result of the accident, as well as for pain and suffering. If, for example, a maintenance worker for the hotel accidentally leaves some tools in the hallway of a hotel, and a guest falls and breaks her watch, the cost of replacing the watch can be easily identified, and the hotel could be expected to reimburse the guest. The same could well be true of any medical bills the guest might incur due to the fall.

Punitive damages seek to serve as a deterrent not only to the one who committed the tort, but also to others not involved in the wrongful act. The principle here is that an individual who was grossly negligent or acted maliciously or intentionally to cause harm should be required to pay damages beyond those actually incurred by the injured party. In this way, society sends a message that such behavior will not be tolerated and that those who commit the act will pay dearly for having done so.

Generally, punitive damages will be awarded only when a defendant's conduct was grossly negligent (the reckless disregard or indifference to the plaintiff's rights and safety) or intentional. In the hospitality industry, a manager could be found to have reckless disregard for the safety of a guest if, for example, the manager knew that a guestroom's lock was defective, yet sold that room to a guest who was subsequently assaulted and seriously injured.

9.4 ANATOMY OF A PERSONAL INJURY LAWSUIT

Hospitality managers do not want to operate their business in a way that will result in legal action being taken against them. In today's litigious society, even for a prudent operator, the threat of loss to the business because of lawsuits is very real. Some of the lawsuits that are filed are frivolous, while others raise serious issues. In either case, the effective hospitality manager must be aware of how lawsuits are filed, how they progress through the court system, and, most important, the role the hospitality manager plays in the process.

LEGALESE

Compensatory damages: Monetary amount awarded to restore the injured party to the position he or she was in prior to the injury (e.g., medical expenses, lost wages, etc.). Also referred to as actual damages.

LEGALESE

Punitive damages: A monetary amount used as punishment and to deter the same wrongful act in the future by the defendant and others.

Personal Injury

Much of your concern as a hospitality manager will focus on the potential for damages that result from *personal injury*. The reason for this is fairly straightforward: Hospitality managers provide guests with food and beverages, lodging accommodations, and entertainment; yet the process of providing these goods and services can place a business in potential jeopardy. The adage "accidents can happen" today can be extended to "accidents can happen, and if they do, the affected parties may sue!"

Certainly, it is best to manage your business in such a way as to avoid accidents. Nevertheless, accidents and injuries will occur, and many times determining where to place the responsibility for the accident is unclear. Consider the case of Norman and Betty Tungett. The Tungetts check into a motel, and at about midnight, Mrs. Tungett goes out to her car to get a piece of luggage. While she is in the parking lot, she is assaulted. In addition to being badly frightened, she suffers physical harm, as well as lingering apprehension about being out after dark by herself. Listed here are just a few of the questions that could be raised in a case such as this:

1. Were the lights in the parking lot working well enough to minimize the chance that a guest would be assaulted?
2. Was management vigilant in eliminating potential hiding places for would-be assailants?
3. Were the Tungetts warned on check-in that the parking lot might not be safe, late at night?
4. Were there any access doors allowing Mrs. Tungett to easily get to her room after visiting the lot?
5. Had the motel experienced similar incidents in the past, and if so, what precautions had been taken?

Notice that, in this example, there is no clear-cut reason for believing the motel is in any way responsible for the Tungetts problem. It is important to remember, however, that the court system gives the Tungetts and their attorney the right to file a personal injury lawsuit in an effort to determine if, in fact, the motel was totally or partially responsible for the assault. In doing so, the Tungetts will seek damages resulting from the assault. Such a lawsuit will, without doubt, be time-consuming for management, and expensive to defend against. Nevertheless, such lawsuits are filed on a daily basis, and it is rare that hospitality managers do not find themselves involved, to some degree, in such a suit at some time in their career. For this reason, we will examine the anatomy of a personal injury lawsuit from its inception to conclusion.

Demand Letter

Typically, a manager will learn that he, she, and/or the business are being sued when a *demand letter* is received. The demand letter comes from an attorney who has been contacted by the injured plaintiff and has agreed to take up the plaintiff's cause. As you can see in Figure 9.1, the typical demand letter sets forth the plaintiff's version of the facts surrounding an alleged personal injury, and might also include the monetary amount of damages being sought and usually a deadline for the manager to respond to the charges.

Attorneys, generally, will accept a personal injury case with one of three payment plans. The first is the hourly fee, whereby the attorney bills his or her client (the plaintiff) at an hourly rate for each hour the attorney works on the personal injury claim. In this case, it is clearly in the best interest of the plaintiff to seek a conclusion to the case as quickly as possible to minimize attorney fees. In a second type of plan,

LEGALESE

Personal injury:
Damage or harm inflicted upon the body, mind, or emotions.

LEGALESE

Demand letter:
Official notification, typically delivered to a defendant via registered or certified mail that details the plaintiff's cause for impending litigation.

January 15, 2000
Via Certified Mail: Z 123 456 789

Nina Phillips, General Manager
XYZ Hotel
Re: My client: Ginny Mayes
Date of Accident: January 1, 2000

Dear Ms. Phillips:

Please be advised that I represent Ginny Mayes. Ms. Mayes has retained my firm to represent her in her claim for damages against the XYZ Hotel and others that might be responsible for causing the incident that led to her injuries.

As you are aware, my client attended the New Year's Eve Gala that was hosted by the XYZ Hotel on December 31, 1999. At midnight, and until a few minutes thereafter, employees of the XYZ Hotel began opening champagne bottles by "popping the corks" (releasing the corks and allowing them to fly into the air).

My client was dancing on the dance floor when she was suddenly struck in her left eye by one of the corks. The cork was traveling at a high rate of speed, and when it struck her eye, she lost her balance and fell, striking her head on the wooden dance floor.

As a result of the negligent acts of the employees/agents of the XYZ Hotel, my client suffered severe injuries including a subdural hematoma, a concussion, facial lacerations, and a permanent partial loss of sight in her left eye.

You are further advised that my client's occupation for the past fifteen (15) years has been as a pilot for a major airline. Airlines require high vision standards to be met by their pilots. Ms. Mayes's physicians have advised her that she will no longer meet the minimum vision standards required to be a pilot (report enclosed), as a direct result of the injuries she sustained while attending the New Year's Eve Gala.

Accordingly, demand is hereby made for the sum of $25,000,000 (twenty-five million dollars) to compensate my client for the injuries she suffered due to the negligence and gross negligence of the employees of XYZ Hotel Company; including past, present, and future pain and suffering; past, present, and future medical expenses for both treatment and rehabilitation; and past, present, and future lost wages.

If you have liability insurance, you are strongly urged to advise the carrier of this claim, as most policies require prompt notification when a claim is made.

Please be advised that in the event this matter is not resolved to my client's satisfaction within ten (10) days of your receipt of this correspondence, that she has authorized me to pursue any and all legal remedies available to her in this regard, including filing suit seeking the recovery of compensatory damages, punitive damages, costs of court, and reasonable attorney fees.

Finally, you are advised that time is of the essence in this regard and that your silence will be deemed an admission. Please contact me or have your attorney contact me as soon as possible if you have any questions.

Thank you for your courtesy and cooperation.

Very Truly Yours,

Ms. Alixandre Caroline, Attorney at Law

Figure 9.1 Demand letter.

the attorney agrees to take the case for one flat fee. In this situation, it is clearly in the best interest of the attorney to seek a quick resolution of the case. The third payment form is the *contingency fee*. Lawyers representing defendants charged with crimes may not charge contingency fees, and in most states, contingency fee agreements must be put in writing. Clearly, in a case where the attorney is representing the client on a contingency basis, it is in the best interest of the plaintiff and the attorney to seek the most favorable, rather than the fastest, settlement possible.

Regardless of the form of payment agreed on between the plaintiff and his or her attorney, the demand letter is the first step in the litigation process. After receiving the demand letter, the defendant is given the opportunity to respond. If the response to the demand letter does not satisfy the plaintiff, he or she will likely instruct the attorney to file suit against the defendant.

Filing a Petition

Filing a petition (also called a pleading or complaint) is the term used to describe the process of initiating a lawsuit. A petition is a document that officially requests a court's assistance in resolving a dispute. The petition will identify specifically the plaintiff and the defendant. In addition, it will describe the matter it wishes for the court to decide. Included in the complaint against the defendant will be the plaintiff's suggestion for settlement of the issue. The plaintiff may, for example, ask for monetary damages. After the petition has been filed with the administrative clerk of the court, the lawsuit officially begins.

Once the complaint is filed with the court, the court will notify the defendant of the plaintiff's charge and will include a copy of the complaint in the notification. Upon receipt of the complaint, the defendant needs to respond in writing within the time specified in the notice from the court.

Discovery

In the discovery phase of a civil lawsuit, both parties seek to learn the facts necessary to best support their position. This can include answering questions via *interrogatories* or *depositions*, requests for records or other evidence, and sometimes visiting the scene of the incident that caused the complaint.

The discovery process can be short or very lengthy. Either side may ask for information from the other, and if necessary, a judge will rule on whether the parties to the suit must comply with these requests. In some instances, one party in a lawsuit may obtain a court order demanding that specific documents be turned over, or that specific individuals be called to testify in court. This order is called a *subpoena*. A subpoena may also be used to obtain further evidence or witnesses while a trial is ongoing.

The plaintiff in the lawsuit has the burden of proving the allegations set forth in the petition. This is the responsibility of proving to the finder of fact (judge or jury) that a particular view of the facts is true. In a civil case, the plaintiff must convince the court "by a preponderance of the evidence," that is, over 50 percent of the believable evidence. In a criminal case, the government has a higher standard, and must convince the court "beyond a reasonable doubt" that a defendant is guilty.

Trial and Appeal

The trial is the portion of the injury suit process during which the plaintiff seeks to persuade the judge or jury that his or her version of the facts and points of law should prevail. In a like manner, the defendant also has an opportunity to persuade for his or

LEGALESE
Contingency fee:
A method of paying for a civil attorney's services where the attorney receives a percentage of any money awarded as a settlement in the case. Typically, these fees range from 20 to 40 percent of the total amount awarded.

LEGALESE
Interrogatories:
Questions that require written answers, given under oath, asked during the discovery phase of a lawsuit.

LEGALESE
Depositions: Oral answers, given under oath, to questions asked during the discovery phase of a lawsuit. Depositions are recorded by a certified court reporter and/or by videotape.

LEGALESE
Subpoena: A court-authorized order to appear in person at a designated time and place, or to produce evidence demanded by the court.

her side. Most personal injury cases are tried in front of a jury. After a jury is selected to hear the trial, the process, while it may vary somewhat from state to state, is as follows:

1. Presentation by plaintiff
2. Presentation by defendant
3. Plaintiff's rebuttal
4. Summation by both parties
5. Judge's instructions about the applicable law and procedures to the jury
6. Jury deliberation
7. Verdict
8. Judgment or award
9. Appeal of verdict and/or award

Either side has the right to appeal a verdict or award. In the personal injury area, it is common for a losing defendant to *appeal* the size of the award if it is considered by the defendant's counsel to be excessive.

LEGALESE

Appeal: A written request to a higher court to modify or reverse the decision of a lower-level court.

LEGALLY MANAGING AT WORK:

The Manager's Role in Litigation

DEMAND LETTER

Upon receipt of a demand letter, turn it over to your insurance company and your attorney for advice. Follow the recommendations of the insurance company and your attorney. Be as cooperative as possible with any investigations that your insurance company or attorney may instigate.

NOTIFICATION OF FILING A LAWSUIT

Ordinarily, a representative of the court (e.g., constable, sheriff, or a private person authorized by the court) will personally hand you the pleading to ensure that the court knows you received it. If you are served with a pleading, you must recognize that these pleadings, and your company's obligations to respond, are time-sensitive. You need to deliver the pleading to your attorney as prescribed; make sure your insurance company gets a copy and that you keep one for future reference.

DISCOVERY

As stated previously, the discovery process enables each party to obtain information from the other party, which will be used as documentary evidence to help prove the facts of a case. Managers will often be asked to turn over records of their business, repair invoices, reports, and information stored electronically. Plaintiffs often must turn over medical records and reports, doctor bills, receipts for damages, and other types of personal information. Often, a manager or staff member may be asked to prepare a personal statement during the discovery process, or even go to court and testify as a witness during the trial.

The cost of responding to discovery requests, either by testifying or preparing documents, can be a very expensive proposition for your operation, not only from a financial perspective but also because of the time involved and the disruption it causes to your staff. Accordingly, the better organized you are at the outset of the incident, the less of a burden the discovery process will be. Work closely with your attorney during this phase, be cooperative, and be sure to meet all time limits imposed for responses, as missing a deadline can be fatal to your side of the case.

TRIAL AND APPEAL

Request that your attorney update you frequently about trial settings (the date the trial will commence). Reciprocally, you need to let your attorney know about any times that you or your employees will be unavailable to testify (such as vacations, scheduled surgeries, etc.).

If your case is appealed, your involvement in the appellate process will be very minimal, if at all. This process rarely requires anything new from you that was not provided before the trial. Nevertheless, you should continue to maintain your records of the case and keep track of any witnesses.

Alternative Dispute Resolution

There are alternatives to resolving personal injury claims in court. The parties at any time during the litigation process can agree on a settlement. Two other common methods used in the hospitality industry are mediation and arbitration. Both can be highly effective alternatives to the time, cost, and stress involved in going through a trial.

In mediation, a trained and neutral individual (the mediator) facilitates negotiation between the parties, in order to achieve a voluntary resolution of the dispute. In most cases, one full day of mediation can result in a compromise acceptable to both the plaintiff and defendant. Mediation can involve sessions jointly held with both parties and their attorneys, or separate meetings with each party, their attorneys, and the mediator. The cost of mediation will vary based on the complexity of the case, but is generally far less than that involved in going to a trial. If the mediation is unsuccessful, the parties may still pursue a trial. If a settlement is made, the parties sign a settlement agreement approved by their attorneys. This agreement, if drafted properly, is an enforceable contract.

In arbitration, a neutral third party (usually chosen by mutual agreement of both parties) makes a binding decision after reviewing the evidence and hearing the arguments of all sides.

Make sure that you and your attorney have established guidelines about what you can say, if anything, and when you can say it. Be patient. To be effective, the negotiation process can sometimes appear tedious, but the art of compromise usually takes time. Be flexible and willing to compromise. Many times, an apology at this point in the process will help pave the way for compromises on other significant issues, including the amount of money to be paid.

9.5 ■ RESPONDING TO AN INCIDENT

Despite all of your careful planning, preparation, and prevention techniques, guests can still be seriously injured on your property. Because of the explosion of litigation in this country and the large jury awards that can result, owners and operators of hospitality facilities have spent great amounts of time, energy, and money to implement training programs and procedures that will reduce accidents. But, when accidents do occur, you must be prepared to act in a way that serves the best interest of both your operation and the injured party.

In his book *Accident Prevention for Hotels, Motels, and Restaurants* (Van Nostrand Reinhold, 1991), author Robert L. Kohr states that the first 15 minutes following an accident are "critical" in eliminating or greatly limiting your legal liability. He is correct. It is your job to know what to do—and, just as important, what not to do—during this critical time period.

The moments following an accident are often confusing and tense. For a manager, they will demand excellent decision-making skills. The steps given in the next Legally Managing at Work box describe how control people (such as people in positions including owners, managers, and supervisors) should react during this crucial time period. Remember, the objective is to act in such a way as to protect both the business and the accident victim. The steps described in Legally Managing at Work will help you accomplish both.

As you can see, it is imperative that control people take charge of the scene immediately after an accident occurs. They should be the only ones talking to the injured party, and they need to be prepared to react and think quickly under pressure. Role-playing is a great way to train people to know how to respond appropriately when an accident or emergency situation arises.

Hospitality operations must continue to undertake serious prevention efforts, but they should also be prepared for reality: Accidents do happen, and the steps taken the first few minutes after an accident can be crucial in minimizing the negative impact of a potential claim.

LEGALLY MANAGING AT WORK:

Responding to an Accident

STEP 1. DO CALL 911.

First and foremost, get qualified, professional help. Do not leave it to the discretion of an untrained person to determine whether an injury requires professional medical treatment. Do not allow the delay of a decision-making process to increase your chance of liability. Call 911.

STEP 2. DO ATTEND TO THE INJURED PARTY.

Let the injured party know that you have requested emergency assistance. Try to make him or her as comfortable as possible. If you have certified care providers on your staff, allow them to administer appropriate aid. Restrict the movement of the injured party as much as possible unless the injury makes immediate movement necessary.

STEP 3. DO BE SENSITIVE AND SINCERE.

Do not treat the injured person as a potential liability claim. If you do, you will probably end up with one. In discussions with many injured patrons who later filed lawsuits, it was found that a significant reason for making their claim was the insensitive treatment exhibited by the establishment after the accident occurred. Treat the injured party with sensitivity, sincerity, and concern.

STEP 4. DO NOT APOLOGIZE FOR THE ACCIDENT.

Being sensitive, sincere, and concerned does not equate to taking responsibility for the accident. Besides, until the investigation is completed, you do not know if an apology by you for the accident is appropriate.

STEP 5. DO NOT ADMIT THAT YOU OR YOUR EMPLOYEES WERE AT FAULT. DO NOT TAKE RESPONSIBILITY FOR THE ACCIDENT.

Statements such as these made immediately following an accident are often based on first impressions, without knowing all of the facts. Unfortunately, making such statements may have a profound impact on the injured party, as well as a judge or jury, who may perceive them to be a credible admission of guilt or liability. Even when the circumstances surrounding an incident seem glaringly obvious, refrain from admitting fault or responsibility. There is no reason to discuss liability, negligence, or responsibility at this time. The focus should be on the guest's injuries, not on the cause of the accident.

STEP 6. DO NOT OFFER TO PAY FOR THE MEDICAL EXPENSES OF THE INJURED PARTY.

By offering or promising to pay for medical expenses, the control person is possibly entering into a contractual arrangement with the injured party or the medical provider to pay for the cost of treatment. This contract might be enforceable even if the outcome of the accident investigation shows that the hospitality operation was not at fault. In minor injury situations, you can offer to call a particular doctor or treatment center for the injured party, but allow him or her to choose the provider. In very limited circumstances, you might want to agree to pay for the initial treatment only, but specify your position in writing with the medical provider.

STEP 7. DO NOT MENTION INSURANCE COVERAGE.

Fortunately, most hospitality operations have insurance for many types of accidents and injuries that occur on their premises. Unfortunately, the fact that an operator has insurance will sometimes be reflected as dollar signs in the eyes of the injured party. Psychologically, it is much easier to pursue a big, cold, indifferent, and unfamiliar insurance company than it is to pursue a very warm, concerned, and well-meaning hospitality manager.

STEP 8. DO NOT DISCUSS THE CAUSE OF THE ACCIDENT.

Discussing the cause of the accident with the injured party is a no-win situation. If the injured party argues or implies that the hospitality operation is at fault for the accident, and the control person agrees, fault has been admitted. If the control person disagrees, it will only create ill feelings and exacerbate the situation. Remaining silent is not an admission of liability, and is preferable to arguing with the injured party. Another alternative is for the control person to reassure the injured party, that he or she will conduct a complete investigation and will be happy to discuss the circumstances upon its completion.

STEP 9. DO NOT CORRECT EMPLOYEES AT THE SCENE.

This immediate reaction can have a very serious negative impact in the future. On-the-scene reprimanding of employees is sometimes interpreted by the injured party that a mistake was made or that the operation caused the accident. Control people need to remember that they cannot change what has already occurred. They can only hope to positively influence the future decision-making process of the injured party. This can best be accomplished by focusing on the injured party, not on the operation. There will be plenty of time to assess each employee's performance and to take appropriate corrective action if it is warranted, after the investigation has been completed.

STEP 10. DO CONDUCT A COMPLETE AND THOROUGH INVESTIGATION.

Although it will take a great deal longer than 15 minutes, a significant amount of the information for a thorough investigation needs to be gathered immediately after the accident. If other guests saw the accident, request that they write down what they saw. Ask them to sign and date their statements, and to leave their address and phone number in case you need to contact them in the future. It may take years for a claim to be resolved. Attorneys and investigators will need to be able to locate the people who gave statements. An incident report, such as the one shown in Figure 9.2, can be used to help gather such information. Remember, evidence wins lawsuits, and the more evidence and documentation you have, the better your chances for a favorable ruling, or one that minimizes the amount of damages you will have to pay.

It is also important to have your employees fill out and sign a written report. Employees may change jobs, voluntarily leave, or be terminated from an operation before an accident claim is resolved. Depending on why they left, employees' perceptions of an accident, or the events leading up to it, may change over time, along with their overall perception of the operation and its owners and supervisors. It is not unusual for an employee to first recount a positive rendition of the events from the employer's perspective, then upon being terminated, to later report information that would make the employer look negligent in the eyes of an attorney or judge.

STEP 11. DO COMPLETE A CLAIM REPORT AND SUBMIT IT TO YOUR INSURANCE COMPANY IMMEDIATELY.

Most insurance policies require prompt notification of any and all potential claims if they are to provide coverage under the policy. The reason is that insurance companies want their experts to become involved in the investigation as early as possible. Your failure to report the claim could cause the claim to be excluded from coverage.

STEP 12. DO NOT DISCUSS THE CIRCUMSTANCES SURROUNDING THE ACCIDENT OR THE INVESTIGATION WITH ANYONE EXCEPT THOSE WHO ABSOLUTELY NEED TO KNOW.

Conversations and opinions given to employees, or even people not associated with the business, can come back to haunt you. Restrict your conversations to the hospitality operation's attorneys or authorized representatives of the insurance company.

STEP 13. DO NOT THROW AWAY RECORDS, STATEMENTS, OR OTHER EVIDENCE UNTIL THE CASE IS FINALIZED.

Cases can be resolved in several different ways: The claim could be settled prior to trial; the case could be tried in court and decided, or perhaps appealed until all avenues for appeal are exhausted. And sometimes a potential injury claim may not be filed as a lawsuit right away. Whatever the circumstance, the case will not be considered closed until the statue of limitations runs out (ordinarily two years from the date of the injury in a personal injury claim). If you are not absolutely certain whether a claim has been finalized, check with your operation's attorney or the insurance company, and request a letter of consent to destroy the evidence.

INCIDENT REPORT

Business _____   Date _____

Address _____   City _____ State _____

Complainant

_____

Last Name   First Name   Initial

_____

Address   City   State   Zip

_____

Home Telephone   Business Telephone

Type of Incident

_____

Theft   Accident   Property Damage   Other

Injury

First aid given?   Yes_____   No_____

First aid refused   Yes_____   No_____

EMS called?   Yes_____   No_____

Taken to emergency?   Yes_____   No_____

Nature of injury _____

_____

_____

Detail of Incident

_____

_____

_____

_____

_____

_____

_____

_____

_____

_____

Property and Value

Damaged/Missing Property Description   Estimated Value

_____   _____

_____   _____

_____   _____

_____   _____

Figure 9.2 Incident reporting form.

Room Entry   **Room Number** _____

Room entered? _____   Time _____

Door locked? _____   Door chained? _____

Entered by _____   Witnessed by _____

Police Report

Police Officer Name _____

Shield # _____   Report # _____

Arrest made? _____ Citation issued? _____

Witnesses:

Name _____ Tel: _____

Address _____ City _____ State _____

Name _____ Tel: _____

Address _____ City _____ State _____

Name _____ Tel: _____

Address _____ City _____ State _____

Comments: _____

_____

_____

_____

_____

_____

_____

_____

Prepared by _____   Reviewed by _____

Date _____   Date _____

Figure 9.2 (*Continued*)

INTERNATIONAL SNAPSHOT

Negligence

Negligence overseas can spell liability at home. The standards used in the United States to determine whether the employees of a hospitality facility exercised reasonable care may apply to the foreign operations of American hospitality companies. Consider the following:

■ Many Americans desire to travel overseas.

■ Many of those Americans are more comfortable staying at a facility that has a familiar name and appearance.

■ The American hospitality industry purposefully seeks to attract the business of those people.

■ Those marketing efforts often succeed because the industry is able to combine the allure of exotic places with the peace of mind that accompanies known corporate brands.

Americans who travel overseas expect that their experience will be consistent with their experiences in the United States. So do U.S. courts. American travelers eventually come home, and when they have suffered losses overseas at facilities operated by American companies, any suit they file is likely to be filed at home. When that happens, U.S. courts usually impose U.S. legal standards. The following factors, either alone or in combination, will be considered:

■ *Whether the parties to the litigation, namely the dissatisfied guest and the U.S. operator of the overseas facility, are United States citizens.* U.S. courts are not comfortable imposing foreign legal standards upon United States citizens.

■ *The nature of the foreign jurisdiction's legal principles.* Some are repugnant to the policy of the U.S. jurisdiction. Similarly, U.S. courts are unaccustomed to analyzing and applying foreign legal standards.

■ *Whether the foreign hospitality facility is under the control of an American company.* For example, American hospitality companies typically impose their corporatewide practices and procedures on their foreign operations. The managers of the foreign operations may have been trained in the United States by the American operator.

Managers of overseas hospitality facilities operated by U.S. companies should strive to meet U.S. standards of care in all aspects of the hospitality operation. U.S. courts evaluating their performance after an American tourist has an unfortunate experience will most likely expect them to do nothing less.

Provided by Perrin Rynders, of the Varnum Riddering Schmidt Howlett Law Firm, in Grand Rapids, Michigan. www.varnumlaw.com

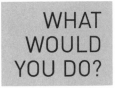

WHAT WOULD YOU DO?

Assume you are a mediator whose job is to help opposing parties limit the expense and time of going to trial in matters of personal injury. In your current case, Jeremy and Anne Hunter have filed a personal injury suit against the Fairview Mayton Hotel's ownership group and its franchisor, Mayton Hotels and Resorts Inc.

According to the Hunters, they checked into their suite at the Fairview Mayton, one of 150 independently owned, franchise-affiliated properties, on a Friday night. Their daughter Susan, who was 8 years old at the time, opened a sliding patio door, and upon seeing the outdoor hot tub that was part of suite, asked her parents if she could get in. They told her yes. Upon entering the tub (it is agreed by both parties that Susan "jumped" into the hot tub), she suffered third-degree burns over 80 percent of her body, and her facial features were permanently disfigured because the water in the hot tub was 160 degrees Fahrenheit, not 102, the maximum recommended by the tub's manufacturer, and well above the 105-degree maximum dictated by local health codes. An investigation determined that the hot tub safety switch, designed to prevent accidental overheating, had been bypassed when some wiring repair was performed by the hotel's maintenance staff. (The Hunters are also suing the franchise company because a mandatory inspection of property safety, which, as part of the franchise agreement was to have been performed annually, had not been done in the three years prior to the accident.)

The hotel's insurance company takes the position that Susan's parents gave her permission to use the tub, despite a written warning on the side of the tub saying it was not to be used by persons under age 14, and thus they bear a majority of the responsibility for the accident.

The Mayton franchise company's insurance company states it is not responsible for the acts of its franchisees, and thus cannot be held accountable. The hotel's manager has been terminated. The Hunters, whose lawyer has accepted the case on a contingency basis, is suing for a total of $5 million.

1. What would you recommend the Fairview Mayton's insurance company do?
2. What would you recommend the franchise company's insurance company do?
3. What would you recommend the Hunters do?

To illustrate the importance of following company policies, consider the case of *Faverty v. McDonald's Rests. of Oregon*, 892 P.2d 703 (Or. Ct. App. 1995).

THE HOSPITALITY INDUSTRY IN COURT

FACTUAL SUMMARY

Matt Theurer (Theurer), an 18-year-old McDonald's employee, was involved in a severe auto accident one morning after work. Theurer fell asleep at the wheel and crossed over into oncoming traffic. His car struck a van driven by Frederic Faverty. Theurer was killed in the accident and Faverty was seriously injured.

The day before the accident, Theurer worked three shifts, for a total of nearly 13 hours, at a McDonald's restaurant. The first shift began after school at 3:30 P.M. and ended at 7:30 P.M. Theurer returned to the restaurant at midnight and worked on a special cleaning project until 5:00 A.M. The final shift of the morning was a continuation of the midnight shift ending at 8:21 A.M. Theurer asked to be excused from his next regular shift and left work, telling the manager he was tired and needed to rest.

On five occasions during the week before the accident, Theurer worked at least until 9:00 P.M. On a few nights he worked past 11:00 P.M., and once past midnight. In addition to working for McDonald's, Theurer was involved in a number of extracurricular activities and served in the National Guard. Many of his friends and family believed he worked too much and was not sleeping enough. McDonald's had a policy of not requiring its high school employees to work past midnight. Additionally, McDonald's policy was to limit the number of shifts worked to two a day. McDonald's controlled the schedules of its employees and knew how many hours each had worked.

The plaintiff Faverty settled the potential claims against the representatives of Theurer's estate. He then sued McDonald's, claiming it was responsible for the acts of an employee even away from the work site. Faverty claimed McDonald's should not have allowed Theurer to work so many hours when it knew Theurer would drive home while tired and pose a risk to himself and others.

QUESTION FOR THE COURT

The question for the court was whether McDonald's was responsible for the acts of its employees outside of the job site. McDonalds initially argued it was Theurer's employer and as such was not responsible for his conduct. As the employer, McDonald's argued, it would only be responsible for Theurer's actions on the job site and would be under no duty to control Theurer away from work. Faverty argued McDonald's had an obligation to avoid conduct that was unreasonable and created a foreseeable risk of harm to a third party. McDonald's next argued that an Oregon State law set the number of hours an employee could work, and the law was not violated. Faverty argued the law did not apply to restaurants and did not establish a maximum number of hours employees could be required to work.

DECISION

The jury ruled for Faverty, finding McDonald's responsible. Faverty was awarded damages for his injuries. The appeals court agreed with the trial court verdict and held McDonald's had an obligation to avoid unreasonable conduct that created a possible risk to third parties. The court also held McDonald's was unreasonable in requiring Theurer to work as many hours as he did, and should have recognized he was tired and posed a risk to the public.

MESSAGE TO MANAGEMENT

This situation possibly could have been avoided if the manager at the restaurant had followed McDonald's policies. Set reasonable policies, follow them, and work hard to be sure your employees comply.

WHAT DID YOU LEARN IN THIS CHAPTER?

All hospitality businesses must operate in a reasonably safe manner or face potential liability for accidents and injuries that occur to their guests. Specific areas (or duties) have been identified in the law that help to define the scope of the business's responsibility to visitors. These include the duty (or obligation) to provide a reasonably safe facility and grounds, to serve food and beverages fit for consumption, and to hire qualified employees. The term "reasonably," however, is sometimes a difficult standard to define, as it is based on current and customary practices in the industry.

If you failed to operate in a reasonably safe manner and damages occur as a result, you might be found to have been negligent and be held liable for damages. If you ignored the safety and well-being of visitors, then you may be found to have been grossly negligent and face greater liability than for ordinary negligence. The visitor also has a responsibility to act reasonably, or he or she may be found to have contributed to the cause of damages.

Types of damages include property loss, medical expenses, lost wages, pain and suffering, punitive fines, and legal fees. Not all types of damages are recoverable in every type of claim.

A personal injury claim is usually initiated with a demand letter. If the situation cannot be resolved amicably, a lawsuit may commence. The steps in a lawsuit include the filing of a petition, the discovery period, and a trial before a judge or jury. You, as a manager, have a crucial role in the litigation and/or resolution process. Claims do not always have to end up in trial; they are sometimes resolved through mediation or arbitration techniques.

If an accident should occur on your property (and one probably will despite your best prevention practices), the way your staff responds can have a significant impact on the consequences that arise from the accident.

RAPID REVIEW

After you have studied this chapter, you should be prepared to:

1. Define and explain the difference between a breach of contract, a crime, and a tort.

2. Describe examples of negligence, gross negligence, and an intentional act that could result in the commission of a tort.

3. Detail the essential difference between a duty of care and a standard of care, using an example of each.

4. Give three examples of strict liability as it may apply to hospitality managers offering food, lodging, and entertainment products.

5. Using the Web or the library, search the hospitality trade press to find an article describing an incident of a jury awarding punitive damages to a plaintiff where a hospitality organization was the defendant. Explain why you believe the jury came to its conclusion.

6. Outline the process involved in initiating a personal injury lawsuit, and discuss the hospitality manager's role in that process.

7. List at least five advantages that result from using an alternative dispute resolution process, as opposed to going to trial in a personal injury lawsuit.

8. Create a checklist that can be used to guide a manager's actions in the first 15 minutes after an accident.

In teams, design a procedural checklist (one-page maximum) for a manager-on-duty to follow when responding to a serious accident in a 1,000-room resort hotel located 100 miles away from the nearest medical center.

TEAM ACTIVITY

CHAPTER 10

YOUR RESPONSIBILITIES AS A HOSPITALITY OPERATOR TO GUESTS

"Good morning, Trisha," said Sheriff Pat Hutting, as he strode into her office. "It's great to see you again. Let me introduce Detective Andy Letonski. Andy is from the city police force, and he is working a case. He asked me to arrange this meeting with you because, frankly, we think you could really help us out."

Trisha Sangus smiled at Sheriff Hutting. He was truly one of her best friends in the business community. He was also the chief law enforcement officer of the county where Trisha managed her hotel. He loved to golf, as did Trisha, and her excellent business and personal relationship with him was extremely helpful in getting a prompt response time when dealing with the occasional guest eviction.

"Good to see you too, Pat," Trisha replied, "and good to meet you, Andy. What's going on?"

"Drugs," replied Andy. "As you know, our area has its share, despite the fact that they go virtually unseen."

"Yes," said Trisha. "Pat and I have helped the school district by holding DARE training sessions at our hotel on several occasions."

"That's right," said Pat as he turned to Andy. "No one in the area is a bigger supporter of our efforts than Trisha—and her property."

"Well," said Andy, "that's why I asked Pat to bring me here. You have a guest in room 417. The guest's name is Marty White."

"That could be," said Trisha. "It's a big hotel, but I really don't think that particular guest has come to my attention before today. Would you like me to check with the front desk to confirm that Mr. White is a guest here?"

"Well," replied the detective, "I was hoping you could assist in another way."

"Andy's men have had Mr. White under surveillance for three days now," said the sheriff.

"We believe Mr. White is involved in drug trafficking in the area," added Andy.

"And what are you asking of me?" inquired Trisha.

"Just to allow us to look at Mr. White's phone records, so we can see whom he is calling," said Andy. "They could be a great help in locating his possible source of supply and delivery. Your telephone call accounting system does record the number of all outgoing phone calls, doesn't it?"

"Yes," replied Trisha, "it does."

"That's great," said Andy. "Those records would be a big help to us."

"Let me be sure I understand your request," said Trisha. "You are convinced that one of our guests is involved with the local drug trade?"

"Absolutely," said Andy.

"Do you have evidence of the involvement?" asked Trisha.

"We have a significant amount. There is no doubt Mr. White is involved. That's why I asked Sheriff Pat to set up this meeting with you," replied Andy. "He told me about your previous involvement in antidrug educational activities in the area."

"And you, Andy, would like to look at, but not copy, our records of the telephone calls that our guest has made since he has been here?" Trisha queried.

"That's correct," said Andy, as the sheriff looked at Trisha somewhat uncomfortably.

"Well," said Trisha, "let me think about a response. I'll get back to you within the hour."

"Can't we look at them now?" asked Andy earnestly.

Trisha looked at him carefully. She knew what she was going to say, but because of her friendship with the sheriff, she wanted to turn this request down carefully, and in a way that would not embarrass the sheriff, who was, she suspected, an unwilling partner in the meeting.

IN THIS CHAPTER, YOU WILL LEARN:

1. To understand your legal responsibility to admit guests and the circumstances when such admission can be denied.
2. To protect the guest's right to privacy.
3. To operate and maintain a facility in a way that maximizes the safety of guests and compliance with the law, including Title III of the Americans with Disabilities Act (ADA).
4. To differentiate among various types of nonguests and understand your obligations toward them.
5. To generate the procedures required to safely and legally remove guests from a property.

10.1 ACCOMMODATING GUESTS

Guests are the lifeblood of any hospitality organization. Guests are so important that management's role could be defined simply as the ability to develop and retain a viable customer base. Without a sufficient number of guests, success and profitability in the hospitality industry is impossible. The reality, however, is that with guests come guest-related challenges; particularly when the legal implications are considered. In this chapter, we will examine guests and their rights, as well as your rights as a manager or proprietor.

Definition of a Guest

The law views a hospitality manager's responsibility to those who come onto a property differently based on the characteristics of the visitor. Consider the case of Eva Barrix. Eva is a motel owner who maintains a pool for the convenience of her guests. Late one night, a robber scales a fence around Eva's property and, because the thief is not familiar with the grounds, accidentally trips, falls, and stumbles into the pool. Clearly, the law does not require that Eva inform would-be criminals about the layout of her facility. In addition, despite the occasional well-publicized personal injury case, thieves would have a difficult time proving to the court that the owner of a business owes a duty of care to them, as discussed in Chapter 9, "Your Responsibilities as a Hospitality Operator." Contrast this example with a guest who may experience a similar fall near the pool area, and you will see why it is important to understand the distinctions involved in determining precisely who is a *guest* and who is not.

Certainly, duties of care apply to guests, and in most cases, to guests of guests. In the restaurant area, a guest is not limited merely to the individual who pays the bill. In fact, all diners are considered to be guests of the facility.

LEGALESE

Guest: A customer who lawfully utilizes a facility's food, beverage, lodging, or entertainment services.

≫ ANALYZE THE SITUATION 10.1

NICOLE FROST AND STEVE Merchand were brother and sister. When their grandfather, Wayne Merchand, was hospitalized for care after a heart attack, the two began to visit him regularly at Laurel Memorial Hospital.

One Sunday afternoon, after visiting with their grandfather, Nicole and Steve went to the hospital's cafeteria for a light lunch. A professional foodservice management company operated the cafeteria under contract to the hospital. Nicole and Steve selected their lunches from an assortment of beverages and prewrapped sandwiches that were displayed unrefrigerated on a tray in the middle of the cafeteria serving line. The sandwiches were made of ham and cheese, with a salad dressing spread, lettuce, and tomato. Steve paid for the sandwiches, beverages, and some chips, and then he and Nicole took a seat in the cafeteria dining room.

Approximately four hours after eating lunch, both Steve and Nicole became ill. They determined that they both had suffered from foodborne illness. The two filed suit against the hospital and its contract foodservice management company. When the facts of the case came out, the hospital maintained that, as visitors, not patients, the hospital had no liability toward Nicole and Steve. The foodservice management company operating the hospital cafeteria maintained that its liability extended only to Steve since he was the only guest who in fact purchased food from its service. Management maintained it should not be held responsible for the illness suffered by an individual that they did not actually serve.

1. Was Nicole a guest of the foodservice facility?

2. Should Steve bear partial responsibility for the damage he and Nicole suffered, given that he purchased the sandwiches?

3. What type of liability (from Chapter 9, "Your Responsibilities as a Hospitality Operator") applies in this case? Why?

LEGALESE

Transient guest: A customer who rents real property for a relatively short period of time (e.g., small number of days with no intent of establishing a permanent residency).

LEGALESE

Tenant: Anyone, including a corporation, who rents real property for an extended period of time with the intent of establishing a permanent occupation or residency.

In the lodging area, guests can be considered to be either a *transient guest* or a *tenant*, and the differences are significant. As can be seen by the definitions, the precise demarcation between transient guests and tenants is not easily established. It is important to do so, however, because the courts make a distinction between the two, even when hospitality managers do not. For example, a transient guest who checks into a hotel for a one-night stay but does not pay for the room by the posted check-out time the next morning may be "locked out." That means, in a hotel with an electronic locking system, the front desk manager could deactivate the guest's key, thus preventing his or her readmittance to the room until such time as the guest settles the account with the front desk. A tenant with a lease, however, could not be locked out so easily, and thus enjoys greater protection under the law.

Whether an individual is a transient guest or tenant is sometimes a matter for the courts to decide, but the following characteristics can help you determine which category an individual might fall into:

■ *Billing format*: Transient guests tend to be charged a daily rate for their stay, while tenants are more likely to be billed on a weekly or monthly basis.

■ *Tax payment*: Transient guests must pay local occupancy taxes, while tenants are ordinarily exempt from such payment.

■ *Address use*: Tenants generally use the facility's address as their permanent address for such things as mail, driver's license, voter registration, and the like. Transient guests generally list another location as their permanent address.

■ *Contract format*: Transient guests generally enter into a rooming agreement via a registration card, while tenants would normally have a lease agreement or specific contract separate from, or in addition to, their registration card.

■ *Existence of deposit*: Tenants are almost always required to give their landlord a deposit. Often this deposit is equal to a specified number of months of rent. Transient guests, by contrast, do not generally put up a deposit. This is true even if the hotel requires a transient guest to present a credit card upon checking into the hotel.

■ *Length of stay*: While it is widely believed that any guest who occupies a room for more than 30 days becomes a tenant, the fact is, length of stay is usually not the sole criterion on which the transient guest/tenant determination is made. In fact, most guests who occupy the same hotel room for over 30 days may do so without affecting their transient status. It is true, however, that the length of stay for a tenant does tend to be longer than that of a transient guest.

Because the line between a transient guest and tenant is unclear, and because the states have addressed this situation differently, if you are a hotel manager and are unsure about the status of a guest/tenant, it is best to seek the advice of a qualified attorney before taking steps to remove the individual from his or her room.

>> ANALYZE THE SITUATION 10.2

KETAN PATEL OPERATED THE Heartworth Suites, an extended-stay, limited-service hotel of 85 rooms. Approximately 40 percent of his guests were extended-stay, which Mr. Pate's company defined as a stay longer than five consecutive days. The remaining rooms were sold to traditional transient guests, whose average stay was approximately 1.8 days.

Bob Thimming was an extended-stay guest at the Heartworth, and an employee of Katy Highway Contractors. Mr. Thimming held the position of construction foreman for a stretch of interstate highway being repaired in the vicinity of the Heartworth Suites. His company signed a contract with the Heartworth confirming that Mr. Thimming would be given a special monthly, rather than daily, rate because he was staying in the hotel for six consecutive months as part of his work assignment.

In the third month of his stay, Mr. Thimming arrived at the hotel from his job site at approximately 5:30 P.M. to find the door to his room ajar. He entered the room and discovered that his $4,000 watch, which he had left on the nightstand, was missing. Mr. Thimming contacted Mr. Patel to complain of the theft. Because the hotel was equipped with electronic locks, Mr. Patel was able to perform a lock audit and retrieved the following information for the day in question:

Time	Key Used	Key Issued To	Results
6:30 A.M.	7J 105–60	Guest	Entry
6:32 A.M.	7J 105–60	Guest	Entry
1:30 P.M.	1M 002–3	Maintenance	Entry

Mr. Thimming maintained that someone negligently left the door open, and as a result his watch was stolen. He contacted his company, whose in-house attorney called Mr. Patel. The attorney stated that Mr. Thimming was a tenant of the hotel, and as a landlord, Mr. Patel was responsible for the negligent acts of his employee and should reimburse Mr. Thimming for his loss. Mr. Patel replied that Mr. Thimming was not a tenant but a transient guest, and thus was subject to a state law that limits an innkeeper's liability in such cases to $350. The attorney disagreed, based on the six-month "lease" signed by Katy Highway Contractors for Mr. Thimming. He demanded that the watch be replaced and threatened to file suit if it was not. Mr. Patel contacted his attorney, who offered, based on his view of the complexity of the case, to defend the Heartworth Suites for $3,000, with a required retaining (down payment) of $2,000.

1. Was Mr. Thimming a transient guest or a tenant?

2. Why is the distinction important in this situation?

3. What should Mr. Patel do in the future to avoid the expense of litigation such as this?

Admitting Guests

LEGALESE

Public accommodation: A facility that provides entertainment, rooms, space, or seating for the use and benefit of the general public.

LEGALESE

Segregate: To separate a group or individual on any basis but especially by race, color, religion, or national origin.

As facilities of *public accommodation*, hotels and restaurants historically were required to admit everyone who sought to come in. More recently, as a result of evolving laws and the changing social environment in which hotels and restaurants operate, and as the protection of guests and employees becomes more complex, the right of the hospitality business to refuse to serve a guest has expanded. At the same time, laws have been enacted at the federal, state, and local levels that prohibit discrimination in public accommodations. Violations of these laws can result in either civil or criminal penalties. Beyond the legal expenses, negative publicity earned from this type of discrimination against guests can also cost a business significant amounts of lost revenue, and can damage a company's reputation for years to come. Consequently, it is important for you to know when you have to admit guests, as well as the circumstances in which you have the right to deny admission.

It is a violation of the Federal Civil Rights Act of 1964 to deny any person admission to a facility of public accommodation on the basis of race, color, religion, or national origin. In addition, it is a violation to admit such guests but then *segregate* them to a specific section(s) of the facility, or discriminate against them in the manner of service they receive or the types of products and services they are provided.

State or local civil rights laws are usually more inclusive in that they expand the "protected classes" to categories not covered under federal law, such as age, marital status, and sexual orientation, and may also have stricter penalties for violations.

Historically, it has been argued that "private" clubs were exempt from the Civil Rights Act and could discriminate in their admission policies because they were not in fact public facilities. However, courts across the United States have slowly dismantled this argument by continuing to broaden the definition of public facilities, and, concomitantly, to narrow the definition of a private club. (For instance, if a country club is very selective about its membership, but nonmembers can rent its facilities for meetings, wedding receptions, and the like, is it really private?) In addition, many cities and towns have passed local ordinances that outlaw discrimination in private clubs, even if those clubs meet the "private" club definition under federal law. Accordingly, most clubs today have opted to comply with the Civil Rights Act and other antidiscriminatory laws.

It is legal, and in fact, in some cases, mandatory, for a facility of public accommodation to separate guests based on some stated or observed characteristic. Some communities, for example, require that restaurants provide distinctly separate spaces for their smoking and nonsmoking guests. It is important to note that such a practice

---

Search the Web 10.1

Log on to www.usconstitution.net.

1. Select: Plain text version of the Constitution, under the head The United States Constitution.
2. Scroll until you reach the Fourteenth Amendment, and read it carefully.
3. Are women specifically mentioned in the Fourteenth Amendment?
4. How does the wording of this amendment impact admission policies in the hospitality industry?
5. Do you believe the amendment prohibits "ladies only" or "men only" nights?

is not illegal, because it does not discriminate against a protected class of individuals as defined by the Civil Rights Act.

Denying Admission to Guests

Although it is illegal to unlawfully discriminate against a potential guest, you do have the right to refuse to admit or serve guests in some situations. A public accommodation may legally deny service to a potential guest when:

1. *The individual cannot show the ability to pay for the services provided.* In this situation, it is important that management be able to clearly show that all potential customers are subjected to the same "ability to pay" test. In a restaurant, for example, if only youths of a specific ethnic background are required to demonstrate ability to pay prior to ordering, the manager of that facility is discriminating on the basis of ethnicity and is in violation of the law.

2. *The individual has a readily communicable disease.* An operator is not required to put the safety of other guests aside to accommodate a guest who could spread a disease to others.

3. *The individual wishes to enter the facility with an item that is prohibited.* It is permissible to refuse service to individuals attempting to bring animals into the premises, with the exception of guide animals for the physically impaired, as well as those carrying guns, knives, or other weapons. Some operators actually post a policy specifically referring to firearms. Figure 10.1 is an example of such a policy.

4. *The individual is intoxicated.* Not only is it legal to deny service to a guest who is visibly under the influence of drugs or alcohol, but also admitting or serving such an individual could put you at great risk. (The duty of care required for an intoxicated person will be discussed more fully in Chapter 12, "Your Responsibilities When Serving Food and Beverages.") It is clear that an individual whose reasoning is impaired by drugs or alcohol poses a significant threat to the safety of others, and thus loses his or her right to be served. Care must be taken in these circumstances to not put the guest or the general public at risk.

5. *The individual presents a threat to employees or other guests.* Obviously, alcohol and drugs need not be present for a guest to pose a threat to other guests or employees. If the guest behaves in any manner that is threatening or intimidating to either employees or other guests, then that individual need not be served, as long as this policy is applied uniformly to all guests. Should such a situation arise, and service is indeed denied, it is best to document the situation using the Incident Report Form from Chapter 9, "Your Responsibilities as a Hospitality Operator," in case your actions are ever called into question. Some operators require guests to sign a "house rules" document that clearly states behaviors that the operator will not permit. Figure 10.2 is an example of such a statement.

It is strictly prohibited for any person to carry a weapon, including but not limited to a handgun, or a concealed weapon anywhere on this property, including parking lots.

We reserve the right to search each person, his or her personal effects, and vehicle as a condition of entry onto or presence on this property.

This policy supersedes any right an employee or guest may believe he or she has to carry a weapon, concealed or otherwise, pursuant to state law.

Violators will be prosecuted.

Figure 10.1 Weapons policy.

The following rules regulate the renting of rooms, suites, and cottages on this property. Occupants will be bound by these rules and policies, and failure to comply will result in termination of agreement and removal from property.

1. Renter is 21 years of age or older.
2. Renter will remain in room and not sublease or turn over room to other parties.
3. Renter will not utilize room for parties or unauthorized social gatherings.
4. Renter will not create noise or other disturbance.
5. Renter will not exceed maximum limit for number of occupants per room (five, or local code).
6. Renter will declare to hotel and pay for all occupants.
7. Renter will be responsible for all damage and excess wear and tear to room and property.

_____   _____
Guest Signature   Date

_____   _____
Property Witness   Date

Figure 10.2 House rules statement.

6. *The individual does not seek to become a guest.* Although hotels and restaurants are considered places of public accommodation, they are also businesses. For example, a guest could enter a coffee shop in a downtown city hotel, order a cup of coffee, and occupy a seat for a reasonable amount of time. However, that same guest would not be permitted to enter the hotel's most exclusive dining room on a busy Friday night and order the same cup of coffee rather than a full meal. A reasonable person would assume that dining tables in a restaurant are reserved for those wishing to eat full meals, and thus denying service to a guest who does not want to do so is allowable.

7. *The individual is too young.* Those businesses that serve alcoholic beverages may be required by law to prohibit individuals under a predetermined age from entering their facilities. It is important to note that laws in this regard tend to be state or local ordinances. In some communities, young people are allowed to eat in a bar as long as a person of legal age accompanies them. In others, that same young person may not be allowed to sit in a dining area that would permit them even to view the bar area. Because the line between a bar or lounge that serves alcohol as its primary product and a restaurant that serves alcohol as an accompaniment to its food can be very unclear, managers should always check with the local or state agency granting liquor permits to ensure that they are up to date on the regulations regarding minors.

   In most states, a hotel may refuse to rent a room to those under a specific age; however, it is important that this not be used as a method for unfairly discriminating against a protected class. To do so would be a violation of federal and state law.

8. *The facility is full.* Obviously, the hotel that is full can deny space to a potential guest. The same is true of a restaurant, bar, or club that has reached its capacity. A hotel or restaurant that is full, however, faces a somewhat different situation when it denies space to a guest with a confirmed reservation. This would be a breach of contract and would, as described in Chapter 4, subject the hotel to possible litigation on the part of the injured party. That said, in the case of a guest who arrives unreasonably late for a dinner reservation, the restaurant is not obligated to seat the guest, because the late arrival would be considered a breach of contract by the guest.

10.2 GUEST PRIVACY

When a guest rents a hotel room, the courts have held that the guest should enjoy many of the same constitutional rights as he or she would in his or her own home. The hotel is, however, allowed to enter the room for routine maintenance, cleaning, and emergency services such as might be required in a fire or other disaster.

Guestroom Privacy

The guest's expectation of privacy should always be respected even when routine intrusions become necessary. In general, you and your staff must be sensitive to guests' needs and expectations at all times. But when the guest is no longer classified as a guest, that is, if a guest unlawfully possesses a room, the courts will allow a hotel manager to remove the guest and his or her belongings in order to make the room rentable to another guest. (The process for legally doing so will be explored later in this chapter.) Additionally, a guest has the right to expect that no unauthorized third party will be allowed to enter his or her guestroom.

Privacy of Guest Records

Just as a guest's room is private, so too are the records created by the hotel that document the guest's stay. Consider the case of Russell Hernandez, the manager of a resort about 50 miles away from a major university. Mr. Russell receives a letter from

›› ANALYZE THE SITUATION 10.3

JESSICA BRISTOL AND HER two young children checked into room 104 of the Travel-In motel at 9:00 P.M. on Friday night. She produced a credit card issued in her name as a form of payment and requested that she be given the room for two nights.

On Saturday afternoon, a man identifying himself as Preston Bristol, Jessica Bristol's husband, presented himself at the front desk and asked for the key that she was supposed to have left for him at the front desk. He stated that he was joining his wife and children at the motel; they were visiting relatives, but he had had to work the day before.

The desk clerk replied that no key had been left and proceeded to call the room to inform Jessica Bristol that her husband was at the front desk. There was no answer in the room.

Preston Bristol then produced his driver's license for the desk clerk, which had the same address that Jessica Bristol had used on her registration card. Mr. Bristol also produced a credit card issued in his name with the same account number as that used by Jessica Bristol at check-in. As the clerk perused the license and credit card, Mr. Bristol offhandedly referred to a picture in his wallet of Jessica Bristol and his two children. Based on the positive identification, the clerk issued Mr. Bristol a key to Jessica Bristol's room.

At approximately 6:00 P.M. on Saturday, a guest in room 105 called the front desk to complain about a loud argument in room 104, Jessica Bristol's room. The desk clerk called room 104 but got no answer.

The clerk then called the local police. When they arrived, they found Jessica Bristol badly beaten and her children missing. A description of Mr. Bristol's car quickly led to his arrest and the recovery of the children by the police.

Jessica Bristol recovered from her injuries and completed the divorce proceedings she had begun against her husband. In addition, she filed assault and battery charges against him. Jessica Bristol also sued the motel's manager, owner, and franchise company for $8 million, stating that the motel was negligent and had violated her right to privacy. The motel's position was that is acted reasonably to ensure Mr. Bristol's identity, and added that it was not an insurer of guest safety and could not have foreseen Mr. Bristol's actions.

1. Did the desk clerk act in a reasonable manner?

2. Did Mr. Bristol have a right to enter the room?

3. What should management do in the future to prevent such an occurrence?

LEGALLY MANAGING AT WORK:

Law Enforcement and Guest Privacy

There are occasions when local law enforcement officers, for reasons they believe are valid, demand entrance to a guestroom. Should such an event occur, it is imperative that hotel management:

1. Attempt to cooperate with a legitimate law enforcement official. You must, however, balance that cooperation with your guests' right to privacy. See the International Snapshot on page 316 for additional consideration under the USA PATRIOT Act.

2. Ask to see a search warrant. The U.S. Supreme Court has ruled that hotel guests have a constitutional right to privacy in their rooms and cannot be subject to illegal search or seizure. Hotel managers should not allow a guest's room to be searched by police without a proper search warrant.

3. Document the event, for the hotel's protection. This would include securing identification information on the law enforcement officer, his or her official police unit, the specifics of the demand, and any witnesses to the demand.

representatives of the National Collegiate Athletic Association (NCAA) stating that they are undertaking an investigation of the local university's football recruiting efforts. They wish to know if a particular person was a registered guest on a date two years ago and, if so, who paid the bill for the room. If Mr. Hernandez provides that information, he does so at the resort's peril, because guests have an expectation of privacy with regard to such records. However, if a court order or subpoena is issued for the records, then the hotel must either provide the records in question or else seek legal counsel to inform the court why it is unable to comply, or should not have to comply, with the court order.

If a law enforcement agent is requesting the information, the USA PATRIOT Act may now control the best practice. See the International Snapshot on page 316 for more details.

Guest privacy is a matter not to be taken lightly in the hospitality industry. Guests have a valid reason to expect that their rights will be protected by management. Ensuring these rights is the morally and legally correct course of action for hospitality managers.

10.3 FACILITY MAINTENANCE

Just as you have a responsibility to protect a guest's privacy, you also have a responsibility to operate your facility properly and safely. Recall in Chapter 9 that we discussed the duty of care that hospitality operators have to provide safe premises. Failure to do so will place your operation at risk for a personal injury lawsuit.

Safe Environment

As a manager, you are responsible for providing a facility that meets the building codes of your local area. In most cases, this involves maintaining a facility in compliance with local, state, and federal laws, as well as the Americans with Disabilities Act. In addition, you are required to operate your facility in a manner that is reasonable and responsive to the safety concerns of guests. You can do this if you remember that a safe facility is a combination of:

- A well-maintained physical facility
- Effective operating policies and procedures

Each year, too many lawsuits are filed against hospitality operations, resulting from accidents that have occurred inside, or on the grounds of, an operation's physical facility. Consider the case of William Oliver from Wisconsin. One January night, Mr. Oliver arrived at a restaurant at 7:30 P.M., well after sundown. On his way from the restaurant parking lot to the front door, he slipped on some ice and hurt himself very badly. If Mr. Oliver decides to sue, the restaurant, in order to defend the lawsuit, will need to demonstrate that it had the proper procedures in place to maintain the safety of its parking lot during the winter. If the restaurant cannot demonstrate and provide documentation of such efforts, it will likely lose the case.

A large number of slip and fall accidents, both inside and outside hospitality facilities, are litigated annually. (Next to motor vehicle accidents, slips and falls are the second leading source of personal injury incidents. They are also a major cause of accidental death and injury in the United States.) The resulting judgments against hospitality companies can be costly. You can help protect your operation against slip and fall and other accident claims if you take the necessary steps to maintain your physical facility, implement effective operating policies and procedures, and document your efforts.

Although it is not the goal of this book to detail all of the preventative maintenance techniques and operating policies used by competent hospitality operations, recall from Chapter 9 that the courts will measure a hospitality operation's negligence based on the standard of care applied by the operation, and the level of reasonable care expected by guests and provided by other facilities.

Establishing the appropriate standard of care might not always be easy. By way of example, let's examine the safety requirements and operating policies for one area of hotel operation that is potentially dangerous, and can subject operators to significant liability: the maintenance of recreational facilities such as pools, spas, and workout areas.

Swimming Pools

Swimming pools and spas can be the source of significant legal liability. The dangers of accidental drowning, diving injuries, or even slipping on a wet surface can pose a significant liability threat to the operators of hotels, amusement parks, and other facilities. While this list is not exhaustive, following these 20 recommendations will go a long way toward reducing the liability related to pools.

1. Pass all local inspections.
2. Train the individual who is maintaining the pool.
3. Supply a trained lifeguard whenever the pool is open. If no lifeguard is supplied, post a sign stating this.
4. Mark the depths of pools accurately.
5. Do not allow guests to dive into the pool. Remove diving boards, post warning signs, and write on the floor area surrounding the pool.
6. Clearly identify the "deep" end of the pool. Use ropes, and keep them in place.
7. Fence off the pool area, even if it is inside the building. Install self-closing and self-latching and/or locking gate doors.
8. Make sure that the pool area, and the pool itself, is well lit, and that all electrical components are regularly inspected and maintained to meet local electrical codes.
9. Provide a pool telephone, with emergency access.
10. Prohibit glass in the pool area.
11. If the pool is outdoors, monitor the weather, and close the pool during inclement weather.
12. Prohibit pool use by nonguests.
13. Strictly prohibit all roughhousing.
14. Restrict use of the pool by young children, by people who are intoxicated, and by those who would put the pool over its occupancy limits.
15. Have lifesaving equipment on hand and easily accessible.
16. Install slip-resistant material on the floor areas around the pool.
17. Post warning signs in the languages of your customers.
18. Do not allow the pool area to be opened unless at least one property employee who has been trained in first aid is on duty.
19. Document all of your pool-care efforts.
20. Make sure your insurance policy specifically includes coverage for your pool.

Spas

Like pools, spa hot tubs are also potential sources of liability. As a manager, it is your job to see that your staff implements the type of signage, physical care, and policies required to safely maintain these areas. The following list can help you maintain your spa in a manner consistent with current best practices:

1. Pass all local inspections.
2. Train the individual who is maintaining the spa.

3. Install a thermometer and check the spa temperature frequently (102 degrees Fahrenheit is the maximum recommended temperature); record your efforts.

4. Mark the depth of the hot tub.

5. Do not allow children under 14 to use the spa at all, and post signs to that effect.

6. Do not allow older children to use the spa alone.

7. Display a sign recommending that the following individuals not use the spa:
   - Pregnant women
   - Elderly
   - Diabetics
   - Those with a heart condition, on medication, or under the influence of drugs or alcohol
   - Children under 14 years of age

8. Install a spa-area telephone, with emergency access.

9. Prohibit glass in the spa area.

10. Prohibit alcohol in the spa area.

11. Prohibit spa use by nonguests and solo use by guests.

12. Install nonslip flooring surfaces around the spa.

13. Display signage indicating maximum spa occupancy.

14. Make sure your insurance policy specifically includes coverage for your spa.

15. Have lifesaving equipment on hand and easily accessible.

16. Check the hot tub's water quality frequently, and document your efforts.

17. Post warning signs in the language of your customers.

18. Do not allow the spa area to be opened unless at least one property employee who has been trained in first aid is on duty.

19. Restrict guest access to spa chemicals and heating elements.

20. Document all of your spa-care efforts.

Workout Areas

Workout rooms can also be a source of potential liability. Many operators of facilities with workout areas post a general "rules" notice, as well as signs governing the use of specific equipment in the workout area. Figure 10.3 is an example of a set of general rules. As you can see, maintaining a pool, spa, or workout area requires great care and attention. Accidents can occur, so the effective manager must take special care to prevent potential liability.

As a hospitality manager, safety should be one of your major concerns. All of your policies, procedures, and maintenance programs should be geared toward providing an environment that maximizes guest safety and security. To stay current in this field and to locate other forms, checklists, and procedures, log on to www.HospitalityLawyer.com.

Bedbugs

Recently, there has been a surge in pest and bedbug-related lawsuits instituted against hotels and apartment complexes. These suits are often quite costly, with some judgments against hotels totaling hundreds of thousands of dollars in compensatory and punitive damages. The most costly aspect of these suits is that it is rare that punitive damages are covered in an insurance policy, and removing a bedbug infestation is extremely costly. Thus, hospitality facilities must institute a quick, effective, and cost manageable procedure in the event an infestation occurs.

1. Equipment in this room is for the use of reasonable adults only. Improper use may result in serious injury.
2. Children under 16 could be seriously injured by improper equipment use or nonsupervision.
3. Please limit workouts to 30 minutes on cardiovascular machines.
4. Only water is allowed in workout area. No other food or beverage is permitted.
5. Please wipe off all equipment after use.
6. Lower and raise all equipment carefully.
7. Because of high risk of injury, you must use a spotter when using free weights.
8. Please replace all weights, dumbbells, bars, and plates when finished.
9. Children not allowed unless accompanied by an adult.

Figure 10.3 Workout area rules.

It is paramount to remove the infestation quickly, because the larger it spreads the more the costs of eradication increase. Consistent inspection and treatment programs are important, as it is difficult to ever totally remove the possibility of a bedbug situation. This is because guests sometimes bring the bedbugs in with them via their clothing and luggage.

Employees should be trained in detecting the signs of infestation, and a reporting procedure should be in place. Furthermore, preventative measures should be taken to eliminate any threat of an infestation before it begins. Proper sanitation and the purchase of products like bedbug-proof mattress covers are all practices a facility can adopt to actively prevent not only an infestation but also a judgment for negligence.

Defibrillators

On November 13, 2000, President Clinton signed the Cardiac Arrest Survival Act into law. The purpose of the act is to improve the survival rates of people who have sudden cardiac arrest in two major ways: (1) by the placement of automated external defibrillators (AEDs) in federal buildings, and (2) in an effort to spur the use of AED devices in the private sector, by establishing protections from civil liability for persons who use AEDs in an emergency situation, except in cases of gross negligence or willful misconduct. The AED device can be utilized by trained, nonmedical personnel in order to increase the survival rate from a cardiac episode. Since enacting the Cardiac Arrest Survival Act, many states have also implemented regulations in order to broaden the use of AEDs. Check with your state to see if providing AED devices is required in your particular establishment.

Americans with Disabilities Act (ADA), Title III

Facilities must not only be safe but also accessible. Title III of the Americans with Disabilities Act addresses the requirements involved with removing barriers to access public accommodations. (Recall that Title I of the ADA addresses making employment accessible to Americans with disabilities.) Title III requirements for existing facilities and alterations became effective on January 26, 1992, and were recently amended on September 15, 2010.

Title III affects businesses that are considered to be places of public accommodation, as defined by the Department of Justice, which is responsible for enforcement of the act. These businesses are facilities operated by a private entity whose operations affect commerce and fall within at least one of the following dozen categories:

1. Place of lodging, except for an establishment located within a facility that contains not more than five rooms for rent or hire, and that actually is occupied by the proprietor of the establishment as the residence of the proprietor. A "place of lodging" includes:
   - An inn, hotel, or motel
   - A facility that provides guest rooms for sleeping for stays that primarily are short-term in nature (generally 30 days or less) where the occupant does not have the right to return to a specific room or unit after the conclusion of his or her stay; and provides guest rooms under conditions and with amenities similar to a hotel, motel, or inn, including the following:
     - On- or off-site management and reservations service
     - Rooms available on a walk-up or call-in basis
     - Availability of housekeeping or linen service
     - Acceptance of reservations for a guest room type without guaranteeing a particular unit or room until check-in, and without a prior lease or security deposit

2. Establishment serving food or drink: restaurant, bar.

3. Place of exhibition or entertainment: theater, cinema, concert hall, stadium.

4. Place of public gathering: auditorium, convention center, lecture hall.

5. Sales or rental establishment: bakery, grocery store, clothing store, shopping mall, video rental store.

6. Service establishment: bank, lawyer's office, gas station, funeral parlor, laundromat, dry cleaner, barber shop, beauty shop, insurance office, hospital, travel service, pharmacy, health-care office.

7. Station used for public transportation: railroad depot, bus station, airport, terminal.

8. Place for public display or collection: museum, library, or gallery.

9. Place of recreation: park, zoo, amusement park.

10. Place of education: preschool, nursery, elementary, secondary, undergraduate, or postgraduate private school.

11. Social service establishment: shelter, hospital, day-care center, independent living center, food bank, senior citizen center, adoption agency.

12. Place of exercise and/or recreation: gymnasium, health club, bowling alley, golf course.

Title III requires places of public accommodation to provide goods and services to people with disabilities on an equal basis with the rest of the general public. The goal is to give everyone the opportunity to benefit from our country's businesses and services, and to allow all businesses the opportunity to benefit from the patronage of all Americans. Under Title III of the ADA, any private entity that owns, leases, leases to, or operates an existing public accommodation has four specific requirements:

1. *Getting guests and employees into the facility.* This involves removing barriers to make facilities available to and usable by people with mobility impairments, to the extent that it is readily achievable. Examples could include parking spaces for the disabled, wheelchair ramps or lifts, and accessible restroom facilities.

2. *Providing auxiliary aids and services so that people with disabilities have access to effective means of communication.* This involves providing aids and services to individuals with vision or hearing impairments. Auxiliary aids include such services or devices as qualified interpreters,

assistive listening headsets, television captioning and decoders, telecommunications devices for deaf persons (TDDs), videotext displays, readers, taped texts, Braille materials, and large-print materials. The auxiliary aid requirement is flexible. For example, a Braille menu is not required if waiters are instructed to read the menu to customers with sight impairments.

3. *Modifying any policies, practices, or procedures that may be discriminatory or have a discriminatory effect.* Such as a front desk policy advising people with disabilities that there is "no room at the inn" rather than attempting to accommodate them, or additional charges for guide animals.

4. *Ensuring that there are no unnecessary eligibility criteria that tend to screen out or segregate individuals with disabilities or limit their full and equal enjoyment of the place of public accommodation.* These include requirements that guests provide a driver's license, for example. Many people with disabilities do not have a driver's license. So the best practice is to request photo identification rather than a driver's license specifically.

As you can see, Title III compliance involves the removal of physical barriers, as well as discriminatory policies. Physical barrier requirements are generally achievable if you consider the following four priorities recommended for Title III compliance:

Priority 1: Accessible approach and entrance
Priority 2: Access to goods and services
Priority 3: Access to restrooms
Priority 4: Any other measures necessary

The recent amendments to Title III address changes in technology, and provide specific requirements to accommodate persons with mobility devices, such as motorized wheelchairs, and video remote interpreting (VRI) communication technology. The amendments also provide for specific exceptions when it is allowable to exclude service animals from a public accommodation, and create accommodation requirements for facilities that allow reservations and ticketed events. Furthermore, the amendments contain a safe harbor provision for public accommodations that have complied with the 1991 requirements. As always, it is important to check that your facility complies with the new Title III requirements, and if there are any questions that arise from the new legislation, you should consult an attorney.

To evaluate a facility for its compliance with these four priorities, you must carefully compare your property with the requirements of Title III. A thorough checklist dealing with Title III can be found online at www.usdoj.gov/crt/ada/racheck.pdf.

It is important to note that changes in your facility must be made where it is "reasonable" to do so. Because reasonability is determined on a case-by-case basis, it is important to plan and document your compliance efforts. To do so, the steps given in the next Legally Managing at Work feature can be of great value.

Laws regarding ADA compliance are complex, so it is a good idea to familiarize yourself with Title III requirements, especially if you are a facility manager. Before building a new facility or renovating an existing one, it is important to select an architect or contractor who is familiar with Title III requirements. And as you learned in Chapter 4, "Contract Basics," it is important to have your construction and/or renovation contract specify who is responsible for ensuring ADA compliance.

LEGALLY MANAGING AT WORK:

Five Steps to Facility Evaluation

1. Plan the evaluation.
   a. Set an evaluation completion date.
   b. Decide who will conduct the survey.
   c. Obtain floor plans.

2. Conduct the survey.
   a. Use a checklist to evaluate the facility.
   b. Use a tape measure.
   c. Record results.

3. Summarize recommendations.
   a. List barriers found, along with ideas for removal.
   b. Consult with building contractors if necessary.
   c. Estimate costs of barrier removal.

4. Plan for improvements.
   a. Prioritize needs.
   b. Make barrier removal decisions.
   c. Establish timetables for completion.

5. Document efforts.
   a. Record what has been done.
   b. Plan for an annual review.
   c. Monitor changes in the law.

Search the Web **10.2**

Log on to www.usdoj.gov/crt/ada/adahom1.htm.

1. Select: 2010 ADA Standards for Accessible Design.
2. Select: 2010 ADA Standards for Accessible Design, either in HTML or PDF format.
3. Browse through the standards established for accessible design and answer the following questions:
   a. How many rooms with a roll-in shower are required for a hotel with 800 rooms?
   b. How many rooms in the same size hotel must be designed to accommodate the visually impaired?
   c. Explain the term equivalent facilitation as it pertains to room charges for disabled guests.

10.4 RESPONSIBILITIES TO NONGUESTS

Guests are not the only individuals who may lawfully enter a hospitality property, of course. Owners, managers, employees, vendors, and a guest's own invited guests will all utilize a hospitality company's facilities or services. Because restaurants, clubs, and hotels are open to the public, people can come in for a variety of reasons, not all of which are for the purpose of becoming a guest. An individual could enter a hospitality facility to visit a friend, ask for directions, use the restroom, use the telephone, or commit a crime. As a manager, you have responsibilities for the safety and well-being of those who are not guests, although that level of responsibility will vary based on the type of nonguest in question. In this section, we will examine three distinct types of nonguests and your responsibilities to each.

Guests of Guests

Most hotels allow guests great freedom in permitting invited friends and family members to visit them in the hotel. Most guests expect, and most hotels allow, guests of guests to enjoy many of the privileges enjoyed by the guest. It is important to note that it is the hotel that allows this practice; it is not a guest's right that is inherent in renting a room. Obviously, it is unlawful for a hotel manager to refuse to allow guests of guests on a discriminatory basis. In addition, hoteliers may impose the same type of reasonable conduct standards on a guest's guest as they do on the guests themselves.

From a personal injury liability point of view, the guests of a guest, if they are on the premises in accordance with hotel policy, should be treated in the same manner as a guest. That is, they should be provided with a safe and secure facility. A question arises, however, as to a hotel's liability for the acts of those not associated with the hotel. Under many state laws, a hotel has no legal responsibility to protect others from the criminal acts of third parties. But a legal responsibility may come into existence if the danger or harm was foreseeable. For example, if dangerous incidents of a similar nature had occurred on or near the premises previously, a jury might find that the hotel could have anticipated such an occurrence again and should have taken reasonable steps to attempt to prevent it.

Because it is not possible to know whether someone is a guest, or a guest of a guest, reasonable precautions should be taken to protect everyone who uses your facility. These precautions will be discussed more fully in Chapter 14, "Safety and Security Issues."

Invitees

A guest is an *invitee* of a hotel. By the same token, many individuals who are not guests can be considered invitees as well. An invitee enters a property because he or she has been expressly invited by the owner, or because his or her intent is to utilize the property in some manner permitted by law and the property's ownership, usually, but not always, for the commercial gain of the property. In either case, the hotel is required to take reasonable care in maintaining its facility and to notify or warn the invitee of any potential danger; also in some cases, the hotel also has the duty to fix and eliminate these potential dangers.

Invitees include employees, managers, contractors, vendors, and individuals such as those entering to ask directions, use a telephone, or make a purchase. Because hotels and restaurants are open to the public, the number of situations in which an invitee enters the premises can be great indeed.

Consider the case of Jeremy Cavendar. Jeremy is the manager of a hotel facility attached to a large shopping mall in a major southwestern city. Because of its location, many shoppers pass through the hotel's lobby as they enter or exit the shopping mall. If an individual were hurt while passing through the lobby, Jeremy would likely be responsible for demonstrating that he and his staff had demonstrated reasonable care in maintaining the hotel lobby. This would be true even though the invitee in this case may have had no intention of utilizing any of the services offered by Jeremy's hotel. The mere fact that the hotel decided to locate within the shopping mall would demonstrate to most juries and personal injury attorneys that the hotel could have reasonably foreseen that a large number of shoppers would be passing through the area, hence that it should take reasonable care in protecting their safety.

Trespassers

Legally, hospitality managers do not owe the same duty of care to an individual who is unauthorized to be on a property as they do to one who is authorized. For example, a restaurant that has its floors mopped nightly has a duty to place "wet floor" signs around any area that is wet and that is likely to have foot traffic passing through it. However, the operator does not have a duty of care to illuminate those signs when the restaurant is closed. So, assuming that access is restricted, a burglar who enters the restaurant after hours has no legal right to expect that the operator will warn him or her of slippery floor conditions.

Some cases of trespass can be more complex, and operators should be very careful to make a distinction between a trespasser and a wandering guest. Consider the example of Deitra Reeves. Ms. Reeves was a guest of the Red Door Lounge, a very quiet and dimly lit club in a large city. One night, while seeking the ladies room, Ms. Reeves accidentally opened the door to a storage room, ran into a storage rack, and was injured in a fall. The lounge's attorney argued that Ms. Reeves was a trespasser since guests are not allowed in storage areas. Ms. Reeves's attorney argued that Ms. Reeves was a guest, and the lounge was negligent because it should have had the storeroom locked. A facility can expect that guests, if allowed, may wander into restricted areas. When they do, they will, in most cases, still be considered guests.

≫ ANALYZE THE SITUATION 10.4

WALTER THOMAS WAS VISITING Jeff Placer, who had registered as a guest at a newly opened Ludger-Inn hotel. The hotel was located off an interstate highway exit; it had been open for only three days. When Mr. Thomas left Mr. Placer's room in the evening, he was assaulted in the hotel's parking lot.

Mr. Thomas contacted an attorney, who threatened to sue the hotel for the injuries. Lashondra Tyson, the attorney for the hotel, replied to Mr. Thomas's attorney that the hotel was not responsible for the acts of third parties, and that the hotel had no history of criminal activity taking place on its grounds; thus, it could not have foreseen any potential problem. In addition, Mr. Thomas was not a registered guest in the hotel.

Mr. Thomas's attorney replied that many hotels experience problems in their parking lots, so the hotel should, in fact, have anticipated potential problems. He also stated that Mr. Thomas was an invitee of the hotel and thus the hotel was required to guard his interest in the same manner as that of a guest.

1. What was the legal status of Mr. Thomas?

2. Why is the distinction important in this situation?

3. What records would Ms. Tyson need from the hotel's manager to give her the best chance of winning any potential lawsuit?

10.5 REMOVAL OF GUESTS

Just as guests must be admitted in accordance with the law, you must also treat those guests who are to be removed from your business in a way that is legally sound. Generally, guests can be removed from the premises for lack of payment, for inappropriate conduct, or for certain conditions of health.

Lack of Payment

When guests check into a hotel, or order food in a restaurant, it is reasonable to assume that they will pay their bill. On occasion, a guest, for a variety of reasons, will not pay.

In a restaurant setting, the manager has few options for collecting. Clearly, the manager can refuse to serve the guest anymore during that visit and can rightfully refuse service in the future, as long as the bill remains outstanding. However, if the guest leaves the premises, there is often little that can be done to recover losses.

It is legal for a hotel to require payment in advance for the use of a room, as long as that requirement is applied uniformly in a manner that does not unlawfully discriminate among guests. If a guest does not present himself or herself at the front desk for payment by the posted check-out time, or authorize a charge to an established credit card or account, that guest can be removed from the hotel for nonpayment. The hotel has a right, subject to local laws, to remove a transient guest from a room for nonpayment of charges due. A tenant with a lease, however, could not be removed or locked out of his or her apartment by a landlord without following state and local laws regarding eviction.

When a guest in a hotel does not pay, or cannot pay, the rightfully due bill, the term *eviction* is often used to denote the guest's removal. Legally, however, a hotel rarely will file a suit of unlawful retainer, which is required in an official tenant eviction. The term eviction continues to be used, however, to refer to a guest who is removed by a variety of means from a hospitality property.

Whether it is in the best interest of the hotel to evict a guest is a judgment call made by the manager. Clearly, lost credit cards or travelers checks, and a variety of other circumstances, might cause a guest to be temporarily unable to pay his or her account. In this situation, it is up to you to protect the financial interest of the hotel while accommodating the guest to the greatest degree possible. When it is clear, however, that the guest either will not or cannot pay, and refuses to vacate the room, it is best to contact the local law enforcement agency to assist in the guest's removal. This protects the hotel in the event that the nonpaying guest claims the hotel used excessive force in the removal of the guest.

Often, the arrival of a law enforcement official at a restaurant or hotel is sufficient to encourage the guest to pay the bill. It is important to note, however, that the police will rarely, if ever, arrest a guest for failure to pay a bill that is owed. Efforts to collect on money owed to a hospitality operation should be pursued according to applicable state and local laws. This would entail filing a suit in *small claims court* or another appropriate court to get a judgment against the debtor (nonpaying guest). The cost of doing so is high in both time and money. Thus, it is best to avoid the situation whenever possible. In Chapter 14, we will discuss several ways that you can protect your operation from guests who have no intention of paying their bill.

Inappropriate Conduct

Guests who pose a threat to the safety and comfort of other guests or employees may be removed from a hotel or restaurant. Indeed, you have a duty of care as a manager to provide a facility that is safe for all guests. Thus, a guest who is extraordinarily

LEGALESE

Eviction: Removal of a tenant from rental property by a law enforcement officer. An eviction is the result of a landlord filing and winning a special lawsuit known as an "unlawful detainer."

LEGALESE

Small claims court: A court designed especially to hear lawsuits entailing relatively small sums of money. They can provide a speedy method of making a claim without the necessity of hiring a lawyer and engaging in a formal trial.

loud, abusive, or threatening to others should be removed. Also, note that inappropriate conduct may be considered a violation of the hotel's or restaurant's house rules (as discussed earlier in the chapter). Thus, a guest's disruptive behavior could be considered a breach of contract, which would give the hospitality establishment the authority to evict. Again, this is a situation best handled jointly by management and local law enforcement officials.

The question of whether such a guest should be refunded any prepaid money or charged for any damages that may occur varies with the situation. In general, it may be said that a guest who has utilized a room and is removed for inappropriate behavior must still pay for the use of that room. Whether management in fact levies such a charge is subject to the principles of sound business judgment.

Overstays

Because a hotel rents rooms on a transient basis, it can also decide not to allow a guest to *overstay* his or her reservation contract. For this reason, guests may be removed from their rooms if they in fact have breached their contractual reservation agreement with the hotel. Although it might appear odd that a hotel would refuse to extend a guest's stay, it does happen. Consider the case of Giovanni Migaldi. Mr. Migaldi operates a hotel in Indianapolis, Indiana. The weekend of the Indianapolis 500 race is always a sellout for Mr. Migaldi, and he is careful to require that all guests reserving rooms for that weekend pay in advance. On the morning before the race, a tour group that was scheduled to leave requests to stay an extra night, after the tour bus experiences mechanical difficulty. Mr. Migaldi is expecting the arrival of another tour bus filled with racing fans coming to town for a three-night stay. If Mr. Migaldi allows the current tour bus passengers to stay, he will have no room for the prepaid racing fans due to arrive. All local hotel rooms are sold out, so Mr. Migaldi has no opportunity to move the race fans, nor does he want to violate his contract with them. Clearly, in this case, Mr. Migaldi will have to use all of his management skills to tactfully achieve the removal of the first group in order to make room for the second, confirmed group. This situation also illustrates the difficulty managers can face in maintaining their legal obligations while attempting to serve guests who encounter unexpected travel delays and difficulties.

Registration cards that are completely filled out, including a space for guest initials verifying arrival and departure dates, can be of great assistance in dealing with the overstay guest. Additionally, the registration card can state that additional nights, if approved by the hotel, will be at the "rack rate" (which is usually significantly higher than the rate a guest is actually paying).

> **LEGALESE**
> **Overstay:** A guest who refuses to vacate his or her room when he or she has exceeded the number of nights originally agreed to at check-in.

Accident, Illness, or Death

A guest stricken with a severe illness, or the death of a guest, creates a traumatic experience for any hospitality facility. Just as people have accidents, get sick, die, attempt suicide, or overdose on drugs in their home, similar situations can also occur in hotels and restaurants. When they do, it is important that everyone in the facility know exactly how to respond. The priority should be to maintain the dignity of the guest while providing the medical attention appropriate for the situation.

If an emergency calls for the removal of a guest, extreme care should be taken. The checklist in the next Legally Managing at Work feature can be helpful in performing the removal in a discreet but effective manner.

LEGALLY MANAGING AT WORK:

Responding to Guest Health Emergencies

1. Train employees on their role in responding to a medical emergency.

2. Instruct employees to contact the manager on duty (MOD) immediately if it appears a guest is seriously ill, unconscious, or nonresponsive.

3. Call 911 or other emergency-care providers. If the circumstances surrounding the incident seem suspicious, also notify the police.

4. Instruct the MOD to survey the situation to determine whether other guests are at risk or the area needs to be secured against entry by others.

5. Designate an individual to keep unauthorized persons away from the area until the emergency medical team arrives.

6. Document the incident, using an incident documentation form.

7. Do not touch the guest unless you are medically trained to provide aid.

8. When the emergency medical team arrives, provide them with any information you have that can help to establish the identity of the guest.

9. If the guest is removed from the property, secure and hold any personal property belonging to the guest. The length of time you must retain personal property and the method of disposing of the property at the expiration of that time will vary from state to state.

10. Report the incident to local law enforcement authorities if required to do so by law.

INTERNATIONAL SNAPSHOT

Should Foreign Governments Adopt Provisions from the USA PATRIOT Act to Combat Terrorist Acts against the Hospitality Industry?

The scene is becoming all too familiar. Terrorists are attacking hotels in greater frequency. First, it was Egypt. On April 18, 1996, terrorists attacked the Hotel Europa in Cairo, killing 18 Greek nationals. Next, it was the island of Bali. On October 12, 2002, in the late evening, a terrorist attack struck a nightclub on the island, murdering over 180, and injuring hundreds. Then, terrorists struck again in Kenya. On November 28, 2002, suicide-bombers attacked the Paradise Hotel, an Israeli-owned hotel, located in Mombasa, killing over 15 people, as two missiles were fired at an Israeli holiday jet that had taken off from Mombasa's airport. Recently, terrorists struck in Morocco. In May 2003, in Casablanca, terrorists targeted a restaurant, a Jewish community center and cemetery, and a five-star hotel, killing 45. Indonesia was the next target. In August 2003, suicide-bombers attacked the J. W. Marriott Hotel in Jakarta, murdering 11 people and injuring 150.

International terrorists will continue to attack nonmilitary installations, known as "soft" targets. Unfortunately for the hospitality industry, today's soft targets include hotels, restaurants, and nightclubs. The central question for the international community, as well as hoteliers, is how to protect the hospitality industry from future terrorist attacks. The answer lies in the introduction of aggressive antiterrorism legislation abroad and increased vigilance by the hospitality industry.

The United States of America is not immune to terrorist attacks against soft targets, as is evident from the suicide-bombing attacks of September 11, 2001. In response to the terrorist attacks, the administration of President George W. Bush proposed sweeping legislation to combat terrorism. President Bush's immortal words to U.S. Attorney General John Ashcroft, "Never let this happen again," resulted in the passage of the USA PATRIOT Act (PATRIOT Act). The Patriot Act, not surprisingly, is applicable to hotels in the United States in several ways.

The Patriot Act provides for the use of emergency warrants to search hotel rooms or to obtain guest information. Under the Patriot Act, federal agents of the U.S. government may, with a search warrant, obtain "tangible records" from a hotel relating to guests or "groups of guests" that registered at the hotel. Even without a search warrant, registration records of a hotel guest may be obtained by a federal agent if proper law enforcement identification is produced and shown to hotel management. Furthermore, records of all electronic transactions relating to a guest at the hotel must be produced if requested by a governmental entity. Those records include telephone records, e-mail correspondence, and transactions involving more than $10,000 in cash.

The Patriot Act grants immunity to hotels that provide voluntary registration information to a governmental entity, if the hotel "reasonably" believes that an emergency involving immediate danger of death or serious physical injury to any person justifies disclosure of the information. In addition, the Patriot Act provides criminal liabilities for individuals that "harbor" or "conceal" a person known, or with reasonable grounds, is believed to have committed or is about to commit an offense of terrorism. If, however, a hotel reports in "good faith" a suspected terrorist directly to the federal government or federal agency (such as the FBI), the hotel will not be subject to liability under the Patriot Act.

The Patriot Act is not the only antiterrorism legislation in the world. Such legislation exists in the United Kingdom, the European Union, and/or other foreign countries as well. But, many countries have limited, or have failed to implement, antiterrorism legislation at all. For instance, it was not until after the J. W. Marriott Hotel in Jakarta was attacked by terrorists that Prime Minister Thaksin Shinawatra rushed into law new antiterrorist legislation before world leaders attended the APEC meeting in October 2003. If the actions of the Thailand government are a barometer of sorts, then the worldwide community has a long way to go in confronting terrorism. Notwithstanding, the international community should consider adopting relevant provisions from the Patriot Act, so that foreign law enforcement agencies may investigate, apprehend, and prosecute terrorists before further hotels are attacked.

Provided by Richard Barrett-Cuetara, Esq., of the Cowles & Thompson Law Firm, in Dallas, Texas. www.cowlesthompson.com.

WHAT WOULD YOU DO?

You are the area vice president of franchising for a quick-service restaurant (QSR) company that serves a unique grilled chicken product, which has become extremely popular. Because of a strong marketing effort and solid operating results, your company's growth has been very rapid. In your five-state area, the company is considering purchasing a small chain of 15 units that sells a comparable chicken product. Those units, consisting of older buildings in excellent locations, are to be converted to units owned and operated by your company. Your immediate supervisor, the company president, has asked you to respond to the following:

1. How will you determine which units are not in compliance with Title III, ADA requirements?
2. What criteria will you use for prioritizing needed improvements?
3. How will you document a good-faith effort to meet Title III, ADA requirements?

Draft answers to your president's questions.

To see how a court views the legal relationship between a hotel operator and its guests, consider two case studies. First, *Young v. Rushmore Plaza Holiday Inn*, 284 F.3d 863 (8ᵗʰ Circuit, 2002).

FACTUAL SUMMARY

Steven Young was a guest at the Rushmore Plaza Holiday Inn in Rapid City, South Dakota. Young and three of his friends rented a suite at the hotel, and after an evening of drinking and bar hopping they returned to the room. Young passed out in the bedroom of the suite, while his two friends continued drinking just outside the door of the suite. Hotel security officers asked the two guests to return to their room or go to a hotel commons area so as to avoid disturbing other guests. The two individuals failed to comply, and hotel security informed them they were being evicted and had ten minutes to pack and leave the premises. Rather than packing and leaving, the two men simply went to the hotel restaurant, leaving the door to the suite partially open and Mr. Young asleep in the room.

The Rapid City police arrived shortly thereafter to remove the three guests from the room. Mr. Young was awakened by the officers, and while disoriented he scuffled with the officers and was arrested for assaulting a police officer. Mr. Young sued the police officers, the city of Rapid City, and the hotel for violating his privacy and for using excessive force in a self-help eviction (carried out by the hotel, rather than authorities).

QUESTION FOR THE COURT

The question for the court was whether hotel guests had the same right to possession of a hotel room as tenants had to a rental property. Young claimed he was a tenant of the hotel and was therefore entitled to the protection of the South Dakota forcible entry and detainer statute. Under the statute, tenants were entitled to three days' notice prior to an eviction and a jury trial to determine if the eviction was justified. The hotel argued the application of the statute would be impractical for hotels, especially in the context of a guest who was only staying for one or two nights.

DECISION

The court held hotel guests were not tenants for the purpose of eviction. Therefore, hotel guests were not entitled to the same protections as tenants in rental properties.

MESSAGE TO MANAGEMENT

There are significant benefits in maintaining the transient status of a guest.

Next, consider *Parr v. L&L Drive-Inn Restaurant* P 96 F.Supp.2d 1065 (D.Hawai'i 2000).

FACTUAL SUMMARY

Plaintiff Eric Parr, a quadriplegic who is able to move exclusively with the aid of a wheelchair, brought suit against L&L Drive-Inn Restaurant (L&L), a franchised fast-food restaurant entity, for violations of Title III of the Americans with Disabilities Act, alleging that L&L had failed to remove architectural barriers to access, which prevented him from utilizing the L&L facility. Specifically, when Parr patronized L&L, he encountered a high entrance threshold, an entrance through the driveway, an incorrectly sloped access ramp, and tables that were too low for wheelchair access. Parr brought suit seeking an injunction against L&L, demanding ADA compliance, and seeking attorney fees and court costs.

QUESTION FOR THE COURT

The question for the court was whether L&L's efforts to accommodate disabled persons amounted to compliance under Title III of the ADA, or if it discriminated against disabled persons. Discrimination under Title III is determined by a defendant's failure to remove architectural barriers that are structural in nature, in existing facilities where such removal is readily achievable. If accommodation is not readily achievable in an existing structure, then discrimination includes the failure to make such goods, services, facilities, and privileges readily available through alternative methods. Parr argued that the barriers he encountered when visiting L&L were all prohibited under the ADA, and that removal of these barriers was readily achievable.

DECISION

The court held that the barriers were in violation of Title III because they did not comply with the specific standards stated in the ADAAG Standard; specifically that the wheelchair accessibility ramp exceeded the allowable slope as defined by ADA standards, which created an incline too steep for wheelchair users to safely traverse, and the public parking spaces were located too far away from the entrance to the L&L facility. However, the court determined that only the accessibility ramps needed to be brought into compliance because, since fixing them would only be at a minimal cost and effort, compliance was readily achievable. As to the parking spaces, although the cost to move the spaces would be minimal, the court found that moving the spaces would reduce the amount of parking space available to L&L, and it would thus be in violation of a Land Use Ordinance. Therefore, the problems associated with parking compliance outweighed the benefit, and the court determined that moving the parking spaces was not readily achievable.

MESSAGE TO MANAGEMENT

Compliance under the ADA is a serious matter, and the courts will require specific adherence to the standards set forth under the act. However, when compliance is found to be unreasonable, or detrimental to the facility, the courts will allow exceptions to compliance on a case-by-case basis.

WHAT DID YOU LEARN IN THIS CHAPTER?

Guest is a term used to describe a transient customer, as opposed to a tenant who may utilize a facility for a longer, or more permanent, time period.

Because most hospitality establishments are considered places of public accommodation, they must observe all applicable federal, state, and local civil rights laws that prohibit discrimination in the admission of guests into a facility, as well as the types of services provided.

Guests in hospitality establishments have expectations of privacy, both personally and for any information about their stay. Hospitality establishments are legally obligated to honor those expectations.

A hospitality operator has a legal obligation to provide a reasonably safe physical facility for its guests. This requires significant attention to potential dangers and preventative maintenance procedures. In addition, Title III of the American with Disabilities Act requires hospitality operators to remove barriers from their facilities to allow access to people with disabilities. Even when someone is not an actual guest, managers still may have a duty of care to provide a reasonably safe premise for individuals on their property.

The process of removing guests from an establishment should be undertaken as a last resort and with caution.

RAPID REVIEW

After you have studied this chapter, you should be prepared to:

1. Identify at least four types of guests who could and/or should be denied service, and the reason for denial in each case.

2. Explain how a guest's room in a hotel is similar to his or her home for purposes of a legal search.

3. Create a ten-minute training program to be used to teach new employees the importance of, and procedures for, cleaning up dining room spills and

slick spots as quickly as possible. Include a testing device to measure the effectiveness of your training.

4. List the four priorities established for ADA compliance, and explain why you agree or disagree with the prioritization.

5. Using the checklist provided in this chapter, evaluate the ADA compliance of a public restroom in your local library, museum, or art gallery.

6. Exculpatory statements (described in Chapter 5, "Significant Hospitality Contracts") are often posted in recreational facilities, exercise rooms, pools, and spas. Explain their purpose and identify their limitations.

7. Contact your local small claims court administrator to determine:
   a. The location of the court
   b. The maximum dollar amount of judgment the court can order
   c. Any fees required to file a claim
   d. The forms required to file a claim

8. Develop a one-page checklist of actions that should be undertaken by a hotel staff to remove an extremely ill or deceased person from a room.

TEAM ACTIVITY   In teams, draft a document (one page) titled "House Rules" for a metropolitan hotel that has historically been frequented by minors for prom and graduation celebrations.

CHAPTER 11

YOUR RESPONSIBILITIES FOR GUESTS' PROPERTY

"GOOD MORNING, LANCE," said Trisha Sangus as she walked into the lobby of the hotel she managed.

"Good morning, Trisha. It's a great day," replied Lance Dani. As the front office manager, Lance was responsible for hiring and training the desk clerks, who checked guests in and out of the hotel, as well as the reservationists, who received reservations from the general public, the hotel's national reservation system, and the sales department. In addition, Lance supervised the guest services area of the hotel, which included bellstaff and shuttle van drivers. In short, Lance's department would be the first and last contact most guests would have with the hotel. Because of that, Trisha spent extra time, whenever she could, helping to develop Lance's skills, as well as those of his staff.

"I see you have rearranged the information," said Trisha. "It looks good." The day before, she had asked Lance to "declutter" the reception desk. The mandatory display of the franchise hotel directory, complimentary newspapers, credit card information, and information on hotel services took up so much space on the front desk that it was often difficult to leave enough room for guests to check in and out. Trisha had asked Lance to review all the materials displayed at the front desk, with an eye toward removing anything that was not absolutely critical. Trisha liked a neat, efficient workspace, but now that he had complied with her request, something was bothering her, and she couldn't quite put a finger on it.

"Tell me what you've done," Trisha began, as her eyes swept across the front desk area.

"Well," replied Lance, "as you asked, I took a look at the material here at the front desk that the guests really use a lot. Then I tried to prioritize, you know, go from most used to least."

"That makes sense," replied Trisha, as she now saw, or rather did not see, the item whose absence had been the source of her uneasiness.

"Well," continued Lance, "after that it was just a matter of removing the things the guests didn't really use and keeping the important ones."

"The important ones?" asked Trisha.

"Right," said Lance, "like the complimentary newspapers and the guest comment cards."

"I notice you moved some signs also," said Trisha.

"Right," replied Lance. "After the desk area looked so good, we decided to move some signs so guests could see them better, such as the check-in and check-out times and the names of the credit cards we accept."

"Which signs did you remove altogether?"

"Just one," said Lance. "I moved the manager-on-duty sign back a bit. The letters are so large the guests can still easily see it. To make room for it, I removed the sign that informed customers we have safety deposit boxes. I talked to the clerks, and they said the guests almost never use the boxes.

"Let me see if I understand you correctly," said Trisha Sangus, in a voice Lance had come to know and did not look forward to hearing, "the desk clerks said that our guests only infrequently use our free safety deposit boxes, so you removed the sign stating we have them?"

"Yes," replied Lance slowly, adding a bit warily. "Is that okay? I made sure that each of our desk clerks knows that if a guest asks to use a safety deposit box, we would certainly accommodate him or her. I mean, we provide lots of guest services without a separate sign—pay-per-view movies, for example. And our guests watch pay-per-views a lot more than they use our safety deposit boxes."

"So, as you see it," continued Trisha, "the sign announcing the availability of safety deposits boxes was simply a convenience to our guests? A nice way to let them know about our services?"

"Right," replied Lance.

"Hmmm," replied Trisha. "Lance, please, come into my office. I want to show you something."

IN THIS CHAPTER, YOU WILL LEARN:

1. To understand fully the responsibility hospitality managers have to safeguard the personal property of their guests.
2. To carry out the procedures needed to limit potential liability for the loss of guest property.
3. To assess the theories of bailment so as to be able to implement policies that limit potential legal liability.
4. To create the procedures required to legally dispose of personal property whose ownership status is in question.

11.1 LIABILITY FOR GUESTS' PROPERTY

Most hotels and restaurants are safe places to visit and work. As explained in Chapter 10, "Your Responsibilities as a Hospitality Operator to Guests," you, as a hospitality manager, have a responsibility to make your facility as safe as possible. This responsibility pertains to the well-being of the guests themselves, and to the security of their property.

Common Law Liability

Historically, under common law, innkeepers were held responsible for the safety of a guest's property. In fact, the inns would often advertise that travelers could rely on their personal protection during their stay. For example, if a traveler stayed at the Heidelberg Arms Inn, he or she was under the protection of the Heidelberg family, including the "arms" (weapons) that the family would muster against any intruders who would dare attack. This was important because, in the past, travel was risky, and those travelers who arrived for a night's lodging needed to know that the innkeeper could provide them with a secure haven during their stopover. Because of the importance of providing protection when traveling, an innkeeper became, under common law, an insurer of the safety of a guest's property. If the common law had not required innkeepers to maintain a protected environment, robbers and bandits would have made the inns unsafe places indeed, and travel would have been greatly restricted.

In today's world, hotel and restaurant guests still face the threat of robbery. The number of crimes reported annually by hotels and restaurants is large and growing. Jewelry, credit cards, and cash, as well as personal property such as cameras, furs, and the like, all entice those who are not honest. Vacationers, business travelers, or simply those dining out are under the threat of an increasingly sophisticated type of thief. Unfortunately, even hospitality employees can also be a threat to guest property.

Hospitality managers must remain vigilant to various threats, from sophisticated con artists to "grab and go" thieves, because today's law may still hold those in the hospitality industry liable for the safety of their guests' property. Consider the case of Evan Gainer. Mr. Gainer checks into a hotel carrying a bag of diamonds valued at $100,000. The bag is stolen from his room. Under common law, the innkeeper could be liable to reimburse Mr. Gainer for the value of his stolen diamonds, even if he or she was unaware that the luggage contained such valuable items.

Of course, property liability extends beyond the threat of theft. Consider the case of Tony Mustafa. Mr. Mustafa allowed a hotel's valet parking staff to park his new Mercedes-Benz convertible in its elevated parking garage. While retrieving the car, a valet driver scraped the side of the car against a concrete pillar, damaging it extensively. As could be expected, Mr. Mustafa was quite upset, and would, in all likelihood, hold the hotel responsible for the damage done to his vehicle. In this case, the guest's property, while not stolen, was clearly damaged while in the possession of the hotel.

In summary, theft, negligent handling, fire, flooding, and a variety of other factors can threaten a guest's property. The general rule of common law is that the innkeeper will be liable for damage to, or loss of, a guest's property; unless an act of nature, civil unrest, or the guest's own negligence caused the damage or loss. Consequently, hospitality managers have an extraordinarily difficult task. Fortunately, in every state, the legislatures have moved to modify, under very specific circumstances, the common law liability requirements placed on innkeepers.

Limits on Common Law Liability

When innkeepers face great liability exposure, they should also have a great deal of control over a guest's possessions. It was this recognition of the great risk taken by innkeepers that moved state legislatures to modify the centuries-old common law liability for innkeepers. Beginning in the mid-1800s, and continuing today, each state has developed its own view of the extent of innkeeper liability for the possessions of their guests. The laws in each state vary considerably, however, so it is extremely important that hotel managers familiarize themselves with the law in their own state.

Section 4721.01 Liability for Loss of Property (GC Section 5981)

An innkeeper, whether a person, partnership, or corporation, having in his [or her] inn a metal safe or vault in good order suitable for the custody of money, bank notes, jewelry, articles of gold and silver manufacture, precious stones, personal ornaments, railroad mileage books or tickets, negotiable or valuable papers, and bullion, and keeping on the doors of the sleeping rooms used by his [or her] guests suitable locks or bolts, and on the transoms and windows of such rooms, suitable fastenings, and keeping a copy of this section printed in distinct type conspicuously suspended in the office, ladies parlor or sitting room, bar room, washroom, and five other conspicuous places in such inn, or not less than 10 conspicuous places in all, shall not be liable for loss or injury suffered by a guest, unless such guest has offered to deliver such property to such innkeeper for custody in such metal safe or vault and the innkeeper has omitted or refused to take and deposit it in the safe or vault for custody and give the guest a receipt therefore.

Section 4721.02 Extent of Liability Agreement (GC Section 5982)

An innkeeper should not be obliged to receive from a guest for deposit in the safe or vault property described in section 4721.01 of the Revised Code exceeding a total value of five hundred dollars, and shall not be liable for such property exceeding such value whether received or not. Such innkeeper, by special arrangement with a guest may receive for deposit in such safe or vault property upon such written terms as may be agreed upon. An innkeeper shall be liable for a loss of any of such property of a guest in his [or her] inn caused by the theft or negligence of the innkeeper or his [or her] servant.

Section 4721.03 Limit of Liability for as to Certain Property (GC Section 5983)

The liability of an innkeeper whether person, partnership, or corporation, for loss of or injury to personal property placed in his [or her] care by his [or her] guests other than that described in section 4721.01 and 4721.02 of the Revised Code shall be that of a depositary for hire. Liability shall not exceed one hundred and fifty dollars for each trunk and it's contents, fifty dollars for each valise and it's contents, and ten dollars for each box, bundle or package and contents, so placed in his [or her] care, unless he [or she] has consented in writing with such guests to assume a greater liability [sic].

Figure 11.1 State of Ohio limitations on innkeeper liability.

Figure 11.1 is a copy of the Innkeepers Liability statute for the state of Ohio. It is an excellent example of the type of law that state legislatures have passed for the benefit of innkeepers. Let's look carefully at several characteristics of the Ohio statute, which are common to most state liability laws.

Posting Notice

When a state legislature modifies the common law liability of innkeepers, it is only right that the guest be notified of the limitation. This is a critical point, and one that must be fully understood by the hospitality manager. Simply put, if a hotel wishes to take advantage of a state's laws limiting its liability for a guest's possessions, the guest must be made aware of the existence and content of that law. Notice that in the Ohio statute, guests must be made aware of the statute by requiring that the innkeeper keep "a copy of this section printed in distinct type conspicuously suspended in the office, ladies parlor or sitting room, bar room, washroom, and five other conspicuous places in such inn, or not less than 10 conspicuous places in all."

A Secure Safe

If a hotel is to limit its liability for a guest's possessions, the hotel must provide a safe where guests can keep their valuables during their stay. Note that the Ohio statute states an innkeeper must provide access to a "metal safe or vault." Hotels in most states are required to provide a safe for guest valuables and to operate the safe in a reasonable manner. That is, the safe should be in good working order, and access to the safe should be restricted and closely monitored.

Suitable Locks on Doors and Windows

Obviously, the hotel that intends to limit its liability must provide a reasonably safe room for its guests. This would include providing functioning locks for doors and windows, or as stated in the Ohio statute, "suitable locks or bolts, and on the transoms and windows of such rooms, suitable fastenings."

Limits on Required Possession

In most states, an innkeeper is not required to accept for safekeeping an unlimited amount of personal property. A hotel is not a bank, and it is not reasonable to assume that it would be as secure as a bank. Note the limitation allowed the innkeeper in the Ohio statute, which states, "An innkeeper should not be obliged to receive from a guest for deposit in the safe or vault property described in . . . the Revised Code exceeding a total value of five hundred dollars, and shall not be liable for such property exceeding such value whether received or not."

Limits on Replacement Values of Luggage

Because it is impossible to know for certain exactly what may have been contained in a lost piece of luggage, most states place a dollar limit on the replacement value of such items. Thus, if a piece of luggage placed in the care of the innkeeper is lost, the hotel's liability will be limited to the dollar value specified in the statute. Note the wording in the Ohio statute: "Liability shall not exceed one hundred and fifty dollars for each trunk and it's [sic] contents, fifty dollars for each valise and it's [sic] contents, and ten dollars for each box, bundle or package and contents."

This limitation provision is very similar to that provided to airlines, by federal law, for lost or damaged luggage. Also, be aware that some limited liability laws also protect the innkeeper (and their insurance companies) in the event of a fire or natural disaster.

Penalty for Negligence

In nearly all states, if an innkeeper is negligent, the statute limiting liability becomes ineffective. As the Ohio statute states, "An innkeeper shall be liable for a loss of any of such property of a guest in his [or her] inn caused by the theft or negligence of the innkeeper or his [or her] servant." Note that the Ohio statute makes an innkeeper responsible for theft, if an employee (servant) commits it. Even more important, the innkeeper becomes liable for the full amount of any property loss resulting from the negligence of the hotel or its staff (subject to the contributory negligence of the guest).

Ensuring the Limitation of Liability

Although it is implied, rather than explicitly stated, in the Ohio statute, failure on the part of the innkeeper to fulfill the statute's requirements will cause the innkeeper to lose the protection of the statute. Simply put, it is the responsibility of the innkeeper to prove that the hotel fully complied with all requirements set forth in the state law (i.e., appropriate notice with the right language, posted in the right number of conspicuous places, in an easy-to-read format, etc.).

≫ ANALYZE THE SITUATION 11.1

TRACI KENNEAR CHECKED INTO the Pullman House Hotel. During her stay, jewelry with an estimated value of $5,000 was stolen from her hotel room. Ms. Kennear maintained that the hotel should be responsible for the jewelry's replacement and sued the hotel for the amount of the stolen jewelry. The hotel stated that its liability was limited to $300 under state law, because Ms. Kennear failed to deposit the jewelry in the safe deposit boxes provided by the hotel.

Ms. Kennear's attorney countered that the notice of the law, which the legislature stated must be "conspicuously posted" in order to be applied, was in fact posted on the inside of a dresser drawer filled with extra blankets for the guestroom, and that, further, the type size was so small that an average person would not be able to read the notice from a distance of 2 feet. The hotel replied that the notice was, in its view, conspicuously posted, and that Ms. Kennear should have asked for help from the hotel if she could not find or read the notice.

1. Did the hotel comply with the state legislature's requirement that the notice be conspicuously posted?

2. How could the hotel manager in this case ensure compliance with the "conspicuous posting" requirement of the state legislature?

11.2 BAILMENTS

There are situations when a hotel or restaurant manager may be entrusted with a guest's property in circumstances not covered directly under a state's liability statute. For example, suppose that a guest arrives at a hotel and is greeted by a bellman who immediately takes the guest's bags and gives the guest a receipt before checking in. Who is responsible for the luggage? In this case, the guest has not had an opportunity to read the posted liability statutes, and has not even technically become a guest yet. However, because the bellman has taken voluntary possession of the bags, the hotel bears some responsibility for the safety of the guest's luggage.

Restaurants are not generally covered under the state laws that limit the liability of innkeepers. Nevertheless, restaurants too have responsibilities for the safety of their guests' property, especially in situations in which the restaurant takes temporary possession of that property.

These responsibilities have been established by the courts through the application of a legal concept known as a *bailment*. In the hospitality industry, bailments are quite common. Coat checks, valet parking, safety deposit boxes, laundry services, luggage storage, and luggage delivery services are all examples of bailments. Restaurant and hotel managers must understand that they are responsible for the safety of a guest's property when a bailment is established.

Bailment Relationship

In a bailment relationship, a person gives property to someone else for safekeeping. For example, a restaurant guest may check his or her coat in a coatroom. The diner assumes that the restaurateur will safely hold the coat until he or she comes back for it. While there may or may not be a charge for the service, the restaurateur assumes responsibility for the safety of the coat when it is received from the guest. In this situation, a bailment has been created.

The word bailment is derived from an old French word *bailler*, which means "to deliver." In a bailment relationship, the person who gives his or her property to another is known as the *bailor*. The person who takes responsibility for the property after receiving it is known as the *bailee*.

To create a bailment, the property must be delivered to the bailee. The bailee has a duty to return the property to the bailor when the bailment relationship ends. Thus, if a guest delivers a suit of clothes to an in-house hotel tailor, the bailment relationship begins when the tailor accepts the clothing and ends when the clothing has been returned to the guest.

It is important to note that a bailment may be for hire; that is, the bailor may have to pay the bailee to hold the property (as in paying for valet parking), the bailee may pay for the privilege of using the property (as is the case when renting a car), or the relationship may take the form of a *gratuitous bailment*.

Types of Bailments

The law surrounding bailments is vast and varied. Essentially, however, bailments are divisible into three kinds:

1. *Bailments for the benefit of the bailor*: In this arrangement, only the bailor gains from the agreement. This arrangement exists, for example, when a refrigeration repairman asks if he can leave his tools in a restaurant's storeroom for the night so they do not have to be reloaded into the repair truck. The tools will be used the next day to finish a repair job covered by the refrigerator's warranty. The restaurant that accepts the tools for safekeeping also accepts the responsibility of a bailment relationship, and so must exercise a high degree of care for the safety of the property (tools). If the restaurant is unwilling to do so, it can, of course, simply refuse to accept possession of the property.

2. *Bailments for the benefit of the bailee*: In some cases, the person holding the property gains from the bailment relationship. When the foodservice director of the local country club borrows chafing dishes from the food and beverage director of the local athletic club in order to service an extremely large wedding, the bailment is for the benefit of the bailee only. Again, it is important to note that this bailment relationship could be a gratuitous one, or the dishes could be rented to the country club. In either case, the bailee who benefits from the relationship is responsible for the safety of the property while it is in his or her possession.

3. *Bailments for the benefit of both parties*: In many cases, a bailment, either for payment or gratuitous, is for the benefit of both parties. This would be the case, for example, when a restaurant agrees to park its guests' cars for them while they dine. The guests (bailors) gain the convenience of having their cars parked for them, and the restaurant (bailee) gains because of the increase in business that comes from providing the parking service.

Although the rule of law varies somewhat in each of these three arrangements, as a manager, you need to realize that guest property, when in your possession, subjects you to the duty of reasonably caring for that property. A simple way to consider your responsibility is to assume that you should exercise as much care for the property of a guest as you would for your own property. If you cannot exercise that degree of care, it is best not to enter into a bailment relationship.

LEGALESE

Bailor: A person or entity that gives property to another in a bailment arrangement.

LEGALESE

Bailee: A person or entity that receives and holds property in a bailment arrangement.

LEGALESE

Gratuitous bailment: One in which there is no payment (consideration) in exchange for the promise to hold the property.

>> **ANALYZE THE SITUATION 11.2**

THE FOX MOUNTAIN COUNTRY Club was a popular location for weddings in a midsized town. In the winter, the country club offered a free coat check service to its guests. A staff member employed by the country club operated the coat check service. The coat checkroom was located just outside the entrance to the club's Crystal Ballroom.

At a wedding held on June 15, Mrs. Kathy Weldo presented her full-length sable coat to the uniformed coat check attendant at the country club. Mrs. Weldo was given a small plastic tag with a number, which she observed corresponded to the number on a coat hanger where her coat was hung. Standing outside the coatroom, Mrs. Weldo had a clear view of her fur as it hung on the coat rack. Mrs. Weldo remarked to the attendant that the coat was "very valuable," and that she hoped the attendant would watch over it carefully.

Upon leaving the club at 1:00 A.M., Mrs. Weldo went to the coat check area to retrieve her coat, only to find that it was missing. When she inquired about the coat's location, the coat check attendant apologized profusely but could not explain the coat's disappearance. The attendant stated that he had left the coatroom unattended only twice that evening, one time for a 15-minute dinner break and the other for a 5-minute cigarette break. The door to the coatroom was left open and unlocked during those periods, so that guests who left early could retrieve their own coats.

Mrs. Weldo returned to the club the next day to speak to Ms. Miles, the club manager. Ms. Miles pointed to a sign prominently displayed near the coatroom door stating, "The club is not responsible for lost or stolen property." She recommended that Mrs. Weldo refer the matter to her insurance company.

1. What was the nature of the bailment relationship in this situation?

2. Did the club exercise reasonable care in the handling of Mrs. Weldo's coat?

3. What should the club manager do in the future to avoid situations such as this?

Liability under a Bailment Relationship

A hospitality facility is liable only if a bailment relationship is established. For example, many restaurants and hotels provide coat racks or unattended coatrooms for their guests. Generally, a restaurant would not be responsible for any theft or damage to a patron's property on an unattended coat rack, because the restaurant did not legally take possession of the property. Thus, a bailment was never created.

This concept also applies to items inside bailed property. For example, a restaurant that offers valet parking would be liable for damage to a guest's automobile. When the guest presents the car keys to the valet, possession of the car is transferred from the guest to the restaurant, and a bailment is established. However, the restaurant would probably not be liable for the loss of an expensive camera that was left inside the car. The restaurant knowingly accepted ownership only of the automobile. No bailment relationship was established for the camera left inside the automobile.

It is important to remember that, in cases where a bailment relationship does not exist, and a hospitality operation does not assume liability, managers should still exercise a degree of care over their guests' property to avoid the risk of a negligence lawsuit.

When a bailment relationship has been established, a hospitality operation will be liable for any loss or damage to a guest's property. In many states, a hotel or restaurant's liability for damage will be limited if the operation (bailee) can prove that it exercised the standard of care required under the law.

A bailee can also reduce its liability by establishing a set liability limit in an express agreement with the bailor, provided the limitation is not in violation of law or public policy. For example, a country club may post a sign stating it will reimburse guests for lost property up to a set amount. Although some states may recognize this type of sign as a reasonable agreement between bailor and bailee to limit liability, other states do not recognize the validity of such a posting. Thus, a hospitality manager should read his or her state law carefully, or consult an attorney, before posting such a sign.

A hotel may also be liable for any bailed property of nonguests using its facilities, such as a hotel guest who has already checked out, or an individual using a hotel's restaurant or meeting room. However, the hotel's liability for such property may be limited under the terms of the state's liability law.

In all cases, if the loss or damage to a guest's property is the result of the hospitality operation's own negligence or fraud, the hospitality operation will be liable for the full amount of that property. By the same token, if a guest's own negligence contributes in some way to the property's loss, the hospitality operation's liability may be reduced, or even eliminated altogether.

Note that, historically, the common law held a hotel liable for the loss of a guest's property if the property and the guest were within the premises of the hotel. This concept was known as *infra hospitium*. Today, most states determine responsibility for lost or stolen items by applying bailment and/or negligence theories.

Consider the case of Alexis Lee. Alexis operates a tailor shop in the city. As part of her business, she makes the rounds of local hotels, seeking alteration and mending jobs. One day, Alexis takes an expensive man's suit from a guest staying at the Ritz hotel. The guest had delivered the suit to the bellstand for pick-up by the alteration company. Unfortunately, in her hurry to finish her collection rounds, Alexis leaves her truck unlocked, and the suit is stolen from the back of it before she returns.

In this situation, it is likely that the guest would expect the hotel to replace the suit. The hotel, of course, may be able to press a case against Alexis if it can be shown that her actions were negligent. However, a bailment was created between the bellman and the hotel guest. Under the law, an outside agent acting as a bailee on behalf of a restaurant or hotel may subject the operation to liability. Even though the suit was outside the physical confines of the hotel, the bailment between the hotel guest and the bellman, and the subsequent bailment established between the bellman and Alexis, served, in effect, to extend the confines of the hotel to include Alexis's truck. Thus, the hotel could be liable for the loss of the suit.

Perhaps the most difficult application of bailment and liability concerns the safekeeping of guests' automobiles. Under common law, innkeepers were responsible for the protection of their guests' means of transportation (which, up until the twentieth century, typically meant the care and feeding of horses). Today, however, the use of automobiles presents a unique challenge, as they generally exceed the state's liability amounts, yet cannot be placed in a safe.

In cases where a restaurant or hotel offers valet parking, the situation is clear. The guest turns over his or her key to the valet, creating a bailment relationship, thereby placing liability for the automobile with the restaurant or hotel. In situations where a hotel has an agreement with an independent parking garage, the hotel may

LEGALESE

Infra hospitium: A Latin term meaning "within the hotel."

still be liable for a guest's automobile, since the garage could be considered to be an agent of the hotel.

Many motels have free parking lots on their premises but accept no liability for their guests' automobiles. Guests are permitted to park on the lot if they so desire, but must keep their car keys with them. Thus, no bailment relationship is established between the guest and the motel that would cover any loss or damage to the automobile; that is, the motel would not be liable. That said, some states consider the availability of a parking lot to be a gratuitous bailment, which would hold the hospitality operation liable for any damage. In cases where guests keep their car keys, but a fee is charged for use of the parking lot, the courts may decide that the charging of a fee creates a bailment relationship, which could hold the parking lot owner liable. The laws covering liability for automobiles vary widely from state to state. As a hospitality manager, you should have a thorough knowledge of all the liability provisions included in your state's laws.

Detained Property

Bailees have significant responsibilities when a bailment is created, but so too do bailors. The bailee has the right to charge a fee to cover any costs that may be associated with holding or protecting property, such as a parking fee or charges for the services of a dry cleaner or tailor. However, the bailor may be required to pay reasonable charges for property requiring special handling or maintenance. If the bailor is unwilling or unable to pay the agreed-on charges, the bailee may detain or keep the goods of the bailment as a lien until full payment is made.

Consider the case of the hotel that operates a parking garage and charges a nightly parking fee for guests. A guest arrives at the front desk to check out one morning and claims to be dissatisfied with the hotel and its services. The guest refuses to pay for either the room charges or the parking fees incurred. The hotel may choose to withhold the automobile from the guest until payment is made. In this situation, the automobile would be considered *detained property*. Of course, during the time the property was being withheld, the hotel, as the bailee, would have an obligation to protect the detained property from harm with the same measure of care it would normally exercise.

The situation just described illustrates not only the concept of detained property, but also why you must use your legal knowledge, as well as good judgment, when operating a hospitality facility. The hotel manager may well be within his or her legal rights to detain the automobile and demand payment, but that action may not be in the hotel's best interest. To maintain good customer relations, and to avoid a lawsuit, the manager may decide that a better approach would be to release the automobile. The procedure of detaining property can subject you to a possible lawsuit if not done properly. It is a course of action that should be pursued only after careful consideration of the legal consequences.

Innkeeper's Lien

The innkeeper's lien is a concept that helps to protect innkeepers from nonpaying guests. Essentially, it enables a hotel to detain certain property that guests may bring with them into the inn if they refuse, or are unable, to pay their bill. Most states allow the innkeeper to hold a guest's property until the appropriate charges have been paid. In the event the guest chooses not to pay the bill, the innkeeper is usually authorized to sell the items and apply the proceeds from the sale to the bill. The innkeeper can also use the proceeds to pay any costs that may have been associated with selling the property. Any surplus left over must be returned to the guest. Certain personal items, such as necessary clothing and wedding rings, have been held to be outside the scope of the innkeeper's lien.

LEGALESE

Detained property: Personal property held by a bailee until lawful payment is made by the bailor.

Ordinarily, the lien can be used only to pay charges incurred by the guest directly with the hotel. So, a charge incurred by the guest at an independent business center, for example, even though located within the hotel, would not qualify. State laws vary, so be sure to consult with the state hotel association for the proper methods to be used. Remember, though, that if at any time a guest pays the bill, the lien is extinguished and the property must be returned immediately.

To see a review of the history of innkeeper statutes, and a proposed uniform statute for all states, go to www.HospitalityLawyer.com and read the article titled "Proposed Model Innkeeper's Limitation of Liability Statute."

Search the Web 11.1

Go online to www.law.cornell.edu/ucc/ucc.table.html. You will arrive at the Uniform Commercial Code.

1. Select: Article Seven from the list of articles available.
2. Scroll to Part 2, Warehouse Receipts: Special Provisions.
3. Select and read: §7-209. Lien of Warehouseman and §7-210. Enforcement of Warehouseman's Lien.
4. What does it mean if a bailee has a lien on a bailor's property?
5. Does a lien permit the possessor of property to sell it to satisfy the lien?
6. What are the implications of section 4 of 7-209 for the hospitality manager proceeding without an attorney?

11.3 PROPERTY WITH UNKNOWN OWNERSHIP

As a manager, you may experience occasions when you and your staff will discover personal property whose ownership is uncertain. Under common law, there are three classifications of property whose ownership is in doubt, each of which carries with it unique responsibilities for the hospitality manager:

1. Mislaid property
2. Lost property
3. Abandoned property

Mislaid Property

Mislaid property comes into existence when the property owner forgets where he or she has placed it. For example, in a restaurant, a guest may enter with an umbrella, place the umbrella in a stand near the door, but upon leaving the restaurant, forget to retrieve it. In this case, the umbrella is considered to be mislaid property, and the restaurant's manager or owner is responsible for the safekeeping of the umbrella until the rightful owner returns. In fact, if the umbrella is given by the manager to someone who claims to be the owner, but who in fact is not, common law would find the manager liable to the true owner for the value of the umbrella.

LEGALESE

Mislaid property: Personal property that has been put aside on purpose but then has been forgotten by the rightful owner.

A manager is required to use reasonable care to protect mislaid property until the rightful owner returns to claim it. If the rightful owner does not return in a reasonable amount of time, ownership of the property would be transferred to the property finder. Most hotels and restaurants require their employees to turn in any mislaid property they find in the normal course of their work. Thus, ownership of the mislaid property would be transferred to the employer, not the employee.

Lost Property

LEGALESE

Lost property: Personal property that has been inadvertently put aside, then forgotten by the rightful owner.

Lost property comes into being when the rightful owner accidentally or inadvertently forgets where he or she has placed the belonging. Under common law, the individual who finds lost property in a public place is allowed to keep it unless the rightful owner returns to claim it. In many states, the finder has a legal obligation to make a reasonable effort to locate the rightful owner of both lost and mislaid property.

Like mislaid property, employees who find lost property in the course of their work must turn the property over to their employer. This is true even if the property was found in a public place. Thus, a hotel lobby cleaning attendant who finds a portable computer on the floor near a chair would be required to turn the property over to the hotel, because the employer could be responsible for the value of the property if the rightful owner were to return to claim it.

A question can arise over the length of time a finder of lost property must retain that property. One would expect the length of time that the property should be held would increase with the value of the property. Thus, a pair of diamond earrings found in a hotel guestroom would likely require a greater holding time than a pair of gym shoes. Many hotel operators solve this problem by requiring that all property be held a minimum length of time before it is given to the employee who found it (as a reward for honesty) or given to charity. Figure 11.2 is a sample form that a hotel or restaurant can use to properly track these lost-and-found items.

Abandoned Property

When an owner abandons property, he or she has no intention of returning to reclaim it. Obviously, it can be difficult for a manager to know when property has been abandoned, and not just misplaced or lost.

LEGALESE

Abandoned property: Personal property that has been deliberately put aside by the rightful owner with no intention of ever returning for it.

Under common law, a finder has no obligation to take care of, or protect, *abandoned property*. In addition, the finder of abandoned property is not required to seek out its true owner. Broken umbrellas, magazines, worn clothing, and inexpensive toilet articles such as razors, toothbrushes, and the like are all common examples of abandoned property found in hotels. The statement that "one man's trash is another man's treasure" certainly holds true in regard to abandoned property. Still, it is a good idea to make sure that any property discarded by the hotel is, in fact, abandoned. When in doubt, it is always best to treat property of doubtful ownership as mislaid, or lost, rather than abandoned.

Disposing of Unclaimed Property

When items of value are found in a hotel or restaurant, your first goal as a manager or owner should be to return the property to its rightful owner. When that is not possible, your next goal should be to safely protect the property until the rightful owner returns for it. Only after it is abundantly clear that the original owner will not be returning should the property be liquidated.

As a guardian of guest property, it is your responsibility as a manager to protect and, when appropriate, properly dispose of property with unknown ownership. If you do so correctly, your guests and your employees will benefit.

Lost-and-Found Ticket

Facility Name _____ Today's Date _____

Item Description _____

_____

_____

_____

_____

_____

_____

Location found: _____ Room Number _____

Name of finder _____

Supervisor who received item(s) _____

_____

DISPOSITION OF PROPERTY

Date item returned to owner _____

Owner Name _____ Owner Address _____

Owner Telephone _____   _____

Returned to owner by _____

Date item:

Returned to finder _____ Disposed of _____

Figure 11.2 Form used to track lost-and-found items.

ANALYZE THE SITUATION 11.3

KARI RENFROE WAS EMPLOYED as a room attendant at the Lodge Inn motel. One day, as she came to work, she discovered an expensive leather jacket stuffed inside a plastic shopping bag in the employee section of the parking lot. The jacket had no ownership marks on it, and neither did the plastic bag. Kari turned the jacket over to the manager of the motel despite the fact that there was no policy in place regarding items found outside the motel.

The jacket was still unclaimed 120 days later, at which time Kari approached the manager and asked if she could have the jacket, since she found it. The manager refused to give Kari the jacket, stating that all unclaimed property found on the motel's premises belonged to the motel.

1. Would the jacket be considered mislaid, lost, or abandoned property?

2. Who is the current, rightful owner of the jacket?

3. How could the motel manager avoid future confusion about handling "found" property?

LEGALLY MANAGING AT WORK:

Disposing of Found Property

The following six guidelines can help you as you devise a policy to protect the rights of original property owners and to reward the honesty of your employees:

1. Review your state's lost-and-found laws to determine any unique requirements that apply to the property in question.

2. Require all employees and management staff to turn in to the property manager or to his or her designee all personal property found in public places (lobbies, foyers, restrooms, etc.), as well as property found in rented areas such as guestrooms, suites, cabins, and campgrounds.

3. Keep a lost-and-found log book, wherein you record the name of the finder, the individual who received the found goods, the location where the property was found, and the date found.

4. If the value of the found item is significant, make all reasonable efforts to locate the rightful owner, and document these efforts.

5. Hold found property for a period of time recommended by your company or a local attorney familiar with the laws in your state regarding found property. Sixty days should be a minimum length for most found property.

6. Permit only the property manager or his or her designee to return found property to purported owners, but only after taking extra care to return the item only to its rightful owner.

If the original owner does not come forward, dispose of the property in accordance with written procedures, which have been shared with all employees and reviewed by your attorney. Many managers give found property to those who found it as a reward for employee honesty. They theorize that it is in the best interest of the facility and its guests to have all property returned promptly, and rewarding employees for doing so is one way to achieve this goal. Other facilities donate all valuable lost property to a local charity, while still others sell lost property once or twice a year to liquidation companies.

INTERNATIONAL SNAPSHOT

Limited Liability of Innkeepers in Canada

In Canada, innkeepers' liability is governed provincially. With the exception of Quebec, all provinces and territories limit liability for damage to a guest's property subject to two exceptions.[1] Innkeepers are liable where goods are stolen or lost through the neglect of the innkeeper or his or her employees, or when goods are deposited for safe custody with the innkeeper (unless the goods were kept in a safe or other sealed device).

[1] While most provinces provide for no liability in circumstances where the exceptions do not exist, in three of the provinces, the liability is capped at a stated amount. For instance, the cap is $200 in Newfoundland, $100 in Saskatchewan, and $40 in Ontario.

Some provinces have additional limitations and exceptions. For example:

- In Quebec, innkeepers can be liable for up to 10 times nightly rate, and where the loss is caused intentionally, the liability can be unlimited.

- In nine jurisdictions,[2] innkeepers can be liable for refusing to receive goods for safe custody or where guests are unable to deposit the goods for safe custody through the fault of the innkeeper. This liability is limited where the establishment does not have a proper safe and the guest is informed of this when the innkeeper refuses to receive the goods.

- Saskatchewan provides that the innkeeper will not be liable for goods lost in a part of the hotel other than the guestroom of the owner of the goods. The innkeeper is also not liable for trunks or their contents or personal effects left by a guest in his or her room, if there is a proper lock and key for the door of the room, unless the room is locked during the absence of the guest and the key is left at the office.

- In Alberta, innkeepers may be liable for property belonging to persons who are not registered guests.

Given the variations between jurisdictions, it is critical to consult the legislation of the relevant province.

Provided by Frank Zaid, a partner, and Jasmine Lew, a student-at-law, with Osler, Hoskin & Harcourt LLP, Barristers and Solicitors, in the firm's Toronto, Ontario, Canada office. www.osler.com.

[2] These clauses were found in the statutes of British Columbia, Ontario, Quebec, Manitoba, Saskatchewan, New Brunswick, Nova Scotia, Newfoundland and Labrador, and the Northwest Territories.

WHAT WOULD YOU DO?

You are the manager of a restaurant in a downtown area of a large city. Because of your location, no parking is available directly adjacent to your facility. For the past five years, you have made valet parking service available to your customers through A-1 Parking. Essentially, A-1 provided valet drivers who would stand outside your restaurant doors, approach cars as they arrived, give guests a claim check for their cars, and deliver the car to a parking garage owned by A-1. The parking garage is located one-fourth of a mile from your restaurant. When guests finish dining, the valet outside your restaurant radios the parking lot with the claim check number, and a driver from A-1 delivers the car to your front door, where guests pay a parking fee before they regain possession of their car. A-1 currently provides this service to several restaurants.

The arrangement has been a good one for both you and A-1. No trouble of any kind has ever been reported. Today, however, the owner of A-1 has announced he is retiring; he approaches you to inquire whether the restaurant would be interested in buying his business.

Draft a letter to the owner of A-1 Parking stating whether or not you wish to buy the parking garage business. In your letter, be sure to address the following points:

1. How operating the valet parking service yourself would change the relationship you have with your restaurant customers.
2. The need for insurance to cover potential damages to automobiles and other areas of liability you might need to insure against.
3. The potential pros and cons of assuming the responsibility for parking your guests' automobiles, as compared to the current situation.
4. The agency, liability, and bailment issues that would arise if the purchase were made.

THE HOSPITALITY INDUSTRY IN COURT

To familiarize yourself with how complying with the requirements of a limited liability statute saved a motel $36,000, read the case of *Emerson v. Super 8 Motel*, 1999 Conn. Super. Lexis 965 (Conn. Super. Ct. 1999).

FACTUAL SUMMARY

Lannell Emerson (Emerson) stayed at a Super 8 Motel (Super 8) in Stamford, Connecticut, on November 12, 1997. Emerson was carrying $36,000 in cash in the glove box of his car. Sometime during the night his car was broken into and the cash was stolen. Emerson sued Super 8 Motel for failure to keep his property safe.

QUESTION FOR THE COURT

The question for the court was whether Super 8 was obligated to keep the personal property of guests safe during their stay. Super 8 argued that under Connecticut law it had no duty to keep Emerson's personal property safe unless he gave the property to the person in charge of the office for safekeeping. The law specifically required motel guests to deliver the property to the person in charge of the office for safekeeping and to take a written receipt. The law also required the motel to post a notice of the availability of a safe in the guestrooms or motel office.

Emerson's only argument was he did not see a notice regarding the safe in either the office or the motel guestroom. He argued that Super 8 failed to comply with the Connecticut law by not posting a notice, hence it could not escape liability for the loss of his property. Super 8 offered evidence showing the notices were in place. Emerson submitted an affidavit stating he did not see the notices, but offered no other evidence.

DECISION

The court found for Super 8 and did not hold it liable for the loss of property suffered by Emerson. The court concluded Emerson failed to offer reliable evidence regarding the notices posted in the guestrooms or office. Super 8 was relieved of liability under the Connecticut law.

MESSAGE TO MANAGEMENT

A hotel must comply precisely with the requirements of the limited liability statutes in each state or face possible liability in situations like this one.

To learn the dire consequences of noncompliance, consider the case of *Frockt v. Goodloe*, 670 F. Supp. 163 (W.D.N.C. 1987).

FACTUAL SUMMARY

Marvin Frockt (Frockt), a traveling jewelry salesman, stayed at a Comfort Inn in North Carolina. Frockt had in his possession a jewelry sample case containing jewelry valued at about $150,000. Upon checking in, Frockt requested the case be placed in a safe at the inn. He also signed his registration card, which contained a statement saying the inn would not be responsible for loss of valuables. The clerk accepted the case to be placed in either the safe or a closet where the petty cash was kept. The clerk was not informed about the contents of the case nor their value. Frockt did state the case was very valuable. The clerk did not offer Frockt a receipt, but Frockt wrote out his own receipt keeping one copy and attaching the other to the case. When Frockt asked for the case the next day, it could not be located. Frockt sued the owners of the Comfort Inn for failing to keep his property safe.

QUESTION FOR THE COURT

The question for the court was whether the Comfort Inn was responsible for the loss of the jewelry case. Frockt argued Comfort Inn was responsible based on North Carolina common law giving innkeepers the duty to receive and safely keep all property at the request of the guest. North Carolina also had a statute dealing with guest personal property. It required innkeepers to receive money, jewelry, and valuables for safekeeping upon the request of a guest. The law limited the value of property required to be held by the inn to $500. The law also required the innkeeper to keep a copy of the law posted in every guestroom and the office of the inn, and stated the law did not apply if the innkeeper failed to post notice. Frockt offered evidence showing Comfort Inn did not post a copy of the statute in the guestroom or the office.

Frockt argued Comfort Inn's failure to post the statute meant it was not applicable to his case. He argued the common law applied and Comfort Inn was unconditionally responsible for all his property.

Comfort Inn argued it was free to place conditions on the receipt of property. Specifically, Comfort Inn argued it could condition acceptance of Frockt's case on his agreement to not hold Comfort Inn responsible for loss. Comfort Inn also argued that Frockt agreed to not hold the inn responsible when he signed his registration card with the release from liability statement on it.

DECISION

The court decided Comfort Inn was responsible for Frockt's lost jewelry case. The release from liability statement on the registration card was void because it violated public policy. Additionally, since Comfort Inn failed to post copies of the statute dealing with valuables, the statute did not apply. The common law of North Carolina held innkeepers completely liable for all property left with the innkeeper for safekeeping.

MESSAGE TO MANAGEMENT

You cannot rely on exculpatory clauses. You need to follow the legal requirements precisely.

As a hospitality operator, you have a responsibility to take reasonable steps to safeguard the personal property that guests bring with them onto your premises. Fortunately, laws have been passed in all states that limit the liability of the operator. There are several requirements that must be met by the operator for the limits to apply. Because the laws vary widely, it is crucial that you become familiar with the requirements of the statute in your state.

From time to time, operators will voluntarily accept possession of guest property (e.g., valet parking, luggage storage, etc.). These are called bailment relationships. Your responsibilities vary, depending on the type of bailment that is created. As innkeeper's lien gives a lodging establishment the right to detain a guest's belongings in the event the guest refuses to pay the bill.

Property can also be mislaid, lost, or abandoned, and a manager must understand the distinctions between those three classifications in order to dispose of the property responsibly.

WHAT DID YOU LEARN IN THIS CHAPTER?

After you have studied this chapter, you should be prepared to:

RAPID REVIEW

1. Discuss the impact that the common law liability of innkeepers had on the development of the early travel industry, and give three reasons why state legislatures have chosen to limit that liability.

2. Using the Internet, contact the offices of your state hotel and motel association to secure a copy of the current innkeeper's liability law. Review the document and create a list of posting/notice requirements that you would implement if you operated a hotel in your state. Explain your rationale for each item on the list and its posting location.

3. Give a restaurant example of a bailment for the benefit of a bailor and one for the benefit of the bailee.

4. Innkeepers are generally held responsible for an even higher degree of care than ordinary bailees. Why do you think this came to be under common law?

5. When a guest places a coat on a coat rack attached to his or her table in a restaurant, is a bailment created? Why or why not?

6. List ten examples of bailment relationships in the hospitality industry.

7. Think of and write out an example you could use to teach employees the difference between mislaid and abandoned property. Why is such an example useful?

8. Create the portion of a lost-and-found policy for a hotel's room attendants that refers to disposition of unclaimed mislaid, lost, or abandoned property. Did you give the property to the employee who found it? Why or why not?

TEAM ACTIVITY

In teams, draft a policy and procedures guide (not to exceed five double-spaced pages) for a large restaurant chain that will instruct employees as to how to handle and protect guest property. Be sure to include bailment issues such as valet parking and coat checks, as well as items that may be left behind by guests and found by an employee. Once you have developed a policy, present it to your class in the form of a ten-minute training session that would be used to educate employees about the new policy.

CHAPTER 12

YOUR RESPONSIBILITIES WHEN SERVING FOOD AND BEVERAGES

" KNOW THE NUMBERS look good," Trisha Sangus said, as she adjusted her glasses. "That's the problem. They look too good." It was a typical second day of the month at the hotel. That meant reviewing the prior month's profit and loss statement. Trisha sat at her desk across from Ahmed Cantonio, the hotel's new controller. Ahmed and Trisha had worked together for three months, and Ahmed had seen this look on the general manager's face before. Usually, Trisha's P&L reviews focused on expense categories that exceeded budget. This time, the focus was on food cost. Those costs were actually below the projection Trisha and Ahmed had made at mid-month, which made Ahmed wonder all the more about Trisha's uneasiness. Usually, expenses below budget or projection were something to celebrate, but Trisha Sangus was not celebrating.

"Are you sure you have accurately reported sales for food and beverage?" asked Trisha. Ahmed was nearly offended. He had answered the same question ten minutes ago. He was positive that all food and beverage sales had been properly recorded.

He replied, "For the month, $273,000. I checked the numbers three times. Banquet sales of $112,000, restaurant sales of $88,000, and bar sales of $73,000. That makes $273,000."

"And our mid-month projection for food and beverage cost of sales?" asked Trisha.

"Well," Ahmed began again, looking up from the P&L, "after we adjusted for the big banquet we picked up on the 22nd, we projected sales of $275,000. Pretty close, if you ask me. Food and beverage costs combined were estimated at 28.5 percent, or $77,800."

"That's true," said Trisha, as she leaned back in her chair and stared at the ceiling. "However, I see an actual expense of only $64,800, and that has me concerned. Did you double-check beginning and ending month inventories as I had asked?"

"Sure did," replied Ahmed. "I know they are accurate. I even spot-checked some of the inventory counts myself. Everything on the inventory is in-house and valued correctly."

"And total food purchases," continued Trisha, "We haven't omitted any invoices from our calculations?"

"No," replied Ahmed, "I am sure we have not. My assistant, Veronica, contacted every supplier this morning. We have all the invoices. I guess the new chef is just doing a great job holding down our costs. We should be pleased."

Trisha looked up at Ahmed. "Ahmed, I like low costs. When Jerry Mekemson was the chef here, before his retirement, we ran great food costs—always in line with my projections. I knew Jerry, and the quality he insisted we . . ."

Before she could finish, Trisha was interrupted by the telephone ringing on her desk. "Hello," said Trisha as she picked up the receiver. "This is Trisha Sangus, how can I help you? . . . Really?" she said. "None at all? But 25 pounds of bleu? By the way, do you happen to know offhand the current price difference between Roquefort and bleu? Okay, thanks, Judy. No problem; yes, I'll be down."

"Well," said Trisha as she hung up the telephone, "that was Judy down in the kitchen storeroom. I called her earlier and asked her if I could get a Cobb salad for lunch. Let's go down to Jill's."

Ahmed was confused. Jill's Tavern was one of two restaurants operated by the hotel. It was a casual, fun-style restaurant that served salads, burgers, steaks, and grilled items—very high quality, and with superb service. But it wasn't like Trisha to leave an unsolved problem, even for lunch. In fact, she was noted for often eating lunch at her desk as she continued to work. And Judy didn't actually work in the dining room. She received and put away the grocery orders as they were delivered to the kitchen that serviced the restaurants.

"Let's go," said Trisha. "A Cobb salad with fresh grilled chicken breast, California avocado slices, Roquefort cheese—makes me hungry just thinking about it," she continued. But she had a look in her eye that told Ahmed she was thinking about more than just lunch. "I think we can have lunch and solve our mystery," she revealed. Let's ask the chef to eat with us, too." Ahmed had a feeling that Trisha was going to enjoy her lunch, but he wasn't quite sure that the new chef would.

IN THIS CHAPTER, YOU WILL LEARN:

1. A foodservice establishment's responsibilities, under the Uniform Commercial Code (UCC) and other laws, to serve wholesome food and beverages.
2. To apply "truth in menu" concepts to the service of food and beverage products.
3. To assess the current legal risks associated with serving alcohol.
4. To implement training programs that result in the responsible service of alcohol.

12.1 SERVING FOOD

People all over the world love to dine out. And when they are not dining out, Americans have increasingly begun to patronize foodservice operations that offer preprepared food they can take home to eat. In fact, 1996 was the first year that takeout occasions exceeded on-premise occasions in the U.S. foodservice industry. Whether the food is eaten in a restaurant or taken home, *Cooking for Profit* magazine estimates that U.S. restaurants post combined sales of nearly $1 billion per day. Some experts predict that fully 75 percent of all food eaten in the United States will be preprepared by restaurants or grocery stores within the first decade of the twenty-first century.

Uniform Commercial Code Warranty

As a hospitality manager involved with the service of food, you have a legal obligation to only sell food that is wholesome, and to deliver that food in a manner that is safe. This responsibility is mandated by the Uniform Commercial Code (UCC), as well as other state and local laws. Figure 12.1 details one section of the UCC that relates to selling safe food. When a foodservice operation sells food, there is an implied warranty that the food is *merchantable*. Simply put, a foodservice manager is required to operate his or her facility in a manner that protects guests from the possibility of *foodborne illness*, or any other injury that may be caused by consuming unwholesome food or beverages. Unfortunately, sometimes, food is served that contains something that the guest normally would not expect to find in the dish (e.g., a small stone in a serving of refried beans). The question that must be answered in these cases is whether or not the food or beverage served was "fit" for consumption.

The courts usually apply one of two different tests to determine whether a foodservice establishment is liable to a guest for any damages suffered from eating the food. (In the case of the stone found in the refried beans, the damage may consist of a broken tooth from biting down on the small stone.) One test seeks to determine whether the object is foreign to the dish or a natural component of it. If the object is foreign, then the implied warranty of merchantability (fitness) under the UCC is breached, and the foodservice operator would be held liable. If it is a natural component, the warranty would not be breached. For example, the stone in the refried beans, though commonly found in large bags of raw beans, would be considered foreign, and thus the foodservice operator would probably be held responsible. If instead the guest had broken a tooth on a piece of clamshell while enjoying a steaming bowl of New England clam chowder, the guest would probably not recover any damages under this test. The clamshell, as a natural component of clams, the court reasons, is also a natural component of clam chowder.

The foreign/natural test is slowly being replaced by the "reasonable expectation" test. This test seeks to determine whether an item could be reasonably expected by a guest to be found in the food. The clamshell situation is a perfect example of why the law (and assessing liability) can be difficult at times. Clamshells are natural parts of clams, but are they really natural components of clam chowder? Put another way, would you, as a guest, reasonably expect to find pieces of clamshell in a bowl of clam chowder that was served to you? If a judge or jury decided that it was not reasonable to expect to find a clamshell in the chowder, then the foodservice operator would be held liable. A tricky situation arises if someone orders a fish filet sandwich. As the word "filet" means boneless, a guest would not expect to find bones in the sandwich. Accordingly, if a bone were present, and the guest choked on that bone, the consequences could be substantial for the foodservice operator.

> **LEGALESE**
>
> **Merchantable:** Suitable for buying and selling.

> **LEGALESE**
>
> **Foodborne illness:** Sickness or harm caused by the consumption of unsafe foods or beverages.

Uniform Commercial Code: IMPLIED WARRANTY

§ 2-314.: Merchantability; Usage of Trade.

1) Unless excluded or modified (Section 2-316), a warranty that the goods shall be merchantable is implied in a contract for their sale if the seller is a merchant with respect to goods of that kind. Under this section the serving for value of food or drink to be consumed either on the premises or elsewhere is a sale.

Figure 12.1 Uniform Commercial Code: Implied Warranty.

Guest Safety

To help foodservice operators prevent foodborne illness, local health departments conduct routine inspections of restaurants and other food production facilities, and may hold training or certification classes for those who handle food. It is important to know the local health department requirements that relate to food handling in your area, and to work diligently to ensure that only safe food is served in your operation. If you do not, the results can be catastrophic.

Consider the case of Kelly Kleitsch. Kelly worked long hours to establish her own successful restaurant. With much hard work and a considerable investment of capital, Kelly built the reputation of her restaurant by serving high-quality food at fair prices. When a careless member of the food preparation team forgot to refrigerate a chicken stock one night, then used the stock the next day to flavor an uncooked sauce, which was later served, several individuals became very ill. The good reputation of Kelly's restaurant disappeared overnight as the local newspapers and television stations reported how one elderly lady was hospitalized after eating at the restaurant. Customer counts plummeted, and Kelly lost her business. And that was before the lawsuit was filed on behalf of the elderly diner.

The law in this area is very clear. Restaurants will be held responsible for the illnesses suffered by their guests, if those illnesses are the direct result of consuming unwholesome food. Thus, managers must make every effort to comply with local ordinances, train staff in effective food-handling and production techniques, and document their efforts. The National Restaurant Association, and its ServSafe program, can be a great asset in managers' efforts to ensure the safety of the food they serve. ServSafe is a national educational program designed to help foodservice operators ensure food safety.

Of course, you should take all reasonable measures to ensure that the food you serve is safe and consumable by your guests. Disclosing ingredients and warning

≫ ANALYZE THE SITUATION 12.1

HARRY DOLINSKI WAS THE executive chef at the Regal House hotel. One of his specialties was a hearty vegetable soup that was featured on the lunch buffet every Thursday. Pauline Guilliard and her friends decided to have lunch at the Regal House one Thursday before attending an art exhibit. Ms. Guilliard read the lighted menu at the front of the buffet line. The chef's specials, including the vegetable soup, were written on the menu with a felt-tip pen.

Ms. Guilliard selected the vegetable soup and a few other items, and consumed one full bowl of the soup. Three hours later, at the art exhibit, she suffered seizures and had difficulty breathing. It turned out that the soup contained MSG—a food additive to which she had severe reactions. Ms. Guilliard recovered, but her attorney contacted the hotel with a demand letter seeking compensation for her suffering.

The hotel's attorney replied that the soup served by the hotel was wholesome and that Ms. Guilliard's reaction to the MSG could not have been reasonably foreseen. In addition, the hotel maintained that MSG is a common seasoning in use worldwide for many years, and thus it would have been the diner's responsibility to inform the foodservice operation of any allergies or allergic reactions. As a result, the liability for Ms. Guilliard's illness was hers alone.

1. Did the hotel have an obligation (or duty as outlined in Chapter 9, "Your Responsibilities as a Hospitality Operator") to notify guests that the soup contained MSG?

2. How do you think a jury would respond to this situation? What level of damages, if any, do you think a jury would be included to award in this case?

3. What should the chef do to avoid similar problems in the future?

guests of potential concerns is the best practice. If a potential incident does occur, however, the steps itemized in the next Legally Managing at Work feature should be taken to ensure the safety of all guests and to prevent further potential liability.

The quality of the food a restaurant serves is important, as you have seen, but how that restaurant serves its food can be just as important from a legal standpoint. Again, the UCC addresses the issue of a restaurant's responsibility to serve food properly. As can be seen in Figure 12.2, a restaurateur is considered an expert—that is, an individual with skill and judgment—when it comes to the proper delivery of prepared food and beverages.

Not only can restaurants be found guilty of serving unwholesome food, but they can also be found liable if they serve wholesome food in an unsafe or negligent manner. Consider Terry Settles. Terry and his wife were guests at the Remington restaurant. He ordered cherries jubilee for dessert. When the server prepared the dish, a small amount of alcohol splashed out of the flambé pan and landed on the arm of Terry's wife. As she jumped back in her chair to try and avoid the burning liquid, she

LEGALLY MANAGING AT WORK:

Steps to Take When a Guest Complains of Foodborne Illness

1. Document the name, address, and telephone number of the guest who complains of an illness, as well as the date and time the guest patronized your facility.

2. Document all items eaten in your facility by the guest during the visit in question.

3. Obtain the name and address of the physician treating the guest. If the guest has not contacted a physician, encourage him or her to do so.

4. Contact the physician to determine if in fact a case of foodborne illness has been diagnosed.

5. Notify the local health department immediately if a foodborne illness outbreak is confirmed, so the staff there can assist you in determining the source of the outbreak, as well as identifying affected guests and employees.

6. Evaluate and, if necessary, modify your training and certification efforts that relate to the areas involved in the incident.

7. Document your efforts, and notify your attorney or company risk manager.

Figure 12.2 Uniform
Commercial Code: General
Obligation and Construction
of Contract.

**Uniform Commercial Code: GENERAL OBLIGATION
AND CONSTRUCTION OF CONTRACT**

§ 2-315. Implied Warranty: Fitness for Particular Purpose.

Where the seller at the time of contracting has reason to know any particular purpose for which the goods are required and that the buyer is relying on the seller's skill or judgment to select or furnish suitable goods, there is unless excluded or modified under the next section an implied warranty that the goods shall be fit for such purpose.

---

fell and severely injured her back. There is little question in this case that the restaurant will face severe penalties for the carelessness of its server.

Management should frequently review all food temperatures, serving containers, food production techniques, and delivery methods. Chipped plates and glasses or poorly washed utensils can present just as much of a legal risk as serving spoiled or unwholesome food. Some states even require restaurants to post signs disclosing the use of microwave ovens when applicable, to caution restaurant patrons who have pacemakers.

In addition, restaurants should strive to accommodate guests who ask that dishes be prepared without a specific ingredient to which they are allergic and to closely supervise the preparation of that dish. In fact, the issue of food allergies has become a topic of increasing importance in recent years. Both the federal and state governments have begun to initiate regulations for foodservice providers, focusing on preventing allergic reactions. For example, the Food Allergen Labeling and Consumer Protection Act, which became effective in 2006, requires the labeling of foods that contain major allergens, such as milk, eggs, fish, shellfish, peanuts, tree nuts, wheat, and soy. These ingredients must be disclosed, even if they are used in

≫ ANALYZE THE SITUATION 12.2

PENNY MANCE WAS A single mother of three children living in an urban apartment complex. She worked as a paralegal in a downtown attorney's office. One morning, Penny was asked to come into work an hour later than her usual time. She used the opportunity to treat her three children to breakfast at a fast-food restaurant near their home. The Mance family arrived at the restaurant at 8:00 A.M. and ordered breakfast. For their beverage selections, Penny ordered hot chocolate and the children selected orange juice.

After the family sat down, Tina, Penny's six-year-old daughter, told her mother that she wanted to try the hot chocolate. The beverage had been served in a Styrofoam cup with a plastic lid. Penny replied that the chocolate was "probably too hot for her to try." This comment was overheard by several guests sitting near the Mance family. Tina reached for the chocolate anyway; her mother, while trying to pull the chocolate away, spilled it on her own hands. Penny suffered second- and third-degree burns from the hot chocolate and was forced to miss work for three weeks. Upon returning, her typing speed was severely reduced as a result of tissue scarring on her left hand.

Penny retained one of the attorneys where she worked to sue the fast-food restaurant. In court depositions later on, it was estimated that the chocolate was served at a temperature of 190 degree Fahrenheit. The restaurant's attorney claimed the chocolate was not unsafe when it was served. He pointed to the fact that Penny knew the beverage was probably too hot for the child as an indication that she was willing to accept the risk of drinking a hot beverage. In addition, the restaurant's attorney maintained that it was the child's action, not the restaurant's, which was the direct cause of the accident. Undeterred, Penny's attorney sued for damages, including medical expenses, lost wages, and a large amount for punitive damages.

1. Did the restaurant act negligently in the serving of the hot chocolate?

2. Do you think that Penny Mance was negligent? If so, how much difference, if any, do you believe that Penny's negligence would make in the size of the jury's award?

3. Whom should the restaurant manager and company look to for guidance on property serving temperatures and techniques? Could you defend this source in court?

minimal amounts, such as a spice blend, or if used as a processing aid in the preparation of a food product, such as peanut oil and soy lectin.

States have also crafted legislation related to food allergies. Massachusetts, for example, requires restaurants to educate their staff on the issue of food allergies, and requires managers to earn certification in a food allergy training course. With the growing notoriety and outbreaks of food allergies, it is likely that more and more regulations will be passed in the future. As a manager, be sure to check with your state laws to make sure that you are in compliance with any regulations that have been, or will be, adopted by your state. Additionally, it is always a good practice to disclose ingredients that are known to cause allergic reactions so that guests can make informed choices. Be sure to train your employees about allergies and to be sensitive to guests with allergies and be patient with their inquires about menu ingredients.

If an incident occurs that involves how a food was served, rather than what was served, the manager should complete an incident report at the earliest opportunity. (Refer back to the Incident Report Form in Figure 9.2.)

12.2 TRUTH IN MENU LAWS

As a hospitality manager, you have a right to advertise your food and beverage products in a way that casts them in their best light. If your hamburgers contain eight ounces of ground beef, you are free to promote that attribute in your advertising, your menu, and as part of your server's verbal descriptions. You are not free, however, to misrepresent your products. To do so is a violation of what has come to be commonly known as *truth in menu laws*. These laws, which could perhaps better be described as "accuracy in menus," are designed to protect consumers from fraudulent food and beverage claims. Many foodservice operators believe that truth in menu laws are recent legislation. They are not. In fact, the federal government, as well as many local communities, have a long history of regulating food advertisement and sales, as can be seen in Figure 12.3.

LEGALESE

Truth in menu laws: The collective name given to various laws and regulations that have been implemented to ensure accuracy in the wording on menus.

2002

The Organic Foods Production Act and the National Organic Program (NOP) are intended to assure consumers that the organic foods they purchase are produced, processed, and certified to consistent national organic standards. The labeling requirements of the new program apply to raw, fresh products and processed foods that contain organic ingredients. Foods that are sold, labeled, or represented as organic will have to be produced and processed in accordance with the NOP standards.

2003

To help consumers choose heart-healthy foods, the Department of Health and Human Services announces that FDA will require **food labels to include trans fat content,** the first substantive change to the nutrition facts panel on foods since the label was changed in 1993.

2004

Passage of the **Food Allergy Labeling and Consumer Protection Act** requires the labeling of any food that contains a protein derived from any one of the following foods that, as a group, account for the vast majority of food allergies: peanuts, soybeans, cow's milk, eggs, fish, crustacean shellfish, tree nuts, and wheat.

Figure 12.3 Laws regulating food labeling and advertising. *(See page 478 for complete figure.)*

⟩⟩ ANALYZE THE SITUATION 12.3

JEFFERY AND LATISHA WILLIAMS arranged a fiftieth anniversary party for Latisha's parents. They reserved a private room at the Tannery, an upscale steak and seafood house located two miles from their suburban home. The Williams hosted a total of ten people. Unfortunately, the service they received from the restaurant staff was not very good. When the check arrived, Mr. Williams noticed that a 15 percent charge had been added to the total price of the bill. When he inquired about the charge, his server informed him that it was the restaurant's policy to assess a 15 percent "tip" to the bill of all parties larger than eight persons. The policy, explained the server, was not printed on the menu, but was to be verbally relayed anytime a guest made a reservation for more than eight people. Mr. Williams replied that the reservation was made by his secretary, and she mentioned no such policy when she informed Mr. Williams of the restaurant's availability.

Mr. Williams refused to pay the extra charge claiming that it should be he, not the restaurant, who determined the amount of the gratuity, if any. When the restaurant manager arrived on the scene, he informed Mr. Williams that the server had misspoken and that the extra charge was in fact a "service charge," and not a tip. Mr. Williams still refused to pay the added charge.

1. Does Mr. Williams owe the extra 15 percent to the restaurant?

2. Does it matter whether the surcharge is called a gratuity or a service charge? How would that be determined?

3. What should the restaurant do to avoid similar problems in the future?

The various truth in menu laws currently in effect run to thousands of pages and are overseen by dozens of agencies and administrative entities; thereby taking the labeling of food to much greater degrees of accuracy. Though these laws are constantly being revised, it is possible for a foodservice operator to stay up to date and in compliance with them. The method is relatively straightforward, and the key is honesty in menu claims, in regard to both the price that is charged and the food that is served.

Certainly, menus should accurately reflect the price to be charged to the customer. If one dozen oysters are to be sold for a given price, one dozen oysters should be delivered on the plate, and the price charged on the bill should match that on the menu. Likewise, if the menu price is to include a mandatory service charge or cover charge, these must be brought to the attention of the guest. If a restaurant advertises a prix fixe dinner with four courses and a choice of entrees, the guest should be told the price of the dinner, which courses are included, and the types of entrees he or she may choose from.

"Accuracy in menu" involves a great deal more than honestly and precisely stating a price. It also entails being careful when describing many food attributes, including the preparation style, ingredients, origin, portion sizes, and health benefits. Because this area is so complex, and because consumers increasingly demand more accurate information from restaurants, the National Restaurant Association (NRA) and many state associations have produced educational material designed to assist foodservice operators as they write and prepare menus. Called *A Practical Guide to the Nutrition Labeling Laws*, this publication is written specifically for the restaurant industry; it outlines everything you need to know about nutrition claims you can make for your menu items. You can secure a copy for a modest charge from the NRA. As discussed earlier, food allergies are another area of concern for hospitality operators. For more information, please visit www.cfsan.fda.gov/~dms/wh-alrgy.html. In addition, the federal government issues food description standards that can be of great assistance. You should pay particular attention to the following areas when you begin writing the menu for your own foodservice establishment.

Preparation Style

Under federal law, certain food items and preparation techniques must be carried out in a very precise way, if that item or technique is to be included on a menu. In many cases, the federal government, through either the Food and Drug Administration or the U.S. Department of Agriculture, has produced guidelines for accurately describing menu items. Consider the following common items and the specificity with which their preparation style is determined by federal guidelines:

Grilled: Items must be grilled, not just mechanically produced with "grill marks," then steamed before service.

Homemade: The product must be prepared on premises, not commercially baked.

Fresh: The product cannot be frozen, canned, dried, or processed.

Breaded shrimp: This includes only the commercial species, Pineaus. The tail portion of the shrimp of the commercial species must comprise 50 percent of the total weight of a finished product labeled "breaded shrimp." To be labeled "lightly breaded shrimp," the shrimp content must be 65 percent by weight of the finished product.

Kosher-style: A product flavored or seasoned in a particular manner; this description has no religious significance.

Kosher: Products that have been prepared or processed to meet the requirements of the orthodox Jewish religion.

Baked ham: A ham that has been heated in an oven for a specified period of time. Many brands of smoked ham are not oven-baked.

It is important that your menu accurately reflect the preparation techniques used in your kitchen, not only because the law requires you to but also to help ensure your operation's credibility with the public.

Ingredients

Perhaps no area of menu accuracy is more important than the listing of ingredients that actually go into making up a food item. Although restaurants are not currently required to divulge their ingredient lists (recipes) to their guests, there are specific situations when the ingredients listed on a menu must precisely match those used to make the item. If, for example, an operator offers Kahlua and cream as a drink on a bar menu, the drink must be made with both the liqueur and the dairy product stated. Kahlua is a specific brand of Mexican coffee liqueur, and cream is defined by the federal government as a product made from milk with a minimum fat content of 18 percent. Of course, a bar manager is free to offer a different, less expensive coffee liqueur to guests, and use half-and-half (which contains 12 percent milkfat) instead of cream, but the drink could not be called a Kahlua and cream. To do so is unethical at best and illegal in most areas.

Whenever a specific ingredient is listed on a menu, that item, and that item alone, should be served. For example, if the menu says maple syrup, then colored table syrup or maple-flavored syrup should not be served. This is especially important when listing brand-name products on a menu. (Recall the discussion of trademarks and brand-name items from Chapter 6, "Legally Managing Property.")

If substitutions of the menu items must be made, the guest should be informed of those substitutions before ordering. As consumers' interest in their own health continues to rise, foodservice operators can expect more involvement and consumer activism in the area of accurate ingredient listings.

Recently, in light of the growing number of obesity-related health issues in the United States, municipal localities and state legislatures have begun to take a stance on what ingredients should not be included in dishes served to the public. Although this issue remains very controversial, these entities, most notably California, have created bans on certain ingredients, and are not allowing them to be served to the public. Specifically, California has legislated a ban on artificial trans fats in restaurants. Trans fats are a type of unsaturated fat that is mostly used to increase the longevity of food products. However, trans fat intake has been related to several dire health issues, such as: coronary artery disease, Alzheimer's, breast cancer, diabetes, and infertility. Hospitality managers need to be aware that such laws may exist, and while there are many opponents that argue the unconstitutionality of the bans on multiple grounds, if your state or local government entity has enacted a law or ordinance that bans certain ingredients, you should be mindful of compliance, unless you wish to pay a fine and copious amounts of legal fees. To learn more about artificial trans fats, and the growing number of laws banning them, go to publichealthlawcenter.org/sites/default/files/resources/phlc-policy-trans-fat.pdf.

Continuing the trend toward bettering the nutrition and health of the American public, legislators have drafted proposed legislation that seeks to set requirements for labeling the nutritional content of food on menus. To read further on the subject of menu labeling laws, go to www.hospitalitylawyer.com/Newsletters/feb11beveragenews.html.

Origin

For many menu items, the origin of the product or its ingredients is very important. Many consumers prefer Colorado trout to generic trout, Washington apples to those from other states, and Bluepoint (Long Island) oysters to those from other areas. It can be tempting to use these terms to describe similar menu items from other places, which may cost less to purchase. But to do so is fraudulent. Moreover, it sends the wrong message to employees who know of the substitutions, as well the guests who ultimately are deprived of the items they thought they purchased. It is also illegal.

Size

Product size is, in many cases, the most important factor in determining how much a guest is willing to pay for a menu item. For example, a steakhouse could offer different cuts of beef and price them appropriately according to size. An 8-ounce steak might sell for $17.95, while the 12-ounce might sell for $23.95 and the 16- ounce for $25.95.

Other types of food products may be harder to associate with precise quantities. For example, "large" East Coast oysters must, by law, contain no more than 160 to 210 oysters per gallon, while "large" Pacific Coast oysters, by law, may contain not more than 64 oysters per gallon. Nevertheless, whether it is the size of eggs sold in a breakfast special, or the use of the term "jumbo" to refer to shrimp, specifying size on a menu is an area that must be approached with the understanding that the law will expect you to deliver what you promise. A simple rule of thumb for avoiding difficulties in this area is: If you say it, serve it.

Health Benefits

For many years, the only menu item most restaurants offered as a healthy one was the "diet" plate, generally consisting of cottage cheese, fruit, perhaps some grilled poultry, and a lettuce leaf. It is no surprise that today's health-conscious consumer demands more. In response, restaurants generally have begun to provide greater detail about the nutritional value of their menu items. The federal government, however, issues very strict guidelines on what you can and cannot say about your menu offerings. Thus, truth in menu laws relate not just to what is charged and what is served, but also to the nutritional claims made by foodservice operators.

According to FDA estimates, well over half of all printed menus in the United States contain some type of nutritional or health benefit claim. There are two types of claims generally found on menus: nutrient claims and health benefit claims. Nutrient claims contain specific information about a menu item's nutrient content. When a dish is described on a menu as being "low-fat" or "high-fiber," the restaurateur is making a nutrient claim. Health benefit claims are claims that do not describe the content of specific menu items, but instead show a relationship between a type of food or menu item and a particular health condition. For example, some restaurants include a note on their menu stating that eating foods low in saturated fat and cholesterol can reduce the risk of heart disease. Other restaurants identify nutritionally modified dishes on their menu using terms such as "heart-healthy" or "light," or use symbols such as a red heart to signify that a dish meets general dietary recommendations.

The Food and Drug Administration (FDA) has issued regulations to ensure that foodservice operators who make health benefit claims on their menus can indeed back them up. These regulations, published in the August 2, 1996, Federal Register, apply the Nutrition Labeling and Education Act (NLEA) of 1990 to restaurant items that carry a claim about a food's nutritional content or health benefits. All eating establishments must comply with these regulations.

Following are two examples of FDA regulations surrounding the use of common menu terms.

Nutrient Claim

A low-sodium, low-fat, low-cholesterol item must not contain amounts greater than FDA guidelines for the term "low." Light, or "lite" items must have fewer calories and less fat than the food to which it is being compared (e.g., "light Italian" dressing). Some restaurants have used the term "lighter fare" to identify dishes containing smaller portions. However, that use of the term must be specified on the menu.

Health Benefit Claim

To be considered "heart-healthy," for example, a menu item must meet one of the following conditions:

■ The item is low in saturated fat, cholesterol, and fat, and provides without fortification significant amounts of one or more of six key nutrients. This claim will indicate that a diet low in saturated fat and cholesterol may reduce the risk of heart disease.

■ The item is low in saturated fat, cholesterol, and fat; provides without fortification significant amounts of one or more of six key nutrients; and is a significant source of soluble fiber (found in fruits, vegetables, and grain products). This claim will indicate that a diet low in saturated fat and cholesterol, and rich in fruits, vegetables, and grain products that contain some types of fiber (particularly soluble fiber), may reduce the risk of heart disease.

When printing health benefit claims on a menu, further information about the claim should be available somewhere on the menu, or be available on request. Restaurants do not have to provide nutrition information about dishes on the menu that have no nutrient content or health claim attached to them. The FDA permits restaurants to back up their menu claims with a "reasonable" base, such as cookbooks, databases, or other secondhand sources that provide nutrition information. (By contrast, the FDA requires food manufacturers to adhere to a much more stringent set of standards. Many food manufacturers perform chemical analyses to determine the nutritional value of their products and to ensure that the information about their product printed on the food label is true.)

The enforcement of truth in menu regulations is undertaken by state and local public health departments, which have direct jurisdiction over restaurants by monitoring their food safety and sanitation practices. The general public can also act as a regulator in this area. In today's litigious society, a restaurant manager should have any menu containing nutritional or health claims reviewed by both an attorney and a dietician.

In addition to carefully developing menus, truth in menu laws require that restaurants truthfully and accurately specify what their servers say about menu items, as well as how their food products are promoted or shown in advertisements, photographs, and promotions.

General Nutrition and Obesity

There is no denying the rising numbers of obesity, morbid obesity, and obesity-related diseases in the United States. Although much debate exists as to what the cause(s) of this increase is, the fact remains that more and more people are dying from obesity-related illness each year. Recently, many states have begun to tackle the obesity problem with regulations that are meant to encourage healthy eating habits and discourage unhealthy ones. You have already learned about one of the ways governments are regulating to promote healthy lifestyles—ingredient bans. However, there are many other ideas circulating throughout legislatures that a hospitality manager needs to be aware of. For example, the so-called Happy Meal laws seek to prevent including toys alongside food that does not meet certain nutritional standards, restrict the use of food stamps to pay for drinks with a high sugar content, and require fast-food restaurants to post the caloric content of food items on the menu.

Regulations enacted to tackle obesity are a quickly moving, controversial, and murky area of the law. Often these laws are newly formed, and there is not much, if any, precedent on which the laws are based; thus, it is difficult to say which laws will be long lasting and which ones will be deemed unconstitutional. However, it is certain that these issues will not go away soon, so it would be wise for a hospitality manager to stay current on any obesity-related movements and legislation.

Search the Web 12.1

Visit www.bk.com.

1. Select: Menu and Nutrition.

2. Select: Any item from the "Select an Item" menu.

3. Review your selected item's nutritional content, then answer the following:

    a. What are the nine nutritional categories about which this company supplies information?

    b. Do you think restaurateurs have a duty of care to provide this level of nutritional information? Why or why not?

    c. What do you think the future holds for the level of nutritional information that foodservice operators will be required to supply?

12.3 SERVING ALCOHOL

Throughout history, alcoholic beverages have played many roles. In some societies, they were thought to possess magical or holy powers. They were also an important part of medical treatment well into the 1800s. In various cultures, alcoholic beverages were considered a basic and essential food. Because beer, ale, and wine did not carry the diseases associated with drinking contaminated water, they became an accepted part of everyday meals. They were particularly valued by travelers, who had to be especially cautious about contracting strange diseases. In fact, most early taverns, as well as hotels, considered the service of alcohol to be a basic traveler's amenity. By the time the first settlers left for the New World, taverns were essential social centers, providing drink, food, and sometimes lodging. The early settlers brought this tradition with them to the New World. In the vast wilderness of the new continent, taverns took on new importance. By the mid-1800s, the largest taverns became the first hotels.

In 1920, Congress passed the Eighteenth Amendment to the Constitution, which prohibited the manufacture, sale, transportation, and importing of alcoholic beverages. The amendment was effective only in stopping the legal manufacture, sale, and transportation of liquor. Many people still drank, but they drank poor-tasting, illegally produced (and in some cases unmerchantable) alcoholic beverages. In 1933, Congress recognized the failure of prohibition and repealed the act with the passage of the Twenty-First Amendment. However, even after the appeal, the consumption of alcohol was not quickly reaccepted into American society.

The Twenty-First Amendment gave individual states, counties, towns, and precincts the authority to control the sale and use of alcoholic beverages within their jurisdiction. As a result, a variety of alcohol-related laws exist throughout the United States today. As a hospitality manager, it is your responsibility to know and carefully follow the applicable laws for your state and community. If you manage a facility that serves alcohol, you should have copies of the state and local laws regulating the service of alcohol in your community.

Privilege of Alcohol Service

Alcohol is a drug. Historically it was used, like other drugs, to treat disease. And like other drugs, it is also a substance to which people can become addicted. Despite the fact that alcohol often creates a euphoric state in the user, it is a *depressant*.

LEGALESE

Depressant: A substance that lowers the rate of vital body activities.

Other depressants include barbiturates, tranquilizers, quaaludes, Librium, and Valium. Interestingly, society very tightly regulates the dispensing of most depressants. Pharmacists must go to school in order to earn the right to legally dispense many types of depressants. In most cases, a depressant can be requested from a pharmacist only after presenting a prescription from a licensed medical doctor. Alcohol, by contrast, can be served by any individual over a state-specified age, who may have had little, if any, mandatory training prior to being employed as a bartender.

All that said, it is important to remember that no hospitality manager has a "right" to serve alcohol; rather, it is a privilege that is carefully regulated by law, and one that cannot be taken lightly.

There is no alcoholic beverage that is safer or more moderate than another. According to the federal government's dietary guidelines, the alcohol content in standard servings (drinks) of beer (12 ounces), table wine (5 ounces), and distilled spirits (1½ ounces in a mixed drink) is equal. Thus, the service of all types of alcoholic beverages must be treated in the same serious manner. Put another way, the major factor in controlling the risks associated with serving alcohol is to realize that it is not what you serve, but how much you serve that is most important.

The amount of alcohol consumed by an individual in a specific time period is measured by the individual's *blood alcohol concentration (BAC)*. Many factors, in addition to the number of drinks consumed, influence the BAC of an individual. Because the liver digests alcohol at the slow, constant rate of about one drink per hour, a 160-pound man may typically reach a BAC of .08 (or 8 percent) by drinking two to four drinks in one hour, which is legally drunk in all 50 states. Ten drinks would produce a BAC of approximately .25 or higher.. Figure 12.4 details some of the effects felt by individuals with increasing BACs.

Alcohol affects different individuals in a variety of ways. Lawmakers commonly use specific BACs to define legal *intoxication*. In October 2000, the federal government passed legislation to establish a .08 BAL as the standard in all states. Although the federal government cannot directly force the states to enact the standard, the threat of withholding federal highway construction funds from any state that did not utilize the .08 standard pretty much guaranteed that all states would comply. Unfortunately, hospitality managers do not have the ability, at this point in time, to easily measure the BAC of their guests. Still, the law prohibits serving alcohol to an intoxicated guest. Thus, a hospitality manager must rely on his or her own knowledge of the law, operational procedures, and staff training programs to avoid doing so.

Alcohol is sold in an amazing variety of hospitality locations. Bars, amusement parks, golf courses, sporting events, and restaurants are just a few of the venues where a guest may legally buy alcohol. Each state regulates the sale of alcohol in the manner it sees fit. Regional differences do exist, but in all cases, those who sell alcohol are required to apply for and obtain a *liquor license* or liquor permit to do so.

Recall our discussion of alcohol regulation from Chapter 2, "Government Agencies That Impact the Hospitality Industry." Every state has an alcoholic beverage commission (ABC), which grants licenses and regulates the sale of alcohol. At the local level, some cities or counties also have a local alcohol control board that works with the state agency to grant licenses and enforce the law. As a hospitality manager, you should request a copy of your state and city's regulations.

LEGALESE

Blood alcohol concentration (BAC): A measurement, expressed in a percentage, of the concentration level of alcohol in the bloodstream. Also known as blood alcohol content or blood alcohol level, or BAL.

LEGALESE

Intoxication: A condition in which an individual's BAC reaches legally established levels. These levels are not uniform across the United States. An intoxicated person may not sell or purchase alcohol, nor operate a motor vehicle.

LEGALESE

Liquor license: A permit issued by a state that allows for the sale and/or service of alcoholic beverages. The entity holding the license is known as the licensee.

Figure 12.4 Effects of increasing blood alcohol concentrations (BACs).

Effects of Increasing BALs	
BAL Level	*Effect*
.06–.10	Significant decrease in reaction time and visual abilities
.11–.15	Slurred speech and volatile emotions
.22–.25	Staggering, difficulty talking, blurred vision
.40	Induced coma
.50	Cessation of breathing and heart failure

Though different types of liquor licenses exist to meet the needs of various types of businesses, they can be divided into two general categories:

1. Licenses for on-premises consumption (required for restaurants, taverns, clubs, etc.)
2. Licenses for off-premises consumption (required for liquor stores and other markets that carry alcohol)

Various types of on-premises licenses also exist, such as a beer-only license, a wine license (which may or may not include beer, but does not include mixed drinks), and a liquor license (which includes, beer, wine, and mixed drinks). In most states, liquor licenses are issued for a period of one year, at the end of which the establishment must apply for a license renewal.

Once an establishment has been granted a liquor license, it is required to operate in accordance with all rules and regulations established by state and local ABCs. Some common areas of operation that are regulated by the states include:

- *Permitted hours of sale:* Local communities may prohibit the sale of alcohol after a specified time of day. Some communities have "blue laws," which restrict or prohibit the sale of alcohol on Sundays.

- *Approved changes for expansion or equipment purchases:* Before a liquor license is issued, the state or local ABC may inspect the applicant's establishment prior to granting approval. Once a premise has been inspected, any further changes to the size of the establishment or the equipment used must first be approved by the state ABC. In some states, establishments that serve alcohol are prohibited from operating in close proximity to a school or a church.

- *Maintaining records:* Establishments that sell alcohol must keep detailed records of the amount of alcohol purchased each day, information on the vendors from which alcohol is purchased (including the vendor's license and other business information), and the establishment's daily sales of alcoholic beverages. A state ABC will perform random audits to determine the accuracy of the information received.

- *Methods of operation:* As discussed previously, employees working as waiters, servers, or in any other capacity where they may be required to handle alcoholic beverages must be above the state's specified minimum age for serving alcohol. Other states have regulations restricting the types of promotions and advertising that a bar can undertake.

In addition to licensing, special rules may apply to specific situations in which alcohol is sold. In each case, however, its service is tightly regulated. Figure 12.5 is an example of one such regulation. Note how precisely the state of Connecticut regulates the sale of alcohol from minibars located in guest hotel rooms.

In order to combat increasing alcohol-related injuries and deaths, many states have enacted happy-hour laws, which are meant to decrease the excessive consumption of alcohol. These statutes vary from state to state, but they all contain some, if not all, of the following prohibitions:

- Distribution of free alcoholic beverages
- Providing additional servings of alcohol until the previous serving has been consumed
- The sale of alcoholic beverages at a reduced price during specified days or times
- Unlimited beverages—the sale of alcoholic beverages at a fixed price during a fixed period of time
- Increasing the volume of alcohol in a beverage without increasing the price
- Giving alcoholic beverages as a prize

States are very careful when granting licenses to sell liquor, and they are generally very aggressive in revoking the licenses of operations that fail to adhere to the

---

Connecticut Permit Law

Sec. 30-37i. Hotel guest bar permit

a) A hotel guest bar permit, available to a hotel permittee, shall allow the retail sale of alcoholic liquor located in registered hotel guest rooms. The annual fee for a hotel guest bar permit shall be fifty dollars for each hotel room equipped for the retail sale of alcoholic liquor. (b) A hotel guest bar shall: (1) be accessible only by key, magnetic card, or similar device provided by the hotel to a registered guest twenty-one years of age or older; and (2) restocked no earlier than nine o'clock A.M. and no later than one o'clock A.M. (c) The Department of Consumer Protection shall adopt regulations, in accordance with the provisions of Chapter 54, for the operation of hotel guest bars.

Figure 12.5 Connecticut permit law.

---

state's required procedures for selling alcohol. In most states, a liquor license can be revoked as a result of:

- Frequent incidents of fighting, disorderly conduct, or generally creating a public nuisance
- Allowing prostitution or solicitation on the premises
- Allowing the sale or use of drugs and narcotics
- Illegal adult entertainment, such as outlawed forms of nude dancing
- Failure to maintain required records
- Sale of alcohol to minors

In some states, representatives from the ABC will conduct unannounced inspections of the premises where alcohol is served and/or intentionally send minors into an establishment to see if the operator will serve them.

Liability Associated with Alcohol Service

Because alcohol can so significantly change the behavior of those who over-indulge in it, society is left to grapple with the question of who should be responsible for the sometimes negative effects of alcohol consumption. In cases where intoxicated individuals have caused damage or injury, either to themselves or others, society has responded with laws that place some portion of responsibility on those who sell or serve alcohol.

Every state has enacted laws to prevent the sale of alcohol to minors, to those who are intoxicated, and to individuals known to be alcoholics. Figure 12.6 is an example of how one state, Texas, has developed laws to discourage minors from drinking and to penalize those who would serve them. It is presented here as an example of how seriously society takes the sale of alcohol to minors.

To understand the complex laws that regulate liability for illegally serving alcohol, it is important to understand that there can be at least three parties involved in an incident resulting from the illegal sale of alcohol.

- *First party:* The individual buying and/or consuming the alcohol.
- *Second party:* The establishment selling or dispensing the alcohol.
- *Third party:* An individual not directly involved in a specific situation having to do with the sale or consumption of alcohol.

There is a misconception by some that the common law did not hold an organization that served alcohol liable for serving an intoxicated person. That is not the case. Under common law, a facility that negligently served alcohol to an obviously

Minor in Possession: If caught with alcohol, a minor will be charged with a Class C misdemeanor. Maximum fine of $500, mandatory attendance at an alcohol awareness class, 8–40 hours community service and 30–180 days loss of driving privilege.

Minor Driving While Intoxicated (DWI): Zero BAL allowed for minor drivers. If caught, a minor will be charged with a Class C misdemeanor. Maximum fine of $500, mandatory attendance at an alcohol awareness class, 20–40 hours community service, and 60 days loss of driving privilege.

Possession of Fake Identification: If caught, a minor will be charged with a Class C misdemeanor. Maximum fine of $500, mandatory attendance at an alcohol awareness class, 8–12 hours community service, and 30 days loss of driver's license for first offense.

Adult Purchase of Alcohol for a Minor: A Class B misdemeanor. Maximum fine of $2,000, confinement in jail for up to 180 days, or both.

Bar That Sells Alcohol to a Minor: Bar owner to receive administrative penalties of 7–20 day liquor license suspension, and a fine not to exceed $25,000 for each day of the suspension. The bartender or employee who sold the alcohol to the minor faces a Class A misdemeanor charge with a maximum punishment of one year in jail and a $4,000 fine.

Figure 12.6 Summary of selected Texas laws that address minors and alcohol.

intoxicated guest could be sued for negligence if harm came to the guest. What is relatively new in many jurisdictions is that *third-party liability* can also be imposed on those that serve alcohol.

Social Host

Historically, courts in the United States have not found that those who host parties where alcohol is served should be liable for the subsequent actions of their intoxicated guests. While this position, like all areas of social law, may change someday, the current feeling of most courts is that a social host has no common law duty to generally avoid making alcohol available to an adult guest.

There are several reasons why a social host is not held to the same standard of care responsibilities as a licensed provider of alcohol. Consider the case of Brad Seeley. Brad is a real estate agent who hosts a party in his home for past customers and potential clients. If you analyze the situation Brad has created by hosting this party, you will see that:

1. Brad's guests will likely make their own decisions on how much to drink.
2. It is unlikely Brad has acquired the knowledge and training to detect those who have become intoxicated.
3. He has no effective means of controlling the number of drinks consumed by his guests.
4. If large numbers of guests attend his party, it will be extremely difficult for Brad to know who, if anyone, is becoming intoxicated.

Despite the court's position on social host liability, the slogan "Friends don't let friends drive drunk," is a good rule to live by. As a responsible party host, Brad should be cautious about allowing his guests unlimited alcohol consumption.

Although courts have not been inclined to impose a duty of care on a social host providing alcohol to a guest, they are less clear on the issue of whether a social host has a common law duty not to allow minors to consume alcohol. A social host does have a responsibility to see to it that they themselves do not serve minors alcohol. Because serving alcohol to a minor is illegal, even a social host could be accused of negligence should he or she allow it.

LEGALESE

Third-party liability: The two areas of liability theory that a hospitality manager should be aware of focus on the duties of a host who holds a party where alcohol is served, and that of an establishment licensed to sell alcohol.

The most important thing for you, as a hospitality manager, to remember about social host liability is that the courts will not view your operation as that of a social host. As a license holder, you and your operation will be held responsible for the service of alcohol in a very different way.

Dram Shop

LEGALESE

Dram shop: A name given to a variety of state laws establishing a liquor licensee's third-party liability.

Prior to the 1990s, most courts did not hold those who were licensed to serve liquor responsible for the damages sustained by a third party that resulted from a customer's intoxication. Today, nearly every state has established *dram shop* laws that impose third-party liability on those who sell or serve alcohol.

Under the dram shop legislation instituted in most states, liquor licenses are responsible for harm and damages to both first and third parties, subject to any contributory negligence offsets by these parties, if three circumstances exist:

1. The individual served was intoxicated.
2. The individual was a clear danger to him- or herself and others.
3. Intoxication was the cause of the subsequent harm.

It is important to understand that there can be criminal liability as well as civil liability when alcohol is sold irresponsibly. Civil liability, under state dram shop laws, could require an alcohol establishment to pay for various expenses to injured or deceased parties, such as medical bills, property damage, lost wages, monetary awards to surviving family members, awards for pain and suffering, and punitive damages. Criminal liability could subject a hospitality operator to a revocation of the liquor license, severe fines, and/or jail time.

Figure 12.7 is an example of the dram shop law for the state of Connecticut. Note the wording that holds alcohol servers responsible for injuries to third parties, the amount of damages they could be liable to pay, and the time limits placed

---

Connecticut Dram Shop Law

Sec. 30-102. Dram Shop Act; liquor seller liable for damage by intoxicated person.

If any person, by himself or his agent, sells any alcoholic liquor to an intoxicated person, and such purchaser, in consequence of such intoxication, thereafter injures the person or property of another, such seller shall pay just damages to the person injured, up to the amount of twenty thousand dollars, or to persons injured in consequence of such intoxication up to an aggregate amount of fifty thousand dollars, to be recovered in an action under this section, provided the aggrieved person or persons shall give written notice to such seller within sixty days of the occurrence of such injury to person or property of his or their intention to bring an action under this section. In computing such sixty-day period, the time between the death or incapacity of any aggrieved person and the appointment of an executor, administrator, conservator or guardian of his estate shall be excluded, except that the time so excluded shall not exceed one hundred twenty days. Such notice shall specify the time, the date and the person to whom such sale was made, the name and address of the person injured or whose property was damaged, and the time, date and place where the injury to person or property occurred. No action under the provisions of this section shall be brought but within one year from the date of the act or omission complained of.

Figure 12.7 Connecticut dram shop law.

on filing a lawsuit. Connecticut is one of several states that places a monetary limit on the amount of damages a hospitality operator would have to pay if found liable. Figure 12.8 summarizes the civil liability for a licensee and a social host with respect to first and third parties who have been harmed by the irresponsible and illegal service of alcohol.

Alcohol Liability

	Licensee Common Law	Licensee Dram Shop	Social Host Common Law
First-Party Liability	Yes	Yes	No
Third-Party Liability	No	Yes	No
Liable If Minors Served	Yes	Yes	Yes, in most cases

Figure 12.8 Alcohol liability.

≫ ANALYZE THE SITUATION 12.4

MARK HADLEY ENTERED THE Squirrel Cage Tavern at 4:00 P.M. on a Thursday afternoon. He sat down at the bar and, according to eyewitnesses, uttered just a single word when approached by the bartender. The one word was "draft."

As the bartender had only one brand of beer on draft, she silently pulled the beer, handed it to Mr. Hadley, and accepted the $5 bill he offered in payment. Mr. Hadley left the bar some 15 minutes later having never said another word to anyone, leaving the change from his $5 on the bar counter.

Subsequently, Mr. Hadley was involved in an auto accident in which a ten-year-old boy was rendered sightless. The boy's parents sued the Squirrel Cage Tavern and another operation, the Dulcimer Bar. The Dulcimer Bar was sued because Mr. Hadley had consumed ten beers in three hours at that establishment prior to leaving it and driving to the Squirrel Cage.

Attorneys for the Squirrel Cage argued that their client could not have known of Mr. Hadley's condition when he entered their establishment, and that they were indeed acting responsibly in that they served him only one beer. Attorneys for the injured boy countered that the Squirrel Cage served alcohol to an intoxicated person, a violation of state law, and thus under the state's dram shop legislation was responsible for Mr. Hadley's subsequent actions.

1. Did the Squirrel Cage violate the liquor laws of its state?

2. Did the Squirrel Cage bartender act responsibly in the service of alcohol to Mr. Hadley? Did she act differently from bartenders in similar situations?

3. What should the owner of the Squirrel Cage do in the future, if anything, to minimize the chances of reoccurrence?

Training for Responsible Service

In many states, legislatures have sought to limit the liability of those who serve alcohol by enacting regulations that insulate, to some degree, those establishments that commit to thoroughly training their employees who are involved in the sale of alcohol. In most jurisdictions, responsible alcohol server training will be either mandated or strongly encouraged. The absence of such training would, without doubt, be a significant hindrance should you ever face a lawsuit that accuses your operation of irresponsible alcohol service. The National Restaurant Association, the American Hotel and Motel Association, and many private organizations provide excellent training materials that can help make your training task easier. Training for Intervention Procedures (TIPS) is one of the most well-recognized responsible server programs. Developed by Dr. Morris Chafetz, founding director of the National Institute of Alcohol Abuse and Alcoholism, TIPS incorporates a common-sense approach to serving alcohol responsibly in a variety of settings. Dr. Chafetz is also the author of the book *Drink Moderately and Live Longer: Understanding the Good of Alcohol* (Scarborough House, May 1995).

Search the Web 12.2

Log on to www.hospitalitylawyer.com.

1. Select: Solutions Store.

2. Select: Alcohol Server Training from the education and training online programs menu.

  a. What are the advantages of online training?

  b. What are the disadvantages of online training?

Regardless of whether you choose to create your own responsible server program, or to purchase and implement one of the many available on the market, you should carefully review your program to ensure that it meets five criteria:

1. *It is an approved training course.* The training program you use will, in all likelihood, need to be approved by the agency that monitors alcohol service in your area. If you create your own training program, it too must be submitted for approval. The best of the nationally available training programs will be preapproved for use in your area, but it is your responsibility to make sure that the one you use is. Never purchase or use a training program that has not been approved. A jury could perceive the use of such a program as an indication that management was not serious about responsible alcohol server training.

2. *It explains the nature of alcohol's absorption into the bloodstream.* A basic understanding of how alcohol is absorbed in the body is crucial for serving responsibly. A variety of factors affect an individual's BAL. These include:

- *Body weight:* The larger the body, the more the alcohol is diluted. Because of this, given the same amount of alcohol, a large person will be less affected by alcohol than a smaller person.
- *Food consumption:* The consumption of food slows the rate at which alcohol is absorbed into the system. In addition, different foods affect absorption rates in different ways.
- *Amount of sleep:* Tired people feel the effects of alcohol more than those who are well rested.
- *Age:* Younger people feel the effects of alcohol more quickly than older people. But the eyesight of older customers is more affected by drinking.
- *Health:* The liver plays an important part in removing alcohol from the system. Customers with liver problems are more apt to become intoxicated.
- *Medication:* Many medications do not mix well with alcohol, and in some instances mixtures can be very dangerous.
- *General metabolism:* Some people's bodies convert alcohol faster than others do.

3. *It extensively instructs servers in the methods of checking for legal identification, as well as for spotting false IDs.* Often, minors who wish to drink secure false identification documents in order to gain access to establishments where they can buy alcoholic beverages. This puts the beverage manager in a difficult legal position. Although a beverage manager is not expected to know whether a minor is presenting false identification, he or she is required to use reasonable care in spotting those who attempt to use a false ID. Because false ID documents are in such widespread use, a major component of any responsible alcohol server program should be instruction in how to identify false IDs. Make sure that your training materials address the following areas:

- Alteration of type style, including font and point size
- Cut-and-paste techniques
- Physical identification/picture match
- Relamination detection
- Random information verification (address, Social Security number, etc.)
- Listing of qualifying ID documents

4. *It emphasizes early intervention when confronted with possible overconsumption by guests.* It is clearly against the law to serve an intoxicated person. The difficulty, of course, lies in identifying when a person is intoxicated. The number of drinks (and/or the amount of alcohol in multishot drinks) served in a given time period gives an indication of possible BAC, but as we have seen, many factors affect BAC. A good, responsible, server-training program will teach your servers to note the observable behavioral changes that occur with advancing stages of intoxication. When these are noted, there are specific techniques that can be employed to limit the quantity of alcohol served to such guests and, if necessary, to refuse service completely.

5. *It provides for documentation of training effectiveness.* It is not enough for employees to attend responsible service training sessions. They must demonstrate a mastery of the material as well. The best of the training

materials on the market have examination components to test trainee competence. The tests should be both reliable and valid. The examinations should be scored by an independent source, and the results should be reported to management in a timely fashion. If you must defend your use of a particular program in court, you almost certainly will be defending its effectiveness as well. The inability to demonstrate your responsible server training results might damage your ability to prove that you have conducted your training in a responsible manner.

≫ ANALYZE THE SITUATION 12.5

MICHELE RODGERS ENTERED THE Golden Spike Bar and Grill on a Friday night at approximately 10:30 P.M. At the door, she was stopped briefly by the bar's security guard. The guard, Luis Sargota, inspected Michele's photo ID, as he had been trained to do during the one-hour orientation class he attended on his first day of work.

The photo ID presented by Michele showed her age to be 21 years and three months. The photo on the picture was clearly her own. She was not asked to remove the ID from her wallet. Michele entered the bar and, over a period of three hours, consumed five fuzzy navel drinks, each containing approximately 1.5 ounces of 80-proof alcohol served with fruit juice.

Upon leaving the bar at 1:30 A.M., Michele was involved in a traffic accident that seriously injured a man who was driving home after working the late shift at a local factory. The family of the injured man sued Michele and the Golden Spike when it was discovered that Michele was, in fact, only 20 years old, and thus was not of legal age to drink alcohol.

The attorney for the Golden Spike maintained that the bar acted responsibly, in that it trained its security guards to check for identification prior to allowing admission to the bar, and that Ms. Rodgers had presented a falsified identification card, which the bar could not reasonably have known was false. In addition, the security guard stated that Ms. Rodgers "looked" at least 21 when she entered the bar. Thus, the bar was not guilty of knowingly serving minors.

1. Is the bar responsible for illegally serving Ms. Rodgers? Was she served excessively?

2. Since the security guard did not serve alcohol, do you think a jury would find one hour of orientation sufficient in his training?

3. What could the owners of the Golden Spike do in the future to prevent a reoccurrence such as this?

≫ ANALYZE THE SITUATION 12.6

SAMUEL VOSOVIC ATTENDED A reception in the ballroom of the Altoona Pike Country Club. Mr. Vosovic was a salesman for a photography studio, and he attended a reception at the invitation of Ronald Thespia, one of the club's well-known members. Mr. Thespia's company sponsored the reception, which consisted of light hors d'oeuvres and an open bar.

Over the course of two and a half hours, it was determined that Mr. Vosovic consumed approximately nine drinks. The reception was large enough to require three bartender stations in the room. No single bartender served Mr. Vosovic more than three drinks in the course of the evening. Lea Tobson, one of the club's bartenders did finally detect a significant change in Mr. Vosovic's behavior and, when Mr. Vosovic requested another drink, refused to serve him and summoned a manager.

The club's food and beverage director determined that Mr. Vosovic was in all likelihood intoxicated. The director asked Mr. Vosovic to turn over his car keys, then instructed one of the club's waitstaff to drive Mr. Vosovic home, give the car keys to his wife, and take a cab back to the club. One hour after being taken home, Mr. Vosovic got back behind the wheel of his car and, still intoxicated, he lost control of the vehicle and crashed into a tree, killing him instantly. His wife brought suit against the country club under dram shop legislation in her state.

The club responded that it had acted responsibly in both refusing to service Mr. Vosovic and in ensuring that he got home safely. Mrs. Vosovic replied that her husband was upset at his treatment by the club when he arrived home and that she "couldn't stop him" when he took the car keys from her, intent on returning to the club. She held the club responsible because, as she stated, "They got him drunk." As additional evidence of the club's irresponsibility, she pointed to the tipping policy in place during open bars; essentially, in an open bar situation, the bartenders at the club were paid a percentage of the sales price of the alcohol consumed. Mrs. Vosovic's attorney claimed that the club's tipping policy encouraged its bartenders to overpour the drinks they served, as they sought to build the sales value of the event and thus their own income.

1. Did the country club act responsibly in this situation?

2. What steps could a responsible beverage manager take to reduce the possibility of such an incident reoccurring?

3. Would the club's tipping policy influence a jury's view of responsible alcohol service by the club if the case went to trial? Why?

4. Was it foreseeable that Mr. Vosovic, once home, would leave the house in his intoxicated condition?

INTERNATIONAL SNAPSHOT

International Perspective on Food and Beverage Litigation

As in the United States, food and beverage litigation internationally involves issues of jurisdiction, substantive law, and burdens of proof. The following is a brief review of these issues.

As for jurisdiction, it was held that when a seaman died onboard a ship in Africa from food poisoning, that the proper jurisdiction was the District of Columbia, the state of registry of the ship instead of Africa (*United States Shipping Board Emergency Fleet Corp. v. Greenwald*, 16 F. 2d 948 (1927)). Courts have also ruled that on international flights, the Warsaw Convention, which provides for uniform rules limiting aviation liability also applies to food and beverage claims (see *Rhodes v. American Airlines*, 1996 U.S. LEXIS 21052 (NY 1996)). Further, when a passenger became sick due to the food he ate on one leg of a round trip from Saudi Arabia, the Warsaw Convention was interpreted as conferring jurisdiction on the location of destination, or in Saudi Arabia and not New York, where the lawsuit was filed (see *Abdulrahman Al-zamil v. British Airways, Inc.*, 770 F. 2d 3 (2d Cir. 1985)). A court also ruled that a French company operating a resort in New Zealand could be sued in New Zealand, with New Zealand law being applied in a case where a guest claimed to have suffered food poisoning at the resort (see *Club Mediterranee NZ v. Wendell*, 1 NZLR 216; 1987 NZLR LEXIS 712 (1987)).

Internationally, suppliers of food and beverage are subject to actions based on reasonable standards of care or negligence (see *McNeil v. Airport Hotel (Halifax) Ltd.*, 1980 A.C.W.S.J. LEXIS 15714, 5 A.C.W.S. (2d) 476); and, under contract and warranty claims, such as for breach of the implied warranty of fitness for a particular purpose, or that the food would be fit for human consumption (see *Lockett v. A & M Charles Ltd.*, 3 AL ER 170, Kings Bench Div. (1938)). A Canadian court held that the manufacturer and seller of a bottle of chocolate milk that contained glass and injured a consumer could be sued under causes of action in negligence and breach of warranty (see *Shandloff v. City Dairy Ltd. and Moscoe*, [1936] O.R. 579; 1936 Ont. Rep. LEXIS 70 (1936)).

The pivotal issue of causation exists under international law as well. In *Berko v. Canada Safeway Ltd.*, 2000 B.C.D. Civ. J. 4810 (2000), the British Columbia Supreme Court held that, to be successful in her lawsuit, a plaintiff must still prove that the food was the cause of her illness. In Berko, the plaintiff became ill within a few hours of consuming food. The medical evidence suggested that the incubation period was too short to support a finding that the food consumed at the restaurant was the cause of her illness. Thus, she could not sustain her burden of proof and her lawsuit was dismissed. However, another Canadian court held that, even though evidence was circumstantial that the food was the cause of illness, the doctrine of *res ipsa loquitur* could be applied when a family became sick after eating a pizza purchased from a restaurant (see *Stewart v. J.M. Investment Ltd.*, 1993 A.C.W.S.J. 581586, 41 A.C.W.S. (3d) 989 (Saskatchewan Provincial Court, (1992)).

Finally, as with many cities in the United States, the City of Toronto's laws require a restaurant operator to disclose the results of a food premise inspection. Toronto's law was recently upheld as constitutionally valid, despite any perceived negative effect on a restaurant (see *Ontario Restaurant Hotel & Motel Association v. Toronto*, [2004] O.J. No. 190; 2004 ON.C. LEXIS 287 (January 22, 2004)).

Provided by James O. Eiler, Esq, partner and chair of the Hospitality Practice Group for Tharpe & Howell, Santa Ana, California; with the assistance of Diane L. Wall, JD. www.tharpe-howell.com

THE HOSPITALITY INDUSTRY IN COURT

To understand how the failure to warn guests of certain ingredients can impact your operation, consider the case of *Livingston v. Marie Callender's, Inc.*, 72 Cal. App. 4th 830 (Cal. Ct. App. 1999).

FACTUAL SUMMARY

David Livingston went to a Marie Callender's restaurant, where he ordered a bowl of vegetable soup. Before ordering, Mr. Livingston asked the waitress whether the soup contained MSG (monosodium glutamate). He explained he had asthma and was allergic to MSG. The waitress assured him MSG was not an ingredient in the soup so Mr. Livingston ordered and consumed the vegetable soup. Thereafter, Mr. Livingston developed MSG symptom complex, which includes respiratory arrest, cardiac arrest, and brain damage, as well as a number of other symptoms. Mr. Livingston subsequently sued the restaurant and its owners for failing to warn him MSG was an ingredient in the vegetable soup.

QUESTION FOR THE COURT

The question for the court was whether Marie Callender's had a duty to warn Mr. Livingston the vegetable soup contained MSG. Mr. Livingston argued a manufacturer has a duty to warn where the harmful ingredient is one that a large number of people are allergic to, and the ingredient must be one whose harmful nature or presence is not generally known to consumers. Where these conditions exist, Mr. Livingston argued, a manufacturer that fails to warn of the presence of such an ingredient should be strictly liable for the injury suffered by the consumer. The court pointed out strict liability was not to be confused with absolute liability. With strict liability, a manufacturer can warn consumers of the potential for harm resulting from an unintended use and be protected from liability. With absolute liability, a manufacturer would be liable for any injury resulting from any use of a product placed on the market.

DECISION

The court held for Mr. Livingston, ruling Marie Callender's could be strictly liable for failing to warn consumers about the presence of MSG in the vegetable soup. The court concluded Marie Callender's knew or should have known of the danger MSG posed to the general public, and hence had a duty to warn the public of the presence of MSG in the vegetable soup.

MESSAGE TO MANAGEMENT

Menu disclosures and warnings such as the one set out here are the best policies:

> Caution: There may be small bones in some fresh fish. Maraschino cherries and nearly all wines contain sulfating agents to protect flavor and color. Certain individuals may be allergic to specific types of food or ingredients used in food items (e.g., MSG). We are not responsible for an individual's allergic reaction to our food or ingredients used in food items. Please alert your server of any food allergies prior to ordering.

> There is a risk associated with consuming raw oysters or any raw animal protein. If you have chronic illness of the liver, stomach, or blood, or have immune disorders, you are at greater risk of illness from raw oysters and should eat oysters fully cooked. If you are unsure of your risk, consult a physician.

For an example of a dram shop lawsuit, see the case of *Jackson v. Cadillac Cowboy, Inc.*, 986 S.W.2d 410 (Ark. 1999).

FACTUAL SUMMARY

On August 31 and September 1, 1994, Kevin Holliday was served alcoholic beverages at the Sundowners Club, a club owned by Cadillac Cowboy, Inc. (Cadillac Cowboy). Mr. Holliday became extremely intoxicated while at the club. Despite his intoxicated state, and with knowledge that he would drive his automobile while intoxicated, the club continued to serve Mr. Holliday. Around 12:45 A.M. on September 1, Mr. Holliday left the club in his pickup truck. His truck collided with a vehicle driven by James Jackson, causing it to roll over and kill Mr. Jackson. Mr. Jackson's wife, Pam (Jackson), sued Cadillac Cowboy Inc. for negligence in failing to refuse service to Mr. Holliday when it was clear he was very intoxicated.

QUESTION FOR THE COURT

The question for the court was whether a licensed alcohol vendor could be liable for selling alcoholic beverages to an intoxicated person who then caused injury to a third person. The plaintiff, Jackson, argued that since the court had already held vendors liable in cases involving the sale of alcoholic beverages to minors, liability should be extended to all persons. Cadillac Cowboy argued it was the job of the legislature to impose liability on alcoholic beverage vendors, and since the legislature had not enacted a civil liability statute, it could not be liable for the death of Jackson. The court examined the rule of law in a number of other states and found only six states that did not impose liability on vendors. The other 46 states all imposed liability in one way or another on state-licensed alcoholic beverage vendors.

DECISION

The court held in favor of Jackson, ruling that a state-licensed alcoholic beverage vendor could be held liable for serving an intoxicated patron who in turn injured a third party.

MESSAGE TO MANAGEMENT

Third-party liability laws exist in almost all states today. Be sure to train all employees and management on the responsible service of alcohol.

WHAT DID YOU LEARN IN THIS CHAPTER?

You are the general manager of a casual theme restaurant. The restaurant includes both a cocktail area and dining room. Average sales per restaurant are $4 million per year, with 30 percent of the sales attributed to alcohol. At the annual conference of managers, sponsored by your company, your supervisor, the district manager, assigns you to a company task force charged with making recommendations on a new liability training program for bartenders working in your operations.

Your specific task is to recommend the length of this portion of a bartender's training, as well as to estimate the costs associated with it.

1. Assuming that bartenders earn $15 per hour, including benefits, and trainers within your company average $40 per hour, develop a short outline of required training concepts, estimate the time to cover each topic, and assign a per-bartender cost, assuming that the bartenders must be trained in a one-on-one setting.

2. Prepare a three- to five-minute presentation for your district manager and the other conference attendees that justifies your costs as developed.

3. Estimate the yearly cost of bartender liability training if your company of 400 restaurants hires 1,100 bartenders per year. Give your opinion on the cost likely to be incurred if no such training is implemented.

RAPID REVIEW

After you have studied this chapter, you should be prepared to:

1. Log on to the website of the National Restaurant Association (www.restaurant.org). Click on the Food Safety tab and then on Foodborne Illnesses. Identify at least three common foodborne illnesses and at least two ways each is spread. Create a ten-minute training session geared to dishwashers that would help them and you prevent these types of outbreaks.

2. Do you think restaurants face greater liability in what they serve or how they serve it? What impact will increased consumer acceptance of takeout foods have on your position?

3. Collect two takeout menus from restaurants near your home. Identify by circling the menu items, any reference to preparation style, brand-name ingredients, origin, size, or health benefits of their menu offerings. Compare the two restaurants' use of these descriptions.

4. Despite its name, "prime rib" does not have to come from prime grade beef. Contact your local butcher or meat purveyor to identify exactly which ribs are contained in prime rib. Check this information against that found in the National Association of Meat Purveyors' *Meat Buyers Guide*.

5. As a drug, alcohol is classified as a depressant. Consult a medical encyclopedia to identify at least two other types of depressants, as well as the following characteristics of depressants:

   Their primary effects on basic metabolism
   Symptoms of excessive dosage
   Symptoms of withdrawal

6. Contact your local police department or state police. Identify the BAC in your state in which a driver is considered legally intoxicated. Discover whether the same BAC applies to minors. Ask for details on how officers identify those that they believe have exceeded the legal limits of alcohol consumption.

7. Assume that you operate a country-western dance club. Create a script for your servers to follow when they must tactfully refuse to serve alcohol to an intoxicated guest. Provide responses that your servers can use to counter the reactions they might reasonably expect from guests.

In teams, brainstorm all of the physical characteristics that an intoxicated person might exhibit. Then develop ten methods to help prevent your servers from serving people who are (or appear to be getting) intoxicated.

TEAM ACTIVITY

LEGAL RESPONSIBILITIES IN TRAVEL AND TOURISM

"YES, I TRULY do understand how unsettling it can be not to get what you expected," said Trisha Sangus politely as she listened patiently to the guest who had identified herself as Ms. Hamilton. Trisha, the general manager, had been walking through the lobby of her hotel moments earlier and had overheard Ms. Hamilton complaining, very loudly, that her room was not at all what she had been promised when she had made her reservation.

Trisha had intervened when she heard Mr. Dani, the hotel's front office manager, explain to the guest that the room types reserved by Tours Deluxe, the bus tour operator managing the trip Ms. Hamilton was taking, were only rooms with king-sized beds, not rooms with two double beds.

"It's not our fault," Mr. Dani had stated to the guest. It was clear from her reaction, however, that Mr. Dani's explanation, though technically accurate, was not being taken well by Ms. Hamilton.

As she continued listening to Ms. Hamilton, the problem this guest was experiencing became clear to Trisha. Trisha also knew Ms. Hamilton's problem would be a difficult one to solve because the hotel was almost fully occupied with a large youth convention, and as a result, the only vacant rooms in the hotel were, undoubtedly, rooms with a king-sized bed. She also knew, as Mr. Dani had stated to the guest, that Tours Deluxe, one of the hotel's best high-volume customers, had, in fact, reserved only king-sized bedded rooms for their Single Seniors tour group, of which Ms. Hamilton was a part. Tours Deluxe had been an account that Trisha and the hotel's director of sales and marketing had worked very hard to land, and the relationship between this tour operator and the hotel had been, up to now, outstanding.

"It's very simple," said Ms. Hamilton, "but you people don't seem to understand. I booked this tour to get away and relax. I specifically told my travel agent that I wanted a room with two double beds because I like to lay my suitcase out on the second bed when I stay in a hotel. That's what I reserved with the Buckeye Travel Agency and that's what I paid them for. Your desk clerk," continued Ms. Hamilton, looking accusingly at Mr. Dani, "claims I have to take a room with a king-sized bed. That's simply not acceptable. I demand that you call my travel agent immediately and get this straightened out!"

"Let me see what I can do to help," replied Trisha, as she motioned for Mr. Dani to join her in the back office.

"Deluxe screwed up," began Mr. Dani as soon as he and Trisha were alone in the office. "It always reserves kings for its single's groups. Always."

"This lady," he continued, referring to Ms. Hamilton, "really has a right to be upset—Deluxe misinformed her and sold her a room type she didn't want."

"That's where you're wrong," replied Trisha. "Deluxe doesn't sell directly to guests; it brokers tours through individual travel agencies. In this case, it sounds like Buckeye Travel is at fault. Besides, Deluxe does three tours a month with us; that's over 2,000 room nights per year. I'm not sure it is in this hotel's best interest, or Deluxe's for that matter, to tell this guest its tour operator 'screwed up.' What's the number to the tour coordinator's room?" asked Trisha as she reached for a telephone.

"Six-one-seven," replied Mr. Dani.

"This is Trisha Sangus," said Trisha as the Deluxe representative accompanying the tour group answered. "I think we are going to need your assistance down here at the desk. It concerns a member of your tour group. Thank you—that's great," said Trisha as she hung up the telephone.

Trisha then turned to Mr. Dani. "We will not, at this time," she said pointedly, "refer to anyone screwing up." "We will," she continued, "deal with this guest's issues and then talk with one of our best customers about how they would like to work with us to handle situations like this one in the future. Let's go see Ms. Hamilton."

IN THIS CHAPTER, YOU WILL LEARN:

1. To identify the components of the travel industry, how they interact, and the complex legal issues that surround this huge industry.

2. To understand fully the roles and potential liabilities of travel agents and tour operators as each fulfills its unique role in marketing and providing travel services.

3. To identify those common carriers typically utilized by the travel industry, as well as the recurrent areas of potential liability inherent in each of them.

4. To evaluate tourism as it relates to gaming, resorts, and timeshares, and theme park operations, based, in part, on the unique liability issues and managerial responsibilities inherent in each of these growing areas.

5. How, from a legal perspective, the unique characteristics of the Internet can impact restaurant and hotel managers' efforts to integrate the power of the Web into their own operations.

13.1 TRAVEL

The word *travel*, which means "to make a journey," is an English variation of the old French word *travailler*, which meant "to labor long and hard in dangerous conditions." In fact, in the earliest days of travel, transportation from place to place was expensive and difficult, dangers to life and limb were plentiful, and risks to personal health were significant. Despite this history, the travel and tourism industry is now, according to the World Travel and Tourism Council (WTTC), the world's largest industry, with an estimated economic value of 3.5 trillion dollars in gross domestic product (GDP); moreover, it employs 1 out of every 12 workers worldwide.[1]

As the global economy continues to make the world smaller, and as declining transportation costs (relative to income) make in-country and international travel available to larger and more diverse segments of society, it is not surprising that the legal issues raised by travel and travelers are significant. Recall that "law" was defined in Chapter 1 of this text, as "the rules of conduct and responsibility established and enforced by society." When members of two very different societies make contact through travel, the possibility that their "rules of conduct" will vary, and even come into direct conflict, can be very high indeed. As a professional hospitality manager, part of your job is to understand which rules of conduct (laws) should be followed. This is, of course, extremely difficult in a world with so many law-making countries, states, regions, regulatory agencies, and international governing bodies to consider.

The Travel Industry

In many parts of the world, the travel industry is referred to as the travel and tourism industry, or even simply the tourism industry. In the United States, few observers would identify businesspeople traveling across their home states to attend a company sales conference as tourists, yet such a journey certainly would expose those travelers to many features and conveniences used by tourists. For purposes of this text, the term *travel industry* will refer to those transportation services (airlines, trains, cruise ships, buses, and rental cars), lodging facilities (hotels, motels, resorts, etc.), eating and drinking places, sightseeing venues, and amusement and recreation activities used by all travelers; as well as to those travel professionals who market these products and services to travelers.

The number of laws, regulations, and standardized procedures used in all of the individual industries that, collectively, make up the travel industry are large indeed. *Travel law* refers to those laws that directly impact the travel industry. The field is so extensive that some attorneys specialize in this field of law. *International travel law* combines aspects of contract law, employment law, tourism and hospitality procedures, antitrust rules, regulatory and agency compliance, and knowledge of certain international agreements and treaties into a comprehensive set of guidelines for the travel industry.

> **LEGALESE**
> **Travel law:** The laws regulating business and individual behavior in the travel industry.

> **LEGALESE**
> **International travel law:** The ordinances, rules, treaties, and agreements used to regulate the international travel industry.

Industry Components

The travel industry is composed of many segments. Consider the case of Benny and June, two American college students who wish to spend their summer break traveling throughout Europe. To examine their entire travel experience, as well as to identify those travel-oriented industries that the students are likely to encounter during their trip, it is useful to view travel as consisting of five key components, as listed in Figure 13.1.

---

[1] WTTC Research Report, March 2003.

> 1. Preplanning Services
> 2. Transportation
> 3. Lodging
> 4. Foodservices
> 5. Attractions and Activities

Figure 13.1 Five key components of the travel industry.

Preplanning Services

To plan their trip, Benny and June may enlist the assistance of a travel agent, a professional whose job is to plan and sell travel-related products and services. Travel agents work, directly and indirectly, with travel service providers and tour operators. Tour operators actually purchase travel services, then market these services directly to travelers or offer them to travel agents, who, in turn, sell them to travelers such as Benny and June.

Search the Web 13.1

Despite the popularity of the Internet as a way to plan your own travel, the services of professional travel agents continue to be in high demand. To view the website of the largest of the travel agent associations, go to www.astanet.com. This is the website of the American Society of Travel Agents (ASTA). When you arrive, click on About ASTA. Select "Who We Are," and then explore the sidebar subcategories to read about the goals of this effective organization.

In addition to selling tours, travel agents also work with transportation providers and those who sell lodging services, as well as those who market attractions and recreational activities.

Transportation

If Benny and June indeed travel to Europe from the United States, the number of transportation services they will use are likely to be extensive. Starting with a taxi cab to the airport, continuing across the Atlantic with an international airline flight or cruise, and culminating, perhaps, in a car rental, bus ride, or trip by rail to their destination of choice, most journeys normally rely, in part, on the services of the very large segment of the travel industry related to transportation.

Lodging

Although Benny and June may decide, as they travel, to stay at traditional hotels, the choices they will encounter as they plan their overnight accommodations will be many. On one extreme, they may choose an extravagant destination resort in a desirable location that, in addition to their sleeping rooms, offers many recreational alternatives, gourmet food and beverage outlets, and numerous other free amenities and activities. Alternatively, they may select a more modestly priced lodging choice housed in a private home that simply provides them with their sleeping rooms and, perhaps, a limited breakfast in the morning.

The lodging segment of the travel industry is sizable and offers travelers a wide range of accommodation choices. In addition to traditional hotels, many private clubs, casinos, cruise ships, timeshare condominiums, and campground sites provide overnight alternatives to travelers. Most of these facilities are open to all of the traveling public. Some other types of facilities offer overnight accommodations for people away from their homes for other reasons. These include schools, colleges and universities offering residential services, health-care (hospital and nursing homes) facilities, correctional institutions (prisons), and military bases.

Foodservices

One of the greatest joys, as well as sometimes one of the most daunting aspects, of traveling is the ability to sample local foods prepared in ways and combinations that are different from those typically found "back home." From the leisurely meal to the hurried snack, the traveling public can choose from a wide variety of food venues. It is likely that Benny and June will find exploring the various cuisines and beverages of Europe one of the most talked-about features of their trip when they return.

Internationally, as well as in the United States, the foodservice industry consists of a plethora of food and beverage outlets that range from the exquisite and expensive to the very modestly priced "eat on the street" meals offered by vendors in most larger cities.

Attractions and Activities

For many travelers, the food and lodging experiences they will encounter are substantially less important than are the sites these travelers will see and the things they will do on their trips. For Benny and June, a walk through Heidelberg Castle in central Germany, a chance to see the masterpieces contained in the famous Louvre museum in Paris, or renting bikes to cycle through the mountains of Switzerland may be the actual reasons for traveling to their chosen destinations.

In well-developed countries, the number of things a traveler can see and do can be extensive. The traveler to New York City, for example, can spend days exploring the sights, sounds, and activities available. In less-developed countries and areas, the natural attractions of beaches, mountains, or forests may be enough to attract significant numbers of travelers. In all cases, however, the attractions and activities offered are likely managed and staffed by local employees, and operated according to the prevailing culture and customs of the area hosting the traveler. This will likely be the case regardless of whether the activity selected involves attending a concert, sporting event, or the theater; visiting a museum, art gallery, or historical site; gambling in a casino; visiting an amusement park; or simply enjoying the area's natural physical setting.

Each of the five major components of the travel industry has developed, over time, its own set of rules, regulations, customs, and laws related to how it does business. Most travelers will not be as aware of how these operational procedures affect their travel experience, as will the managers working in the areas. As a result, an important part of many travel industry managers' jobs is to communicate these specific procedures to the individual travelers they encounter.

Economic Breadth and Impact

The travel industry is big business. In 2010, U.S. Travel Association reported that travel and tourism is the nation's largest services export industry, with a $32 billion balance of trade surplus for the United States. In 2010, the U.S. travel

Total Domestic U.S. Person-Trips	704.4 Billion
Purpose of Trip	
Leisure Travel	489.7 Billion
Business/Convention	214.7 Billion
Combined Business and Pleasure	704.4 Billion
Sources of Travel Spending	
Food Services	179.4 Billion
Lodging	126.6 Billion
Public Transportation	124.6 Billion
Auto Transportation	113.2 Billion
Recreation/Amusement	82.9 Billion
Retail	77.7 Billion

Person-trip is defined as one person on a trip away from home overnight in paid accommodations or on a day or overnight trip to places 50 miles or more [one-way] away from home.

Source: U.S. Travel Association

Figure 13.2 U.S. domestic travel in 2009.

industry generated sales of more than $750 billion, including airfares from domestic and international travelers. These travel expenditures, in turn, supported more than 14 million jobs for Americans (7.4 million directly in the travel industry), with nearly $188 billion in payroll income. Approximately 1 out of 9 jobs in the United States depend on travel and tourism.[2]

Travel is popular. As shown in Figure 13.2, in 2009, domestic travelers took over 1 billion trips on which they traveled more than 50 miles from home.

The financial impact of international travelers is also great. In 2001, international visitors to the United States spent $260 billion traveling in the country, including international passenger fares. Just as the travel professionals in the United States recognize the magnitude and impact of travel on the national economy, so do travel professionals worldwide. The World Travel and Tourism Council (WTTC) is the association created by global business leaders in travel and tourism. Its members are chairs and chief executive officers from 100 of the industry's foremost companies, including airlines and other passenger transport, hospitality, manufacturing, entertainment, tour operators, car rental, and other travel-related services. Founded in 1990, the WTTC is headquartered in London. Its mission is to raise awareness of the impact of travel and tourism, and to persuade governments to make it an economic and job-creating priority. Travel and tourism helps local economies in many ways:

▪ *Export earnings:* Currency earned by tourism results in the addition of "new" money in a local economy. For many countries and geographic areas, especially those that are not rich in natural resources, tourism dollars may be the single largest source of new income.

---

[2]U.S. Travel Association, "Talking Points and Facts," April 2011. www.ustravel.org/marketing/national-travel-and-tourism-week/talking-points-and-facts. Accessed June 2011.

Search the Web **13.2**

The U.S. Travel Association helps connect, promote, advocate, and research all aspects of travel; including foreign and domestic. To view its website, go to www.ustravel.org. When you arrive at the site, click on About U.S. Travel to read about its goals and activities.

- *Enhancement of rural areas:* Tourism jobs and businesses are usually created in the most underdeveloped regions of a country, helping to equalize economic opportunities throughout a nation and providing an incentive for residents to remain in rural areas, rather than move to cities that may already be overcrowded and unable to easily support additions to the population.

- *Employment:* Travel and tourism is an important job creator. In addition, it is essential to understand that the vast majority of tourism jobs are in small or medium-sized, family-owned enterprises such as restaurants, shops, and the management/provision of tourism-related leisure activities.

- *Development of infrastructure:* Travel and tourism encourages enormous investments in new infrastructure, most of which helps to improve the living conditions of local residents, as well as the enjoyment of the tourists. Tourism development projects include airports, roads, sewage systems, water treatment plants, restoration of cultural monuments, and the creation or expansion of museums.

- *Tax collections:* The tourism industry provides local governments with hundreds of millions of dollars in tax revenues each year through hotel occupancy and restaurant taxes, airport users' fees, sales taxes, park entrance fees, and employee income taxes.

Complexity of Legal Issues

The travel industry is large and complex; thus, its legal issues are as well. Travel law is unique, in that it encompasses many countries, industries, regulatory agencies, and even traditions. Returning to the example of Benny and June, and given your understanding of sources of potential liability, imagine the complications that might arise if these two travelers bought a 21-day package tour of Europe (operated by a tour company based in Amsterdam) and that the tour company then subcontracted meals and accommodations for the tour with hotels and restaurants in a variety of European cities. Assume further that they purchased the tour from a New York state travel agent and that the two travelers took an Amtrak train to get to their departure city, where they stayed in a hotel that they reserved through an Internet booking site operated by a travel wholesaler located in Atlanta, and the next day, they flew on a transatlantic airline (operated by a non-U.S. company) to reach their destination. Finally, assume that their plane arrived late, and they missed the assigned departure time for their tour. No doubt you can begin to see the potential difficulties faced by consumers, as well as those who do business in a specific travel segment.

Travel law is complicated for a variety of reasons, including:

■ *Interconnectivity:* When one travel-related business controls the sale and delivery of a complete travel product or service, the liability for poor or nonperformance may be easily assessed. When one business is dependent on the performance of another business, however, liability for poor performance is more difficult to determine. For example, assume that a travel services seller, relying on the promise made by a resort developer that a new resort would be ready to accept business on January 1 of a given year, sells a three-night stay at the resort; but upon the guests' arrival, the swimming pools, tennis courts, and golf course are not yet fully operational. Is fault to be assigned to the travel seller, the resort operator, or both? The interconnectivity of travel services makes it critical for hospitality managers to understand travel law.

■ *Jurisdiction:* By its very nature, much of the activity in the travel industry occurs in a variety of legal settings. Does a New Jersey traveler who books a night's stay at a hotel in Dallas, via an Internet site operating out of Florida, and who ultimately feels that the hotel did not deliver the services promised, seek relief through the New Jersey, Texas, or Florida courts? Where many travel-related legal issues are concerned, the question of precisely which court has *jurisdiction* is crucial to understanding the applicable law.

■ *Variation in terminology and resulting expectations:* In the United States, the term *first class* has a specific meaning to most travelers. But is it realistic for American travelers to assume that the rest of the world is bound by the same expectations when the term *first class* is used? Clearly, everyone in the world is not required to think exactly as Americans do. Alternatively, what if unscrupulous travel salespeople, knowing the ambiguity of the term *first class*, seek to defraud unwitting travelers? The question of honest differences in terminology and resulting expectation is complicated by multiple languages and multiple translations of travel-related words, phrases, and concepts.

■ *Identity of the actual service provider:* Travel services are often packaged; that is, travelers will, in many cases, buy a complete travel experience that includes transportation, meals, and lodging, as well as leisure activities. When a component part of that travel experience is defective, it may be very challenging to determine exactly who is responsible to the traveler. For example, if a company that puts tours together purchases, at a discount, 100 sleeping rooms from a hotel and then uses those rooms to lodge a tour group, is the hotel's customer the tour company or the individual traveler? If the hotel does not operate in the manner the tour company promised the travelers purchasing the tour, and if monetary compensation is due for that poor hotel service, is the compensation more appropriately refunded to the tour operator that purchased the rooms, or the guest who stayed in the room? In complicated cases, it may well require a court to sort out a resolution.

■ *Uncontrollable forces:* Travel is affected by many factors beyond the control of travel services providers. Severe weather, civil unrest, war, disease, and a variety of other variables can serve to make travel either unpleasant or impossible. Most observers would say that these forces should not generally be used to hold a travel services provider responsible for nonperformance of a contract. But what is the responsibility of the travel services provider that knowingly subjects travelers to these forces? For example, if a cruise ship captain knowingly sails his or her ship into waters that are in the direct path of a hurricane, that captain will likely, in most traveler's opinions, assume some level of liability for the potential outcome. A jury may be required to determine the actual degree of the cruise operator's responsibility.

LEGALESE

Jurisdiction: The authority given by law or treaty to a court to try cases and make decisions about legal matters within a particular geographic area and/or over certain types of cases.

In the remaining sections of this chapter, you will learn about some of the governmental and quasigovernmental groups that help regulate and set national and worldwide policy for the travel industry. You will also become familiar with the travel agents, wholesalers, and tour group operators that make up the distribution segment of the travel industry. In addition, we will examine those industries that provide the means of passenger transportation, (i.e., buses, trains, planes, etc.) for their unique regulation and liability issues. The intent is to demonstrate the interconnectivity of the travel industry, and to direct you to sources of further information in those areas that entail specialized legal knowledge appropriate for hospitality managers.

13.2 TRAVEL AGENTS AND TOUR OPERATORS

Not all travelers need the help of travel professionals when they decide to take a trip. For many, however, the knowledge and skills of such professionals are extremely important to the success of their trip. As a result, travel agents, tour companies, and travel wholesalers are essential components of today's travel industry, making it critical to understand how each operates and how travel law relates to them individually, and to the hospitality industry as a whole.

Travel Agents

Historically, and despite the increased popularity of the Internet, individual and corporate travel agents remain the primary distributors of travel services. They offer customers packages or services provided by tour companies, organize tailor-made travel on request, and sell services such as vacation packages, air tickets, train tickets, cruises, hotel bookings, car rentals, and other services. Whether individual or corporate, as travel experts, their job is to inform and advise travelers. In the hospitality industry, hotel managers interact with travel agents on a daily basis because, in most hotels, a high percentage of the reservations made in the hotel will be booked by travel agents via the global distribution system (GDS) that electronically links travel agents worldwide to individual hotel reservation systems.

Search the Web **13.3**

Important travel-related news affects travel agents throughout the world. Log on to the Internet and enter www.travelagents.com.

1. Select: Travel News from an area of the world in which you have an interest.

Compensation

Travel agents contract for travel services on behalf of their clients. Accordingly, they have a *fiduciary* responsibility to those clients. This is an important concept because travel agents are expected to act in the best interests of their clients, not those of the hotels, airlines, or other travel organizations that may actually compensate the travel agent.

LEGALESE

Fiduciary: A relationship based on trust and the responsibility to act in the best interest of another when performing tasks.

Travel agents are expected to be knowledgeable about the products they sell and to exhibit reasonable care in their dealings with clients. When they do not, they risk assuming liability for their own actions, as well as for the service levels and behavior of the third-party travel services suppliers with which they affiliate. For example, assume that a travel agent books a room for a client at a hotel in a large city. The agent represents to the client that the hotel is of "four-star" quality in a "safe" part of the city. In fact, the agent knows that the hotel is a "two-star" hotel in a high-crime area of the city. In this case, the travel agent's client is likely to have cause for legal action against the travel agent because of misrepresentation, even if the travel agent was compensated for the booking by the hotel, not the agent's actual client.

Travel agents have historically worked on a commission basis for the hotels, airlines, and other travel suppliers with which they do business. Even when travel agents are paid their commission by a third party, a hotel, or airline, they still owe a fiduciary responsibility to their client, the traveler. More recently, as airlines have reduced travel agent commissions, and as the Internet has made it increasingly popular to book travel without the assistance of a travel agent, some agents are directly charging their clients fees for services provided. When a travel agent charges to a client a fee for booking a hotel or airline reservation, it is clear that the travel agent has a fiduciary responsibility to that client.

Responsibilities

Travel agents routinely perform a variety of tasks. Essentially, however, a manager in the travel agent industry has a duty to train and inform his or her in-office and outside sales staff on all phases of travel offered to the public so that these individuals are in a position to provide professional travel advice, and to secure the most appropriate travel services available for each client. To that end, travel agents should make every effort to provide accurate information so that their clients can make an informed choice as to travel services. In particular, travel agents who work with clients wishing to travel internationally have a responsibility to advise their clients of the necessary passport and visa requirements for the trip to be undertaken. In addition, travel agents are required, at the time of booking any travel service on behalf of a client, to inform that client about any cancellation fee, revision fee, supplier service charge, or other administration charges, and the amount of these fees. When possible, agents must also inform clients of the existence of cancellation protection and/or insurance.

Regulatory Structure

Travel agents and their actions are, of course, subject to the same rules of law as any other business; at this time, there is no federal licensing requirements specifically for travel agents. State regulation does vary, however; currently, 14 states have regulations that mention travel sellers specifically. And because different departments and agencies are responsible for the oversight of these agents in these states, regulations may vary widely indeed, as shown in Figure 13.3.

For those states not listed in Figure 13.3, the individual state's office of attorney general or the Department of Commerce is the most likely source of information regarding specialized state laws affecting travel agents.

Like professionals in many other businesses, travel agents have traditionally been primarily responsible for the regulation of their own industry and its members. And though the American Society of Travel Agents (ASTS), in conjunction with the Institute of Certified Travel Agents (ICTA), administers the Travel Agent Proficiency (TAP) test, there are not, at this time, any educational or experiential requirements that agents must meet before registering to take the exam, nor must they complete the TAP before being allowed to sell travel services.

State	Agency with Regulations Related to Travel Sellers
California	Department of Justice
Delaware	Division of Revenue
Florida	Division of Consumer Services
Hawaii	Department of Commerce and Consumer Affairs
Illinois	Attorney General
Iowa	Office of the Secretary of State; Corporations Division
Massachusetts	Attorney General, Anti-Trust and Consumer Protection Division
New York	Office of the Attorney General
Ohio	State Fire Marshall
Oregon	Department of Consumer and Business Services
Pennsylvania	Bureau of Transportation and Safety
Rhode Island	Department of Business Regulation
Virginia	Department of Agricultural and Consumer Service, Consumers Affairs Office
Washington	Department of Licensing

Figure 13.3 Travel-regulation agencies for various states.

Potential Liability Issues

Constantly changing airfares and schedules, literally thousands of available vacation packages, and a vast amount of travel information on the Internet can make travel planning frustrating and time-consuming for travelers. To sort out their options, tourists and businesspeople often turn to travel agents. These professionals are truly "agents" in the agent/principal relationship defined in Chapter 3; that is, they act on behalf of a principal. For example, when a travel agent acts on behalf of a tour company (the principal) when selling a tour to the travel agent's client, the principal will be bound by the actions of the travel agent. In turn, the travel agent will be responsible for informing the client about the identity of the tour company.

Travel agents routinely act as agents for airlines, hotels, car rental agencies, and others. Thus, they have a duty to both their clients and their principals. Common areas of potential travel agent liability, and, as a result, possible litigation, have revolved around five issues:

1. *Failure to provide promised services.* When a travel agent books a service for its client (the traveler) from a travel services provider, the agent should be confident about the ability of the provider to deliver as promised. That said, not all failures to provide services result in travel agent liability. For example, if a travel agent, in good faith, books a client at a Hilton hotel that normally operates a swimming pool, yet at check-in the guest discovers that the pool is closed for repairs, the agent is unlikely to be held responsible for this event because the client could reasonably foresee that such events happen at hotels. If, on the other hand, the travel agent booked, for the same client, a whirlpool suite at the hotel knowing that the hotel did not have whirlpool suites, the travel agent would likely be held liable for the inability of the hotel to provide

the promised services. Travel agents have a duty to exercise reasonable care when promising specific travel services will be available from specific travel service providers.

2. *Failure to honor agreed-upon pricing.* The ability of a travel agent in one part of the world to control the pricing behavior of a travel service provider in another part of the world is often quite limited. As a result, the traveler who paid a travel agent $100 to secure a hotel room reservation in a foreign country could, upon arrival at the hotel, be forced to pay additional monies before the hotel will actually honor the reservation. In such a situation, the traveler might have no immediate option except to pay the additional amount. He or she would likely, however, have a claim against the travel agent for failure to secure the services purchased at the agreed-on price. To avoid such situations, travel agents should deal only with reputable hotels, as well as any other providers of travel services.

3. *Misrepresentation.* Travel agents generally are paid only upon the sale of a travel service. Unfortunately, this causes unscrupulous travel agents to intentionally misrepresent the services they market in order to make more sales, and thus more personal income. When they do so and are caught, they face potential liability. However, actual liability in this area is not always easy to determine. For example, Florida is known worldwide as the sunshine state, yet it rains there in some months more than in others. If a travel agent represents to a client living in Vermont that a vacation to Florida during one of the rainy months, would be a chance to "escape to the sunshine," it might be unclear as to whether this statement constituted actual misrepresentation on the agent's part or was in fact a legal marketing effort designed to generate vacation sales, and thus agent commissions. It is highly unlikely that a jury would hold a travel agent responsible for the weather in Florida, but that same agent might be held responsible if it could be established that the agent willfully misrepresented the facts about Florida weather during a specific time period in order to sell more Florida tours.

4. *Failure to discover and disclose.* Travel agents generally are not held liable for the negligent acts of the hotels, restaurants, airlines, and other travel service providers they represent, but they are responsible for informing clients about known hazards and risks. Thus, the travel agent who sells an excursion package for a rafting trip down a river would be required to disclose, if it were known, that, typically, several couples, per rafting season, drown on the same trip. The failure to discover and disclose such information puts the travel agent (as well as the clients!) at risk. To avoid this risk, travel agents must become knowledgeable about the products they sell, then they must be forthright with their clients about what they know. In addition, travel agents are liable for disclosing information that could be interpreted as creating a conflict of interest, which could be detrimental to the interests of their client. For example, if the travel agent is also acting as a tour operator selling its own packages to its travel agent clients, it must disclose this fact.

5. *Negligence.* Faced with the difficulties involved with relying on other parties to provide the services they sell, travel agents have, commonly, sought to limit their liability exposure through the use of contracts that include exculpatory clauses or disclaimers. As noted in Chapter 2, however, the courts are not likely to limit a travel agent's liability via the use of exculpatory clauses or disclaimers when it can be proved that the agent exhibited negligence or gross negligence when interacting with his or her clients.

Of course, consumers who feel they have been treated unfairly by a travel agent have the ability to file a lawsuit against the agent. When large numbers of consumers experience the same alleged breach of law, it is often to their advantage to combine their complaints into a *class action lawsuit*. This is frequently the case when the same incident affects many potential plaintiffs in the same manner. If a class action lawsuit is successful, a period of time is generally established by the court to allow people who can prove they fit the class (suffered the same or similar damages due to the same or similar treatment) to file claims to share in any judgment amounts.

To illustrate, assume that a cruise ship returns to port after four days of what was to be a seven-day cruise. The ship does so because 300 of the 1,500 passengers became ill with a Norwalk-type virus. In this case, all 300 passengers, as well as the 1,200 who had their cruise cut short, may be able to file a successful class action lawsuit if it is determined that there was negligence on the part of the cruise ship's owners or operators that contributed to the viral outbreak.

> **LEGALESE**
> **Class action lawsuit:** A lawsuit filed by one or more people on behalf of themselves and a larger group of people who were similarly affected by an event.

Search the Web 13.4

The world's oldest travel agency is the Thomas Cook Agency. Log on to the Internet, and enter www.thomascook.com.

1. When you arrive, scroll almost all the way down, and click on About Us.
2. Next select Thomas Cook History.
3. Read about Cook's international operations and development.

Tour Operators

Tour operators are an important part of the travel industry, and while they often work closely with travel agencies, they are, from a legal perspective, distinctly different. Hospitality managers will generally encounter both travel agents and tour operators in their normal course of work.

Tour operator is the broad term used to identify those varied companies that purchase travel services in large quantity and then market those same services to individual travelers. In many cases, tour operators, because they purchase travel services in bulk, are able to buy them at a significant discount, add a mark-up that represents the tour operator's profit margin, and still offer travelers lower prices for these travel services than the individual traveler could negotiate on his or her own.

Sometimes travel agencies serve a dual role and also function as tour operators. Legally, however, a tour operator is not an agent, but rather is the principal in the provision of travel services. As a result, the tour operator is directly responsible for the delivery of the travel services they have marketed and sold. This distinction is an important one because principals are responsible for the failure to deliver services as promised, while agents are generally not held responsible, unless they knew or should have known at the time of the booking that services could not be delivered as promised.

Another difference between travel agents and tour operators is the way they earn their income. Tour operators do not work on commission; travel agents do. The tour operator's profit must come from the sale of travel services they

> **LEGALESE**
> **Tour operator:** A company whose primary activity is the planning, packaging, and marketing of travel services, including transportation, meals, accommodations, and activities.

themselves have previously purchased. For example, if a tour operator purchases 100 tickets to the Super Bowl, with the intention of packaging those tickets with airfare and overnight accommodations to create a "Super Bowl Extravaganza" vacation package, the tour operator will have incurred the cost of the football tickets, whether the sale of the vacation packages is successful or not. Thus, while travel agents may lose an unearned commission when a vacation package they offer for sale does not sell, the tour operator will likely face an out-of-pocket monetary loss.

Tour operating companies can offer either a limited or a large number of services. Thus, one tour operator may simply market self-guided trips, relying on selected transportation, hotels, and attractions to make up the trip's itinerary. For example, a tour package from such an operator might consist of airline tickets to a large city, hotel reservations, and tickets to the theater. In this case, the tour itself is not guided or managed by the tour operator. Other tour operators elect to offer full-service tours that include transportation, accommodations, meals, attractions, and the actual tour guides or leaders who serve as escorts. Of course, from a legal perspective, the potential for misunderstandings and litigation increases as the number of services offered by the tour operator increases.

Regulatory Structure

Just as travel agents are regulated primarily at the state level, so too are tour operators. In most cases, the states are concerned about the financial stability of the tour operator. Since tour operators must generally purchase travel services ahead of their actual use, the financial risk taken by tour operators can be great. Some tour operators overextend themselves and then face financial difficulties that result in nonperformance or nondelivery of promised services for which they have previously received client monies. The state statutes that seek to protect consumers in these situations are varied, but all contain provisions designed to ensure that tour operators can provide the services promised, or that consumers can recover money they have paid when the contracted-for services are not provided. Figure 13.4 is an example of this type of law in Hawaii. Note that Hawaiian travel agencies, as well as tour operators, are affected by this statute.

Trust Account. §§468L-5, 468L-23

Travel agencies and charter tour operators must maintain a trust account in a federally insured financial institution located in Hawaii. The account will be established and maintained for the benefit of those paying money to the seller. Payments received for travel services must be deposited in the trust account within five business days.

Withdrawals from the account are permitted for:

■ Payments to the entity directly providing the travel services;
■ Refunds as required by this law;
■ Sales commission;
■ Interest earned and credited to the account;
■ Remaining funds of a purchaser once all travel services have been provided or once tickets or other similar documentation binding upon the ultimate provider of the travel services have been provided.

Charter Tour Operator - Additional Security §468L-22

In addition to the trust account, charter tour operators offering seven or more air charters per year must provide a bond or letter of credit of $300,000 -$1,000,000

Figure 13.4 Hawaii Revised Statutes, Chapter 468L.

Generally, when a person agrees to buy from a tour operator services or products that include transportation, lodging, an interest or investment in a timeshare plan, travel investments, or other travel services, the travel operator must provide the buyer with written disclosure of all terms of the purchase within five business days. After receiving full written disclosure, typically the buyer may cancel such an agreement until midnight of the third business day after the disclosure is received.

Contracts made between tour operators and hospitality services suppliers such as hotels or restaurants will generally be governed by basic contract law. As a result, hospitality managers who do business with tour operators should become familiar with the laws and regulatory requirements that affect their own operations and those of tour operators. One such source of information is the National Tour Association, (NTA), a 4,000-member group consisting of travel professionals working in the packaged travel and tour segment of the industry. The association membership includes tour operators, travel suppliers, and individuals representing destinations and attractions.

Search the Web 13.5

The National Tour Association (NTA) monitors travel law related to tour operators. Go to www.ntaonline.com.

1. When you arrive, click on the For Members tab.
2. Under the Government Relations category (left margin), select Seller of Travel laws.
3. Select: Guide to U.S. and Canadian Seller of Travel Laws.
4. Read the Travel Sellers law in the state that is closest to you.

Potential Liability Issues

Tour operators have specific responsibilities to those from whom they purchase travel services, as well as to those persons actually using the services. Common areas of potential tour operator liability and, as a result, possible litigation, have revolved around five issues:

1. *Nonpayment for prearranged services.* As a hospitality manager, you are most likely to interact with tour operators when they contract with you for food or lodging services. In most cases, the terms of such agreements are subject to the traditional tenets of contract law. Nevertheless, disagreements can arise, so the best practice for restaurant and hotel managers is to seek payment from tour operators for the services they are to render before those services are supplied. Clearly, it is more difficult for a hotel or restaurant to collect payments due to them after services have been provided than it would be if payment were required in advance. Payment terms of contracts with tour operators should be clearly spelled out in any agreements made.

2. *Nondelivery of promised services.* Most travel supplier and consumer-oriented complaints about tour operators revolve around the question of whether the travel services supplied were, in fact, those promised. Honest differences of opinion can easily exist in this area. As noted, tour operators usually concentrate on selling travel services—they rarely provide them.

Thus, these businesses rely on others to transport, feed, and house their travelers. Inevitably, disputes can arise when promised services are not delivered. For example, did a restaurant selected by a tour operator actually provide tour participants "delicious" meals, as promised in a travel advertisement? Was a rafting trip "exciting"? Was a tour guide "qualified"? Often, the courts are asked to decide these issues because the actual written contracts including such terms are difficult to interpret and quantify.

3. *Adhesion contracts.* An *adhesion contract* exists when one party to the contract dictates its nonnegotiable terms to the other party. If the terms of the contract are so one-sided as to be deemed unconscionable by the courts, the offending portion—or, in some cases, all of the contract terms—will be set aside, and the contract interpreted as the court sees appropriate. Because a tour operator's booking conditions often fit the profile of an adhesion contract—that is, tour buyers are often offered a "take it or leave it" form to sign when selecting a tour—it is important that tour operators offer contracts that will be deemed by the courts to be fair to both parties. Thus, excessive cancellation or change fees, broad liability disclaimers, and unreadable fine print (so small it can be assumed to have been used to put off buyers) should be avoided in tour operator contracts.

4. *Liability for injury or accident.* Despite all the advances made by the travel industry, travel can still be dangerous. This is especially true in this day of worldwide terrorist activities that are purportedly directed toward specific governments, but inevitably strike individual travelers on a random basis. In addition, many tour activities such as rock or mountain climbing, skiing, motorized sports, or hunting are all inherently risky, regardless of the safety precautions taken. In cases such as these, and even in tours that involve no more strenuous or dangerous an activity than walking, accidents will happen, dangerous unforeseen as well as foreseen events will occur, and even the weather may cause injury or accident. All these raise the question of liability, especially for tour operators who, in most cases, contract for, rather than directly provide, the services they sell. Generally, the courts will not hold tour operators liable for the negligent actions of travel services suppliers unless they are owned by the tour operator. Tour operators will be held liable, however, for their own negligence.

5. *Misrepresentation.* Most tour operators are honest, but some are not. Misrepresentation can occur whenever a tour operator knowingly misrepresents the fares and charges for their services, knowingly sells transportation when the tour operator has not made a binding commitment with the carrier designated in the agreement sold to the buyer, or knowingly misrepresents other travel services to be provided in an unscrupulous effort to entice buyers to buy. Unfortunately, misrepresentation can be difficult to prove. Therefore, as a hospitality manager doing business with a tour operator, you should strive to understand exactly what you have been contracted to supply, as well as how your company will be presented in the marketing efforts of the tour operator.

Corporate and Government Travel

Many legal issues arise during the domestic and international travel of corporate and government employees. When employees who travel domestically or internationally are faced with a volatile situation, employers need to be aware of their responsibility to extract their employees from the volatile or unsafe situation. Specifically, corporations and governments have a duty of care to their employees when they travel, and have been found liable for the injuries, medical evacuation, and medical treatment when employees are working either domestically or overseas. This duty of care is similar to that of a negligence standard, and it is assessed by asking whether the actions taken by the corporation or government were reasonable—a sort of reasonable person standard for corporate managers.

To keep employees safe and secure and to reduce liability, as well as further injury to employees, corporate managers and government travel managers should enact internal protocols for mobile employees and specify the steps to be taken when an emergency happens that affects an employee while traveling. There are many organizations that offer education and assistance to corporations and government travel managers in the area of employee travel. A few of these are the Association of Corporate Travel Executives, the Global Business Travel Association, and the Society of Government Travel Professionals. You can learn more about these groups by accessing their websites at www.acte.org, www.gbta.org, and www.shtp.org, respectively.

(Search the Web **13.6**)

The Global Congress on Legal, Safety, and Security Solutions in Travel is an annual event where professionals from all aspects of the travel industry can come together to discuss their legal, safety, and security experiences and best practices. To learn more about the Global Congress's mission, and learn how to participate, visit its website at www.globalcongressontravel.com.

≫ ANALYZE THE SITUATION 13.1

AS PART OF A three-day "Mystery Tour," Joan Larson of Apex Travel, Inc., a Wisconsin-based tour operator, contacted the Ragin Cajun restaurant in Illinois, for the purpose of reserving 120 seats for dinner on a Friday night in September. The tour group arrived, and one male group member, after three drinks, began making rude and suggestive comments to one of the restaurant's female servers. When Steve, the restaurant manager approached Gene, the Apex tour leader, about the situation, Gene maintained the comments were probably made in harmless fun and should be overlooked by the restaurant. "Besides," stated Gene, "our bus is leaving to go back to our hotel in one hour and that particular tour group member lives several hundred miles away and is unlikely to ever see that server again." As the Ragin Cajun's restaurant manager:

1. What are your legal responsibilities to your server?

2. Who is responsible for controlling this guest's behavior?

3. How would you respond to Gene, the tour operator?

4. What potential liability does Apex face in this situation?

13.3 TRANSPORTATION AND COMMON CARRIERS

The method of transportation travelers select for their trip is typically one of the most important decisions they make. Speed, comfort and safety, and cost are all factors that determine which method of transportation they will choose. Of those, the reduction in the cost of transportation is a primary factor contributing to the total amount of world travel and, subsequently, to the rise in the number of *common carriers.*

Travel-related common carriers have a responsibility to service the transportation needs of most any passenger who wishes to travel. Generally, these carriers have no more right to refuse a passenger, if they have sufficient room, than an innkeeper has to refuse a guest (see Chapter 10). A common carrier has a special duty to its passengers to see that they arrive at their destination safely, which includes using the highest degree of care to protect them against physical harm. This is so important that the quality of a country or region's common carriers determines, in large part, the amount of tourism activity in that area, as well as how much others in the travel industry want to invest in and develop the area's tourism infrastructure.

The Transportation Industry

The transportation industry includes both those businesses carrying people and those moving freight. This is true because manufacturers need to safely transport their goods from one place to another in the same way that passengers must be transported. Historically, stagecoaches, steamships, and railroads developed operating systems that accommodated mail, freight, and passengers. Today, some businesses in the transportation industry, such as United Parcel Service (UPS) and Federal Express (FedEx), specialize in the transportation of freight, others emphasize passenger transportation, and still others provide both. For the hospitality manager, knowledge of the laws related to the passenger transportation industries is very important. These include the airlines, as well as rail, cruise ship, bus, and—although they are not technically common carriers—car rental companies.

International travel has become an important topic, particularly as it relates to common carriers. As technology advances, and people are able to move around the world with much ease and little cost, the U.S. and foreign governments have worked together in order to find ways to more safely and effectively administer international travel. Specifically, there are numerous international travel treaties that have been executed between the U.S. and other foreign governments; two of the major treaties being the Warsaw Convention, and the Montreal Convention. *The Warsaw Convention,* or the Convention for the Unification of Certain Rules Relating to International Transportation by Air, seeks to create a uniform body of law pertaining the rights and responsibilities of international passengers, shippers, and air carriers. The main purpose of the Warsaw Convention is to limit the liability of air carriers by fixing the liability of carriers for harm to passengers, baggage, and goods; as well as creating uniform documentation, procedures, and law for claims arising out of international air carriage.

The Warsaw Convention was subsequently amended by the Convention for the Unification of Certain Rules for International Carriage by Air drafted in Montreal, called the Montreal Convention. The Montreal Convention has been described as favoring passengers rather than the air carriers. Specifically, the Montreal Convention provides that a carrier is liable for damages sustained in cases of death or bodily injury of a passenger if the injury occurred aboard the aircraft or at any time during embarking or disembarking. To read more about the Warsaw and Montreal Conventions, go to: www.dot.gov/ost/ogc/Warsaw1929, and www.dot.gov/ost/ogc/ProtocolNo4.

Airlines

U.S. airlines carry over 500 million passengers per year. In most cases, airplanes are the preferred method of long-distance travel for both leisure and business travelers—despite the tragic events of 9/11. Since 1954, the total number of passengers served by the airline industry has increased significantly each year, because of the speed and relatively low cost. Of course, with large numbers of travelers comes the potential for large numbers of legal issues, especially given the number of factors that can affect on-time arrivals and departures, along with the inconvenience and difficulty caused by missed connections, damaged luggage, or physical injury. While it is rare, airplanes can and do crash, and lawsuits inevitably result. In all cases, the cause of the crash is investigated thoroughly, and the findings are used to assist in the assignment of liability for the accident, and to determine the law that applies to the particulars of the crash.

Precisely which laws apply to the relationship between a service provider and a consumer depends, in large measure, on what each party has promised and agreed to. The same is true of the relationship between airlines and their passengers. The details of the contract made between an airline and the passengers it carries is called the *tariff*, which, by law, must be made available, in its entirety, from the airline. To enforce the terms of its tariff, an airline must:

- Ensure that passengers can receive an explanation of key terms identified on the ticket from any location where the carrier's tickets are sold, including travel agencies.

- Make available for inspection the full text of its contract (tariff) at each of its own airport and city ticket offices.

- Mail a free copy of the full text of its tariff to the passenger upon request.

The terms of the tariffs affect how passengers are treated. For example, each airline has its own policies about what it will do for passengers whose flights are delayed. There are no federal laws or requirements in this area. Some airlines, especially those charging very low fares, do not provide any amenities to stranded passengers. Others may not offer amenities if the delay is caused by bad weather, or something else beyond the airline's control. Contrary to popular belief, airlines are not required to compensate passengers whose flights are delayed or canceled. Compensation is required by law only when a passenger is "bumped" from a flight that has been overbooked.

U.S. airlines operate flights regionally, nationally, and internationally. When operating solely within the borders of the United States, federal law applies. This is because the U.S. Supreme Court has ruled that the Airline Deregulation Act of 1978 and the Federal Aviation Act 1958 preempt all state statutory and common law claims related to rates, routes, or services of air carriers.

In a similar manner, when airlines operate internationally, they are subject to the rules and liability limitations of the Warsaw Convention. The agreements made at the Warsaw Convention have been amended and updated several times. Today, as modified by subsequent agreements, it governs claims arising from international air transportation, and preempts common law and those laws created by various countries in which airlines operate. The Warsaw Convention applies to all international transportation supplied to persons, baggage, or goods by any aircraft for hire. It sets forth a comprehensive scheme that defines the liability of international air carriers for personal injuries, damage, loss of baggage and goods, and damage caused by delay. The United States is a *signatory* of the Warsaw Convention, which means that, for international flights, U.S. consumer protection laws are preempted by its terms.

LEGALESE
Tariff: The agreement between an airline and its passengers. When purchasing a ticket, the passenger agrees to the terms of the tariff.

LEGALESE
Signatory: An entity that signs and agrees to abide by the terms of a document.

Trains

Train transportation was instrumental in the early development of the United States, but today its role is far smaller than that of airplanes and automobiles. Although rail companies can move freight efficiently, and make money doing so, given the present structure of the rail system in this country, it is simply unprofitable in most cases to operate trains for the purpose of passenger transportation. This should come as no surprise. Public dollars are routinely used to build airports, and the airlines that utilize them profit from doing so. In a similar manner, the automobile industry has benefited from the immense investment in public roads and highways undertaken by federal, state, and local governments. The average U.S. citizen has been less enthusiastic, however, about using tax dollars to invest in the land, track, signals, and equipment needed to build and maintain a reliable passenger rail system. Consequently, with the exception of specific areas or routes, especially in highly populated regions, passenger rail service is not routinely available. There are, however, still nationwide passenger rail routes operated by Amtrak.

Despite a widely held belief to the contrary, Amtrak—whose name is a blend of the words "American" and "track"—is not a part of the federal government. Officially the National Railroad Passenger Corporation, Amtrak is, ostensibly, the nation's for-profit passenger rail service. However, since its inception in 1971, it has been dependent on the federal government (as well as some state governments) for grants that enable it to continue offering its services. In 2010, Amtrak employed about 20,000. More than 28 million passengers rode Amtrak in fiscal year 2010, a ridership record that was 5.7 percent higher than the previous year, which earned Amtrak $1.74 billion in ticket revenue.[3]

Since its inception, New York City, Philadelphia, and Washington, DC, are the most popular boarding and disembarkment points for Amtrak rail travelers, reflecting actual use of the railroad for large-city commuting rather than long-distance travel.

Amtrak, like all other common carriers, is responsible for the safe delivery of its travelers and can be held liable for its negligence. And as on airplanes, train delays can occur and travelers can be inconvenienced, and as a common carrier, Amtrak may bear some responsibility for the resulting impact on travelers. As can be seen in Figure 13.5, Amtrak's liability disclaimer seeks to limit its liability for the effects of traveler inconvenience by carefully detailing its responsibility in the event of a travel disruption.

Amtrak's fares, time schedules, equipment, routing, services and accessibility information are not guaranteed, are subject to change without notice, and form no part of the contract between Amtrak and a passenger. Amtrak reserves the right to change its policies without notice. Amtrak disclaims liability for inconvenience, expense, or damage resulting from errors in its timetable, shortages of equipment, or delayed trains, except when such a delay causes a passenger to miss a guaranteed connection. When a guaranteed connection is missed, Amtrak will provide alternate transportation on Amtrak, another carrier, or overnight hotel accommodations at Amtrak's discretion. It may be necessary for Amtrak to provide substitute transportation and to cancel service when necessitated by operational or safety conditions. (Effective 9/2003)

Figure 13.5 Amtrak liability disclaimer.

---

[3] "Amtrak Sets New Ridership Record Thanks Passengers for Taking the Train," Amtrak News Release, October 11, 2010. www.amtrak.com/servlet/BlobServer?blobcol=urldata& blobtable=MungoBlobs&blobkey=id&blobwhere=1249216336898&blobheader=applic ation%2Fpdf&blobheadername1=Content-disposition&blobheadervalue1=attachment; filename=Amtrak_ATK-10-134_AmtrakRidershipRecordFY10.pdf.

Search the Web **13.7**

Rail travel takes longer than air travel, but passenger fares, in some cases, make it more cost-effective. Log on to the Internet and enter www.amtrak.com.

1. At the site, price a passenger fare between New York City and Chicago.
2. Now price the same trip by airplane on www.Travelocity.com.
3. Compare the travel time involved with the fare savings. To whom do you believe train travel would be most appealing?

Cruise Ships

Before the advent of airplanes, ships and luxury liners were the only available method of traveling from one continent to another. While the use of ships for business and vacation travel has generally decreased from the early 1900s through today, the use of cruise ships for, specifically, vacation travel has increased steadily. According to the Cruise Lines International Association (CLIA), about 13.5 million passengers took a cruise in 2009.[4]

The U.S. government also keeps statistics on cruise lines. The Maritime Administration (MARAD, www.marad.dot.gov), which is part of the U.S. Department of Transportation, is responsible for the U.S. maritime transportation system of freight cargo and cruise travel. MARAD's statistics cover the major cruise lines that offer North American cruises with a U.S. port of call. They include Azamara, Carnival, Celebrity, Costa, Crystal, Cunard, Disney, Fred Olsen, Holland America, MSC, Norwegian (NCL), Oceania, Princess, Regent, Royal Caribbean, Seabourn, Seadream, Silversea, and Windstar. For vacation cruises, Miami is the largest departure port in the United States; Ft. Lauderdale is second. The western Caribbean was the most visited destination in 2010, with the Bahamas in second place and Alaska finishing third. Cruises typically range in length from three days to three months, with those cruises in the six- to eight-day category having the largest share of both number of cruises and passengers.

Perhaps part of the reason for the increase in cruise ship popularity is that cruise itineraries include some of the calmest waters in the world. In addition, stabilizers on modern ships, the availability of advance weather information, and the development of effective preventative medications have, for the most part, eliminated the incidence of motion (sea) sickness. In 2010, the North America cruise market added four huge ships: Royal Caribbean's *Oasis of the Seas* (5,400 passenger capacity) and *Allure of the Seas* (5,400 passengers), NCL's *Norwegian Epic* (4,200 passengers), and Carnival's *Carnival Dream* (3,646 passengers). Together, these four accounted for 10 percent of the fourth quarter 2010 North America cruise passenger capacity.[5]

---

[4] Cruise Lines International Association, "Profile of the U.S. Cruise Industry," 2010, www2.cruising.org/Press/sourcebook2010/profile_cruise_industry.cfm. Accessed June 2011.
[5] U.S. Department of Transportation, *Maritime Administration*, *North American Cruise Statistical Snapshots, 2010*, March 2011, pp. 9, 13. Accessed October 5, 2010, at www.marad.dot.gov/documents/North_American_Cruise_Statistics_Quarterly_Snapshot.pdf.

LEGALESE

Maritime law: Also called "admiralty law" or "the law of admiralty," the laws, regulations, international agreements, and treaties that govern activities in navigable waters.

Legal issues related to cruise travel have not similarly disappeared. In many respects, a cruise ship is very much like a floating full-service hotel. Thus, managers working in the cruise industry face many of the same guest safety, security, and liability issues as their land-based hospitality management counterparts. Like all common carriers, those who operate cruise ships are subject to many local, state, national, and international laws. Cruise ships and their passengers are also subject to *maritime laws*, many of which may preempt more localized laws.

Buses

Buses are still an extremely important mode of transport for the travel and tourism industry. True, their use for long-distance travel is substantially less than that of either airplanes or automobiles, yet they play an important role in many areas, including shuttle services from train stations, bus depots, and parking lots. Buses are also widely used for charters on routes between destinations within 200 or 300 miles of each other. On these routes, buses may actually be faster than air travel, especially considering new time-consuming airport security measures. Transporting groups to hotels, restaurants, and nightclubs; visiting historic sites and local attractions; attending concerts, sporting events, and competitions; and the going on group shopping trips are additional popular ways groups make use of bus travel.

The federal government defines a bus as a passenger-carrying vehicle designed to seat at least 16 people, including the driver. The U.S. Department of Transportation's Motor Carrier Safety Administration is the major regulatory agency responsible for bus safety. The agency develops rules and regulations in an effort to ensure the safety of bus passengers. Such rules include the hours a bus driver may be required to drive, safety features of buses, and operator license requirements.

In the hospitality industry, the term *bus* is sometimes misunderstood, and that misunderstanding can lead to contract disputes. Consider, for example, the corporate executive who contracts with a bus operator for a bus to transport 30 high-level managers to and from a pro football game. Greytrails Bus Lines agrees to supply a bus for the trip; however, when the day of the trip arrives, the bus provided turns out to be a school bus. Clearly, it is unlikely that the desired bus and the bus provided are one and the same in the mind of the executive arranging the travel. Although no mandated definitions exist, those in the bus industry generally recognize the following bus types:

- *Economy:* School-type buses represent the basic, lowest-cost option for group travelers wishing to minimize their expense. These buses typically are arranged with bench (not individual) seating, and contain no restroom facilities.

- *Deluxe motor coach:* This type of tour bus is most often selected for longer trips, or for those groups seeking greater comfort than is afforded by economy buses. The typical seating is 47 to 55 individual seats, with VCR/DVD capability, multiple monitors, advanced sound systems, and restroom facilities.

- *Executive motor coach:* This top-of-the-line bus is chosen by those who prefer extra-luxurious bus travel. Executive coaches are custom-made, so options vary, but typically they include full bedrooms, showers, social and meeting space, and state-of-the-art telecommunications. The maximum capacity for buses of this type range from 5 to 20 persons.

- *Specialty:* In some cases, trolley or double-decker buses are appropriate and are contracted for on a special-case basis.

For managers in the hospitality industry, bus travelers can be a significant source of income. Restaurant managers encourage buses to stop at their restaurants for meals, and hotel managers seek to contract with bus operators for the overnight hotel stays required in long-distance bus travel.

Car Rentals

Car rental companies are not technically common carriers because they lease cars rather than transport passengers. The car rental business is, however, an important component of the transportation industry, and it comprises establishments primarily engaged in renting or leasing passenger cars, vans, trucks, and utility trailers. There are more than 10,000 such operations within the United States alone. These businesses generally operate from a retail facility. Some establishments offer only short-term rental, others only longer-term leases, and still others provide both types of services. Not surprisingly, California, Florida, and Texas are the three states that host the greatest number of car rental outlets and lease the most vehicles.

Rental car companies operate under laws within the states they do business. The terms of the rental agreements made must be clear to the person renting the vehicle, and rental companies are held responsible for renting safe vehicles to persons qualified to drive them. When they are not, the car rental company may, under a variety of statutes, be held liable for the accidents that ensue, or the consumer rights violated.

Regulation in the Transportation Industry

The transportation industry is one of the most highly regulated industries in the world. In the United States, for example, local and state laws may govern the terms of transportation service that can be provided (e.g., at what speed a bus may drive when transporting passengers on a state-maintained highway), federal law may dictate how those in the transportation business must maintain their equipment (e.g., the Federal Aviation Administration requirements for plane maintenance). Similarly, international maritime law may dictate the responsibilities of an internationally registered cruise ship docked in a U.S. port.

In addition to various state and local regulation enforcement agencies, at the federal level, those agencies that impose requirements on various businesses in the transportation industry include the FAA, DOT, NTSB, U.S. Postal Service, EPA, IRS, Interstate Commerce Commission, Department of Labor, Bureau of Citizenship and Immigration Services, Department of Agriculture, and other federal agencies; as well as nonfederal governmental agencies such as local airport authorities.

For those businesses in the transportation industry that operate across national borders, compliance with international law is critical. To facilitate the legal conformity of these businesses, each industry segment maintains its own voluntary compliance enforcement group. For example, in the airline industry, those companies that transport passengers internationally belong to the International Air Transport Association (IATA). The IATA was founded in Havana, Cuba, in April 1945. It is the prime vehicle for interairline cooperation in promoting safe, reliable, secure, and economical air services. At its founding, IATA had 57 members from 31 nations, mostly in Europe and North America. Today it has over 230 members from more than 130 nations. Since January 1, 2000, all airlines joining IATA have been required to demonstrate, as part of the membership eligibility process, that they operate according to an existing set of recognized international operational quality standards (OQS). These standards encompass not only flight safety but also engineering, maintenance, security, and flight operations.

Potential Liability Issues

A myriad of legal issues confront consumers and those who do business in the transportation industry. Those of most interest to hospitality managers are discussed in the following subsections.

Legal Jurisdiction

One of the most difficult issues to resolve in a legal dispute related to transportation is the identification of the appropriate court to hear the complaint. If, for example, a traveler residing in Texas purchased, from a Texas-based travel agent, an airline ticket for an intrastate (within the state) flight operated by an airline incorporated in Texas, and that traveler experienced difficulty, it is likely the traveler's complaint would be heard in a Texas court. But, if, instead, the traveler were an Israeli citizen who purchased via a London-based travel agent a vacation cruise operated by a Scandinavian cruise line that docked in the Bahamas, and, while docked there, the traveler was injured on the ship, the question of which court of law should hear this traveler's complaint would, of course, be much more complex. Often, the contracts themselves will specify which location will have jurisdiction should a dispute arise, but others may not, and the battles can be fierce; as "home-field" jurisdictions often provide the same advantages in litigation as they do in sporting events.

The hospitality manager involved in international travel and venues must be certain to operate under the applicable laws at the appropriate times.

Overbooking

Just as hotels can sometimes miscalculate their occupancy forecasts and oversell their capacity, so too can airlines and rental car companies. Thus, hotel managers often find themselves housing guests who are affected by the overbooking of a transportation provider. In many such cases, guests are understandably upset and, consequently, may express much more dissatisfaction with their accommodations than would a guest whose travel plans had not been disrupted by overbooking. When this happens, it is important for the hotel manager to understand that the client paying for the hotel's services (generally, the transportation provider) is in an unfortunate situation, as is the guest staying in the hotel, and that both parties should be accommodated in the best manner possible.

U.S. federal regulations do not require any compensation be made for a delayed or canceled flight if the delay or cancellation is due to circumstances beyond the airline's control, such as inclement weather. For other kinds of delays and schedule interruptions, each airline has its own policies on offering compensation for a passenger. Those policies are either included with the paperwork associated with passenger tickets or are available from an airline's airport or ticket offices. Typical compensation offered for a delayed flight may range from free meals to hotel accommodations. When faced with a delay, passengers should either review the airline's policy or obtain a copy of the policy to see what compensation is available.

Federal law specifically allows airlines to overbook flights to allow for no-show passengers. But when passengers are involuntarily bumped, airlines are first required to request volunteers to give up their seats in exchange for compensation. Involuntarily bumped passengers are subject to minimum compensation as follows:

■ No compensation if alternative transportation is available to get the passenger to his or her destination within one hour of the original scheduled arrival.

■ The equivalent of the passenger's one-way fare up to a maximum of $200 for substitute domestic flights that arrive between one and two hours after the original scheduled arrival time, or for substitute international flights that arrive between one and four hours after the original scheduled arrival time.

■ If the substitute transportation is scheduled to get the passenger to his or her destination more than two hours later (four hours internationally), or if the airline does not make any substitute travel arrangements, the compensation doubles, to a maximum of $400.

The compensation schedule does not apply to charter flights or scheduled flights operated with planes that hold 60 or fewer passengers, or international flights inbound to the United States.

Responsibility for Baggage

With millions of people traveling each year, it is inevitable that some of those travelers get separated from their luggage. Also, despite their best efforts, common carriers may damage baggage that has been entrusted to them. Airlines, by far, handle the greatest amount of passenger luggage. Thus, airlines flying domestic routes may, as part of their tariffs, set limits on the amount they will pay for lost or damaged bags. For travel wholly between U.S. points, federal rules require any limit on an airline's total baggage liability to be at least $2,500 per passenger; and this information must be communicated to the passenger. For international flights, provisions of the Warsaw Convention limit liability for lost or damaged baggage unless a higher value is declared in advance and additional charges are paid. The limit for most international travel is approximately $9 per pound for checked baggage and $400 for unchecked baggage.

Baggage that has been lost is an inconvenience to both the traveler and the business responsible for the loss. Hospitality managers hosting travelers who have lost their luggage should, of course, ensure that their operations will do all they can to assist these travelers.

Unplanned Changes in Itinerary

Travel plans can be disrupted by a variety of factors, some controllable, some not. Inclement weather, mechanical failures, traffic congestion, and human error can all disrupt travel plans, resulting in losses of both time and money. For example, if a couple's flight delay means they miss a cruise ship departure, an entire vacation may be in jeopardy. Regardless of who is responsible, when travel plans are disrupted, those in the restaurant and hotel business may be affected. Meals may be delayed or canceled, hotel rooms may go unused, or, when travel departure plans are disrupted, a hotel may be overbooked.

Managers must be sensitive to the needs of the inconvenienced traveler, as well as the needs of their own business. The best time to address the potential difficulties that could result from unanticipated itinerary changes is prior to signing a contract with a service provider. For example, assume that a restaurant agrees to serve dinner to a sports team traveling from one state to another. The 45-person team is scheduled to arrive at the restaurant at 6:00 P.M. The food for the group is prepared and the dining area reserved. But due to mechanical trouble with the bus used to transport the players, the team is stranded 100 miles away and elects to eat dinner in the town where the bus has broken down. The terms of the contract signed between the restaurant and the team's representative will dictate what level, if any, of charges will be assessed by the restaurant.

Industry-specific Issues

Because the transportation industry is so diverse, certain laws will apply only to specific segments of it. This is especially true with regard to catastrophic events. Catastrophic events involving common carriers include plane crashes, train derailments, bus accidents, and maritime accidents. Additionally, a common carrier might be liable for other noncatastrophic incidents such as a slip and fall on a cruise ship, a sexual assault by a cruise ship employee or passenger, and other occurrences. Generally, common carriers are held to a very high safety standard, and hence may be liable for even the slightest amount of neglect. Moreover, laws have been passed in direct response to specific incidents. For example, in 1996, after the

TWA crash that killed 230 people off Long Island, New York, Congress passed the Aviation Disaster Family Assistance Act, which provides that, after a crash involving fatalities:

■ Family members must be given time to notify other relatives before the names of passengers are made public.

■ The airline must offer crisis counseling.

■ The airline must make hotel rooms and food available for relatives.

■ The airlines must help family members retrieve dental records and X-rays to identify the victims.

■ The airlines must provide transportation to families to and from the crash site.

Hotel and restaurant managers are not, of course, expected to be experts in all areas of travel law; nevertheless, managers whose jobs bring them in regular contact with specific segments of the transportation industry are well advised to familiarize themselves with the industry-specific legislation that directly affects their hospitality operations.

13.4   TOURISM

The terms *travel* and *tourism* are not synonymous. Travel, especially business-related, is conducted for a specific commercial purpose. Much business travel is undertaken strictly to advance commerce, and travelers typically have little or no time to take in the sights and attractions of the places to which they travel. Tourism, in contrast, consists of the activities directly related to pleasure travel. Tourists, in most cases, select their destinations based on what they want to see and do when they get there. There is, of course, some crossover between the two definitions. Business groups, for example, may choose their meeting locations based on what attendees can do after their scheduled daily activities have concluded. As noted earlier in this chapter, tourism can have a major impact on local economies and ecologies. As a result, circumstances often arise that can result in legal conflict, related to zoning, taxation, environmental impact, and human resources management, to name but a few.

For those hospitality managers working in areas that cater to large numbers of tourists, tourism may represent a substantial portion of the total income generated by their business. Many legal issues specifically related to tourism are important to hospitality managers, but three areas are of particular interest: the *gaming* industry, the resort industry (including *timeshares*), and the *amusement park* industry.

Unique Responsibilities of Gaming Operations

Few segments of the travel and tourism industry elicit a more passionate response from both its advocates and adversaries than the gaming industry. Not surprisingly, the litigation surrounding gaming is significant and continues to grow as gaming, as a form of recreational activity, expands both in the United States and internationally. The result, for those working in the industry, is a unique set of regulatory requirements, as well as potential liability issues.

History of the Gaming Industry

Gambling is not a recent phenomenon. The Chinese, Japanese, Greeks, and Romans all were known to play games of chance as early as 2300 B.C. Gambling is not new to the United States, either. Both Native Americans and colonists brought a history of gambling from their own cultures that helped shape America's gaming views and practices. Native Americans even developed language to describe gambling, and in 1643, the explorer Roger Williams wrote about the games of chance developed by the Narragansett Indians of Rhode Island.

Government-approved gambling, and the idea of using gaming proceeds to pay for societal projects is also a concept with a long history in the United States. Lotteries, a popular form of voluntary taxation in England during the Georgian era (1720–1750), subsequently became popular in America as European settlers arrived here. Lotteries sponsored by prominent individuals such as Ben Franklin, John Hancock, and George Washington operated in each of the 13 colonies to raise funds for building projects. Between 1765 and 1806, the state of Massachusetts authorized lotteries to help build dormitories and supply equipment for Harvard College (now Harvard University), as well as many other institutions of higher learning. Dartmouth, Yale, and Columbia are all examples of educational institutions whose early development was financed, in large part, through lotteries. A lottery was even approved to provide funds for the American Revolution.

Today, the gaming industry in the United States is large and growing. Its exact size is difficult to establish; thus, estimates can vary widely. Though there are many ways to measure the size of an industry, conventional standards include using the number of employees, the output of products, tax receipts, or customer count. The most common measure, however, is gross revenues, or sales. When gross revenue is used to gauge the size of the gaming industry, it is common to measure either how much consumers bet or how much the gaming operator wins on legal gambling games. This undertaking is more complex than it may first appear.

For example, assume that Bessie Hale, a retired schoolteacher, elects to visit a local casino with her friends. Bessie intends to play some slot machines and attend a Doug Stone concert held in the casino's ballroom. While at the casino, Bessie exchanges $100 in cash for 100 $1 tokens to use in the slot machines. One token at a time, Bessie bets all of the original 100 tokens. Based on the machine's payout, Bessie will win some of her $1 bets, and because the average slot machine pays out 90 cents for every dollar put in, Bessie will end up with about 90 tokens. She continues to bet one token at a time, until she has gone through her 90 remaining tokens. Again Bessie wins about 90 percent of her bets, and thus, after betting each of her tokens, retains about 81 tokens (90 percent win rate times 90 tokens equals 81 tokens). By this time, the concert is about to begin, and so Bessie cashes in her 81 tokens and goes to the concert. Of her original $100, Bessie has $81 left. She will have, in the opinion of most observers, spent $19 on the slot machines. The slot machine records, however, $190 in total wagers (her original $100 plus $90 winnings). The casino's winnings are, of course, only Bessie's actual "loss" of $19.

Confusion between the amount actually bet, which is sometimes referred to as the "handle," and the amount actually spent (lost) accounts for the widely varying estimates of the size of the legalized gaming industry. But most observers agree that the amount actually spent (lost) by customers, not the total amount they may have wagered repeatedly over the course of an evening, is the best way to measure the industry's size. Based on that approach, legalized gambling is an industry with revenue estimates exceeding $75 billion per year. The industry encompasses state-operated lotteries, casinos, horse and dog tracks, and other locations where gambling is legally allowed (such as off-track betting parlors—OTBs).

Gaming Regulation and Control

All states that allow gaming regulate it. The federal government also regulates gaming through the U.S. Justice Department, the U.S. Treasury Department, and the Department of the Interior. Other agencies with oversight relationships to gaming include the FBI, the IRS, the U.S. Attorney General's Office, the U.S. Marshals, the Secret Service, and the Bureau of Indian Affairs. Gaming is also allowed, under strict control, in casinos operated by Native Americans (Indians). The Indian Gaming

Regulatory Act of 1988 (IGRA), which provides for a thorough system of regulation of Indian gaming, divides gaming activity into three categories:

Class I: Social or traditional and cultural forms of Indian gaming, conducted for minimal prizes or in connection with ceremonies or celebrations, and solely regulated by the tribes.

Class II: Includes bingo and related games, as well as nonbanking card games, if those games are otherwise lawful within the states where tribes conduct those activities. This gaming is regulated by the National Indian Gaming Commission and Tribes through the Tribal Gaming Commissions (TGC). TGCs are established and operated by Indian nations to regulate gaming activities on reservations. There are some 186 TGCs in full operation nationwide.

Class III: All other gaming, including casino gaming. Class III gaming is regulated according to the terms of compacts tribes negotiate with the governments of the states where they are located. These compacts often give tribal gaming commissions the primary, on-site regulatory responsibility for gaming.

Gaming is one of the most highly regulated industries in the United States. The governmental agencies involved with gaming regulation have their own professional association, called the North American Gaming Regulators Association (NAGRA). Formed in 1984, NAGRA is composed of federal, state, local, tribal, and provincial government agencies that are responsible primarily for the regulation of legalized gaming activities.

Search the Web 13.8

Log on to the Internet and enter www.nagra.org.

1. At the site, click on About NAGRA.

2. Next, click on Vision & Goals.

3. Why would standardization among regulations be important for the continued development of the gaming industry?

Potential Liability Issues

Hospitality managers operating hotels or food and beverage outlets within casinos, or near other gambling venues face a number of liability issues. Those managers should continually monitor the legal environment surrounding gaming. There are three current issues of significance in this area:

1. *Accountability for reckless gaming behavior.* If a society allows gaming, does it follow that an individual should have the right to wage (and lose) all of his or her family possessions? This question is one with both ethical and legal implications. It also raises the question: What responsibility does a gaming operator have to prevent excessive or reckless wagering by those who are compulsive gamblers, visibly intoxicated, or underage? These are difficult questions to answer. To avoid problems, well-managed casino operations train their employees to watch for telltale signs that indicate threats to responsible gaming and might result in litigation in which the gaming operator is accused of irresponsible behavior. Harrah's casinos

have pioneered efforts in this area through their "Operation Bet Smart" program, designed to alert Harrah's employees to gamblers who may have problems controlling their behavior. And Harrah's "Project 21" is designed to help employees enforce regulations related to the minimum legal age requirements of gamblers.

2. *Employee working conditions.* The operation of gaming facilities involves legal issues that affect employees as well as consumers. One such issue is smoking. Many casinos allow smoking throughout their premises. Increasingly, employee rights groups, as well as state and local communities, are restricting smoking in casinos because of the dangers of second-hand smoke. Currently, 25 states fully or partially ban smoking in public places such as casinos. Those casino operators who continue to allow smoking where it is prohibited do so at some legal risk.

   Other current issues affecting casino employees are sexual harassment of workers by guests, the legality of extensive employee background checks, and level of training and experience required by employees to demonstrate that reasonable care standards in operations are met.

3. *Internet gambling.* Bricks-and-mortar casinos in the United States are subject to federal corporate taxes; publicly traded companies must comply with Securities and Exchange Commission rules; and casinos must report large winnings with the IRS, as well as withhold federal taxes on certain winnings. In addition, "land-based" casinos must adhere to anti-money-laundering statutes and regulations administered by the U.S. Treasury Department. In contrast, currently, gaming operators engaged in the business of taking Internet wagers from U.S. citizens are not currently subject to such federal and state legal requirements. And though it is unlikely that the U.S. governments will ban all Internet gaming, probably Internet gaming operators will become subject to state and federal gaming oversight in the future. Legislation addressing the differences between currently "approved" gaming and Internet gaming is taking shape and is well worth monitoring by those managers working in the gaming industry.

Gaming remains an activity that is enjoyed by millions in this country, and it is an area within the travel and tourism industry that carries with it the potential for a great deal of enjoyment. But it also presents complex legal challenges for the businesspeople, lawmakers, and the public at large.

Unique Responsibilities of Resort/Timeshare Operations

For many travelers, a resort is the ideal location for a vacation or holiday. There is no universally accepted definition for the term *resort*, but in the hospitality industry, it generally refers to an operation offering food and beverages, lodging, and entertainment and/or recreation. Thus, resorts are found in many locations. Favorite resort types include:

- Summer resorts
- Winter resorts
- Beach resorts
- Ski resorts
- Spa and health-related resorts
- Fishing resorts
- Recreational resorts (e.g., golf, tennis, etc.)

Some travelers became so enamored with a specific resort that they seek to reserve space at it year after year. This gave rise to the development of the timeshare concept, whereby a buyer acquires the right to occupy a piece of real estate, such as an apartment or condominium in a resort area, for a specific period of time each year. From this grew the practice of timeshare owners trading their occupancy rights with others.

Background to the Resort/Timeshare Industry

In most respects, the resort industry is not unlike the mainstream hotel industry, with two significant differences. The first is that guests at resorts are likely to engage in activities that can, potentially, put them at some level of physical risk. Resorts typically offer their guests the chance to participate in optional recreational activities. Whereas a show or concert presents minimal physical risk, others are not so benign. For example, assume that a couple elects to visit a Western-style "working ranch," which features outdoor camping, as well as the opportunity to herd cattle while on horseback. Obviously, these activities raise the risk for numerous kinds of accidents and injuries.

The second major difference is that the resort industry has embraced timeshare as a method of development and expansion. There are essentially two main types of time-sharing plans: "deeded" and "undeeded." Under the deeded plan, a buyer purchases an ownership interest in a piece of real estate. Under the undeeded plan, buyers purchase a lease, license, or club membership that lets them use the property for a specific amount of time each year for a specific number of years. Under both plans, the cost of the unit is related to the dates and length of time the property will be occupied.

Potential Liability Issues

Liability issues raised by the resort and timeshare industry revolve around the impact of resorts on their local communities, and the sales techniques used to sell timeshare units. On the face of it, the process of selling timeshares appears to be fairly straightforward, but the tactics used in some real estate transactions have resulted in major legal difficulties in this segment of the resort market. Consider three possible liability issues:

1. *Economic and environmental impact of resorts and resort activities.* Resorts, especially those in countries with underdeveloped economies, can have a tremendously positive financial impact. There are more than 7 million timeshare owners, in more than 100 countries.[6] Jobs, improvements to utilities, construction of roads and other infrastructure components can all result when a resort is developed. But resort development can also drive up the cost of living for local residents, damage ecosystems, and consume a disproportionately large share of natural resources. In some local economies, other businesses cannot compete with resorts for available labor, and so these communities come to depend almost entirely on the resort(s) for their livelihood. The result is litigation between the entities operating the resorts and residents and governments seeking to control the impact of the resort on the local area.

2. *Deceptive sales tactics.* With over 5,700 resorts worldwide participating in timeshare sales, it is inevitable that some would employ unscrupulous means to sell their products. Most states regulate time-sharing sales either under existing state real estate laws or under laws that were specifically enacted to address time-sharing. The regulating authority is usually the real estate commission in the state where the timeshare is located. In the past, problems have arisen with regard to sales deception in the areas of total costs, exchange programs, and facility operations.

---

[6] Timeshare Consumers Guide, "Timeshare Statistics," 2009, www.timeshareconsumerguide.org/statistics.htm. Accessed June 2011.

Search the Web **13.9**

The timeshare industry has been helped tremendously by the entrance of large and well-established hotel companies seeking to promote the resorts they own and operate.

Go to www.hiltongrandvacations.com.

1. Click on Learn About Ownership.

2. Do you believe Hilton does a good job explaining the advantages and limitations of a timeshare purchase?

The cost of buying a timeshare includes its purchase price, as well as any required monthly or annual maintenance fees. Maintenance fees are related to the normal upkeep of common ownership property areas such as pools, tennis courts, and the like. These fees typically rise at rates that equal or exceed inflation, though some timeshare operators have used increases in annual maintenance fees to generate exorbitant profits.

For many vacationers, the chance to participate in exchange programs is a major factor in their buying decision. Exchange programs offer the opportunity to arrange trades with the owners of other resort units in different locations. But promises about the specifics of such exchange programs can be exaggerated, and hence result in litigation alleging deceptive sales practices.

In sum, timeshares can be good investments if they are operated properly. And buyers must consider the track record of the seller, developer, and management company before making a purchase. In short, they must do their homework.

3. *Rights in event of default.* Perhaps the worst-case scenario for timeshare purchasers (or managers!) is the closure or bankruptcy of the resort they partially "own." If a developer, builder, or management company defaults on its financial obligations for a resort, the impact on the individual timeshare owners of that resort can be significant. To help ensure against problems of this type, timeshare buyers should insist that their contracts include a *nondisturbance clause.* A nondisturbance provision ensures that individual timeshare owners will continue to have the use of their timeshare unit in the event of default and subsequent third-party claims against the resort's developer or management firm.

LEGALESE

Nondisturbance clause:
A clause in a contract that stipulates that leases or other ownership investments in the property will be allowed to continue uninterrupted in the event of a default or insolvency by the landlord/seller.

Given the popularity of resorts and the perceived advantages of timeshare ownership, these two components of the travel and tourism industry will continue to grow. Those hospitality managers involved in these industry segments should, as appropriate, monitor the legal environment related to them.

Unique Responsibilities of Amusement Park Operations

Amusement parks are extremely popular with visitors of all ages. The International Association of Amusement Parks and Attractions (IAAPA) estimates that over 325 million people visit amusement parks each year, and while there, these visitors spend over $10.8 billion. Hospitality managers working within these parks typically provide food, beverage, and lodging services, and many hospitality managers work in communities whose travel patterns and economies are heavily influenced by the amusement parks in their area.

History of the Amusement Park Industry

The amusement park industry began in medieval Europe when pleasure gardens were developed on the outskirts of major European cities. These gardens, forerunners of today's amusement parks, featured live entertainment, fireworks, dancing, games, and even some primitive amusement rides. Pleasure gardens remained extremely popular until the 1700s, when the political environment caused most of them to close. But one such park still exists, in Bakken, north of Copenhagen. It opened in 1583 and now enjoys the status of being the world's oldest operating amusement park.

In the late 1800s, the growth of the amusement industry shifted to the United States and the amusement park entered what many say was its golden era, culminating with the 1893 World's Columbian Exposition in Chicago. This world's fair introduced the Ferris wheel and the midway to the world. The midway, with its wide array of rides and concessions, was a huge success. The following year, Captain Paul Boyton borrowed the midway concept and opened the world's first modern amusement park on the south side of Chicago. The success of his Chicago park inspired him to open a similar facility at the then-fledgling Coney Island resort in New York City, in 1895. That, too, was a great success, and subsequently, many amusement parks were developed following the Coney Island model. In 1929, when America entered the Great Depression, spending declined, and by 1935, those amusement parks that still remained were struggling to survive.

The end of World War II brought a brief resurgence to amusement parks, but by the 1950s, television began replacing the amusement park as a major source of entertainment. Thus, when Walt Disney opened Disneyland in 1955, many were skeptical that an amusement park without any of the traditional attractions would succeed. But Disneyland, as everyone knows, proved the skeptics wrong. Instead of a midway, Disneyland offered five distinct themed areas, providing visitors with the fantasy of travel to different lands and times. It also offered many activities that could be enjoyed by the very young and the young at heart. An immediate success, Disneyland gave rise to the theme park era.

But by the 1980s, while the theme park boom began spreading around the world, the industry growth had slowed considerably in the United States, due to high operational costs and a lack of markets large enough to support a theme park. Today, those parks that remain are very large and thus have substantial impact on the economies of those communities in which they are located.

Potential Liability Issues

In addition to issues related to food and beverage service, hospitality managers working at or near major amusement parks may face three amusement park–specific legal challenges:

1. *Safety of activities.* Accidents related to amusement park rides, though they typically receive widespread publicity, are actually quite rare. Injury figures are but a small fraction of those attributed to other recreational activities. In fact, in 2009, 1,181 ride accidents were reported to the National Safety Council,[7] most of which were minor bruises, strains, and sprains. In comparison, each year, an estimated 20,000 people are treated for injuries sustained at concerts. Nevertheless, amusement park operators implicated in the injury of a visitor will be expected to have exhibited an appropriate

---

[7] National Safety Council Research and Statistical Services Group, "Fixed-Site Amusement Ride Injury Survey, 2009 Update," Prepared for the International Association of Amusement Parks and Attractions, Alexandria, Virginia, August 2010, www.iaapa.org/safety/RideSafetyReports .asp. Accessed June 2011.

amount of care in the maintenance and operation of their rides. If they do not, probably they will be held all or partially liable for the damages.

2. *Performance expectations.* When guests are charged an admission fee to enter a park, there are expectations on the part of the park's operators that guests will behave appropriately. If guests do not, they can be removed from the park. In a similar manner, guests will have expectations, too; for example, that advertised rides will be available, that appropriate facilities such as restrooms and food and beverage outlets will be provided, and that these will be maintained in an appropriate manner. If they are not, guests may have a legitimate basis for legal action against the park.

3. *Litigation related to employee training.* Much of the work required to appropriately maintain amusement type rides can be dangerous if not performed properly. Thus, adequate staff training programs are critical if park employees are to safely perform their required tasks. If such training, as well as the proper tools and safety devices, are not provided by a park's management, potential lawsuits related to resulting accident or injury are very likely to occur.

» ANALYZE THE SITUATION 13.2

SANDRA WILKENS WAS A roller-coaster enthusiast who, along with others, attended the Harley Amusement park's "Roller Fest," a POP (pay one price) event featuring unlimited roller-coaster riding by all attendees. Sandra, 25 years old, paid the $50 admission fee and was, at the time of her fatal accident, riding the Superman, a wooden double-loop coaster. On the final loop, Sandra was thrown from the coaster and killed. Witnesses say she was standing in the coaster car as it approached the final loop.

Sandra's family filed suit against the park and its state ride inspectors, claiming negligence because Sandra was placed in a car where she had the ability to stand up. Park officials countered that all riders were informed, via a public address system, not to stand during the ride's operation. In addition, they pointed to posted signs that warned riders not to stand up during the entire length of the ride. Further, they said, the ride was operating properly, all rider restraints had been inspected and approved that morning, and Sandra had taken inadvisable action to defeat the restraining devices built into the ride.

1. What level of responsibility should the park operators be assigned for Sandra's behavior?

2. List five specific actions the park management could take, or institute, to help eliminate such guest behavior in the future.

3. What similar situations might you face in your own area of hospitality where responsibility for guest injury may be all or partially related to guest behavior?

13.5 ONLINE TRAVEL SALES

Online travel sales are those that are completed via use of the Internet and the World Wide Web. They include the sale of hotel rooms, car rentals, and other transportation services such as airline tickets and cruise reservations. Travelers who use online services tend to be computer-savvy, using the Internet at a higher rate than the general public, according to a Travel Industry Association of America "Travelers' Use of the Internet" study. Currently, over 100 million travelers use the Internet to seek travel information or to book travel. This number includes both business and leisure travelers.

The online travel sales segment is also one of the Internet's largest components. By most industry estimates, travel accounts for 30 to 40 percent of all Internet consumer sales. And this segment of the travel industry continues to grow, posting a 47 percent increase in online travel sales revenue in 2002, despite an overall travel industry sales decline of 5 percent.

Background of the Online Travel Sales Industry

In 1995, the total revenue generated by the online travel sales industry was close to zero. According to eMarketer, 2010 sales exceeded $92.5 billion. That year, 162 million people in the United States will research products online, and much of this research will lead to in-store purchases. More than 82 percent, or 133 million people, who research travel options online end up making online purchases.[8]

The enhanced accessibility of last-minute travel specials via the Internet, coupled with everyday low prices, have resulted in a tremendous increase in online travel sales. Whether true or not, the majority of travelers believe that the best travel "deals" can be found on the Internet, and for these travel buyers, price is a very important decision factor. As a result, the online travel sales industry will likely continue to play a larger and larger role in the overall travel industry.

Essentially, there are two basic types of websites used to sell online travel services. The first are those that serve as electronic brochures (e-brochures) and in this capacity display information about one or more travel products. An e-brochure might include, for example, pictures of a hotel room, departure and arrival schedules of a common carrier, or details of a travel package. These websites also act as catalogs, basically displaying information about a business and include, in most cases, a method (typically email) that enables the website visitor to ask for additional information about ordering products or services, or about communicating directly with the entity identified on the site.

The second type of website enables consumers to make a purchase or reservation online. Thus, an airline ticket can be purchased, a hotel reservation made, or a rental car reserved directly at the website. These e-commerce sites allow the traveler to see the product offered, as well as buy and pay for it online. In order to do so, however, the site must have several features not required by an e-brochure site, and it is the use of these features that raise the legal issues surrounding the use of e-commerce sites. These features include:

- *A bank account that can process Internet purchases:* This means an Internet merchant account, which is different from a typical business bank account because it is designed specifically to handle Internet purchases. Funds from Internet purchases are deposited in these accounts.

- *An agreement with a credit (bank) card processor:* A credit or bank card processing company is responsible for collecting funds from the buyer and depositing those funds into the Internet merchant's bank account. For this

---

[8]Jeffrey Grau, "U.S. Retail E-Commerce Forecast: Room to Grow," *eMarketer*, March 2010, www.emarketer.com/Report.aspx?code=emarketer_2000672. Accessed June 2011.

Search the Web **13.10**

E-commerce sites, by definition, must allow consumers to buy while at the sites. PayPal is one example of a credit card processing company required to allow such purchasing. Log on to the Internet, and enter www.paypal.com.

1. When you arrive, click on Business.

2. Next, review the different payment options.

3. Describe the differences between these options.

4. Which do you believe would be the best choice for a business in the hospitality industry?

---

service, the processor will take, from the revenue generated by the merchant, an agreed-on fee for each purchase. This fee will vary, based on the type of bank card used by the purchaser.

- *A secure connection:* When a website takes private and sensitive information like a credit card number from a visitor, it must provide a level of security to protect it from unscrupulous individuals. To do so, an e-commerce website must have a "secure" connection. Sites can purchase their own secure connection or share the use of one with others for a small percentage of the sold item's purchase price.

The total cost of developing and maintaining an e-commerce site is, because of the fees involved, higher than that of maintaining an e-brochure site. Thus, some travel providers elect to allow online purchases, while others prefer the brochure approach. Each type is involved in a rapidly developing and specialized area of law associated with the online travel sales industry.

Legal Issues Related to Online Travel Sales

The advent of the online travel industry has raised some new issues, and caused the modification of some older legal issues. Here are five of the most important:

1. *Parties to the contract.* On websites, it is sometimes difficult to determine exactly who is party to a consumer transaction. For example, assume that a business traveler, utilizing the Internet, logs on to the Priceline.com travel site. While there, the traveler bids for a room and is successful in getting a reservation for the Chicago Hilton. Upon arrival, however, the Chicago Hilton has no record of the traveler's reservation. If, indeed, the error was on the part of Priceline.com, the traveler's legal action would likely be, all or in part, with Priceline.com. In this scenario, a judge would likely rule that Priceline advertised the ability to secure for the traveler a reservation that, in this example, it did not. Alternatively, if the traveler had made the same reservation on Hilton's own website, the responsibility for providing the room, and hence the responsibility for failure to provide it, would ultimately rest with the hotel. With multiple third-party websites, and with the ownership of websites frequently shared by members of the travel industry, the entity responsible for performing the terms of a web-initiated contract may not be readily apparent to any but the most sophisticated of users.

LEGALESE

Global distribution system (GDS): An interconnected computer system that connects travel professionals worldwide to those companies selling travel services.

2. *Data interface issues.* When airlines, hotels, cruise lines, and others take reservations on the Internet, the potential for problems, and thus litigation, increases. The reason is that reservation systems on the Internet are often not directly connected (interfaced) with the service provider. To clearly understand the problem, it is important to understand that an independent hotel in, say, Manhattan is not likely to directly connect its reservation systems with the thousands of websites offering hotel rooms for sale. Such direct connections are expensive and frequently technologically unwieldy. As a result, if a third-party-operated website advertising hotel reservations for a specific hotel is not interfaced with the hotel's reservation system through the *global distribution system (GDS)*, it must communicate with the hotel via fax or email to confirm that a room has been sold via the website. The problem, of course, is that in the time between the sale of the room on the website and the hotel's notification (and acknowledgment) of the sale, the same room may have been sold by the hotel itself, or even on another website. The result may be either an oversold situation, or that the product reserved (and in many cases confirmed on the website making the sale) is not available upon the guest's arrival.

Hospitality managers entering into sales agreements with websites that are not interfaced with their own product inventories should have a very clear understanding with the website provider as to responsibility in the event guests arrive with reservations erroneously made due to an absence of real-time interfacing.

3. *Data security/ownership issues.* When a reservation for a hotel room, cruise, or airline flight is made, personal information is typically gathered from travelers. Other businesses in the travel industry are often interested in this information, especially as it relates to the latest economic data on travel to an area, where those travelers come from, and their spending patterns. Consumers, on the other hand, have a right to privacy, and when personal information is accessed by organizations unknown to them, or unapproved by them, they may have cause for concern and complaint.

Even within a single company, sharing personal guest information can be cause for litigation. For example, consider the case of Marques Johnson. He is a hotel franchisee who owns and operates a Best Sleep hotel. Best Sleep is one of five hotel brands franchised by United Hotels Inc., a large franchise company. United instructs all franchisees that they are to begin collecting email addresses from guests and then make the database of those email addresses available to United so that corporate advertising efforts can be better targeted. Mr. Johnson objects on three grounds: First, that it is his staff, not the franchisor's who will collect the information, and thus it rightfully belongs to Johnson's company, not United Hotels. Second, he is concerned that the addresses of his guests will be shared, by United, with other

---

(Search the Web **13.11**)

Hospitality managers and service providers seeking to offer consumers the ability to reserve online can choose from a variety of options. Log on to the Internet, and enter www.webervations.com.

1. When you arrive, scroll down to Online Reservations.
2. Describe the differences between a "reservation request" and a "real-time reservation."
3. Why would a hotel manager elect to choose one or the other?

United franchisees operating different United brands in the same city as Johnson's franchise. These hotels, in many cases, compete directly with Johnson's hotel. Therefore, sharing data on his guests would, in his opinion, unfairly assist these other hotels in competing with him. Last, Johnson states, his guests have a right to know when he is sharing their email addresses with others; thus, ethically, unless he has these guests' preapproval, he does not believe he should share their email addresses. The franchisor maintains that he must, to remain a franchise in good standing, collect and share the addresses.

Lost in this disagreement, of course, is the issue of the guests' right to privacy. Although the law in this area is still developing, the best practice today is that personal data related to guests should not be shared with organizations that did not directly collect the data, unless the guest has been explicitly informed about the sharing arrangement prior to the information's collection. In addition, those who collect personal data on guests have a responsibility to take reasonable care in securing that data from theft or misuse by others.

4. *Forum (venue) selection issues.* "Forum" refers to the location in which a lawsuit may properly be filed. In many cases, where a legal dispute has taken place, and thus should be settled, is relatively straightforward. For example, assume that a restaurant manager working in Alabama hires a local electrician to install additional lighting in the restaurant's parking area. If the restaurateur does not believe the electrician has adequately performed the terms of his contract, the dispute would be resolved, in all likelihood, by a court in Alabama and in accordance with Alabama law.

Now assume that the same restaurateur purchased, online, a cruise for herself and her husband. The cruise was advertised on a website managed by a New York state travel agency. It offered a ten-day Caribbean cruise departing from Miami. The cruise ship itself is operated by an Italian cruise line company. If, ultimately, the cruise supplied did not meet the expectations of the restaurateur, the proper venue for her potential legal action would be less clear. But there would be no question if the contract agreed to by the restaurant manager included information about the appropriate location for any needed legal action. A *forum (venue) selection clause* is a statement in a contract specifically identifying the court or entity authorized to hear disputes related to a contract's terms.

> **LEGALESE**
>
> **Forum (venue) selection clause:** A statement in a contract identifying the agreed-on tribunal for resolving legal disputes related to the contract's terms.

Those travel companies doing business on the Web will typically insert forum selection clauses into their contracts in an effort to preclude having to defend against lawsuits that might be filed anywhere in the world. The courts will generally enforce Internet forum selection clauses if they are clearly communicated to purchasers. But though forum selection clauses are commonly used by hotels and international cruise line operators, it is important to point out that the U.S. Department of Transportation (DOT) has prohibited the use of these clauses for the purchase of airline tickets.

In addition to identifying the location of potential litigation, website travel providers may, for instance, insert contract clauses that require buyers to agree that any dispute arising would be resolved before an arbitration tribunal, rather than a court.

5. *Lawful advertising.* Internet travel advertising, like all advertising, is subject to regulation through state consumer protection statutes, state and federal telemarketing statutes, the Federal Trade Commission (FTC), the Department of Transportation (DOT), and the Sellers of Travel statutes enacted by some states. Many of these are intended to address the problem of deceptive advertising versus "puffing." Puffing is a common, and allowable, advertising technique used by both e-brochure and e-commerce sites. It is, essentially, the act of "accentuating the positive" when promoting a travel product. Thus, a hotel site may claim that its rooms are "beautiful," "modern," or "spacious," and the assumption by law is that consumers should recognize such terms as an attempt by the advertiser

to encourage sales. But when such superlatives are considered sufficiently misleading and deceiving, they may fall under deceptive advertising or actionable misrepresentation statutes; depending on the specific conditions of the accommodations, or actual inferiority of the services purchased online. Certainly, puffing makes for interesting and effective advertising copy, but truth in advertising is as effective a practice when describing products and services on a website as it is on a restaurant menu.

For the most part, websites are just another form of advertisement, and thus the developed law related to advertising applies to them as well. Some special managerial considerations about website advertising are given in the next Legally Managing at Work section.

LEGALLY MANAGING AT WORK:

Internet Advertising Checklist

The Federal Trade Commission (FTC) considers as deceptive any ad that is likely to mislead consumers acting reasonably and that is material (i.e., important) to a consumer's decision to buy the product or service. To avoid charges of deceptive or illegal advertising, hospitality managers should review with its website developers the following Internet advertising checklist. If the answer to any of the checklisted items is no, the site content should be revised until the answer is yes.

1. **Are all statements and claims true?**

   A claim is a legal advertising term referring to any provable statement contained in an advertisement. It is the responsibility of the advertiser to be able to "prove" all claims made. Hospitality managers should ensure that they have the ability and proof required to substantiate all claims made before they are published on the website. If there is any doubt about the validity of the claim, it should not be posted on the Internet.

2. **Are prices accurate?**

   Prices, if given, must be stated accurately. If taxes or local assessments will be added, these too must be identified. In addition, any conditions that must be met to get the advertised price must also be disclosed.

3. **Are conditions spelled out clearly?**

   It is best to disclose all conditions necessary to enable the buyer to fully understand what is offered for sale. For example, a hotel offering "free breakfast" with the price of a room would be well advised to detail whether there are limits to the number of guests per room who are allowed to eat, as well as when the breakfast is offered. In general, the use of the word free should be avoided when there are, in fact, conditions that must first be met, unless those conditions are prominently disclosed. In addition, the words sale or discount should be avoided, unless there have been substantial and recent real-life sales made at a higher price.

4. Is inappropriate puffery avoided?

The development of an Internet site typically involves the use of sight, sound, and text on a webpage. Although puffery is allowed, the information that is presented must be carefully reviewed to ensure that it is within acceptable bounds. It is difficult, for example, to claim that a web ad contains allowable puffery, when a hotel displays the picture of one very nice room, and uses the phrase "great rooms," when, in fact, other rooms of the same quality do not exist within the hotel.

The Web has spawned some new views toward puffery. In a recent lawsuit against a college textbook retailer that on its site that its store was "the globe's largest college bookstore," the website owners claimed that the statement was puffery and thus allowable. The National Advertising Division of the Council of Better Business Bureaus Inc. disagreed, stating that claims like this might have been puffery in a non-Web context, but online, which is accessible worldwide, and where the website owner can appear large or small with few obvious clues to actual size, statements such as this one appear, on their face, to be believable, and thus are no longer puffery.

5. Have web-specific advertising issues been considered?

The Federal Trade Commission has developed some web-specific standards for advertising. Some of those standards include:

- Placing disclosures near, or on the same screen as, the related claims.
- Ensuring that, when using links or hyperlinks to disclosures, the links are obvious and easy to find.
- Ensuring that text, graphics, or sound is not used to distract attention from disclosure information.
- Ensuring that disclosures are repeated, as needed, on lengthy websites.

6. Are proper marks, logos, and business names used correctly?

Are proper symbols, such as the trademark symbol, used where appropriate? Are trademarks and logos accurate and used only when written, prior approval has been granted? Many website developers create a style manual that details the approval procedures to be used before including such marks, logos, or business names on their sites.

7. Have photos and drawings used been cleared for intellectual property rights?

The Internet abounds with pictures and images that can be easily copied or downloaded. The best rule to follow when creating your own website is quite simple: If your organization did not directly create or pay for the creation of the image you wish to use, you should obtain written permission from the owner of that image prior to its use, unless its reproduction and sharing has been authorized by the owner.

WHAT WOULD YOU DO?

You are the manager of a franchised, 90-room limited-service hotel property located across the highway from 7 Flags, a major amusement park that is extremely busy in the summer. One of the most popular family packages your hotel sells includes a two-night stay (in on Friday night, out on Sunday morning), complimentary breakfast, and tickets to 7 Flags. You purchase the tickets, in quantity, from the 7 Flags group sales department. Your packages are marketed directly by your hotel and sold through select travel agents to whom you pay a sales commission.

At 3:00 P.M. on a Saturday afternoon in July, lightning from a severe summer thunderstorm strikes a major electrical transformer in the area, causing an area power outage that includes the amusement park and results in the park's immediate closure. Your hotel is sold out. The power company is unsure how long it will take to fully restore power, but its estimate is hours, not minutes. Your own hotel has a backup generator—thus, essential hotel services such as emergency lighting and power to the property management system (PMS) are maintained.

Your lobby, however, is filled with families seeking to check out (it is 4:30 P.M.) so they can leave the area and drive back to their homes (where most of them will have power.) Approximately 60 guests want to check out. None of these guests believe they should have to pay for their Saturday night stay because, due to the power outage, they will not use their reserved rooms. Some want a refund for Friday night as well, claiming the hotel did not provide the complete two-day "package" that was promised.

1. Would you bill these 60 guests for Saturday night's stay, even if they elect to leave?

2. Would you give the guests any other compensation?

3. Would your course of action be affected if you learned the theme park had made the decision to refund the price of admission to all those who entered the park on that day?

4. If the theme park had made the refund mentioned, do you believe the amount of the refund belongs to the disappointed park attendee or to your hotel?

5. Describe briefly how the decision you make will affect:

   a. Your relationship with the theme park's management

   b. The relationship with your franchisor

   c. Your relationship with travel agents marketing your packages

---

THE HOSPITALITY INDUSTRY IN COURT

For an example of a case on matters of jurisdiction, consider the case of *Decker v. Circus Circus Hotel*, 49 F.Supp. 2d 743 (Dist. N.J.).

FACTUAL SUMMARY

Janice and Robert Decker (the Deckers), New Jersey residents, were guests at the Circus Circus Hotel (the Hotel) in Las Vegas, Nevada. The Hotel was part of a Nevada corporation doing business in Nevada. One or both of the Deckers were injured while at the hotel, and they sued Circus Circus for negligence in New Jersey Federal District Court.

QUESTION FOR THE COURT

The question for the court was whether the New Jersey court had jurisdiction or the power to adjudicate the matter. A court can exercise jurisdiction over a defendant if the defendant has a certain level of contact with the geographical area where the court sits. This level of contact is referred to as minimum contact, and the resulting jurisdiction is personal or specific jurisdiction. The Deckers argued that the Hotel had enough contact with the state of New Jersey to allow the court to exercise jurisdiction. Specifically, the Deckers pointed to national television campaigns, which aired in New Jersey, and advertisements printed in national print media such as *USA Today* and *People* magazine. The Hotel first contended the ads used in New Jersey were isolated, one-time television spots. The Hotel also argued the lawsuit brought by the Deckers did not arise from the television or magazine ads, so the contact between the Hotel and New Jersey would not meet the minimum contacts standard.

DECISION

The court held in favor of the Hotel and found there was not enough contact between the Hotel and the state of New Jersey to give the New Jersey court jurisdiction. Instead, the case was transferred to the U.S. District Court in Las Vegas, Nevada, since the Hotel was a Nevada corporation, hence jurisdiction would be proper for the state of incorporation.

MESSAGE TO MANAGEMENT

Plaintiffs want to sue in the most convenient (and sometimes favorable) location possible. Potential defendants want to reduce the number of locations in which they can be sued due to the expense and uncertainty involved.

For an example of an international jurisdiction case, consider the case of *Bernardi v. Apple Vacations*, 236 F.Supp. 2d 465 (E.D. Penn., 2002).

FACTUAL SUMMARY

Karen Bernardi, a resident of Pennsylvania, was a passenger on a Lineas Aereas Allegro S.A. de C.V. (Allegro) flight from Cancun, Mexico, to Newark, New Jersey. Bernardi and several other passengers alleged they were treated inhumanely during their flight. Bernardi and the other plaintiffs sued Allegro for violations of the Pennsylvania Unfair Trade Practices and Consumer Protection Law, misrepresentation, false imprisonment, intentional infliction of emotional distress, and negligence, all of which are state law causes of action. The original suit was filed in the Court of Common Pleas of Delaware County, a Pennsylvania State Court. Allegro requested the case be moved to the United States District Court for the Eastern District of Pennsylvania, which was granted. At that time, Allegro requested to have the case dismissed since the Warsaw Convention governs injuries suffered by passengers on international airline flights.

QUESTION FOR THE COURT

The question for the court was whether the Warsaw Convention, an international treaty signed and ratified by the United States, preempts or overrules state law dealing with injuries suffered on international flights. Bernardi argued the Warsaw Convention only applied to acts of negligence, not willful misconduct. Therefore, the claims based on the willful misconduct of the defendant should be allowed to proceed under Pennsylvania state law. Allegro first argued the language of the Warsaw Convention expressly included provisions relating to willful misconduct. There were specific causes of action contained in the Warsaw Convention for willful misconduct. Allegro also argued the purpose of the Warsaw Convention was to achieve uniformity in international airline litigation; to allow state law claims for willful misconduct would be counterproductive. The defendant also pointed out the recent U.S. Supreme Court cases where the Warsaw Convention was found to apply to willful misconduct claims. Finally, Allegro argued the plaintiffs were misreading a provision, which allowed the determination as to whether conduct was willful misconduct to be made using local (state) law.

DECISION

The court held for the defendant, Allegro, and dismissed the claims brought by Bernardi. The court did point out, however, that Bernardi could bring suit against Allegro for any cause of action allowed under the Warsaw Convention.

MESSAGE TO MANAGEMENT

Be sure to put venue and jurisdiction clauses in all contracts for passage, as these issues can be very expensive to litigate and may require the carrier to defend itself around the world.

WHAT DID YOU LEARN IN THIS CHAPTER?

The hospitality industry is one component of the larger travel (and tourism) industry, which is heavily regulated. Because it is so large and diverse, the number of groups and organizations responsible for the legal oversight of travel activities is large. Some of the most notable of these include governmental agencies, at both the federal and the state level, as well as nongovernmental groups that operate internationally to coordinate travel policies.

The travel industry has historically relied on travel experts (travel agents) to assist travelers in planning their trips. These agents, who have a fiduciary responsibility to travelers, are a highly professional group. Tour operators, whose role is to develop travel and vacation packages, typically use travel agents to market these packages, thus creating a special, mutually dependent relationship between travel agents and tour operators.

The transportation industry also plays a critical role in the travel industry. It consists primarily of common carriers, which include those entities providing transportation services to all travelers. These companies, providing airline, bus, cruise ship, and train services, are a large and highly regulated segment of the travel industry. The rental car portion of the transportation industry, while not technically a common carrier, also plays a critical role in the U.S. travel market, as well as in those countries with well-developed road and highway systems.

Because so many people travel for enjoyment, the tourism business is, for many communities, a critical factor in the local economy. Gaming establishments, resorts, and amusement parks are all popular leisure-time venues, but they are also potential sites of legal entanglements for those who operate them, as well as for those who visit them.

The Internet has emerged as a major force in the travel and tourism industry. It has affected how industry products are marketed and sold and has raised new legal questions relating to the uniqueness of the electronic product distribution systems now in widespread use on the World Wide Web.

After you have studied this chapter, you should be prepared to:

1. Identify the five major components of the travel industry.

2. Detail the legal relationship that exists between the three parties when a travel agent sells to a client a travel package marketed by a tour operator.

3. Specify at least two legal issues that would be considered unique to the transportation industry.

4. Tribal gaming is a controversial issue in many communities. Prepare a list of five points explaining your support for or opposition to its expansion.

5. Write a paragraph explaining why you might seek employment in the gaming, resort, or amusement park industries. What might be some disadvantages of such employment?

6. The Internet is popular among travelers. Discuss your view of how the Internet will impact the travel agent and tour operator segments of the travel industry in the coming years.

In teams of four, collect and review at least eight "legal disclaimers and legal acknowledgment notices" from online reservation sources (both from branded sites such as Hilton.com and third-party sites such as Expedia.com). Using this information, the discussion in the book, and input from the class, in two pages or less, create a model disclaimer and notice provision for a branded online reservation site.

CHAPTER **14**

SAFETY AND SECURITY ISSUES

"THAT WAS INCREDIBLE," thought Trisha Sangus. She collapsed in her office chair, truly exhausted after a 15-hour day at the hotel. Lance Dani sat in the chair opposite hers on the other side of her desk. Between the fire itself, the media, guest telephone calls, and numerous meetings with the hotel's employees and department heads, Trisha barely had time to take a five-minute break. She had been awakened in the middle of the night by Lance, the hotel manager on duty, when the fire broke out in a guestroom on the second floor.

As Lance had explained it, the guests in room 232 had been burning an open-flame candle on the wooden nightstand when they fell asleep. They were awakened by the smoke alarm in their room, and shortly thereafter, the entire hotel was awakened by the hotel's fire alarm system.

"We were lucky," said Lance.

"Lucky? You mean that the fire didn't spread, and that no one was injured?" asked Trisha.

"Well, yes, that," said Lance, "but more than that. I mean, the fire department got here so quickly, and the evacuation plan worked without a hitch. I remember you meeting with the chief just last month to review the department's response plan."

"Yes," replied Trisha, "the firefighters did a great job."

"They sure did," said Lance, "and you did a great job letting the media know we had everything under control. And your idea of having a manager visit each guestroom afterward to ensure everyone was all right. Wow. What could have been a real disaster turned out just fine. That's what I mean, we were lucky."

No, thought Trisha, *they had not really been lucky. What they had been was rewarded for hours of planning for just such a time as this.* The fire department had not responded quickly due merely to luck, and Trisha made a mental note to call her good friend Fire Chief Stanley to thank him. Her relationship with the chief had always been a top priority for Trisha, and she was sure he had taken every measure to ensure that his group responded quickly when the hotel's alarm system activated.

The evacuation plan that had been so painstakingly prepared and revised by Trisha was also not a piece of luck. Trisha had spent many hours with her corporate director of safety and security preparing a total emergency response plan they both hoped would never be used, but knew would be critical if it were.

Many of the hotel's department heads had also worked hard on the plan. The hard work was apparent today when everyone knew what to do, and for the most part, were able to do it quickly and efficiently. The monthly safety and security inspections had helped, too. In addition to providing a regular self-inspection check, they kept safety in the forefront of the hotel's department heads' and staff's minds. It had paid off.

Trisha had expected the media to show up. Fires were news; the news media monitored the police and fire stations' activities, and she knew she would be expected to address the press. She had been prepared.

The "idea" of visiting each guestroom was not, she knew, her own. She picked it up when reading an article in her trade association magazine that emphasized the importance of both checking for injured guests and calming any potential fears caused by the incident. It had worked well, and she was pleased. She spent many hours a month keeping current by reading her trade magazine and by attending continuing education seminars. These activities had paid off.

"We weren't lucky, Lance, we were ready," said Trisha. But she knew that being ready was not a static condition. Rather, it was a state maintained only by the constant process of observing, coaching, and training both herself and the staff.

As she reflected on the excellent performance of her coworkers, the telephone rang. Trisha's secretary told her that the corporate office was on the phone. It was a call Trisha had been anticipating since she notified her boss's office of the fire earlier in the day. She was ready. The company president was on the line.

"Trisha, I understand your team performed like clockwork! Great job!" Trisha smiled and replied, "Yes, they did. And I have some ideas for how we could do even better in the future. Let me tell you about today, and what I have planned for tomorrow."

"Great, I'm anxious to hear all about it. Then I want you to let me tell you about the regional vice president's job in your area that just became vacant. Supervising 25 hotels in five states, Trisha. It's a big responsibility, and a big raise. You're perfect for it. Let me tell you why. . . ."

IN THIS CHAPTER, YOU WILL LEARN:

1. To recognize the responsibility hospitality managers have to protect the safety and security of guests and employees in hospitality operations.
2. To carry out the procedures needed to limit the potential liability of safety risks and security risks.
3. To minimize the risk of crimes against your own business operation.
4. To recognize the need for and benefit of implementing an effective crisis management plan.

14.1 THE IMPORTANCE OF A PROTECTED ENVIRONMENT

As you have seen in previous chapters, you are responsible for taking reasonable care that people are not hurt when they enter or stay in your establishment, and for ensuring that their possessions are safe during their stay. In Chapter 10, "Your Responsibilities as a Hospitality Operator to Guests," we used examples of recreational facilities, such as pools and fitness facilities, to show you one way that hospitality operations can demonstrate reasonable care for the safety of their guests. Of course, safety extends beyond guests to include management, staff, and the general public.

The courts will not expect you to protect everyone who comes into contact with your operation against all possible calamities. They will, however, expect you to use good judgment in carrying out the procedures necessary to show you care about the well-being of your guests, employees, and visitors, as well as the security of their property. In this chapter, we will examine some procedures used to protect people and assets in the hospitality environment; as well as the procedures used before, during, and after a period of potentially devastating circumstances, such as a fire, storm, criminal activity, or other threatening activity.

Safety and Security Management

As the manager of your facility, you will be responsible for a large number of activities designed to protect people and property. All of these activities can be grouped under the commonly used terms of *safety programs* and *security programs*. In order for a safety and security program to be effective, hospitality managers must make sure that the program covers every component of a guest's visit and every aspect of their facility's operation. Effective managers may implement several different policies, procedures, and training programs that together make up a comprehensive safety and security program.

> **LEGALESE**
> **Safety program:** Those procedures and activities designed to ensure the physical protection and good health of guests and employees.

›› ANALYZE THE SITUATION 14.1

MR. AND MRS. ANGELO were frequent diners at the Buffet World restaurant, a moderately priced operation that featured an all-you-can-eat lunch and dinner buffet. Jessie Carroll was the manager of the restaurant. On a busy Sunday, Mr. and Mrs. Angelo entered the restaurant, paid for their meal, and were directed to their table by the dining room greeter. As Mrs. Angelo sat down, the wooden dining room chair snapped under her weight. Her neck was injured as she fell on the restaurant's tile floor.

The Angelos sued Buffet World, charging negligence in the operation of the restaurant. Their attorney argued that the normal wear and tear of chairs was a foreseeable event, and thus an inspection program should have been in place. No such program could be shown by the restaurant to have existed.

The attorney for the restaurant countered that Mrs. Angelo was "larger" than the average guest, and therefore Buffet World could not have foreseen that she would be seated in a chair that was not capable of holding her weight. The restaurant's attorney also noted that Buffet World had never experienced a problem like this before.

> **1.** Is Mrs. Angelo's weight a relevant issue in her case against the restaurant?
>
> **2.** What evidence could the restaurant have provided to its attorney to demonstrate reasonable care in the inspection of its dining room furniture?
>
> **3.** If it were independently owned, who would be responsible for designing and implementing an effective furniture inspection program for Buffet World?

Large restaurant and hotel companies generally employ directors of safety or directors of safety and security. It is the job of these individuals to design safety and security programs, and then to encourage on-site managers to implement and maintain them. In smaller or independent hospitality operations, you may be the individual responsible for developing and maintaining your own safety and security programs. In later portions of this chapter, we will show you how to implement and evaluate a safety program.

Crisis Management

LEGALESE

Crisis: An occurrence that holds the potential to jeopardize the health of individuals and or the business.

Hospitality managers face a myriad of routine, but generally minor, challenges and problems in the day-to-day operation of their facilities. In some situations, however, the challenges are anything but minor. Many types of circumstances have the potential to cause devastating damage to a hospitality operation. These are called *crisis* situations. Examples include:

Power outages
Vandalism
Arson/fire
Bomb threats
Robbery
Looting

Severe storms, including:

- Hurricanes
- Tornadoes
- Earthquakes
- Floods

Snow and Ice
Accident/injury
Drug overdose
Medical emergency
Need for rescue breathing/cardiopulmonary resuscitation (CPR)
Death/suicide of guest or employee
Intense media scrutiny
Adversarial governmental agency investigation
Civil disturbance

Although it is reasonable to assume that you might not have much control during a crisis such as a snowstorm, it is also reasonable to assume that, prior to the storm, you would have preplanned for the difficulties your operation might face during such

>> ANALYZE THE SITUATION 14.2

WAYNE DOBINION WAS THE district manager for a franchised quick-service Mexican-style restaurant in a large city. On a Friday night at 11:30 P.M., just after the restaurant locked its front doors to the general public, three masked men entered the store through the unlocked back kitchen door. They demanded that the assistant manager on duty at the time turn over all the restaurant's cash. Nervously, the 19-year-old assistant manager explained that all the cash had been deposited in a safe in the manager's office and that he had no ability to open it.

Angry at their inability to rob the restaurant, the gunmen shot two of the restaurant workers, including the assistant manager, as they fled the restaurant. The assistant manager later died from his wounds. The attempted robbery and shooting make that night's local television news.

A lawsuit filed by the assistant manager's parents charged that the restaurant lacked proper alarms and locks on the back door. In addition, they charged that the restaurant owners and the franchise company failed to provide any training to its staff regarding the proper response to an armed robbery. The lawsuit was reported in a front-page article in the local paper.

An investigative reporter from another television station in the city called the restaurant's manager to request an on-air interview regarding the training the restaurant's employees receive related to robberies. The manager referred the call to Mr. Dobinion.

1. What issues will the courts and jury likely consider as they evaluate the legitimacy of the parents' lawsuit?

2. What legal position might the franchisor take if it had provided training materials to the local franchisee, but the franchisee had never utilized those materials?

3. What is the likely outcome if Mr. Dobinion refuses to meet with the investigative reporter? What if Mr. Dobinion has not been trained to do so?

a storm. Crisis management consists of (1) preplanning before a crisis, (2) responding properly during a crisis, and (3) assessing your operation's performance after the crisis to see how your response could be improved for the next time.

Advantages of Preplanning

By preplanning for certain types of accidents and events, you will be able to minimize the possibility of injury or loss, demonstrate reasonable care, and show a jury that you were able to foresee a potentially dangerous situation, as well as take appropriate steps to prevent the harm from occurring or to mitigate the consequences. (Recall the importance of "foreseeability" in personal injury lawsuits, as discussed in Chapter 9, "Your Responsibilities as a Hospitality Operator.") There are also at least 11 other advantages for considering ahead of time how your operation could be made safer and what types of actions you and your staff can take on a daily basis to keep it safe:

1. *Improved employee morale.* When employees see you implementing safety and security programs, they know that there is a direct benefit to them. In an age of increasing workplace violence, employees have a legitimate concern for their own security.

2. *Improved management image.* Often, managers are accused, directly or indirectly, of putting the needs of the business ahead of those of the individual worker. Regardless of the legitimacy of such criticism, the implementation of safety and security programs demonstrates management's concern for staff and guests in a way that is both visible and undeniable.

3. *Improved employee recruiting effectiveness.* For prospective employees, the mention of effective safety and security programs can often mean the difference between accepting or rejecting a position. Consider the parents of a teenage worker helping to counsel their son or daughter to look for an after-school job. Having a safety-oriented workplace will clearly be important in the decision-making process of the potential employee and his or her parents.

4. *Reduced insurance rates.* In many cases, your insurance company will reward your safety and security efforts with reduced insurance premiums. It simply makes sense for them to do so. Just as auto insurance companies provide lower rates for safe drivers, business insurers look at the potential for loss when establishing rates for providing coverage.

5. *Reduced employee costs.* Employees who avoid injury are more productive and reliable than those who do not. Because that is true, it is up to you as a manager to help employees avert accidents. Workers' compensation claims are lower in a safe work environment, and lost productivity due to injury-related absence is reduced. No one wins when workers are injured on the job.

6. *Improved operating ratios.* When theft by guests or employees is reduced, profitability increases. Restaurants and hotels particularly have inventory items that many employees and guests find desirable, because they can be used or consumed in their own homes. Well-conceived programs that reduce theft or raise awareness about security measures result in lower operating costs, and thus enhance gross operating profits.

7. *Reduced penalty costs for violations.* Hospitality establishments are visited by federal and state inspectors from a variety of agencies to ensure compliance with the different laws that regulate the industry. Often the inspections are unannounced, and the fines for violating the law, as we have shown you, can be severe. The best way to avoid expensive fines and penalties is by operating safely and legally at all times. An effective safety and security program can help ensure your compliance with the law.

8. *Support in the event of an accident.* When accidents happen, attorneys and upper management will look to the hospitality manager to provide documented evidence that safety and training programs were in place to reduce the chance of a mishap. This evidence is crucial because, as we have seen, juries will be interested in whether or not the manager exercised reasonable care in the operation of his or her facility. If the manager cannot do so, the chances of successfully defending the operation in court are greatly reduced.

9. *Increased guest satisfaction.* Today's traveling public is sophisticated. Guests have come to expect that their personal safety and the safety of their possessions will be protected to the greatest degree possible by hospitality managers who care about their repeat business. The hotel that does not provide adequate locks on its guestrooms, for example, neglects to do so at its own peril. Potential guests will simply find other, safer, lodging options. The restaurant that does not protect its inventory from employee theft, and then runs out of a needed ingredient on a busy Saturday night, faces the same probability of guest dissatisfaction. Dissatisfied customers seldom return.

10. *Marketing advantages.* All hospitality facilities, even those in the nonprofit sector, compete for customers or resources. When an operation can legitimately represent itself as one that takes a genuine and documented proactive stance in the area of safety and security, it becomes easier to market that facility to the general public. For example, the tour bus operator selecting a hotel for a tour group's overnight accommodations will, all other things being equal, select the hotel that raises the least risk to the group's safety, and thus the least likelihood of adverse guest experiences. To do so is merely good business judgment on the part of the tour operator.

11. *Reduced likelihood of negative press.* Few events can have as adverse an impact on the success of a business as sustained negative press. Although such press is often undeserved, the reality is that today's media will sensationalize some misfortunes in a way that casts the business owner in the least favorable light. As we will see later in this chapter, your ability to deal honestly with the media in a time of turmoil is very important, but it is always easier to avoid accidents than to defend yourself in the press. Many managers have the attitude, "It can't happen to me." It can, and the results can be crippling to your business.

14.2 SAFETY AND SECURITY PROGRAMS: FOUR-STEP SAFETY AND SECURITY MANAGEMENT METHOD

Because the safety and security needs of hospitality organizations vary so widely, it is difficult to provide one all-purpose, step-by-step, list of activities that should be implemented to minimize the chances of accident, injury, or loss. That said, from a legal perspective, your basic obligation is to act responsibly in the face of threats to people and property. One way to analyze and respond to those responsibilities is illustrated by a four-step safety and security management method presented in Figure 14.1.

Four-Step Safety and Security Management Method

1. Recognition of threat
2. Program development (response to threat)
3. Program implementation
4. Monitoring of program results

Figure 14.1 Four-step safety and security management method.

Areas of Safety and Security Concern

Guests

Parking lots
Guestrooms
Public areas
Dining rooms
Bars and lounges

Guest Properly In

Coatrooms
Guestrooms
In-room safes
Parking lots
Safety deposit boxes

Employees

Work site safety
Workplace violance
Worker accidents
Employee locker rooms

Facility Assets

Cash and cash equivalents
Operating supplies
Food inventories
Beverage/mini-bar inventories
Vending income/equipment
Telephone access

All People and Property

Medical emergency
Criminal activity
Natural disaster
Utility outages

Figure 14.2 Areas of safety and security concern.

Recognition of Threat

Safety and security programs generally start with the recognition of a need, that is, a realization that a threat to people or property exists. Consider the case of Garth Rivers. Garth is the manager of a popular pizza parlor that also serves beer and wine. Over the past six months, Garth has had four guests and two employees complain of vandalism to their cars. The damage ranged from scratched paint to broken windows, and in it least one case, it appeared that the vandals attempted to break into the car. Before these six incidents, Garth never had a problem. Now, however, he realizes that he must act responsibly to serve the interests of his guests and employees, and protect their property. A need for security has surfaced.

Figure 14.2 lists the most common areas of security concern in the hospitality industry. The list is not intended to be exhaustive, but it does give some indication of the vast number of areas within a facility that must be considered when developing an overall safety and security program. Note the five major areas into which this list is divided: guests, employees, property, facility assets, and crisis situations.

Program Development

Once a threat to safety or security has been identified, managers and security personnel can develop an appropriate response to address that threat. Figure 14.3 details the many different components of an effective hotel safety and security program, which would have to be addressed by management. Responses, or programs, can take a variety of forms, as follows.

Training for Threat Prevention

In many cases, the proper response to a safety and security threat is proper training for employees. If, for example, employee safety is threatened by a large number of back injuries caused by the use of improper lifting techniques, training employees in proper lifting techniques could reduce or eliminate that threat.

Significant Elements of a Hotel Security Program

▶ Key controls

▶ Effective guestroom lock system

▶ Proper and adequate training of security staff

▶ Guestroom doors with one-way viewers and chain/latch bars

▶ Adequate lighting and ongoing maintenance

▶ Perimeter controls

▶ Employee background checks

▶ Employee education

▶ Guest safety education (safety videos on TV, safety literature in guest directory, recommended hiking/jogging paths, recommended vendors)

▶ Written security policies and procedures

▶ Established responses to incidents and corrective action

▶ Liaison with local authorities

Figure 14.3 Elements of a hotel security program.

Other examples include training room attendants in the proper manner for disposing of bloody items found in rooms, teaching cooks the proper way to use a meat slicer, or instructing employees and guests in what should be done in the event of a fire emergency.

Increased Surveillance and/or Patrol

In some cases, the best response to a threat simply involves monitoring the activities in a particular area with greater frequency; and, as mentioned in Chapter 9, you can even be found negligent for not doing so. In the parking lot problem just described, one of Garth's best responses could be to increase surveillance of the parking lot of his pizza parlor. Routine patrols carried out by management, employees, an outside security firm, or the police may serve as a significant deterrent to vandals.

Other safety and security threats can be addressed by installing video cameras in public areas to record activity. Stairwells, halls, and storerooms are appropriate areas for the installation of these devices. In many cases, the presence of the camera itself can help deter crime. Video camera systems can either record action to tape or simply display the activity of a specific area in real time, with no recording of the events. In all cases, however, if a camera is installed to view a specific problem area in a hospitality organization, then that camera must be adequately monitored. Many organizations have actually chosen to forgo the use of video cameras as a guest-safety tool if they cannot be monitored, because the presence of the camera could give the guest a false sense of security.

It is important to understand that an owner's right to unlimited monitoring and surveillance, even on his or her own property, is not absolute. In today's computer age, illegally monitoring the behavior of guests, and especially that of employees, can dramatically increase an employer's liability.

Systematic Inspections

In some cases, holding a routine and comprehensive inspection of facilities can help identify possible threats to safety and security. As a professional hospitality manager, you will be expected to carefully monitor your facility's compliance with accepted standards of a safe and secure operation. It is important that you not only regularly monitor your facility for compliance but also document your efforts.

Figure 14.4 is an example of a checklist that can be used to do both: monitor compliance and document the effort. Many sophisticated travel agency companies concerned about the safety of their clients, as well as corporations concerned about the safety of their employees, have developed their own safety and security checklists.

Hospitality Facilities Safety and Security Checklist

Operation _____   Manager _____

Month/Year Inspected _____   Inspected by _____

Mark "OK" by any item that is in compliance. For those items not in compliance, assign an individual to correct the problem, along with a target date for its completion. For any item appearing two months in a row, attach a sheet explaining progress toward the problem's solution.

OK	Not OK	Facility Section	Correction Assigned to	Target Correction Date
		Outside/Parking Areas		
_____	_____	Paved areas free of cracks, uneven surfaces	_____	_____
_____	_____	Walkways uncluttered, unobstructed	_____	_____
_____	_____	Lighting adequate in working condition	_____	_____
_____	_____	Required warning, caution signage in place	_____	_____
_____	_____	Landscape void of hiding areas	_____	_____
_____	_____	Fences in good repair	_____	_____
		Transportation/Valet		
_____	_____	Driving records of drivers on file	_____	_____
_____	_____	Daily vehicle inspection on file	_____	_____
_____	_____	Vehicle maintenance records on file	_____	_____
		Lobby/Entrance Areas		
_____	_____	Steps/stairways marked, in good repair	_____	_____
_____	_____	Handrails installed	_____	_____
_____	_____	Floors, carpets in good condition	_____	_____
_____	_____	Lighting levels adequate	_____	_____
		Fire and Safety		
_____	_____	Fire alarm system tested, documented	_____	_____
_____	_____	Sprinkler system tested, documented	_____	_____
_____	_____	Fire extinguisher tests current	_____	_____
_____	_____	Kitchen hood ANSUL system tested, documented	_____	_____
_____	_____	All Exit signs illuminated	_____	_____
_____	_____	Smoke alarms tested, documented	_____	_____
_____	_____	Meeting with local fire officials held, documented	_____	_____

Figure 14.4 Safety and security checklist.

Elevators

_____ _____ Lights operational _____ _____

_____ _____ Telephones operational _____ _____

_____ _____ Elevator inspection current, posted _____ _____

_____ _____ Signage includes Braille _____ _____

Restaurant

_____ _____ Floor covering in good repair _____ _____

_____ _____ Adequate lighting _____ _____

_____ _____ Seating inspected _____ _____

_____ _____ Tables inspected _____ _____

_____ _____ Signage appropriate _____ _____

_____ _____ Evaluation plan posted (if required) _____ _____

_____ _____ Room capacity posted (if required) _____ _____

_____ _____ Wiring on public space equipment inspected _____ _____

Kitchen

_____ _____ Floor tile in good repair _____ _____

_____ _____ Chemicals stored away from food _____ _____

_____ _____ Safe food storage practices _____ _____

_____ _____ GFI installed on outlets _____ _____

_____ _____ Hood ducts and filters cleaned, documented _____ _____

_____ _____ ANSUL system inspection posted _____ _____

_____ _____ Kitchen inspection scores reviewed with manager _____ _____

_____ _____ Fire extinguisher training held/documented _____ _____

_____ _____ MSDS in place _____ _____

Laundry

_____ _____ Dryer vents cleaned/documented _____ _____

_____ _____ Chemicals stored properly _____ _____

_____ _____ MSDS in place _____ _____

Swimming Pools/Spas

_____ _____ Floor nonslip, no cracks _____ _____

_____ _____ Self-closing gate _____ _____

_____ _____ Depth markings in feet and meters _____ _____

_____ _____ Lifesaving equipment in place _____ _____

_____ _____ Appropriate signage _____ _____

_____ _____ Lights installed and operable _____ _____

_____ _____ Hot tub thermometer in place _____ _____

Figure 14.4 (_Continued_)

Private Meeting Rooms/Ballrooms

_____ _____	Floor covering in good condition	_____ _____
_____ _____	Entrance doors open/close properly	_____ _____
_____ _____	Kitchen doors open/close properly	_____ _____
_____ _____	Evaluation procedures posted	_____ _____
_____ _____	Appropriate signage	_____ _____
_____ _____	Lights installed and operable	_____ _____

Back of House

_____ _____	Floor covering in good condition	_____ _____
_____ _____	Proper storage techniques used	_____ _____
_____ _____	Hot water temperature tested	_____ _____
_____ _____	Power shut-off identified/labeled	_____ _____
_____ _____	Gas shut-off identified/labeled	_____ _____
_____ _____	Appropriate signage	_____ _____
_____ _____	Lights installed and operable	_____ _____

General/Additional Comments _____

_____

_____

_____

_____

_____

_____

Inspected filed on _____

Reviewed By _____   Title _____

Figure 14.4 (_Continued_)

As a manager, these can be very instructive because they let you know what travel agents think is important in a facility they would recommend to their clients.

Modification of Facilities

When the facility itself contributes to a threatening situation, that facility may require modification. For example, worn carpets should be replaced before a guest falls; sidewalk curbs should be painted if they are not visible to pedestrians; and extra lighting might have to be added in specific areas to increase safety and security. It is important to remember that facility defects that have been recognized or should have been foreseen by management, but not corrected, can be very damaging in the event of a lawsuit.

Establishing Standard Procedures

Routine policies and procedures can also serve as an effective response to threats to safety and security. Consider the case of the hotel that offers guests the use of a safety deposit box. Obviously, procedures should be in place to ensure the security of the items placed on deposit with the hotel. In a similar way, a restaurant must have appropriate procedures in place for counting and depositing the cash it takes in on a daily basis. Periodic product inventories, plate counts on buffet meals, and signing in and out of management keys are all examples of standard operating procedures that directly impact the safety and security of an operation.

» ANALYZE THE SITUATION 14.3

THE COMMODORE HOTEL WAS owned by the First Community Insurance Company, and managed by Fieldstone Hospitality Management. After two separate guest assaults occurred inside the hotel rooms, Fieldstone Management approached First Community Insurance with the idea of either installing a closed circuit video camera (CCVC) system in all hallways or increasing the lighting levels of the hotel's corridors. First Community Insurance authorized Fieldstone Management to purchase a video surveillance system consisting of six cameras and a central location to view them. The events shown by the cameras were not committed to tape.

Late on the evening of February 6, Mrs. Cynthia Larson checked into the Commodore and was assigned a room at the end of one of the hotel's corridors. As she attempted to insert her electronic key into the door lock, she was assaulted.

Mrs. Larson sued both Fieldstone Management and First Community Insurance, claiming that both companies' failure to monitor their cameras was a direct cause of her assault. In addition, she claimed that the cameras' use was deceptive, in that it gave her a false sense of security. As she stated, "The cameras showed me the hotel cared about my security, and I wanted to stay in a safe location." According to timesheets provided under subpoena by the hotel, an employee was assigned to view the cameras in the central location for an average of two hours per night between the hours of 8:00 P.M. and 6:00 A.M. The assault occurred at a time when no employee was monitoring the cameras.

The attorney for First Community Insurance stated that the company was merely the owner of the hotel and not responsible for day-to-day management; thus, is should not be held responsible for Mrs. Larson's injuries. Fieldstone Management maintained that it too should not be held responsible just because the cameras installed were not monitored at all times. The presence of the cameras themselves and electronic locks on their doors demonstrated that the company used reasonable care in the protection of its guests.

1. Will First Community Insurance be held partially responsible for the actions of Fieldstone Management?

2. Did Fieldstone Management use reasonable care in the installation and operation of the camera system? Would it matter if the cameras were recording to tape?

3. What could the hotel owners do in the future to help avoid a similar situation with a guest?

Program Implementation

Once a hospitality firm has identified the threats to its operation, and designed a safety and security program that addresses those threats, it must put the program into action. Large hospitality facilities may have individuals specifically designated for these tasks, while in smaller properties every employee may have implementation responsibilities. Both large and small properties may find the need for temporary or longer-term security assistance, which may be provided by a security guard company. In all cases, local law enforcement officials should be a vital component of a property's safety and security program.

Safety and Security Departments

In a large hospitality facility, a safety and security department may exist. The department head would ordinarily report to the general manager of the facility. Staff members in the department would be responsible for routine duties such as patrolling the facility for unauthorized people or suspicious activity, performing inspections, assisting the police with crime reports, and serving as a liaison with insurance carriers. In addition, the department might advise the general manager on topics related to safety and security. The Educational Institute of the American Hotel and Motel Association offers an excellent certification program for members of a safety and security department.

Safety and Security Guards

If yours is a small facility, you may decide that it makes sense to contract with a security guard company to hire a guard to implement all or a portion of your safety and security program. Consider the case of Teddy Ross. Teddy manages a resort that includes lodging, foodservice, and entertainment facilities. Teddy decides to renovate his 200 hotel rooms. All of the furniture for the renovation is to be delivered to Teddy's facility at the same time, but it will be stored in tractor-trailers in his parking lot until the building contractor finishes the room renovation. The process is expected to take 10 weeks, with 20 rooms per week being furnished from the items in the trailers. Because Teddy does not have the extra staff required to guard the trailers at night, it might make good economic sense for him to contract with a security company that could provide such a guard.

Generally it is the role of the security guard to:

1. Monitor the facility.
2. Report observations to management or the police if needed.
3. Intervene only if it can be done safely or to protect the life of a guest or employee.
4. Record activities and findings.

Security guards are an excellent choice when additional help is needed—for example, in the event of a large party or whenever management expects that additional safety or security protection is warranted. They are not, however, a substitute for a comprehensive and ongoing safety and security program. If such guards are to be used, it is a good idea to insist that the security guard company:

■ Provide an acceptable indemnity/hold-harmless agreement.
■ Supply proof of liability insurance that names your operation as an additional insured.
■ Demonstrate proof that it carries workers' compensation insurance.
■ Supply a copy of its hiring standards/procedures.
■ Draw up a written agreement detailing the specific services it will provide.

Safety Committees

Many managers find that property safety committees can play a valuable role in the identification and correction of safety and security problem areas. Ideally, a safety committee should consist of members from each of a property's departments. For example, a large restaurant might have members from the preproduction, production, and clean-up areas in the back of the house, and bartenders, servers, and hosts in the front of the house. A hotel's safety committee might have one or more members from housekeeping, laundry, maintenance, food and beverage, front desk, guest services, and the administrative offices.

Once a committee is established, regular meetings should be scheduled on a weekly, biweekly, or monthly basis. The meetings need not be long; typically, one hour is sufficient. An agenda for a property-level safety and security committee meeting might include:

- *Safety or security instruction:* Training videos, new policies and procedures, and related instruction can be presented. It is critical that the committee members see their role as that of a teacher, not just a police officer, because a worker's peers can often best reinforce the dissemination of important safety and security information.

- *Review of safety concerns:* Members should be informed of the actions that were taken in response to safety and security concerns raised in prior meetings. If, for example, a member of the dishwashing crew expressed concern in a previous meeting that the chemical sanitizer in the automatic dispenser was not working properly, he or she should be informed of the actions that have been taken to correct the problem. In addition, any new concerns of the group should be discussed at this time, with each department having an opportunity to contribute. Suggestions, corrections, and improvements to the property's safety and security programs should all be encouraged.

- *Effectiveness report by manager:* If accidents have decreased, committee members should be made aware of that fact. If accidents have increased, that too should be shared. The meeting is also a good time to let committee members know how important you consider their contribution to the overall success of your facility.

The most significant resource you have for reducing safety and security liability is the commitment of your staff. Safety committees are an exemplary way to demonstrate your own safety and security commitment, and an excellent way to utilize your staff's eyes, ears, and ideas for the betterment of your operation.

Law Enforcement Relationships

In addition to your own staff, local law enforcement officials are an important part of any safety and security effort. Establishing and maintaining a good working relationship with them is an integral part of your job. Law enforcement organizations can interact with your business in five key ways:

1. *Regularly scheduled meetings.* It is a good idea to meet on a regular basis with the chief law enforcement official in your area. This can be a time of sharing mutual concerns and ideas for support. If the time comes that you need the help of your local law enforcement officials, a personal working relationship with them is a tremendous asset in resolving any difficulties quickly and efficiently.

2. *Neighborhood business watch programs.* These programs involve business owners who report any suspicious individuals or activities encountered within their place of business.

3. *Property safety and security reviews.* Many law enforcement officials will conduct a courtesy "walk-through" of your property to help detect possible security threats or problems, and offer suggestions for improvement. Because the police are familiar with the difficulties encountered by other businesses, they are in a unique position to point out problems you may have but might not easily recognize. In most cases, law enforcement officials are quite willing to identify areas for improvement.

4. *Interdiction programs.* These special programs involve law enforcement officers who are assigned to a specific area of crime prevention. In many communities, drug enforcement and other officials create *interdiction programs* that allow hospitality managers and employees to inform members of the interdiction team in the event that they observe specific behaviors previously identified by the interdiction team. When you make a call to an interdiction program, you are calling as a concerned citizen, not as a police agent. By working together, hospitality organizations and police officials can help prevent crimes and look out for the safety interests of their customers and their business.

5. *Training programs.* Some police departments offer training programs for crime detection and deterrence. These classes are usually offered free of charge or at very little cost, and can be attended by management and staff employees alike. Many police departments have a variety of training programs that cover topics such as personal safety, preventing employee theft, credit card fraud, identifying counterfeit money, and detecting drug trafficking.

LEGALLY MANAGING AT WORK:

Establishing an Effective Guestroom Lock Policy

The following steps outline an effective policy to protect the security of hotel guests by controlling the distribution of room keys and to ensure the effectiveness of guestroom locks. It also serves as a good example of how a safety program should be implemented. Notice the number of different components of a hotel's operation that contribute to the effectiveness of this policy, from the use of technology (by installing electronic locking systems) to staff training (following procedures such as never announcing room numbers out loud) to management functions (performing a lock audit).

1. Install an electronic locking system.

   Essentially, an electronic locking system uses a computer to generate a room key for each guest. At the conclusion of the guest's stay, the key "expires," or is made inoperable. In addition, the key system computer records the number of times a key is used to enter each room, as well as to whom the key used for entry was issued. For example, if a room attendant is issued a submaster key to all rooms on the first floor of a hotel, each time the room attendant uses the key, the time of use, as well as the identification number of the key, will be recorded in the computer's memory, where it may be retrieved if needed.

   Traditional mechanical locking devices do not help ensure guest safety, nor do they allow you to monitor the use of the key. Guest safety is compromised because any guest could make a copy of his or her room key, and return after he or she has checked out of the hotel to gain access to his or her old room. Employees could also make duplicate keys. Management cannot monitor key usage in any way because a mechanical lock does not record the identification number of the key used to open the door.

2. **Train all new employees on the procedures used to ensure key security.**

   Every new hotel employee needs to understand the importance of guest safety and key control. Housekeepers, maintenance staff, front desk staff, and even food and beverage staff should all be trained prior to beginning work. Excellent key control and guest privacy training materials can be secured from the Educational Institute of the American Hotel and Lodging Association at a very reasonable cost. And, remember, it is important to document your training efforts.

3. **Never announce guestroom numbers out loud.**

   When guests check into a hotel, it is never appropriate to say their room number out loud. The number should be written on the envelope or key cardholder containing the guest's room key. Also, it is important never to give a guest's room number to a caller or other guests in the hotel, regardless of their relationship to the original guest.

4. **Never mark the room number directly on the key.**

   Guestroom keys should never be imprinted with the guestroom number.

5. **Do not identify the hotel with the key.**

   Despite the widespread practice of customizing electronic key cards, it is never a good idea to "market" the hotel by printing property-specific information on the key card itself. If lost or stolen, potential thieves should not be able to determine where the key originated. It may be good marketing to custom print key cards, but it makes for poor security. Avoid the practice.

6. **Do not reissue keys to guests without a positive ID check.**

   When guests lock themselves out of a room, or lose their keys, they must be required to positively identify themselves before they are issued a duplicate key. This rule simply cannot be broken. If a guest maintains that he or she has left his or her identification in the guestroom and thus cannot produce it, the guest should be escorted by management to the room, where the proper identification can be secured. Employee violations of this rule should lead to immediate disciplinary action, because requesting and receiving an unauthorized key to a room is the primary way a thief can foil an electronic locking system.

7. **Do not issue duplicate keys to anyone except the registered guest.**

   The registered guest, and only the guest, should be able to request and receive a duplicate or replacement room key. Keys should not be issued to either spouses or children. Remember that it is the guest, not the hotel, who has the right to determine who is to be allowed access to his or her room.

8. Minimize the number of master keys.

Electronic locking systems preclude the making of master keys. In addition, master keys with restrictions can be created. That is, a housekeeping supervisor may be issued a submaster key that opens all guestroom doors on the first floor, but not the electronic lock to the liquor storeroom, which is also on the first floor. A master key should be available to the manager on duty, in case of emergency.

9. Keep a log of all existing masters and submasters.

All master and submaster keys that are issued should be recorded. The key identification number, the individual receiving the key, and the key's expiration date should be noted. In all cases, the number of master and submaster keys should be limited and accounted for on a regular basis. In addition, all such keys should be voided and reissued on a regular basis. The regulation of these key types should be well documented.

10. Train all managers on duty (MODs) on the procedures to conduct a lock audit. Record the results of any audits performed.

When it is necessary to determine who has gained access to a room, an audit of all keys used to open a guestroom door should be performed. Possible instances that could necessitate an audit include a guest report of theft from a room, reports of poor service to a room, and so on. In all cases, a record should be kept of who performed the audit and the results of the audit, including any subsequent action taken by management. Every MOD should be trained in how to perform the lock audit and how to record the results.

Monitoring Program Results

If a safety program is not working—that is, if it is not reducing or eliminating the threats to people or property you have identified—then the program must be reviewed for modification. Consider the case of Dave Berger. Dave is a regional manager for a chain of 30 delicatessens. The restaurants serve sandwiches and homemade soups. While reviewing his stores' performance, Dave noticed that each store averaged three critical sanitation violations per health inspector visit. In response to this, Dave purchased a food safety video and required each store manager to view it. Six months later, the number of sanitation violations reported per store remained unchanged. From this information, Dave learns that he will have to do more than show a video to ensure food safety in his stores.

Legally, you are in a much stronger position if you can document not only that you have a safety and security program, but also that the program has proven effective. There are a variety of ways to measure your program's effectiveness. Some tangible measurements include:

- Number of inspections performed
- Inspection or quality scores
- Number of incidents reported
- Dollar amount of losses sustained
- Number of insurance claims filed

- Number of lawsuits filed
- Number of serious or minor accidents
- Number of lost workdays by employees
- Insurance premium increases
- Number of drills or training exercises correctly performed

Less tangible measures include guest satisfaction scores, improved employee morale, and enhanced product marketability. The important point to remember is that a program has been successfully designed for implementation only after an appropriate evaluation component has been developed. Unless you know a program has made a measurable difference, you may be lured into a false sense of security about the program's effectiveness.

≫ ANALYZE THE SITUATION 14.4

PEGGI SHULKEY MANAGED A commissary for a large cafeteria company. Her facility prepared food products for 75 company restaurants. Although her operation did not have a tremendous number of work-related accidents, Peggi believed the number of accidents could be reduced. To that end, she formed a safety committee made up of employees and management, and charged them with the task of developing a model program to reduce employee injuries. The committee proposed the six-step plan presented here, along with their rationale for each step.

1. **Proper selection of employees.**

   An employee with a drug problem is dangerous; therefore, applicants should be required to take a drug test before being hired. The applicant must also execute a continuous authorization for drug testing, which permits the employer to administer a drug test in the event of an accident.

2. **Designation of a safety/injury coordinator.**

   The safety/injury coordinator will review past accident records and implement programs to reduce situations that may result in accidents. The safety coordinator will maintain a logbook of incidents, which each department supervisor can review for incident trends.

3. **Implementation of mandatory safety training.**

   Each employee will be trained in safety related to his or her job.

4. **Increased awareness of safety.**

   Through the implementation of programs, games, and posters, employees will be reminded to think intelligently and safely.

5. **Implementation of incentive programs for safety.**

   To further encourage safety, rewards and incentives will be given to employees who practice such behavior.

6. **Measurement of results.**

   To be determined by the general manager.

1. What specific measurements might Peggi use to gauge the effectiveness of the group's plan?

2. How effective is training likely to be in reducing this particular threat to safety?

3. Analyze the committee's plan for thoroughness. Are there potential liabilities that still need to be addressed?

≫ ANALYZE THE SITUATION 14.5

KARIN PELLEY WAS EMPLOYED as a district manager by Ron's Roast Beef, a regional chain of 150 quick-service restaurants serving sandwiches, soups, and soft drinks. Most of the stores were located in shopping mall food courts or strip malls. Ms. Pelley worked out of her home office, traveling to visit her 12 assigned stores on a regular basis.

Ms. Pelley communicated with the corporate office via telephone, fax machine, and modem, all of which were installed in her home by Advance Technology, a telecommunications company selected by Ron's Roast Beef to supply telecommunications equipment and services to employees. As part of its contract with Ron's Roast Beef, Advance Technology serviced the machines used by Ms. Pelley in her daily work.

When Ms. Pelley's modem stopped working one day, she contacted her home office, which then called Advance Technology to request that a service technician be dispatched to Ms. Pelley's home. In the course of his visit, the technician assaulted Ms. Pelley. The technician was later apprehended by the police and convicted of felony assault, his third such conviction in three years.

Ms. Pelley sued Advanced Technology, claiming negligent hiring. In addition, her attorney submitted a demand letter to Ron's Roast Beef, requesting a $400,000 settlement from the company for negligence in contracting its telecommunications services from Advance Technology. The attorney for Ron's Roast Beef refused to pay the claim stating that:

■ Ron's had no control over the hiring practices of Advance Technology.

■ Ms. Pelley was prohibited by law from pursuing any injury claim against her employer other than workers' compensation, because the assault occurred in Ms. Pelley's "office."

1. What responsibility did Ron's Roast Beef have for providing a safe home working environment for Ms. Pelley?

2. Will Ron's Roast Beef be held liable for the damages suffered by Ms. Pelley? Will Advance Technology be held liable?

3. What should Ron's do in the future to avoid potential liability in situations such as this?

14.3 CRIMES AGAINST HOSPITALITY BUSINESSES

Most of our discussion so far has centered on the protection of guests and employees from outside threats, but hospitality managers also need to be aware of threats and criminal activities aimed directly at their own operation. The three most common threats are as follows:

1. Consumer theft of services, which involves a guest who leaves without paying a bill, or one who refuses to pay it
2. Fraudulent payment of a bill through the use of an unauthorized credit card (stolen, canceled, or revoked), a bad check, or counterfeit money
3. Internal theft of assets, committed by your own staff

Undoubtedly, your safety and security plan has provisions to protect your business from some types of property theft; often, however, additional measures for preventing theft of services, fraudulent payment, and internal theft will be required. These measures may involve a different set of procedures and extra vigilance on the part of you and your employees. It's also important to be aware of legislation that addresses these types of criminal behavior.

The federal government has passed a law prohibiting the fraudulent use of credit cards. Individuals who fraudulently use credit cards in interstate commerce to obtain goods or services of $1,000 or more in any given year could be subject to fines of up to $10,000 and prison terms of up to 15 years. Recently, technology has advanced in the prevention and detection of credit card fraud. New technologies, such as PCI DSS, are making it easier for merchants to proactively protect consumer account data. PCI DSS, or Payment Card Industry Data Security Standard, is a multifaceted security standard that includes requirements for security management, policies, procedures, network architecture, software design and other critical protective measures. More specifically, PCI DSS helps protect guest's privacy by creating an additional level of protection for card issuers, like Visa, MasterCard, and Discover, by ensuring that merchants meet minimum levels of security when they store, process, and transmit credit card data. For more information on PCI DSS, visit the Payment Card Industries Security Standard Council website (the organization that administers PCI DSS) at www.pcisecuritystandards.org.

In addition, every state has passed laws prohibiting individuals from taking advantage of hospitality services without paying for them. These laws are strict and often carry large fines or prison terms for those found guilty. As in many areas of the law, the specific provisions of these state statutes vary widely, so check with your attorney to learn the specifics of your state's law. Interestingly, many of these laws favor the hospitality operation by requiring an accused defendant to prove that he or she did not intentionally try to avoid payment of a bill. The responsibility for security in these three important areas, however, still falls on you and your staff, and thus is examined in detail next.

Consumer Theft of Services

When guests are legitimately unhappy with the level of service they have received during a meal or an overnight stay, they may become angry and protest all or a portion of their bill. As a manager, you must help calm the customer and fashion a solution that is fair to both the customer and the business. But when unprincipled and devious individuals consume services with no intention of paying for them, the action you take will be entirely different. In the foodservice industry, these customers are said to have "skipped," meaning that they have evaded the process of paying the cashier; in the lodging industry, a guest of this type is said to have "walked" his or her bill, because he or she has left the hotel without paying.

In either case, the loss of revenue to your business can be substantial if you do not take the necessary steps to reduce this type of theft. Unfortunately, in a busy restaurant or hotel, it can sometimes be relatively easy for a guest or an entire party to leave without settling their bill, unless everyone on the staff is extremely vigilant. The following Legally Managing at Work feature details some of the steps you should implement to help reduce the instance of food and beverage skips.

Hotel room "walks" are best addressed at check-in, because it is impossible to know when hotel guests are leaving their rooms for a legitimate reason, as opposed to intending to walk their bill. Because this is so, employee intervention techniques are less successful in hotels than in a food and beverage situation. The best way to limit the possibility of a guest walking the bill is to verify the guest's payment information and identity at check-in. If the guest intends to pay by credit card, the card should be authorized for an appropriate amount. If a cash payment will be used, it should be taken in advance. If the guest writes a check, the check should be authorized using the facility's established policy. Some facilities also require a verifiable form of positive identification when a guest pays with cash or check (usually a copy of a driver's license or some other generally accepted form of identification). When guests know that the hotel is aware of their true identity and can contact them after their stay, the likelihood of walking an entire folio (charge) is greatly reduced.

LEGALLY MANAGING AT WORK:

Procedures to Reduce the Incidence of Skipping

1. If the custom of the restaurant is to allow the ordering of food prior to receiving payment, present the bill for the food promptly when the guests have finished eating.

2. If the facility has a cashier in a central location in the dining area, make sure that person is available and visible at all times.

3. If the facility operates in such a manner that each server collects for his or her own guests' charges, instruct the servers to return to the table promptly after presenting each guest's bill to secure a form of payment.

4. Be observant of exit doors near restrooms or other areas of the facility that may give an unscrupulous guest an easy "out."

5. In a hotel dining situation, if it is the custom of the restaurant to allow food and beverage purchases to be charged to a room or master bill, verify the identity of the guest with both a printed and signed name. Guest identity verification may take a variety of forms, but in all cases should firmly establish that the guest requesting credit privileges is indeed authorized to do so.

6. If an employee sees a guest leave without paying the bill, he or she should notify management immediately.

7. Upon approaching a guest who has left without paying the bill, the manager should ask if the guest has inadvertently "forgotten" to pay. In most cases, the guest will then pay the bill.

8. Should a guest refuse to pay or flee the scene, the manager should note the following on an incident report:

a. Number of guests involved

b. Amount of the bill

c. Physical description of the guest(s)

d. Vehicle description, if the guests flee in a car, as well as the license plate number, if possible

e. Time and date of the incident

f. Name of the server(s) who waited on the guest

g. Name of the server who notified management of the skip

If the guest is successful in fleeing the scene, the police should be notified. In no case should staff members or managers be instructed to attempt to physically detain the guest. The liability that could be involved should an employee be hurt in such an attempt is far greater than the value of a food and beverage bill.

Fraudulent Payment

In the United States, credit cards, cash, and personal checks are the most common forms of payment for hospitality services. Unfortunately, all three can be used fraudulently by deceitful guests.

Credit Cards

Credit card security has come a long way since the cards' introduction. Today, credit cards are issued with holographic images, magnetic strips, encoded numbers, or other features that reduce the chance of consumer fraud. In addition, today's electronic credit card verification systems are fast, accurate, and designed to reduce the chances of loss by businesses.

Hospitality operations should use a credit card verification service, even if credit cards are used infrequently for payment. These verification services charge a fee, but they guarantee that the business will receive its money for a legitimate credit card charge, even if the cardholder does not pay the bank that issues the monthly statement. In many cases, businesses face challenges with credit card holders who pay the full bill using their card but later voice dissatisfaction and protest all or part of that bill. Unless the guest can be placated, the business may well face the prospect of defending its procedures.

Each major credit card issuer has its own procedures, and hospitality managers should become familiar with those of each card they accept. It is also important that managers realize that credit card companies have a responsibility to both the hospitality business and the cardholder. To be fair to both, the card issuer will require a business to follow its procedures for accepting cards and billing for services. This is to ensure both that when a guest has a legitimate complaint, he or she is treated fairly, and that any fraudulent intent on a guest's part is resolved in a way that protects the business.

The next Legally Managing at Work details ten general procedures that should be followed by employees when accepting any type of credit card.

LEGALLY MANAGING AT WORK:

Guidelines for Handling Credit Cards

1. Confirm that the name on the card is the same as that of the individual presenting the card for payment. Use a driver's license or other acceptable form of identification for this purpose.

2. Examine the card for any obvious signs of alteration.

3. Confirm that the card is valid; that is, that the card has not expired and is in effect.

4. Compare the signature on the back of the card with the one produced by the guest paying with the card.

5. Initial the credit card receipt. This should be done by the employee processing the charge.

6. Destroy carbon paper, if used.

7. Keep credit card charges that have not yet been processed in a secure place, to limit the possibility that they could be stolen.

8. Do not issue cash in exchange for credit card charges.

9. Do not write in tip amounts for the guest. These should be supplied by the guest only, unless the tip is mandatory and that fact has been communicated in advance to the guest.

10. Tally credit card charges on a daily basis, making sure to check that the preceding procedures have been followed. If they have not, take immediate corrective action to ensure compliance.

Cash

Guests who use cash to defraud a business usually fall into two categories. The first is the so-called quick-change artist, an individual who intentionally tries to confuse or distract the cashier when tendering payment for a bill. The best defense against such an attempt is to instruct cashiers to take their time and make change carefully. Handling cash is confusing only when cashiers do so too quickly or carelessly. It is this type of cashier that the quick-change artist seeks out.

The second type is one who attempts to use counterfeit money to pay his or her bills. Fortunately, as with credit cards, great strides have been made by the issuer—in this case the federal government—to reduce the likelihood of creating passable counterfeit U.S. currency. Redesigned bills printed by the federal government began to be circulated in the late 1990s, and they have made the counterfeiter's task much more difficult. Even so, managers should enroll in one of the counterfeit-detection training programs generally offered by local law enforcement officials. And, if possible, those staff members who routinely accept cash for payment should also attend such instructional programs.

Personal Checks

In many hospitality businesses, personal checks are a popular form of payment, but their use raises a number of risks. Guests may either deliberately or through an oversight write checks that they guests do not have sufficient funds to cover.

Also, fraudulent customers may attempt to write checks on closed accounts, on accounts at nonexistent banks, or on a legitimate checking account owned by another individual.

Although there are services that can be used to preauthorize the validity of personal checks, similarly to credit cards, these services do not generally agree to reimburse the business for the value of the check should it be returned as unpayable by a bank. To minimize the number of such occurrences at your business, implement the procedures in the next Legally Managing at Work feature.

If a check is returned to you because the account either does not exist or has insufficient funds to cover the amount, contact your local law enforcement officials for help in collection. Accepting partial payment of the check's original amount in exchange for not prosecuting the check writer is usually not a good idea. Doing so indicates your acceptance of treating the check amount as a "loan" that is to be paid back, rather than as a debt that must be paid at once. Local laws vary in this area, so take the time to become familiar with them.

LEGALLY MANAGING AT WORK:

Personal Check Verification

1. Ask for a form of identity verification, to ensure that the name on the check is the same as that of the individual presenting the check for payment.

2. Make a notation on the check of the identification source and identifier used to verify the individual presenting the check as payment (e.g., driver's license number, student identification number, etc.)

3. Establish a maximum on the amount for which the check can be written without preauthorization directly from the bank named on the check.

4. Ensure that the check has:

    Correct name of your business

    Correct date

    Correct dollar amount

    The same numerical dollar amount and written dollar amount

    A clearly identifiable issuing bank address

    A signature that matches the name on the check

5. Examine the check carefully for any obvious signs of alteration.

6. Deposit all checks you receive promptly with your own bank.

7. Keep a list of individuals who have passed uncollectable checks to you previously, and require cashiers to refer to this list each time they accept a check.

8. Insist that all checks include a local telephone number and address.

9. Accept out-of-town checks with caution or not at all, as these checks may be more difficult to collect upon.

10. Instruct all employees accepting checks for payment to initial and date them.

Internal Theft of Assets

The internal theft of assets by employees generally takes one of two forms: the theft of financial assets, a crime known as embezzlement, or the theft of company property.

Embezzlement

Guarding your business against embezzlement consists of implementing and maintaining financial controls that will verify the following:

> Product sales receipts
> Services sales receipts
> Deposits
> Accounts receivable
> Accounts payable

For a detailed discussion of the procedures involved in income control, consult your accountant, or one of the many cost control or income control books on the market today.[1] One procedure many hospitality operators employ to protect themselves against embezzlement is to *bond* employees whose tasks include the handling of financial assets.

In addition to theft of a business's financial assets, the hospitality industry presents opportunities for employees to defraud guests as well. Some common techniques in this regard include the following:

■ Charging guests for items not purchased, then keeping the overcharge

■ Changing the totals on credit card charges after the guest has left, or imprinting additional credit card charges and pocketing the cash difference

■ Overcharging, with the intent of keeping the excess

■ Purposely shortchanging guests when giving back change, and then keeping the extra change

■ Charging higher-than-authorized prices for products or services, recording the proper price, and then keeping the overcharge

Theft of Company Property

The potential for theft of company property in the hospitality industry is high for the simple reason that employees can easily use so many typical hospitality-related items in their own homes. Food, trash bags, and guestroom supplies are common targets of employee theft. It is impossible to prevent every instance of employee theft, but best-practice preventative measures will reduce the number. These measures fall into three main categories:

1. Screening employees at the hiring stage

2. Creating an environment that discourages theft

3. Eliminating the opportunity to commit theft

Figure 14.5 details some of the activities that can be undertaken in each of these areas.

Theft, whether by guests or employees, greatly impacts your ability to operate a profitable business. Although there are laws in place to help you protect your operation against theft, and perhaps even recover damages, it is important to understand that being the plaintiff in a lawsuit you initiate can be just as costly and disruptive as defending your business against one brought against it. Thus, the best way to protect your operation is by establishing safeguards and procedures that prevent

---

LEGALESE

Bond(ing): An insurance agreement in which the insurer guarantees payment to an employer in the event of financial loss caused by the actions of a specific employee.

[1]One helpful book in this area, which you might have used in another course, is *Food and Beverage Cost Control*, by Lea R. Dopson and David K. Hayes (Hoboken, NJ: John Wiley & Sons, Inc., 2011).

Employee Theft Prevention	Activities
Screen employees.	Do preemployment reference checks. Do criminal background checks. Consider psychological prescreeing tests.
Create an antitheft atmosphere.	Enforce all theft-related policies fairly and consistently. Let employees know the real cost of theft and how it relates to them personally. Reward employees for their efforts to reduce theft.
Eliminate the opportunities to steal.	Do not let "off-the-clock" employees loiter around the property. Allow employee purchases of products only by a manager. Consider a policy to eliminate the opportunity to enter with or leave with unexamined packages, bags, knapsacks and the like. Implement effective inventory controls.

Figure 14.5 Activities to reduce employee theft.

these types of activities from happening in the first place. Some police departments offer training sessions that demonstrate how to recognize forgeries, bad checks, counterfeit money, and stolen credit cards, as well as how to identify threats to internal assets. Services such as these, along with your own vigilance and effective antitheft procedures, can be of tremendous assistance as you train employees in the proper procedures required to avoid and prevent problems of consumer theft of services, fraudulent payment, and internal theft problems.

14.4 CRISIS MANAGEMENT PROGRAMS

Just as the safety and security needs of hospitality organizations vary widely, so too do their crisis management needs. Hotels, for example, would more likely face challenges associated with evacuating guests during a weather-related crisis than would the manager of a take-out restaurant. A property's physical location is another factor in crisis preparations. Hospitality managers in the midwestern part of the United States, for example, might not have to worry about preparing for a hurricane, but they would have to be ready for snow and ice storms that can be just as disruptive and threatening. And there are certain circumstances that could cause a crisis situation no matter where your property is located, such as power failures, criminal acts, fires, and workplace violence. If any of these should occur, it is up to you, as the manager, to be ready.

Essentially, crisis management consists of these distinct activities:

- Precrisis planning
- Crisis response
- Postcrisis assessment

Precrisis Planning

Obviously, it's too late to prepare for a crisis when you are experiencing one. If you are unprepared, not only will you respond poorly, but you may also be held legally responsible for your lack of planning. Consider the case of Roland Naimo. While eating dinner at a steakhouse, a piece of steak became lodged in his throat, and he began to choke. No one on the restaurant staff had been trained to deal with such an emergency, and had it not been for a fellow diner who administered the Heimlich maneuver, Mr. Naimo might have died. Had that been the case, no doubt the restaurant would have faced a lawsuit, along with the associated expenses and negative publicity. Everyone involved would have asked: Why wasn't the restaurant prepared for such an occurrence? Why wasn't someone employed by the restaurant trying to help?

To prepare for a crisis effectively, a hospitality manager should develop and practice an *emergency plan.* An emergency plan, simply, identifies likely crisis situations, and then details how the operation will respond to them. Finally, that plan must be practiced, so that should it be necessary, everyone on the site will know what to do, and when.

Emergency Plan Development

Needless to say, no one can prepare for every crisis that could occur in a hospitality facility. But it is possible to be ready for those you can foresee. Moreover, many crises will require similar responses. For example, training employees in the proper procedures for handling general medical emergencies will prepare them for responding to slips and falls, employee accidents, guest injuries, and other threats to safety that could require medical attention. Similarly, preparing a facility evacuation plan will be helpful not only in case of a fire, but also during a weather-related disaster or power outage. The point is, you will find that by developing responses to a relatively small number of circumstances, you and your staff will be well equipped to address a wide variety of potential crises, because all crises have some characteristics in common:

- Urgency
- Halt in normal operations
- Human suffering and/or financial loss
- Potential scrutiny by the media
- Threat to the reputation or health of the business

You must commit your emergency plan to writing. This is important for two reasons: First, a written plan will clarify precisely what is expected of management and employees in times of crisis; second, if you are involved in a lawsuit, the written emergency plan can serve as evidence to support your defense. A judge or jury would readily acknowledge that a policy was in place, indicating reasonable care on the part of your operation.

That said, an emergency plan need not be complicated. In fact, it is best if it is not. A crisis is a stressful time, during which confusion itself is a real threat. Thus, any planned response to an emergency should be clear and simple, regardless of the number of steps required. In its simplest form, a written emergency plan should address:

- The nature of the crisis
- Who is to be informed when the crisis occurs
- What is to be done in response to the crisis
- When is it to be done
- Who is to do it
- Who will communicate to whom regarding the crisis

Though the specific threats that you may encounter will vary widely based on the type of facility you operate, and where, the following should be covered in any effective emergency plan:

- Emergency telephone numbers
- Fire procedures
- Storms
  - Hurricanes
  - Tornadoes
  - Earthquakes
  - Snow and ice storms

- Power failure
- Injury/accident
- Illness of guest or employee
- Death of guest or employee
- Evacuation of nonworking elevator
- Robbery
- Bomb threat
- Media relations

After the emergency plan has been finalized, each manager and affected employee should be given a copy of it or have immediate access to it. Subsequently, it is important to review, revise, and practice the emergency plan on a regular basis. Figure 14.6 is an example of the type of information required in an emergency telephone list, one component of a comprehensive emergency plan.

EMERGENCY TELEPHONE NUMBERS

Property Manager _____

Emergency Services

Fire Department   _____

Fire Alarm Service Provider _____

Police Department _____

Ambulance _____

Paramedics _____

Elevator Service Company _____

Insurance Company Representative _____

Telephone Repair Service _____

Utility Services

Gas _____

Electric _____

Water _____

Property-Specific Numbers

District Manager _____

Owner (with approval) _____

Other _____   _____

Other _____   _____

Other _____   _____

Figure 14.6 Emergency telephone list.

Emergency Plan Practice

Once your emergency plan has been developed, the next step is to practice the procedures you have included in it. Obviously, it is not possible to create, for example, a snowstorm in order to practice your staff's response to it. But you can practice your response to such a storm. Practicing your emergency plan might include verbal plan review to an actual run-through. Figure 14.7 shows a section of an emergency plan related to a fire crisis. Here, the emergency plan itself becomes a blueprint for practice sessions.

FIRE ALARM PROCEDURES

1. When an alarm sounds: All nonemergency committee personnel will go out the first available exit that is safe and then to the parking lot.
2. Room attendants will push their carts into the nearest vacant room before exiting to clear hallways.
3. Front office manager/supervisor will examine the fire panel to determine location of the smoke/fire.
4. Front desk will call fire department (after receiving signal from manager on duty) and notify them of alarm and approximate location of fire (if the fire department is not wired directly to the hotel).

FIRE RESPONSE INSTRUCTIONS

1. Without endangering yourself, notify any employees or guests in immediate danger of smoke, heat, or fire.
2. Close all doors to prevent the spread of the fire.
3. If possible, and trained to do so, help extinguish the fire by using one of the public/department fire extinguishers.
4. Never permit the fire and or smoke to come between you and your route of escape.
5. Via telephone or direct council, advise all guests/employees of the nearest safe fire exit.
6. Immediately notify all disabled guests in rooms marked with a red marker on the bucket registration cards). If a guest does not answer by phone, direct someone to make an attempt to physically assist the guest out of the room, if it can be done safely. It unable to reach guest, notify firelighters when they arrive.
7. Do not attempt to use the elevator under any circumstances.
8. If you or a guest are inside a room with smoke/fire, *do not open* the door. Stuff wet towels under the door and call for help. Place wet towels over your head and shoulders and stay low until help arrives.
9. If you encounter smoke in a hallway, stairwell, anywhere, *stop*; go back to a safe area and look for another means of escape.
10. Keep doors and windows in the area of the fire closed. To minimize further fire spreading.

EVACUATION

Evacuation of the building should be done quickly and calmly. Safety of guests should be the primary concern. Each department will appoint one of its staff to oversee fellow staff members' evacuation from the building. This employee will be responsible for needed supplies and the general safety of the department's staff members.

Time permitting, the manager in the following departments will be respoinsible for:

Food and Beverage
1. Secure food, storage, and liquor rooms.
2. Place cash in a sealed envelope and drop into safe.
3. Take kitchen keys.

Figure 14.7 Fire crisis emergency plan.

Accounting

1. Back up computer programs onto disks.
2. Take current payroll register.
3. Take all master keys.

Sales

1. Take banquet event book and group/function book binder.

Engineering

1. Take master key log.
2. Deactivate all gas-operated equipment.
3. Shut down elevators.

Front Office

1. Take bucket (guest registration files).
2. Take blankets from the supply cabinet.
3. Pull off current guest list by PBX.
4. Seal up cash in envelopes; drop in safe.

Housekeeping

1. Take all time cards for roll call.
2. Take all master keys and floor keys.
3. Fill laundry cart with blankets.

General Manager (GM)/Manager on Duty (MOD)

1. Meet the department outside and advise them of the current situation.
2. Assist police/fire personnel to secure exit and entrance to the hotel.

Figure 14.7 (*Continued*)

Of course, the question of which sections of the emergency plan to practice, and how often, can only be answered by management. The objective in developing a schedule for practicing your emergency plan should be to emphasize the most likely and serious threats, and to allow each staff member with responsibilities during the crisis to fully understand his or her role. The aftermath of a crisis, especially one that results in injury or loss of life, will inevitably lead to finger-pointing and intense scrutiny of you and your staff's actions. As a manager concerned with the safety and security of your staff and guests, and the potential liability resulting from poor execution of an emergency plan, you must always ensure that your operation knows how to perform in a crisis.

Crisis Response

No matter how well prepared you and your staff are, when a crisis does occur, you will nevertheless be faced with an overwhelming number of reactions and responses, from your staff, your guests, and perhaps even the media. Your ability to properly manage and control these responses will, in great part, determine the ultimate impact of the crisis on the reputation, potential legal liability, and financial health of your business.

Management Response

During a crisis, events unfold at an extremely rapid pace. Managers who have done their homework, by preparing and practicing an emergency plan, are more likely to behave professionally than those who have not. That said, a manager's particular

---

LEGALLY MANAGING AT WORK:

The Manager's Responsibilities in a Crisis

1. Take the immediate action required to ensure the safety of guests and employees.

2. Contact the appropriate source of assistance; for example, the fire department, police, or a medical professional.

3. Implement the relevant portion of your emergency plan.

4. Contact those within the organization who need to be informed of the crisis. This might include your supervisor, the owners, insurance companies, and company safety and security professionals.

5. Assume the leadership role expected of management during a crisis. Demonstrate your competence and professionalism by showing a genuine concern for the well-being of those affected by the crisis.

6. Communicate with your employees about the crisis.

7. Inform those guests who need to know what is being done and what will be done to deal with the crisis.

8. Secure organizational property, but only if it can **be done** without risking injury to guests or employees.

9. Prepare for and make yourself available to the media.

10. Using an incident report form or a narrative style document in writing your efforts and activities during the crisis.

---

response will depend, of course, on the nature of the crisis. The specific steps you would take to investigate a guest's claim of a coat stolen from your dining room would be very different from those you would take if the National Weather Service issued a warning that a hurricane was bearing down on the city in which your hospitality operation is located.

The checklist in the next Legally Managing at Work feature is a helpful guide for recalling the major duties of management during a crisis. These steps can be modified as needed to apply more specifically to your own hospitality operation, and they should become a part of each manager and supervisor's orientation training program.

Staff Response

Your staff's response to a crisis is just as important as yours. Essentially, the role of your staff in a crisis is to help you protect people and property without risking danger to themselves. In a fire, for example, staff can play a crucial role in notifying guests, helping to evacuate a building, securing assets if time permits, and helping to calm distraught and shaken guests. Remember, you, as a manager, simply cannot be everywhere during a time of crisis. In the case of a robbery or suicide attempt in your facility, you may not even be aware of the crisis until it has essentially passed. The crisis preparedness of your employees in such a case, therefore, will determine how your entire property responds.

It is also vital in a crisis that employees do nothing to further endanger guests or the business. Consider the case of the restaurant employee who refuses to immediately summon medical help for an injured guest because he or she fears that by doing so, the restaurant will be admitting responsibility for the guest's injury and might be held liable. But, if the guest dies, and it can be shown that the actions of the employee contributed directly to that death, the operation will face far greater exposure to liability and cost than if the employee had called an ambulance in the first place. Remember that the courts will hold you and your employees to the standard of reasonable care. Reasonable people do not value money above life. No piece of property or amount of money is worth risking personal harm to employees or other individuals on the property. An important concept to teach employees is this: Protect people before property.

Unfortunately, workers themselves can become victims in a crisis. The threat of harm from robbery, vandalism, and even other coworkers is very real. Good employees will not stay long with an organization that does not actively demonstrate concern for their safety. Effective managers take the training and security steps needed to help protect employees while on the job.

If a crisis of any type does occur, it is important that you keep employees informed about the status of the situation. In a serious situation, daily briefings may be required. Employees will want to know how the crisis will affect them and their

---

Search the Web 14.1

Go online to www.cdc.gov/niosh/topics/violence/. You will arrive at a website developed and operated by the National Institute for Occupational Safety and Health (NIOSH). NIOSH is operated by the federal government's Centers for Disease Control (CDC).

At the site, scroll down, locate, and read NIOSH Publication No. 93–109, then do the following:

1. Currently, only the operation of motor vehicles and machinery caused more workplace deaths than homicides. List five explanations you believe can be used to help understand the proliferation of homicides taking place in the workplace.

2. Identify the ten occupations that most put workers at risk of serious workplace violence.

3. List five actions suggested by NIOSH to reduce life-threatening situations at work.

4. Address the question of how a serious incident of workplace violence would impact:

   a. Other employees

   b. Guests

   c. The business itself

For additional information on preventing workplace violence, visit the NIOSH home page.

families. If the business will close for a time, will they continue to be paid? If not, what alternative assistance might be available? Will additional hours be required of staff? If so, of whom?

Realize that a crisis will affect your employees both in the short and long run. Experiencing a crisis, especially one that entails injury or loss of life, can be very stressful. Negative effects on employees can include anxiety, depression, nightmares, flashbacks, and even physical effects such as insomnia, loss of appetite, and headaches. Collectively, these and related symptoms are known as *post-traumatic stress disorder (PTSD)*. Increasingly, employers have been called on to recognize and respond to the post-traumatic stress disorder symptoms of employees following their exposure to a crisis.

Guest Response

When a crisis occurs, guests may be involved in a variety of ways. They might be witnesses to crimes or accidents, they themselves might be victims, or they might simply be innocent and concerned bystanders. You cannot control a guest's reaction to a crisis situation; what you can control is your response to the guest, and that can have a major impact on the ultimate reaction of the guest.

Never forget that a guest in a crisis situation will, in all probability, be upset, scared, angry, and sometimes all three. Consider, for example, Mr. and Mrs. Rahshad, two elderly hotel guests who were awakened in the middle of the night when a fire alarm went off. Though it was a false alarm, understandably, they were agitated by the interruption of their sleep, concerned whether there was an actual fire, and somewhat angry at both the hotel and the travel agency that had arranged for their stay. Most likely they would demand to speak with a manager, and perhaps even threaten a lawsuit. And if the hotel is full of guests who feel just like Mr. and Mrs. Rahshad, it will be your job, as the manager, to calm them and diffuse a difficult situation. If you find yourself in this position, remember the points in the following Legally Managing at Work feature. Your objective is to show genuine concern, treat the guests fairly, and avoid any needless legal fallout.

LEGALLY MANAGING AT WORK:

Guest Relations in a Crisis Situation

1. Recognize that the guest may be agitated and feel confused, scared, or angry. Accept these feelings as legitimate, and take them into consideration when speaking to the guest.

2. Introduce yourself, and state your position title. Immediately ask for the guest's name, and repeat it to make sure you say it correctly. Use the guest's name in your conversation with him or her.

3. Give the guest your undivided attention, maintain eye contact, and avoid interrupting the guest. Listen more than you talk.

4. Stay calm. Do not lose your temper, regardless of the guest's comments.

5. Apologize for the inconvenience suffered by the guest. Be genuine. Put yourself in the guest's position, and treat the guest as you would want someone you care for very much to be treated.

6. Tell the guest what is currently being done or what will be done to alleviate the crisis.

7. Arrange for medical treatment if needed. This can be done without accepting blame for the accident, because the responsibility for the problem may be unclear at the time of your conversation. What can be made clear, however, is your real concern for the safety of the guest.

8. Offer alternative solutions to the problem, if possible, and seek a solution that satisfies the needs of the guest to whom you are talking.

9. Let the guest know that you will follow up to ensure that all you have promised will be done.

10. Thank the guest for talking with you; afterward, make notes of the conversation if you feel they are needed.

Often, plaintiffs in lawsuits state that they would not have sued an establishment if they had received an expression of sincere concern from the establishment about their inconvenience. Even in a crisis caused by severe weather, which is completely beyond the control of management, it is likely that some guests will become upset, and they may, from fear or anger, blame management. Let those guests know that you are genuinely concerned about their plight and that you are doing everything possible to ease the difficulties of the situation.

Media Relations

When a crisis occurs at your property, it, and your business, may become the news story of the day. When, for example, a restaurant is robbed at gunpoint, newspaper, radio, and television reporters may call or descend on the property to find out what happened. Although most reporters are fair and even-handed in their coverage of a story, some are not. And, remember, a poorly prepared management statement or *press release* can magnify a crisis rather than help diffuse it.

Unfortunately, even the best preparation cannot turn bad news into good. During a crisis, you can, however, help ensure that you are allowed to tell your side of the story on behalf of the company and the property, and in so doing preserve your image as an organization that is professional, caring, and concerned. If you do not achieve this goal, not only might your liability for the crisis increase, but you might also face litigation simply because you did not express an appropriate amount of concern for the victims of the crisis. The guidelines in the next Legally Managing at Work feature can be helpful if you are called on to serve as the spokesperson for your organization during a crisis.

Some managers feel that they and their operations are treated unfairly by reporters during a crisis. Certainly, when a crisis occurs, the potential for negative publicity is great, and it is natural not to want to see yourself or your operation cast in a negative light. It is important, however, that you not do anything to make a difficult situation worse by attacking the media. You cannot control the actions of reporters; you can only conduct yourself in a positive, professional manner while expressing genuine concern for crisis victims. As a professional manager, it is your responsibility to do so.

LEGALESE
Press release: An announcement made by an organization or individual distributed for use by the media.

LEGALLY MANAGING AT WORK:

Guidelines for Dealing with the Media during a Crisis

1. Be professional. And remember that your picture may be taken or you may appear on television, so dress appropriately.

2. Update the press regularly. Be proactive. If you prepare a press release, distribute copies to all interested reporters.

3. Clearly identify yourself and your position prior to any exchange with the media.

4. Speak calmly and clearly. Project the image that you are a professional who knows how to deal properly with a difficult situation.

5. Avoid speculating as to the causes or outcomes of the crisis. Speak only to those items about which you have factual knowledge.

6. Express genuine concern for the suffering of the victims.

7. Avoid graphic descriptions of events or injuries.

8. Do not release the names of victims or suspects. Refer these questions to the appropriate party, such as the police or medical facilities.

9. Never reply to a question with "no comment." If you truly cannot comment, give the honest reason why you cannot. Legitimate reasons not to respond to a specific question include:

   a. Pending legal investigation

   b. Incomplete information

   c. Responsibility to respond falls to another (give that person's name)

10. Remember that your primary responsibility to the media during a crisis is to provide factual information and to express genuine concern for any crisis victims. But you also have an opportunity to emphasize the positives of your organization even in the face of the crisis. Mention, for example, safety and security efforts in place, training programs implemented that relate to the crisis, and your commitment to cooperate fully with all investigating authorities.

11. Expect tough questions, and practice your answers to them. Do not become belligerent or hostile to reporters.

12. Never demand to see or review a reporter's story before it is printed. Never agree to speak *off the record*.

13. If you feel that you or your organization has been unfairly depicted in the reporting of the crisis, contact the reporter to calmly retell the factual side of the story.

14. Temporarily suspend advertising for a period of time appropriate for the crisis endured.

15. Consider creating a publicity campaign to counteract any negative impact caused by the crisis.

LEGALESE

Off the record: An oral agreement between a reporter and an interviewee wherein the reporter promises not to quote the interviewee's comments for publication.

Postcrisis Assessment

As stated previously, evaluating your emergency plan should be an ongoing process, but in the aftermath of a crisis, it is imperative to do so. At this time you will be able to review your performance and that of your staff and guests, as well as your effectiveness in dealing with the media.

A variety of approaches may be used to do a postcrisis analysis of performance. The STEM model introduced in Chapter 1, "Prevention Philosophy," is a good place to start. Consider the case of Brenda Mendez. Brenda managed a 64-room limited-service hotel near the airport. Her largest customer, Northeast Airlines, housed its crew members in her hotel during their layovers. One night, as her van driver was returning from the airport with a crew, a serious accident occurred, severely injuring four crew members and the driver. Although the cause of the accident was not initially apparent, negative publicity ensued and threatened to damage the safety reputation of the hotel, and, of course, relations with Northeast Airlines were strained. Fortunately, Brenda had a plan in place to deal with the crash. Afterward, however, she felt that certain elements of the plan could be improved, so she decided to undertake a postcrisis assessment. Using the STEM approach, Brenda reviewed:

- **Selecting:** Were procedures in place to ensure that the drivers were qualified for the job? Had background checks on licenses been performed? Were vision tests required as a part of the selection process, and corrective glasses mandated if needed? If an opposing attorney sued the hotel for negligence, the answers to these questions and others would be required. It might be too late to correct any deficiencies related to a current crisis, but it certainly is not too late to prepare for, and attempt to prevent, a second occurrence.

- **Teaching:** Part of the STEM approach involves teaching employees properly, which includes using feedback devices such as competency testing to ensure that the training was effective. In the van accident just described, the number of employees who would have required training in anticipation of such a crisis is large indeed. Certainly, the van drivers would need to be trained in administering first aid. Additionally, front desk and night audit staff would need to be trained in how to field possible calls from the media, the airline, and families of the victims. Those involved in sales would certainly be called on to reassure customers of the hotel's safety. When employees know what to expect, and have been trained how to react, the chance of their making a mistake that would exacerbate the crisis is greatly reduced.

- **Educating:** Remember that managers too must continuously educate themselves. If a lawsuit results from a crisis, a plaintiff's attorney will want to know the competency level of management. Employee selection and employee training are ultimately a management responsibility. Therefore, an effective postcrisis assessment also includes an examination of management's competency. Proof of continuing education, certification, and expertise in the specific safety and security area involved in the crisis can be crucial in reducing legal liability. In addition, management's performance in handling the press should be reviewed. Were employees told who would serve as the media spokesperson in the event of a crisis? Was the spokesperson/manager well studied and prepared? Was anything said by management or the staff that could increase the operation's potential liability?

- **Managing:** Management is a process. It includes the actions of the manager as well as the processes and procedures established and enforced by management. A postcrisis assessment necessarily involves reviewing those processes and procedures for improvement. For the van accident, a review would involve an examination of all hiring and training practices related to van drivers, training of employees affected by the crisis, and the processes and procedures related to management's emergency response. In addition, an analysis of diverse areas such as the availability of first-aid supplies, insurance coverage, and the property's relationships with law enforcement agencies would be undertaken. The goal, of course, is to use what is learned in one crisis to help prevent future crises, and to utilize your knowledge of the law to respond in a more effective manner should a similar crisis arise in the future.

⟫ ANALYZE THE SITUATION 14.6

IRVING NASH MANAGED A 24-hour table-service restaurant that specialized in breakfast items. Lendal Ketchar, a customer, arrived at the restaurant at approximately 2:00 A.M. one morning. Upon entering the restaurant, Mr. Ketchar tripped over the curb alongside the sidewalk and broke his hip. Because Mr. Ketchar was a city councilman, the incident was reported in the local paper.

Mr. Nash was interviewed extensively about the cause of the accident. He specifically mentioned to reporters that the curb had not been painted bright yellow as a warning to guests, nor were lighting levels very high at the entrance area where Mr. Ketchar fell. Mr. Nash later read the interviews and shared them with his two assistant managers. Both suggested that the restaurant paint the curb area, install additional lighting, and inform the media that these actions were undertaken. Mr. Nash's boss vetoed this idea, however, stating that any action such as painting the curb and installing better lighting could imply previous negligence on the part of the organization and thus could increase the organization's potential legal liability.

1. Which factors would influence the potential liability of Mr. Nash's restaurant for the accident?

2. Is the future liability of the restaurant greater under the proposed actions of Mr. Nash's assistant managers or those of his boss?

3. What effective safety and security programs could be undertaken to limit legal liability if Mr. Nash is required to follow the advice of his boss?

4. As a professional hospitality manager, is Mr. Nash ethically obligated to take action to prevent a further occurrence of this type?

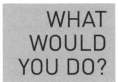

WHAT WOULD YOU DO?

You are the manager of a 150-room limited-service, all-suite hotel located off the interstate highway near a large metropolitan area. Kate Roessler is your executive housekeeper. Ms. Roessler asks you to go with her to inspect room 415, which is occupied by a guest, Mr. Barney.

Ms. Roessler explains that the guest has been checked in for ten days and has had a "Do Not Disturb" sign on the door for all but two of those days. She asks you to view the room before it is cleaned, because she says she is concerned for the safety of her housekeepers in their routine cleaning tasks.

Upon entering the room, you observe several ripped plastic baggies, money wrappers, large quantities of empty fast-food containers, a scale, and a pistol holster partially hidden under a mattress. You recall that this is the same man who arrived by cab to the hotel and paid cash up front for a two-week stay.

1. Write a memo to your executive housekeeper outlining the steps she is to take for servicing Mr. Barney's room.

2. Assuming a drug interdiction program is in place in your city, would you contact that program to report Mr. Barney?

3. Regardless of your decision in regard to question 2, if the police asked to use the room next to that of Mr. Barney for an undercover operation, would you allow them to do so?

4. Write a memo to the chief of police stating your position in question 3, along with your rationale for the decision.

THE HOSPITALITY INDUSTRY IN COURT

To understand the sometimes difficult line drawn between workers' compensation and negligence in a failure to provide adequate security, read the case of *Holshouser v. Shaner Hotel Group*, 518 S.E.2d 17 (N.C. Ct. App. 1999).

FACTUAL SUMMARY

Fredericka Holshouser (Holshouser) worked as a waitress at a Holiday Inn Select Hotel in Winston-Salem, North Carolina, owned by Shaner Hotel Group (the Hotel). Holshouser arrived at the hotel for work around 4:40 A.M. on October 23, 1996. She parked in the employee parking lot at the rear of the Hotel. Just before she reached the back door of the Hotel, an unknown attacker grabbed her from behind, forced her into an area overgrown with trees and shrubs, and then raped her. She brought suit against the Hotel for failure to keep the shrubbery and trees properly cut back, and for failure to provide adequate lighting and security behind the Hotel. She also sued Loss Prevention Services (LPS), the security firm hired by the Hotel to provide security for the premises for failure to do so adequately.

QUESTION FOR THE COURT

There were two questions for the court in this particular case. The first was whether LPS had a duty to provide security for Holshouser, an employee of the Hotel. Holshouser argued that LPS had a duty to protect her from criminal attacks under the terms of the contract negotiated between the Hotel and LPS. LPS argued there was no specific promise within the contract to protect hotel employees from harm. The court held the terms of the contract were ambiguous and that outside evidence could be used to determine whether LPS was required to protect hotel employees under the contract. Under the "Rules and Regulations Governing Loss Prevention Services Security Officers," security guards were required to "... at all times preserve the peace, protect life and property, prevent crime, apprehend violators, and enforce all Loss Prevention Services rules. ..."

The second question for the court was whether Holshouser was limited to the damages allowed under a Workers' Compensation Act claim against the Hotel. The Hotel argued Holshouser's injury was: (1) an accident, (2) arose out of her employment at the Hotel, and (3) was within the course of her employment. According to the Hotel, she could only collect damages under the Workers' Compensation Act (WCA) and could not sue for negligence against the Hotel. Holshouser argued her injury did not arise out of her employment so her claim was not eligible under the WCA, giving her the option to sue the Hotel for negligence.

DECISION

On the first question, the court found there was sufficient evidence to create a duty on the part of LPS to protect Holshouser. The ambiguous nature of the contract and the clause in the Rules and Regulations manual was enough to impose a duty to on LPS protect hotel employees.

On the second question, the court held in favor of Holshouser, finding the assault on her was not a "natural and probable consequence of the nature of her employment." She was therefore not eligible under the WCA but could instead sue the Hotel for negligence.

MESSAGE TO MANAGEMENT

Frequent inspections for safety and security concerns are a must. Adequate lighting and clear lines of sight help prevent circumstances like this from happening.

To familiarize yourself with the types of arguments a complaining customer might make in a failure to respond adequately to a crisis case, read the case of *Mauro v. GNLV Corp.*, 982 S. W. 2d 530 (Tex. App.–Texarkana 1998).

FACTUAL SUMMARY

Joseph and Maria Mauro (Mauros) were playing the slot machines in the Golden Nugget (GNLV) casino when a man approached them and stole two rolls of coins. The Mauros both gave chase and apprehended the man. In the process of apprehending the thief, the Mauros were both injured. They then sued the casino for negligence in failing to provide adequate security.

QUESTION FOR THE COURT

The question for the court was whether GNLV was negligent by failing to provide adequate security on the casino floor. More specifically, the court examined whether the GNLV had a duty to provide security. In general, the owner of a business or the party in control has no duty to protect patrons from the criminal act of another. The owner owes a duty to the patron only if the owner knows or should have known of an unreasonable and foreseeable risk. For risks such as injury from criminal activity, the plaintiff must show evidence of previous crimes near the premises. The Mauros argued robberies and thefts are common occurrences at casinos so GNLV knew or should have known of the risk. GNLV argued the Mauros had no evidence of specific previous crimes at the Golden Nugget. Without evidence of specific previous crimes, the Mauros could not show GNLV had a duty to provide security.

DECISION

The court ruled in favor of GNLV, finding no evidence of prior specific crimes. Absent such evidence, the Mauros could not prove GNLV had a duty to provide adequate security.

MESSAGE TO MANAGEMENT
Liability for the intentional acts (criminal in nature) is an evolving area of the law. The best practice is to be vigilant in your exercise of safety and security procedures. And if criminal activity becomes foreseeable, then specifically address that area of concern.

This chapter emphasized the need to prevent liabilities from occurring and to be prepared for events that give rise to liabilities. A four-step safety and security management method was introduced:

WHAT DID YOU LEARN IN THIS CHAPTER?

1. Recognize the threat.
2. Develop the response to particular threats.
3. Implement the program.
4. Monitor the program results.

It is crucial to develop emergency plans so that you and your staff are prepared in the event of a crisis, and to practice those plans regularly. During a crisis you have a responsibility to respond to the community at large via the media, to your staff, and to your guests. The way you respond can have a major impact on your future reputation once the crisis has subsided. It is always important to assess your performance in any situation, and an assessment following a crisis is vital.

After you have studied this chapter, you should be prepared to:

RAPID REVIEW

1. Describe three threats to safety and three threats to security in the hospitality organization with which you are most familiar. Explain how management currently addresses (manages) these threats.

2. Assume that you are the foodservice manager of a college dormitory. You are asked to address parents regarding the impact your facility will make on the overall educational experience of their children. Compose a five-minute presentation that addresses your safety and security philosophy and its relation to the well-being and educational experience of your residents.

3. Analyze the four-step safety and security management method. Select one of the steps and prepare a three-minute presentation that could be delivered to members of your safety committee, in which you emphasize the importance of this step.

4. Assume that you have implemented a safety program designed to reduce employee accidents resulting from improper lifting techniques. Identify at least three different measurable outcomes that could be used to evaluate the program's effectiveness. Explain which of these three you would use, and why.

5. Contact your local law enforcement officials to determine what training programs are offered to businesses for the purpose of assisting those businesses in their safety and security efforts. Determine the cost, if any, of the programs and the frequency with which they will be offered in the coming 12 months.

6. The Educational Institute of the American Hotel and Lodging Association (EI) certifies hospitality security guards. Log on to its Web site at www.ei-ahla.org and identify the methods of qualifying for the designation of Certified Lodging Security Director (CLSD). Assume that your property is considering such a program for the head of your safety and security department. Prepare a memo for your immediate supervisor detailing the advantages and disadvantages of using the EI program, as opposed to one you would develop yourself.

7. Assume that a bomb threat has forced you to evacuate your restaurant. The police have arrived; no one has been hurt, but the press is at your property. Create an outline of a one-page press release that would address the items about which the media would be most interested.

8. An employee who burned himself while working did not seek medical treatment. The employee missed five days of work, then later filed, and won, a workers' compensation claim, because the burn became infected. Draft a memo outlining the criteria your mangers should use in the future for determining which employee accidents will result in mandatory medical treatment.

TEAM ACTIVITY   The director of risk management has asked your team to evaluate the number of lawsuits and workers' compensation claims that have occurred at your three-hotel chain in the last year and to create an action plan to reduce the number by 75 percent. Your analysis shows more than 50 lawsuits and comp claims. The reasons for the lawsuits vary from slips and falls to alcohol-related injuries to theft of guest property and assaults in the parking lot. The comp claims are primarily due to back injuries suffered by employees in the kitchen and housekeeping and those working banquets. How can you meet your goal? Does it matter if one of your properties is in a high-crime area? Be prepared to present your recommendations at the next executive council meeting.

MANAGING INSURANCE

"THAT WAS TRULY a great meal!" said Trisha Sangus as she left the lobby area of Chez Louise, one of her favorite restaurants in the city. Trisha was in a festive mood, as she walked back to the restaurant's parking lot with Bob Zaccarelli, editor of *The Community News,* her city's largest newspaper. Trisha and Bob had just enjoyed dinner while they worked together on planning the print advertising for the city's annual Taste of the Town festival. As they approached Bob's car, he shouted, "What the . . . !!!!"

Trisha looked at Bob's brand-new sports car. The driver's side window had been smashed. Shattered glass was everywhere, and Trisha noticed on the ground beneath the car window that it included the distinctive brown glass of a beer bottle with its wrapper still partially attached.

"Did they take anything?" asked Trisha, as Bob examined the inside of the car.

"No, I don't think so. My CD player's still here," replied Bob still angry. "I can't believe this. We were only inside for an hour! I thought this restaurant was in a safe neighborhood. It will take me a week to order a new window and get this fixed! I'll have to rent a car in the meantime."

Trisha looked up at one of the halogen lamps in the well-lighted parking lot. Nearby, other cars passed on a busy commercial street.

"I'm really sorry, Bob," she said. "It looks like the work of some kids with nothing better to do. If they had been car thieves, you would have lost the whole car! By the looks of things, I would guess someone drove by and threw the bottle from the street. I'm sure the police will be able to determine what happened better than we can. I have my cell phone. Would you like me to call them?"

"Don't bother," replied Bob. "The police are not going to be able to fix my window. Besides, as you say, it looks like vandalism. It's unfortunate, but I guess it goes with doing business in the city. Anyway, I'm sure the restaurant has insurance for this type of thing."

"The restaurant?" asked Trisha quizzically. "Won't you file a claim with your own auto insurer?"

"No way," said Bob. "This happened in a restaurant parking lot. The owners' insurance should pay. My car is supposed to be safe here. It wasn't, and that's their responsibility. Just as if the car had been vandalized in your hotel parking lot, it would be your responsibility. It's as clear-cut a case of liability as I have ever seen. I'm going back in to see the manager!"

"Clear-cut," repeated Trisha to herself. She wondered what type of reception Bob would get from the manager at Chez Louise. She had never seen Bob so upset. She wondered how the hotel managers on her own staff would react if Bob approached them with a similar complaint. She knew what she would say, but what about her manager on duty? Just as important, if they said the wrong things, she wondered what impact that might have on the hotel's liability insurance coverage. Trisha made a mental note to add this issue to the top of her agenda for tomorrow's staff meeting.

IN THIS CHAPTER, YOU WILL LEARN:

1. To understand the value of insurance in protecting a business from financial loss.
2. To become familiar with the different types of insurance required of hospitality operations.
3. To understand the role of workers' compensation and the requirements of an employer.
4. To critically evaluate the financial rating of an insurance company and other information to help you select an insurance carrier.
5. To distinguish between the terms "primary" and "umbrella" insurance coverage, and determine appropriate amounts of coverage.
6. To analyze an insurance policy and determine what types of claims will be covered and what types of claims will not be covered.

15.1 INTRODUCTION TO INSURANCE

LEGALESE

Insure (insurance): To protect from risk.

Every individual faces risk. Illness, accidents, the acts of others, and even death, are all potential hazards each of us faces in life. Your business will face possible calamities, also. Floods, fire, and the acts of guests, employees, and others can all put your business at risk. To guard against the financial loss these risks can bring, both individuals and businesses need to *insure* themselves. In its simplest form, insurance involves the spreading of risk from one person or business to a larger group.

Hospitality businesses seek *insurance*, or protection from risk, for two basic reasons. First, because doing so makes good financial sense. Second, some types of insurance coverage are required either by law (such as workers' compensation) or by lenders to protect their collateral. Consider, for example, the restaurateur who owns a business that provides her with a salary of $100,000 per year. The restaurant is her sole source of income. If the restaurant were to burn down, she would lose this source of income. To protect her business, and her income, she would want to buy a fire insurance policy that would pay to completely replace the restaurant in the event of a fire, provided that the cost of the insurance was reasonable. Not buying the insurance would put this restaurateur and her family at great financial risk. Buying the insurance would provide the restaurateur with both financial security, in the event of an accidental fire, and the peace of mind that such security brings.

To be protected from risk does not mean that hazardous events will not occur. Insurance does mean, however, that the person with insurance is provided some protection against the financial loss he or she may incur as a result of a hazardous event. The insurance industry is built on four fundamental premises:

1. The type of hazard the insurance company is underwriting must be faced by a large enough number of individuals or businesses so that statisticians can use actuarial (*actuary*) methods to predict the average frequency of loss involved in the risk.

2. The monetary value of the loss must be calculable against an accepted standard. For example, if a hotel seeks coverage for broken windows caused by vandals, it must be possible for the *insurer* to fairly determine the cost of replacing such a window.

3. The *premiums* (fees) for the insurance must be low enough to attract those who seek to be *insured* but high enough to support the number of losses that will be incurred by the insurer.

4. The risk must not have the possibility of occurring so frequently during any given time period that the insurer cannot pay all legitimate claims. Insurance companies spend millions of dollars annually researching industries to determine the risk factor of providing insurance for a specific market, such as hospitality. Obviously, the fewer number of casualty losses, workers injured, lawsuits, and so on, the lower the risk that the insurance company may have to pay out money on a claim. Logically, then, the safer the operation, and the safer the industry as a whole, the lower the cost of insurance.

The insurance contract between an insurer and an insured is called a *policy*. There are a variety of policy types, but they can be conveniently grouped into three categories:

1. Life insurance
2. Health insurance
3. Property-casualty (often referred to as "property-liability")

Life insurance policies generally are written to pay a certain amount of money at the time of the insured's death, or to pay the insured an *annuity* upon the insured's reaching a specified age. Health insurance is generally created to pay for hospital and doctor bills, as well as annuity payments for those who are disabled. In the hospitality industry, it would be common for you, as a manager, to receive some level of both life and health insurance as part of your compensation package.

Property-liability insurance provides financial protection (*indemnification*) in the event of occurrences such as floods, fires, lawsuits, and automobile accidents. As a manager, it is important to know the types of insurance policies that make sense for your operation, and how to evaluate the quality of the companies that offer insurance, as well as the merits of the actual policies.

It is also important to remember that insurance companies, like hospitality companies, are in business to make a profit. Profits in the insurance industry are the result of increasing premium amounts, increased return from the investment of premiums, and the reduction of costs, including the payment of insurance *claims*. Because this is true, insurers are very careful to pay only those claims that are proven to be legitimate and within the terms of the insurance policy.

Because insurance protects against risk at an agreed-upon price, it is critical that you as a hospitality manager know:

■ The risks you are insuring against
■ The amount of coverage you will receive
■ Any exceptions to your coverage that are written into your policy

LEGALESE

Actuary: A mathematician or statistician who computes insurance risks and establishes premium rates.

LEGALESE

Insurer: The entity that provides insurance.

LEGALESE

Premium: The amount paid for insurance coverage; it can be paid in one lump sum or over time, such as monthly.

LEGALESE

Insured: The individual or business that purchases insurance against a risk.

LEGALESE

Policy (insurance): The contract for insurance agreed upon by the insurer and insured.

LEGALESE

Annuity: Fixed payments, made on a regular basis, for an agreed-upon period of time or until the death of the recipient.

LEGALESE

Indemnification: To insure against possible liability and loss, and/or to compensate financially for losses incurred.

LEGALESE

Claim: Demand for money, property, or repairs to property.

- How much the insurance will cost
- The likelihood that the insurance company is financially sound enough to pay, if it becomes necessary

To purchase insurance, a potential buyer must demonstrate that he or she has an insurable interest in the premises to be insured. That is, he or she must demonstrate that a loss would, in fact, affect him or her in a material way. This insurance concept is fundamental and helps protect against possible intentional acts of destruction or fraud. In addition, an insured must honestly divulge information needed by the insurer to enable the insurer to establish appropriate premium rates.

» ANALYZE THE SITUATION 15.1

SAMUEL RENKO, PRESIDENT OF Senframe Hotel Management Company, authorized the purchase of a $2 million fidelity insurance policy, the purpose of which was to protect the company in the event of employee theft or fraud. In discussing the purchase with the insurance agent, Jana Foster, Mr. Renko assured Ms. Foster that all hotel controllers were subject to a thorough background check before they were hired. As a specific condition of the insurance policy, background checks on controller candidates were required prior to employment.

The insurance policy was purchased and went into effect on January 1, 2011. On June 1, 2011, the Senframe Hotel Management Company took over the management and operation of the Roosevelt Hotel, a 300-room property in a resort area. As part of the operating agreement with the Roosevelt Hotel's owners, the hotel's controller and its director of sales were retained by Senframe. On December 20, 2011, Senframe management discovered that the Roosevelt Hotel's controller had been creating and submitting false invoices. The invoice payments were deposited in a bank account he had established for himself five years earlier. Total losses for the five-year period that the falsification occurred were over $500,000.

The controller resigned, but the hotel owners sued Senframe for the portion of misappropriated fund ($70,000) taken during the period the hotel was under Senframe's management. Ms. Foster maintained that her insurance company was not liable to indemnify Senframe, because the controller had not been subjected to a background check, as Mr. Renko had promised. Mr. Renko countered that the controller, although not background-checked, had no criminal record of any kind, and thus a background check would not have prevented the hotel from hiring the controller.

1. Must Ms. Foster's company defend Senframe in the litigation brought by the hotel's ownership?

2. If you were on a jury, would you hold Senframe responsible for the employee theft?

3. Regardless of the outcome of this situation, what changes in operational procedure should be implemented by Mr. Renko and the Senframe Hotel Management Company?

As with any purchase, careful comparison shopping before selecting insurance is a very good idea. Because insurance is a contract between the insurer and the insured, it is also a good idea to read the contract carefully, or to have an expert evaluate it for you. As with any type of contract, it is critical that the insurance policies be kept in a safe, secure location.

Purchasing insurance is often complex and can be confusing. You may find it easier if you think of buying insurance as a three-step process:

1. Determine the type of insurance coverage you need. Here, you are looking at various aspects of your operation and deciding which risks to protect against.

2. Determine the ideal monetary amount of insurance coverage, and the type of policy you will require. Remember, as the dollar value of your coverage increases, so will the premiums you have to pay.

3. Select a specific insurance company from which you will buy your policy.

The next three sections of this chapter examine each of these steps in detail, and offer some guidelines for helping you determine the appropriate type of insurance coverage.

15.2 TYPES OF COVERAGE

Because the hospitality industry is made up of a variety of operations in different locations, the insurance needs of restaurants and hotels will vary considerably. A hospitality establishment's insurance policies will reflect the unique characteristics of the type of business being operated and the location in which it does business. For example, a restaurant on the United States Gulf Coast may well feel that hurricane insurance makes sense, while the same type of operation in South Dakota would not. Similarly, the resort that offers overnight camping excursions for families may desire insurance against animal attacks, while the yogurt store in a shopping mall would be hard-pressed to justify purchasing such a policy.

Insurance companies offer a wide variety of products designed to meet the needs of their customers. Because this is true, hospitality managers must be very careful to make sure that they select the proper insurance coverage for their specific situation. With too much coverage, or with coverage that is not necessary, operational profits are reduced because premium payments are unnecessarily high. With no insurance, or too little insurance of the right type, however, the economic survival of the hospitality operation and its members may be at risk.

Many states have laws requiring businesses to carry certain types of insurance, at specified minimum amounts, in order to conduct business within the state. In addition, when hospitality firms lease space in buildings, the lease agreement may also require them to carry minimum amounts of insurance.

Although the specific types and amounts of insurance needed for any given hospitality operation will vary, the following types of insurance coverage are common.

Property-Casualty

Just as its name indicates, property-casualty insurance is purchased to protect against the loss of property. These losses include damages incurred due to a fire, flood, or storm. Some insurance companies will classify threats to property in different ways, but in all cases, property-casualty insurance protects property and its contents. The determination of which risks to insure against must be made on the basis of each hospitality operation's special circumstances.

Consider the case of Ralph Escobar. Ralph operates a seafood restaurant that is housed on a ship that is permanently docked on one of the Great Lakes. Ralph, unlike many other restaurateurs, must insure his operation against a variety of water-related events that could destroy his business. These include accidentally being hit by another boat, high- or low-water damage, and seasonal storms that could damage his floating restaurant. Ralph must select casualty insurance that will cover these incidents and reimburse him for the cost of repairs and any potential loss of business.

Property-casualty insurance, in its many forms, is the most common type of business insurance purchased. It may be purchased in policies covering losses as small as a few hundred dollars or as large as many millions of dollars.

Liability

General liability insurance is selected when you wish to protect against injuries to other people resulting from the operation of your own hospitality facility. For example, Diane Sulayman operates a French fine-dining establishment that serves a variety of items, including flamed desserts. One evening, her server accidentally sloshes flaming alcohol out of a flambé pan and it splashes onto the suit of a diner. The diner is not injured seriously, but suffers some minor burns and is quite upset. Should the diner elect to bring a lawsuit against Diane, her general liability insurance would help cover the expenses and potential damages that might be awarded in such a lawsuit.

There are a variety of liability insurance types on the market today. The following are some of the most popular:

■ Property damage liability coverage is selected when you wish to protect against claims resulting from damage to the property of others.

■ Personal injury liability coverage provides you with protection for such offenses as false arrest, libel, slander, invasion of privacy, and food poisoning.

■ Advertising injury liability coverage helps cover your legal liability for offenses arising out of the advertising of your business's goods and services.

Insurance companies have the right and obligation to defend any lawsuit against their insured customers that seeks damages for bodily injury or property damage, even if the allegations in the suit are groundless, false, or fraudulent. The insurance company can also enter into any settlement agreement it deems expedient. It is important to remember, however, that the company is not obligated to pay any claim or judgment or to defend any suit after the applicable limit of the company's liability has been reached, or that falls outside the coverage of the policy.

Consider the case of Roger Kuhlman. Roger owns and operates a hotel in which a guest accidentally discharges a pistol in one of the guestrooms. The shot passes through the wall of the room and injures a guest in the next room. The injured guest sues both Roger and the guest responsible for the accidental shooting. Roger's insurance company defends his hotel in the lawsuit. In the resulting jury trial, Roger's hotel is deemed to be partially responsible for the accident, and is ordered to pay the victim $3 million. The hotel's insurance policy provides only $1 million of coverage. In this case, Roger's hotel is responsible for paying the remaining $2 million.

With the increasing monetary value of awards resulting from litigation today, wise hospitality managers are attempting to confirm they have sufficient liability coverage. This is not an easy task. You must weigh the cost of coverage (the premium payments) versus the risk (possible damages), and assess your ability to absorb or pass on these insurance costs to your customers.

Employee Liability

An employee liability policy is selected when, as an owner or manager, you wish to supplement your general liability coverage with additional coverage for any harmful acts your employees may commit in the course of their employment. Some areas of coverage to be considered include those related to:

Wrongful termination
Workplace harassment
Sexual harassment
Breach of employment contract
Discrimination
Failure to employ or promote
Deprivation of a career opportunity
Negligent evaluation
Employment-related misrepresentation
Defamation
Theft

Dram Shop

Liquor liability, or dram shop, insurance provides establishments that sell alcohol coverage for bodily injury or property damage that may result from any or all of the following acts:

- Causing or contributing to the intoxication of a person

- Serving alcoholic beverages to a person under the legal drinking age

- Serving alcohol to an intoxicated person

- Violating any statute, ordinance, or regulation relating to the sale, gift, distribution, or use of alcoholic beverages

Serving alcoholic beverages in today's society makes a hospitality manager subject to great risk. Dram shop insurance is truly a necessity in today's legal environment, and states may require it as a condition for granting a liquor license.

Health/Dental/Vision

One of a hospitality manager's greatest costs, and one that continues to rise dramatically, is that of employee medical insurance. Although medical coverage such as health, dental, and vision insurance is not a requirement, the degree to which it is offered can have a significant effect on a manager's ability to retain and maintain a quality workforce.

Like all types of insurance, the varieties of coverage available for medical insurance are tremendous. In addition, this is one area of insurance where the cost is generally split, in some manner, between the employer and the employee. Employers can choose from contributing 100 percent of medical insurance premiums for their employees to simply making such coverage available to employees on a voluntary basis. Employees often depend on such coverage for their families and can maintain that insurance even if they lose their jobs.

The Consolidated Omnibus Budget Reconciliation Act (COBRA), passed by the federal government in 1986, requires employers to continue providing health, dental, and optical coverage benefits to employees who have resigned or been terminated, and to family members of employees who have lost their health insurance due to death, divorce, or dropping out of school. COBRA participants may continue their benefits for up to 18 months, with possible extensions to a maximum of 36 months, following the loss of their insurance; although they are responsible for paying the entire cost of their premiums.

In March 2010, President Barack Obama signed the Affordable Care Act into law. This legislation seeks to give individuals better health security by passing comprehensive reforms that hold health insurance companies accountable, lower health care costs, guarantee more choice to Americans, and enhance the quality of healthcare for all Americans. The bill is comprehensive and extremely detailed, and any possible effects that the law will have on your particular hospitality entity should be discussed with competent counsel. The important thing to note about the law is that the changes it implements will be done on a staggered scale constituting five main phases that will take place periodically through 2018.

Workers' Compensation

The Workmen's Compensation Act of 1908 was the first effort to provide injury-related insurance to those workers who were hurt while on the job. This law, passed by Congress, which covers federal employees, spurred the states to enact similar legislation covering workers in their states. Today, all states require public- and private-sector employers to provide some form of mandatory workers' compensation insurance.

Workers' compensation policies provide payments to workers or their families in the event of an employee's injury or death. Coverage normally includes medical expenses and a significant portion of the wages lost by the employee being unable to work due to the injury. In more serious cases, lump-sum payments can be made to those workers who have been partially or permanently disabled. In addition, if a worker is killed while on the job, payments may be made to the worker's family. The injury must have happened in the "*course and scope*" of employment. The courts have broadly defined course and scope to sometimes include commuting to and from the place of employment, during mealtimes, or on or off the work site.

Injured employees are generally prohibited from suing their employer for damages beyond those awarded by workers' compensation. Only in the case of gross negligence or an intentional act will an employer potentially be subject to paying greater damages than those normally imposed by workers' compensation.

It is important to know that some states will designate specific doctors who will examine those employees who appear to have been injured. This is an effort on the part of the state to hold down premium costs and reduce incidents of fraud. It is also important to remember that employers cannot claim the negligence of the worker as a defense for a work-related injury. Usually, only in cases where the worker has been proven to be under the influence of drugs or alcohol at the time of the injury, or if the injury was fraudulent, will an employer be able to mount a legally valid defense against a workers' compensation claim.

In cases where another employee or third party has caused a worker injury, or when the employer challenges the legality of a worker's claim for compensation, a hearing is held before the state workers' compensation board. A judge will determine whether the claim has merit and how much compensation the worker is entitled to receive, if any. Both parties have the right to appeal the judge's decision, if they choose.

Because some form of workers' compensation is mandatory in every state, the failure on the part of management to provide it is punishable by fines and/or imprisonment. Employers are also required by law to accurately report on-the-job accidents to the state agency overseeing the workers' compensation program. This information is significant, as the cost of providing workers' compensation insurance varies based on the safety history of the employer, and the potential risk of injury to employees working for a specific employer. For example, a restaurant manager who does not encourage the immediate clean-up of spills in the kitchen, and thus experiences a greater-than-average number of employee injuries due to slips and falls, will pay a higher premium than an employer in an identical situation whose internal policies help prevent such accidents. Many state workers' compensation boards use experience ratings, which categorize businesses by the number of injury claims that are paid out, to determine the amount of insurance premiums that will be assessed.

Depending on the state in which they are operating, an employer may provide workers' compensation insurance through a private insurance company, a state

LEGALESE

Course and scope: The sum total of all common, job-related employee activities dictated or allowed by the employer.

agency, or itself. If the state allows a self-insurance option, the security deposit required can be substantial since, under the self-insurance option, an employer might be solely responsible for the payment of large awards in the case of a serious accident.

» ANALYZE THE SITUATION 15.2

CHRISTINA FLEISCHER WAS 16 years old when she was hired to work as a busser for a private country club. On Sundays, the club operated a popular brunch that served 500 to 1,000 people between the hours of 9:00 A.M. and 3:00 P.M. On Christina's first day of work, her supervisor quickly detailed the job requirements. As part of her job, Christina was to remove the guests' used dishes from the table, take the dishes to a bussing station, and scrape any leftover food from the dishes into a garbage receptacle lined with a plastic trash bag. Periodically, she was to bring the dishes to the kitchen to be washed and take the garbage receptacle to a designated area, where she would then remove the plastic trash bag and replace it with an empty one. The filled bags were left in the designated area until they could be taken out to a dumpster by a member of the dishroom staff. The garbage receptacles would often get very heavy, and all bussers were instructed to replace the plastic bags in them when they were half-full. Christina's supervisor made it a point of mentioning that during their 15-minute training session.

The club was very busy with Sunday morning brunch patrons on Christina's first day of work. Halfway through her shift, Christina forgot to replace one of the garbage bags until it was nearly full. She placed the garbage bag with the others in the designated location. Later that afternoon, a dishroom attendant, while taking out the 20 plastic garbage bags filled from the brunch, attempted to lift the bag that Christina had accidentally overfilled. The dishroom attendant seriously injured his back.

The injury was deemed within the scope of his work, so the dishroom attendant was awarded a monetary settlement by the workers' compensation board in his state. However, he then threatened to sue the country club, claiming negligence in Christina's training, and stated that this negligence was the direct cause of his accident. He also stated that management had provided workers with garbage receptacles that were too large and thus directly contributed to the accident.

1. Was management negligent?

2. Does the dishroom attendant have a viable claim against the club?

3. Do you feel the workers' compensation premiums for the club should be increased because of this incident?

4. What steps might the country club take to avoid paying higher premiums?

15.3 SELECTING AN INSURANCE CARRIER

Most insurance companies sell their products through agents, rather than directly to the public. Some companies use agents that represent them exclusively, while others use independent agents. These independent agents may represent several insurance companies, and can be a real asset in selecting the best policy at the best price. The premium rate, however, is set by the insurance company, and generally it cannot be changed by the agent.

An insurance agent does not provide insurance. The agent merely represents the insurance company that *underwrites* the actual insurance policy. When you buy an insurance policy, it is critical that you purchase it from a credible insurance company, and not just from an agent who is an effective salesperson.

If an insurance company is to protect against risk, it must have the financial capability to pay any and all claims you are held responsible for during the coverage period. The last thing you want is to buy an insurance policy, then relax, believing you have coverage, only to find out after a claim has been filed that your insurance company does not have the assets to pay the claim. It is important to remember that if your insurance company will not, or cannot, pay a claim, you will be held responsible for payment.

Insurance companies are rated based on their financial capability to pay claims. According to analysts, the stronger the rating, the more financially solvent the company is projected to be. Rating categories vary based on the organization doing the rating, but generally use either an A1, A, A2, B1, and so on, system, or an AAA, AA, A, BBB, and so on, system. Today, it would be difficult to justify purchasing an insurance policy from an underwriter with a rating of less than A2 or AA. It is best to buy from those companies that have achieved a rating of A1 or AAA.

Ratings can be verified by contacting the rating companies directly. A.M. Best and Standard & Poor's are two such companies. Alternatively, you can contact your state's insurance regulatory department. It can also provide you with a list of complaints filed against the insurance companies for failure to pay claims in a timely fashion or to act in good faith. This is information you need to know before you buy your policy.

> **LEGALESE**
>
> **Underwrite:** To assume agreed-upon maximum levels of liability in the event of a loss or damages.

Search the Web 15.1

Log on to www.insure.com.

1. Click on: Insurance Company Ratings under the "Insurance Tools" section.
2. Select: What the Ratings Mean.
3. Read the definitions of AAA through B insurance ratings.
4. Select: Access Ratings Lookup Tool.
5. Type the name of your own automobile or life insurance company into the search box, and click OK to find the rating of your own automobile or life insurance company.
6. What is your insurance company's rating?
7. How does it rank among the insurance companies in your state?

15.4 SELECTING THE INSURANCE POLICY

Once you have found two or three companies that you feel are financially sound, the next step is to get quotes, or bids, to provide coverage from each of the companies.

Consider the case of Vasal Bakar. Mr. Bakar is seeking to add a dental plan to his employees' health coverage. He selects three companies, all of which are rated AA, and proceeds to request a bid from each. When he asks for dental insurance bids to cover his 240 employees, he gets the following response:

Dental Insurance Quote for Vasal Bakar	
Insurance Company	**Coverage Cost per Employee**
Company One	$45.00/month
Company Two	$43.25/month
Company Three	$17.80/month

While at first glance it might appear that Company Three is offering the best policy price, it will be important to determine whether the level of dental coverage is the same under the terms of all three policies. When Mr. Bakal investigated further, he found that in the proposals of the first two companies, annual per-employee maximum benefits were $3,000, while in the case of Company Three, the per-employee annual maximum was only $1,000. Under these circumstances, the price for each $1,000 of employee dental insurance provided was actually highest from Company Three. The decision of whether to pay for the higher amounts of coverage, and whether the employees would be asked to contribute partial payments, is of course, left to Mr. Bakal.

To understand how much insurance you are actually purchasing for your premium dollar, and to realize how much total insurance you have for the period of time covered by the policy, it is critical that you understand the terms used in marketing insurance products.

Tina Shulky, the owner of a bagel franchise, is seeking liability coverage for her business. She selects some potential insurance providers, based on their financial ratings, then requests quotes on a *primary policy* with a *per-occurrence* amount of $500,000, an *aggregate* of $1 million, and an additional *umbrella* policy of $1 million.

If the policy that Ms. Shulky ultimately selects states that she has $500,000 of coverage per occurrence, it means that for each and every incident that occurs for which Ms. Shulky could be held liable, her insurance company will pay up to $500,000 on her behalf, less any *deductible*. If the judgment exceeds that amount, she would be responsible for anything over and above $500,000.

If her insurance policy has the term *aggregate* after the amount, it means that this is the total amount her insurance company will pay for all incidents and damages incurred during the coverage period. Thus, if she had a $500,000 per-occurrence policy and $1 million aggregate, two claims of $500,000 would wipe out her total insurance coverage (as would four claims of $250,000).

It's also important to understand how a deductible affects your total insurance costs. The deductible is an amount of money you are responsible for paying on a claim before your insurance company will begin paying for it. If you choose a high deductible, your premium payments will be lower, because you are assuming more risk by agreeing to pay a higher share of any claim filed against you. Managers must learn to factor the cost of the deductible into their insurance buying decision, and balance the needs of having a set amount of coverage that will be paid out by their insurance company with the amount of premium payments they are willing to make.

LEGALESE
Primary policy: The main insurance policy that provides basic coverage and the amount of insurance provided by the policy.

LEGALESE
Per occurrence: The maximum amount that can or will be paid by an insurer in the event of a single claim.

LEGALESE
Aggregate: The maximum amount that can or will be paid by an insurer for all claims during a policy period.

LEGALESE
Umbrella: Insurance coverage purchased to supplement primary coverage. Sometimes referred to as excess insurance.

LEGALESE
Deductible: The amount of money the insured has to pay before the insurance coverage will begin to pay. Accordingly, the higher the deductible, the less risk to the insurance company, which should equal lower premiums.

Basic coverage is referred to as primary coverage. In addition, you can purchase an umbrella, or what is commonly referred to as excess coverage. Be aware that umbrella coverage ordinarily pays only when and if your primary per-occurrence coverage is completely exhausted from a single claim.

To illustrate this point, assume the following scenario: You have a $500,000 per-occurrence policy with $500,000 aggregate, plus you have $1 million in umbrella, or excess coverage. The policy period runs from January 1, 2012, to December 31, 2012. An accident occurs on January 20, 2012, and the claim is settled for $750,000. The primary coverage will pay the first $500,000, less any deductible you might have. Your umbrella policy will pay the remaining $250,000. However, if you have a subsequent claim from an incident that occurs on February 15, 2012, how much coverage do you have available to pay this claim? The answer is zero. You have depleted your coverage under your primary policy because it has a $500,000 aggregate. Your umbrella policy is not available, because it pays only if you have exhausted your primary per-occurrence amount on a given claim. If you do not have any primary per-occurrence coverage left, the conditions for coverage of your umbrella policy cannot be met, unless you are able to pay out of your pocket the first $500,000. If you find yourself in this situation, you need to buy additional primary coverage.

15.5 POLICY ANALYSIS

LEGALESE

Face sheet: A one-page document briefly describing the type and amount of insurance coverage contained in an insurance policy. Sometimes referred to as a declaration page.

Analyzing an insurance policy consists of determining both what is and what is not covered. You are responsible for knowing and understanding the types and amounts of coverage that are written into your insurance policy. Additionally, be aware that when you purchase insurance, you ordinarily do not immediately receive a copy of the actual policy, because it takes some time for the insurance company to put the formal policy together with your unique coverages and exclusions. Instead, you receive a one-page *face sheet*, which generally sets out the types and amounts of coverage; it does not contain detailed information on what is specifically included and excluded from the policy's coverage. The actual policy will contain this information, but usually, you will not receive it until 30 to 60 days from the date of purchase. In other words, the face sheet contains the large print, or overview, while the actual policy contains the fine print, and you won't get the latter until after you buy.

Figure 15.1 shows a segment of language taken from an actual insurance policy. It is important to remember that, despite the difficulty of reading documents such as this, the courts will hold an insured party responsible for reading and understanding his or her policy. If you are at all unclear about what your final insurance policy will and will not cover, have your attorney review a sample policy, which can be provided by the insurance company.

Because you will not receive the actual insurance policy until after you purchase the policy, it is imperative that you discuss any unclear issues with the insurance agent before you buy. Ask for written answers to your questions, and continue to request information until you are satisfied with your comprehension of the details. Once the policy arrives, read it and make sure you fully understand:

LEGALESE

Exclusions: Liability claims that are not covered in an insurance policy.

▪ The policy's language, and whether it is consistent with your agent's earlier explanations.

▪ The policy's coverage, *exclusions*, *exceptions*, and clarifying language.

Most insurance policies will have both exclusions and exceptions. The insurer will almost always retain the right to exclude certain types of liability claims. If, for instance, a restaurateur has purchased fire insurance, but proceeds to intentionally set fire to his or her own restaurant, the insurance company would exclude, or refuse to cover, the cost of replacing the restaurant. Common exclusions include those involving intentional acts and fraud by the insured.

LEGALESE

Exceptions: Insurance coverage that is normally included in the insurance policy, but that will be excluded if the insured fails to comply with performance terms specifically mentioned in the policy.

Exceptions are also common in insurance policies, and it is best to be well aware of all that apply. An exception is a statement by the insurer that it will not pay for an otherwise legitimate claim if certain conditions have not been met. For example, the

> **B.   Limits of Liability**
>
> Regardless of the number of persons or entities insured or included in Part I.D. Covered Persons or Entities, or the number of claimants or Claims made:
>
> 1.   The maximum liability of the Company for **Damages and Claim Expenses** resulting from each **Claim** first made against the Insured during the **Policy Period** and the Extended reporting Period, if purchased, shall not exceed the amount shown in the Declarations as each Claim;
>
> 2.   The maximum liability of the Company for all **Damages and Claim Expenses** as a result of all **Claims** first made against the Insured during the **Policy Period** and the Extended Reporting Period, if purchased, shall not exceed the amount shown in the Declarations as Aggregate.
>
> The Company shall not be obligated to pay any **Claim** for **Damages** or defend any **Claim** after the applicable Limit of Liability has been exhausted by payment of judgments, settlements, **Claim Expenses** or any combination thereof. **Claim Expenses** are a part of and not in addition to the applicable Limits of Liability. Payment of **Claim Expenses** by the Company reduces the applicable Limits of Liability.
>
> The inclusion of more than one Insured, or the making of **Claims** by more than one person or organization, does not increase the company's Limit of Liability. In the event two or more **Claims** arise out of a single negligent act, error or omission, or a series of related negligent acts, errors or omissions, all such **Claims** shall be treated as a single **Claim**. Whenever made, all such **Claims** shall be considered first made and reported to the Company during the **Policy Period** in which the earliest **Claim** arising out of such negligent act, error or omission was first made and reported to the Company, and all such **Claims** shall be subject to the same Limit of Liability.

Figure 15.1 Insurance policy language.

insurance company may require a restaurant to have a valid license to serve food, in order to protect that restaurant in the event a guest claims damages resulting from food poisoning. Likewise, a fire insurance policy may require that an operator purchase and install specific types of fire suppression equipment, and that the equipment be inspected and approved on a regular basis by a qualified inspector.

In most cases, your insurer will require you to notify the company immediately if a claim is made by you, or if you believe something has occurred that might lead to litigation. In addition, if an attorney serves you with notification of intent to sue you, you must contact your insurance carrier. Some insurance policies are "claims made" policies. This term means that the coverage is available only if an actual claim is brought to the attention of the insurance company during the policy period. Most insurance policies, however, cover claims that occur during the policy period, even though they are not brought to the attention of the insurance company until after the coverage period has elapsed. Obviously, this type of policy is preferable to the "claims made" policy.

In spite of the problems and expense involved, insurance is not an option; it is a protection needed to operate your businesses with a sense of comfort and peace. You can avoid unpleasant surprises by taking the proper care when selecting insurance. This includes speaking and listening to your colleagues and asking those questions that will make it easier for you to purchase the right coverage in the right amount from the right insurance company.

Most policies are issued for a one-year period. Generally, new policies are issued annually, assuming that there is mutual satisfaction with the coverage, claim responsiveness by the carrier, and an agreement as to the premium (or cost) paid for the amount of insurance.

In Chapter 9, "Your Responsibilities as a Hospitality Operator," we examined how you can take steps to reduce insurance costs through the effective management and training of staff. Prevention of insurance claims, like the prevention of all legal claims, should be the goal of every hospitality manager.

INTERNATIONAL SNAPSHOT

Hotels Operating Internationally Need to Think Globally about Their Insurance Programs

Due to a number of factors, international insurance issues typically lag behind the U.S. insurance market by several years. These factors include:

■ Less litigious claims environment

■ Lower claims counts

■ Absence of punitive damages

■ Social environment, as respects claims

Because of this, international insurance pricing has remained lower than that in the U.S. insurance market. Quite often, this has led multinational hotel chains to place more emphasis on claims and risk control in the United States. Most hotels, especially those chains with large properties, are fairly adept at the basics of risk management that will allow them to control claims costs, minimize litigation potential, and maximize safety and risk mitigation. Too often, these concepts are not pushed out to the overseas locations on a consistent basis due to cost or internal operational hurdles.

Meanwhile, as the hotel industry was focused on the tight insurance market in the United States, the international insurance market and global legal climate changed in ways that are critical to the way a hotel operates. Over the past five years, the international insurance industry has started to drive the development of more sophisticated risk management programs throughout the world through market selection and pricing. The increasingly tight and limited international insurance capacity for both property and casualty lines is going to force multinational hotel chains to take more risk and to manage that risk in more countries.

WHY IS THIS HAPPENING?

A number of changes within the global insurance market and global legal climate are forcing underwriters and hotels alike to reexamine international insurance:

Market capacity: Because hotels have traditionally been loss leaders in the insurance marketplace, there have always been a fairly small number of insurance carriers that are willing to look at a hospitality risk.

Additionally, in the past five years, numerous insurance companies that have done multinational programs have left the market—Kemper, Royal US, and others. More international carriers have moved away from doing hospitality risks at all. This puts fewer markets in play for a hotel risk and forces pricing and selectivity up.

Legal changes: The world legal climate still remains well behind the litigious environment in the United States. However, there have been significant increases in "claims awareness" in a number of countries. While the systems are not as developed, they are nevertheless making large strides and increasing claims for the hospitality industry. There is also a growth of global case law—that is, legal decisions in countries such as Australia have cited California case law.

Claims counts: Around the world, we are seeing sharp increases in the claims counts being recorded on hospitality business. Since underwriting pricing is traditionally much lower on international accounts, as compared to U.S. accounts, this increase will put an immediate strain on insurer profitability and insured's costs.

Social change: More and more, we are becoming a global economy. People travel the world and expect the legal system to keep up with them—not the other way around. Legislation such as the European Union's Tour Operators Liability is globally focused. Hotels need to protect every location they have in every country of the world, not just those where the claims occur.

WHAT SHOULD BE DONE?

Hospitality companies need to start managing the risk worldwide more aggressively than ever before. The basics of risk management need to be adhered to by all locations. Additional strategies would include:

Claims and litigation management: Hotel chains should settle claims worldwide in the same manner, whether they are self-insured or not. A claim settled in Germany should be settled in the same manner as a claim in California. This will allow a hotel to create precedent in a lawsuit situation, not be surprised by it.

Program management: Many international programs stand alone from a domestic program and may or may not require participation from all locations. This should be managed very closely: as carriers fail or exit the hospitality business, it will be much harder to be reactive to a program change than be proactive to it. Brand-name protection: All locations bearing the company name should be required to carry the same levels of insurance or carry a documented exception. All franchises should be required to carry U.S. suits no matter where they are in the world. Since that is not available in most countries, they should be required to purchase this as part of a program that the parent company sponsors. As lawsuits go global, companies need to ensure that the brand is protected in any court in the world.

Information management: The key to underwriting and managing insurance risk is information flow. Standardize the forms for information on property and liability risks. Enforce the forms and collect them annually. Although this is an administrative burden, it is critical to managing the insurances.

Insurance programs should help a hotel manage its risk. Historically, most international hotels have used insurance as a reason *not* to manage their risk, since it did not cost them to have claims. As the changes evolve, a hotel chain must be a step ahead of its carrier to allow it to control its own insurance destiny.

Provided by Elizabeth Francy Demaret, Managing Director, Worldwide Risk Services Group, Arthur J. Gallagher & Co. in Itasca, IL. www.ajg.com.

WHAT WOULD YOU DO?

Assume that you are an insurance agent with the Arizona Business Insurance Company (ABIC). You sell ABIC products exclusively. Your company, which is rated AA, offers insurance coverage against a variety of risks, including workers' compensation, and specializes in the hospitality industry.

You are approached by Ted Betz, the operational vice president of J-Town Smokies, a chain of pit barbeque restaurants. Mr. Betz would like to purchase workers' compensation insurance from your company because he will be opening five stores in the Southwest in the coming year. A review of his application and claim history indicates that J-Town Smokies has experienced a rather large number of worker injuries in its four years of existence. In fact, the rate of worker injury per man-hour worked is nearly two times that of the restaurant industry average. Further investigation indicates that most of these injuries resulted from cutting meat prior to or after the barbeque process.

A review of the U.S. Department of Labor statistics reveals the following highest injury rate industries for this year and last.

	Employees (in thousands)	Accident Rate per Thousand This Year	Accident Rate per Thousand Last Year
Meat-packing plants	147.2	36.6	30.3
Ship-building and repairing	102.5	32.7	27.4
Steel foundries	26.6	26.4	26.4
Mobile homes	68.0	24.3	26.2
Automotive stamping	117.7	23.8	23.2
Restaurants	250.0	16.1	16.6

1. What type of information would you want to see from Mr. Betz before you offer to sell him a workers' compensation policy from your company?

2. Do you believe Mr. Betz's restaurants should pay the same amount for workers' compensation coverage as other restaurants, or should he be charged rates consistent with those in the meat-packing industry?

To review a case that involves the distinction between furniture and permanent fixtures, as discussed in Chapter 6, and to learn how insurance policies are closely analyzed by the courts when there is a dispute, consider the case of *Prytania Park Hotel v. General Star Indem.*, 179 F.3d 169 (5th Cir. 1999).

FACTUAL SUMMARY

The Prytania Park Hotel (Prytania) in New Orleans, Louisiana, was heavily damaged by a fire in one of the hotel buildings. The guestrooms in the hotel contained custom-made furniture, which was attached by screws and bolts to the walls of the rooms. A significant amount of the furniture was destroyed by the fire. The owners of the Prytania submitted a claim to General Star Indemnity Company (General Star), the insurer of the hotel.

The insurance policy for the Prytania covered loss or damage to the building, loss or damage to business personal property, and loss of business income resulting from business interruption. The provision in the policy for loss or damage to the building included permanently installed fixtures, machinery, and equipment. Prytania was entitled to the full replacement value of permanently installed items under the terms of the policy.

The business personal property provision in the policy included furniture and fixtures, and limited the amount of a claim to the actual cash value of items lost or destroyed. The owners of the Prytania submitted a building claim to General Star for $276,687.96. This amount included the damaged hotel building and all the hotel furniture at full replacement value. A contents claim was also submitted in the amount of $85,888.10, covering business personal property, but not the hotel furniture. Prytania also submitted a claim $75,000.00 for loss of income.

General Star adjusted the claims and paid $186,448.47 on the building claim, which did not include compensation for furniture; $68,273.93 on the contents claim; and $34,988.00 for loss of business income. The owners of the Prytania sued General Star to recover the unpaid portions of the claims.

QUESTION FOR THE COURT

The question for the court concerned the definition of permanently installed fixtures under the building provision and furniture and fixtures under the business personal property provision. Prytania argued the hotel furniture was permanently installed fixtures since removal from the walls would cause considerable damage to the furniture and walls. Prytania also argued the room furnishings were permanently installed fixtures based on the dictionary definition of each word. Since the owners intended the furniture to stay in one place and it had been secured to the wall, they argued it was permanently installed.

General Star argued the hotel furniture was clearly covered under the business personal property provision since the word "furniture" was used there and not in the building provision. Additionally General Star offered evidence showing removal of the furniture would cause no damage to either the furniture or the room.

DECISION

The court held the guestroom furniture was not permanently installed fixtures under the building provision of the policy. The furniture was covered under the business personal property provision since furniture was explicitly listed under the category. The court also found the furniture was not permanently attached since removal was possible without damage to the room walls or furniture.

MESSAGE TO MANAGEMENT

In insurance policies, leases, and other legal documents, it pays to clearly describe personal property, fixtures, and real property.

Insurance is a valuable tool to help protect a business and its owners from financial loss. There are many different types of insurance coverage, including property/casualty, liability, health/life, and that for injuries to workers. Not all insurance companies are the same, so an owner/operator should research a company's reputation, claims-paying record, and financial strength prior to purchasing the needed coverage for the business. A thorough understanding of the terms used in the insurance industry—such as primary, umbrella, exclusions, and exceptions—is crucial for an owner/operator to make informed decisions about coverage and pricing.

WHAT DID YOU LEARN IN THIS CHAPTER?

After you have studied this chapter, you should be prepared to:

RAPID REVIEW

1. Describe the importance of mathematics and statistics to the insurance industry.
2. Identify at least five types of insurance that would be needed by a nightclub or bar owner, and discuss the importance of each.
3. Assess the pros and cons of self-insurance in the area of workers' compensation.
4. Use the Internet to find a company that will likely provide liability coverage for your new hotel. Assume that the hotel is to be built in Berlin, Germany, and that your company requires a minimum of an AA Standard & Poor's financial-strength rating.
5. Assess the legal climate today, and then determine the amount of umbrella coverage your hospitality company would need to defend itself against a wrongful death suit brought about by dram shop legislation. Assume that you have $1 million in primary coverage. Be prepared to discuss the factors that influenced your decision.
6. Describe the function and limitations of a face sheet, or declaration page.
7. Develop a checklist for purchasing insurance, beginning with the recognition of the need for insurance to the evaluation of the face sheet and actual policy.
8. Describe, in detail, an example of both an exclusion and an exception that might be in effect with a workers' compensation policy at a hospitality operation where you have worked.

In teams, identify and evaluate Internet sites that would enable a prospective purchaser of insurance to discover information about various types of insurance coverage, the financial status of the companies offering the coverage, and the cost for the coverage. Present to the class the top three sites, and describe why your team selected them (e.g., scope and depth of information, ease of navigation, etc.).

TEAM ACTIVITY

GLOSSARY

Abandoned property Personal property that has been deliberately put aside by the rightful owner with no intention of ever returning for it.

Acceptance Unconditional agreement to the precise terms and conditions of an offer.

Actuary A mathematician or statistician who computes insurance risks and establishes premium rates.

Adhesion contract A contract whose terms were not truly negotiated or bargained and, as a result, may be so one-sided in favor of the stronger party that the contract is often deemed unenforceable by the courts.

Affirmative action A federally mandated requirement that employers who meet certain criteria must actively seek to fairly employ recognized classes of workers. (Some state and local legislatures have also enacted affirmative action requirements.)

Agent A person authorized to act for or to represent another, usually referred to as the principal.

Aggregate The maximum amount that can or will be paid by an insurer for all claims during a policy period.

Americans with Disabilities Act Federal legislation (law) that protects the rights of people with disabilities so that they may be treated fairly in the workplace and have access to places of public accommodation, such as hotels, restaurants, and airplanes.

Amusement park An entertainment facility featuring rides, games, food, and sometimes shows. Theme parks are amusements parks in which the rides, attractions, shows, and buildings revolve around a central theme or group of themes. Examples include the Disney- and Universal Studios–owned amusement parks.

Annuity Fixed payments, made on a regular basis, for an agreed-upon period of time or until the death of the recipient.

Appeal A written request to a higher court to modify or reverse the decision of a lower-level court.

Arbitration A process in which an agreed-on, independent, neutral third party (the arbitrator) renders a final and binding resolution to a dispute. The decision of the arbitrator is known as the "award."

Attorney Any person trained and legally authorized to act on behalf of others in matters of the law.

Attrition Reduction in the number of projected participants or attendees.

At-will employment An employment relationship whereby employers have a right to hire any employee, whenever they choose, and to dismiss an employee for or without cause, at any time; the employee also has the right to work for the employer or not, or to terminate the relationship at any time.

Bailee A person or entity that receives and holds property in a bailment arrangement.

Bailment The delivery of an item of property, for some purpose, with the expressed or implied understanding that the person receiving it shall return it in the same or similar condition in which it was received, when the purpose has been completed. Examples include coat checks, valet parking, safety deposit boxes, laundry, luggage storage, and delivery.

Bailor A person or entity that gives property to another in a bailment arrangement.

Bill of sale A document under which personal property is transferred from a seller to a buyer.

Blood alcohol concentration (BAC) A measurement, expressed in a percentage, of the concentration level of alcohol in the bloodstream. Also known as blood alcohol content or blood alcohol level, or BAL.

Bona fide occupational qualification A job qualification, established in good faith and fairness, that is necessary to safely or adequately perform the job.

Bond(ing) An insurance agreement in which the insurer guarantees payment to an employer in the event of financial loss caused by the actions of a specific employee.

Breach of contract Failure to keep the promises or agreements of a contract.

Capital improvement The purchase or upgrade of real or personal property that results in an increased depreciable asset base.

Caveat emptor A Latin phrase meaning "let the buyer beware." The phrase implies that the burden of determining the relative quality and price of a product falls on the buyer, not the seller.

Chattel Personal property, movable or immovable, that is not considered real property.

Civil law The body of law (usually in the form of codes or statutes) created by governmental entities that are concerned with private rights and remedies, as opposed to criminal matters.

Claim Demand for money, property, or repairs to property.

Class action lawsuit A lawsuit filed by one or more people on behalf of themselves and a larger group of people who were similarly affected by an event.

Clause (contract) A distinct contract provision or stipulation.

Collateral Property that is pledged to secure the repayment of a debt.

Collective bargaining agreement (CBA) A formal contract between an employer and a group of employees that establishes the rights and responsibilities of both parties in their employment relationship.

Commercial lease A lease that applies to business property.

Common carrier A company or individual that is in the regular business of transporting people and/or freight for a fee. Examples include airlines, cruise lines, trains, and buses.

Common law Laws derived from the historical customs and usage of a society, and the decisions by courts when interpreting those customs and usages.

Comparative negligence Shared responsibility for the harm that results from negligence. The comparison of negligence by the defendant with the contributory negligence of the plaintiff. Also known as comparative fault.

Compensatory damages Monetary amount awarded to restore the injured party to the position he or she was in prior to the injury (e.g., medical expenses, lost wages, etc.). Also referred to as actual damages.

Condominium A multiple-unit complex (i.e., hotel, apartment house, office building), the units of which are individually owned with each owner receiving a recordable deed to the individual unit purchased, including the right to sell that unit and sharing in joint ownership of all common grounds, hallways, and on-site facilities.

Condominium homeowners' association (CHOA) A group of condo owners, elected by all of the condo owners in a project, to interpret, develop, and implement the policies and procedures required to effectively manage their condominium complex.

Conference services contract An agreement that details the space, products, and services to be provided to a group before, during, and after its meeting.

Confirmed reservation A contract to provide a reservation in which the provider guarantees the guest's reservation will be honored until a mutually agreeable time. A confirmed reservation may be either guaranteed or nonguaranteed.

Consideration The payment/value exchanged for the promise(s) contained in a contract.

Contingency fee A method of paying for a civil attorney's services where the attorney receives a percentage of any money awarded as a settlement in the case. Typically, these fees range from 20 to 40 percent of the total amount awarded.

Contract An agreement or promise made between two or more parties that the courts will enforce.

Contributory negligence Negligent conduct by the complaining party (plaintiff) that contributes to the cause of his or her injuries.

Copyright The legal and exclusive right to copy or reproduce intellectual property.

Copyright owner A person or entity that legally holds a right to intellectual property under the copyright laws.

Corporation A group of individuals granted a charter, legally recognizing them as a separate entity with rights and liabilities distinct from those of its members.

Counteroffer Conditional agreement to the terms and conditions of an offer that includes a change to those terms, creating a new offer.

Course and scope The sum total of all common, job-related employee activities dictated or allowed by the employer.

Crisis An occurrence that holds the potential to jeopardize the health of individuals and or the business.

Cut-off date The date on which any rooms contracted, and thus held for sale, but not yet picked up (reserved) by the group are returned to the hotel's general rooms inventory.

Damages Losses or costs incurred due to another's wrongful act.

Deductible The amount of money the insured has to pay before the insurance coverage will begin to pay. Accordingly, the higher the deductible, the less risk to the insurance company, which should equal lower premiums.

Deed A written document for the transfer of land or other real property from one person to another.

Deed of trust Used in some states instead of a mortgage. A deed of trust places legal title to a real property in the hands of a trustee until the debtor has completed paying for the property.

Defamation False statements that cause someone to be held in contempt, lowered in the estimation of the community, or to lose employment status or earnings or otherwise suffer a damaged reputation.

Defendant The person or entity against which litigation is initiated. Sometimes referred to as the respondent.

Demand letter Official notification, typically delivered to a defendant via registered or certified mail that details the plaintiff's cause for impending litigation.

Depositions Oral answers, given under oath, to questions asked during the discovery phase of a lawsuit. Depositions are recorded by a certified court reporter and/or by videotape.

Depreciation The decrease in value of a piece of property due to age and/or wear and tear.

Depressant A substance that lowers the rate of vital body activities.

Detained property Personal property held by a bailee until lawful payment is made by the bailor.

Disclosure To reveal fully and honestly.

Dividend A portion of profits received by a shareholder, usually in relation to his or her ownership (shares) of a corporation.

Dram shop A name given to a variety of state laws establishing a liquor licensee's third-party liability.

Dram shop acts Legislation, passed in a variety of forms and in many states, that imposes liability for the acts of others on those who serve alcohol negligently, recklessly, or illegally.

Duty of care A legal obligation that requires a particular standard of conduct.

Emergency plan A procedure or series of procedures to be implemented in response to a crisis.

Employee An individual who is hired to provide services to an employer in exchange for wages or a salary.

Employee evaluation A review of an employee's performance, including strengths and shortcomings; typically completed by the employee's direct supervisor.

Employee manual A document written to detail the policies, benefits, and employment practices of an employer.

Employer An individual or entity that pays wages or a salary in exchange for a worker's services.

Employment agreement The terms of the employment relationship between an employer and employee that specifies the rights and obligations of each party to the agreement.

Enforceable contract A contract recognized as valid by the courts and subject to the court's ability to compel compliance with its terms.

Ethics Choices of proper conduct made by an individual in his or her relationships with others.

Eviction Removal of a tenant from rental property by a law enforcement officer. An eviction is the result of a landlord filing and winning a special lawsuit known as an "unlawful detainer." The procedure that a lessor uses to remove a lessee from physical possession of leased real property, usually for violation of a significant lease provision, such as nonpayment of rent.

Exceptions Insurance coverage that is normally included in the insurance policy, but that will be excluded if the insured fails to comply with performance terms specifically mentioned in the policy.

Exclusions Liability claims that are not covered in an insurance policy.

Exculpatory clause (or contract) A contract, or a clause in a contract, that releases one of the parties from liability for his or her wrongdoings.

Express contract A contract in which the components of the agreement are explicitly stated, either orally or in writing.

Face sheet A one-page document briefly describing the type and amount of insurance coverage contained in an insurance policy. Sometimes referred to as a declaration page.

Fiduciary A relationship based on trust and the responsibility to act in the best interest of another when performing tasks.

Fiduciary responsibility The requirement that agents act in the best interest of their principals.

Financing statement A formal notice of a lien being held on personal property, required under the Uniform Commercial Code in most cases. Also called a UCC-1 because of its form number in the UCC.

Fixture(s) An article that was once a chattel but that has become a part of the real property because the article is permanently attached to the soil or to something attached to the soil.

Foodborne illness Sickness or harm caused by the consumption of unsafe foods or beverages.

Force majeure Greater force; a natural or human-induced disaster, through no fault of the parties to the contract, that causes a contract to not be performed.

Forum (venue) selection clause A statement in a contract identifying the agreed-on tribunal for resolving legal disputes related to the contract's terms.

Fractional ownership A purchase arrangement in which a condominium owner purchases the use of his or her unit for a portion (fraction) of a year. The fraction may be defined in terms of the number of days per year (e.g., 30, 60, etc.) or very specific days and/or months (e.g., January 1 through March 31). Individual units purchased under such an arrangement are commonly known as fractionals.

Franchise A contract between a parent company (franchisor) and an operating company (franchisee) to allow the franchisee to run a business with the brand name of the parent company, as long as the terms of the contract concerning methods of operation are followed.

Franchise agreement A special hospitality contract that details the responsibilities of both parties (franchisor and franchisee) involved in the operation of a franchise.

Franchisee The person or business that has purchased and/or received a franchise.

Franchisor The person or business that has sold and/or granted a franchise.

Gaming Legalized gambling.

Garnish A court-ordered method of debt collection in which a portion of a person's salary is paid to a creditor.

General (or managing) partner The entity in a limited partnership relationship that makes the management decisions and can be held responsible for all debts and legal claims against the business.

General partnership A business organization in which two or more owners agree to share the profits of the business but are also jointly and severally liable for its debts.

Global distribution system (GDS) An interconnected computer system that connects travel professionals worldwide to those companies selling travel services.

Gratuitous bailment One in which there is no payment (consideration) in exchange for the promise to hold the property.

Gross negligence The reckless or willful failure of an individual or an organization to use even the slightest amount of reasonable care.

Guaranteed reservation A contract to provide a confirmed reservation in which the provider guarantees the guest's reservation will be honored regardless of time of arrival, but stating that the guest will be charged if he or she no-shows the reservation. Prepayment or payment authorization is required.

Guest A customer who lawfully utilizes a facility's food, beverage, lodging, or entertainment services.

Hospitality law Those laws that relate to the industry involved with the provision of food, lodging, travel, and entertainment services to its guests and clients.

Implied warranty An unwritten expectation that a product purchased is free of defects.

Improvements An addition to real estate that ordinarily enhances its value.

Indemnification To insure against possible liability and loss, and/or to compensate financially for losses incurred.

Independent contractor A person or entity that contracts with another to perform a particular task but whose work is not directed or controlled by the hiring party.

Infra hospitium A Latin term meaning "within the hotel."

In-house dispute resolution A program, funded by employers, that encourages the equitable settlement of an employee's claim of unfair employment, prior to or without resorting to litigation.

Insure (insurance) To protect from risk.

Insured The individual or business that purchases insurance against a risk.

Insurer The entity that provides insurance.

Intangible property Personal property that cannot be held or touched. Examples include patent rights, copyrights, and concept rights.

Intellectual property Personal property that has been created through the intellectual efforts of its original owner.

Intentional act A willful action undertaken with or without full understanding of its consequences.

Interdiction program An arrangement whereby citizens contact police to report suspected criminal activity before a crime is committed.

International travel law The ordinances, rules, treaties, and agreements used to regulate the international travel industry.

Interrogatories Questions that require written answers, given under oath, asked during the discovery phase of a lawsuit.

Interstate commerce Commercial trading or the transportation of persons or property between or among states.

Intoxication A condition in which an individual's BAC reaches legally established levels. These levels are not uniform across the United States. An intoxicated person may not sell or purchase alcohol, nor operate a motor vehicle.

Invitee An individual who is on a property at the expressed or implied consent of the owner.

Job description A written, itemized listing of a specific job's basic responsibilities and reporting relationships.

Job qualifications The knowledge or skill(s) required to perform the responsibilities and tasks listed in a job description.

Jurisdiction The authority given by law or treaty to a court to try cases and make decisions about legal matters within a particular geographic area and/or over certain types of cases.

Kickback A secret rebate of part of a purchase price, given by the seller, to the buyer, in exchange for the buyer's influence in the purchasing decision.

Landlord The lessor in a real property lease.

Law The rules of conduct and responsibility established and enforced by a society.

Lease A contract that establishes the rights and obligations of each party with respect to property owned by one entity but occupied or used by another.

Lessee The entity that occupies or uses the property covered in a lease.

Lessor The entity that owns the property covered in a lease.

Liable To be legally responsible or obligated.

License Legal permission to do a certain thing or operate in a certain way.

Licensee One who is granted a license.

Licensing agreement A legal document that details the specifics of a license.

Licensor One who grants a license.

Lien A claim against property that gives the creditor (lien holder) the right to repossess and/or sell that property if the debtor does not repay his or her debt in a timely manner.

Limited liability company (LLC) A type of business organization that protects the owners from liability for debts incurred by the business, without the need for some of the formal incorporation requirements. The federal government does not tax the profits of LLCs; however, some states do, while others do not.

Limited partner The entity in a limited partnership relationship who is liable only to the extent of his or her investment. Limited partners have no right to manage the partnership.

Limited partnership (LP) A business organization with two classes of owners. The limited partner invests in the business but may not exercise control over its operation, in return for protection from liability. The general or managing partner assumes full control of the business operation but can also be held liable for any debts the operation incurs.

Liquor license A permit issued by a state that allows for the sale and/or service of alcoholic beverages. The entity holding the license is known as the licensee.

Litigation The act of initiating and carrying on a lawsuit. Often, used to refer to the lawsuit itself.

Lost property Personal property that has been inadvertently put aside, then forgotten by the rightful owner.

Management agreement The legal agreement that defines the responsibilities of a business owner and the management company chosen to operate the owner's business. Also known as a "management contract."

Management company An entity that, for a fee, assumes responsibility for the day-to-day operation of a business.

Management contract The legal agreement that defines the responsibilities of a business owner and the management company chosen to operate the owner's business.

Maritime law Also called "admiralty law" or "the law of admiralty," the laws, regulations, international agreements, and treaties that govern activities in navigable waters.

Master bill A single folio (bill) established for a group that includes specifically agreed-on group charges. Sometimes called a "master folio," "group folio," or "group bill."

Mediation A process in which an appointed, neutral third party (the mediator) assists those involved in a dispute with resolving their differences. The result of mediation, when successful, is known as the "settlement."

Meeting planners A group of professionals that plan and organize meetings and events for their employers and clients.

Merchantable Suitable for buying and selling.

Minimum wage The least amount of wages that an employee covered by the FLSA or state law may be paid by his or her employer.

Mislaid property Personal property that has been put aside on purpose but then has been forgotten by the rightful owner.

Mortgage The pledging of real property by a debtor to a creditor to secure payment of a debt.

Negligence per se When a rule of law is violated by the operator; such violation of a rule of law is considered to be so far outside the scope of reasonable behavior that the violator is assumed to be negligent.

Negligent (negligence) The failure to use reasonable care.

Negligent hiring Failure on the part of an employer to exercise reasonable care in the selection of employees.

Nondisturbance clause A clause in a contract that stipulates that leases or other ownership investments in the property will be allowed to continue uninterrupted in the event of a default or insolvency by the landlord/seller.

Nonguaranteed reservation A contract to provide a confirmed reservation where no prepayment or authorization is required.

Off the record An oral agreement between a reporter and an interviewee wherein the reporter promises not to quote the interviewee's comments for publication.

Offer A proposal to perform an act or to pay an amount that, if accepted, constitutes a legally valid contract.

Ombudsperson A company official appointed to investigate and resolve worker complaints.

Operating agreement A contract that details the areas of responsibilities of the owner of a business and the entity selected by the owner to operate the business. Also referred to as a "management contract."

Operating structure The relationship between a business's ownership and its management.

Organizational structure The legal entity that owns a business.

Overstay A guest who refuses to vacate his or her room when he or she has exceeded the number of nights originally agreed to at check-in.

Owner-operator A type of operating structure in which the owners of a business are directly responsible for its day-to-day operation. Also known, in some cases, as an "independent."

Patent A grant issued by a governmental entity ensuring an inventor the right to exclusive production and sale of his or her invention for a fixed period of time.

Perfect a lien To make a public record of a lien, or to take possession of the collateral.

Per occurrence The maximum amount that can or will be paid by an insurer in the event of a single claim.

Personal injury Damage or harm inflicted upon the body, mind, or emotions.

Personal property Tangible and intangible items that are not real property.

Plaintiff The person or entity that initiates litigation against another. Sometimes referred to as the claimant, petitioner, or applicant.

Policy (insurance) The contract for insurance agreed upon by the insurer and insured.

Post-traumatic stress disorder (PTSD) A severe reaction to an event that threatened an individual's physical or emotional health.

Premium The amount paid for insurance coverage; it can be paid in one lump sum or over time, such as monthly.

Press release An announcement made by an organization or individual distributed for use by the media.

Primary policy The main insurance policy that provides basic coverage and the amount of insurance provided by the policy.

Principal Employer, the person hiring and directing employees (agents) to perform his/her/its business.

Progressive discipline An employee development process that provides increasingly severe consequences for continued violation of workplace rules.

Proximate cause The event or activity that directly contributes to (causes) the injury or harm.

Public accommodation A facility that provides entertainment, rooms, space, or seating for the use and benefit of the general public.

Public domain Property that is owned by all citizens, not an individual.

Punitive damages A monetary amount used as punishment and to deter the same wrongful act in the future by the defendant and others.

Quid pro quo Latin term for "giving one thing in return or exchange for another."

Quitclaim deed A deed that conveys only such rights as the grantor has. This type of deed transfers the owner's interest to a buyer, but does not guarantee that there are no other claims against the property or that the property is indeed legally owned by the seller.

Real estate Land, including soil and water, buildings, trees, crops, improvements, and the rights to the air above, and the minerals below, the land.

Real property Land and all the things that are permanently attached to it.

Reasonable care The degree of care that a reasonably prudent person would use in a similar situation.

REIT Short for "real estate investment trust," a very special form of business structure in which the owners of a business are generally prohibited from operating it.

Respondeat superior Literally; "let the master respond," a legal theory that holds the employer (master) responsible for the acts of the employee.

Right of first refusal A clause in a contractual agreement between two parties in a business relationship in which one party, upon termination of the business relationship, can exercise the right to buy the interest of the other party before those rights can be offered for sale to another.

S corporation A type of business entity that offers liability protection to its owners and is exempt from corporate taxation on its profits. Some restrictions limit the circumstances under which an S corporation can be formed.

Safety program Those procedures and activities designed to ensure the physical protection and good health of guests and employees.

Security agreement A contract between a lender and borrower that states that the lender can repossess the personal property a person has offered as collateral if the loan is not paid as agreed.

Security interest A legal ownership right to property.

Segregate To separate a group or individual on any basis but especially by race, color, religion, or national origin.

Service charge An amount added to a guest's bill in exchange for services provided.

Shares Fractional portions of a company in which the owner of the portion has voting rights and rights to a respective fraction of the assets of the company.

Signatory An entity that signs and agrees to abide by the terms of a document.

Small claims court A court designed especially to hear lawsuits entailing relatively small sums of money. They can provide a speedy method of making a claim without the necessity of hiring a lawyer and engaging in a formal trial.

Sole proprietorship A business organization in which one person owns and, often, operates the business.

Standard of care The industry-recognized, reasonably accepted level of performance used in fulfilling a duty of care.

Stare decisis The principle of following prior case law.

Statute of limitations Various laws that set maximum time periods in which lawsuits must be initiated. If the suit is not initiated (or filed) before the expiration of the maximum period allowed, then the law prohibits the use of the courts for recovery.

Strict liability Responsibility arising from the nature of a dangerous activity rather than negligence or an intentional act. Also known as absolute liability or liability without fault.

Sublet To rent property one possesses by a lease, to another. Also called subleasing.

Subpoena A court-authorized order to appear in person at a designated time and place, or to produce evidence demanded by the court.

Tangible property Personal property that has physical substance and can be held or touched. Examples include furniture, equipment, and inventories of goods.

Tariff The agreement between an airline and its passengers. When purchasing a ticket, the passenger agrees to the terms of the tariff.

Tenant Anyone, including a corporation, who rents real property for an extended period of time with the intent of establishing a permanent occupation or residency. The lessee in a real property lease.

Third-party liability The two areas of liability theory that a hospitality manager should be aware of focus on the duties of a host who holds a party where alcohol is served, and that of an establishment licensed to sell alcohol.

Timeshare A form of shared property ownership in which a buyer acquires the right to occupy a piece of real estate, such as a condominium in a resort area, for a specific period of time each year.

Tip credit The amount an employer is allowed to consider as a supplement to employer-paid wages in meeting the requirements of applicable minimum wage laws.

Tip pooling/sharing An arrangement whereby service providers share their tips with each other on a predetermined basis.

Tip A gratuity given in exchange for a service performed. Literally an acronym for "to improve service."

Title search A review of land records to determine the ownership and description of a piece of real property.

Title The sum total of all legally recognized rights to the possession and ownership of property.

Tort An act or failure to act (not involving a breach of contract) that results in injury, loss, or damage to another (e.g., negligence is an unintentional tort, whereas battery, physically touching someone, is usually an intentional tort).

Tour operator A company whose primary activity is the planning, packaging, and marketing of travel services, including transportation, meals, accommodations, and activities.

Trade dress A distinct visual image created for and identified with a specific product.

Trademark A word, name, symbol, or combination of these that indicates the source or producer of an item. Sometimes called a mark.

Transient guest A customer who rents real property for a relatively short period of time (e.g., small number of days with no intent of establishing a permanent residency).

Travel law The laws regulating business and individual behavior in the travel industry.

Truth in menu laws The collective name given to various laws and regulations that have been implemented to ensure accuracy in the wording on menus.

Umbrella Insurance coverage purchased to supplement primary coverage. Sometimes referred to as excess insurance.

Underwrite To assume agreed-upon maximum levels of liability in the event of a loss or damages.

Unemployment benefits A benefit paid to an employee who involuntarily loses his or her employment without just cause.

Unemployment claim A petition, submitted by an unemployed worker to his or her state unemployment agency, which asserts that the worker is eligible to receive unemployment benefits.

Unemployment insurance A program, funded by employers, that provides temporary monetary benefits for employees who have lost their jobs.

Uniform Commercial Code (UCC) A model statute covering such issues as the sale of goods, credit, and bank transactions.

Vicarious liability A party's responsibility for the acts of another that result in an injury, harm, or damage. (See also *respondeat superior.*)

Warranty A promise about a product made by either a manufacturer or a seller that is a part of the sales contract.

Warranty deed A deed that provides that the person granting the deed agrees to defend the title from claims of others. In general, the seller is representing that he or she fully owns the property and will stand behind this promise.

Warsaw Convention Short for the Convention for the Unification of Certain Rules Relating to International Carriage by Air, signed at Warsaw on October 12, 1929, this agreement set limits on the liabilities of airlines that follow established guidelines for the safe operation of international airline flights.

Whistle-blowers protection acts Laws that protect employees who have reported illegal employer acts from retaliation by that employer.

Workers' compensation A benefit paid to an employee who suffers a work-related injury or illness.

Wrongful termination A violation, by the employer, of the employment relationship resulting in the unlawful firing of the employee.

1906

The Federal Food and Drugs Act and the Federal Meat Inspection Act authorize the federal government to regulate the safety and quality of food. The responsibility falls to the U.S. Department of Agriculture (USDA) and the Bureau of Chemistry, the Food and Drug Administration's predecessor.

1913

The GOULD Amendment requires food packages to state the quantity of contents.

1924

In *U.S. v. 95 Barrels Alleged Apple Cider Vinegar,* the Supreme Court rules that the Food and Drug Act condemns every statement, design, or device that may mislead, misdirect, or deceive, even if technically true.

1938

The Federal Food, Drug, and Cosmetic Act replaces the 1906 Food and Drugs Act. Among other things, it requires the label of every processed packaged food to contain the name and address of the manufacturer or distributor. A list of ingredients also is required on certain products. The law also prohibits statements in food labeling that are false or misleading.

1957

The Poultry Products Inspection Act authorizes the USDA to regulate, among other things, the labeling of poultry products.

1966

The Fair Packaging and Labeling Act requires all consumer products in the interstate commerce to contain accurate information and to facilitate value comparisons.

1974

The Safe Drinking Water Act authorizes the Environmental Protection Association (EPA) to establish standards for drinking water safety and water quality. (Mineral water, seltzer, and club soda are exempt from these provisions, because the FDA classifies them as soft drinks.) In addition, the FDA has established strict criteria and labeling requirements for all types of bottled water, mineral water, and sparkling water.

1990

Congress passes the Nutrition Labeling and Education Act (NLEA), which makes nutrition information mandatory for most foods. Among the few foods exempted were restaurant items, unless they carried a nutrient or health claim.

1993

The FDA issues regulations under NLEA that require restaurants to comply with regulations for nutrient and health claims that appear on signs and placards. Menu claims are exempt.

1996

The U.S. District Court in Washington, DC, rules that Congress had intended restaurant menus to be covered by NLEA, and orders the FDA to amend its nutrition labeling and claims regulations to include menu items about which claims are made.

1997

The FDA's regulations for nutrition labeling of restaurant menu items that bear a nutrition or health benefit claim take effect.

2002

The Organic Foods Production Act and the National Organic Program (NOP) are intended to assure consumers that the organic foods they purchase are produced, processed, and certified to consistent national organic standards. The labeling requirements of the new program apply to raw, fresh products and processed foods that contain organic ingredients. Foods that are sold, labeled, or represented as organic will have to be produced and processed in accordance with the NOP standards.

2003

To help consumers choose heart-healthy foods, the Department of Health and Human Services announces that FDA will require **food labels to include trans fat content**, the first substantive change to the nutrition facts panel on foods since the label was changed in 1993.

2004

Passage of the **Food Allergy Labeling and Consumer Protection Act** requires the labeling of any food that contains a protein derived from any one of the following foods that, as a group, account for the vast majority of food allergies: peanuts, soybeans, cow's milk, eggs, fish, crustacean shellfish, tree nuts, and wheat.

This is the complete version of Figure 12.3 which appears on page 346 in Chapter 12.

INDEX